The Brown and Benchmark Reader In
INTERNATIONAL RELATIONS 1992

Edited by

Dr. Jeffrey M. Elliot
North Carolina Central University

Brown &
Benchmark

a division of Wm. C. Brown Communications, Inc.
Dubuque, Iowa

Book Team

Editor *Edgar J. Laube*
Project Editor *Roger B. Wolkoff*
Production Manager *Joanne L. Cooper*
Permissions Editor *Vicki Krug*

Wm. C. Brown Publishers

President *G. Franklin Lewis*
Vice President, Publisher *Thomas E. Doran*
Vice President, Operations and Production *Beverly Kolz*
National Sales Manager *Virginia S. Moffat*
Group Sales Manager *Eric Ziegler*
Executive Editor *Edgar J. Laube*
Director of Marketing *Kathy Law Laube*
Marketing Manager *Kathleen Nietzke*
Managing Editor, Production *Colleen A. Yonda*
Manager of Visuals and Design *Faye M. Schilling*
Production Editorial Manager *Julie A. Kennedy*
Production Editorial Manager *Ann Fuerste*
Publishing Services Manager *Karen J. Slaght*

WCB Group

President and Chief Executive Officer *Mark C. Falb*
Chairman of the Board *Wm. C. Brown*

Copyeditor Kathleen Childers

Permissions Editor Karen Dorman

Cover Design Kay D. Fulton

Cover Image © Nicholas Foster/The Image Bank

Printed in the United States of America by Wm. C. Brown Publishers,
2460 Kerper Boulevard, Dubuque, IA 52001

10 9 8 7 6 5 4 3 2 1

Contents

ABOUT THE EDITOR

Dr. Jeffrey M. Elliot is a professor of political science at North Carolina Central University, as well as a free-lance writer and editor. He received his bachelor of arts degree in 1969, and his master of arts in 1970, from the University of Southern California, and his doctor of arts degree from the Claremont Graduate School in 1978. In 1985, he was awarded an honorary doctor of humane letters degree from Shaw University, and in 1986 California State University, San Bernardino, established "The Jeffrey M. Elliot Collection," a permanent archive of his published works. Dr. Elliot is the author of over sixty published books and five hundred articles, reviews, and interviews. His work has appeared in more than 250 publications, both in the United States and abroad, and has been nominated for numerous academic and literary awards. In 1991, he was selected as one of North Carolina Central University's "Most Outstanding Researchers." Recent book titles include: *The Trilemma of World Oil Politics* (Borgo Press, 1991); *Third World* (Dushkin Publishing Group, 1991); *Urban Society* (Dushkin Publishing Group, 1991); *Voices of Zaire: Rhetoric or Reality?* (Washington Institute Press, 1990); *The Arms Control, Disarmament, and Military Security Dictionary* (ABC-Clio, 1989); *The State and Local Government Political Dictionary* (ABC-Clio, 1987); *Fidel Castro: Nothing Can Stop the Course of History* (Pathfinder Press, 1986); *Black Voices in American Politics* (Harcourt Brace Jovanovich, 1985); *The Presidential-Congressional Political Dictionary* (ABC-Clio, 1984); and *Tempest in a Teapot: The Falkland Islands War* (Borgo Press, 1983).

Dubbed the "Boswell of Modern America," Dr. Elliot has conducted over 350 interviews, among them: President Jimmy Carter, Nobel Prize winner Bishop Desmond Tutu, Cuban president Fidel Castro, Zairian president Mobutu Sese Seko, UNITA president Jonas Savimbi, PLO chairman Yasir Arafat, Contra leader Adolfo Calero, and Jamaican prime minister Michael Manley. In addition to his academic duties, he serves as Distinguished Advisor on Foreign Affairs to Congressman Mervyn M. Dymally (D-Calif.), editor or contributing editor to six journals, chairperson of the Durham County Youth Services Advisory Board, vice president and a member of the board of directors of the Academic Help Center, and a member of the Durham Housing Authority Crime Prevention Board. He is the subject of a book-length study, *The Work of Jeffrey M. Elliot: An Annotated Bibliography and Guide* (Borgo Press, 1986).

TO THE READER

Many years ago, Hans J. Morganthau, a distinguished political scientist, opined: "In the life of nations, as in the life of individuals, a great crisis can be a boon if it reveals in the contours of the abyss the stark and simple outlines of the eternal verities which men and women neglect only at their peril." Clearly, Morganthau's observation is as true today as it was then. With the collapse of the Soviet Empire—and the demise of communism—the international community faces a new set of challenges and opportunities. Now that the euphoria surrounding the end of the Cold War has subsided, the superpowers must devise a new world order. Ultimately, one question remains: How can the United States and the Soviet Union move from chaos to cooperation, from competing superpowers to prospering superpartners?

The Cold War has dominated superpower relations from 1945 until only recently. During this period, the United States and the Soviet Union—for vastly different reasons—engaged in an intense rivalry that served to undermine international peace and stability. In addition, they encouraged the development of a military technology that now threatens all human life. In the process, the two superpowers plunged humankind into a crisis of unprecedented proportions—one that was characterized by a monstrous and dangerous paradox. In our zeal to protect our interests—and advance the cause of peace and freedom—we developed the most sophisticated scientific arsenal the world has ever known, but our very technology and those who controlled it concocted a world which threatened to obliterate the planet. Indeed, we set into action economic, political, and technical forces that should have promoted international cooperation. Yet, never was the world community more divided. In the process, the two superpowers created two mighty political blocs, each armed to ensure the ascendancy of its own objectives, its own ideology, and its own interests.

Today, we know that neither side can achieve preeminence without destroying the other, and perhaps even the human race. At its zenith, both sides stepped dangerously close to the precipice edge. All the while, both nations knew, or should have known, that there was no defense, no safety, no salvation, in the path they had chosen. With the Cold War now behind us—and the present high-stakes scramble to define the future and reshape the world—it has become all the more important to capitalize on recent events by fashioning a new world order—one that is free of political oppression, social injustice, authoritarian rule, ethnic and religious strife, and military aggression.

As we assess the future—replete with the opportunites and dangers that lie in wait—we should be reminded that the problems we now face, nations in various ways have faced before. What we must dare, others have dared in earlier days and lands, though under different names and against different enemies. To the dweller in the ancient Mesopotamian city of Lagash, menaced by the spearmen and charioteers of King Lugalagezi of Umma in about 2400 B.C., the end of the world must have seemed as imminent and as terrible as ever it seemed to us. To the Israelite threatened by the armies of the Assyrian emperor Sennacherib in 701 B.C., or to the Roman of the fifth century A.D., who dreaded the hordes of Attila the Hun, or to the native of Constantinople, helpless before the might of the Turkish sultan Mohammed II in 1453, or to the sixteenth-century Dutchman, beseiged in the city of Haarlem by the Spaniards, the face of doom surely stared as huge and frightful as if humankind foresaw a nuclear assault.

Fortunately, the moral and ethical climate has, in some ways, improved. Today, we no longer automatically look upon the Individual beyond the next hill as a probable enemy, as did the early Greeks. We no longer rush to the woods at the sight of a strange approaching vessel, which in years past may have been teeming with slave-taking marauders. The concept of international law, if not its practical realization, has been with us long enough to command respect, as has the idea of the oneness of humankind, while the ideal of universal justice has gained new believers even in the face of immoral ideologies and unparalleled massacres and wartime crimes. Whereas in ancient Sumer or in classical Greece or in early Italy it was commonplace for any small city to attack its neighbors, in our world the idea of peace among local communities is well established. Not only that, but the desire for peace—and sometimes even the belief that peace is possible—has grown among nations, at least in part because of the appalling nature of the alternative.

This book is about international relations, which is the study of interactions among states and other actors in the international sphere. It has three main goals: First, to give students in an introductory course in international relations a basic understanding of the history of the international system from the First World War up to the present. Second, to help students understand the current issues and crises in the global arena that are likely to have the greatest impact on the future. Third, to assist students in developing generalizations about and discerning patterns in the conduct of foreign affairs. Specifically, it seeks to foster a heightened understanding of the dynamics of international relations; to identify the salient trends and developments in world politics with which policymakers must deal; to examine the principal questions that will confront the international community over the next decade or so; and to foster an informed discussion of war, peace, and world politics.

This book, which contains fifty-eight readings—selected from more than 250 newspapers, magazines, and journals—is divided into seven sections: The International Environment; The Cold War and Beyond; Peace, War, and Crisis; The Balance of Terror; The Path to Peace; The Economic Challenge; and A World in Ferment. The articles themselves—which are authored by a wide variety of scholars, policy analysts, journalists, and political officials—raise a wealth of important and challenging questions. Along with the readings, each section features a brief overview, discussion questions, a glossary of key terms, and a selected bibliography. In selecting the contents, the editor was guided by five main criteria: scholarship, readability, balance, relevance, and currency. At the same time, no one book—however well conceived or organized—can possibly do justice to the full range of issues and concerns which dominate the study of international relations. For this reason, the editor invites you, the reader, to provide that feedback which will be so essential in compiling the second edition. In this regard, your comments, suggestions, and criticisms are welcome. After all, it was for you that this book was published. It is our hope that you will complete the questionnaire at the end of the book, so that we will better know your feelings about the selections contained in the reader to help us prepare the next edition of the Brown & Benchmark Reader in International Relations.

Dr. Jeffrey M. Elliot
Editor

THE INTERNATIONAL ENVIRONMENT

International relations is significantly different from domestic relations, in that the latter typically occur within a system in which there is an accepted central authority and a set of mechanisms for making decisions and resolving conflicts. For example, a democracy is, by definition, a system of government in which political authority is vested in the people, and in which citizens enjoy a high degree of access to and influence over their government. On the other hand, in a totalitarian government, the people have little or no control over the actions of their leaders, who have typically seized power by extraconstitutional means. In such cases, changes in government can come about only by resignation, death, revolution, coup d'etat, or war. Still, whether the government is democratic or totalitarian, most political systems boast some kind of recognized authority. By contrast, this is not true in the field of international relations, since individual states have no one arbiter or institution to which they can turn to resolve disputes, enforce their rights, or protect their security.

For this reason, all states inevitably face a "security dilemma," in which they feel obligated to protect their interests by arming themselves. At the same time, they do not necessarily guarantee their own security, because their neighbors and foes are also forced to resort to the same means. Although conflict and war historically have characterized international relations, few could have envisaged such twentieth-century dangers as large-scale guerrilla warfare, international terrorism, and nuclear annihilation, which threaten not only the security of individual states but that of the entire world.

The imperatives of the security dilemma have given rise to a dangerous arms race, in which nations compete to maintain their real or perceived military superiority. Arms races have been part of the political landscape since steel weapons supplanted bronze in the ancient world. In the post-World War II era, the United States and the Soviet Union initiated a massive arms race, even though both understood the dangers inherent in an armed confrontation. Yet, this did not stop them from building their arsenals, including nuclear weapons, nor did it prevent other countries from increasing their military stockpiles far beyond any real need for self-defense.

After 1945, the world arms race assumed new dimensions with the advent of nuclear weapons. Prior to this, most arms races invariably resulted in war, with one side eventually prevailing. However, the discovery of the atomic bomb changed the nature of modern warfare. Following World War II, the superpowers engaged in a kind of "global chess match," in which they sought ultimate security by building large numbers of nuclear weapons, with each seeking to intimidate the other into not using their respective arsenals. Ironically, neither side seemed to appreciate that greater numbers of warheads do not a safer world make. The fact that war could no longer be conducted between nuclear states without the ultimate destruction of both parties was not publicly acknowledged by either government until the 1980s, when the "nuclear winter" scenario and the Chernobyl nuclear power plant disaster suddenly exposed the civil defense plans of both sides as self-delusional charades. By then, the United States and the Soviet Union possessed the means to destroy each other a hundred times over.

As a fact of international life, the quest for and maintenance of power plays a salient role in the relations between nations. Today, power is a major aspect of interstate politics. In general terms, it refers to the ability of one nation to influence or control the behavior of others. However, power is an elusive concept. One must draw a distinction between actual power and perceived power. In most cases, a country's power is unknowable—that is, until or unless it wins a decisive military victory. With the advent of nuclear weapons, and their enormous destructive potential, the power of most nations remains untested. As a result, a country's "perceived power" will often confer power, whether or not that nation has actually demonstrated its strength on the battlefield.

Despite these facts, the problem of war—both conventional and nuclear—remains real. The causes of war are many and varied, not to mention puzzling and complex. In 1925, for example, the Conference on the Cause and Cure of War identified over 250 reasons for war, grouped under four major categories: political, economic, social, and psychological. In his seminal study of international conflict, Quincy Wright concluded that "war has politico-technological, juro-ideological, socio-religious, and psycho-economic causes." Specifically, major explanations include: (1) war is inherent in the nation-state system; (2) war is caused by conflicting beliefs and values; (3) war is innate in human nature; and (4) war is a natural by-product of a turbulent social environment. Other explanations are equally compelling. For example, political scientist John Spanier contends that war derives from the failure of nations to bridge the gap between their search for peace and preparations for war; states' inability to maintain order and security; and war's effectiveness for achieving national and international objectives. Despite popular folklore, a case can be made that war is neither irrational, immoral, nor impractical—that is, it is a viable instrument of state policy, which is why many nations are willing to forego the benefits of peace in favor of armed confrontation.

Sadly, conflict appears to be an inherent feature of interstate relations. Despite its importance, there is no single theory of conflict which is acceptable to both theorists and practitioners of international relations. As a result, most of the discussion about conflict focuses on moralistlc or pragmatic explanations of human nature or national self-interest. Forest L. Grieves, a specialist in world affairs, offers four explanations of the nature of conflict: First, human conflict is a fact of modern social life and is likely to remain so for the indefinite future. Second, the abolition of war is a dream. Third, theories of Armageddon are likely to be not only empty but even dangerous. Fourth, wars may be inevitable, but nuclear war is unthinkable.

Interestingly, some experts, like social scientist Lewis Coser, believe that conflict may actually serve several positive purposes. These include: enhancing social solidarity, clarifying values, stimulating growth, and promoting learning. In many cases, however, conflict is mismanaged. When this occurs, the result may be violence or war. Ultimately, interstate conflict is not so much the product of misperception but the fact that nations harbor conflicting objectives. John Spanier echoes this view, stating: "Human beings may well be alike, in spite of their different languages, clothing, and manner. But politics starts where the commonalities of humanity stop, and it starts here because of the different interests, values, ideologies, and histories of the many nation-states. All want peace—but only on their terms." Obviously, peace is attainable if one state accedes to the demands of the other. However, few nations have adopted this course. Thus, conflict cannot be explained simply as a failure of communication. By itself, communication is not necessarily a potent antidote to conflict. In the end, the problem is not conflict—which is inevitable—but how to manage conflict, so as to avoid the carnage of war.

Section I, "The International Environment," is divided into three chapters. The first chapter, "Imperialism and Intervention," examines the question of U.S. self-interest in the context of internationalism, which the author claims is antithetical to national security, lasting peace, and sustained prosperity. After critiquing the failures of globalism, he proposes a new foreign policy agenda, which is predicated on interest-based thinking which, he maintains, is rooted in common sense and classical theory. The second selection analyzes the causes and consequences of the gulf war, arguing that the success of the U.S.-led coalition is directly attributable to the decline of Soviet power. Absent recent developments in the USSR, the Kremlin might have prevented Saddam Hussein's attack on Kuwait, or forced the U.S. to weigh the risks of a possible confrontation with the Soviets if it chose to intervene in the face of Soviet opposition.

In Chapter 2, "Ethnic and Nationalist Conflict," the author explores the nature and causes of the resurgence of nationalism, which he contends is, at best, a mixed blessing. Focusing on recent changes in Eastern Europe, he applauds the revival of democratic politics and cultural diversity but warns that nationalism is itself laden with countless myths and dangers. The second article describes the resurgence of nationalism in Yugoslavia, which the author insists will not necessarily produce a liberal democracy. As he views it, Yugoslavia will continue to be plagued by ethnic rights issues, which are likely to erupt into major territorial, linguistic, and demographic disputes.

Chapter 3, "Revolution and Civil Strife," deals with the 1989 Tiananmen Square massacre in China, in which that country's aging leadership ordered the People's Liberation Army to beat, maim, and murder student demonstrators who had taken to the streets to demand democratic rights and economic reform. The article reviews the issues behind the protests, the history of student demonstrations, the forces of revolution, the response of the Chinese government, and the likelihood of future uprisings. The second selection compares and contrasts the statelessness of the Kurds with that of the Palestinians, concluding that the world response to both groups is fraught with contradictions. He attacks the Bush administration and, for that matter, the international community, for betraying the Kurds, whose claims to nationhood are as valid, if not more valid, than those of the Palestinians, who have garnered worldwide support.

DISCUSSION QUESTIONS

1. What principles have motivated American foreign policy since World War II?
2. Is internationalism relevant in today's world?
3. Should America adopt an interest-based foreign policy?
4. Did the decline of the Soviet Union as a superpower make the gulf war possible? If so, how?
5. In what sense, if any, was the gulf conflict a victory for the capitalist world?
6. Is the gulf war an expression of American imperialism? Why, or why not?
7. Is the United States ever justified in supporting a dictatorship?
8. What explains the current revival of nationalism?
9. Is nationalism compatible with democratic rule? Why, or why not?
10. What are the chief myths of nationalism?
11. What factors led to the Tiananmen Square uprising?
12. Did Deng Xiaoping err in using force to put down the protests?
13. In what sense, if any, does the Chinese revolution remain unfinished?
14. Why did Saddam Hussein force the Kurds to flee Iraq?
15. Did the world abandon the Kurds by pushing them into "safe havens" in Iraq?
16. In what sense, if any, can the plight of the Palestinians be compared to that of the Kurds?

KEY TERMS

BALANCE OF POWER   A relationship in which countries attempt to achieve national security in an environment of shifting alignments and alliances by maintaining an approximate power equilibrium in the state system.

BIPOLARITY   A balance system, dominated by two superpowers, each with its own political ideology, bloc of supporters, and client states.

CENTRAL INTELLIGENCE AGENCY   The primary U.S. agency charged with gathering and assessing information, acquired by the intelligence community, that may contribute to effective foreign and defense policies.

COLD WAR   The state of fierce rivalry and tension that has characterized U.S.-Soviet relations from the end of World War II until the recent present.

COMMUNISM   An ideology that opposes capitalist institutions in favor of a collectivist society, in which land and capital are socially owned and in which class conflict and coercive state power no longer exist.

CONVENTIONAL WEAPONS   Personnel, equipment, or armaments used in defensive or offensive warfare, which do not directly require the use of nuclear weapons.

COUP D'ETAT   A sudden forcible internal uprising by a military or political group to wrest power from the established regime.

DEMOCRACY   A political system in which ultimate authority rests with the people, and which is characterized by such liberal values as individual freedom, limited government, human dignity, political eguality, and the rule of law.

FOREIGN POLICY   A nation's external goals and the strategies and tactics used to achieve them.

INTELLIGENCE COMMUNITY   Those executive branch agencies and organizations that conduct the intelligence activities that comprise the overall U.S. intelligence effort.

INTERNATIONALISM   A global strategy, whereby a nation seeks to advance its political, economic, and military interests by supporting or opposing leaders, regimes, or movements that enhance its safety and well-being.

INTERVENTIONISM   Political and/or military interference in the affairs of a state by another state or group of states to affect the internal or external policies of that state.

ISOLATIONISM   A doctrine which views the national interest of the United States as best served by avoiding foreign entanglements.

KURDS   An ancient people who inhabit a region of the Middle East that extends from Kermanshah in Iran to the northeastern section of Iraq and the eastern provinces of Turkey, and who are divided into many tribal communities and speak Indo-European dialects of their distinct Kurdish language.

NATIONAL INTEREST   An issue of paramount importance to a country's security or well-being.

NATIONALISM   Overriding attachments to one's country, reflecting a spirit of pride and a desire to preserve the identity of a group by institutionalizing it in the form of a state.

NATIONAL SECURITY   The freedom—both relative and absolute—of a country from possible armed attack or political or economic sabotage, combined with that nation's ability to respond with deadly effectiveness if attacked.

PALESTINIANS   Arabs who vacated land and homes now in or controlled by the state of Israel, many of whom reside in refugee camps in Jordan, the West Bank territory, Lebanon, and Syria, and who today seek their own independent state and an end to Israeli occupation.

REVOLUTION   A radical transformation of a state's social, political, and economic institutions, resulting from a major upheaval or the overthrow of an established government.

THIRD WORLD   The economically underdeveloped and developing countries that comprise Africa, Asia, Latin America, and the Middle East.

Chapter 1

Imperialism and Intervention

Article 1.1.   What Is the National Interest?

For the past half century, argues Alan Tonelson, America's foreign policy has been based on the principle of internationalism, a policy which the author contends has resulted in enormous costs and risks. Now, with the end of the Cold War, the United States must redefine its foreign policy, placing renewed emphasis on rebuilding its own economic and political strength. It can no longer guarantee the security and prosperity of the world while neglecting its own safety and well-being.

WHAT IS THE
NATIONAL INTEREST?

BY ALAN TONELSON

For almost half a century U.S. foreign policy has been based on internationalism—on the assumption that the security and prosperity of every place on earth is vital to America's own. Internationalism, the author argues, has entailed enormous risks and costs—more than we can continue to bear or need to pay—and offers scant promise of success. It is time, he argues, for a new foreign-policy blueprint—a stripped-down strategy whereby the United States looks out for itself and recognizes that building its own strength, not creating a perfect world, is the best guarantor of its safety and well-being

★   ★   ★   ★

FOR THE FIRST TIME SINCE THE END OF THE Second World War the United States faces the need to redefine the international requirements for its security and prosperity. Circumstances today demand that the United States rethink the ends of its foreign policy—that is to say, its national interests.

With the recent victories in the Cold War and the Gulf War, those who have been responsible for U.S. foreign policy are in a triumphant mood. There is little reason for it. The world continues to fray; ever more threatening weapons become ever more widely available. The gap between the stated ends of U.S. foreign policy and the means to achieve and pay for them remains wide and unbridgeable, as it has been for decades. Nor is it clear that the ends of U.S. foreign policy, when they are achieved, do more good than harm—for ourselves or for those we seek to assist. Perhaps most important, the recent victories have brought few benefits to the home front; indeed,

From *The Atlantic Monthly*, July 1991, pp. 35-52. Reprinted by permission.

they seem scarcely relevant to the daily lives and pressing concerns of most Americans today, or to the economic and social problems that bedevil the nation. The disconnection between the nation's needs at home and its ambitions abroad is at once bizarre and dangerous.

And yet, faced with all these facts, much of the nation's foreign-policy elite has chosen variously to ignore them or to berate those who have called attention to them.

Since the end of the Second World War, Americans have by and large defined their foreign-policy objectives in what may be called globalist or internationalist terms. Internationalism has been protean enough—liberal and conservative, hawkish and dovish, unilateralist and multilateralist—to have commanded the loyalty of figures as different as Ronald Reagan and Jimmy Carter. But its essence springs from three crucial lessons learned by most Americans and their leaders from the Great Depression and the rise of fascism during the 1930s, from the global conflagration that those events helped produce, and from the emergence of a new totalitarian threat almost immediately after that war.

The first lesson was that the United States would never know genuine security, lasting peace, and sustained prosperity unless the rest of the world also became secure, peaceful, and prosperous. The second lesson was that international security was indivisible—that the discontent that produced political extremism and, inevitably, aggression was highly contagious and bound to spread around the world no matter where it broke out. The third lesson was that the only way to achieve these fundamental goals and prevent these deadly dangers was to eliminate the conditions that breed extremism wherever they exist, and somehow to impose norms of peaceful behavior on all states.

The result of all this was a global definition of vital U.S. foreign-policy interests, with globalist international-security and economic structures to back it up. The United States supported the United Nations and forged alliances with scores of countries to guarantee security in all major regions and to deter aggression everywhere. In the process Washington expanded the definition of the U.S. defense perimeter to encompass literally every country outside the Communist world. At the same time, the imperative of resisting subversion as well as aggression everywhere in the world created an equally vital interest in the political and economic health of all these countries, which was fostered by U.S. foreign-aid programs and by an international economic system built on such mechanisms as the International Monetary Fund, the World Bank, and the General Agreement on Tariffs and Trade.

The internationalist approach led U.S. foreign-policy makers to insist that no corner of the world was so remote or insignificant that it could be ignored. Of course, not all parts of the world were given equal attention or resources. But disparities emerged not because foreign-policy makers viewed certain regions as expendable but because they perceived no serious threat either to these regions per se or to crucial international norms at the moment. Whenever a serious threat did appear, America's leaders usually favored a prompt response. The power of internationalist impulses has been underscored by military interventions, paramilitary operations, peace-keeping missions, and diplomatic initiatives in marginal countries and regions such as Angola, the Horn of Africa, and Lebanon, and also by a foreign-aid program that continuously sprinkles funds on virtually every Third World mini-state, micro-state, and basket case that has won its independence since 1945.

Internationalism has insisted that U.S. foreign policy should aim at manipulating and shaping the global environment as a whole rather than at securing or protecting a finite number of assets within that environment. It has yoked America's safety and well-being not to surviving and prospering in the here and now but to turning the world into something significantly better in the indefinite future—into a place where the forces that drive nations to clash in the first place no longer exist. Internationalism, moreover, has insisted that America has no choice but to "pay any price, bear any burden" to achieve these conditions, even though humanity has never come close to bringing them about. In so doing internationalism has sidestepped all questions of risk and cost. In fact, it has defined them out of existence.

YET EVEN BEFORE THE GORBACHEV REVOLUTION IN Soviet foreign policy—during the Cold War years, when the case could be made for a total response to the ostensibly total Soviet threat—the problems created by the internationalist approach to foreign policy were beginning to loom as large as those that it was meant to solve. Militarily and strategically, internationalism identified America's foreign-policy challenges in such a way as to turn any instance of aggression into an intolerable threat to America's own security, whether or not tangible U.S. interests were at stake, and no matter how greatly the costs of intervention may have outweighed any specific benefits that the United States could plausibly have realized. Vietnam is the classic example. Internationalism also drew America into nuclear alliances—notably, in Europe—deliberately structured to entrap the country in nuclear conflict even in cases when our own national security had not been directly affected.

Economically, as early as the late 1960s internationalism showed signs of turning into a formula for exhaustion. Richard Nixon brought the post–Second World War international monetary system to an end, in 1971, precisely because America could no longer meet its foreign-policy obligations and its domestic obligations simultaneously. Politically, the internationalist strategies and rhetoric employed by U.S. leaders throughout the postwar era generated tremendous pressures on these same leaders to follow through. Remembering the political fire storms that followed the "losses" of China and Cuba, they repeatedly resolved to prove the nation's mettle when the next outbreak of trouble occurred, reducing to almost nil the possibility that non-involvement would even be considered as an option, much less chosen.

Now, in the post–Cold War era, internationalism has become even more problematic. As our chronic budget gap shows, our foreign policy is politically unaffordable in today's America—as opposed to the America of the 1950s, when popular satisfaction with the barest skeleton of a welfare state and the country's economic predominance permitted levels of military spending two and three times as high as those of today (as a proportion of total federal spending). Internationalism continues to deny us a strategic basis for selectivity, a way of thinking about our international goals that would enable our leaders to resist the temptation to plunge into every crisis and right every wrong that life brings along, and to stand aside without being perceived by the American people as impotent or callous.

In fact, internationalism dismisses as morally reprehensible questions that other nations ask routinely in order to inject some discipline into their decision-making: What is it that we need to do in the world to secure a certain level of material and psychological well-being? What is it that we simply would like to do in the world? What are we able to do? How can we pursue our objectives without wrecking our economy, overloading our political system, or convulsing our society?

At best, post–Cold War internationalism is a recipe for intense, genuinely worrisome domestic political frustrations. Repeated failure to achieve declared foreign-policy goals and especially to avert foreign-policy outcomes officially characterized as intolerable or disastrous could poison and destabilize American politics and democracy. A string of such failures could bring calamitous international consequences by undermining America's ability to conduct a minimally responsible, rational foreign policy. At worst, internationalism raises the threat of drawing the nation into dangerous conflicts for the slightest of stakes. And even if such political and military disasters are somehow avoided, internationalism will continue to drain the nation to its core, especially if U.S. allies do not lend enough help.

Internationalism has not only locked the foreign policy of this nation of self-avowed pragmatists into a utopian mold; it has led directly to the primacy of foreign policy in American life and to the consequent neglect of domestic problems which has characterized the past fifty years. Internationalism encourages us to think more about the possible world of tomorrow than about the real world of today. Thus the strange irrelevance of our recent foreign policy, and even its victories, to the concerns of most Americans.

A New Foreign-Policy Blueprint

IF INTERNATIONALISM IS NO longer an acceptable guide for U.S. foreign policy, what should take its place? What *can* take its place? Assuming that the means available to U.S. foreign-policy makers will not change significantly anytime soon—that American scientists will not devise a new ultimate weapon and preserve monopoly control of it; that U.S. allies will remain reluctant to increase their military and foreign-aid spending dramatically or to compensate the United States for its leadership role in other ways; that the American public will remain unwilling to make the sacrifices needed to carry out an internationalist foreign policy effectively (through some combination of higher taxes, reduced consumption, and reduced demand for public services); and that the unprecedented increases in national economic productivity needed to finance such a foreign policy soundly will remain nowhere in sight—the United States will have to make some profound adjustments.

If the United States cannot hope to achieve the desired level of security and prosperity by underwriting the security and prosperity of countries all over the world, and by enforcing whatever global norms of economic and political behavior this ambition requires, then it must anchor its security and prosperity in a less-than-utopian set of objectives. It must therefore distinguish between what it must do that is absolutely essential for achieving this more modest set of objectives and those things it might do that are not essential. It must, in other words, begin to think in terms not of the whole world's well-being but rather of purely national interests.

The adjustments that are required would produce a foreign policy largely unrecognizable to Americans today. The U.S. government would still be a major force in world affairs, and the American people would still trade with, invest in, work in, and travel to other lands. But the preferred instruments of the new foreign policy would differ radically from those of internationalism. And the policy itself would spring from a completely different vision of America, of its strengths and weaknesses and, most important, its basic purposes. The new orientation, moreover, would reflect the manifest (if seldom articulated) wishes of the great majority of Americans, rather than those of the small, privileged caste of government officials, former government officials, professors, think-tank denizens, and journalists whose dreamy agenda has long dominated foreign-policy decision-making in America. For surely American foreign policy has been conducted with utter disregard for the home front largely because it has been made by people whose lives and needs have almost nothing in common with those of the mass of their countrymen.

Unlike internationalism, interest-based thinking rests on a series of assumptions drawn both from common sense and from classical strategic maxims; and it can help prevent counterproductive outcomes by forcing decision-makers continually to examine the impact of their policies on national security and well-being within a finite time frame. In the first place, a foreign policy derived from interest-based thinking would accept today's anarchic system of competing nation-states as a given. It would neither seek to change the nature of this system nor assume the system's imminent transformation. Instead, the new policy would confine itself to securing certain specific objectives that are intrinsically important to America's security and welfare—for example, the protection of regions that are important sources of raw materials or critical manufactured goods, those that are major loci of investment or prime markets, and those that by virtue of their location are strategically vital.

Interest-based thinking holds that in such a world U.S. national interests can and must be distinguished from the interests of the international system itself and from those of other individual states. This is just common sense. Because states differ in location, size, strength, natural wealth, historical experience, values, economic systems, degree and type of social organization, and many other particulars, their foreign-policy needs and wants—their interests—cannot always be identical or harmonious, and will in fact sometimes clash with those of certain other countries and those of whatever larger international community those states are supposed to belong to. Internationalism's assumption of an ultimate harmony of interests among states and between states and the larger system often obscures these critical truths.

In addition, interest-based thinking assumes that since the world lacks a commonly accepted referee or means of resolving clashes of interests, states cannot count on other states or entities to define their interests or to protect them. States therefore need the means to accomplish these tasks on their own. Interest-based thinking assumes that because countries can in the end rely only on their own devices, national self-reliance and freedom of action are intrinsic goods. With an internationalist foreign policy, these imperatives tend to get lost in the shuffle.

Further, interest-based thinking maintains that because resources are always relatively scarce (if they were not, the discipline of economics would not exist), once foreign policy moves beyond the quest for what strategists call core security—the nation's physical, biological survival, and the preservation of its territorial integrity and political independence—the specific, concrete benefits sought must be brought into some sustainable alignment with the policy's economic, social, and political costs. And the payoff of policies cannot be put off into the long-term future. A country with finite available resources simply does not have the luxury of infinite patience.

THUS AN INTEREST-BASED FOREIGN POLICY WOULD tend to rule out economic initiatives deemed necessary for the international system's health if those initiatives wound up siphoning more wealth out of this country (in the form of net investment, interest on debt, military expenditures, foreign aid, trade credits, jobs destroyed by imports versus those created by exports, and so forth) than they brought in. Similarly, it would oppose economic policies that actually destroyed wealth—for example, by stimulating inflation, by committing excessive resources to economically unproductive military spending and research and development, by necessitating excessive currency devaluations, by requiring exorbitant interest rates that discourage productive investment, or by blithely accepting the loss of industries that have been technology and productivity leaders for the sake of free-trade ideology or alliance unity.

Unlike internationalism, an interest-based foreign policy would not emphasize alliances and multilateral institutions, or promote worldwide economic efficiency to the point at which U.S. dependence on other countries is seen as a good in and of itself. Rather, the new policy would recognize the importance of maintaining the maximum degree of freedom of action and self-reliance in a still dangerous world. Indeed, an interest-based policy would also recognize that the related realms of economics and technology are as nakedly strategic as the military-political realm. While the Cold War was raging, internationalists viewed economic initiatives and technology as little more than assets to deny the Communist world or as a collection of baubles, to be doled out periodically as political favors to allies and neutrals. The end of the Cold

INTERNATIONALISM
CONTINUES TO DENY US A WAY OF THINKING ABOUT OUR INTERNATIONAL GOALS THAT WOULD ENABLE OUR LEADERS TO RESIST THE TEMPTATION TO PLUNGE INTO EVERY CRISIS AND RIGHT EVERY WRONG.

War has produced many acknowledgments by internationalists of the rising importance of economic power. But even this outlook still tends to be nonstrategic. Internationalists still assume that, economically speaking, winning and losing have no meaning whatever—unless one cares about national pride—so long as the competition takes place among nonhostile states. And they continue to believe that economic competition can always be kept reasonable and constructive, as if it were an athletic contest.

Despite its heightened sensitivity to questions involving resources, the new foreign policy would proceed from an assumption of American strength, not weakness. While conceding that the United States is neither powerful nor wealthy enough to remake the world in its own image, or to achieve security and prosperity for itself by securing these benefits for every country on the planet, it would recognize that America is powerful, wealthy, and geopolitically secure enough to flourish without carrying out this ambitious agenda. And it would understand that the cultivation of America's economic and military strength, not the creation of international institutions or global norms of behavior, is the best guarantor of national independence and well-being over the long run. The emergence of transnational threats such as environmental destruction and drug trafficking does nothing to reduce the importance of national power. The nations whose preferred solutions are adopted will be those bringing the most chips to the table.

PERHAPS MOST IMPORTANT, AN INTEREST-BASED U.S. foreign policy would firmly subordinate international activism and the drive for world leadership to domestic concerns. Indeed, it would spring from new and more realistic ideas about what can be expected of a country's official foreign policy in the first place. The new approach would acknowledge that the modest policy tools actually at a government's command—weapons, money, and suasion—cannot build a fundamentally new and more benign or congenial world political order, or change the millennia-old patterns of poverty, tradition, and misrule in which so much of humanity is trapped. Such changes can occur only on the organic level of international relations, as the result of informal social, cultural, and economic interactions over long stretches of time. And even if modern science and technology have greatly accelerated the pace of change, there is little reason to think that change can be controlled or manipulated at the operational level of international relations—by a state's day-to-day foreign policy.

The interest-based approach would also eschew any notion of foreign policy as first and foremost a vehicle for spreading American values, for building national character, for expressing any individual's or group's emotional, philosophical, or political preferences, or for carrying out any of a series of additional overseas missions that, however appealing, bear only marginally on protecting and enriching the nation: promoting peace, stability, democracy, and development around the world; protecting human rights; establishing international law; building collective security; exercising something called leadership; creating a new world order; competing globally with the Soviets (or whomever) for power and influence. None of these sweeping, inspiring, quintessentially internationalist goals can serve as guides for U.S. foreign policy. They are simply free-floating ideals. From time to time they may represent ways of advancing particular and advanceable American interests. But first we have to know what interests we want to advance. An interest-based approach would also reject the idea that meeting a set of global responsibilities can be the lodestar of U.S. foreign policy. Whose definition of this unavoidably subjective notion would be chosen? And on what basis?

Nevertheless, the interest-based approach would recognize that in a democracy such views—that is, simple national preferences—frequently influence foreign policy. That is to say, Americans from time to time favor a course of action (invading Grenada, for example, or aiding the Kurds) not because it serves vital national interests but simply because they like it. An interest-based foreign policy would acknowledge that the citizens of a democracy have every right to choose whatever foreign policy they please; certainly they are answerable to no one but themselves. And it would hold that there is nothing intrinsically wrong with sometimes basing a foreign policy on the whim or preference of the majority. The new approach would insist, however, that the American public be willing to finance its whims soundly—something the United States government has not done for decades. If the public favors aid to insurgents around the world, or fighting poverty in developing countries, or helping new democracies in Eastern Europe or Latin

America, or defending certain parts of the world because of a shared cultural heritage, then it should be willing to raise the revenues needed to pay for these policies. If the revenues are not forthcoming, the whims are probably not very strong to begin with and are probably best ignored.

The new foreign policy certainly would not preclude acting on principle. But it would greatly de-emphasize conforming to abstract standards of behavior. In fact, the new foreign policy would shy away from any overarching strategy of or conceptual approach to international relations. Unlike isolationism, for instance, it would not elevate non-intervention to the status of a commandment. And it would view other popular doctrines of American foreign policy—containment, détente, multilateralism, unilateralism, idealism, realism, the achievement of a global balance of power—with skepticism. It would be free to use whatever approach or combination of approaches seemed likeliest to achieve the best ends for the United States in a given situation. Its only rule of thumb would be "whatever works" to preserve or enhance America's security and prosperity and—provided that Americans are willing to pay the bills—what the country collectively wishes to define as its psychological well-being.

Internationalists worrying about this policy's potential lack of moral content might think harder about channeling more of their compassion into good works at home—where there is no shortage of grievous wrongs to be righted and where, as is not the case in many other countries, the social and institutional wherewithal for successful reform actually exists.

As for the issue of defining the ends of U.S. foreign policy beyond core security, there are no magic formulas to rely on. Once national survival and independence are assured, all the major objectives of U.S. foreign policy must be subjected to a rigorous cost-risk analysis. If objectives are truly vital—if physical survival or the continuance of America's democratic values and institutions are at stake—costs and risks can never exceed benefits. But if objectives are less than vital, costs and risks can exceed benefits. For a country with America's built-in geopolitical and economic advantages—with its capacity for achieving security, prosperity, and independence—the top priority is not to settle on a fixed definition of vital interests. It is much more important to learn to think rigorously and strategically about foreign policy, in order to ensure that whatever set of interests is chosen is not so ambitious that it exposes the country to more risks than it repulses, drains it of more strength than it adds, and makes Americans feel bad about themselves and their nation more than it makes them feel good.

The new policy's aversion to grand doctrines and frameworks would be in keeping with the conviction that the fundamental purpose of U.S. foreign policy should be nothing more glamorous than attempting to cope with whatever discrete developments arise abroad that could endanger American security and prosperity. The stress would not be on comprehensive initiatives to get at the root causes of the world's ills and conflicts, on promoting greater international cooperation or integration, or on getting on the right side of history—for these favorite internationalist aims entail enormous costs and offer scant promise of success. In a perilous strategic world, it is usually a mistake to consider foreign policy to be an activist instrument at all. Rather, Americans should start thinking of foreign policy in terms of avoiding problems, reducing vulnerabilities and costs, maximizing options, buying time, and muddling through—objectives that may be uninspiring but that are well suited to a strong, wealthy, geographically isolated country.

Still, how might the new approach affect specific aspects of U.S. foreign policy? What alternatives would it entail?

THE SOVIET UNION: ONLY TREAT THE SYMPTOMS

THE INTERNATIONALISTS' utopianism has been evident even where utopia has seemed furthest away—in dealings with the Soviet Union. Since the beginning of the Cold War, Washington has been striving to achieve genuine, durable superpower cooperation. For all the hostility and conflict that has marked U.S.-Soviet relations in the postwar era, American leaders have aimed to create a relationship that would have the capacity to elicit desired Soviet behavior irrespective of power considerations. Yet even in the Gorbachev era this objective is badly misconceived.

It may seem strange to describe postwar U.S. policy toward the Soviets as a quest for community. Through the mid-1980s America built a vast, globe-girdling military machine to contain Soviet power, fought what it viewed as Moscow's proxies in the Third World, placed tight clamps on Western economic dealing with the Soviet bloc, and fenced with the Soviets diplomatically in countless forums. Yet from its inception Soviet containment has been portrayed as the first stage in a process aimed at ending East-West hostility by transforming the USSR and other Communist countries into model international citizens.

Since 1985 the revolution in Soviet

foreign policy sparked by Mikhail Gorbachev has created a widespread impression that Moscow has been converted to American ways of thinking, even to the point of denouncing the militarism of its past foreign policy and spouting the rhetoric of international law and common security. Internationalism's goal seems closer than ever.

Nothing, however, could be further from the truth. Moscow's unconditional acquiescence in German unification should have made this obvious. A country that accepts the rebirth of a mortal enemy because its political survival may depend on substantial foreign aid from that erstwhile enemy is not a country that has seen the light but one that has been defeated. Since the late 1980s the West has not been negotiating with a sovereign equal but has been unwittingly dictating the terms of surrender. Moscow is de-emphasizing classical concepts of strategic and economic self-interest because those options are no longer available. It speaks of transcending power because it has none—at least none to prevent outcomes that it has understandably dreaded for decades. It is taking a leap not of faith but of desperation.

The moment the Soviets become stronger, or feel stronger, the cooperative veneer will be stripped away. And even if a candidate endorsed by Mother Teresa were to win power in Moscow, geography alone would guarantee that Soviet and U.S. aims will not always be compatible. Recall the U.S.-Soviet tiff that developed near the end of the Gulf War. Whatever they thought of Saddam Hussein, Soviet leaders were understandably uncomfortable with a Western and Arab force of half a million soldiers, armed with aircraft carriers, tanks, self-propelled artillery pieces, bombers, cruise missiles, and a swarm of other smart weapons, perched close to their southern doorstep.

How can internationalism cope with such problems? The theory behind our quest for East-West community holds that such tensions aren't supposed to break out anymore. How can this provide helpful guidance for policy-makers? Here internationalism's shortcomings result from its assumption that viable U.S. policies can be based on analyzing international threats and conditions rather than on identifying U.S. interests. The Bush Administration and most outside analysts have justified a new course for America's Soviet policy—notably involving cuts in defense spending—by pointing to Gorbachev's foreign-policy spectaculars and, to a lesser extent, his domestic reforms. By the fall of last year, however, the pace of Soviet diplomatic surrender began to slow. The cause of domestic reform also began to lose ground. If the situation worsens, the internationalist method of divining U.S. interests indirectly might dictate reversing the current modest decline in U.S. military budgets. But

who believes that an increase in the Pentagon's budget will occur, even after the Gulf War? And which internationalists will call for the tax increases or domestic-spending cuts needed to finance a new military buildup responsibly? The alternative internationalist recipe for Soviet policy holds no more promise: promoting reform by aiding the Soviet economy. Even most internationalists admit that Moscow's problems are so vast that no realistically available amount of American or even Western resources can suffice to solve them—assuming that the main problem is lack of resources.

Thus the quandary looming before us, thanks to internationalism: We supposedly have a vital stake in bringing democracy and capitalism to the Soviet Union, but we are powerless to do so. And we will not go back to a Cold War military posture if reform fails. It's hard to imagine clearer proof of policy breakdown.

A POLICY THAT DERIVED FROM SERIOUS THINKING about national interests would look very different. Because the United States, acting on the basis of such a policy, would regard the root causes of international conflicts as basically uncontrollable even in a post-Communist age, and because it would doubt that in achieving important foreign-policy goals any arrangements or institutions could adequately substitute for power, it would concern itself primarily with the symptoms of U.S.-Soviet rivalry should this rivalry heat up again. Moreover, because it would be acutely conscious of the cost of and limits on U.S. power, it would address only those symptoms that directly affected regions or activities important to the United States. Thus the United States would concern itself with the activities of the Soviets (or other hostile powers) in Third World trouble spots mainly when the fate of such trouble spots bore directly on America's core security (for example, Mexico and the Caribbean Basin). Regarding countries that represent major markets or sources of critical raw materials or manufactures, the new policy toward the Soviets would require officials to ask whether the costs and risks of securing these assets outweighed the benefits of non-internationalist solutions. Because the United States under the new policy would not see international peace and security as a seamless web, it would respond to many instances of Soviet (or any other) troublemaking by doing nothing at all.

The new policy would also strictly curb U.S. objectives when responses to Soviet or other hostile challenges were necessary. Unlike internationalism, it would not see every one of these challenges as a golden opportunity to advance the cause of global cooperation or to go after the roots of the troubles that hostile powers were seeking to exploit. An interest-based policy would view such crises as discrete problems that, no matter how alarming, America could realistically hope only to deter or beat back as they arose.

The new policy toward the Soviets would not rule out aiding Moscow economically or technically—provided that U.S. taxpayers were willing to foot the bill or take the revenues out of other programs. But it would focus on ensuring that America could tolerate the consequences if Soviet reform fails. In this respect, Washington's top priority must be coping with the possibility that a breakdown of order in the Soviet Union will fragment control over Soviet nuclear weapons and increase the odds of an accidental launch or a launch by extremists. A non-internationalist policy would address this specific military problem not by vainly trying to hold the Soviet Union together but by constructing the kind of thin missile-defense system that seems technologically within our grasp. Above all, it would recognize that without nuclear weapons the Soviet Union is itself today little more than what Walter Lippmann, in 1947, described the regions adjacent to the Soviet Union as consisting of: a collection of "disorganized, disunited, feeble or disorderly nations, tribes and factions." For America, the only available option worse than strategic detachment would be futile engagement.

In essence, America's Soviet policy should be to have no overarching Soviet policy as such. Rather than seeking positive objectives, the policy's goals would be predominantly negative—to make sure that Soviet actions do not damage the security or welfare of the United States or interfere with any ambitions that it truly holds dear.

FRIENDS AND ALLIES: AN END TO SMOTHERING

IF U.S. INTERNATIONALISTS have viewed relations with the Soviet Union as the wilderness they have been trying to civilize, they have seen relations with major treaty allies as a promised land they have already reached. Nevertheless, U.S. policy toward Western Europe, Japan, and the countries where we maintain military bases vividly represents how the internationalist approach to securing U.S. interests can heighten more security risks than it neutralizes and drain America of more wealth than it brings in.

Since 1945 this internationalist alliance strategy—especially regarding Western Europe and Japan—has aimed at more complex, even more grandiose, goals than has generally been realized. The objectives have involved far more than protecting Western Europe and Japan against Soviet military aggression and political intimidation, as should now be clear from Washington's insistence that sizable U.S. nuclear and conventional forces remain in place in these regions even after most Soviet forces pull back. Nor does U.S. alliance strategy limit itself to that task of protection plus the task of preventing German and Japanese revanchism. Instead, both aims flow from a larger strategy: one of meeting all the major needs—principally those for security and prosperity—that historically led the Western European countries and Japan to conduct their own foreign policies in the first place.

This is why America has been determined to provide an enormous, guaranteed market for these now wealthy, heavily trade-dependent, and heavily protected countries (often at considerable cost to its own fortunes) as well as to cover them with a nuclear shield. In the case of Japan, the strategy has gone even further. Not only did America write the constitution that was instrumental in turning Japan into a political and military midget. (Unlike the members of NATO, Japan is not obliged by its security treaty with Washington to come to America's aid in the event of attack.) It provided the economic blueprint that Japan followed to become a highly bureaucratized, monomaniacal, mercantilist powerhouse, and encouraged Japan to rely on America, not the rest of Asia, for most of its export market. Since 1945, then, the United States has been struggling to contain not only the Soviet Union but all the world's great nations—to do nothing less than prevent them from acting like great nations in the first place.

This strategy of smothering the foreign-policy (and economic) independence of Western Europe and Japan initially constituted an effort to balance two deeply held but conflicting goals set by U.S. foreign-policy makers shortly after the Second World War. On the one hand, they were determined to put these regions back on their feet—in order to create both markets for American goods and powerful allies capable of resisting Soviet power and of helping the United States manage the rest of the globe. On the other hand, U.S. officials knew that rebuilding these nations raised the possibility of restoring the pre-1914 global balance of power, which had proved highly unstable and in fact had collapsed into two terrible conflicts. In a nuclear age the next world war might very well be the last.

As the Cold War intensified, American internationalists convinced themselves that they could have it both ways: their allies could be strong enough to help in the struggle against the Soviets but not so strong as to challenge U.S. world leadership. Smothering, the means to

IN A PERILOUS STRATEGIC WORLD, AMERICANS SHOULD START THINKING OF FOREIGN POLICY IN TERMS OF AVOIDING PROBLEMS, REDUCING VULNERABILITIES AND COSTS, MAXIMIZING OPTIONS, AND MUDDLING THROUGH.

this end, was conceived of gradually during the 1950s and involved a huge forward deployment of U.S. conventional and nuclear forces in Europe and the Far East; guaranteeing the allies' prosperity by opening U.S. markets wide to their exports; tolerating and even encouraging their own protectionism (the European Community, a discriminatory trade bloc, was avidly promoted by Washington); and upholding a stable international monetary order.

The most obvious problems with this strategy have been difficult enough. America has paid the lion's share of the free world's defense costs. And it has borne the lion's share of the nuclear risks in its major alliances as well. In Europe, in particular, the strategy of "coupling," by deploying nuclear weapons in such a way as to deny Washington any choice in whether or not to use them, has sought to convince the Soviets that the United States would indeed use nuclear weapons if necessary to repel an attack and run the risk of all-out nuclear war—something that U.S. leaders have understandably been loath to tell the public. In fact, from the signing of the first U.S.-Soviet strategic-arms agreement, in 1972, to the breakdown of communism in Eastern Europe, in 1989, the story of intra-alliance relations was the story of Western Europe and America trying to foist the bulk of this risk onto each other. Meanwhile, Washington's indifference to maintaining U.S. economic strength led America to make most of the near-term sacrifices demanded by the allies to hold the common military front together and to keep the Western economy stable.

This strategy has entailed a less obvious but more troubling long-range cost. Numerous analysts have written—and many Europeans have complained—that America has frequently exploited the dollar's key currency role in the world economy for its own advantage. Specifically, the United States has been able to lean on its allies to finance the huge balance-of-payments deficits it has run, and thus to avoid the painful discipline imposed by the international economic system on other deficit countries, ranging from Brazil to Britain. What these complaints have overlooked, however, is that this arrangement has been bad for the United States in the long run. It is at most a second-best strategy, a substitute for repairing the mounting structural problems of the U.S. economy. It is second-best because it suffers a fatal inter-

nal flaw: ultimately, the real political and military clout on which it is based cannot be wielded without that real economic strength which it neglects, and has in fact squandered.

Mainly because the circumstances that made it possible have changed, the smothering strategy needs to change. The overwhelming nuclear superiority that enabled America to deter Soviet conventional attacks without worrying about Soviet retaliatory strikes is gone, and Europe has known this ever since the goal of superpower strategic parity was formally endorsed in the U.S.-Soviet strategic-arms agreement of 1972. Gone, too, is the overwhelming relative economic strength that enabled the United States literally to buy Western European and Japanese cooperation without requiring visible sacrifices from the American people—or exacting tribute from the allies themselves. In fact, by the late 1960s the smothering strategy had turned hegemonic in all but name. The United States brazenly exported first inflation and then sky-high interest rates in order to run larger and larger budget and overall payments deficits. As the price of alliance has risen for Western Europe and Japan, their willingness to accept subordinate status and entrust their fate to U.S. leadership has understandably diminished. And the three power centers will surely continue to drift apart strategically as the Soviet threat that helped hold them together fades. Worse, the short-term gains reaped by the United States came at the expense of its long-term ability to create wealth.

Internationalists advance powerful arguments for persisting in adherence to the smothering strategy. Stability in Europe and the Far East has indeed been achieved, and America has undeniably benefited. But, as usual, internationalists miss the main question. It is not whether smothering is necessary, a so-called vital interest. Smothering is not in fact necessary, because the stability of Europe and the Far East no longer bears on America's physical survival; our nuclear arsenal affords whatever military protection we need. The main question is whether these benefits of smothering can be achieved at tolerable cost, and for two related reasons the answer increasingly is no.

One reason is that the strategy is now completely unsustainable for America. The military budgets required to provide the degree of military protection or stabilizing

13

"assurance" that the allies still want are a formula for the continued hemorrhaging of U.S. economic strength and the fall of American living standards vis-à-vis these countries'. This decline has become unacceptable. The other reason is that although Western Europe and Japan and the rest of the Far East plainly wish to remain stable, they no longer wish to be contained. However these regions wind up organizing themselves, they will increasingly assert control over their own destinies no matter what America wants or does, cultivating their own strengths, pursuing their own goals, and placing their own interests above everyone else's. This increased Western European and Japanese independence will undoubtedly make the world less stable. Will the United States continue to try to stop the inevitable? Or will it focus on coping with the consequences of a less stable world?

The Bush Administration currently seems torn between two inconsistent beliefs. One is that there is no alternative to smothering—hence the President's repeated insistence that smaller but still sizable American conventional and nuclear forces will remain in Europe and the Far East. The other is that institutional arrangements—for example, a U.S.-European-Japanese troika—can be devised to make up at least partly for a diminished American military presence. Neither belief seems promising as a basis for policy. The first assumes that a level of military deployments in Europe and the Far East can be found which is low enough to grant the United States real budgetary relief and just high enough to provide real assurance and stability for those regions. The second suffers from a practical flaw: institutional arrangements cannot substitute for a power shortage. Had such arrangements been important in shaping America's alliances, in theory they could be rejiggered—burdens and risks could be shifted. But U.S. alliances have been predominantly creations of power—the power to smother. The burden of proof rests on internationalists to show that the leap to true cooperation can be made—that America can get from here to there.

In fact, one danger created by the Gulf War is that America's smashing victory will tempt Washington into a new burst of hegemonism. After all, the current European and Japanese weakness outside the economic sphere has been exposed anew. The allies' willingness to join or finance a U.S.-dominated military operation has been demonstrated—even in a case when all except the United Kingdom obviously had serious misgivings. Add in that George Bush is manifestly uninterested in domestic economic revitalization, and it is easy to envision him concluding that he has given new life to an internationalist arm-twisting strategy.

YET EVEN IN A POST–SADDAM HUSSEIN WORLD THE fatal flaw of smothering remains: a strategy of manipulation and arm-twisting is not viable because it neglects and even fritters away the economic strength that it depends on. A new, non-internationalist approach would reorient U.S. policy around two objectives. The first would be to decouple America's security from that of its allies, and above all to eliminate—not reduce but eliminate—the automatic nuclear risks built into the alliances. There is nothing intrinsically wrong with a decision by the American people to help their allies resist aggression militarily. But they should be free to make this choice. Coupling and forward-deployment strategies (deploying enough U.S. troops and their families on allied soil to make the threat of nuclear response credible) are designed to lock Americans into what is by far the most important decision they could ever face as a people—the decision to precipitate a nuclear war. Once America's overwhelming nuclear superiority faded, adherence to this strategy became nothing less than depraved, especially since it grows out of the Western European countries' refusal to pay for an adequate conventional defense. The United States should announce the unilateral withdrawal of all of its nuclear forces and all but token conventional forces from Europe within a fixed period—say, two years. And the vast majority of these forces should be demobilized. Removing most of our armed forces from Europe is doubly important given the new potential for instability on the Continent caused by the fall of the Soviet empire. If order breaks down in Eastern Europe, the last thing we should want is large numbers of American soldiers and nuclear weapons right next door.

Second, the United States should seek to maintain access to European and East Asian markets not by wielding military and political clout but by the much more reliable strategy of insisting on complete reciprocity in trade and investment and restoring our leadership in a wide range of major industries. The aim must be to produce goods of such high quality that even the most protectionist nations will be forced to buy them or fall behind economically and technologically. The savings achievable through troop cuts could provide much of the financing that a domestic-revitalization strategy would need. Of course, it would still be up to Americans to spend this money wisely. But first we have to give ourselves the option.

Regarding the Far East, the coupling problem is less serious, since the U.S. allies (except Korea) lie offshore and therefore have never been vulnerable to sudden ground attacks from the Soviet Union or China. Moreover, the cost of maintaining America's forces in the Far East is lower than the cost of maintaining its forces in Europe. Still, the prime mission of the Far East forces, especially in a post–Cold War era, is completely misconceived. Japan can no longer be contained at a reasonable cost to the United States. Until that distant day when China attains modernity, Japan will be the region's natural predominant power. It is already East Asia's leading supplier of private capital and foreign aid, by far. And despite America's historical opposition to the emergence of anything like Japan's wartime Greater East Asia Co-Prosperity Sphere, the Japanese-supervised integration of the region is well under way.

If Japan (which has every interest in using its power peacefully and constructively in the Far East) and its neighbors (who still fear the Japanese, even as they pursue Tokyo's economic vision) want U.S. forces in the region to ease their anxieties, Washington should provide them—as long as the local countries pick up the tab (including the "rent" that America pays for its Philippine bases, if maintaining those bases is something the local countries want). If they refuse, the United States should simply go home (and in the process end the degrading practice of submitting to Philippine blackmail for something that Manila needs much more than we do). What-

ever U.S. forces remain in the region, moreover, should be deployed so as to maximize America's freedom of choice in using them. And any U.S. nuclear weapons should be deployed in naval units well offshore, especially from Korea, which remains the region's most dangerous flashpoint.

U.S. alliance policy should vigorously seek opportunities for cooperation with the countries of Europe and East Asia. But advancing U.S. national interests will depend on keeping this cooperation ad hoc—abandoning the illusion of restoring perfect control and establishing idyllic relationships—and on our maintaining the strength to drive hard bargains. We need both the diplomatic skill to create healthy partnerships when specific interests coincide and the street smarts to protect our interests when they do not.

THE THIRD WORLD: TIME TO DISENGAGE

INTERNATIONALISM'S GENIUS for focusing U.S. attention on sideshows has nowhere been more evident than in America's relations with the generally weak, poor, politically fragile nations of the Third World. During the Cold War, internationalism's characteristically exaggerated fears—of Soviet power and prestige, and of losing valuable military bases, raw-material deposits, and export markets to hostile forces—turned the Third World into the only theater in which U.S. and Soviet ambitions clashed violently, and the theater in which these conflicts most often threatened to ignite wider war, from Korea to Indochina, from Cuba to the Middle East, from Afghanistan to Central America. Meanwhile, internationalism's equally excessive hopes led U.S. policy-makers to try to combat the Soviet threat not only by helping protect these countries militarily and organizing them into facsimiles of alliances but also by spending hundreds of billions of dollars trying to turn them into modern, subversion-resistant societies.

The Cold War is over, but similar fears continue to drive U.S. policy in the Third World. The specter of local tyrants armed with weapons of mass destruction and long-range delivery systems has replaced the specter of the Soviets, while access to the same markets and raw materials and even most of the same bases is considered as vital as ever. Archetypal internationalist policies—regional security arrangements, multilateral arms and technology export curbs, and aid programs to promote eco-

nomic development and democracy—are still being proposed to deal with potential Third World problems.

With or without the Soviet threat, internationalists have portrayed America's extensive involvement in Third World countries as a security and economic imperative, resulting from tight, indissoluble links between the Third World's fate and our own. To the extent that these links exist, however, they are largely artificial—the products of internationalist policy. Since well before the Cold War ended, the importance of the Third World to the United States has been shrinking steadily. America's internationalist foreign policy perversely has sought to reverse this process, and to bind America's future ever more closely to these generally woebegone lands and their desperate problems. Worse, where troubles in the Third World do cause America difficulties, internationalism has prevented the United States from pursuing superior non-internationalist solutions.

With respect to security, the value to America of most Third World military bases on the Soviet periphery has been eliminated by the deployment of intercontinental nuclear weapons, which enable U.S. nuclear warheads to strike any spot on earth. And although the military arsenals of many Third World countries will continue to expand, America's military edge over the developing world will probably widen for the foreseeable future, as the latest advances in microelectronics and other technologies are built into American weapons systems. The

Gulf War should have made that clear. In this vein, the Vietnam debacle should have taught us only that the United States will have problems using its military to serve its interests in the Third World when those interests are absurdly peripheral, and also when its objectives (in this case, nation-building) are utopian.

As for America's economic stakes in the Third World, they have always been small and they continue to shrink. Take the idea of the Third World and its teeming billions as the world's last great untapped market and the potential salvation of U.S. industry. Meaningless aggregate figures make this broader version of the myth of the China market seem credible. In fact America's Third World trade is dominated by a handful of countries—the so-called newly industrialized countries (the South Koreas and Taiwans of the world), Mexico, and the OPEC oil producers. U.S. trade with the rest of the Third World rose impressively during the 1970s, but only because the West lent those countries so much money that some increase in their purchasing power was inevitable. Unfortunately, when the loans came due, it became clear that the money had been used not to encourage sound, self-sustaining growth—and thus the creation of reliable markets for U.S. products—but to line rulers' pockets and to finance politically popular national shopping sprees. The resulting debt crisis represents simply the return of those nations to their historical state of economic stagnation following an artificially induced spending boom. Consequently, private U.S. and other Western banks are falling all over themselves to cut their losses and get out of the business of making new loans to most Third World countries (except for loans made involuntarily, as part of government-mandated rescue packages). Indeed, on the whole, all forms of private foreign investment in the Third World are in relative decline. In 1956–1960 direct Western private investments in the Third World amounted to 27.4 percent of the $126.5 billion (in constant dollars) in net Western financial flows to those countries. In 1981–1985 such investments represented only 11.1 percent of the total Western financial flow of $442.4 billion—and this period included some of the peak foreign-lending years.

The United States is heavily reliant on Third World countries for many strategically and economically critical raw materials. But resource availability is hardly a cut-and-dried concept. Appearances to the contrary, statistics on the availability of such resources as petroleum and metals do not tell us definitively how much of these substances remains in the ground. Geologists simply do not know enough to provide credible numbers. And the domination of world production of certain resources by certain countries does not mean that those countries possess the planet's sole deposits. It simply means that their easily accessible supplies can be extracted and refined at costs that the market considers profitable at a given time. Import dependence, moreover, is not the same thing as

vulnerability to supply cutoffs. Specifically, the more countries that supply a given material, the less likely it is that a price increase or a supply interruption from any single source will be damaging to the United States.

In addition, materials science today is an exceptionally promising research field, and many new forms of plastics, ceramics, and composites are superior to naturally occurring metals and the alloys made from them. As a result, the smokestack industries now use decreasing amounts of Third World raw materials in their products. (The new information-intensive industries, of course, have never relied heavily on Third World raw materials.) And the development of synthetics will only accelerate, further lessening our reliance on Third World raw materials.

AMERICAN INTERESTS IN THE THIRD WORLD IN FACT boil down to a handful of concrete issues. On the security side the United States needs to worry about only one region: the Caribbean Basin. And in this region it has only two important concerns: that no hostile outside force establish any significant military or intelligence presence, and that Mexico not fall apart economically and socially.

The United States cannot live with social and economic chaos on its southern border, or insulate itself from the consequences. Yet turning such an enormous, corruption-ridden country as Mexico into a success story seems impossible using standard internationalist tools like economic- and political-development programs. The United States might do better to abandon the dream of remaking Mexico and aim instead at keeping the lid on—helping Mexico muddle through as long as possible. Desperation has forced the Mexican government to make some promising economic-liberalization moves. It should be pressured to make more. The proposed U.S.-Mexico free-trade agreement might help as well, provided that Mexico is not permitted to become either an export platform that gives European and Asian companies easy access to the U.S. market, or more of a sweatshop for American firms seeking to evade strict U.S. environmental, child-labor, and occupational-safety laws.

America's policy toward the Caribbean Basin in general has been wasteful and roundabout. Thus, for a decade after the Sandinista revolution, in 1979, liberal and conservative internationalists alike convinced themselves that securing U.S. interests in Central America required turning that region's countries into something they had never been—stable, democratic, and prosperous societies that would never think of hosting unfriendly foreign presences. The Carter and Reagan Administrations both pumped hundreds of millions in aid into the region and oversaw reform programs down to the village level.

Central America isn't in great demand today as a base for operations against the United States, but if this threat returns, Washington should remember that the lack of

THE NEW APPROACH WOULD ACKNOWLEDGE THAT THE MODEST POLICY TOOLS ACTUALLY AT A GOVERNMENT'S COMMAND—WEAPONS, MONEY, AND SUASION—CANNOT BUILD A FUNDAMENTALLY NEW AND MORE BENIGN WORLD POLITICAL ORDER.

democracy, development, and social justice in Central America—however unfortunate for people who have to live there—has never appreciably affected U.S. fortunes. We are strong enough to rely on simpler responses than those chosen by Jimmy Carter and Ronald Reagan. The United States should keep unfriendly foreign powers out of the hemisphere by using and threatening to use force unilaterally. Washington could implicitly propose a new regional compact: local populations would be allowed to mismanage themselves to their hearts' content, provided that no foreign-policy decisions were made that America deemed troublesome. Washington alone would be judge, jury, and court of appeals. Countries that disobeyed would be punished—perhaps in the form of air or naval bombardment, or full economic embargoes. Countries that obeyed would be left alone, no matter which political faction happened to be in power in a given week.

The United States also needs to think about the proliferation of advanced weapons and long-range delivery systems throughout the Third World. Even after the Gulf War, however, the most commonly proposed internationalist solution to the threat of missile attack from Third World countries is one that has already failed: multilateral controls on the military and commercial technologies needed to make missile weapons. This solution has failed for entirely predictable reasons. The worldwide economic integration to which internationalists love to point means that technology—knowledge—is excruciatingly difficult to contain. It is all the more so when the line between military and civilian technology in the crucial high-tech sectors is blurry, when, consequently, many of the key technologies are in private hands (or heads), and when demand is high. In other words, the problem cannot be legislated out of existence. It is hard to see that diplomacy can do much either. How could the West possibly convince Third World countries that nuclear and other high-tech weapons are not valuable assets, especially in the dangerous regions in which many of the countries are located? And regional security agreements aimed at obviating the need for such weapons are little more than pieces of paper. If states felt secure enough to rely on such arrangements, they wouldn't want the weapons so desperately.

Therefore, it's time for approaches recognizing that the genies are out of the bottle. One approach would replace denial with destruction. Israel understood this first:

its bombing of Iraq's nuclear facilities in 1981 bought the world ten years of valuable time. Operation Desert Storm has bought much more. Better yet, such operations—especially if they are restricted to bombing runs over weapons factories—can easily be repeated against militarily and technologically inferior nations whenever necessary. The United States could also replace denial with protection. Ronald Reagan's dream of shielding Americans from the kind of mammoth nuclear strike that the Soviets could launch was never attainable. But a thin-shield defense against the kinds of much smaller strikes that developing countries can launch would be fairly easy, and if we lack the capability now, we should hurry up and get it. Financing would require only a small fraction of the money currently spent on protecting Western Europe and Japan.

ON THE ECONOMIC SIDE, AMERICA NEEDS TO MAKE sure that its banking system is not damaged by further Third World stagnation, and it needs more-reliable supplies of key raw materials found in the Third World. In each case, the internationalist solution has been more complicated, more expensive, less direct, and less reliable over the long term than non-internationalist alternatives. Creating flourishing Third World markets for American goods where none currently exist would be marvelous, but it does not seem possible at any cost that the United States could afford. It is true, as foreign-aid advocates note, that America spends a pittance, in relative terms, on development assistance. But aid has been the same kind of bargain as one on a used car with a bum engine. The prospect of any return at all on the money is so remote that the waste is likely to be total.

Moreover, the chief obstacle to modernization and self-sustaining growth in most of the Third World is not lack of money but, rather, the social, economic, and political disorganization and the official corruption from which Third World countries suffer. Indeed, many of these places are not real countries—at least not in the sense that states in the industrialized free world and parts of the Far East are. Third World countries may belong to the UN, they may have their own flags and airlines and armies and postage stamps, but many of them lack the critical attributes of statehood—the institutional structures and the bedrock cohesion needed both to generate resources and to use them productively.

Rather than persist in trying to solve problems that may be unsolvable, the United States should make the best of a less-than-ideal but eminently tolerable situation, and focus on insulating itself as completely as possible from the consequences of prolonged economic stagnation in the Third World. However significant, the costs could be a bargain compared with the costs and the uncertainties of continued bailout attempts and conventional aid programs. The United States should assume that any real economic promise shown by any of these countries will eventually be recognized by the private sector, however gun-shy it is now.

Since the end of the Second World War the United States has generally accepted its dependence on Third World supplies of strategic materials and has sought to secure them through a combination of military and political means—fielding the forces needed to protect the supplies from hostile powers, using foreign aid and diplomacy to court the regimes that controlled the resources, and, when necessary, helping the regimes fend off internal challenges. These national-security programs represent costs that must be added to the price tag of Third World raw materials. In fact, when one considers all the costs and uncertainties of securing access to these materials, the entire policy equation changes. It becomes clear that many "cheap" Third World raw materials are not cheap at all. In some cases the true cost of these materials may approach or even exceed the true costs of supposedly uneconomical alternatives. Oil provides the most striking example. The cost of the U.S. military forces maintained even in peacetime primarily to protect the flow of oil from the Middle East, together with the cost of U.S. regional-aid programs—not to mention the cost of the Gulf War—increase the real price of Middle Eastern oil to U.S. taxpayers by a staggering sum. Estimates of the actual amount vary, and preoccupy a small cottage indus-try; the estimates *start* at tens of billions of dollars a year.

These hidden costs of "cheap" foreign raw materials mean that in many cases the United States has the option of greater self-sufficiency. And because in a strategic world self-sufficiency and freedom of action are intrinsic goods that are worth much, Washington should be aggressively exploring alternatives to Third World supplies. The United States should be looking into developing artificial substitutes for both fuel and nonfuel minerals, stimulating alternative international sources of supply, encouraging exploration for new domestic supplies, and more fully exploiting low-grade domestic deposits.

In the Third World as elsewhere, internationalism has its hopes and fears backward. The modernization of most Third World societies may be out of the question for the time being. As a result, integrating those societies into the tightly interconnected, efficiency-oriented global economy envisioned by internationalism may be indefinitely delayed. Those countries cannot be counted on as strategic assets or substantial markets anytime soon. The United States must not concentrate on turning the situation around, and risk its own exhaustion in the process. Strategic and economic disengagement from the Third World, which has already begun, should be allowed to continue unimpeded.

The greatest obstacles to adopting this new Third World policy are plainly psychological. It is difficult in this era of Spaceship Earth, amid rampant talk of interdependence and globalization, to envision a future in which the developed and developing halves of the world are largely decoupled—in which one half continues to make great economic, social, and scientific progress while the other languishes in decrepitude and anarchy. Tragically, it is even more difficult to envision the kind of effort that would be needed to prevent this scenario from unfolding.

DOING FOR OURSELVES

A TIGHTER FOCUS ON AMERI-ca's national interests could remove many of the political and institutional influences responsible for the seeming otherworldliness of our internationalist foreign policy. If internationalism has not been serving the interests of the nation as a whole especially well lately, it may be, as noted, because few influential internationalists have to live with the domestic consequences of their positions. Many—probably most—are affluent enough to bear a heavy tax load and to secure the best financial advice money can buy. Their children have not, for the most part, been the ones who have fought in the military conflicts of the past. Their jobs rarely are eliminated when predatory foreign trade practices close American factories. They can also shield themselves from the impact of internationalism's indifference to domestic decay. Their neighborhoods are not haunted by violent crime and drugs. Their sons and daughters are not educated at ineffective public schools. They are not struggling to pay medical bills and send their children to college.

Surely one explanation for internationalists' success at making their priorities those of U.S. foreign policy at large involves their belief that, given our perilous world and America's particular vulnerabilities, a democratically made foreign policy could be a dangerous luxury. The notions of globalization and interdependence and the indivisibility of peace and security all reinforce the belief that foreign-policy makers cannot waste time playing by the rules and seeking the consensus that democratic governance rests on. National security in particular, the internationalists seem to believe, is too important to entrust to the ignorant, fickle masses and their only slightly less ignorant, fickle representatives in Congress.

A foreign policy cognizant of America's considerable strengths and dedicated to enhancing them would automatically allow domestic quality-of-life issues priority on the national agenda. And it would also no longer implicitly accept the need for control by an elite. In this more relaxed environment internationalists would find it harder to portray their prejudices and obsessions as urgent national needs. Their priorities would no longer command automatic assent. Their world-order ideas would enjoy no automatic claims on the country's resources, its attention, or the lives of its young men and women.

After half a century of predominance, internationalism would be superseded by a foreign policy for the rest of us. □

Article 1.2.   Imperialism and the Gulf War

Tom Mayer contends that the gulf war was a product of the new American imperialism, which was made possible, in large part, by the ideological, political, and military decline of the Soviet Union. In the author's view, the conflict occurred because of the USSR's diminished role as a superpower, as that country had little choice but to accede to U.S. demands. Further, the collapse of the Soviet Union portends even greater obstacles for revolutionary movements in the Third World. It is likely, he suggests, that the United States will embark on more frequent and destructive military interventions against movements or nations that threaten America's imperialist objectives. Although the Bush administration continues to rejoice over its recent victory in the gulf, it is highly unlikely that the war will strengthen the U.S.'s control over the region and its resources. Rather, it will produce a new wave of instability and chaos that will severely undermine the new American imperialism.

IMPERIALISM AND THE GULF WAR

by TOM MAYER

The decline of the Soviet Union as a world power and the emergence of significant economic competitors to the United States have ushered in a new phase of capitalist imperialism. The war in the Persian Gulf is an expression of these revised imperial circumstances.

Although the United States has been the world's leading

Tom Mayer teaches sociology at the University of Colorado. He thanks Sara and Bernie Mayer for their comments on a previous draft of this paper.

imperialist power since the end of the Second World War, its management of world capitalism over the last two decades has been constrained in three important ways: (1) by the military power of the Soviet Union, (2) by the opposition of a significant share of the American people to foreign wars, largely as a result of the Vietnam disaster, and (3) by the high cost of major imperialist adventures, which has aggravated structural problems of the U.S. economy. Facing these constraints, even Ronald Reagan, a president equipped with a starkly Manichean outlook on international affairs, did not undertake any major imperialist military offensives. But the international context has been transformed by the erosion of Soviet power and the steady emergence of economic competition to the United States.

Soviet Decline

The decline of the Soviet Union has an ideological as well as a political meaning. Not only did the Soviet capacity to influence international affairs diminish drastically, but the rejection of the Soviet political system by large sections of its citizenry undermined the socialist alternative to capitalism. This ideological aspect of Soviet decline weakened—at least temporarily—virtually all revolutionary challenges to capitalism and, conversely, enormously strengthened the self-confidence of the dominant classes within capitalist societies. Although the U.S. capitalist class is by no means unified about the political advisability of the Persian Gulf war, its bolstered self-confidence establishes the subjective context within which new strategies of imperial assertiveness become feasible.

But ideological factors notwithstanding, the war in the Persian Gulf could not have occurred if the Soviet Union were still a superpower. With its former political clout, Moscow might have restrained Saddam Hussein from taking such a dangerous initiative. On the other hand, if the Soviet Union were still a superpower, the risk of confrontation with the USSR might have restrained Washington, which most likely would have remained content with alternative means of forcing Iraq out of Kuwait.

For ideological and opportunistic reasons, the Soviet Union has sometimes allied itself with revolutionary movements or with third world countries seeking some degree of isolation from the world capitalist system. But the Soviet connection never provided anything like a bulletproof shield against imperialist retaliation because Soviet resources were limited and cautiously used. Soviet protection was real, however, as the survival of the Cuban Revolution attests.

The precipitous decline of Soviet power places revolutionary movements and independently inclined third world countries in greater jeopardy than they have been at any time since 1945. In the new phase of imperialism, we can expect more frequent and more crushing military interventions against movements or countries which challenge the rules of

20

the imperialist system. These interventions are likely to be conducted directly by the United States, still the dominant military power of the world capitalist system, rather than indirectly by way of intermediaries. Such intermediaries have often proved militarily ineffective, and reliance upon them has often led to political difficulties.

Rising and Declining Capitalist Powers

Over the first five centuries of world capitalism, no nation exercised the degree of dominance enjoyed by the United States at the end of the Second World War. All conceivable competitors were physically destroyed, economically ruined, or politically subjugated. Such overwhelming dominance could not last very long in a complex and highly dynamic system like world capitalism. The United States, however, speeded up the erosion of its own economic position by maintaining a huge military establishment and by excessive emphasis on weapons research and production. Over the last two decades, foreign competitors have surpassed U.S. nonmilitary technology in one field after another and have captured ever larger shares of domestic and international markets.

Germany and Japan are rising economic powers, while Britain and the United States are declining. In the global economy, rising powers usually believe that unfettered economic processes will work to their advantage and hence discourage political interference with international markets. Declining powers, more pessimistic about the results of uncontrolled economic interaction, are more inclined to protect their economic interests via political intervention.

This distinction between rising and declining economic powers helps explain the differing reactions of the major capitalist countries to the Persian Gulf crisis. As rising powers, Germany and Japan were not particularly threatened by Iraq's seizure of Kuwaiti oil resources. Their robust economies could afford the oil price increases resulting from the Iraqi invasion and any associated economic shocks. Fortified by such confidence, Germany and Japan have been distinctly unenthusiastic about a military solution to the Persian Gulf crisis with all its attendant political dangers.

Britain and the United States have had exactly the opposite reaction. As declining powers they cannot be so sanguine about the effects of rising oil prices and changing investment patterns on their respective economies. The United States, in particular, covets the economic advantages of its political relationship with Kuwait, Saudi Arabia, and the oil emirates. The lion's share of the oil profits accruing to these politically dependent countries is currently reinvested in the U.S. economy, so it hardly matters that formal ownership resides elsewhere. If these oil profits were to be invested within the Middle East itself and oil prices substantially increased, the consequences for the U.S. American economy—seldom far from recession—could be most unpleasant.

In the environment of renewed economic competition which has emerged over the past two decades, the fixing of international oil prices in dollars is a great advantage to the United States, strengthening the position of the dollar in the world market. The abolition of American suzerainty over oil-producing states of the Persian Gulf would threaten this arrangement and weaken the competitive position of the United States relative to its principal commercial rivals.

Given these economic advantages, it is hardly surprising that the United States government should resort to war to repel a challenge to the imperial status quo. In the traditional fashion of declining economic powers (e.g. fourth-century imperial Rome, late fifteenth-century Spain, pre-First World War Britain), U.S. leaders are continually tempted to compensate for economic weakness with military force.

The rising capitalist powers in the current period are economically strong but militarily weak; their economic success is linked to small military budgets and modest weapons industries. The declining capitalist powers, however, are militarily powerful notwithstanding the dwindling competitiveness of their industries in international markets. Because of this imbalance the rising powers become dependent upon the declining powers in times of crisis when military force is threatened or used. This helps explain the frequent willingness of U.S. political elites to intervene militarily in other countries well beyond the minimum necessary to defend the imperialist system.

The imbalance between military and economic strength also suggests how the financial constraints on foreign adventures may be overcome during the new phase of imperialism. If the war in the Persian Gulf is any indication, the United States plans to make the economically strong but militarily weak capitalist countries shoulder a considerable share of the costs of a more assertive imperialism. Exacting tribute in this form will encounter considerable resistance. United Nations approval or some other ideological legitimation for imperialist enterprises will be necessary, if not always sufficient. But as long as the dominant classes within the economically strong capitalist countries feel they require external military protection, the United States will retain considerable political leverage over them.

Iraq

The imperialist countries at the center of world capitalism have democratic political systems, but they rarely foster democracy in the third world regions over which they exercise dominion. Democratic governments in the third world are insufficiently attentive to imperialist interests and regularly run afoul of the major capitalist powers. Constant open and covert interventions from abroad undermine democracy, while the booming arms trade and disproportionate growth of military institutions sow the seeds of dictatorship.

Americans have been told over and over again that Saddam Hussein is a brutal tyrant, which is certainly true. Less frequently are we told that Washington ignored or abetted many of Hussein's most abominable deeds—including the war against the Kurds, the attack upon Iran, and the use of poison gas. And even more rarely is the American public confronted with the human rights records of American allies in the Persian Gulf conflict (or elsewhere in the third world).

The ideological preparation for the war against Iraq was no mere sideshow. Its task was to sweep away the Vietnam syndrome: the reluctance of many Americans to support military intervention. If this reluctance could be overcome, even in one crucial case, a formidable barrier to the new phase of imperialism would be eliminated.

The first step was to exaggerate vastly the danger posed by the regime of Saddam Hussein. Iraq—with its 19 million people, oil dependent economy, lack of significant industrial base, and gaping wounds from war with Iran—was proclaimed a dire threat to the entire Middle East, soon to Europe, and in the foreseeable future to the entire world. But while Iraq cannot now produce a nuclear explosive and has uncertain prospects of developing such a weapon, it must contend with Israel's substantial nuclear capacity and now confronts the United States with over 10,000 nuclear weapons and a demonstrated willingness to use them. Cultural stereotypes about Arabs increase the potency of imperialist propaganda about Iraq.

In order to make Saddam Hussein a suitable target for unlimited violence, all positive achievements of his government are ignored. We hear almost nothing about the growth of literacy in Iraq, the increased availability of housing, women's rights, religious freedom, improved transportation facilities, lack of government corruption, or the fact that Iraq invests far more of its oil revenues internally than other Arab states of the Persian Gulf. We hear very little about several reasonable-sounding Iraqi proposals seeking to avoid war. And the U.S. left, repelled by the tyranny of the Hussein regime and burdened with a guilty conscience from its blindness to the infamies of "actually existing socialism," remains largely silent on these issues.

Israel

Support for U.S. policy in the Persian Gulf is often expressed in terms of concern about the welfare of Israel. Much has been written about Israel as an ally and agent of American imperialism, but less attention has been given to its ideological function within the imperialist system. Many people, and not only Jews, feel a strong identification with Israel, partly as a reaction to the Holocaust, partly due to traces of grassroots socialism they perceive in Israeli society, partly due to the striking disparity between its geographic smallness and military success. This identification has survived both 23 years of Israeli military rule in the occupied territories and the racism of the Israeli state towards the Arabs.

The number of people affected by such intense and highly emotional identification with Israel is probably not large, but many of them are crucially located in the ideology-producing apparatus of contemporary imperialism. A large number of most hawkish journalists and public intellectuals seem motivated by this identification, and it saps the anti-imperialist vitality of much academic scholarship on the Middle East. Moreover, identification with Israel is the most common ideological route away from radical politics. At certain critical junctures (e.g., the Six Day War of 1967, the 1982 invasion of Lebanon) a misguided sense of loyalty to Israel within the U.S. left has caused confusion about the very meaning of imperialism and hesitancy in adopting principled anti-imperialist positions.

Whatever admirable characteristics Israeli society may have, the state of Israel could not have been created without imperialist control of the Middle East, and throughout its existence Israel has chosen to ally itself closely with the dominant imperial power. But the collaboration between the Israeli state and imperialism runs squarely against the basic historical trajectory of the Middle East region in the modern era, which entails struggle against foreign domination. Military power alone cannot protect Israel forever in a profoundly anti-imperialist context. Long term survival requires that it weaken its ties with the imperialist powers and become more closely identified with the broad historical movement of other people in the Middle East. Unfortunately, the rulers of Israel and their U.S. supporters have no tolerance for such policies.

If the war against Iraq is longer and more painful than George Bush has bargained for, it will not increase the security of Israel. Iraqi military power will be destroyed, but the awareness of the Arab people from Morocco to Oman that they are controlled, exploited, and killed by foreign powers will grow by leaps and bounds. By comparison with this overwhelming injustice, the brutalities and transgressions of Saddam Hussein will seem trivial. Most Arab people will increasingly identify with Iraq and increasingly focus their anger upon Israel as the local representative of capitalist imperialism.

Why War?

Political leaders choose war, but not under circumstances of their own making. In choosing war, George Bush probably sought to divert attention from such domestic problems as the savings and loans fiasco and to gain the kind of popularity Margaret Thatcher acquired through the Falkland/Malvinas War. But the logic of imperialism also played a part in Bush's decision to attack.

Nothing short of a war which secured overwhelming acceptance by the American people, could overcome the "Vietnam syndrome" that had restricted imperialist activity for almost two decades. Driving Iraq out of Kuwait by non-military means would not suffice.

The awesome violence of the U.S. military machine's air war against Iraq provides a fitting inauguration to the new phase of capitalist imperialism. This outpouring of brutal force is designed to intimidate any foreign challenges to the restructured imperialist order, while simultaneously overwhelming lingering domestic doubts about the viability of the renewed U.S. military assertiveness. By choosing war, George Bush has maneuvered international politics onto the terrain where the United States has the greatest relative advantage— one of the few arenas in which it can still exercise unchallenged world leadership.

The Persian Gulf War arrived just in time to rescue the so-called military-industrial complex and the economic strategy known as military Keynesianism, both of which were seriously threatened by the collapse of state socialism in Eastern Europe and the end of the Cold War. The essence of military Keynesianism is the effort to steer a capitalist economy structured along oligopolistic lines by means of massive government military expenditures. Although this strategy generates strong inflationary pressures, is of diminishing effectiveness as a means of stimulating demand and controlling unemployment, and erodes the international competitiveness of American industry, it has powerful institutional support among corporations engaged in military production, in Congress and sectors of the state bureaucracy, within branches of organized labor, and in the military establishment.

The military-industrial complex and military Keynesianism fit nicely with the new phase of imperialism inaugurated by the Persian Gulf war. They are essential components of the assertive unilateralism through which the current rulers of the United States expect to deter displays of local autonomy or, failing that, to crush them by swift and overwhelming application of military force.

Contradictions of the New Imperialism

I have called the new imperialism a phase rather than a stage to emphasize that it will be short-lived. The new imperialism could meet disaster in its very first public outing: the effort to assert direct American military control over the Persian Gulf. Even if this does not happen, however, the new imperialism is rife with debilitating contradictions which bid fair to make its tenure brief.

The most fundamental contradiction derives from the relative economic weakness of the United States. The U.S. economy is simply not strong enough to support the political and military ambitions of the group which currently controls the state. The effort to implement the new imperialism will beget severe economic dysfunctions, probably leading to broad popular opposition and ultimately to defection by part of the capitalist class itself.

In the absence of either strong anti-capitalist movements or a large state socialist bloc, the other major capitalist powers have little incentive to accept American political leadership or to foot the bill for dangerous and unnecessary military adventures. Applications of the new imperialism are likely to stimulate emphatic declarations of political independence by European countries and Japan. Efforts to implement a policy of military unilateralism will politically isolate the United States and undermine its credibility as leader of the world capitalist system.

The political and economic future of the Soviet Union is unclear. It will not constitute a significant challenge to world capitalism in the foreseeable future, but its current weakness is strictly temporary. While the Soviet Union is not headed for anything like socialism, neither is it destined for political oblivion. Whatever social form it assumes, the Soviet Union or its successor states will be a force to reckon with in international affairs and an important constraint on the new imperialism.

The constellation of ideas and feelings called the Vietnam syndrome will not be easily erased from American consciousness, not by rhetoric, not by media hype, not even by a triumphant war. The Vietnam syndrome is anchored by painful reality: modern imperialism offers scant benefits and high—possibly fatal—costs to large sectors of the U.S. population.

Moreover, massive military intervention is a crude device with which to control a complex political system. Whatever the military outcome, the current war will not give imperialism greater control over the Persian Gulf and its resources. On the contrary, the war will probably initiate a period of chaos and instability that will severely tax the effectiveness of imperial control.

Article 2.1.   Nationalism Is Not Necessarily the Path to a Democratic World

The current resurgence of nationalism signals a revival of freedom, self-determination, and cultural diversity, particularly in Eastern Europe and the Soviet Union. However, according to Fred Halliday, nationalism is predicated on three major myths. First, that nations have long, rich histories. Second, that in certain ways, nations correspond to something real—that the contemporary political map reflects the diversity of peoples in the world. Third, that in some way, all people belong to one national identity. The author eschews nationalism, which, he argues, is fraught with danger, in favor of internationalism, which is still relevant in today's world.

Nationalism is not necessarily the path to a democratic world

FRED HALLIDAY/*NEW STATESMAN & SOCIETY*

Across much of the contemporary world, we are witnessing a supposedly welcome revival of nationalism. Nationalism, it is said, is the driving force behind the new political movements in Eastern Europe, responsible for the unification of Germany as well as for the likely breakup of the USSR. Flags, languages, cultures long suppressed (or supposedly forgotten) have now been revived.

There are two welcome aspects of this phenomenon. First, what we are seeing in Eastern Europe and the USSR is the development of democracy, increased freedom for peoples who have long been denied it. Because nationalism asserts the rights of distinct peoples to independence, it plays an important role in democratic politics.

The changes in Eastern Europe are also reasserting a cultural diversity—in language, writing, music—that draws on the richness of traditions among these peoples. Insofar as "internationalism," as imposed by the USSR, denied these two things, the world is well rid of it. But to welcome greater democracy and self-determination, and the extension of cultural diversity, is not to welcome nationalism itself. Nationalism may well incorporate such positive forces, but it is not identical with them and is itself beset with myths and dangers.

For all the emphasis that nationalism in its various forms places on uniqueness and special character of a country, nationalism in different countries is in many respects all the same, and it rests on three recurrent ideas, each of which is unfounded.

The first is that nations have existed for a long time. Peoples, cultures, communities—with varying degrees of continuity and homogeneity—have existed for centuries and more. But nations, in the sense of communities practicing the right to self-rule, are all less than 200 years old. It is only since the French Revolution that the values and ideology of nationalism have become part of political life.

The second myth of nationalism is that in some way nations correspond to something real—to a history, a tradition, a common race, language, territory, fate, and, in some cases, a divine order. All

From *New Statesman & Society*, March 30, 1990, as it appeared in *Utne Reader*, November/December 1990, pp. 99-100.
Reprinted with permission of *New Statesman & Society*.

this is nonsense. Counting newly independent Namibia, there are now 170 sovereign entities in the world that we dignify with the term *nation-state*. But there is nothing "given," by history, God, or anything else, that makes our contemporary political map correspond with the diversity of peoples in the world. Language, the first try of anyone trying to define a nation, defines very few—not just in the Third World, but in many parts of Europe too, not least Switzerland and Belgium. There are more than 4,000 languages in the world. Perhaps there should be 4,000 states?

Race, the other most common criteria for what constitutes a nation, is a dangerous concept at best. Even if it were not, it would not get very far with most of the nations in the world. None of the societies created since the year 1500 make much sense in terms of race. The United States, Australia, Brazil, and dozens of others actually represent a vigorous mingling of races. Even in more settled continents, the dividing lines of the contemporary international system fell haphazardly, with little respect for existing communities and peoples.

The third myth of the nation is that in some way we all belong to one. But many people in the world have more than one national identity. My father was a Yorkshire Quaker, my mother an Irish Catholic. Having lived in England and Ireland, I find much in each that I like, and feel a refreshing degree of non-belonging in both.

In many nation-states of the world, the official nationalism is that of one dominant group using its

---

True internationalists must question the terms on which the world is being internationalized today.

---

supposed legitimacy to enforce the subordination of others. It is conventional to say that this is true of Third World states, but it is equally true of the United Kingdom, a multinational state forged by conquest and long maintained by force.

But even for people who qualify, the idea of belonging is equally bogus. For what is the entity to which they are supposed to belong? How is its identity defined? Here the ready answers of nationalism draw upon tradition in one form or another, as if what constitutes the nation is handed down by earlier generations. This is an absurdity. Tradition

is an artifact, a selective collection of myths and inventions made for contemporary purposes; and what constitutes tradition is defined by those with power.

It is these myths that underlie all nationalism. In themselves these myths might be seen as innocuous, necessary for identity and a sense of security in the modern age. Yet once accepted they provide a basis for oppressing those within the community who dissent, and they provide an excuse for arrogance (or worse) toward those seen as foreign or alien.

The dangers of nationalism are not confined to oppressor states. Other peoples, including those currently or recently oppressed on national and ethnic grounds, may well reply in kind, and often against other oppressed peoples. The current upheavals in the USSR and Eastern Europe have already unleashed their own crop of ethnic and communal conflicts in Bulgaria, Romania, Armenia, and Azerbaijan as well as the rise of anti-Semitism in Russia and Poland.

In recent years many political activists around the world have abandoned the idealistic notion of internationalism. I believe that internationalism is still relevant in the contemporary world, particularly in two respects: the rejection of nationalist myths (whether these be the myths of "others" or of one's "own" people) and support for democratic forms of international cooperation in the face of international trends that are neither.

Yet true internationalists must question the terms on which the world is being internationalized today. A question arises: On whose terms is this internationalization taking place? In the media, for instance, we can see a growing concentration of power at the international level. The same thing is happening in many other sectors of our world economy. The release of Eastern Europe from Soviet political domination may be replaced by the less overt but equally tenacious economic domination by West German capital. The questions that arise with regard to both nationalism and internationalism are the same: How far do they lead to greater or lesser democracy, and how far do they promote or preclude cultural diversity? On their own, both can be instruments of control by social classes, states, genders, or dominant ethnic groups. ∎

Reproduced with permission of New Stateman & Society *(March 30, 1990). Subscriptions available from New Statesman & Society, 38 Kingsland Rd., London, England E2 8DQ.*

Tomislav Sunic insists that the demise of communism in Yugoslavia has given rise to a new sense of nationalism, which views the future in terms of competing ethnic rights. It is highly unlikely that Yugoslavia will choose to model itself after Federal Germany or the United States, whose people each share a national language and a set of common political beliefs. In the case of Yugoslavia, it is more likely that that nation will continue to be plagued by major territorial, linguistic, and demographic divisions. To survive, it must attempt to reconcile what many experts believe are irreconcilable ethnic aspirations.

Yugoslavia: The End of Communism, The Return of Nationalism

By TOMISLAV SUNIC

Many wonder whether Yugoslavia can still be salvaged, and many more ponder what impact Yugoslavia's collapse might have on neighboring states.

THE END OF COMMUNISM in Yugoslavia has brought about the return of nationalism. The notion of human rights—hailed by many Westerners as the linchpin of liberal democracy—is frequently perceived by disparate Yugoslav peoples through the prism of ethnic rights. Representative democracy and one-man-one-vote electoral procedure, as attractive and functional as they may be in the relatively homogeneous societies of the West, have little chance of success in the fractured Yugoslav state. Turning Yugoslavia into a replica of Federal Germany or into the American melting pot would first and foremost presuppose a homogeneous nation speaking the same language, sharing the same destiny and professing the same political beliefs. Any implementation of such a democracy in Yugoslavia will continue to be hindered by the issues of major territorial, linguistic and demographic differences. The only democracy that can possibly function in Yugoslavia is one that first takes root within the ethnic confines of each of its constituent peoples.

Regardless of their size and the number of people, most Yugoslav ethnic groups perceive themselves as victims of an international order in which some ethnic groups were able to acquire their state while others were deprived of it. While the end of World War I benefited Serbia, which received a mandate to create the future Yugoslavia, other ethnic groups found themselves unwilling agents in building a state deemed from the outset to be hostile to their own ethnic and historical aspirations. Consequently, contrary to the widespread current belief that rapid introduction of liberalism and the free market system will spell the end of ethnic passions, it is only too likely that each additional breath of liberalism will unleash more ethnic resentments and lead to more instability. To imagine, as many Western well-wishers do, that multinational countries can democratize by reciting the newly found slogans of liberal democracy is to ignore the lessons of history and to repeat the blunders of the architects of the Versailles treaty. In all of Eastern Europe, and particularly in Yugoslavia, ethnic rights have traditionally played a prominent role, which, although put on hold during the age of Communism, have recovered their strength in the era of liberal reform. The independent-minded Slovenes, Croats and Albanians remind us that political theologies and ideologies come and go, but ethnic identities have an extraordinarily long life.

From *America*, April 20, 1991, pp. 438-440. Reprinted with permission of America Press Inc., 106 West 56th Street, New York, NY 10019. © 1991 All Rights Reserved.

As long as the spirit of Yalta prevailed and Europe remained divided into two blocs, the non-aligned Yugoslavia was seen as a geopolitical asset by both superpowers. With the fall of the Iron Curtain and the concomitant breakup of the Soviet Union, Yugoslavia's continued existence appears to have lost legal ground. Today, even its former supporters admit that the country poses an awkward threat to the process of Europe's bloc-free consolidation. Its multi-ethnic turmoil, pitting the Catholic Slovenes and Croats against the Christian Orthodox Serbs, could, if prolonged, once again sweep Europe into another cycle of dangerous uncertainty. Unfortunately, if there is still something that binds the Yugoslav peoples together, it is the bond of seething, mutual hatred.

For Serbia, Yugoslavia's largest and most important republic, the vocation of "Yugoslavianism" has historically been understood as a special mission to forge a regional melting pot, even if that meant bringing in line the Catholic Croats and Slovenes in the north, or punishing the "infidel" Albanians and Muslims in the south. Following World War I, this mandate was garbed in pan-Slavic messianism and wrapped in the banners of Orthodox Christianity. In the wake of World War II, with the Communists in power, this mandate turned into a "covenant" blended with Marxian secular universalism that effectively legitimized Serbian dominance in the Communist *apparat*, the military and the diplomatic corps. In this context, then, it is little wonder that the Orthodox Church in Serbia has not shown much enthusiasm for the anti-Communist reforms that have already taken place in other parts of Eastern Europe.

The first cracks in the Yugoslav structure appeared last year when, in free elections, Croats and Slovenes ousted the local Communists from power and replaced them with central rightist parties. In turn, as if it wished to brave the winds of change throughout Eastern Europe, Serbia voted overwhelmingly in December of last year for Communism and its hardline standard-bearer Slobodan Milosevic. Henceforth, in the eyes of Catholic Croats and Slovenes, as well as in the mind of rebellious ethnic Albanians, Yugoslavia effectively ceased to exist. In its place "Serboslavia" was born.

HOW CAN Slovenia and Croatia leave Yugoslavia and how can Serbia retain Yugoslavia, or is there something in between that could satisfy both the secessionist West and the unitarist East? For Alpine Slovenia to pry itself out of Yugoslavia is relatively easy. With two million culturally homogeneous citizens it does not have to worry about accommodating other ethnic groups. Quite different is the story of Croatia, also home to half a million Serbs who still harbor bitter memories that go back to the Second World War when Croatia was ruled by local fascists. But more than anything else Serbs in Croatia resent the loss of the postwar status that conferred on them a role of political and colonial overseers in Croatia as well as in other non-Serbian republics. Today, Serbs are loudly conjuring up the specter of a resurgent Croatian

fascism in the hopes that they can discredit Croatia's longstanding claim to a separate state. And so far they have been able to make their point. The setting of road blocks and acts of highway banditry in Serbian-populated enclaves in Croatia last year were designed, as in the past, to provoke Croatia and Slovenia into armed resistance. A violent Croatian reaction, it was hoped, would deflect world attention from Serbia's siege of the Albanian Kosovo region. The Croatian Government under (the now deposed) President Franjo Tudjman, in an attempt to heal the wounds dating back to World War II, had repeatedly urged Croatia-based Serbian representatives to iron out their grievances in the Croatian Parliament. This appeal fell on deaf ears among the Serbs—who prefer to receive orders from the strongman Milosevic in Serbia, and who for all practical purposes tend to see in each Croat an unrepentant fascist agent.

ALTHOUGH Serbia continues to insist on annexing the part of Croatia populated by ethnic Serbs on the grounds that their distant countrymen are being threatened by "neo-fascists," it does not flinch a bit from cracking down on the majority of ethnic Albanians in Kosovo. Hundreds of murdered Albanians, mass layoffs and the deployment of formidable Serbian paramilitary units in the regional capital of Pristina have been part and parcel of Serbia's Kosovo scenario since the early 1980's—a scenario that I fear is now on its way to neighboring Croatia. Even if one assumes that the Serbs will one day hammer out some deal with the Croats, they are unlikely ever to patch things up with the Albanians. The mistrust and hatred between these two communities is so strong that it will take generations before it goes away. Moreover, with the prospect of Communism's collapse in neighboring Albania, the ethnic Albanians in Kosovo may find valiant allies across the border who will help them to secede. In sum, Serbian actions, meant initially as an attempt to preserve national unity at all costs, are ironically speeding up the disintegration of Yugoslavia. Henceforth, the survival of Yugoslavia no longer depends on how to bring Slovenia or Croatia back to the Yugoslav fold, but rather on how to change Serbia's own mindless policy of ethnic exclusion that may soon result in a war of all against all.

THE Belgrade-based Federal Presidency under Slobodan Milosevic, although always alert to signs of separatism in other constitutional republics, hardly ever mentions the continuing Serbian repression of the Kosovo Albanians. This double standard, although not difficult to grasp, is nonetheless difficult to redress. For the remnants of the Yugoslav Federal Government have proved powerless to check Mr. Milosevic—and as long as he can count on the tacit support of the Serbian-dominated officer corps in the Federal army, his ambition to redesign the Yugoslav provincial borders will have no bounds.

The Army officers, seconded today by Milosevic's

With the prospect of Communism's collapse in neighboring Albania, the ethnic Albanians in Kosovo may find valiant allies across the border who will help them to secede.

zealots, relentlessly portray Croatia and Slovenia as run by fascist cliques bent on undermining Yugoslav unity. To underscore this point the top ten Serbian generals recently accused the Croatian Government of receiving funds from the Vatican, the Comintern and the C.I.A. Moreover, day after day the Belgrade newspapers run ghastly articles signed by retired generals alleging that the Pope is plotting a world fascist revolution! Underneath, however, not much remains of the vaunted ideological and ethnic "superglue" of the Yugoslav National Army. Its officer corps continues to issue orders to the majority of non-Serbian recruits whose hatred of Serbia is well known. Mr. Milosevic may be miscalculating.

The simmering mistrust between Serbs and Croats has now become so tense that it may yet result in bloody civil war. To an average Croatian the Federal Army and Presidency have always appeared as a fig leaf for Serbia's hegemonic interests against other republics. To Serbian generals, by contrast, the end of Communism in Croatia and Slovenia means the end of Yugoslavia, which could strip them not just of their rank but of vested interests as well. Isolated from the rest of the world, it is small wonder that the Serbian Communist hardliners, with their power base in the army, continue to mask their political ineptitude by championing the "idea" of Yugoslavia—an idea which, to all practical purposes for the rest of Yugoslavs, has become synonymous with "Serboslavia."

But the reality is that Yugoslavia is not only ethnically fragmented beyond repair; it is also ideologically and religiously polarized to the breaking point.

Many wonder whether Yugoslavia can still be salvaged, and many more ponder what impact Yugoslavia's collapse might have on neighboring states. All agree, however, that even if a third Yugoslavia emerges, it will be something quite different, possibly a confederated state with only a semblance of central government. But in the light of mutual animosity and outright hatred that have poisoned the relationship among Yugoslav peoples, it is more likely that its breakup is imminent. This may not be as dangerous as it once was. For ethnic strife in the Balkans has ceased to be the athletic field on which the great powers play out their rivalries against each other.

LITTLE BY LITTLE, as Eastern Europe recovers from Yalta, it is beginning to realize that it still suffers from the malady of Versailles. And nowhere is this malady more acute than in the artificially created Yugoslavia—a country once hailed as a promising melting pot, but today seen as a boiling and dangerous cauldron. Western illusions that peace and stability could be achieved through the creation of hybrid states such as Yugoslavia have foundered again on the reality of irreconcilable ethnic aspirations. Communism has receded, but in its place the ethnic issues have surfaced. It is time now for Eurocrats in Bonn and Brussels to cease dreaming of an opulent and unified Western Europe living side by side with its pesky secessionist neighbors. One thing the two Europes need to learn quickly is that before democracy can arrive, ethnic questions must be faced—and resolved. ∎

Chapter 3

Revolution and Civil Strife

Article 3.1.   China: The Unfinished Revolution

Although the Chinese government—with the assistance of the People's Liberation Army—succeeded in repelling the 1989 student revolt in Tiananmen Square, China's aged leaders have not extinguished the desire for democratic change. Indeed, as recent events in Eastern Europe proved, the government cannot hope to permanently suppress the pro-democracy movement, which still enjoys widespread support throughout China. Ultimately, the future of China—and the fate of the revolution—will depend on how the next generation of Chinese leaders responds to demands for change.

CHINA:
The Unfinished Revolution

by Allen B. Linden

LATE Saturday evening, June 3, 1989, a tragedy began to unfold in the streets around Tiananmen Square in the heart of Beijing, the capital of the People's Republic of China. From Saturday evening through Sunday morning, soldiers of the People's Liberation Army beat, maimed, and murdered demonstrators who were calling for democracy and economic reform. Due to a historical coincidence, many Americans were witnesses to that event.

We knew that Chinese students and their numerous supporters had occupied Tiananmen Square and were seeking change in their country because television crews from CNN and CBS had been broadcasting from Beijing daily since May 15. The coincidence was that the networks had sent their people to China to cover a different story—the summit conference between Deng Xiaoping and Mikhail Gorbachev.

The revival of full diplomatic relations with the Soviet Union was to be Deng Xiaoping's final triumph. He had initiated economic reforms in 1978, had renewed diplomatic relations with the U.S., and believed that the resumption of ties with the U.S.S.R. would secure China's position in world affairs. Deng looked forward to retiring as the great reformer. His dream remains unfulfilled. Students and their supporters have exposed the inadequacies of the government's reforms and the decline of respect for the Communist Party of China. They are living testimony that the Chinese revolution remains unfinished.

To place the tragedy at Tiananmen in the history of China's modern revolution, it must be recognized that this is an Asian revolution in which a single generation has lived through the change of their political structure from an empire to a people's republic, and the transformation of their civilization from a deep-rooted blend of elite Confucian traditions and peasant folk-ways to a volatile mixture of ideals transplanted from Europe, Japan, and the U.S.

The first overt act of the Chinese revolution was the collapse of the Qing Empire in 1911. For the Manchu rulers, who had given their court the Chinese title, Qing, the 1800's had been disastrous. Peasant rebellions and defeats in wars with the Western powers had revealed that China was suffering from economic decline and that its imperial administration was corrupt and incompetent. A mutiny by a small contingent of soldiers in Wuhan in October, 1911, initiated a series of revolts that led to the abdication of the ruling family in the following year. In 1911, Jiang Kaishek, who became the leader of the Guomindang and President of the Republic of China from 1928 to 1949, was a 24-year-old army officer serving Sun Yatsen, one of the leaders of the revolution. In that same year, Mao Zedong, who became Jiang's rival in the 1930's and replaced him as China's ruler from 1949 to 1976, was a 17-year-old student in Chang-

Dr. Linden is associate professor of history, University of New Hampshire, Durham.

Reprinted from *USA Today Magazine*, September copyright 1990 by the Society for the Advancement of Education.

sha, Hunan province, who was seeking to decide what sort of career he should pursue; Deng Xiaoping was nine years old, in elementary school in his home province, Siquan.

One must remember that these men and others of their generation were born in an agrarian China in which the political and cultural institutions of modern nation-states did not exist. Even the words to describe the ideals and organizations which had spread from Europe and America to Asia were lacking in the Chinese language. *Geming*, the term which Chinese now use to translate "revolution," had meant only the replacement of one ruling dynasty by another until the late 1800's. Chinese revolutionaries had to transform themselves as they sought to transform their country.

The May Fourth Movement of 1919 accelerated political and cultural change. Every schoolchild is taught that this movement marked the beginning of China's contemporary history. When students occupying Tiananmen Square marked the 70th anniversary of the May Fourth Movement in 1989, they knew the symbolic power of that event. On May 4, 1919, some 3,000 students from 13 colleges and universities in Beijing stood before the Tiananmen, a gate of the Imperial Palace, to protest against the awarding of special privileges in Shandong province to Japan by the powers at the peace conference in Versailles. The protesters sought much more than the righting of a diplomatic wrong. They used this demonstration as the first step in their march to transform their country. For slogans, the students borrowed terms coined by one of their professors, Chen Duxiu, stating that China must follow "Mr. Democracy" and "Mr. Science." On May 4, 1989, thousands of students stood before Tiananmen and, once again, demanded greater participation in government and a more rational society.

In 1919, student demonstrators could not establish democracy and science. In an impoverished peasant society in which po-

USA LOOKS AT THE WORLD

litical power was divided among dozens of local militarists, frustrated revolutionaries concluded that establishing democracy would be impossible. Teachers and students read about the manner in which a small, determined group of Russian revolutionaries—the Bolsheviks led by Lenin—were changing their country.

Russia, like China, had been ruled by a corrupt autocracy, and, like China, the majority of the population was a poor peasantry. Some educated Chinese concluded that the fastest way to unify and modernize their country was to adopt the Leninist model. The college professor who had call-

ed for democracy and science before 1919, Chen Duxiu, became one of the founders of the Communist Party of China by 1921.

Lenin's successes impressed Sun Yatsen and Jiang Kaishek, too. To strengthen his party, the Guomindang, Sun Yatsen welcomed advisers from the Soviet Union and invited members of the Communist Party of China to join him. Sun adopted a new party constitution which was modeled on that of the Communist Party of the Soviet Union and set up a military academy outside Guangzhou [Canton] to train officers for a party-army which would function like the Red Army. In 1927, two years after Sun's death, Jiang Kaishek gained control of the Guomindang and sought to destroy the Communist Party of China, but he maintained the Leninist principle of one-party rule throughout his life. The ideal of democracy was put aside in the political and military struggles which dominated Chinese life between 1927 and 1949.

In 1949, as a consequence of the victories of the People's Liberation Army during the war with Japan, the People's Republic of China was established. At that time, Mao was 56 and Deng 47. They had experienced conflicts with the armies of Jiang Kaishek and local militarists in the 1920's and 1930's; had developed their military capabilities and refined their techniques for political organization during the 1937-45 war with Japan; and had used their experience effectively in defeating the forces of Jiang Kaishek in the 1945-49 civil war, which brought them to power. As they celebrated their victory, however, the leaders of the Communist Party knew that they faced a new challenge. They had to transform a peasant-based revolutionary organization into an effective ruling party that could implement policies to promote economic development, improve people's lives, and establish China as an equal in the world community.

In their efforts to achieve these goals, the Communist Party split into competing factions by 1965, a split which changed the lives of Mao and Deng. They became advocates of two quite different approaches to the development of a productive, prosperous China in which socialist values would permeate people's daily lives. After several years of seeking to implement the Soviet models of party organization and central planning for the economy in the 1950's, Mao concluded that China had to reject the Russian way. He believed such a system was leading to the bureaucratization of the party. Furthermore, he criticized Soviet-style economic planning for two reasons: first, it was failing to promote rapid economic growth; and second, through differential rewards and bonuses, it was creating an elite of managers in what was supposed to be an egalitarian society.

Deng disagreed. He believed that the

key to building socialism was economic development. In the short run, that meant that China had to train talented managers, engineers, and technicians to use limited resources wisely. It is necessary to reward specialists, Deng argued, because of the responsibilities they bear. As the economy developed, he believed, its rewards could be distributed more broadly.

The disagreements between Mao and his supporters and those who agreed with Deng culminated in the Great Proletarian Cultural Revolution which began in 1966 and ended, according to Chinese communist authorities, in 1976 after Mao's death. Mao initiated the Cultural Revolution in 1966 in order to purge his critics from the Chinese Communist Party and to convert the nation's youth to his vision of China's future. He urged university and high school students to criticize their teachers and administrators and to challenge the policies of local party authorities. Students responded eagerly. Calling themselves "Red Guards," with little guidance or direction, they not only criticized school and party authorities, but disrupted society. Deng was one of the early victims of Mao's purge, condemned in 1967 as a counterrevolutionary and sent off to the countryside for re-education through labor.

However, Mao was unable to consolidate his victory over his rivals. In 1967, the Cultural Revolution was getting out of hand. Groups throughout Chinese society—workers as well as students—took advantage of the disruption of party control to proclaim their grievances and demand changes. Mao concluded that he was facing anarchy. To restore order, he had to rely upon a coalition of officers of the People's Liberation Army and rehabilitated party veterans. He even accepted the return of Deng to a leadership role in the Communist Party in 1972.

In 1976, another event occurred in Tiananmen Square in Beijing which influenced the youth who would occupy that same area in 1989. On Jan. 8, Zhou Enlai, the popular head of the state administration, died. It was Zhou who had stepped in after the Cultural Revolution's violence had been halted to promote moderate internal policies, to take steps to reopen diplomatic ties with the U.S., and to rehabilitate Deng. The people revered Zhou. In March and early April of 1976, individuals and groups brought flowers and poems to Tiananmen Square in his memory. The memorials for Zhou were a clear criticism of those in the party leadership who sought to revive Mao's stress on egalitarian enthusiasm, the Maoists. During the night of April 4, the wreaths and poems were removed from the square. On April 5, when people saw what had happened, they demonstrated in protest, which the government labeled a riot. The Maoists aciused Deng of instigating the "riot," and he was purged again.

The re-emergence of Deng

The ascendancy of the Maoists was relatively brief. On Sept. 9, 1976, Chairman Mao died. Hua Guofeng, a little-known member of the party leadership, was selected to replace him, a compromise choice made among the party's factions. One month after Mao's death, Hua ordered the arrest of the leading Maoists—Jiang Qing, Mao's widow; Zhang Chunqiao; Yao Wenyuan; and Wang Hongwen. The "Gang of Four" became the scapegoats for all of China's problems. One of the beneficiaries of the change in party policy was Deng. By the summer of 1977, he was Vice President of the Communist Party of China, Vice Chairman of the Central Military Commission, and Vice Premier of the People's Republic of China.

The re-emergence of Deng encouraged those who sought reform. Educated Chinese who read the newspapers carefully were aware that a struggle for control of the party and the direction of national policy was taking place. In November, 1977, while the intra-party conflict was being fought, posters calling for democratic reforms began appearing on a wall in the Xidan district of Beijing. On "Democracy Wall," Chinese expressed their bitterness each day at the suffering caused by the Cultural Revolution. Only democratic reforms, they wrote, could curb the excesses that were the products of one-party rule. One of the popular writers was a young electrician in Beijing, Wei Jingsheng, whose articles in underground magazines were read widely. The contributors to "Democracy Wall" hoped that their essays and poems would influence the outcome of the struggle for control of the party.

In December, 1978, the Central Committee of the Communist Party of China met. When its decisions were announced, it seemed as if a new era of reform was about to begin. Deng emerged as the leader of the party, and he promised that economic development, not class struggle, would be its guiding policy. To symbolize the new era, Deng traveled to the U.S. in January, 1979, to complete the reopening of diplomatic relations, which had been suspended since 1949.

In the course of 1979, Chinese learned that Deng and his supporters believed it was possible to carry out sweeping economic reform without comparable political change. While private profits for farmers and incentives for foreign capitalists to invest in China were approved, the right to freedom of speech was curbed. On March 27, Wei Jingsheng was arrested as a counterrevolutionary. In October, he was sentenced to 15 years in prison. On Dec. 6, the Beijing government banned the placing of posters on "Democracy Wall."

Deng had authorized the arrest of Wei Jingsheng and the closing of "Democracy Wall." On March 30, 1979, three days after the arrest of Wei Jingsheng, he issued a statement that Chinese had to accept the "Four Cardinal Principles"—that they would promote socialism, maintain the dictatorship of the proletariat, accept the leadership of the Communist Party, and be guided by Marxism-Leninism-Mao Zedong Thought. In short, the party would not give up its authority. Political liberalization was not part of Deng's program. As he consolidated his power in 1980 and 1981, Deng put two loyal supporters into major posts. Deng placed Hu Yaobang as head of the party and Zhao Ziyang as head of the government. Both Hu and Zhao, in time, concluded that some political liberalization was necessary in order to promote economic and administrative reforms. Both suffered for straying from Deng's insistence on one-party rule.

Hu was the first to fall from power. He had been impatient with the slow progress of reforms in the early 1980's, believing that only by bold action in political, as well as economic, affairs could effective reform be accomplished. Hu encouraged young intellectuals to express their views. One of those who did speak out was an astrophysicist, Fang Lizhi. In 1986, Fang delivered speeches on various university campuses in which he criticized the Communist Party's monopoly of political power and called for democracy in China.

The texts of Fang's speeches were circulated widely, which indicated to students that some of China's leaders were supporting him. In December, 1986, and January, 1987, students at a number of universities held demonstrations calling for party reform and democracy. These pro-democracy demonstrations were not covered by the world's television networks. By the end of January, the demonstrations were stopped. Hu was held responsible for failing to curb the student protests and was forced to resign as head of the party, but he was not purged. Fang and several other intellectuals, however, were expelled from the party.

In the reshuffling of leadership after Hu's removal, Zhao Zhiyang became the leader of the party and Li Peng, the candidate of the conservatives, was appointed head of the government. In 1987 and 1988, economic problems, particularly inflation, became serious. Conservatives within the party leadership used these problems as a justification for curtailing whatever reforms had been accomplished.

The rise of student discontent

Among those who were upset by the lack of change were groups of students on university campuses. At Beijing University, for example, they organized discussion groups, which they called salons, to talk about China's future. They were aware that 1989 would be an important year in the nation's history. Two milestones would be celebrated—the 70th anniversary of the May Fourth Movement and the 40th anniversary of the establishment of the People's Republic of China. Students discussed ways in which to use these events to promote change in China.

In January, 1989, the potential for confrontation between Communist Party veterans and college students existed because the gap between the aspirations of each group had widened. Deng is one of the few survivors of a generation of Chinese communists who were born in imperial times and who lived through the defeats and victories which brought them to the 40th anniversary of the state they helped create. While Deng may accept reforms in the economy, he believes that only the party can direct China's political life.

Among the students leaders who would confront Deng and his associates in the spring of 1989 were Wang Dan, 20 years old; Chai Ling, 23; and Wuer Kaishi, 21. These students were born in the 1960's and grew up in the aftermath of the Cultural Revolution. They learned of the miscarriages of justice and the violence that had erupted in the name of creating a "proletarian culture." For them, neither the Communist Party nor the government was infallible. As they matured, the new generation of college students believed that the programs outlined by Hu Yaobang and his supporters could lead to genuine reform. By January, 1989, student leaders were frustrated by the gap between the promises of the Communist Party and the actual conditions in which they lived. The discontent of college youth, the group who were to be China's new leaders, demonstrated that the Chinese revolution remained unfinished in 1989.

The push that set the pro-democracy movement of 1989 in motion was an unanticipated event. On April 15, Hu passed away. On the following day, students in Beijing organized the first of several demonstrations to mourn his death. They knew that their memorials for Hu would remind many of the memorials for Zhou Enlai in 1976 and that honoring Hu was a way to criticize the party's conservatives.

As more and more people joined their activities, the student leaders formulated a number of demands. To press for freedom of speech, they called for the release of Wei Jingsheng from prison and a reassessment of the party's expulsion of participants in the "pro-democracy movement" of 1986-87. To protest against corruption and nepotism in the Communist Party, demonstrators demanded that the incomes of sons and daughters of party leaders be investigated. In more general terms, they called for a Chinese version of democracy which never was defined clearly.

On April 26, 1989, the leaders of the Communist Party rejected the students' demands in an editorial in the offical newspaper, *People's Daily*. The writer of the editorial alleged that "a handful of individuals in Beijing fabricated rumors against the Party and state leaders and incited people to attempt to storm into Communist Party Headquarters and shout reactionary slogans like 'Down with the Communist Party.' . . . This is a planned conspiracy which aims at negating Party leadership and the socialist system."

From this point, the confrontation between the party and the demonstrators escalated. The students found ways to rally supporters. On May 4, the 70th anniversary of the student demonstration for democracy and science, more than 100,000 people joined the students in Tiananmen Square to renew that call. On May 18, American television crews transmitted pictures of more than 1,000,000 protestors in the streets of Beijing. Demonstrations in cities throughout China took place. The student leaders had won support of people from all walks of life, but they didn't have the means to win the support of the People's Liberation Army, nor could they change the balance of power in the Communist Party leadership.

From the first outbreak of the demonstrations, Deng believed that the students had to be suppressed, even if violence was necessary. He had closed down "Democracy Wall" in 1979 and had removed his own protege, Hu Yaobang, from office for failing to suppress the pro-democracy demonstrations in 1986-87. There were some party leaders, however, who hesitated to use force against the demonstrators. When Zhao Zhiyang recommended leniency in mid-May, Deng lost patience. Zhao was removed as party head, martial law was proclaimed, and party leaders agreed that use of the military was necessary to suppress the demonstrators. Deng always had believed that a disciplined Communist Party must control China. In his 80's, he knows no other way to rule. The tragedy of June 3-4 was the result.

The bankruptcy of the Chinese Communist Party today is revealed by the fact that the only way its aged leaders can impose their will is by using the People's Liberation Army to maintain order. Today, the generals obey Deng Xiaoping. To whom will they turn after he passes away? The answer to that question will influence the course of China's unfinished revolution.

Article 3.2.   Unpromised Lands

This article compares and contrasts the plight of the Kurds with that of the Palestinians, both of whom are stateless peoples. In the case of the Kurds, a despised, betrayed, and long-suffering minority—who are neither Semites nor Arabs—the future remains bleak. Without national rights or human rights, the Iraqi government has little interest in their welfare, preferring instead to "liquidate" the problem by forcing them to flee. Sadly, as the author notes, in the recent war with Iraq, the world turned its back on the Kurds, offering them only humanitarian aid and "safe havens" in Iraq. On the other hand, the Palestinians, whose cause is no more immediate or just, enjoy widespread political support, owing more to the creation of a Jewish state in Palestine and less to their ambiguous identity. Although many nations are sympathetic to the Kurds, few support an independent state, while these same nations are quick to support such an option for the Palestinians. Why? Because the Palestinians will accept nothing less.

UNPROMISED LANDS

By Martin Peretz

Among the national minorities in the Middle East that have been kept from political self-expression, the Kurds are not alone. But they are the largest such minority. Neither Arabs nor Semites, they are an ancient, distinct people who can honestly trace their history back to the time of Cyrus the Great. They speak an Indo-European language all their own. Twenty-odd million of them, roughly as many as ethnic Persians, live in the contiguous territory of what was once called Kurdistan. The Kurds, unlike the tribes of Lebanon or some of the nationalities trapped in the Soviet Union, do not claim independence to the exclusion of other indigenous groups. They have a homogeneous country and a history of their own. Few people deserve the sobriquet "nation" more richly than these people, who have run their own daily affairs on their own lands for millennia.

Twice in this century the Kurds were given auguries

From *The New Republic*, June 3, 1991, pp. 20-23. Reprinted by permission of *The New Republic*, © 1991, The New Republic, Inc.

of self-determination, and twice were betrayed. The Treaty of Sèvres, which in 1920 allocated the vast territories of the defeated Ottoman Empire, envisaged an autonomous Kurdish state leading to independence. But it was never ratified by the Turks, and the decisive ally, Britain, whose troops had occupied all of Mesopotamia since 1918, became increasingly committed to its new satrapy of Iraq. At the behest of Britain, the League of Nations awarded Iraq the Kurdish area of Mosul and, more to the point, the oil riches around it. With that act, the future of Kurdish prosperity was handed to their future oppressors.

After the Second World War, a Kurdish republic was proclaimed by rebels in the part of Iran then occupied by the Soviet Union. The republic lasted a year. After the Red Army's retreat in 1946, and with the collusion of Britain and the United States, Tehran crushed the Kurds. Although there have been various risings in Kurdistan in the intervening forty-five years, they all seemed forlorn. The Kurds' fate echoed again and again their initial betrayal after the First World War. They had had no friends then to argue for them in Western capitals. They have few such friends now.

Nowhere has the Kurdish agony been more excruciating and unremitting than in Iraq. There, ever since the British in 1921 handed over political power to a feeble Sunni chieftain from the Arabian desert (the French had just ousted him, after one year, as ruler of Damascus), the Kurds have been the targets of relentless, routine persecution. In 1969 sixty-seven Kurdish women and children were burned alive in a cave into which they had escaped to seek refuge from shelling. Two years later some 40,000 Kurds were expelled from the country. During 1974 and 1975 the regime napalmed Kurdish villages and dispossessed many thousands of civilians. Samir al-Khalil's scrupulous book, *Republic of Fear*, testifies to summary executions, assassinations, and public hangings.

This bloody history somehow eluded President Bush and Secretary of State Baker. They were thus dumbfounded by Baghdad's recent brutalities. The hatreds mystified them, and did not truly outrage them. The crimes did not cross formal borders, after all; nor did they correlate with the traditional idea of a civil war, where brother fights against brother. But they were crimes nonetheless; and crimes that would have been particularly noxious to a new world order with any genuine claims to moral or historical seriousness.

In the aftermath of Desert Storm, we pushed the Shiites' suffering out of our minds. But the Kurds did not go so gently. They fled by the hundreds of thousands, their dead and dying paraded for weeks on end in prime time. So, despite his efforts to evade responsibility, George Bush was finally forced to acknowledge that the United States had to do something for them. What he did not acknowledge—because he did not grasp it— was what it was precisely that we owed them.

Humanitarian aid is not enough. The Kurds of Iraq are not survivors of an earthquake. They are the permanently endangered victims of a government that won't integrate them into the body politic as long as they are Kurds and can't integrate them precisely because they are Kurds. That is to say, their plight is hopeless because they are not Arabs. And Iraq is an Arab state: a Sunni Arab state, at that. As Hannah Arendt pointed out once after self-determination replaced empire in Eastern Europe, in many cultures only nationals can truly "be citizens, only people of the same national origin could enjoy the full protection of legal institutions." Nowhere is this truer than in the Middle East.

This is a notion difficult for Americans to grasp. Ours, after all, is ostensibly a nationality of nationalities: our ideal and imperfect practice is a citizenship devoid of ethnic or cultural determinism. Or at least it has been until recently when everything from public contracts to the composition of juries, from the character of election districts to academic appointments, is constrained by these considerations. But the Arendtian proposition is axiomatic in those regions where modern liberalism has yet to permeate, where men are either kin or enemies. It is true today among peoples in the Soviet empire and in Yugoslavia, in Romania and Czechoslovakia, in India and Indonesia, in Ireland and South Africa. The Middle East is hardly a more open and inclusive place than these.

Arendt argued further—and in a vein still more alien to American sensibilities—what she thought leaders of the great nations "knew only too well, that minorities within nation-states must sooner or later be either assimilated or liquidated." It is an unbearable thought, but borne out across the globe. In the Arab world there is the added irony that the dominant "state people" are often themselves minorities, numerically weaker and sometimes culturally less coherent than the groups they rule. Assimilating the majorities is neither enticing to them nor, history tells them, feasible. Total liquidation ordinarily being impossible, mass murders are common measures of temporary pacification. That's why the Arab wars are forever.

There are many examples of this, but take Syria. There the "state people" and especially its ruling elites are drawn not simply from the schismatic Alawite Muslim sect (12 percent of the population) but more narrowly from the Matawira tribe and, even more narrowly, from the Numailatiyya clan. Indeed, those who hail from Qardaha, Hafez Assad's birthplace, are the most favored among the tiny cohort that rises to the top. These Alawites are joined by a myth of common unity, as distinct from the Sunnis, the Druze, and the remnant Christian sects. Other Syrians are just that: "other." In states where one group routinely wields the whip over another—even where they may both be Arab—citizenship is an abstraction connoting neither loyalty nor rights. Aside from those in the ruling group, there are no citizens, merely stateless people.

There are two major stateless peoples in Iraq, its Kurds and its Shiites, and several smaller sects and ethnicities. The regime itself is run by an ideological kleptocracy drawn, as in Syria, from a "state people," which is a fragment of a fragment of the populace. This group brutalizes because nothing but brutality would sustain its power. Indeed, the Iraqi ruling group is far more ferocious than the Alawites in Syria. The Alawites, a heretic creed made up mostly of rural believers, brutalize because of their own fear. The Sunni elites in Iraq, however, brutalize with the swagger that comes from the knowledge that, although they make up only one-fifth of their country, they are of the dominant branch of Islam. But even in Baghdad itself the Sunnis are a small minority, which is why, had the coalition forces gone on to the capital, they would have been welcomed as liberators.

There is no mystery here. As the Shiite historian Abas Kelidar has written, almost no one "accepts the state of Iraq in its present form . . . it remains an artificial political entity . . . nationalism as advocated by the Iraqi political elite could appeal to only one community." The identity cards of the Shiites named them as Iranians, regardless of where they had been born. Thus, it was easy to expel them, and expelled they were. In the late 1970s, 200,000 of them were put across the border with nary a peep from anyone in the West.

Saddam Hussein preferred to liquidate his Kurdish problem by inducing them to flee. Let them, he thought, vex his old enemy Turgut Ozal of Turkey, already burdened by more than 9 million Kurds who do not think of themselves as Turks. Saddam has now been forced to pretend that he welcomes his Kurds back and that he will grant them some measure of self-rule. He has even produced from the Talabani family of longtime and certified Kurdish quislings some mountaineers quick to cut a deal with Baghdad. But Saddam's refusal to accept U.N.-supervised safe havens betrays his enduring motives. And the Kurds' seasoned instincts tell them that they are being brought to the slaughter. Most of them, of course, are not going home. They are going to hastily constructed refugee camps where they will linger until the protecting coalition forces leave. Then the safety of the Kurds will depend for the long haul on U.N. forces—hardened troops from places such as Finland and Fiji—like those who kept the peace so well in Lebanon.

This is not, then, the end of a problem but its beginning. When the short haul is over, the worst is likely to happen again. Modest estimates put the Kurdish civilian death toll at 250,000 in the decade before the current atrocities. It is in the very logic of Iraq's pan-Arab ambitions that the Kurds shall be such objects once more, the more so in that Baghdad's more grandiose plans have, for the moment at least, been frustrated.

Pushing the Kurds into "safe havens" in an unchanged Iraq is no way out. The coaxing of the Kurds back into Iraq is really bullying them back into the areas of danger. It is an example of what Arendt described in *The Origins of Totalitarianism*: "Non-recognition of statelessness always means repatriation, i.e., deportation to a country of origin, which either refuses to recognize the prospective repatriate as a citizen or, on the contrary, urgently wants him back for punishment." The sin of the Kurds was not some particular acts or thoughts but, as with other stateless peoples, "what they unchangeably were."

Without national rights, in short, the Kurds are without human rights. The Bush administration won't for a moment acknowledge this awful truth. It is true nonetheless, because the political culture of Iraq makes it a case *in extremis* of a state that is not an instrument of law but an instrument of the "state people," this minority of the Sunni minority. There is an important distinction between human rights and national rights that is illumined by the Iraqi case. Many peoples in the world crave political expressions of their national rights. But, failing to achieve these, they are not everywhere without human rights, which are the elementary freedoms—to physical safety, to work, to opinions—said to be inalienable and independent of citizenship and nationality. The Basques have these in Spain without national rights, as do Irish nationalists in the United Kingdom, and, if I dare say so, the Palestinian Arabs in Israel. But in Iraq the most elementary freedoms depend on both citizenship and nationality. When the administration let stand the structure of Iraqi power it let stand the utter rightslessness of the Kurds.

The complicity of the administration in the forfeiting of the human rights of the Kurds is a direct consequence of its calamitous and callous endgame in the war against Iraq. It is a remarkable spectacle. Within hours the United States abdicated the power it had won in the Gulf, leaving behind incalculable anguish in Kurdistan and in southern Iraq: demolished homes, razed villages, disintegrated social structures, and, of course, the irreplaceable dead. To have won a war against a monstrous regime and nonetheless to have permitted it the mass murder of civilians is a debacle that will sully American policy for years to come. The tragedy, moreover, is not yet finished. The Baath is still on good behavior, and will be as long as American soldiers remain in place. The food, the blankets, the medical inoculations provided by coalition personnel have only temporarily impeded Baghdad's objectives.

But what is more remarkable is the rationale for this abandonment of the national cause and human rights of the Kurds. Neither the president nor the secretary of state has conceded what is obvious to serious observers: the United States turned its back on the Kurds of the north and the Shiites of the south, before we even knew quite what was actually occurring there, out of deference to Saudi anxieties and sensibilities. Saudi Arabia is the ally that the Bush administration values most highly. (Neither Bush nor Baker has ever felt that special tie that has bonded Americans to Israel through thick and thin.) And if the Saudis feared a non-Arab state in Kurdistan and a non-Sunni state in the Shiite areas of Iraq, we'd do everything to prevent these from coming to pass. So the administration, in an extraordinary military achievement, had won a unique opportunity for the liberation of the Kurds, but chose instead to betray them in order to take up another cause—a cause tangential to the events of the Gulf war and far from the region where the United States wields the most leverage. The cause was the plight of a people whose claims to nationhood are less profound than the Kurds', and whose lonely role in the Gulf war was vociferously to support our enemy. I mean, of course, the Palestinian Arabs, James Baker's perennial obsession.

To compare the claims to nationhood of the Kurds and the Palestinian Arabs makes for some interesting ironies in the politics of the Middle East. The passion for a distinctive Palestinian state among the Arabs, unlike that among Kurds for a Kurdish state, is derived less from that people's intrinsic history than from their intimate encounter with the Jews. It is no longer politically correct to say that without Zionism there is no Palestinian people, but it contains a good deal of truth. Until 1948, as Professor Aziz Haidar of Bir Zeit University on the West Bank put it, the Palestinians "did not constitute a group that had any sort of crystallized ethnic identity—cultural, religious, or based on community, life-style, or language. Instead, they were a part of the Middle Eastern Arab population. Actually, the differences between the Palestinians and the bordering peoples of the region were less obvious than the differences within the Palestinian population itself." A more apologetic scholar, Muhammad Y. Muslih, concedes the same: until the 1920s "there is no Arabic name for Palestinian nationalism." And even after there was a nationalist nomenclature, the particular idea remained in constant struggle with more generalized pan-Arab aspirations. The establishment of the Jewish state in Palestine after the war was, of course, made possible by the fact that a large amount of land in Palestine was already owned by Jewish national institutions. Much of it had been sold by Arab notables. One can understand poor Arab peasants doing that for cash. It is slightly harder to comprehend why members of the Arab Executive and the Arab Higher Committee—many of them ostensibly militant nationalists, some of whom had actually organized riots against the Jews—sold land to the Zionists. Lists of such sellers go on for many pages in the scholarly studies dealing with this matter. One thing you cannot say about the Kurds is that they sold or abandoned their patrimony.

This does not mean, of course, that the Palestinians do not deserve some form of autonomy, along the lines of the Camp David accords. They do. Some species of subsovereignty, like the paradigm proposed for the Kurds by Brian Uruquart, former undersecretary general of the United Nations, would allow the Palestinians self-rule and reassure the Israelis on security issues. My comparison between the two stateless peoples is intended simply to raise the question of why an ancient historic people like the Kurds can be effortlessly sidetracked, while the Palestinians, with a newer and more ambiguous identity, press on everybody's agenda.

Even those sympathetic to the plight of the Kurds, such as Harvard professor Stanley Hoffmann, rarely go so far as to support their right to an independent state. But they do not flinch at such options for the Palestinians. At a recent Harvard meeting, Professor Hoffmann preferred to offer the Kurds succor under international "Minority Treaties," the kind through which the League of Nations was so effective in protecting the Jews, Slavs, and Gypsies from their tormentors. Why such meager measures for the Kurds and such urgency for the Palestinians? "Because the Palestinians won't settle for less." It does not make for a particularly convincing moral—or prudential—argument.

The administration was certain the epilogue to the Gulf war would be a prologue to Arab-Israeli peace. So certain, in fact, that it blinded itself to the actual epilogue taking place in the north of Iraq. We were told that Saudi Arabia and Kuwait had shown new flexibility and new openness toward Israel. Baker would produce these valued allies at the beginning of the process. And they would produce not only conciliatory Syrians but also Palestinians who were more than mere marionettes of the PLO in Tunis. Reassured about a changing climate in the Arab world, Israel would then be expected to be forthcoming toward the Palestinians. But, as an old Arab proverb has it, "The words of the night are erased by the day." Baker has been able to deliver almost nothing of what he had promised from the salient Arabs. Instead of Saudi Arabia taking the lead in the accommodation of the Arab world to Israel, it has chosen to hide behind the robes of the Gulf Cooperation Council, and to do this only after frantic pleas from America.

In retrospect, one wonders why any of us believed that the Saudis would come out from the shadows to sit with the Jews. Saudi Arabia is not central, the secretary now opines, because it is not a front-line state. Well, in every war it was a front-line state, and more than symbolically. It always sent troops and, more important, it always sent money. So having rescued the Saudi monarchy from the clutches of Saddam, the administration still has precious little leverage over it. It prefers to use its leverage over Israel: the financial power to make the Soviet migration a success or a failure. Even a hard-line government like Shamir's cannot be altogether indifferent to these realities.

It is a curious logic that abdicates power in the Gulf

and asserts it in Israeli-Palestinian affairs. The United States fought linkage all along in the Gulf, and yet now linkage is the cornerstone of its postwar policy. We defeated Saddam only to keep him in play. We thwarted Saddamism only to give a new lease on life to its deadly and cherished illusions. And one of those illusions is that the Palestinian Arabs deserve so much more, and deserve it so much more urgently, than the people whose future we accidentally brightened, only to condemn to sudden and certain eclipse. ●

SELECTED BIBLIOGRAPHY—SECTION I

Arian, Asher. *Politics in Israel: The Second Generation*. Chatham, N.J.: Chatham House, 1989.

Barme, Geremic, and John Minford. *Seeds of Fire: Chinese Voices of Conscience*. New York: Noonday Press, 1989.

Benewick, Robert, and Paul Wingrove. *Reforming the Revolution: China in Transition*. Pacific Grove, Calif.: Brooks/Cole, 1989.

Buckley, Kevin. *Panama: The Whole Story*. New York: Simon & Schuster, 1991.

Chomsky, Noam. *Deterring Democracy*. New York: Verso, 1991.

Cohen, Benjamin. *The Question of Imperialism*. New York: Basic Books, 1973.

Fromkin, David. *The Independence of Nations*. New York: Praeger Publishers, 1981.

Gwertzman, Bernard, and Michael T. Kaufman, *The Collapse of Communism*. New York: Times Books, 1990.

Hilsman, Roger. *The Politics of Policymaking in Defense and Foreign Affairs*. Englewood Cliffs, N.J.: Prentice-Hall, 1987.

Hoover, Kenneth R. *Ideology and Political Life*. Pacific Grove, Calif.: Brooks/Cole, 1991.

Jones, Walter S. *The Logic of International Relations*. Glenview, Ill.: Scott, Foresman, 1988.

Kegley, Charles W., Jr., and Eugene R. Wittkopf. *American Foreign Policy: Pattern and Process*. New York: St. Martin's, 1987.

Krasner, Stephen D. *Defending the National Interest*. Princeton, N.J.: Princeton University Press, 1978.

Nathan, James A., and James K. Oliver. *United States Foreign Policy and World Order*. Boston: Little, Brown, 1985.

Papp, Daniel S. *Contemporary International Relations: Frameworks for Understanding*. New York: Macmillan, 1991.

Peretz, Don. *Intifada: The Palestinian Uprising*. Boulder, Colo.: Westview Press, 1990.

Segal, Jerome M. *Creating the Palestinian State*. Chicago: Lawrence Hill Books, 1989.

Spanier, John. *Games Nations Play*. Washington, D.C.: Congressional Quarterly Press, 1987.

Wang, James C. *Contemporary Chinese Politics: An Introduction*. Englewood Cliffs, N.J.: Prentice-Hall, 1980.

Ziegler, David W. *War, Peace, and International Politics*. New York: HarperCollins, 1991.

Zinn, Howard. *Declarations of Independence: Cross-Examining American Ideology*. New York: HarperCollins, 1991.

THE COLD WAR AND BEYOND

Since 1945—and the end of World War II—U.S.-Soviet relations have been marked by extreme tension and hostility. Often referred to as a "cold war," it differs from a "hot war" or a "shooting war," which involves an actual state of war between two nations. The origins of the Cold War have been the subject of bitter debate. Some scholars believe that it began in 1917 with the Bolshevik Revolution, while others contend that it developed following World War II.

Although the United States and the Soviet Union were wartime allies, the Soviets became increasingly suspicious of the West, owing, in part, to Western intervention in the Soviet civil war, attempts to reduce Soviet influence in Central Europe, and Western appeasement of Adolf Hitler (specifically, the Munich Agreement), all of which led the Soviets to conclude that the West sought to "open the gates to the East." On the other hand, President Franklin Roosevelt felt that U.S.-Soviet cooperation during World War II had diminished Soviet mistrust of Western motives and had created a new atmosphere based on mutual understanding and respect that would ensure that future disputes could be settled in an amicable manner.

The Cold War, argue most orthodox political scientists and historians, was the inevitable result of a precipitous confrontation in Central Europe, which was intensified by two diametrically opposed economic and political systems, each competing to establish its own sphere of influence. These experts blame the Soviets for the Cold War, claiming that Soviet belligerence and aggression were responsible for destroying superpower relations.

In recent years, however, revisionist scholars such as William Appleman Williams, D.F. Fleming, Gar Alperovitz, and Gabriel Kolko have suggested that the Cold War could have been averted if the United States had pursued an alternative course of action. Although the revisionists disagree among themselves, many attribute the Cold War to the actions of President Harry S Truman and his advisers, whom they criticize for abandoning President Roosevelt's attempts to understand and maintain friendly relations with the Soviet Union. Other revisionists fault U.S. capitalism, the decision of the United States to drop the atomic bomb on Japan, and the absence of strong U.S. diplomatic initiatives aimed at influencing Soviet behavior.

The Cold War, for sundry reasons, continued to dominate U.S.-Soviet relations for the next four decades. Clearly, both nations represent different cultural, historical, political, and economic backgrounds, are geographically situated at opposite ends of the world, and are motivated by divergent national and international objectives. Inevitably, this clash of interests was certain to produce unfriendly relations. Moreover, both the United States and the Soviet Union were driven by totally opposite ideological goals, possessed vast human and materiel resources, and were determined to pursue their aims with dedication and resolve.

Increasingly, however, many Americans became disillusioned with the Cold War policies of the past forty years. This dissatisfaction was fueled by a spiraling arms race and the possibility of a major nuclear confrontation. Likewise, the Soviets became equally cognizant of the enormous political and economic costs of the Cold War, which were evident in their ever-deteriorating economy. Like the Americans, they feared the consequences of a suicidal war, which is why, under President Mikhail Gorbachev, Soviet leaders proposed a series of measures to improve relations and reduce tensions between the two superpowers.

Today, the world is a very different place. The forces of glastnost, perestroika, and democratization have unleashed previously unthinkable changes within the Soviet Union—what some have called a "Second Russian Revolution." Before it is over, its impact on the Soviet social, political, and economic system may prove no less eventful than the revolution of 1917, which brought the Bolsheviks to power. Many years ago, Voltaire opined that the Holy Roman Empire was neither holy nor an empire. In assessing the current changes in the Soviet Union, it is increasingly likely that it will neither be a union nor Soviet nor socialist.

In early 1991, what appeared to many in the West to be an unrelenting, irreversible march toward liberalization at home and "new thinking" abroad suddenly became mired down in the muck of economic indecision, the nationalities problem, and general political chaos. The changes came quickly. First, Eduard Shevardnadze, the Soviet foreign minister and Gorbachev's longtime associate, announced his resignation and, in an historic speech, warned the world about a possible Soviet dictatorship. Then Boris Yeltsin demanded that Gorbachev resign, urging his supporters to take to the streets to defy the government. Not long thereafter, one republic after another expressed their desire to secede—to become sovereign independent states. In open defiance of Soviet authority, the republics established interim governments, approved new constitutions, held free elections, and declared themselves independent. Then, with the situation worsening—and Gorbachev away on vacation—a group of Communist hard-liners staged a coup, ousting the president from power, and declaring martial law. Within three days, the coup collapsed, and Gorbachev was returned to power, only to discover that he had been mortally wounded and had to share power with Boris Yeltsin, his longtime nemesis and recently elected Russian president and who, during the coup, urged his countrymen to oppose the new government.

Today, Gorbachev is desperately seeking to hang on, begging the West to save his country from total disintegration and collapse. In fact, during the past two years Gorbachev has proposed no less than eight rescue plans. To date, neither the Soviet Union nor the West have a very clear idea of what kind of large-scale support is wanted or needed. Straddling a fine line between economics and politics, Gorbachev has asked the West for billions of dollars in exchange for sweeping reforms—deliberately vague. The Bush administration has endorsed the principle of humanitarian aid, but refuses to provide the millions hoped for until sweeping economic changes are implemented, leading to a market economy.

According to public opinion polls, most Americans are amenable to Soviet requests for assistance, but in the form of lowered trade barriers and not cash handouts. This attitude reflects one of pride and generosity—that is, why shouldn't we help the Soviets if they want to become more like us? At the same time, other bigger issues trouble Washington, chief of which is the fear that Soviet disintegration could spawn a new group of smaller, unstable nuclear powers or even spark a nuclear civil war. Indeed, the Soviets are already exploiting that fear. Still, most experts discount the threat, noting that all Soviet weapons—an estimated 30,000 warheads—are protected by electronic cipher locks with codes tightly held in Moscow. Their confidence was shaken, however, when, during the three-day coup, it was reported that the hardliners had access to or were in possession of the secret codes. Despite this fact, they continue to maintain that even the officers trained to use the weapons could not activate them on their own. In addition, the warheads are designed to self-destruct should anyone attempt to dismantle them to discover their nuclear material or the secrets of their design. According to these top officials, the breakaway republics may be able to seize the nuclear warheads, but they would not be able to deploy them against each other or the United States.

Presently, the Bush administration fears that a Soviet implosion would result in an undeniable social and political disaster, precipitating a refugee crisis that would dwarf that of the Kurds. Perhaps that is why many European leaders appear more enthusiastic than Bush about finding a way to provide immediate aid to Gorbachev. In fact, some insiders say that pressure from European heads of state persuaded Bush to reverse himself and agree to Gorbachev's attendance at the London economic summit.

Clearly, President Bush is still committed to keeping the Soviets and Gorbachev fully engaged. For all of its problems, Bush still views the Soviets as a military superpower with a permanent seat on the United Nations Security Council. In addition, White House aides report that Bush credits his close working relationship with the Soviet leader for many of his foreign policy triumphs, including the recent gulf war. Gorbachev is someone Bush can deal with and, for that reason alone, the president is unlikely to turn a deaf ear on the Soviet leader's calls for help.

Perhaps more complicated is whether any amount of external help can solve the Soviets' economic crisis and whether the United States can afford to help the Soviet Union at a time when its own economy is so depressed and urgent domestic needs are not being met. Washington insiders contend that peace can best be maintained by helping Gobachev to remain in power and keeping the Soviet Union on the road to reform. Although Bush would like to help the Soviets as much as possible, he recognizes that the United States can afford to give little more than agricultural credits or trade concessions—at least for now.

In the long run, whether the Soviets can be helped depends, in large measure, on how far the reforms go toward removing the bureaucratic obstacles that threaten to sabotage any major investments in programs for long-term economic revitalization. Clearly, Gorbachev's own record on reform is hardly flawless. To survive, he will have to continue to make strong overtures to both the republics and the

West. At present, the Soviet system lacks the laws, banks, markets, and tax regulations so essential to a market economy. This lack, argue the reformers, is the best argument for a swift and total overhaul. However, they are opposed by the old-guard, who contend that any sudden move would result in total chaos.

Obviously, without a major shakeup in the Soviet bureaucracy, no significant reform—economic or political—is possible. Critics argue, rightly or not, that nothing short of "bankruptcy" will force the Soviets to slash military spending, curtail all future aid to Cuba, and initiate other changes that would strengthen U.S. interests and solve the Soviets' economic problems. At this point, the Bush administration is faced with a difficult dilemma: will Gorbachev be able to deliver the order that he promises or will he fall victim to the chaos of the moment. At this point, the verdict is still out.

Section II, "The Cold War and Beyond," is comprised of four chapters. Chapter 4, "The Soviet Collapse," examines the disintegration of the Soviet Union. The first article contends that Gorbachev's problems—and they are many—are due in large part to his failure to solve the nationality problem. This, maintains the author, has weakened his authority, cost him the support of many supporters, sabotaged his reform programs, and led to disillusionment and violence. In the second selection, the authors focus on the recent coup, Boris Yeltsin's increasing influence, the status of the breakaway republics, and fears of Russian domination in any new confederation. Special attention is paid to the Baltic republics who, the authors contend, have solid claims to sovereignty. All of these issues are examined against the backdrop of the chaos and disorder that is sweeping the Soviet Union following the collapse of the Communist Party and other institutions of state.

Chapter 5, "East-West Relations," focuses on the new U.S.-Soviet relationship that has emerged in the wake of the Cold War. The first article advocates that the United States restructure its foreign policy and defense system to reflect the realities of the new order. The author proposes a series of sweeping changes, concluding that no real progress can occur unless the United States develops a clear-cut vision of the kind of world it would like to see and a strategy for bringing it about. The moment is right, he suggests, to end the arms race. In this regard, he calls upon the Bush administration to abandon nuclear deterrence as the cornerstone of U.S. defense policy, adopt a policy of "no first use" of nuclear weapons, hasten the elimination of nuclear weapons, and end production of new strategic weapons. The second selection reviews the history of the Soviet reform movement, concluding that both Gorbachev and Yeltsin need one another. For example, Yeltsin needs Gorbachev to assure a smooth transition to a less centralized, more democratic state, as well as to provide some protection for Yeltsin and the other radical reformers. Likewise, Gorbachev needs Yeltsin to help maintain order, encourage the reform process, increase his legitimacy, and hold the Soviet Union together—at least in some form.

Chapter 6, "American Foreign Policy," explores the profound changes that have altered the course of superpower relations in the past three years. The author advocates a new national consensus, predicated on the principles of cooperative interaction, economic interdependence, diplomatic problem-solving, burden sharing, and the neutralization of conflict. The U.S. should also attempt to resolve the numerous problems resulting from changes in the global distribution of power, encourage the Western Europeans to develop and strengthen their identity, exhort the Japanese to become more involved in the developing world, and strengthen international and regional organizations. In the second article, the author argues that the Bush administration must abandon its assumption that only the U.S. can deter aggression, an assumption that may have been valid in the post-World War II era but is clearly irrelevant today. In this regard, he urges Washington to transfer this responsibility to other world powers, several of whom are quite capable of shouldering the responsibility. The U.S. must also reduce its military spending, downsize its defense establishment, and phase out its global network of alliances.

Chapter 7, "The New World Order," examines the meaning of the phrase both in terms of America's international purpose and domestic agenda. The first article analyzes President Bush's often-repeated phrase by asking three different writers—each of whom represents a different political perspective—to assess the "New World Order." One calls it a political illusion; the second, a call for international morality; and the third, a cruel hoax. In the second selection, the author critiques Bush's "New World Order," suggesting that the gulf war clearly illustrates the president's true motives, which are to build a new world order based on military supremacy over its market-based competitors and to protect and cultivate client regimes whose interests are reflective of those of the United States. In the author's view, it is a global imperial vision that is inherently flawed—one that is certain to court disaster. This new imperialism seeks to exploit the American public—who have pressing domestic concerns—in order to expand militarily abroad.

DISCUSSION QUESTIONS

1. How did President Gorbachev's inexperience with nationality relations undermine his position?
2. Why did Gorbachev fail to set out a specific program to deal with nationality problems?
3. To what extent did the relaxation of political controls lead to popular pressure for political reform in the Soviet Union?
4. What factors gave rise to the independence movements in the Baltic republics?
5. In what sense did Lithuania play the most pivotal role in the battle for independence in the Baltic region?
6. What problems is Gorbachev likely to face in bringing about a more free and democratic society?
7. Have the hard-line communists been displaced since their unsuccessful coup attempt?
8. What, if anything, remains of the now-defunct Communist Party?
9. How has the coup affected Gorbachev and contributed to his loss of power and influence?
10. Is Russia likely to dominate what remains of the USSR? Why, or why not?
11. To what extent has Gorbachev been reduced to a figurehead, with Russian president Boris Yeltsin wielding the real power?
12. Can the Soviet Union survive without some sort of confederation? Why, or why not?
13. Is the principle of nuclear deterrence a valid concept in today's world?
14. Should the United States provide direct financial assistance to the Soviet Union? If so, what kind?
15. How, if at all, should America revamp its foreign policy to reflect current political realities?
16. What should be the key elements in a new U.S. defense strategy?
17. In what sense, if any, does Gorbachev deserve credit for accelerating the transition to democracy and a market economy?
18. What role should the United States play in the new post-Cold War world?
19. To what extent, if any, has the Cold War contributed to America's debtor status?
20. Should the U.S. openly embrace Yeltsin, even if that means contributing to Gorbachev's fall from power?
21. Can the United States continue to play the role of "world policeman"? Why, or why not?
22. Is the time right for the U.S. to phase out its global network of alliances?
23. How does President Bush define his often-repeated phrase "New World Order"?
24. Is Bush's New Economic Order rooted in a realistic understanding of the post-Cold War world?
25. What political values are reflected in the president's New World Order?
26. Does President Bush's New World Order imply a new Pax Americana? Why, or why not?
27. Is the gulf war an apt example of Bush's New World Order?
28. To what extent, if any, has the gulf war served to "militarize" American society?
29. Does the president's New World Order seek to subordinate Europe and Japan to U.S. global aims?
30. Would it be a mistake for the United States to pursue a global imperial vision following its success in the gulf? Why, or why not?

KEY TERMS

BALTIC REPUBLICS   The states of Estonia, Latvia, and Lithuania, which were forcibly annexed as Soviet republics in 1940 and recently declared their independence.

BRINKMANSHIP   The strategy of deliberately provoking a crisis to the point of conflict to force the other side to withdraw.

CONGRESS OF PEOPLE'S DEPUTIES   The newly formed reformist Soviet parliament.

CONTAINMENT   The foreign policy of the United States in the period after World War II, designed to prevent the spread of Soviet power.

DEMOCRATIC REFORM MOVEMENT   An umbrella group of well known Soviet politicians who favor radical change.

DIPLOMACY   The practice of conducting international relations between nations through official representatives.

EAST-WEST CONFLICT   A term used to describe the Cold War or the U.S.-Soviet conflict and rivalry for global influence.

FEDERALISM   The division of power between the Soviet state and its union republics.

GLASNOST   A Russian word meaning "openness," which under President Mikhail Gorbachev has come to signify increased candor in public discourse of problems and events in the USSR.

HARD-LINER   One who is unwilling to compromise in regard to foreign policy aims.

IMPERIALISM   A superior-inferior relationship, in which one nation dominates or controls, politically or economically, another nation.

IRON CURTAIN   A term, popularized by Winston Churchill, to describe the division of Europe between the Soviet Union and the West.

MANIFEST DESTINY   A nineteenth-century American doctrine which held that it was the destiny of the United States to expand its territories across North America and beyond.

MONROE DOCTRINE   A policy statement enunciated by President James Monroe in 1823 which asserted that the United States would not interfere in the affairs of European countries. European nations should not create new colonies in the Western Hemisphere; European countries should not intervene in the affairs of independent nations of the Western Hemisphere.

NIXON DOCTRINE   The policy articulated by President Richard Nixon that although the United States would help to defend its allies, those nations would have to bear the major burden of their own security.

PEACE THROUGH STRENGTH   The belief that America should pursue a policy of nuclear superiority and oppose arms control with the USSR.

PERESTROIKA   A Russian word meaning "restructuring," the term was used by Soviet leader Gorbachev to signify a basic shift in Soviet economic policy from centralized state planning and control to a market-based economy, as well as to describe the recent political changes that have swept the USSR since the late 1980s.

POLITBURO   The Political Bureau of the Central Committee, the principal political organization and institution in the Soviet Union.

PRIVATIZATION   The substitution of government paid-for products and services by private industry.

SECESSION   The right of states to retain their sovereignty and, if desired, to leave the nation.

SOVEREIGNTY   The principal decision-making authority enjoyed exclusively by the state.

STALINISM   The theoretical and practical interpretations of Marxism by Josef Stalin who, as party secretary and premier, dominated the Soviet state from 1928 to 1953.

SUPREME SOVIET   The bicameral national legislation, which is the highest organ of state power and possesses the authority to make laws and approve constitutional amendments.

TRUMAN DOCTRINE   As articulated by President Harry Truman, a declaration that American security and world peace depended on halting communist expansion in southeastern Europe.

VIETNAM SYNDROME   The reluctance of U.S. leaders and the American public to intervene militarily in any foreign country for any reason in any way as a result of the U.S. experience in Vietnam.

Chapter 4

The Soviet Collapse

Article 4.1.   The Soviet (Dis) Union

Although the Soviet collapse was precipitated by economic decline, it was fundamentally the result of ideological and moral failure. It was also hastened by Gorbachev's inability and inexperience to deal with the nationality problem, which cost him valuable allies and crippled his reform programs. Following a policy of concealment and concession, Gorbachev was forced to relax his earlier hard-line policies to appease the non-Russian nationalities. This policy of temporary retreat was subsequently replaced by his new binding Treaty of Union, which promised to work out relations between the republics and the center. Too little, too late, Gorbachev's policy misjudged public opinion, and Gorbachev ultimately decided to crack down on the independence movements, which served to destroy his credibility as a political reformer. In the end, Gorbachev sacrificed his political legitimacy in favor of preserving the union by force, thereby ensuring his downfall.

THE SOVIET (DIS)UNION

by Martha Brill Olcott

When he took office in 1985, Mikhail Gorbachev never contemplated the breakup of the Soviet Union. By Gorbachev's own reckoning, his most pressing task was to get the USSR's stalled economy through a series of economic and political reforms. Yet Gorbachev did not anticipate that overhauling the Soviet system would lead millions of Soviet citizens to reject the legitimacy of Communist party rule and Russian political hegemony that had been masquerading as "communist internationalism" for more than 70 years.

Gorbachev's inexperience with nationality relations has cost him dearly. It has undermined his authority, cost him the support of close political allies, crippled his reform programs, resulted in the deaths of what some estimate to be more than a thousand citizens, and could well lead to the bloody dissolution of the country that he is seeking to preserve.

In developing his policies of reform, Gorbachev accepted former General Secretary Yuri

MARTHA BRILL OLCOTT, *professor of political science at Colgate University, is working on a book on nationality problems in the Gorbachev era.*

Andropov's premise that, although national sensibilities had to be respected, the interests of the state as a whole must be placed above those of any individual republic or nationality. Gorbachev did not see these ideas as potentially contentious. He expected opposition from entrenched political elites in the various republics, but he also expected "rational" reformers, regardless of nationality, to realize that everyone would benefit if the economy were strengthened and arbitrary political rule eliminated.

Gorbachev mounted a two-pronged attack: complex bureaucratic maneuvers against Brezhnev-era politicians coupled with political reforms to mobilize popular support. *Glasnost* and *perestroika* were designed to provide Gorbachev's government with the political legitimacy of Lenin and the USSR's founding principles. Although Gorbachev understood that official communist ideology had warped the development of Russian culture, he failed to appreciate that most non-Russians felt similarly thwarted, not just by communism but also by Russian rule. The relaxation of political controls did lead to popular pressure for reform. But the popular movements that developed in most non-Russian areas have been unacceptable to a Soviet patriot like Gorbachev.

Over the past four years Gorbachev has tried to slow gathering political momentum with promises of political and economic decentralization and opportunities for greater individual involvement in political life. Although Gor-

Reprinted with permission from *Foreign Policy 82* (Spring 1991), pp. 118-136. Copyright 1991 by the Carnegie Endowment for International Peace.

bachev's policies have changed, his basic political premise has not: The preservation of the USSR is paramount. When persuasion fails, coercion will be used. As Gorbachev warned repeatedly in December 1990, "national extremism" will be combated at all costs; the "crazies" who seek to dissolve the union cannot get their way.

Gorbachev's nationality crisis dawned on December 16, 1986, when Moscow announced that Gennadi Kolbin, the Russian who headed the Ulyanovsk Communist party, would replace "retired" Kazakh party boss and Politburo member Dinmukhamed Kunayev. The news triggered three days of demonstrations in Alma Ata, in which at least 58 people were killed by special Interior Ministry (MVD) troops brought in to quell the riots.

Moscow's response to the killings was one of concealment and concession. Official accounts claimed three deaths, including one policeman. Fifty-eight people, however, reportedly were secretly buried. Although the riots were condemned, Gorbachev learned from them. Over the next few years he reversed earlier hard-line policies and offered a stream of concessions to appease the non-Russian nationalities.

Since the mid-1970s Communist party conservatives have complained that power has been oozing from the center to the republics. During the drafting of the 1977 constitution some had even tried to eliminate republics in favor of a unitary state. Gorbachev accepted that republics should be retained but insisted that they be purged of their corrupt leaderships. At the 27th Communist Party Congress in early 1986 he made clear that republic interests would be defined in Moscow and the party cadre would be rotated throughout the country to insure that national or regional biases did not affect personnel policies.

The protests that followed Kunayev's dismissal demonstrated the risks of this cadre policy. Recognizing this, Gorbachev continued to attack "localism" and political corruption, but he never again appointed someone to local office who had no regional ties. Instead, whenever possible he named local nationals, such as diplomats, who lacked close ties with wayward communist parties.

Moreover, Gorbachev softened his public stand on nationality issues. National chauvinism would not be tolerated, but neither would intolerance of the legitimate sensibilities of the USSR's national minorities. *Glasnost* and *perestroika* must be applied to nationality relations in a way that returned the party to its Leninist roots.

Gorbachev's inexperience with nationality relations has cost him dearly.

Gorbachev, however, was reluctant to set out a specific program for the redirection of nationality problems. The 19th Communist Party Conference in June 1988 skirted the issue by making vague promises of future "home rule" and the need to respect the cultural rights of all nationalities. A promised Central Committee session on nationality relations was repeatedly postponed. When finally held, in September 1989, it passed an ambiguous resolution promising a new national compact in which sovereign republics would be joined on a contractual basis. By then Gorbachev was trying to deal with near civil war conditions in Azerbaijan and Armenia and the impending obliteration of Communist party rule in the three Baltic republics.

Glasnost focused public attention on Joseph Stalin's crimes and the historic injustices perpetrated against the Soviet Union's ethnic minorities. Crimean Tatar activists, for example, demonstrated in summer 1987 for the right of return to the Crimea, from which they were deported en masse during World War II. Harassed and roughed up, the demonstrators were otherwise not interfered with, and they were even promised a hearing by a Supreme Soviet commission.

Baltic nationalists then organized their own protests, against the Ribbentrop-Molotov Pact—the 1939 agreement with Nazi Germany that led to the incorporation of the Baltic states into the USSR. Although the demonstrators were clubbed by police and assailed in the press, many unpopular local party leaders were quietly replaced. The Estonians then became the first to take advantage of the newly granted right to organize informal groups, creating the National Front in early 1988. In the following months similar groups developed in Latvia and Lithuania.

These organizations advocated the devolution of political power to the republics. Throughout 1989, Moscow gradually ceded control of culture to the republics. Throughout the USSR local languages became state languages, causing ethnic Russians living outside the Russian republic to launch their own political action groups. Gorbachev promised economic autonomy to the republics, and assigned the task of drafting legislation to the newly formed Congress of People's Deputies.

Yet the Baltic republics were impatient with Moscow's pace of addressing their grievances. Baltic voters rejected the overwhelming majority of party candidates in the spring 1989 elections to the USSR Congress of People's Deputies, and local Baltic legislators, reacting to the nationalist sentiment, passed laws on economic autonomy, sovereignty, and republic citizenship. The campaigns in early 1990 for the Baltic republic's Supreme Soviets turned into referenda on independence.

Demands for the transfer of power proceeded less peacefully in the Caucasus. The dispute over control of the Nagorno-Karabakh autonomous province in Azerbaijan dates back to Stalin, who as commissar of nationalities in the early 1920s awarded this territory first to Armenia and then to Azerbaijan. In February 1988 the local Armenian-dominated government demanded that the province be transferred back to the Armenian republic. The Azerbaijanis rejected the request. Later in February inter-ethnic fighting resumed—and more than 31 Armenian civilians were massacred in Sumgait, just outside of Baku. Nagorno-Karabakh was placed under Moscow's "special administrative control," but armed skirmishes remained a regular occurrence and eventually hundreds of thousands of Armenians and Azerbaijanis fled from each others' jurisdictions.

In November 1989 Moscow decided to return Nagorno-Karabakh to Azerbaijani control. This decision, which was immediately rejected by Armenia, exacerbated tensions. The situation turned violent in January, when Azerbaijani nationalists tore down guard posts and wire fencing along a stretch of the Iranian-Azerbaijani border and fighting between Armenians and Azerbaijanis broke out in Baku. The National Front was blamed for the disturbances, though the Front claimed to have restored order, something that the discredited Azerbaijani Communist party clearly was unable to do.

On January 19, 1990, a presidential decree declared a state of emergency in Baku, and additional tanks and troops were sent to support Soviet Army and MVD troops that were already in the area. The accounts of what happened on January 20 are sharply contradictory, but Azerbaijani nationalists claim that, as in April 1989 in Tbilisi, Georgia, a peaceful crowd was provoked and attacked by Soviet troops. At least 19 had died in Tbilisi, and more than 100 were killed in Baku—an action that the Bush administration said fell under the legitimate right of a state to maintain order.

Most Soviet nationalist leaders saw the events in Baku as part of a consistent pattern of excessive use of force by Moscow to defeat and discredit political opposition. Unlike the Tbilisi attack, there was no full-scale public investigation designed to distance Gorbachev from the deaths in Baku. Shortly after the declaration of martial law, prominent members of the National Front of Azerbaijan were arrested for provoking the disturbances. As of early 1991 several Azerbaijani National Front activists remained in jail.

The Lithuanians closely monitored the situation in Azerbaijan. During the election campaign in March 1990, Vytautas Landsbergis, then leader of the Lithuanian nationalist movement, *Sajudis*, promised that if *Sajudis* took control of the new Lithuanian Supreme Soviet, he would push for an immediate declaration of independence. Otherwise, he feared, Gorbachev would either outmaneuver the anticommunist Baltic leadership or manufacture an excuse to crush them militarily, as seemed to have been done in Baku and then again a month later in Dushanbe, the capital of Tajikistan. *Sajudis* activists monitoring the election campaign in Lithuania complained of vast campaign chests that newly organized Polish political groups had suddenly accumulated and of anti-Lithuanian provocations in Russian-staffed factories.

Landsbergis was convinced that Gorbachev did not appreciate the seriousness of the Baltic independence movement, even after the Soviet leader's January 1990 tour of the republic. Others who met with Gorbachev during his barnstorming visit spoke of the general secretary's blindness on the question of nationalities. Some Lithuanian nationalists reported that, while in Lithuania, Gorbachev made vague promises of "special arrangements" that would govern relations between Moscow and the Baltic republics. But a major speech on nationality policy made to a party gathering three weeks later contained no reference to any such arrangements. Instead, Gorbachev proposed writing a new union treaty to govern relations between Moscow and the republics, implying the application of an egalitarian formula to all.

By March 1990 Gorbachev's international reputation had reached an all-time high. The regimes in Eastern Europe had been allowed to go their own ways. The Berlin Wall—the symbol of the Cold War—had been breached permanently, and Gorbachev was signaling that he would even permit the reunification of Germany. The USSR was showing itself prepared to give up its post-World War II acquisitions. But it showed no flexibility with regard to Estonia, Latvia, and Lithuania, nor toward its other prewar territorial conquests.

The USSR's incorporation of Estonia, Latvia, and Lithuania in 1940 has never been recognized by the United States or most Western powers. This gave Baltic nationalists hope that they would gain foreign support for their independence bids. Yet Western leaders were unwilling to get directly involved in the dispute that developed between Moscow and Vilnius after the newly elected Lithuanian Supreme Soviet announced its independent status on March 11, 1990.

Western leaders feared that direct intervention in the Baltics would threaten negotiations with the Soviet Union over German reunification, and believed that Moscow would gradually move to grant the Baltic states independence. Thus American, British, French, and German leaders counseled moderation and pushed for a negotiated settlement during Moscow's subsequent campaign of military harassment and economic embargo.

Although Moscow felt that a political compromise would create unacceptable precedents for other potentially secessionist nationalities, the three Baltic republics feared that delay would ensure defeat. The lack of direct Western support crippled the Lithuanian republic economically and led Gorbachev to expect that he had a free hand in the region.

Lithuania's strategy to attain independence was far more daring than that of the other Baltic republics. All three republics recognized that the future independence of the region would be decided in Lithuania. In late spring 1990 the three republics joined in a Baltic Council, but even earlier the leaders of the three national fronts held monthly meetings and kept in close contact. With an ethnic Lithuanian population of about 80 per cent, there was a chance for a public groundswell for independence in this republic not possible for the Latvians and Estonians, who made up roughly 50 and 60 per cent of the populations of their respective republics.

Gorbachev would later criticize Landsbergis and the new Lithuanian government for severing 50 years of ties during a single weekend of furious parliamentary activity. The Lithuanians, however, felt that they had to reestablish their claim to independence before Gorbachev substantially expanded his political powers by be-

coming president of the USSR. In fact, one of the new president's first actions after taking office on March 15 was to get the Congress of People's Deputies to declare Lithuania's "secessionist" legislation null and void and to invoke strong presidential emergency powers.

The Soviet legislature also adopted a law on secession, which took effect upon ratification on April 3, 1990. The procedure prescribed was elaborate: a two-thirds vote for secession in a republic-wide referendum, followed by a five-year period for exit to be negotiated with each of the Soviet republics. The three Baltic republics rejected this measure as inapplicable to them. On March 30, 1990, the newly elected Estonian Supreme Soviet declared its intention to gradually restore full independence, and on April 3 passed a bill recognizing Lithuania's independent status.

Gorbachev tried to threaten the new Lithuanian government into submission even before his new presidential powers were affirmed. During the last two weeks in March he authorized a series of military maneuvers through Vilnius streets, including tank drills, and used troops to seize control of several key downtown buildings. These tactics only increased Landsbergis's support among his constituents.

In mid-April Gorbachev changed tactics, introducing an economic embargo designed to starve out the republic. Natural gas and oil shipments to Lithuanian consumers were cut off, but the Lithuanians defied Moscow by taking to bicycles and horse carts. Lithuania later charged that Moscow pressured the West European countries to recognize the embargo.

During their travels in April and May, then Lithuanian Prime Minister Kazimiera Prunskiene and her deputy prime minister, Algirdas Brazauskas, had little luck in securing either diplomatic recognition or economic aid. Prunskiene received polite refusals from heads of state in Canada, France, Great Britain, and the United States while Brazauskas failed to gain support from Germany and Switzerland. In every case the message was similar: Diplomatic and financial support would only be extended once the Lithuanians demonstrated that they were in control of their own territory.

Prunskiene got a more sympathetic hearing in Oslo, where the Norwegians agreed to permit oil sales to the Lithuanians for hard currency. However, when the Nordic Council foreign ministers met in late May, they too declined to formally recognize the Sajudis regime.

Czechoslovakian President Vaclav Havel was willing to recognize the new Lithuanian government, offering to mediate between Soviet and Lithuanian leaders, though he never officially did so. The Polish government did not offer official diplomatic recognition to the Lithuanians, but Solidarity in particular made clear that its sympathies were with the break-away regime. Warsaw did not support Moscow's claims of unfair Lithuanian treatment of their Polish minority, and even signed a limited trade agreement with Vilnius and promised to draw up similar agreements with the nationalist-led local governments in the western Ukraine. However, Soviet railroad authorities prevented fuel shipments from Poland to Lithuania and denied port rights at Kleipeda to a Dutch freighter filled with oil that Vilnius had purchased.

Although the Vilnius regime remained isolated internationally, the Landsbergis government became a sensation among democratic reformers within the USSR. Lithuania's resistance demonstrated the fragility of Moscow's political hegemony. Gorbachev and the Kremlin leadership were booed off the podium during spontaneous 1990 May Day demonstrations, in which scores of marchers carried pro-Lithuanian placards. Critics of Moscow's policies were helping the Lithuanians break the blockade. Pro-reform city councils in Moscow and Leningrad were contracting for Baltic beef; the Byelorussian National Front had helped arrange gasoline shipments to the republic; and Georgian nationalists were airlifting in medical supplies.

New Declarations of Sovereignty

More serious, from Gorbachev's point of view, was that political leaders who supported his reform program were losing control in a number of other republics. On May 4 the Latvians declared their independence. Elections in Moldova (formerly Moldavia) produced a split between pro-independence Moldovans and pro-Moscow Russians, robbing the new leadership of the republic of Moldova of its ability to govern. The Ukranian nationalist party, *Rukh*, won just over a quarter of the seats in the heavily orchestrated Ukrainian Supreme Soviet elections, but dominated the regional elections in the western Ukraine. Vychaslav Chernovil, the leader of the Ukrainian Helsinki Union who had spent 10 years in Soviet prison camps, became head of the Lvov provincial council, whereupon he declared that sovereignty within the Soviet federation was a contradiction in terms.

While Gorbachev pondered a new strategy for dealing with the increasingly influential independence movements, Boris Yeltsin was elected head of the Supreme Soviet of the Russian republic on May 29, 1990. A day later, Yeltsin stated that a sovereign Russia would be willing to trade with the Baltic republics. This promise significantly altered Moscow's Baltic policy. When the Russian republic declared its sovereignty on June 12, Yeltsin loomed as a more threatening figure than Landsbergis. Moscow seemed defeated; any Soviet economic boycott would be an empty gesture if Russia traded with Lithuania. In late June both Moscow and Vilnius accepted terms akin to those of the failed Kohl-Mitterrand initiative of late April: Lithuania would suspend its independence decree for three months to negotiate with Moscow.

Gorbachev's nationality policy throughout summer and early autumn of 1990 was clearly one of temporary retreat. In May, Gorbachev fought with Yeltsin over the proposed terms of the Russian republic's decree that Russia's laws should take precedence over those of the union. Then in June, Gorbachev announced his own countermeasure: a new binding Treaty of Union between sovereign republics, which would work out the relations between republics and the center.

In the next few weeks the presidents of Byelorussia, Kazakhstan, the Ukraine, and Uzbekistan, all loyal to Gorbachev, announced plans to draft their own declarations of sovereignty. Each of these decrees violated the Soviet constitution by declaring the preeminence of republic laws and claiming ownership of all mineral rights, including gold reserves. But with the principal ports of entry to the USSR under Moscow's firm control, the republics had little opportunity to exercise their newly claimed rights.

These declarations of sovereignty allowed Gorbachev's supporters to usurp the local nationalists' agenda and helped stabilize political conditions in the nation. The strategy worked best in Byelorussia, Kazakhstan, and Uzbekistan, though it was not successful in other republics. Several weeks of large and sometimes violent public demonstrations in Kiev, for example, forced the resignation of Ukrainian Prime Minister Vitaliy Masol, who was replaced by Vitold Fokin, a former communist party official more acceptable to the nationalists.

The situation in the Russian republic was more confusing as more than 20 autonomous regions also declared their sovereignty, asserting the right to control their own natural resources.

Some cynical but experienced Soviet Kremlin watchers speculated that Gorbachev might have encouraged the sovereignty movements within the small subnational communities in order to cripple Yeltsin and demonstrate the nonviability of republic sovereignty.

These declarations of sovereignty, however, worsened the economic situation. Most of the republics established their own trade barriers, as did many of the principal economic regions within the Russian republic. This exacerbated food shortages in industrial areas like Moscow and Leningrad, which lack farm belts within their territorial jurisdiction.

Yet one advantage of encouraging the republics and autonomous formations of the USSR to declare their own sovereignty has been to make popularly supported independence movements harder to distinguish from state-sponsored sovereignty movements. As one Soviet journalist noted in November 1990, in the "parade of sovereignty. . . Latvia's claims to statehood have become indistingishable from those of the medieval Khanate of Kazan." Tatars might argue that their claims, in fact, are indistinguishable from those of the Baltic states, but the grounds on which the Chukchis, Chuvash, Maris, and Udmurts have "reclaimed" their sovereignty would persuade no international court.

All the newly sovereign republics have also begun developing their own foreign policies, which in some cases could work to Moscow's benefit, while in others it will not. Certainly Moscow gains by the resultant overshadowing of the Baltic republics' claims, since there is no immediately obvious difference between Baltic efforts to secure foreign recognition of their independence and Kazakhstan's announcement that it plans to form its own diplomatic corps and set up foreign consular legations.

But the intents of the two actions are clearly different. Kazakhstan has signed contracts with Western petroleum companies for the development of the Tengiz oil fields and is willing to share the proceeds of the oil sale with Moscow. The Baltic states, however, are looking for foreign economic aid and investment to separate themselves from Moscow. They will not allow Moscow to speak for them in international settings, and have refused to join representatives of Armenia, Byelorussia, Russia, and the Ukraine in the Soviet delegation when the Baltic states were denied separate representation at the November 1990 Conference on Security and Cooperation in Europe (CSCE) talks in Paris.

The Baltic republics term their relations with the USSR their "Eastern Policy." Lithuania, for example, now handles relations with Moscow solely through its diplomatic legation, yet formal talks on Lithuania's withdrawal from the union, which did not begin until October 1990, quickly stalled in preparatory discussions. All three Baltic republics have signed treaties of cooperation with a number of Soviet republics, but they report that deliveries of foodstuffs and certain raw materials covered in some of these agreements have been blocked by the central government.

Economic Sovereignty

The Baltic republics are also trying to demonstrate their statehood in other ways. All three have established home guards and customs posts on their respective borders with the Russian republic. The Lithuanians have issued stamps, and both Lithuania and Estonia have announced plans to introduce their own currency in 1991. The Estonian currency is to be minted in cooperation with Finland.

The Baltic leadership believes that economic assistance from the Scandinavian states is critical to achieve their economic independence. For example, economic links between Estonia and Finland have increased. The two have always enjoyed a special relationship; however, Finland, like the other members of the Nordic Council, has tried to carve out a policy of cautious support for Baltic independence. The Nordic states are providing moral encouragement, increasing their diplomatic presence in the region, and working on programs of long-term cooperation. But they have not formally recognized these states, nor provided the financial support the Baltic republics will need to keep their economies afloat in 1991, when much of their Soviet as well as foreign trade will be hard-currency transactions.

The East European countries are following a similarly judicious policy with regard to the Baltic states, Moldova, and the Ukraine. The new president of Hungary, Árpád Göncz, has promised that Hungary will treat Lithuania and the Ukraine as independent states. Göncz has even visited the Ukraine, making stops in Kiev and the Carpathian region in the western Ukraine.

The Polish government has also announced a new "Eastern Policy" of direct relations with all the "nations and republics" on their border and has signed a declaration of cooperation with the Ukraine that will entail an exchange of diplomatic representatives. Their policy seems designed to promote cooperation with whatever government is in charge of that republic: The Poles are staying in regular contact with the government in Kiev, as well as with its critics in Lvov. The Polish government has also disavowed territorial claims on Byelorussia, the Ukraine, and Russia.

Romania's relations with Moldova are more ambiguous. The instability of Ion Iliescu's pro-Moscow government in Bucharest has made both sides cautious in seeking ties with one another. In August 1990 Romania announced plans to help Moldova develop a national police force, and a month later the two signed a treaty of cooperation. Although each side has disavowed Romanian-Moldovan reunification, groups are lobbying for it in both republics.

A number of other neighboring states have also become more deeply involved in Soviet republic affairs. Turkey, for example, is now a major trading partner of both Armenia and Azerbaijan and plans more formal ties with the latter republic. Turkey has also been negotiating direct economic relations with the various Central Asian republics.

Iran has also been seeking direct ties with the various Muslim republics, particularly with neighboring Azerbaijan and Persian-speaking Tajikistan. These ties may speed the pace of local economic development but over the long run could help advance Islamic separatism. The same is true of the smaller but growing economic presence of Saudi Arabian business interests, which have offered to fund the development of Islamic banks in several Muslim republics. Saudi Arabia is also helping to fund the distribution of Korans, the rebuilding of religious schools, and mass pilgrimages to Mecca.

The introduction of more direct ties between Kazakhstan and the Muslim minority population in China has been far more in line with Moscow's basic interests. In addition, the Russian republic has been actively seeking agreements of economic cooperation with Eastern Europe and, more important, with its Pacific neighbors. South Korean investment has been promised to Russia, as well as to Kazakhstan.

In many ways, having the republics act independently has worked to Moscow's advantage, since a whole variety of state-to-state investment programs are now planned that might not have developed had Moscow been the sole bargaining agent. Moreover, republic-to-republic agreements are helping distribute resources and manufactured goods in a potentially more efficient way than occurred under the former hypercentralized system. However, at some point the USSR's international legitimacy will be weakened by a perceived inability to pursue a unified foreign policy. Economic investors also need to be confident that those who have guaranteed them certain rights do indeed control them.

Gorbachev has usually been an acute judge of international public opinion. Immediately after the conclusion of the CSCE treaty he made clear that he was no longer going to be a willing party to the further decentralization of Soviet domestic and foreign policy. On November 24, 1990, his draft of a union treaty was published—a plan for a union of "sovereign" republics that would be subordinate to Moscow on questions of finance, defense, and foreign policy. The treaty would leave the USSR's gold, diamond, and other strategic reserves in the hands of the central government.

Gorbachev used the strengthened presidential powers to threaten fractious republics, and appointed a new hard-line minister of internal affairs, Boris Pugo. The war of words was renewed against the Baltic republics, and the whole country was put on warning that the terms of delivery previously set for 1991 were going to be enforced. All foreign trade agreements not submitted for Moscow's approval were declared null and void. Gorbachev wanted to keep control of foreign trade until January 1, 1991, when virtually all transactions would be based on hard currency exchanges. The Soviet republics have essentially been denied the ability to maintain their own hard currency reserves, without which their sovereignty will be sharply restricted.

Gorbachev's conduct at the Fourth Congress of People's Deputies in mid-December 1990 made clear that his commitment to democratic reform was secondary to that of keeping the USSR intact. Gorbachev asked for expanded presidential powers to ensure that the central government's decisions were enforced. He then stated that these new powers would be used against republics that failed to observe the nation's laws. The Treaty of Union was approved by the Congress, as was a proposal to bypass the republic legislatures and ratify the treaty in national referenda. Republics that voted down the treaty were further warned that they would have to meet the terms of exit from the USSR that the Congress had previously established.

Indeed, the policies announced at the Fourth Congress had immediate consequences. In the midst of the December 1990 conference, then Foreign Minister Eduard Shevardnadze delivered a passionate resignation speech, citing fears

All three Baltic republics recognized that the future independence of the region would be decided in Lithuania.

of an encroaching dictatorship. Shevardnadze's warnings were soon borne out.

Tensions in the Baltic republics increased steadily in December 1990 and early January 1991. The considerable pro-Soviet Russian-speaking minority in Latvia and Estonia as well as Russians in all three republics began to complain loudly of the hardships brought by the "illegal" actions of their republics. The local Soviet military, always a strong presence in the region, also stepped up its criticism of these regimes, which were determined to deny ethnic Russians special access to housing, food, or schooling for their children. For their part, the Baltic republics refused to bow to the renewed pressure and continued to pursue policies that reinforced their aim of peacefully devolving into fully independent states.

On January 7, 1991, Moscow signaled that it would no longer tolerate the Baltic republics' assumption of a special status. The conscription of youths into the Soviet Army would be forcibly implemented nationwide. Moscow announced that the overwhelming majority of youths had failed to show up for conscription in Armenia, Estonia, Georgia, Latvia, and Lithuania. Elite "Black Beret" troops were going to the Baltic republics to insure adherence to a January 13 deadline for youths to turn up for service.

Efforts by the Landsbergis government to continue with business as usual faltered. A threefold price increase on food provoked massive public demonstrations, and the decision to rescind it prompted the resignation of Prime Minister Prunskiene. While Landsbergis struggled to find a new prime minister, Moscow announced that a shadowy Committee of National Salvation had been formed in Vilnius, with unnamed membership, that was committed to restoring "constitutional order" to Lithuania.

The first efforts to restore this order were taken on January 13, when tanks and troops were used to "retake" the television tower in Vilnius, which was guarded by unarmed civilians. At least 14 Lithuanians were killed in the assault, and more than a hundred were injured. While Moscow has claimed that the local military commander made the decision for the attack, it has shown its de facto support by, among other things, offering falsified reporting of the events.

The Latvians and Lithuanians both feared that their duly elected governments would be forced to resign. Parliaments in both republics were barricaded against possible attack. But while Gorbachev sought to allay fears that force would be used again, the three pro-independence Baltic governments were convinced that they faced uncertain futures.

The situation also remains volatile in Georgia, where some estimate that there are at least 17,000 members of paramilitary organizations and, in addition, the KGB and MVD have been placed under local control. The Georgians seem prepared to defend the continued existence of their own pro-independence government and to defy Moscow by forcibly integrating southern Ossetia into Georgia. The situation in Armenia is also unpredictable. President Levon Ter Petrossian is pursuing a more moderate course toward an independent or non-Soviet Armenia, but Armenians, too, are likely to resist forced conscription and the suspension of republic laws.

The government of Moldova has demanded that its citizens submit to Gorbachev's presidential decree, which demands the reintegration of the republic, now split into three parts. But Moldovan nationalists will not quietly submit to curbs on the use of the Moldovan language and calls to disband their local police force and national guard. Yet, unless they do so, the Turkic-Christian Gagauz minority and local Russians will continue to reject the authority of the government in Kishinev. Prospects for peace in the Ukraine are even less certain; the republic will hold together only if secessionist-minded western Ukrainians are convinced that their republic is fully sovereign.

Gorbachev has enough dependable troops to send to a number of trouble spots concurrently. But it would be difficult to send, let alone maintain, occupation forces in all of these regions simultaneously.

Gorbachev's decision to crack down on the independence drives has seriously reduced his credibility as a political reformer and can offer only a temporary solution to the USSR's nationality problem. Gorbachev may be able to reestablish the central government's authority among most of the population of the Russian republic, particularly if emergency food shipments are strategically distributed among the large cities of European Russia and Siberia.

Nonetheless, Russian "liberals" feel betrayed by Gorbachev's actions in Lithuania and his apparent move away from guaranteeing Soviet citizens basic civil liberties, such as freedom of the press, speech, and assembly. Demonstrations and political strikes seem sure to continue, particularly if the liberals continue to receive at least tacit support from Yeltsin. However, Gorbachev can surely count on the support of most of the nearly 30 million Russians who live outside the republic as well as ethnic minorities who fear that they will be involuntarily joined to secessionist states.

The support of other non-Russians—who make up close to half the country's population—will be more difficult to sustain. Four years after the violence in Alma Ata, Gorbachev still thinks that waving both the carrot of foreign goods and the stick of threatened force will get people to pursue their "rational" self-interest, rebuilding the shattered Soviet economy in unison.

The events of the past several years, however, should have clearly demonstrated that the idea of a single union—even a loosely defined one—is unacceptable, not just to millions of Soviet citizens but to whole national communities. For many, economic concerns are no longer primary; others distrust an economic recovery that is not backed by political guarantees. For significant numbers of non-Russians, independence and political autonomy are worth dying for. So far no one is expressing any willingness to risk dying for the union.

Gorbachev might have the stronger hand for now. However, time seems destined to prove him a transitional figure, a leader with the ability to question but not reject his own formative political values. Many of today's republic leaders suffer from the same defect. They are balanced between the unsteady leadership in Moscow and a populace who feel tricked by false promises of sovereignty. Anticommunist republic leaders who fail to deliver either independence or prosperity will prove vulnerable to the will of the people.

Western leaders rightfully fear the destabiliz-ing impact of the disintegration of the Soviet Union. The border states that are rushing to cement ties with the frontier republics realize that regional strategic balances could shift in their favor. If the Soviet western border changes, all the borders in Central Europe will become less stable. The secession of the Caucasian republics could affect the power balance in Southwest Asia, and the breakaway of Central Asia certainly would. No responsible leader wants to face these problems, but they may be unavoidable.

The preservation of the Soviet Union may be in the best interests of the Western powers and the USSR's neighbors, and in the economic self-interest of the Soviet citizens themselves; but stable states require the consent of the governed. Majority rule is not synonymous with consensual government. Carefully worded national referenda do not denote popular confidence in a political system. There is no way that the West can confer upon Gorbachev the political legitimacy that his own people have denied him.

Gorbachev has been crippled politically by his nationality crisis. He has failed to demonstrate the creative vision at home that he has shown in the international arena. He has sacrificed democratic reforms in favor of preserving the union by force. He no longer enjoys the confidence of the Soviet people. Thus while it is all well and good to provide humanitarian assistance to Soviet citizens, aid should not be tied directly to Gorbachev's political future or to any of today's Soviet leaders, lest their downfall limit future U.S. relations with successor regimes in Moscow or in the republics.

The principle behind the Bush administration's advice to the Vilnius government in March 1990 should guide American policy toward the Soviet Union more generally: The United States will help only those who can demonstrate they are exercising legitimate authority.

Article 4.2. Soviet Disunion

The authors analyze the political changes sweeping the USSR, which continue unabated. Badly shaken by the recent coup against him, Soviet president Gorbachev finds himself increasingly weakened and vulnerable, to the point that he has been forced to accede to a list of demands from Russian president Boris Yeltsin—demands which have further undermined the central Soviet government and the Supreme Soviet, suggesting that Gorbachev will be little more than a figurehead in the future. With Russia as the new center, the Soviet Union is certain to be a looser confederation of states. At the same time, many Soviets fear increased Russian domination and total disintegration in the days ahead.

SOVIET DISUNION

In 1917, as the czar's power faltered and chaos grew, the Russian writer Maxim Gorky observed with disgust that his countrymen seemed to have "an inborn inclination toward anarchism."

As the changes sweeping the U.S.S.R. spread with unstoppable force last week, they took on that especially Russian character that Gorky would have had no trouble recognizing—less about building a new society of freedom and democracy, more about simply tearing down the old and fighting over whatever is left.

The leadership of Byelorussia, which had seemed hard-line communist before the coup attempt, became converts to the nationalist cause and joined the other Soviet states that have declared independence and laid claim to the assets of the defunct Communist Party and the near defunct central government. With the fight over the remnants of central power intensifying, Russian President Boris Yeltsin each day seemed to discover yet another item that be-

longed to his own increasingly powerful republic. He claimed as Russia's the property of the Russian Communist Party, the property of the Soviet Communist Party within Russia, the ethnic Russian areas of neighboring republics, the coal-rich areas of the Crimea, the KGB, even the Kremlin buildings themselves.

Soviet President Mikhail Gorbachev, badly shaken by the coup against him, pulled himself together last week but seemed increasingly impotent and irrelevant as the pace of change quickened.

"The whole question now is Russia and the republics," argues Seweryn Bialer of Columbia University. "There is no central Soviet government. There is no central Supreme Soviet. What remains in the center is only a vacuum." It is primarily Russian Republic leader Yeltsin and other republic leaders, not Gorbachev, who will decide what happens next.

By the end of last week, Yeltsin had already negotiated interim economic and mili-

tary pacts with the Ukraine and Kazakhstan that all but ignore the central Soviet authority. Citing "the inability of union state structures to provide vital interests of the peoples," the Ukraine-Russia agreement calls upon other states of the "former U.S.S.R." to join in economic agreements and expresses a commitment to abide by arms-control treaties signed by the U.S.S.R. The pact calls for new military arrangements, including joint control by local governors and the central government over troops stationed in each republic. "The old union does not exist and there can be no return to it," said Leningrad Mayor Anatoly Sobchak, who sat in on the Ukraine-Russia talks as Gorbachev's observer.

Clearly, Yeltsin hopes that in any new union, his own Russian state will be calling the shots. "The collapse of the Kremlin does not mean the collapse of the center," he suggested. In fact, as Russia's power has grown in the wake of the failed coup, Gorbachev has lost both power and legitimacy, and the Soviet leader last week found himself reduced to repeating his threat to resign if the union is not preserved. The Supreme Soviet, which stripped Gorbachev of his emergency economic powers, was elected more than two years ago and packed with communists; when the more representative and

Copyright, September 9, 1991, *U.S. News & World Report.*

55

reformist Congress of People's Deputies convenes this week, it is likely to unleash a new torrent of criticism on Gorbachev and his discredited government.

In promoting Russia as the new center, however, Yeltsin is guaranteeing a much looser confederation of states — something more than the European Economic Community but less than the United States. Resentment of Russian ethnic chauvinism and centuries-old memories of enslavement to Muscovy have already caused sparks to fly from the non-Russian republics. "Russia will end up as the de facto center," says James Brusstar, a Soviet military specialist at the National Defense University, "but it won't be able to dictate to the republics."

The Big Four. But balancing any fears of Russian domination are fears of total disintegration into chaos, a taste of which has been provided already. Although the situation remains extremely volatile, some sort of loose confederation centered on the four most important states — Russia, Byelorussia, the Ukraine and Kazakhstan — seems likely to emerge ultimately, if for no other reason than economic necessity. Kazakhstan President Nursultan Nazarbayev has already called for a meeting of all 15 republics to work out future economic and political relations. He has pointedly not invited Gorbachev. "It would be better if Gorbachev were not there because otherwise it would look as though the center were dominating matters once again," he explained.

With the major exceptions of the Baltic States, whose claims to sovereignty are widely accepted in Europe and the United States, and Moldavia, which has historical, linguistic and ethnic links to Romania, at least some of the independence declarations by the Soviet republics seemed more tactical than an expression of genuine national aspiration: The old-guard communist leaders of many of the republics, anxious to dissociate themselves from the discredited central party and eager, too, to stake out the most advantageous bargaining position in the coming negotiations divvying up the assets and powers of the center, have jumped on the independence bandwagon. Nationalist drives in Byelorussia, Azerbaijan and Central Asia — led by the conservative communist presidents of those republics — may have more to do with political survival than democracy and more to do with looting than liberation. Huge wealth once controlled by the center, such as California-size state farms, is now up for grabs.

Economic reality. Even those republics driven by genuine nationalistic senti-

ment, such as Georgia and Armenia, are likely to find that they cannot survive economically outside some confederation. "The republics know that they need to buy and sell from each other. They're not crazy," says Roman Szporluk, professor of Ukrainian history at Harvard University. "What they don't want is to have people in Moscow give them orders."

So far Yeltsin has preferred to negotiate with the republics instead of trying to give them orders. He has let it be known, for example, that if the rights of the Russian minorities in other republics are respected, Russia will make no territorial claims on its neighbors. But if Russians are mistreated or expelled, Russia may seek to redraw the artificial boundaries drawn by the Bolsheviks and Stalin, most of which are in dispute anyway. And Russia has both carrots and sticks at its disposal: The bulk of the Army and the KGB will be loyal to Russia, and the largest republic has enormous economic leverage it can use to prevent the union from disintegrating completely.

But the nationalist genie, even if summoned for cynical ends, may not be so easy to recork. Experts on Soviet nationalities suggest that some of the republics may even be willing to descend to subsistence-level economies rather than submit to Russian economic and political domination. The nationalist fever may have to run its course — with full independence, the establishment of separate currencies, and so on — before a confederation will re-emerge.

The Baltic States are, on several scores, well ahead of the other breakaway republics. Their historical claims to independence are on much more solid ground than are, say, Byelorussia's. France and Germany, in extending full recognition to the Baltics — which were wiped off the map in 1940 when they were annexed by the Soviet Union as the result of a secret agreement between Hitler and Stalin — emphasized that the three countries were a "special case," which set no precedent for recognizing the other Soviet republics. The Baltics are a special case in another sense: They have geographic and ethnic ties to the Scandinavian countries that may allow for quick economic assimilation outside the Soviet sphere.

As recriminations over the August 19 coup continued, with the dismissal of the entire governing council of the KGB and the indictment of 13 top officials on the capital charge of high treason, it became increasingly clear that the conspiracy failed not only as a result of "people power" but because of old-fashioned power politics. It was organized by a

clique of Communist Party politicians, not military men. In fact, the coup leaders had been counting on the support of three Army divisions; all three balked. At first it appeared that individual soldiers were refusing to fire on the Russian people, but soon it was clear that entire units were switching allegiance to the Russian Federation.

The swift descent into chaos and national disintegration following the collapse of the Communist Party and the state's traditional organs of repression revealed the limits of Gorbachev's political reforms. By the same token, it showed just how much power the KGB, the military and the party had retained, even under *perestroika*. "Gorbachev had sought to preserve both the union and the Communist Party, the only structure capable of governing it," observes Yale historian Michael Howard.

For a nation that was so long governed by absolute and arbitrary rule, there are few ready-made sources of legitimacy to take the place of the discredited institutions that, until last week, continued to exercise power. One that the people may turn to — and that has many non-Russians worried — is old-fashioned Russian imperialism. Yeltsin, who unlike Gorbachev was popularly elected, nevertheless rushed into the vacuum left by the collapse of the center and immediately began issuing a series of decrees.

Yeltsin's order to shut down six Communist Party newspapers stirred one *Pravda* correspondent to retort that the authorities were "acting like Bolsheviks" — a comment echoed by Anatoly Vavilov, a director of Moscow's communist Party High School, who found the front entrance to the school sealed by Moscow city officials. "Suddenly today we found ourselves without a job," said Pavel Zlobin, a director of the school.

But the collapse of the Communist Party — and the suspension last week of all its activities by the Supreme Soviet — means more than just lost jobs for party hacks. The seizure of party bank accounts and some 5,000 party buildings throughout the country, including the gray stone headquarters of the Central Committee near the Kremlin, ripped the moorings from a highly centralized society that for 70 years ran everything from factories and farms to the military and the media on orders from above.

Although weakened by *perestroika*, the power of the party had by no means been eliminated by Gorbachev, who tried to walk a fine line between the new reformers and the old guard. While trimming the power of the party and the KGB, he had, until last week, found them too helpful to his own cause to eliminate completely.

Most clearly, Gorbachev's unwavering support of the party, which outlasted even the coup attempt by several days, had stifled the rise of any meaningful opposition. "Outside of the Baltics, there's no real alternative to the political elite," says Martha Olcott of Colgate University. "And even in the Baltics, half of the new leadership are old Communist Party functionaries."

The old KGB. The enormous power of the KGB over Soviet political and social life is now becoming clearer. While curtailing its worst abuses of the past, the KGB has continued to keep an eye on Soviet citizens and to manipulate the flow of information. "The KGB only changed on the surface," says KGB defector Stanislav Levchenko, who now is an international security consultant. "[It] is literally everywhere. Every collective farm, every nuclear submarine has at least one KGB officer."

While eliminating its notorious Fifth Directorate, which had dealt with political dissent, the KGB under Gorbachev continued many of the same activities through its new Directorate for the Protection of the Soviet Constitution. Gorbachev just this spring pushed through a new law—suspended last week—that codified the agency's enormous powers, including such "rights" as controlling postal dispatches and telephone conversations and detaining for 30 days persons "spreading provocative rumors." As it turned out, of course, by trying to use old, discredited institutions as his vehicle for reform, Gorbachev preserved the very power structures that nearly unseated him.

In decrees signed last week, Gorbachev removed the government's communication system from KGB control and ordered the transfer of hundreds of thousands of KGB troops, who had been responsible for maintaining internal order and guarding borders, to the Defense Ministry. Yegor Yakovlev, the new head of Gostelradio, the state broadcasting company, said he contacted the new KGB chief, Vadim Bakatin, who confirmed his suspicions that many KGB agents were working as news correspondents and in the TV personnel department. "I got Bakatin's agreement that all those agents won't be working here tomorrow," he said. And last week, Bakatin called the agency a "huge monopoly that must be done away with." He said he wants to eliminate all the political functions of the agency and transform it into a Western-style intelligence agency.

The KGB will hardly be missed. But the sudden collapse of central power

The real nuclear problem

The Soviet Union proved that command economies are a disaster. But when it comes to controlling nuclear weapons, central authority still has a lot to recommend it.

Moscow recognized that it had to ensure the security of its 27,000-warhead arsenal as early as 1990. After violence erupted in the Baltics and in the warring republics of Azerbaijan and Armenia, the Ministry of Defense withdrew tactical nuclear weapons from supply depots in those areas.

But that has left thousands of strategic weapons—bombs and missiles—in the Ukraine, Byelorussia and Kazakhstan. U.S. experts insist that unauthorized use of the weapons is extremely unlikely. Bruce Blair of the Brookings Institution, a former Minuteman launch-control officer, says no individual could give the order to launch a nuclear weapon. The Soviet president and the Ministry of Defense must each provide special codes to start the process; probably fewer than a half-dozen officials have access to the codes.

On bases, warheads are guarded separately from the missiles that carry them. To arm a warhead, a 12-digit number must be punched into an electronic cipher lock. Punching in the wrong code permanently disables the warhead. Moreover, each code is good for only one warhead or one small group of missiles. And commanders can override subordinates preparing to launch. During the coup, the commander in charge of mobile SS-25 ICBMs reportedly sheltered them in garrisons where they could not be used.

Then there is the potential problem of short-range missiles, bombs and artillery shells, which may have fewer safeguards than strategic weapons. At present, these are under Russian control in the other republics. But some experts wonder whether they will all be returned to Russia as promised.

The real problem may be sorting out who has legal authority over nuclear forces. Twelve of the 16 Soviet bases for intercontinental ballistic missiles are in Russia, as are 10 of 12 mobile ICBM bases, all six ballistic missile submarine bases and 11 of 26 strategic bomber bases. But that still leaves thousands of warheads in the Ukraine, Kazakhstan and Byelorussia.

As the Soviet Union disintegrates, Russia may inherit its nuclear arsenal. The new Soviet defense minister, Air Force Marshal Yevgeny Shaposhnikov, has hinted that equipment like tanks might be handed over to Ukrainian control but that nuclear weapons are another matter.

The other republics may not even want nuclear weapons. The Ukraine, where the Chernobyl accident galvanized an anti-nuclear movement, has called for the removal of nuclear weapons from its territory; in Kazakhstan, site of most of the 500 Soviet nuclear tests conducted since 1949, there also is strong anti-nuclear sentiment. A popular backlash, sparked by radioactive leaks during 1989 tests, has shut down the test site at Semipalatinsk.

The most likely outcome is a transfer of weapons from Kazakhstan and the Ukraine to Russia. Blair says SS-19 and SS-24 ICBM fields in the Ukraine may have been slated for decommissioning even before the failed coup. And the new START agreement specifically allows for the removal of SS-18s from Kazakhstan to new bases in Russia.

Will that make Russia the new nuclear superpower? Not quite. Divorced from the other republics, it will lose defensive facilities such as early-warning systems, and it can't afford to replace them on Russian soil. And a new chain of command may prove cumbersome: Yeltsin's aides' call for dual control of all weapons on Russian soil would give the republic a veto over use of the Soviet nuclear force.

BY BRUCE B. AUSTER

has raised questions about the future of other institutions much more vital to the functioning of the new state or states. The biggest upheavals may come in the workplace, where party cells not only attempted to enforce ideological conformity but, even under Gorbachev's economic reforms, continued to play a vital role in obtaining supplies through the vast party networks. "It will be easier to extricate the party from political and social life than from the economy," says Joel Hellman of Columbia University. "The network of party officials was created over 70 years and may not just fold."

Productivity gains. Some industries are by their nature more able to adapt to the sudden lifting of party control than others. Urged on by Yeltsin, Gorbachev issued a decree last week that in one stroke shattered the party's media empire, which employed 80,000 people in 144 publications and 81 publishing houses. Almost overnight, a string of independent newspapers were created that, in most cases, were given to employees. "We are finally able to write what we think," said Michael Berger, a specialist on economics for the evening newspaper *Izvestia.* "Productivity is soaring. People are working all morning and all night."

But the outlook for the bureaucracy-bound indus-

The secrets in the basement

For more than 70 years, the trail of some of the most enduring mysteries of the 20th century—from the fate of Raoul Wallenberg to the plot to kill Pope John Paul II—stopped cold at the front door of Lubyanka, the KGB's yellow-and-gray stone headquarters on Moscow's Dzerzhinsky Square. But now, the once untouchable Committee on State Security is being forced to surrender its secret archives.

Last week the new KGB chief, former Interior Minister Vadim Bakatin, ordered the archives, which are buried in the bowels of the former insurance office that has served as KGB headquarters for 53 years, "frozen" to prevent their destruction. "I am not against making public all the archives that deal with our history," Bakatin said, "but I will categorically oppose . . . demands for access to archives on agents."

Was there a CIA mole? The documents inside the locked file cabinets could solve an array of tantalizing cases: What Western politicians were on the Soviet payroll? Was there a "fifth man" who worked with British spy Kim Philby? Is there new evidence on Alger Hiss? Did the KGB help plan the assassination attempt on the pope? What relationship, if any, did Lee Harvey Oswald have with the KGB? Was Soviet defector Yuri Nosenko, who claimed to have information on Oswald, genuine or a plant? Was there a high-level KGB mole in the CIA?

The records cover the whole bloody history of the Soviet secret police, from its founding in 1917 as the Cheka, through its Stalinist reincarnation as the NKVD, to its present status as the KGB. Although they are a treasure-trove of information on all the years since the Bolshevik Revolution, the KGB refused to open its files even to the most prominent Soviet historians, including the author of an official military history of World War II. Soviet journalist Alexander Milchakov, who rankled the KGB by locating 11 mass grave sites of Stalin's victims around Moscow, says he was never allowed to see the archives, even after the KGB agreed to cooperate in his search. But a KGB officer assigned to help Milchakov said in an interview that when he examined the documents for the period, he found that even the names of victims dumped in mass graves had been meticulously recorded.

The files almost certainly would shed light on the nagging case of Swedish diplomat Raoul Wallenberg, who saved the lives of thousands of Jews in Nazi-controlled Hungary and was arrested by the Soviets in Budapest at the end of World War II. Soviet officials insist that Wallenberg died in 1947 but have produced little convincing evidence of his fate. Last year, then Interior Minister Bakatin allowed an international team to examine some non-KGB prison records, but officials made it clear that if a full dossier on Wallenberg existed, the KGB had it. Now Bakatin, considered a reformer, is the head of the KGB. Wallenberg's half brother, Guy von Dardel, was planning a visit to Moscow this week, so a break in the case could be near.

But Bakatin's order freezing the files has come too late to uncover evidence of crimes committed by KGB officers who are still serving. Angry Latvians attacked the KGB office in Riga and destroyed files. Oleg Kalugin, a dissident former KGB major general, said he believes the KGB destroyed much of the evidence of the suppression of Soviet dissidents during the past two years. In addition, according to the Soviet newspaper *Kommersant,* KGB officers, fearing a mob attack on headquarters after the coup collapsed, began stuffing classified documents into special burn bags.

BY DOUGLAS STANGLIN IN MOSCOW

trial, transportation and agricultural sectors is not so bright in the short run. President Bush and British Prime Minister John Major announced that the two nations would accelerate food aid to the Soviet Union in anticipation of severe shortages forecast for this winter. At least some of the aid would be sent directly to the republics, bypassing the central authorities.

Whose military power? The Soviet Army is another institution unlikely to survive intact. The loss of the Baltics and the potential loss of the Ukraine pose enormous strategic problems for military planners. According to Edward Warner of the Rand Corp., all five branches of the Soviet military maintain substantial forces in the Ukraine, including 29 divisions, two ICBM fields, bomber bases and the Black Sea fleet.

In talks with Ukrainian leaders, the new Soviet defense minister, Air Force Marshal Yevgeny Shaposhnikov, has already signaled Moscow's recognition that control of ground forces could be shared. Pentagon analysts believe that Soviet ground forces will most likely be split up into local militias, with total force numbers dropping substantially from 4 million today to 2½ million, with only half of those under central control. Shaposhnikov predicted last week that an all-volunteer force will ultimately take the place of the current conscript Army.

The Air Force, the Navy and the ICBM forces may have less trouble adapting to change than the ground forces. Their ranks are already predominantly Russian, and the bases of those forces that are outside Russia could probably be relocated into Russia proper without too great a disruption.

Air defenses may be the thorniest problem. They can only function as a nationwide, integrated system; loss of air defense radars and interceptor bases in the Baltics and the eastern republics could shorten the warning time of an attack on Moscow by 10 minutes or more.

One thing is certain: Whatever is left will be a shadow of the military force that struck fear into the hearts of Western military planners for four decades. Reformist Soviet officers who had advocated a posture of "minimum sufficiency" — the smallest force that could defend the country — are now finding their ideas in the mainstream. "Everything has changed," says one Pentagon official of the new Soviet military leadership. "If they weren't reformers before, they'll have to become reformers now." ■

BY STEPHEN BUDIANSKY WITH DOUGLAS STANGLIN IN MOSCOW, JULIE CORWIN AND BRUCE B. AUSTER

Article 5.1.   Reaching Out to Moscow

Advocating a new foreign and defense policy, Marshall Brement contends that recent events in the Soviet Union and Eastern Europe underscore the two major fallacies—namely, that nuclear deterrence prevented a Soviet attack on the United States and its allies, and that in the event that deterrence proves inadequate, the West has only a matter of weeks to prepare for war. The author rejects both of these assumptions, insisting that the United States should reject the doctrine of nuclear deterrence in favor of cooperation, which would not only reduce the risks of nuclear war but allow the U.S. to spend some of the savings in defense on more pressing domestic problems.

REACHING OUT TO MOSCOW

by Marshall Brement

The time has come for a radical restructuring of American foreign policy and the defense system that supports it. The U.S. military posture has been based on two fallacies: that only nuclear deterrence prevents a Soviet attack on America and its allies, and that if deterrence should fail the West has at most several weeks to get ready for war.

Both of these suppositions were always dubious, but profound changes in the Soviet Union and Eastern Europe have now deprived them of even the most marginal plausibility. The West would have many months, not weeks, to prepare for war. And the political changes necessary before the Kremlin decided to go to war would require not months, but years.

This gives the United States time. Washington should use it to reorganize its defenses, to bring its alliances into line with twenty-first century realities, to discard the scare doctrine of nuclear deterrence, and thereby to change its relationship from competition to cooperation with the only nation that has the physical power to destroy America. This would not

MARSHALL BREMENT, *former U.S. ambassador to Iceland and senior National Security Council staff member in charge of Soviet affairs, served two tours in the U.S. Embassy in Moscow and is currently a guest scholar at the Woodrow Wilson International Center for Scholars.*

only immeasurably enhance U.S. security, but would also allow a transfer of hundreds of billions of dollars to urgent domestic needs. The United States spent almost $2 trillion to defend itself and its allies against Moscow during the past decade. It cannot afford to spend the same sum during the next.

Americans first must recognize that a determined reduction of international tensions is not just the policy of Soviet President Mikhail Gorbachev. It is the likely policy of even the most hardline of his possible successors. It was, in fact, the general policy of his short-lived predecessors Yuri Andropov and Konstantin Chernenko, who learned from Leonid Brezhnev that détente could not be maintained in tandem with a series of confrontations in the Third World.

A pervasive apathy and cynicism throughout the Soviet political and social system and economic stagnation were the root causes of Gorbachev's program of *perestroika*, *glasnost*, and *democratizatsiya* (democratization). But it also was not lost on the Soviets that the annual U.S. defense budget grew from $144 billion to $289 billion in the six years after they invaded Afghanistan. By this budgetary commitment the United States conclusively demonstrated that confrontation resulted in a defense competition that the USSR could not maintain.

As Communist party general secretary, Gorbachev has faced a barrage of criticism unparalleled in Soviet history. But very little of it has focused on his foreign policy, on the new thinking about the importance of mutual security with the United States, or on his conviction that the Soviet Union must abandon "outmoded views on the world revolutionary process," end "isolation of socialist countries from the mainstream of world civilization," and abandon "the understanding of progress as a permanent confrontation with a socially different world." Complaints are growing among his conservative opponents that Gorbachev has been maladroit, that he has given too much away without getting enough in return. But these are complaints about tactics, not about the basic strategy of achieving a consensus with the West on security questions.

The fact is that there is now no political group in the Soviet Union—however radical, however nationalistic, however conservative—and no potential successor on the horizon that has come up with an alternative foreign policy or that would oppose the Gorbachev program of rapprochement with Washington, of reducing support for Third World clients, of abandoning dreams of a genuine blue water navy, and of withdrawing forces not only from Hungary and Czechoslovakia but also from Cam Ranh Bay and Socotra. This phenomenon is a result of the Soviet Union's inward focus, which will endure for a long time. It has become impossible to convince the Soviet public that events in Benin, Mozambique, or North Yemen really matter.

The Politburo and the Central Committee that selected Gorbachev in March 1985 were extremely orthodox conservative bodies. Yet only the most hard-nosed ideologues within the leadership failed to grasp that the Soviet system was in crisis and that a radical shakeup was desperately needed. At that time *glasnost* and *democratizatsiya* were probably not on anyone's agenda other than Gorbachev's, and possibly not even on his. But some form of *perestroika*—a radical organizational and economic transformation—would have taken place no matter who was running the USSR. And *perestroika* requires relaxation of tensions with the United States and its allies.

Further, *perestroika* is a road that will take decades to travel. Before it reaches its end it will—as has already been seen—lead to imbalance, instability, and enormous popular grumbling at empty shelves, corrupt officials, rising prices, and broken dreams. In order to allay such dissatisfaction and keep the process moving, Gorbachev needs some quick economic fixes. These can only be obtained through direct help from the West and, even more important, through a massive internal transfer of investment and resources from the military to the civilian economy.

Yet this also requires assistance from the United States in the form of strategic cooperation to demonstrate that the perceived threat to the Soviet Union is genuinely diminishing. *Perestroika* depends in both the short and the long run on using the resources of the military economy, which account for 15–17 per cent of the Soviet gross national product according to the CIA, and more than twice that amount according to estimates by other observers, including the late Soviet dissident Andrei Sakharov. It therefore requires an extended period of relaxed tensions in the international arena.

Thus for at least the coming decade and perhaps longer the West can operate under the assumption that Gorbachev and his successors will do everything in their power to avoid jangling the international environment and that when problems arise they will try to settle them skillfully and fairly. A decade of benign behavior is not just a prediction. It is a factual description of what has actually happened not only during Gorbachev's time in office—a period already substantially longer than an American presidential term—but also during the five years that preceded it. For the first time in 50 years, Soviet policy initiatives during a decade —the 1980s—could receive at least passing grades, in fact a high B+, from Washington.

Much Soviet conduct over the past decade has been objectionable—not least the inexcusable destruction of a Korean civilian airliner. But such actions either resulted from decisions made before 1980 or were aberrations such as the Korean Airlines incident. Despite continued production of both nuclear and conventional weapons far in excess of any legitimate defense needs, the Kremlin in this period has initiated no egregiously objectionable new policies anywhere in the world. This is the dog that did not bark. It is the most important fact of our time. It gives the United States a chance to change the world.

A Time to Act

Yet Washington is not picking up the challenge. Instead of acting, it is constantly reacting. Having finally concluded that Gorbachev is not really—in the words of presidential spokesman Marlin Fitzwater—a "drugstore cowboy," the Bush administration now clearly wishes him well and is looking for ways to help. But the U.S. reaction is still piecemeal and tentative. Washington is being pushed by events rather than making them happen. Missing is a strategic concept of what it wants a U.S.-Soviet relationship to be and how far it should go to obtain one. Caution is understandable, especially in the face of Soviet history and the enormous military power still at the Kremlin's disposal. But there are important reasons to act decisively, and to act now. The United States cannot afford to sit back and wait for good things to happen.

First, the United States has urgent needs of its own. It must reshape its society, restore its environment, build up its tattered economic infrastructure, resolve its fiscal crisis, and improve the scandalous state of its educational system. Second, even the benign intentions of an inward-focused USSR cannot entirely eliminate the danger of conflict between two powerful nations that keep vast nuclear arsenals pointed at each other on hair-trigger alert. The tragic destruction of Korean Airlines flight 007 illustrated the dangers of failures of communication between the superpowers.

Third, key aspects of America's own foreign and defense policies themselves obstruct changes it wants from the Soviets. There is a critical contradiction between whipping up American popular support for nuclear deterrence and ending the confrontational relationship with Moscow. Americans must distinguish between a USSR that is too absorbed by its own problems to be the kind of troublemaker it was in the past and one willing and able to take the decisive and irreversible actions that would allow a fundamental and permanent transformation of U.S.-Soviet relations. Already, rising direct criticism of Gorbachev himself and the harder line taken by Soviet arms control negotiators suggest that he may run out of room to make significant unilateral concessions. To transform the role of the military in society, for instance, he will need to demonstrate to critics at home that the threat from the West is being substantially reduced.

Moreover, the United States cannot go on conceding the moral high ground to Gorbachev indefinitely without suffering permanent damage to America's role in the world and without undercutting public support for American involvement in international affairs. If the administration digs its heels in and focuses so much on the maintenance of outmoded security arrangements, it will become increasingly irrelevant to European concerns. The United States may miss the opportunity to lead the world into the next century.

Finally, by its reluctance to overcome its rivalry with the USSR in the face of inevitable decreases in its defense budget, the United States in effect is making a whole series of strategic decisions by default. Washington must not be caught in the trap of dealing piecemeal with issues such as arms control, defense realignment, trade, and burden sharing. The United States is building weapons platforms that are intended to be the mainstay of its armed forces 30 or 40 years from now.

This means that unless policymakers evaluate such purchases in a strategic framework they risk not only wasting billions of dollars, but also compromising strategic goals. Closing a base in Arizona may save a great deal of money, but it has no effect in Moscow. Cancelling the MX missile, on the other hand, carries a strong message to both Gorbachev and the general staff. Now is the time to think through what U.S. defense reductions ought to convey to the Kremlin and how they can be fitted into the structure of *perestroika* so that the United States benefits strategically as well as financially.

But altering patterns that have been woven into place and have endured for decades is no simple matter, especially when such patterns are now widely credited with "winning the Cold War." Myth and misconception permeate the entire fabric of U.S.-Soviet relations. Permanent hostility between the superpowers is, in fact, an axiom underpinning a national security framework that consumes a quarter of the federal budget, provides the livelihoods of millions of Americans, and is central to America's alliance structure and to its role in the world. This framework is based on the tenet that only the military strength of the United States has deterred the Soviet Union from attacking the West—a highly debatable proposition.

It is a framework whose components—the U.S. system of defense, the Soviet system of defense, America's alliance system, and the doctrine of nuclear deterrence—form four strands of a rope that have been wound together by five decades of history and the expenditure of trillions of dollars. These disparate strands cannot be successfully unraveled one by one, deferring basic changes in United States security policy or alliance relationships until a fundamentally new bond with the Kremlin is firmly established. All should be disentangled simultaneously and for this the United States must have an overarching strategy, a major key to which each section of the orchestra plays in relative harmony.

Washington must first decide precisely what new U.S.-Soviet relationship it wants. The administration should begin by articulating what more the Soviets must do in order to persuade it that they no longer pose a threat to America's vital interests. Gorbachev has already come a long way in this direction. But even in terms of his own stated goals the road ahead remains long. If the Cold War is over, what need does Moscow have for tens of thousands of nuclear warheads and standing armed forces of 4–5 million troops?

The unilateral cuts in manpower and equipment announced by Gorbachev in December 1988 were bold measures. A Conventional Forces in Europe treaty will further slash the most threatening conventional weapons west of the Urals. But the Urals are no magic barrier; it is a week's train trip from Irkutsk to Berlin. And the Soviet capacity for generating forces, their cadre system of reserves, and their mobilization capabilities remain very impressive.

Even with markedly reduced forces the Soviets will remain the dominant land power in Europe. So if the United States is to transform its relations with the USSR, it is reasonable for Washington to ask Moscow to declare its intentions. The United States should ask the Soviet Union to commit itself to a program approximating the following 17 points:
• roughly 50 per cent cuts in total Soviet armed forces, or from the 4 million troops Moscow now claims to about 2 million;
• an end to conscription;
• conversion of a significant portion of Soviet military industry to civilian purposes;
• acceptance of foreign inspectors at appropriate command and control centers, arms depots, airfields, railheads, and fuel dumps who could detect preparations for war;
• establishment of a date for the promised removal of all Soviet forces from foreign soil, including Mongolia and Kuril islands as well as Eastern Europe;
• a halt to production and deployment of all land-based intercontinental ballistic missiles (ICBMs) and their destruction or reconfiguration for space launch purposes (You cannot build a relationship of trust with a neighbor who has a loaded 50-caliber machine gun pointed at your bedroom.);
• publication of accurate data on the Soviet military budget in accordance with agreed cost accounting methods;
• an end to meddling in trouble spots throughout the world, particularly in Central America and the Middle East, and cooperation with the West in constructive efforts to settle these problems in an equitable fashion;
• substantiation of fine words about preventing chemical warfare and nuclear and missile proliferation with tough action against clients and friends bent on acquiring such capabilities;
• limitation of lethal arms shipments to participants in Third World conflicts;
• reasonable and convincing guarantees for Soviet citizens that their fundamental rights will be respected;
• integration of the USSR into the world economy, including rational pricing and foreign exchange controls, with the ultimate objective of making the ruble fully convertible;
• increased cooperation in the spheres of science and space, and an end to classification of information on spurious grounds of national security;
• permission for foreign institutions of higher education to be established in the USSR;
• expansion of exchanges to include tens of thousands of students;
• termination of official disinformation programs designed to discredit the United States (Contrary to claims by Soviet government-controlled media, the AIDS virus was not invented in U.S. Defense Department biological warfare laboratories.); and
• an end to espionage and the massive government-sponsored program to steal commercial and technological secrets. (Government theft of patents, copyrights, and machinery is unacceptable, particularly when the victim is expected to be a co-signer on the thief's next mortgage application.)

U.S. Policy Changes

To ask the Soviets to commit themselves to such a program, and thereby to lay down a series of benchmarks by which to measure progress in U.S.-Soviet relations, would have seemed hopelessly unrealistic two or three years ago. Had Washington done so, however, it would have seen by now that Moscow has moved forward—in some cases substantially—on every one of these points. It is no longer unrealistic, or even unduly optimistic, to expect eventual satisfaction on all of them.

If such a program were adopted, each of these Soviet moves would require a corresponding American response. The administration, too, would have to accept inspectors at comparable points of importance in the United States. Washington would have to be prepared to let Moscow participate in international economic institutions if it made the necessary economic reforms. Perhaps most difficult, the United States would have to limit lethal arms shipments to its own friends engaged in Third World conflict and take stronger action to hinder the chemical, biological, or nuclear weapons programs of such U.S. allies as Israel and Pakistan.

But matching Soviet moves should not be just a matter of tit-for-tat, since the United States and the USSR do not share all the same fears. Moscow might, for example, be more interested in the elimination of nuclear-armed cruise missiles and airplanes from U.S. naval vessels, or in a drawdown of American submarine-launched ballistic missiles (SLBMs) to the Soviet level, or even in a dignified role in pan-European security organizations, than in cutting the U.S. Army by half or in getting all United States forces off foreign soil. Indeed, it is far from clear that at this point the Soviets want the American military entirely out of Germany or South Korea.

Thus the United States must understand what a Soviet Union that is willing to pursue a program like that sketched above can legitimately ask; what aspects of America's defense program the Soviets consider threatening and a barrier to change on their part; and what Moscow's legitimate security interests are in the countries on its periphery, particularly those across which Russia repeatedly has been invaded.

No doubt Moscow would have its own list of U.S. policies and actions that it deems threatening to its legitimate interests. Some are easy to anticipate. Soviet military leaders would not be earning their salaries if they did not paint a rather grim picture of the U.S. threat to the Soviet Union. It was no accident that former Chief of Staff Sergei Akhromeyev, when he visited his American counterpart in July 1988, was carrying a map that showed the ring of U.S. bases encircling his homeland. On these and other bases are enough nuclear weapons with enough megatonnage to destroy the Soviet Union many times over. Much of this force is kept on a hair-trigger alert, and the United States and its allies still refuse to renounce the threat of first use of nuclear weapons in response to conventional attack by the Soviet Union. In fact, the United States has no credible nonnuclear defenses, which suggests to the Soviet military that the United States believes any conflict will inevitably escalate into Armageddon.

At the root of the problem is the theory of nuclear deterrence, which underlies all aspects of U.S. defense policy. Axiomatic to that theory is the assumption that if the United States did not possess such a massive nuclear arsenal the Soviet Union would engage in unacceptable behavior, including an invasion of Western Europe. The doctrine of nuclear deterrence therefore locks the United States into the status quo. Winning congressional and public support for the staggering costs involved requires depiction of a hostile Soviet Union restrained from wrecking the American way of life only by U.S. maintenance of at least nuclear parity, accompanied by a relentless drive for technical if not numerical superiority.

The credibility of deterrence depends not just on possession of such weapons, but upon forces that are trained in their use through war games and military exercises. These offer convincing evidence to the other side of its opponent's aggressive intentions, further fueling fear and hostility. Scenarios for the use of nuclear weapons impel the kind of thinking behind the U.S. Single Integrated Operations Plan, the kind of thinking that causes the commander-in-chief of the Strategic Air Command to certify every year, in a document that historians will one day surely regard as one of the most bizarre of the twentieth century, that the roughly 10,000 nuclear weapons at his disposal are not sufficient to carry out his mission. Since the Soviets see things in much the same way, continued U.S.-Soviet hostility is assured.

To overcome this, both sides must change their outlooks and policies simultaneously—not sequentially. The United States must come up with a realistic program that commits it to the elimination of nuclear weapons or, failing that, to an end to their deployment and their reduction to the lowest possible levels.

Nuclear deterrence has always been a con game. While it is impossible to prove a negative, there is no reason to believe that if nuclear weapons had not existed either superpower would have seriously contemplated attacking the other, or that the Soviets would have invaded Western Europe. Indeed, numerous defectors and émigrés in recent years have testified that Soviet leaders have believed the USSR to be far weaker throughout the postwar era than Western analysts had supposed. What was most frightening about the Soviet invasion of Afghanistan was that for the first time since

World War II the Soviets believed the correlation of forces in the world permitted them to engage in a direct war, rather than one by proxy. Soviet military as well as political leaders now concede how tragic a mistake that was.

Proponents of nuclear deterrence have also asserted that the superpower nuclear standoff has made the United States and the Soviet Union less willing to risk a direct engagement with each other in Third World conflict and deterred Third World nations from challenging the superpowers' vital interests. In theory, this is logical. But in practice the experience of the past 40 years strongly suggests that the horrors of nuclear holocaust deprive such weapons of their deterrent value because the presumed victim fully understands the physical, political, and psychological penalties that a nuclear aggressor must pay. Stalin knew that the United States would not use its nuclear monopoly to stop his seizure of Eastern Europe. Beijing and Hanoi inflicted hundreds of thousands of casualties on American forces in Korea and Vietnam despite America's possession of nuclear weapons. Arab states more than once attacked Israel despite America's commitment to that country's survival.

Yet another argument advanced on behalf of nuclear deterrence is that without the U.S. nuclear umbrella America's allies in Europe and elsewhere would have been intimidated into making political, economic, or security concessions to the USSR. But proponents of this dubious theory have never been able to come up with a single example or credible scenario to back it up, or to explain precisely what Moscow would have bullied the West Europeans into doing. Moreover, since the newly independent East European nations will soon serve as a physical buffer between the Soviet Union and Western Europe, any temptations Moscow may feel to practice "Finlandization" and its practical opportunities to do so will shrink further.

On the other hand, West Europeans have liked to believe themselves more secure because of the American nuclear guarantee, though leaders from Charles de Gaulle to Henry Kissinger have pointed out its lack of credibility. The nuclear guarantee was an excuse European leaders gave themselves not to pay the political as well as economic costs of raising conventional forces to match those of the USSR. And Washington's role as nuclear guarantor ce-

mented its claim to leadership of the Western world. The arrangement thus served both European and American political ends. But that is a very different thing from being essential to America's security. Indeed, the more Americans warned the West Europeans of the dangers they would confront in the absence of a credible American nuclear guarantee, the more the United States created the very sense of vulnerability to Soviet pressure it claimed to want to avoid. Insofar as it ever existed outside American minds, the "Finlandization syndrome" probably was a self-inflicted wound. In any case, it is a thing of the past, not the future.

Not only do nuclear weapons have little deterrent value but they place the United States at a military disadvantage. Their use could undercut what is perhaps America's greatest single military advantage: the ability of the U.S. Navy to control the seas. And in a Third World conflict their possession by a Khomeini or a Qaddafi would neutralize U.S. conventional superiority. Would the United States have taken action against Libya in 1986 or Panama in 1989 if Qadaffi or Noriega had possessed nuclear weapons?

For the United States, nuclear weapons have served a political rather than a military function; they have increased U.S. influence over the policies of allied states that believed America's protection was necessary. But the price has been high—not least in that it has allowed West Europeans and Japanese to devote their resources to domestic concerns and to outdistance the United States economically. In any case, a Western Europe that no longer fears the Soviet Union has begun to question its need for U.S. protection.

A Conventional Deterrence

Conventional wisdom holds that the genie cannot be put back in the bottle—that since nuclear weapons cannot be uninvented, the United States must keep them in its arsenal for deterrence purposes. Conventional wisdom is wrong. Modern nonnuclear weapons in the hands of a superpower are accurate and powerful enough to deter anyone from attacking Washington or Moscow with nuclear or conventional weapons and to keep either superpower from attacking the other. This will be doubly true of the exotic weapons of the next century.

Advanced conventional weapons cannot threaten to destroy whole cities or an entire civilization, although Dresden, Manila, and An Loc were bombed just as flat as Nagasaki. They will not deter by terror as nuclear weapons do, and they will lack the latter's psychological cachet, at least until their full destructive power is understood. But Reconnaissance Strike Platforms and conventional weapons now on the drawing board and in development, such as Fuel Air Explosives, the Precision Location Strike System, and the Sadarm Cluster Projectile, combine extremely long range, pinpoint accuracy, and vastly greater explosive power than currently available weapons.

They will give the battlefield commander of the twenty-first century all of the warfighting advantages of nuclear weapons without their accompanying drawbacks. They will be able to destroy up to an entire division of tanks with one hit. Within the decade such weapons could reach deep into the Soviet Union from ships or aircraft well beyond its borders, making it impossible for Soviet forces to mass their armor for an invasion of Western Europe. And because advanced conventional weapons could be fired from the same ships and planes that now carry nuclear weapons, they would be just as capable of surviving any first-strike attack.

By depriving a Soviet leadership of the hope of mobilizing offensive forces before they were annihilated, such conventional weapons could provide a deterrent different in kind, but no less effective, than the threat to wipe out their civilization. Such a deterrent would in reality be far more credible than the counterthreat of unleashing Armageddon. If the United States wants to preserve deterrence in the twenty-first century, it should be looking for a means other than a professed willingness to commit suttee on a European funeral pyre.

Since deterrence is largely in the eye of the beholder, it is significant that for more than a decade the Soviet military has been sounding the alarm about the revolutionary nature of emerging conventional weapons. Soviet military literature, in fact, is replete with articles that demonstrate the revolutionary capacities of *visokotochnie oruzhia* "high-precision weapons" (sometimes translated as "precision conventional arms") and "weapons based on new physical principles" (such as lasers and directed energy beams). As long ago as May 1984, Marshal Nikolai Ogarkov, then Chief of the Soviet General Staff, noted that

automated reconnaissance-and-strike complexes, long-range, high-precision remotely

controlled weapons, pilotless aircraft, and qualitatively new electronic controls systems are making many types of armaments global and are making it possible to increase sharply by at least ten times the strike force of conventional weapons, bringing it close, as it were, to the effectiveness of weapons of mass destruction.

Even if U.S. officials continue to believe that nuclear deterrence is necessary, they can have it without nuclear weapons themselves. The current Soviet leadership paid heavily in lives, money, and prestige as a result of the April 26, 1986, nuclear accident at Chernobyl and the subsequent evacuation of more than 100,000 people. The recent elections in the Ukraine and the demonstrations that took place on the accident's fourth anniversary show that the bill is still coming due for a disaster that over time may cost more than $300 billion. And since the United States has the capacity to hit nuclear reactors with conventional weapons, it can create a hundred Chernobyls without the use of a single nuclear weapon.

Others will argue that the United States could never be sure that the Soviet Union had scrapped all of its nuclear weapons. But if nuclear weapons cannot be deployed, used in exercises, or tested, no power will long have confidence in their utility. The problem of verification can best be solved by eliminating whole classes of weapons and deployments—or better still, by doing away with all nuclear weapons. The zero solution is the best solution.

Still others will object that proliferation is inevitable, that irresponsible Third World leaders will still have nuclear weapons, whatever the Americans and the Soviets do, and that therefore the United States must maintain a nuclear capability to deter them from nuclear attacks or blackmail. But the deterrent value of modern conventional weapons will prove even more persuasive to a Third World state than to the Soviet Union and more credible than the threat of retaliation with nuclear weapons. Small states with nuclear weapons might feel somewhat more confident that a major power would hesitate to attack them, but they would know that a decision on their part to initiate a nuclear attack against a superpower would be suicidal—dooming their country's infrastructure and perhaps a significant share of its population.

Further, a restructuring of superpower relations and mutual renunciation of weapons of mass destruction could allow Washington and Moscow to declare jointly that they would consider the use of nuclear, chemical, or biological weapons against any nation an act of war against both of them as well. Concrete plans for a jointly enforced total military and economic blockade of any outlaw nation could give such a declaration real teeth. This would not necessarily solve the problem of nuclear proliferation. Iraq, for instance, might hope that its mere possession of nuclear weapons would cow its neighbors. But a concerted effort by superpowers that were "clean" themselves on the nuclear issue could give nonproliferation a boost and help make such blackmail less credible.

New Defense Strategy

Nuclear weapons, of course, are just one aspect of the military threat each superpower poses to the other. Rightly or wrongly, the Soviets also perceive a conventional threat from the United States and its allies and are concerned about the long-term vulnerability of their Pacific maritime provinces. Given the decline of the Soviet threat in Europe and East Asia and the much greater warning time the West can expect for any attack, it would now both reassure Moscow and make far more military sense to reduce U.S. forces in Europe and the Far East. If any remain in Europe, they should serve as a strategic mobile reserve, rather than being permanently positioned to defend a major segment of NATO's front line.

Former Secretary of the Navy John Lehman, even before the remarkable developments in Eastern Europe in 1989, had already suggested that the United States revise its military structure to field fewer active forces, but maintain greater reserves and increase capacities for mobilization. Both the Gorbachev phenomenon and inevitable cuts in the defense budget, Lehman argued, make these changes necessary. The only alternative will be to make cuts piecemeal.

Lehman argued that the United States should keep the present force structure, but:
• shift one-third of U.S. forces to the reserves, thereby saving between $30 and $45 billion annually;
• convert the army from its present 18 active and 10 reserve divisions to 10 active and 18 reserve divisions;
• reorganize the air force from its present ratio of two-thirds active wings and one-third reserve wings to half active and half reserve;
• change the navy from 550 active and 50 reserve ships to 450 active and 150 reserve;
• change the marines from three active and one reserve division to two active and two reserve divisions;
• fill the ready reserve with a skeleton force of regular active-duty personnel, thereby setting up a cadre system similar to the one used by Israel, the Soviet Union, and some West European allies;
• emulate the West Europeans by having the reserves train for several weeks at a time on the most modern equipment and on the best training ranges; and
• return to the traditional concept of the American citizen soldier.

In view of the extraordinary changes since Lehman first made this proposal, it would now be reasonable to transfer still more U.S. military strength from the active forces into the reserves. The army could consist of 6 active and 20 reserve and cadre divisions. This would not result in weaker conventional forces so long as the United States accepted the obligation to strengthen its reserves seriously. To allay Soviet fears, in tandem with such a force restructuring the United States should close most American bases overseas and bring ground combat units home, leaving air force, navy, and support forces in place, at least for now. The United States could also rely on stored heavy equipment and air facilities maintained by U.S. allies in Europe, Israel, South Korea, and Japan. In addition, the United States could increase its air- and sealift capacity to transport troops and equipment overseas should the need arise.

Such a program, if matched by the USSR, would reassure both the United States and the Soviet Union that they were not only spending hundreds of billions less on defense, but also getting more security in the bargain. It would require a number of changes in defense strategy. For instance, the navy would need to pay more attention to sea control, to protection of sea lines of communication, to its ability to mount a blockade, and to mining and countermining.

The military would also have to evaluate its hardware needs with a focus on contingencies other than a war with the Soviet Union; this might include smaller diesel submarines and carriers, a different kind of bomber without a primary strategic mission, and a tank more suitable for Third World conflict. These other contingencies include terrorism, international crime, and the more limited threat from Third World countries. National leaders may also need to embark on the creation of an industrial policy to handle a shrinking defense industry. The basic goals would be to prevent the marketplace from dissipating pools of irreplaceable talent and to maintain the U.S. lead in military high-technology, particularly in communications, targeting, and intelligence.

Such a shift in U.S. defense policy should cause no military concern to America's allies, who will be facing a far less threatening Soviet Union. Warning time of any attack from the East will have increased from weeks to months —plenty of time for the United States to come to their assistance. It is time in any case for the West Europeans to take primary responsibility for their own defense.

But this obviously will have profound effects on broader U.S. relations with Western Europe, which heretofore have relied so heavily on the desire of European governments for an American military presence. It will also exacerbate European nervousness about a united Germany. These are not trivial problems. But they will not abate if the United States tries to force European security issues into a bloc-to-bloc framework that Europeans increasingly consider irrelevant or that causes the Germans to feel that forces are staying in their country to control rather than to defend them. Economic and political integration into the European Community is the best way to anchor Germany to the West. If the United States tries to base its role in Europe primarily on military might, it will become increasingly irrelevant to more basic European concerns.

What is needed from American leaders is a broad, overarching strategic framework. Washington cannot deal effectively with its place in the world or with the U.S.-Soviet relationship without a coherent vision of the kind of world it wants and a strategy for bringing it about. American policymakers must first recognize that if they merely go on responding to Gorbachev's prodding rather than offering new ideas and proposals of their own, they could lose the worldwide public relations battle—a battle that is bound to have important effects over the long run on democratic states.

The doctrine of nuclear deterrence locks the United States into the status quo.

But this is not just a problem of public relations. The United States has the first serious chance of the postwar era both for major improvements in European security, and for fundamental changes in U.S.-Soviet relations. The Bush administration should seize the initiative by articulating its concept of a changed U.S.-Soviet relationship, and of what will be required from both states to achieve it. The 17 points sketched above are useful benchmarks by which Soviet progress can be judged. But the United States should make clear at the outset its conviction that change cannot be one-sided. Its willingness to abandon the doctrine of nuclear deterrence and to change other key aspects of its defense posture that the Soviets consider threatening should be part of the concept the administration initially lays out.

In the case of nuclear weapons, the administration should declare an unequivocal willingness, if the Soviets will match it, to embark upon a carefully phased and reciprocal program that for the United States should include
• abandoning nuclear deterrence as a bedrock theory and as the rationale for a major share of the U.S. defense budget;
• adopting a policy of "no first use" of nuclear weapons;
• reaffirming the stated intentions of former Presidents Jimmy Carter and Ronald Reagan to eliminate nuclear weapons and beginning negotiations with the USSR to achieve that end;
• ending production of new strategic weapons;
• halting routine Strategic Air Command and Trident deployments; and
• agreeing to a testing moratorium.

While reciprocity and careful phasing are important, too many officials see negotiations as a way to slow down changes that are moving too fast. To proceed cautiously in a series of mutually agreed, lockstep negotiations, trading narrow concession for narrow concession, being infinitely careful not to mix apples and oranges, giving both bureaucracies a piece of the action, will be the preference of even those bureaucrats, arms controllers, diplomats, and alliance managers who sincerely want results. Negotiations are a formula for stagnation and will be used by opponents of change on both sides to block innovations.

Major disputes can only be resolved at the top, often even without prior knowledge of most officials. It is usually a mistake to wait for solutions to emerge from the great dismal swamp of the Washington "interagency process" or the negotiations droning on in Geneva and Vienna. After agreement in principle is reached at the top, officials can work out the details; but even that will require constant presidential vigilance to keep guerrilla warfare among government agencies, or outright sabotage efforts, from gumming up the works. There also is considerable opportunity for moves outside the negotiating arena. In important areas the United States can take unilateral action and challenge Moscow to reciprocate with radical changes.

The United States could, for example, propose to begin the process of eliminating nuclear weapons by doing away with all U.S. and Soviet land-based ICBMs and reducing American SLBMs to Soviet levels by a specific date and on a specific drawdown schedule, if Moscow will join Washington in this task. To jump-start the proposal (and incidentally, save billions of taxpayer dollars) the United States could halt work on the Midgetman and the MX land-based ICBMs, pending a Soviet response. Both the United States and the USSR would retain more than enough nuclear weapons at sea and in the air to ensure nuclear deterrence until, as trust builds, all nuclear weapons could be stockpiled and then eliminated.

At some point, before final elimination of all American and Soviet nuclear weapons, the British, French, and Chinese weapons must be brought into the process. And while the United States might end the deployment of nuclear weapons relatively quickly, some would undoubtedly have to remain stockpiled for an extended period before being destroyed. But Washington should first seize the initiative with a comprehensive proposal; it should go well beyond fine words about wanting a different U.S.-Soviet relationship and move to a concrete and equitable program for getting from here to there.

It is of course possible that Gorbachev (or a successor) may not be willing to undertake so radical a restructuring of superpower relations, or that he will face the kind of internal chaos that could make change impossible. Thus we must insist on careful, phased implementation of key agreements to ensure that U.S. security interests are protected at each stage as a hedge against Soviet reversals. Moscow will have its own reasons for careful phasing, including the problem of absorbing millions of soldiers into the civilian economy.

But uncertainty about the Soviet Union's future course also reinforces the need to boldly and rapidly articulate a vision of what a new relationship with the USSR will require from both countries, and to lock in agreements while the Kremlin can still deliver. The United States should be leading this process, not tagging along. And if what now seems so promising proves to be yet another false dawn, it should be apparent to all that the reason was not lack of American vision or will.

Article 5.2.   Balancing the New Order

This article reviews U.S.-Soviet relations, both during the Cold War and its aftermath. The author believes that Soviet President Gorbachev will prove to be a transitional figure who will be remembered for having helped to unleash the forces of reform. At this point, the United States should start to build permanent ties to the newly independent states, which are permitted under the draft Union Treaty. Although the Gorbachev government may oppose such agreements, they are not likely to damage Washington's relationship with the Kremlin. Gorbachev himself should seize the moment to accelerate the transition to democracy and a market economy, which would serve to strengthen his position. At the same time, while the United States should remain supportive of the Soviet president, it would be a mistake to permit American policy to be dictated by a misplaced sense of loyalty to Gorbachev or by an undue fear of who might succeed him.

Balancing the New Order

The United States must carefully juggle relations with the Kremlin and reformers in the new strategic triangle emerging in the post-Cold War period.

by Dimitri Simes

After months of despair and disarray, Soviet reformers have finally been able to get their act together and regain political momentum. One sign of their new self-confidence is the creation of the Democratic Reform Movement, an umbrella group of prominent politicians who favor radical change.

Although the radical reformers are still in the opposition in the central government and the Soviet parliament (the Congress of People's Deputies), they now control several key positions at both the republic and local levels. Moreover, with newly elected Russian President Boris Yeltsin at their center, the radical reformers have gained a meaningful role in running the Soviet Union as a whole. This was made possible in part by the new Union Treaty. Often referred to as nine-plus-one, the agreement was discussed at a country mansion in the Moscow suburb of Novo-Oga-revo and signed by Soviet President Mikhail Gorbachev and the leaders of nine republics.

A variety of factors have contributed to the change in fortune of the proponents of reform. First, Gorbachev's experimental attempt to stabilize the country through a semi-alliance with nostalgic reactionaries has been a dismal failure. The perception in the republics that the Gorbachev government was turning against their national aspirations only accelerated the disintegration of the Soviet Union. Also, the highly advertised economic stabilization measures introduced by Prime Minister Valentin Pavlov had precisely the opposite effect and were quite destabilizing. His antiinflationary measures lacked coherence and were introduced so clumsily that they only contributed to further economic deterioration. Anyway, Pavlov's widely unpopular government lacked the legitimacy needed to introduce the essential but painful market oriented reforms.

After Gorbachev rejected the 500-day radical reform economic program last September, he gave the impression that brute force could become his instrument for governing. However, Gorbachev proved to be a reluctant wielder of power—prepared to go just far enough to irritate and alarm his opponents, but not far enough to make a real difference. Gorbachev looked as uncomfortable and out of place in his role as savior of the old system and empire as he had looked earlier as their destroyer. The Soviet president initially gave the green light for a show of force, first against the se-cessionist governments in the Baltic republics and then against the democratic forces in Moscow itself. But, when the targets of intimidation refused to surrender and the first drop of blood was shed thereby raising fears of a major confrontation, he pulled back and disclaimed responsibility.

Both the democrats and the reactionaries gradually recognized Gorbachev's indecision and drew appropriate conclusions. The military, the security services, and the remnants of the party apparatus that had become the Soviet president's temporary partners, soon lost any illusions they may have had regarding his ability to establish law and order, Soviet-imperial style. Yet, the reactionaries had neither power nor courage to proceed with an outright coup. Instead, they were increasingly reduced to complaining and making idle threats in an attempt to force Gorbachev's resignation. This only reinforced the impression that their bark was worse than their bite.

Eventually this indecisiveness encouraged the democrats to challenge the conservative onslaught. They still had some serious concerns about the possibility of a right-wing dictatorship; however, even the most dedicated supporters of radical change had to acknowledge that Gorbachev's warnings about the country sliding into chaos had some validity. In the fall of 1990, prominent democrats such as Leningrad's mayor, Anatoly Sobchak, and Moscow's vice mayor (vice chairman of the Moscow City Council), Sergei Stankevich, had considered that perhaps making the government more authoritarian was the only alternative to the Soviet Union's becoming ungovernable. By the spring of 1991, however, that view changed. Appalled by repression in the Baltic republics, official attacks on freedom of the media (particularly television), and the inconsistent and clumsy economic policies of the Pavlov government, they began to argue that a democratic solution was preferable to an authoritarian one.

Communists at crossroads

The pro-Yeltsin demonstrations in Moscow last March 28 were the turning point in the USSR's political dynamics. These demonstrations were in response to an attempt by a hard-line faction, the Communists of Russia, to remove Boris Yeltsin from the chairmanship of the Russian parliament. Organized by the prore-form coalition, Democratic Russia, they were clearly designed to influence members of the Russian Congress of People's Deputies that was scheduled to open in the Kremlin the following day. However, this was not the first demonstration sponsored by Democratic Russia, and thus far such demonstrations had proceeded peacefully without any serious problems in terms of law and order.

Despite lack of imminent danger, the central government went on alert as if a coup were in the making. The Minister of Interior, Boris Pugo, ominously warned that the demonstrators planned to take over the capital. Prime Minister Pavlov issued a decree removing the Moscow police department from the supervision of the City Council with its radical majority and banned any public meetings in Moscow until April 15. When organizers of the demonstration refused to budge

and announced their intention to proceed on schedule, the authorities brought 50,000 troops in full battle gear equipped with water cannons and armored vehicles to the capital.

Yet when the demonstration's sponsors from Democratic Russia refused to be intimidated, Gorbachev—according to a number of his associates—personally intervened to ensure that the conflict would be settled peacefully. His vice president, Gennady Yanayev, met with representatives of the Democratic Russia and cautioned them against penetrating Red Square and other areas adjoining the Kremlin. The message was unambiguous: The government would not use force as long as the demonstrators acted with restraint and did not get too close to the Kremlin. Yanayev's conditions were easily accepted and the demonstrations, involving up to 300,000 people, took place without incident.

The impact of the government's failure to deliver on its threats cannot be underestimated. Very few people were willing to entertain the possibility that Gorbachev (to say nothing about the Pavlov cabinet) was too humane to spill Russian blood in the streets of Moscow. Instead, the government looked brutal but weak, provocative but impotent. Meanwhile, Gorbachev's aides began spreading the story that their boss had not been aware of Pavlov's and Pugo's actions and regretted them. These accounts were widely disbelieved. They only made the public even more suspicious of the Soviet president's earlier disclaimer regarding his prior approval of the January crackdowns in Vilnius and Riga.

The democrats' anger mobilized them into action. The Russian Congress of People's Deputies suspended its sessions until the troops were withdrawn from

Moscow. More important, in its new defiant mood, the Russian congress refused to discuss Yeltsin's removal from power as planned and, instead, gave him broad executive powers. Furthermore, the congress, while stopping short of formally scheduling Russian presidential elections, passed a resolution authorizing the preparations for them. There was little doubt that Yeltsin was the most likely candidate to become the first democratically elected president in Russian history. Nor was there much question that, once elected, Yeltsin would have a very powerful base from which to strengthen his control over Russia and expand his influence in the Soviet Union as a whole.

In addition to the new prominence of the radical reformers in Russia, Gorbachev had to cope with the failure of his efforts to reestablish central control over the republics. Six of them—Estonia, Latvia, Lithuania, Armenia, Georgia, and Moldavia—refused to take part in the March 17 referendum on the preservation of the Union. On March 31, Georgia conducted its own referendum on independence from the USSR. More than 80 percent of the votes cast were in favor of secession. Of course, the Soviet military and interior troops had enough brute force to establish emergency rule in the republics. But Gorbachev has consistently shied away from this extreme option. His preference for a peaceful and legal solution may be a partial explanation for such relative timidity.

Besides, nobody could have been sure that the Soviet army—based on conscription, weakened by draft dodging and defections, dispirited and divided along ethnic lines—could withstand a bloody struggle with nationalist forces in the republics. In Armenia and Georgia, at least, it was apparent that paramilitary units under the control of local governments would not surrender without a bitter fight in a difficult mountainous terrain that favored guerrilla warfare. Also, a wholesale armed assault on the six independence-minded republics would certainly have led to a profound conflict not only between Gorbachev and Yeltsin, and his allies among the radical reformers, but also with the powerful governments of Ukraine and Kazakhstan, the largest of the other Soviet republics. Their leaders, Leonid Kravchuk and Nursultan Nazarbayev respectively (still members of the Communist Party and eager to stay on good terms with Gorbachev), have been careful to maintain their nationalist credentials. Yet, both were critical of Moscow's pressure on the Baltics. Putting the proindependence republics under emergency rules would likely have pushed them closer to Yeltsin and created, in the process, a powerful united front against the central government.

Reformed decision making

After engaging in a holding operation for months, Gorbachev has had to face the fact that, during times of revolutionary change, centrism is not a credible political option. He had accepted a semi-alliance with the reactionaries in the name of saving some of the foundations of communism, preserving the empire, and maintaining law and order. Opponents of communist rule had won in Russia and in some of the other republics. The empire was collapsing, and the government was quickly losing what little remained of its authority.

Back in February, Yanayev, who gradually began acting as Gorbachev's de facto chief of staff, started informal discussion with the Deputy Chairman of the Russian Supreme Soviet Ruslan Khazbulatov on putting an end to their principals' bitter feud. At that time, however, Gorbachev was still on the offensive against the democrats whom he had been accusing of destructive extremism. Yeltsin, in turn, had

> After months of despair and disarray, Soviet reformers have finally been able to get their act together and regain political momentum.

been calling for the Soviet president's resignation. Therefore, the Yanayev-Khazbulatov dialogue did not get very far. Now, with radical reformers regaining their fighting spirit and obtaining a specific objective, to assure Yeltsin's election as Russian president, the political dynamics had changed. On April 23, the Yanayev-Khazbulatov effort culminated in the so-called nine-plus-one agreement.

The nine-plus-one agreement provided the democrats with a role in running the Soviet Union. It created an informal framework for regular discussions between Gorbachev and the republican leaders not only in the union treaty, but on most of the key national, political, and economic issues. As the Soviet president has become increasingly disenchanted with the established centers of power such as the Pavlov cabinet, the Communist Party apparatus, and the Supreme Soviet, the treaty process has pro-

vided a forum for collective decision making by Gorbachev, Yeltsin, and the leaders of other republics. It was through this process that the Soviet and Russian presidents have been able, at least temporarily, to bury the hatchet and to begin their unprecedented cooperation.

Yeltsin's support for Gorbachev—particularly his July 9 endorsement of his arch rival for the Soviet presidency—has come as something of a shock to the more radical elements in the proreform coalition, since only six months ago he had been calling for his resignation. Yeltsin has explained that his move was the result of changes in Gorbachev's conduct, the shift from reactionary to progressive policies. This shift has been real and has undoubtedly played a role in the Russian president's calculations. First, Yeltsin was endorsing Gorbachev for the Soviet presidency that will be established by the new Soviet constitution. This, in turn, will be based on the Union treaty currently being negotiated in Novo-Ogarevo and debated in the legislatures of the nine participating republics. While some crucial features of this treaty remain in doubt, it is already certain that the new union government—including the president—will end up with vastly reduced powers.

Second, now that Yeltsin is the undisputed chief executive of the Russian republic, the nature of his interaction with Gorbachev has changed. Previously, when the Russian leader was promising to destroy the old regime, the Soviet president performed a useful political role for Yeltsin as its symbol. But now that the Russian president has acquired governing responsibility, he finds himself in the same boat as his Soviet counterpart. Endlessly checkmating each other would almost certainly result in a catastrophic economic downslide and lead to a major political explosion.

Finally, with political dynamics now on his side, Yeltsin needs Gorbachev to smooth the transition to a less centralized, more democratic state. Although the danger of a reactionary coup has receded, few in the Soviet Union dismiss it entirely. As Gorbachev's adviser and one of the founding fathers of the Democratic Reform Movement, Aleksandr Yakovlev, wrote in *Izvestia* on July 3: "It is impossible to disregard the possibility that the forces of right-wing extremism and reaction will attempt to dispose of the ideas behind the transformations and their initiators. And the point is not that the implementation of such an attempt is technically and politically possible but that, in my view, it is highly likely."

Having President Gorbachev, who is also General Secretary of the Communist Party on their side, obviously would buy some protection for Yeltsin and the other radical reformers. Whatever their long-term intentions for cooperation with the Soviet president, it certainly makes sense to work with him during this interim period of painful transition to a qualitatively different political and economic system.

Today, the radical reformers' immediate plans include convening a congress of the Demo-cratic Reform Movement in September and perhaps creating a new political party to challenge the communists. The next step would be the election of mayors throughout the Russian republic which, presumably, would remove the remnants of the party apparatus from power in the Russian provinces and put in charge the representatives of the newly created democratic party. This would be followed by the signing of the new Union Treaty, the adoption of a new constitution and, after that, national parliamentary and presidential elections that will finally establish democratic rule in a new federation of states that voluntarily choose to live together.

The road to this bright tomorrow is bound to be bumpy at best. The economic situation continues to deteriorate. And nobody, radical reformers included, seems to have the solutions that could improve the situation quickly. Yeltsin and his supporters are firmly in favor of privatization and a shift to a market economy. But they did not really level with the people about the inevitable social costs of such an historic transformation. It is unclear, for instance, how they would deal with the miners who played such an important role in persuading Gorbachev to seek a compromise with the reformist forces. Now the miners expect economic compensation that goes far beyond what is economically justified by the pitiful level of productivity in an obsolete industry. Either the Yeltsin government will have to disappoint the miners or offer them some kind of subsidy, which could be inflationary and trigger unfulfillable demands from workers in other industries.

Chances are that the necessary radical reforms will be so controversial that only a democratically elected government that has popular confidence would be in a position to carry them out. But that means, even with Gorbachev and Yeltsin working together, the pattern of economic half measures will have to continue for months. And that might open a window of opportunity for political polarization and a new counteroffensive by the reactionaries who could capitalize on populist slogans.

Another potential problem for the proponents of change is the fact that there is no unity in their ranks. Sources of tension go far beyond the personal competition between Yeltsin and Gorbachev, which is likely to resume in the not so distant future once the tactical reasons that brought them together are no longer present. The Democratic Reform Movement includes groups and individuals with very different political philosophies and conflicting ambitions. Taking into account that the word *compromise* has a derogatory connotation in Russian, clashes among reformers are easy to predict.

Still, reformers have been able to demonstrate their vitality. And, with each day of reform, the process of transformation becomes more and more irreversible. Many of their leaders, like Gorbachev, will prove to be transitional figures overwhelmed by the historic changes they have helped to unleash. But it is already apparent that, at this point, these changes themselves are much more than a temporary interlude in the tragic history of the communist Soviet Union. In terms of destroying the old totalitarian rule, Yeltsin and the other democratic reformers have already made a permanent contribution.

Gorbachev's rediscovered reformist orientation helps the United States to start building ties to the independence-minded republics without generating a confrontation with the central government. After all, Gorbachev personally endorsed Yeltsin's trip to the United States. And the draft Union Treaty gives the republics—even those that intend to stay in the USSR—the right to establish full diplomatic relations and enter into political and economic agreements with other countries. At the current stage of internal Soviet political interplay, the Gorbachev government does not realistically expect to maintain a monopoly on foreign relations. It, for obvious reasons, will not welcome U.S. approaches to the republics, but—unless they are particularly provocative and intrusive—it will not allow them to spoil the relationship with Washington.

In more general terms, it is time to recognize that the alternative for Gorbachev may not be a reactionary dictatorship or civil war, but rather an accelerated transition to democracy and market economy. It would be reckless and unfair, of course, for America to do anything intentionally to un-dermine the position of the founding father of perestroika, who still—as Yeltsin's rapprochement with Gorbachev suggests—may be indispensable for the orderly transition from imperial totalitarianism. Still, as this transition moves forward, it would also

Even with Gorbachev and Yeltsin working together, continued economic half measures might open the window of opportunity for a new counteroffensive by reactionaries.

be a mistake to allow American policy toward the Soviet Union to become unduly influenced by the combination of an excessive loyalty to yesterday's hero and an undue fear of the consequences of his departure from the center stage of Soviet politics.

The United States has a stake in ensuring that the other nuclear superpower turns into a democratic and stable state with a benign foreign policy. It would be ironic if, in the process of offering Gorbachev a helping hand, America turned a cold shoulder toward the radical reformers who are trying to push the Soviet Union precisely in that direction and do so without his hesitations and zigzags.∎

Dimitri Simes is a senior associate at the Carnegie Endowment for International Peace where he directs the U.S.-Soviet Project.

Article 6.1.   After the Cold War: What Should the U.S. Do?

In this article, the author argues that the United States should reevaluate its foreign policy, which was, until recently, dictated by the principle of containment. Indeed, the logic of the Cold War—with its emphasis on survival, security, and access—drove American foreign policy in the Cold War era. Today, the United States must redefine its interests to reflect the goals of mutual understanding, economic interdependence, and global leadership. Although he admits that his recommendations will face formidable domestic obstacles, the author believes that a strongly engaged president, bolstered by high approval ratings at home, can bring about such changes.

AFTER THE COLD WAR
WHAT SHOULD THE U.S. DO?
STANLEY HOFFMANN

Mr. Hoffmann is the chairman of the Center for European Studies at Harvard University. From "What Should We Do in the World?" by Stanley Hoffmann, The Atlantic Monthly, October 1989, pages 84–96:

There are periods of history when profound changes occur all of a sudden, and the acceleration of events is such that much of what experts write is obsolete before it gets into print. We are now in one of those periods, which obliges the United States to rethink its role in the world, just as it was forced to do by the cataclysmic changes that followed the end of the Second World War.

For more than forty years American foreign policy has been dominated by the contest with the Soviet Union. The strategy of containment, defined by George F. Kennan in 1946–1947 and applied by all American administrations since, often in a manner that displeased Kennan, may not have been an adequate compass at all times. The Soviet Union found ways of leaping across the barriers that the United States tried to erect, with military alliances and bases, all around the Soviet empire. Moreover, the imperative of containment failed to provide clear guidance for dealing with a host of regional and internal conflicts, especially in developing areas. Nevertheless, containment proved to be an extraordinarily sturdy concept. It was flexible enough to serve such diverse policies as the original strategy of alliance-building and confrontation, the détente of the early 1970s (aimed at providing Moscow with incentives for self-containment), and occasional attempts at "rollback," including the Reagan doctrine. And while there were constant clashes over the Third World between "globalists," keen on interpreting the politics and conflicts of, say, the Middle East, Central America, and southern Africa strictly in terms of the Soviet-American contest, and "regionalists," who believed that we had to deal with the local sources of trouble, the two groups agreed that the main goal of American diplomacy was to prevent the expansion of Soviet influence. In the view of the globalists, this goal required reliance on friendly clients and stern opposition to the Soviet Union and its allies; in that of the regionalists, it required the avoidance of moves that could push local nationalists into the arms of Moscow. Similarly, in the 1970s there were those (led by Zbigniew Brzezinski) who wanted a Washington-Beijing anti-Soviet entente, and those (led by Henry Kissinger) who wanted a triangular game that would allow the United States to be closer to both Moscow and Beijing than the two were to each other. Still, containment of Moscow was the aim of both groups.

The momentous changes of the past three years have done more than any other trends or events since 1947 to deprive U.S. foreign policy of this overriding rationale. The détente of the early 1970s was a limited rapprochement between superpowers that were continuing to arm even while seeking to control jointly some parts of the arms race. It was a shaky convergence of contradictory calculations, in which the United States was trying to impose its version of stability and its own predominance on the Soviets, while the Soviets were hoping for condominium. Despite the defection of China, Moscow was still the center of a powerful empire. Today this empire is in serious trouble, China appears the more repressive and cruel of the two Communist giants, and Mikhail Gorbachev has gone far toward fulfilling the prophecy of Gyorgy Arbatov, the head of Moscow's Institute of USA and Canadian Affairs, who said that the new Soviet Union would deprive the United States of its main enemy.

As if stupefied by the pace of events, many members of the American foreign-policy establishment behave like the orphans of containment—clinging to the remains of an obsolete strategy and incapable of defining a new one. And yet this is the moment coolly to re-evaluate American interests in the world. For many years our perceptions (often mistaken) of the Soviet threat drove our policy and defined, or distorted, our interests. Any great power has fundamental concerns, such as survival, physical security, and access to essential sources of energy, raw materials, and markets. In addition it has what specialists in international relations call milieu goals: promoting its values abroad, or at least preserving chances for the flowering of those values, and shaping international agreements and institutions in such a way that the nation's fundamental objectives and values are served. These very general interests are translated into something that can be called the national interest—a more precise list of concerns that takes into account external factors, such as the distribution of power in specific areas between friends and foes, and internal ones, such as the imperatives and prohibitions set by domestic political and economic forces. In periods of extreme international tension, when there appears to be one global enemy, any move made by the adversary tends to be seen as a threat, creating a national interest in repelling it. A bipolar conflict thus serves as a Procrustean bed: each side's definition of its interests is dictated by the image of the enemy. Now that the enemy recedes, a redefinition of those interests becomes possible, and necessary.

In order to understand what the United States ought to do now, we have to begin by taking stock of where we are—of the main features of the international system in which we operate, and of the main perils it contains.

THE TWO WORLD SYSTEMS

The traditional theory of international relations which professors have taught their students, and which statesmen have practiced, treats international politics as if it were exclusively the strategic and diplomatic game of states as it was played in the days of Thucydides or in the eighteenth century. But the key reality of the post-1945 period is that states play in two arenas. The first is the traditional strategic and diplomatic one, in which there is no broad international consensus, and in which power tends to be used in the way it always has been, usually as a contest in which my gain is your loss. The second is the economic arena, in which a variety of games are played —about trade, finance, energy, raw materials, the environment, and so forth—and most countries, but not all of them, are closely linked; they are interdependent in the sense that even the more powerful and less vulnerable are affected by what happens elsewhere. Here states combine the usual attempts to gain relative advantages with an awareness that this is not a zero-sum game, and that every country has an interest in the prosperity of the global economy and of the other players. Here the logic of "anarchy"— the fragmentation of the world into sovereign states—is checked by the logic of, and a broad consensus on, an open global economy. While international organizations are all fragile, and none of them has power over the major states, they are more numerous and effective in the second arena than in the first.

Each arena has its own distribution of power. *POLARITIES* In the strategic and diplomatic arena, we have *OF POWER* been blessed or cursed, depending on one's point of view, by bipolarity—by the dominance of the United States and the Soviet Union. The economic arena, however, has been marked for a very long time by American hegemony. This is still largely the case, although increasingly important roles are, of course, being played by West Germany and Japan. What's more, here there are major players that are not states but, rather, regional organizations and multinational corporations, banks, and speculators, whose capital movements, investments, and loans deeply affect the world economy and contradict the efforts of states to preserve, singly or jointly, some control.

Moreover, each arena has its own, unprecedented restraints upon it. In the strategic and diplomatic field restraint has been imposed by nuclear weapons. What is new here, as McGeorge Bundy has shown in his recent book, *Danger and Survival*, is that above a certain level of force, superiority does not make any difference, because there is nothing one can *do* with those weapons (as Robert McNamara has been telling us ever since he stopped being Secretary of Defense). Nuclear weapons have restrained the superpowers from all direct military confrontation, which is quite an unprecedented achievement. In addition, these weapons are largely unusable for political blackmail (for it is hard to wrest gains by brandishing weapons that one doesn't want to use), and the result is that on the very field that is dominated by two powers, they are often impotent. What we find, therefore, is a downgrading of the great powers, a relative pacification at the top, and a continuation of the traditional "state of war" among other powers at lower levels, because despite prophecies about the obsolescence of war, nuclear restraints certainly have not eliminated violence altogether.

In the economic arena the restraints are different but perhaps even more interesting: they are the shackles of economic interdependence. The economies of the main players have become so thoroughly intertwined that any state that tries to exert its power for competitive, immediate, or hostile gains risks creating formidable boomerang effects, as we have seen, for instance, in the case of OPEC, and may be seeing in the future with Japan. To be sure, there is a constant tension between the forces of protectionism—interest groups harmed by open borders and external competitors, bureaucracies trying to save their fiscal policy and other instruments of domestic control—and the imperatives of the open capitalist economy. But, paradoxically, the fact that the agenda for this arena is set by the demands of domestic consumers and producers tends to make those imperatives prevail over the occasional domestic backlash against interdependence or the occasional temptation of states to use their economic power belligerently. This is so because very few states, including the biggest ones, are capable of reaching their economic objectives by what has been the basic principle of international affairs: self-help.

Finally, the internationalization of production—the fact that when you buy a product these days it is hard to know what its nationality is—and the global nature of financial markets result in even more restraints on the manipulation of economic power by any given state. Because the use of force is irrelevant in this realm, its politics are, in fact, an unstable hybrid of international politics without war and domestic politics without central power.

THE DIFFUSION OF POWER

These features have been visible for a while. But some changes have taken place only in recent years. On the strategic and diplomatic front the most interesting trend has been the beginning of the end of the Cold War. Some of the reasons for this trend are external, or international, the main one being the extensive limitations on the effectiveness of force to which I have already alluded. In addition to the nuclear restraint, we must consider the increasing capacity for resistance among the victims of external force, especially if those victims get support from the outside, as usually happens, or if, like the Palestinians in the occupied territories, they fight at a level that makes successful repression difficult. Here recent experiences are telling. We have witnessed remarkably parallel American experiences in Vietnam and Soviet experiences in Afghanistan; the Israelis have been thwarted in Lebanon (which also gives Syria much trouble); the Vietnamese are calling it quits in Cambodia; and so on. Plainly there exists a wide inability to use force abroad for the control of a foreign people. These frustrations lead one to a conclusion once expressed by a former French Foreign Minister (a very shrewd man who liked to talk in apparent banalities): if you can't win a war, you might as well make peace. Thus the bizarre epidemic of peace in 1988. There is another external reason for the beginning of the end of the Cold War. Over time, inevitably, there had to be some loosening of the two blocs that have confronted each other; the compression of all the internal divergences and conflicts within them could not last forever. It was largely artificial: they were compressed as long as there was a cold-war condition, a kind of mimicked state of war; once it became clear that war was being postponed indefinitely, there was no reason for the blocs to remain as rigid as they once had been.

Of course the dominant reasons for the ending of the Cold War are internal. In the United States, apart from economic factors to which we will come, there is what is quite improperly

INTERNAL REASONS

called the Vietnam syndrome, which is simply the marked reluctance of the American public to become engaged in protracted, uncertain wars for unclear purposes in secondary parts of the world. After all, Ronald Reagan, a rather popular President, did not succeed in getting the U.S. public to support the contra war against Nicaragua, nor did the American public support the presence of the United States Marines in Lebanon, once the awful cost become visible. In the Soviet Union the internal situation is far more serious, and there is a rather desperate need for retrenchment because of the economic predicament.

In the realm of economic interdependence, the evolution of recent years has two main characteristics. One is that despite the considerable difficulties of the past two decades, the economic relations among the advanced countries have developed successfully. To be sure, there has been a creeping erosion of the international principles of free trade established after the Second World War. Nevertheless, a relatively open and growing international economy has been preserved despite the economic shocks of the 1970s—no mean achievement, especially if one compares this with the situation that prevailed between the wars. The second trend, which is much more disturbing, has occurred in North-South relations; there we have not been so successful. An increasing differentiation has taken place between the developing countries that have been able to join the industrial world, and whose economic take-off has been spectacular, and the many other countries that have failed, and have fallen more and more deeply into debt. Between the latter countries and the rest of the world the gap has grown ever wider.

Behind this evolution in both fields there is one very important trend, which concerns the distribution of power. The surface manifestation is a diffusion away from the superpowers. But we are not moving back to the traditional world in which *several* great powers had reasonably equal weight. In the strategic and diplomatic field we now find a coexistence of weakened global superpowers and regional balances of power, which are often unstable and where an important role is played by what are sometimes called regional influentials. In the arena of interdependence an increasing role is being played by a tightening European Community, by Japan, in some areas by Saudi Arabia. The aspect of this diffusion of power that is most significant for us here is the relative decline of the United States, to use the obligatory cliché of the past two years (after all, a cliché is simply a truth that too many people have uttered and that many resist). Many public officials and academics have wrapped themselves in the American flag in the long debate

on decline. They keep saying, quite rightly, that—if one compares the United States in the world today with the United States in the world of 1945–1950—a major part of this decline is not only normal but has been planned by the United States. Since 1945, when, after all, the world situation was completely abnormal, the United States has done its best to help the economies of Western Europe, Japan, South Korea, and Taiwan; as a result the American share of world GNP was bound to decrease.

However, there is more to it than that. The United States has become a debtor nation that depends on the willingness of others to provide the funds necessary to finance its budget deficit; we are going to be burdened for a long time by that debt. The United States has also seen its competitiveness decline for reasons that are largely internal and that cannot simply be dismissed by referring to the inevitable growth of other countries. The phenomena of overconsumption and underinvestment; insufficient industrial productivity; rigidity, waste, and shortsightedness in industry; and the problems in American education, particularly technical education, which have been much discussed though not much has been done about them, are the main culprits here. As a result the United States is simply no longer the leader in a number of key sectors in the world economy. Granted, this is less significant than it would have been in past international systems, where declining in key sectors meant a dangerous advantage for a major new military challenger. In the current system the United States faces no military challenger that is in better shape than it is. Nevertheless, this decline means that the American capacity to mold the international system of the future is not what it used to be, insofar as technological predominance often leads to wide influence abroad, and technological decline reduces the dependence of others on American civilian and military goods.

NO LONGER THE LEADER

BEYOND THE COLD WAR

Given these features and trends of the world of the late 1980s, what ought American foreign policy to be? The point of departure must the recognition of a paradox. The United States remains the only "complete" great power, the possessor of the largest military arsenal and of the most powerful economy in the world. On the other hand, both the diffusion of power in recent years and the partial impotence of military and economic power because of the restraints on its uses make it much more difficult for the United States to impose its will on others and to shape outcomes according to its preferences. We can still lead, toward goals that have a reasonable chance of being deemed by others compatible with their own interests. But we can no longer rule. Games of skill must replace tests of will. Our waning power to command and control needs to be supplemented by the new kind of power that the international system requires: the power to convince and to deal. In order to be effective, we have to define our national interest in a way that has a chance both of preserving a national capacity for steering toward world order (not because we are wiser than other nations but because there is no other candidate for the job) and of persuading others that their long-term concerns and ours mesh.

We cannot replace a fading vision—that of containment—with mere short-term management and avoidance of trouble, because the present offers opportunities for a decisive change in direction, and because there are simply too many dangers ahead to allow us to stumble from issue to issue in a "pragmatic" way. Nor can we follow the advice of neo-isolationists who believe that the United States ought not only to reduce its commitments and its military presence abroad, now that the Cold War is ending, but also to transfer to other powers the responsibility for dealing with the world's perils. That a great deal of what some call "devolution" needs to take place is not in doubt, but there is a gap between devolution and abdication. The truth is that only our continuing involvement is likely to draw other powers into an effort for world order, precisely because our past predominance has led others to rely on our initiatives and has led us to hug political control even as we rhetorically deplore the costs and burdens that come with it.

We have to define first our goals, then our strategy. Our first goal ought to be the rearrangement of our relationship with the Soviet Union, away from both the old Cold War and the rather misleading exchange of misunderstandings that was the détente of the 1970s. This new relationship will inevitably be partly competitive, because our two nations will continue to have conflicting interests in many parts of the world, but it ought to be competitive without excessive militarization, and partly cooperative on issues in which there will be or already are converging interests.

A second goal ought to be to facilitate a transition to a world in which major new threats to world order will be neutralized. One is the threat of fragmentary violence resulting from sharp internal conflict in many of the weak countries of the world—conflicts in which others will be tempted to intervene—and from the regional conflicts that still rage in many parts of the world. Some conflicts are likely to surface or to worsen once the discipline exerted on each camp by the Cold War is no longer there, once often centrifugal or nos-talgic nationalisms (in Eastern Europe, for instance) replace artificial and defunct ideological solidarities. Another new threat is the threat of chaos in world economic relations, because of mismanagement by states (of the huge problem of Third World debt, for instance), or because of a victory of economic nationalism over the constraints of interdependence, or because of states' lack of control over the economic activities of private parties whose moves could provoke financial panics. Therefore, our third goal ought to be to bring about more order and more justice—to coin a phrase, a kinder and gentler world.

The domestic precondition for these new foreign-policy goals must be, of course, putting our economic house in order. What needs to be done in this sphere is too familiar from books and articles for me to repeat it here. I would only point to the price that our continuing budget crisis exacts from the pursuit of U.S. interests abroad. In Poland, for example, the pace and reach of reform will be less than if we had been able to make more money available to promote political pluralism and a market economy.

Goals are easy to describe. What matters more is a strategy for reaching them.

THE GORBACHEV OPENING

Even though the Bush administration appears to have emerged from its inauspiciously long initial phase of skepticism toward Gorbachev and grudging annoyance at the pace of his moves, much of what calls itself the enlightened public remains extraordinarily hesitant about what to do with the Soviet Union. The doubt takes two forms: fear that Soviet efforts at reform are still very much reversible, and questioning whether the United States really has an interest in "helping" Gorbachev. My answer is that of course much is reversible—in human affairs many things always are, and in politics nothing, not even totalitarianism, is ever definitive—but a great deal of the new thinking about foreign affairs which is going on in the Soviet Union is not tied exclusively to Gorbachev. It appears to be shared by much of a political generation, because it corresponds to almost desperate domestic necessities that are being proclaimed by a large number of Soviet people who have, by traveling around the world and by reading foreign works, been able to compare the Soviet performance with what goes on abroad. This is one of the interesting, welcome, and unexpected by-products of the détente of the 1970s. Also, the new thinking corresponds to a realistic reading by many Soviet leaders and experts of an international system in which the traditional Soviet mode of behavior—the attempt to impose political control and ideological conformity on others by

A REALISTIC READING

force—yields limited results, often at exorbitant cost; in which the arms and the logic of "absolute security" lead only to a higher, more expensive plateau of stalemate and to new forms of insecurity; and in which, in particular, the contest with the United States for influence in the Third World has turned out to be extraordinarily unrewarding. Thus, while Gorbachev may ultimately fail and be replaced, while some of his daring foreign-policy moves may be reversible, and while we may have only limited leverage over what happens in the Soviet Union, the important question is whether it is at all in our interest to undermine Gorbachev's innovations. The answer is obviously no, because the alternatives that one can think of are worse: a return to the militarized foreign policy that prevailed in the years of Leonid Brezhnev or a domestic triumph of the sort of Russian fundamentalism—anti-Western, chauvinism, anti-Semitic, nationalist—that would make any kind of cooperation with the USSR much more difficult.

Thus it would be foolish for the United States to contribute to Gorbachev's fall, even if the contribution took the form of merely responding too grudgingly to some of his initiatives, and especially if it took the form of setting intemperate or untimely preconditions about internal changes or external retrenchment which could only embarrass and help derail him. Moreover, if Gorbachev should succeed, the result would not be a Soviet Union so much more efficient that it was more dangerous than the one we have known; in fact it would be less dangerous. *Glasnost* and *perestroika* are likely to produce a more open society, with a better informed and less manipulable public, with a greater role in the arena of interdependence and a smaller role in the military arena—precisely what we have always said we really wanted. Moreover, should Gorbachev fall after the United States had tried to cooperate with him, we would still have the means to return to our second nature—the Cold War—especially if we preserve our alliances while pursuing a new policy.

Therefore, it is in our interest to respond to Gorbachev's overtures, for all kinds of reasons. First of all, it is probably the best way of preserving the Western alliance; as the instructive few weeks before the NATO summit last spring showed, the more we drag our feet, the more divided we will be from at least some of our major allies—West Germany in particular.

IMPORTANCE OF INFLUENCE And, then, we should respond in order to prevent the Soviets from getting too far ahead of us in a competition that Gorbachev seems to understand is more important than the classic military contest or the struggle for physical control of governments, peoples, and resources: the competition for influence. We should,

when we celebrate the end of the Cold War as a victory for our past strategy and for our values, be careful not to nurture the illusion that Gorbachev wants to preside over the shrinking of Soviet foreign influence and the liquidation of the Soviet empire. In Europe, in the Middle East, in his relations with China, he acts like a man who understands that his country's best chances for affecting the course of world affairs lie in shedding counterproductive or fruitless burdens and attracting strong support, so that even suspicious powers (say, Israel and South Africa) will be willing to acknowledge a Soviet role. U.S. passivity would only play into his hands. Also, we have a chance, while Gorbachev is in power, of achieving with the Soviet Union not only a nonhostile relationship, which already would not be so bad, but also a number of cooperative arrangements in several areas.

Finally, we and the Soviets have a remarkably convergent interest in reducing the burden of arms that are very difficult to use and whose main purpose is to deter the other side from doing something that it has no particular desire to do. First, in arms control, the time has come to close the famous grand deal on strategic nuclear reductions that we might have obtained toward the end of the Reagan Administration, and that a large number of players in that administration wanted. It was blocked by the President, because he would not give up his Star Wars dream, even in exchange for drastic cuts in Soviet offensive weapons. The Strategic Defense Initiative may have been a clever bargaining chip, which contributed to Gorbachev's reversal of previous Soviet positions of verification and on cuts in heavy missiles, but the time has come to agree to limits on SDI in exchange for these reductions. Such limits would amount simply to recognizing the fact that the "Astrodome" concept is unrealizable, that no reliable deployment is conceivable for many years anyhow, and that there are ways of preserving land-based missiles that are cheaper and better than antiballistic defenses. A START agreement has also become snagged on the issue of sea-launched cruise missiles. The United States should agree to the Soviet proposal to limit these weapons, which might otherwise multiply threateningly and without any foreseeable possibility of verification. And the two sides should agree to ban antisatellite weapons.

The reduction of NATO and Warsaw Pact conventional forces, which experts have tended to present as a formidably difficult undertaking, appears far less so since the Soviets' agreement to the framework proposed by NATO and President Bush's decision to accept the inclusion of aircraft, on which the Soviets had insisted. The coming negotiations are still likely to be complicated, if only because of the number of parties engaged in them and the disagreements on the types of aircraft to be included and on the number of states that will have to reduce their armed forces. But the two sides have agreed to concentrate on those forces that are capable of surprise attack and on those weapons—such as tanks and armored personnel carriers—that are primarily offensive, and they have agreed to try to stabilize the restructured alliance forces at levels much lower than the present ones.

CONTINUED COOPERATION

As for regional conflicts, whether in Afghanistan, the Middle East, or Central America, the imperative is clear: we must continue to cooperate with the Soviet Union in resolving them without being handicapped by the needless fear that by engaging the Soviets in such negotiations we legitimize their presence in those regions. They are there anyhow, whether we legitimize them or not. The "Finlandization" of Eastern Europe—the granting of internal autonomy in exchange for continuing membership in the Warsaw Pact—is not a fit subject for Soviet-American negotiations: the Soviets appear already to have granted Poland and Hungary the right to proceed in this direction, and evolution in East Germany and Czechoslovakia depends on the domestic situations there more than on Soviet, or Soviet-American, decisions. As for another suggestion that is sometimes made, that we negotiate the neutralization of Eastern Europe with the Soviets, it is most unlikely that they would accept this, and its necessary consequence, a total withdrawal of Soviet forces, without asking for at least a partial neutralization of Western Europe—including West Germany—and the departure of American troops and weapons. It would be unwise for us to accept this, because American forces would be even more difficult to send back to Europe in case of a crisis than Soviet forces would, and because neither great power has much interest in severing the ties that bind "its" Germany to it and to the other countries of its alliance. (Also, could two neutralized Germanys remain separate for so long? And would not a reunified Germany, even if formally neutralized, be a far more powerful and unpredictable independent actor than, say, a neutral Austria or Switzerland is?)

In the economic realm, the real question is not whether we should provide our chief military rival with high-tech goods and military technology; obviously the answer is no. But what the Soviet Union mainly needs is consumer goods, and the kinds of industries that can produce consumer goods. These are not strategically dangerous goods and industries, and are something we ought to be able to provide, in exchange for evidence of progress toward a more decentralized economy. If we don't act in this realm, our allies will anyhow. Finally, we

should take advantage of the Soviets' cooperative strategy in order to involve them more, as they say they are willing to be involved, in international and regional organizations—including those that promote human rights.

AGAINST VIOLENCE

In the long run, strategy on the global front outside the Cold War is likely to be most important, and needs to become our main foreign-affairs priority. Much of what we will need to do between now and the end of the century can be grouped under three headings. The first of these is "Against Violence" in international affairs. Here the most urgent task ought to be the liquidation of the acute, dangerous, and lasting regional conflicts that are still with us.

In Central America we are a major part of the problem; we should leave the initiative as much as possible to the regional powers themselves. With respect to Nicaragua they seem to be doing a little better than we have done: our goal has been to overthrow the Sandinista regime, and it appears that we have finally given up on it, whereas President Oscar Arias Sanchez, of Costa Rica, and his colleagues can be counted on to keep applying pressure for democratization. In El Salvador it is up to us to make further military aid to the government contingent on the elimination of human-rights violations and the opening of serious negotiations with the opposition; the alternative is endless war and horror.

In the Middle East we are perhaps not a major part of the problem, but we are certainly a major part of the potential solution. There will be no solution if we continue to exert only mild pressure on Israel. The Israeli government's proposal for elections in the occupied territories is one more detour to avoid negotiating with the Palestine Liberation Organization and reaching a comprehensive settlement by means of an international conference. But if we want such elections, they will have, in order to be acceptable to the PLO, to include East Jerusalem and to occur in the absence of Israeli military control and without crippling restrictions being placed on the role of the elected representatives. If we succeed in obtaining free and open-ended elections, we will still ultimately need an international conference, because it is only with such a conference that some of the decisive parties—the PLO and Syria—could be involved and that each superpower would have an opportunity to exert some moderating influence on its allies or clients. If there should finally be a settlement of the Palestinian issue, which inevitably will be a Palestinian state (for the choice is either continuing occupation, repression and violence and the internal corruption of Israel, or a Palestinian state), the other

American role will be to provide security guarantees for Israel after the state is established.

Another important priority in the area of violence will be to try to limit the risk of contagion from the fragmentary violence described earlier. This means taking more seriously, and backing with collective sanctions, the reinforcement of the nuclear nonproliferation regime, signing and enforcing a treaty against chemical warfare, and gradually negotiating both with the Soviet Union and with our allies (the latter being likely to prove resistant) limitations on the indiscriminate export of high-tech conventional weapons and missiles. These exports are already making even more dangerous a world in which many states have reached the stage of producing their own weapons—something about which we can do little. Both dynamics of the arena of economic interdependence—the traditional drive of states for comparative economic advantage and the logic of an open market that treats the trade in lethal goods like any other trade—threaten to make the strategic and diplomatic arena more deadly. Contrary to Kant's prediction, commerce detracts in this respect from the pacification of world affairs, which Kant thought would result from economic interdependence and the increasing horror of modern war.

AGAINST INJUSTICE

Under this second heading, "Against Injustice," we have a double mission. Some of what we should do derives from self-interest. In matters of distributive justice among states, economic interdependence means that we have an interest in the progress toward prosperity of many of the poorer societies, for they can provide us either with markets or with refugees. Moreover, if their states should collapse under the weight of debts, our international financial system might collapse also. But some of our duties go beyond self-interest. We have values, and it is perfectly normal to seek to promote them. In an increasingly open world of instant communications the claim of states to exert unlimited jurisdiction over the lives of their subjects is anachronistic and repugnant, because there is a connection between such a claim and the external behavior of a government, and because there is a constant demand by the American public in the realm of human rights abroad—an unease with any amoral foreign policy. This demand sometimes (as currently, with China) conflicts with the cold calculations of realpolitik, or else absolves the United States of its own exactions abroad, yet it cannot be ignored by American statesmen who seek legitimacy at home for their diplomatic course. We do not have to be apologetic about a human-rights policy as long as it is pursued without either hubris or illusions.

The main areas of policy against injustice would be the following: First, we continue to face the problem of the debt of numerous developing countries; here what is needed is, in the short term, extensive relief measures that will allow developing countries to concentrate on exports and to afford imports, rather than having to spend their resources on servicing their debt. We also need a reform of the conditions ritually imposed by the International Monetary Fund, because those conditions have so often turned out to be politically disastrous and recessionary. Any American policy on human rights must seek to be an international strategy; the United States cannot by itself redress injustices against human beings all over the world. If we look at South Africa, we realize quickly how limited American leverage is: American sanctions are not insignificant, but by themselves, they are not very effective. The United States *can* stop providing military and economic support to, or encouraging its companies to invest in, countries where serious human-rights violations take place. Moreover, there are many parts of the world where the United States by itself can have a considerable influence on the fact of human rights: those areas where it continues to be dominant and where it could use the tools of policy at its disposal to prod clients toward democracy and freedom.

FOR A MORE BALANCED ORDER

Under this last heading, "For A More Balanced Order," come the steps we must take in the 1990s to resolve numerous problems resulting from changes in the global distribution of power over the past fifteen or twenty years. We ought to adjust our burdens and privileges to our (relatively shrinking) power, and encourage others to play the roles and carry the responsibilities their power now requires. We should encourage the Western Europeans to develop and strengthen their identity. Whether or not they succeed in establishing a unified market by 1992 is a detail; it is not the timetable that matters but the process itself. It may take a little longer, because the issues of pooling sovereignty over money, taxation, and fiscal policy, for instance, are very complicated, and because Margaret Thatcher exists, but even without Thatcher the issues would be difficult, and what counts is that things are again in motion. Fears that a "Fortress Europe" will exclude American goods are not justified; many powerful forces in Europe, including Great Britain and West Germany, and many multinational businesses operating in Europe, will not allow this to happen. It is in the American interest, in the long run, to encourage the European Community to play a larger role in diplomatic and security affairs, an arena where

THE EUROPEAN COMMUNITY

progress among the twelve members has so far been very limited. If we succeed in lowering the level of armaments in Europe, in agreement with the Soviets, the moment will come when we will indeed be able to withdraw a part of our forces. The NATO alliance will then become more of an even partnership between the United States and its European associates. They are more likely to cooperate with one another on defense if the level of defense is lower overall than the present one. The situation that President Dwight D. Eisenhower, many years ago, thought would come very quickly will finally arrive: we will be able to disengage somewhat, and our allies will engage more. Western Europe has an extremely important diplomatic role to play in the eastern half of the continent. There the American and European objective ought to be to encourage as much Finlandization as possible. Each country in Eastern Europe is different, and it is much easier for the Western Europeans to pursue a discriminating policy—helping with economic ties and cultural agreements those countries that liberalize most convincingly—than it has ever been for the United States.

We should encourage Japan to be more active in international organizations, particularly in world institutions of assistance, development, and finance. Greater Japanese efforts at helping the developing countries would allow a partial reorientation of Japanese trade away from the developed world, where resistance to the volume of Japanese exports has been growing. Japanese consumers are likely to demand that their nation's economy also shift from the conquest of new external markets to the satisfaction of long-repressed domestic needs.

The last part of a policy toward a more balanced order should consist of deliberately strengthening international and regional organizations. Their decision-making machinery—especially that of world economic and financial organizations—needs to be reformed, so that the distribution of power, which now reflects the realities of the 1950s, will express the realities of the 1980s and 1990s. This means more power for Japan and Western Europe in the World Bank, the International Monetary Fund, and the General Agreement on Tariffs and Trade. We will need international and regional organizations as peacekeepers in areas of conflict. We will need them for information and for inspection. And we will need them on all the economic fronts, where self-help no longer gets one anywhere. There, such collective frameworks for bargaining are likely over time to affect the way in which states define their interests—by injecting a concern for the long term and for the survival of international institutions. A collective defense of the environment is inconceivable without them. But we will also need to strengthen and spread such institutions in the field of security, in particular, for the prevention and limitation of regional conflicts and the monitoring of agreements against the proliferation of conventional and nuclear arms.

A PUBLIC AHEAD OF THE ESTABLISHMENT

There are formidable domestic obstacles to the policy I have sketchily described here. One —with us for so long that it is pointless to pin the blame on any administration—is the disjointed way in which American foreign policy is made. We can deplore this, but we could also try to do something about it, so that the amount of disorganization and fragmentation that inevitably results from our constitutional system is minimized. This requires a strongly engaged President (not one like Reagan, who concentrated on only a few, largely ideological concerns), a State Department that tries to balance the need to pursue a strategy abroad and the need to cooperate with Congress (instead of sacrificing one to the other), and a National Security Council staff that can effectively coordinate, but avoids making, policy. It also requires a sharp reduction in the covert role of the Central Intelligence Agency, a role that not only creates more bad will than successes abroad but also often threatens to divert American policy into uncontrolled, harebrained schemes.

Another obstacle is the disorientation of the foreign-policy establishment. It has become accustomed to American predominance and to the comforting ideas that only the United States has a sense of "world responsibility" and that it has a single permanent enemy and a number of reliable but dependent allies. A world that is more fluid, in which we remain "No. 1" but without the ability to control, is unsettling. A world in which the main perils are abstract—damage to the environment, the risk of a global recession, the possibility of regional arms races—is less easy to understand than a world dominated by a contest between two countries representing rival value systems. The Bush Administration is largely made up of conservative men, whose formative experiences occurred from the 1950s to the 1970s, and while their pragmatism has been evident, they seem, as in the case of the NATO summit, to have been pushed and pulled into the new world, rather than to have devised a coherent and long-term strategy for dealing with it.

However, there is at least one element favorable to the redirection of American foreign policy, and it has to do with the public. If one looks at opinion polls, one sees that the public, while quite wisely cautious toward the Soviet Union, is less mired in old modes of thinking than it has been in a long time. It is sufficiently worried about domestic economic trends to believe that the first priority is indeed putting our house in order. The shackles that opinion sometimes puts on the perceptions of leaders are not apparent for the time being.

In conclusion, in the world we have entered there will be many things that the United States can do nothing about. We should accept this state of affairs and, incidentally, perhaps even be grateful for it. It is a world in which war is no longer the principal and often inevitable mode of change; change comes more often now from domestic revolutions, about which we can and should do very little, because usually we do not understand the political cultures and trends of other countries and often we make mistakes. Change also, now that the pressures exerted by the Cold War are easing, comes from the rebirth of nationalisms. Many of the new forces of nationalism may lead to explosions and revolutions, about which, again, there will be very little that we or anybody else in the West can do. The task therefore is not to eliminate trouble everywhere in the world. Instead, we must devise what could be described as a new containment: not of the Soviet Union (although this will be part of it,

insofar as conflicts of interest with the Soviets will continue) but of the various forms of violence and chaos that a world no longer dominated by the Cold War will entail. It is a complicated agenda, but it is at least different from the agenda we have had for so long.

If, as I have indicated, statesmen and citizens now operate not in a single international system but in two different fields, with different logics, actors, and hierarchies and tools of power, the question remains whether this duality can persist. An imperative for the United States is to prevent it from ending in the wrong way, as in the 1930s, when economic power was widely used for either self-protection or aggression. This is why we need to strive for the devaluation of hostile forms and uses of power in the strategic and diplomatic arena, and against a major recession in the field of economic interdependence. Our new strategy must aim at spreading the sense of common interests in the former and at strengthening it in the latter. It will require more "internationalism" than before, and the novel experience of cooperating widely with associates who are no longer satellites or dependents—as well as with the enemy of the past forty years.

Article 6.2. Uncle Sam as the World's Policeman: Time for Change?

American political leaders must learn, suggests Ted Galen Carpenter, to distinguish between vital and peripheral security interests. Since World War II, the United States has tended to view even the most minor crisis as a threat to its security. The United States can no longer assume the role of "global policeman" in the new post-Cold War world. Real threats are those that jeopardize America's physical survival and political independence. These threats, concludes Carpenter, are likely to be rare in the future, as no potential adversary is capable of achieving global domination. In addition, the United States should rethink its Cold War system of alliances and commitments, which are both expensive and dangerous. Finally, the time has come to transfer America's security burdens to other prosperous and capable world powers.

UNCLE SAM AS THE WORLD'S POLICEMAN:

TIME FOR A CHANGE? by Ted Galen Carpenter

It no longer is necessary or desirable for the U.S. to carry the security burdens of the planet.

THE BUSH Administration apparently intends to preserve the principal features of America's activist Cold War strategy in a post-Cold War world and to maintain unnecessarily high levels of military spending. Its proposed $306,000,000,000 1991 defense authorization bill is 16% higher in real terms than was the 1981 budget adopted immediately after the Soviet invasion of Afghanistan and the collapse of détente. Even the original projections for the 1995 budget were nearly eight percent higher. The Bush Administration gradually has been retreating from that position, with the President announcing plans for a 25% reduction in military personnel. That action is a belated step in the right direction, but we can and should make far deeper cuts, both in personnel and weapon systems.

More disturbing than the grudging nature of the Administration's budget cuts has been the pervasive attitude that the fundamentals of America's Cold War strategy of global interventionism should remain intact despite vastly altered international conditions. Typical of the reasoning is the comment in Secretary of Defense Richard B. Cheney's 1990 report to the President and Congress that the U.S. must strive to "attain the same basic strategic objectives with a somewhat smaller defense budget." The President himself has sought to preserve venerable Cold War institutions such as

Mr. Carpenter is director of foreign policy studies, the Cato Institute, Washington, D.C.

NATO by formulating vague alternative missions. NATO and the U.S. military presence in Europe, he affirms, will be needed for decades, not to deter a Warsaw Pact invasion (which even he concedes is now utterly improbable), but to prevent "instability and unpredictability."

That approach is a blueprint for the indefinite prolongation of expensive and risky U.S. military commitments around the globe. The international system always has been quite unstable and unpredictable, and there is little evidence that the future will be significantly different. However, instability *per se* does not threaten America's security. Indeed, in a post-Cold War world, there may be many local or regional disputes that are (or at least should be) irrelevant to the security interests of the U.S.

Iraq's invasion of Kuwait is a case in point. Baghdad's aggression unquestionably is odious, but that expansionist drive, however unpleasant it may be for Kuwait and other nations in the region, does not threaten vital American interests. Even the most "realistic" reason for the U.S. intervention—the supposed need to protect the Persian Gulf oil supply—fails to withstand scrutiny. The takeover of Kuwait gives Iraq control of only seven percent of world oil production; a subsequent conquest of Saudi Arabia would have increased the total to 15.7%. That degree of control might be enough to nudge up oil prices, but it hardly would give Saddam Hussein a stranglehold on the economies of the West. Because any major rise in oil prices would have to be predicated on Iraq's will-

ingness to withdraw a substantial portion of existing supplies from the market—a most unlikely step since oil is its only significant source of revenue—even a worst-case scenario of Iraqi preeminence in the Persian Gulf region would have meant an increase in oil prices to approximately $30 a barrel. By leading the fight to impose an embargo on Iraqi and Kuwaiti oil exports, and by creating the prospect of a war in the Middle East (with the disruption of the oil flow war would cause), Washington has succeeded in driving prices far higher.

Even assuming the U.S. can thwart the "threat" to Persian Gulf oil supplies by taking military action against Iraq—and by no means will success be assured—such a victory must be measured against the probable cost of achieving it. Just maintaining forces to protect the Persian Gulf oil flow in peacetime is extremely expensive—nearly $40,000,000,000 per year. These ongoing deployments in the Gulf region are costing an additional $1,200,000,000 to $1,500,000,000 per month, and sustained combat operations would be vastly more expensive. Some defense experts estimate that combat expenses could approach $1,000,000,000 *per day.* If those military costs are factored into the price of oil, it is far less expensive to risk a price increase resulting from the unpredictability of Persian Gulf supplies, and that is only taking into consideration the financial factors—not the inevitable loss of life that will ensue if the U.S. goes to war against Iraq. In short, the stakes in the Persian Gulf are not worth the costs or risks that American military action would entail.

U.S. leaders must learn to distinguish between vital and peripheral—much less nonexistent—security interests. During the Cold War, American policymakers tended to regard even the most trivial geopolitical assets as essential. However, to be considered a threat to a vital interest, a development should have a direct, immediate, and substantial, connection with America's physical survival, its political independence, or the preservation of its domestic freedoms. Threats to truly vital interests are relatively rare, and they may be even rarer in a post-Cold War setting where no potential adversary is capable of making a bid for global domination.

In that context, the preservation of America's Cold War system of alliances is ill-advised. Not only are such commitments expensive, they are profoundly dangerous. As Cato Institute senior fellow Earl C. Ravenal has noted, alliances are "lethal transmission belts for war," converting what should be minor, localized conflicts into wider confrontations between great powers.

There are various flash points around the world where Cold War-era commitments to clients could entangle the U.S. In addition to the volatile Persian Gulf, the tense situations involving Pakistan and India, Syria and Israel, and the two Koreas are the most visible examples. The Balkans and other portions of Eastern Europe also could become caldrons of ethnic strife.

There has been much discussion of a "peace dividend" emerging from the end of the Cold War, but without an entirely new defense strategy, there will be no such dividend for Americans to enjoy. Instead, Washington will perpetuate a vast array of increasingly irrelevant commitments and the military forces to defend them. The statements of Secretary of State James A. Baker III and other Administration officials that the U.S. will need a long-term military presence in the Persian Gulf even if Iraq's expansionist bid is stymied exemplify both the logic and the consequences of global interventionism.

The pursuit of stability is a chimera. Even when a problem is "solved" and stability in a particular region is restored, it is rarely more than a temporary achievement. New revisionist powers invariably arise, revolutions can replace pliant regimes with hostile ones, and the maneuvering for advantage on the part of rival states continues unabated. That is especially true of the volatile Middle East, but it also applies to most regions. If the U.S. insists on linking its security interests to the achievement of global stability, and thereby injects itself into a host of regional quarrels, it will need military forces that are larger, more diverse, and more expensive than those maintained to wage the Cold War.

The connection between force levels and commitments is crucial. Military units do not exist for their own sake, but to fulfill specific missions, and creating and maintaining those forces is inherently costly. For example, 11 of the Army's 18 divisions exist to help defend Western Europe from a Warsaw Pact invasion. Similarly, the Navy's alleged need for 14 aircraft carrier battle groups is predicated on the continuation of U.S. commitments to allies and clients in Europe, the Far East, and the Persian Gulf. Even the size of the U.S. strategic arsenal is largely the result of embracing the doctrine of extended deterrence—shielding other nations with our nuclear umbrella.

The pertinent question is whether such commitments serve America's security interests, especially now that the Cold War is over. With the decline of the Soviet threat and no other would-be hegemonic power on the horizon, a global network of U.S.-dominated alliances appears to make little sense—particularly given its enormous expense. NATO alone costs American taxpayers more than $130,000,000,000 each year. Washington's commitments to Japan, South Korea, and other nations in the Far East run $40,000,000,000, and our Persian Gulf commitments add another $40,000,000,000.

It was one thing to undertake such expensive and risky obligations to prevent Soviet global domination, as improbable as that danger may seem in retrospect. It is quite another to perpetuate those obligations merely to prevent vaguely defined instability or discourage the outbreak of local quarrels that have little or no relevance to America's security interests.

It's time to transfer power

Washington fails to recognize that other democratic powers are now important actors in the global arena—the Bush Administration proceeds on the assumption that only the U.S. can deter aggression. That may have had some validity in the years following World War II when Europe lay in ruins, Germany and Japan were occupied and disarmed, and the geostrategic environment was starkly bipolar, but today the situation is changed radically. It no longer is necessary or desirable for the U.S. to play the role of Atlas, carrying the security burdens of the planet on its shoulders. The time has come—indeed, it is long overdue—to transfer the entire responsibility for their own defense to prosperous and capable world powers.

It is quite clear, however, that those nations will not volunteer to protect their own security interests as long as the U.S. is willing to do so on their behalf. That point has been underscored by the meager allied support for the U.S. military intervention in the Persian Gulf. The so-called multinational force arrayed against Iraq is an overwhelmingly American enterprise, with little more than token military contributions from Japan, the members of the European Community, and even the Middle Eastern nations that would seem to be the most directly threatened by Iraqi expansionism. Those countries exhibit little inclination to accept meaningful financial burden-sharing and even less inclination to undertake meaningful risk-sharing.

Instead of attempting to preserve expensive and dangerous alliances and other military commitments, the U.S. should adopt a new policy of strategic independence for the post-Cold War era. This would be based on three factors: a recognition that the Soviet threat has declined, a narrower and more rigorous definition of America's vital security interests, and the appreciation that other nations now have the economic strength to provide for their own defense needs without a U.S. subsidy.

By phasing out its global network of alliances and adopting a course of strategic independence, the U.S. radically could downsize its military establishment. The most important changes would include reducing the number of aircraft carrier battle groups from 14 to six and tactical air wings from 40 to 17; cutting the number of Army divisions from 18 to two and combining the remaining units with the Marine Corps in a new mobile strike force; scaling down the strategic arsenal from more than 12,000 warheads to 3,000-3,500; eliminating such unnecessary systems as the MX and Midgetman missiles, the B-2 Stealth bomber, and the C-17 transport plane; and placing greater emphasis on defending American territory and lives than on power projection in distant regions, which requires the development of an effective defense against ballistic missiles.

Under a regime of strategic independence, the U.S. eventually could defend its legitimate security interests with a military force of only 905,000, compared with the 2,044,000 proposed in the Administration's 1991 budget—and the force of 1,635,000 contemplated in the revised 1995 projections. Adopting that strategy would enable the U.S. to reduce its military spending to $120,000,000,000 within five years. That is a sizable peace dividend by any definition. It not only would eliminate the alleged need for a tax increase to narrow the budget deficit, it could (and should) lead to substantial tax reductions. The American people have borne great risks and burdens throughout the Cold War; they now deserve to reap the benefits from the end of that long, twilight struggle.

Chapter 7

The New World Order

Article 7.1.   Defining the New World Order

In his now-famous September 11, 1990 address. in which he outlined the reasons for the conflict with Iraq, President Bush first used the phrase, "New World Order," a phrase which he has since repeated many times. This article presents the views of three distinguished writers, with different political perspectives. Each was asked to define the term, as he understands it, and to assess its meaning in the wake of recent world developments. Owen Harries, editor of *The National Interest*, views it as a political impossibility, a term which is likely to encourage a utopian vision of the new American role in international affairs; Ian Buruma, foreign editor for *The Spectator* in London, hopes that it will force the United States to reevaluate its commitment to democratic values and human rights; and Richard Barnet, co-founder of the Institute for Policy Studies, in Washington, D.C., sees it as a political illusion, a partisan ploy, and a dangerous distraction from the real problems that face America.

DEFINING THE NEW WORLD ORDER

In a speech on September 11, 1990, when President Bush explained to the public the reasons for the conflict with Iraq, he used for the first time a phrase he would repeat throughout the winter: "New World Order." Since then it seems to have attracted as many meanings as victory has fathers. The President's critics say the phrase is a cobbling of three nice, vague words intended to give a sense of international purpose to a war whose true motive was oil, say, or a diversion from domestic politics. They believe the phrase has a half-life comparable to Gerald Ford's "Whip Inflation Now" or Jimmy Carter's "New Foundation."

Others argue that, because the events of the past two years have so altered the constellation of national alliances and the structures of power, a New World Order holds actual promise—as a Pax Americana, or a United Nations with teeth, or born-again international law, or a nuclear nonproliferation police force. In order to plumb the term's depth of meaning, *Harper's Magazine* asked three writers of differing political outlook to answer the question implied by the President's phrase: What is the New World Order and, in terms of realpolitik, whose is it?

OWEN HARRIES *is editor of* The National Interest. *He has served as Australian ambassador to UNESCO and as foreign-policy adviser to the Australian prime minister. He recently edited a collection of essays entitled* America's Purpose: New Visions of U.S. Foreign Policy.

AN IMPOSSIBILITY

In 1933 Franklin Roosevelt launched his New Deal. In 1960 John Kennedy asked Americans to be pioneers on the New Frontier. Now another generation later, George Bush offers us a New World Order.

"New" is a potent word in American politics, promising not merely change but sweeping and transforming progress. It offers escape from the constraints and problems of the past, and a fresh start. After forty years in the realm of necessity occasioned by the Cold War, that is not an unattractive prospect.

But what exactly is to be the content of the proclaimed New World Order? To date, President Bush has been vague and unforthcoming on the subject. From the general proclamations, though, four different models emerge:

The Interdependence–Global Village Model. This view holds that the countries of the world are now so closely intermeshed, with such a density of transactions, that the old zero-sum games of power politics no longer apply. Conflict and competition will soon be replaced by harmony and complementarity. Instead of the separation that fostered ignorance and suspicion, there will be growing familiarity and understanding.

The trouble with those who idealize the Global Village in this way is that they seem to have never lived in a real village. They are unaware of the envy, meanness, rivalry, and cruelty that the intimacy of village life can, and often does, accommodate. Or, to put it another way, the most interdependent social organization

that men and women enter into is the family; and it is in families that most murders occur. Interdependence, in other words, is no guarantee of international harmony.

The Pax Democratica Model. In order to hold this view, one must make two assumptions: first, that a democratic revolution is sweeping the world; second, that democracies don't fight one another. Therefore, we are heading toward a much more benign and peaceful world in which sweetness and light shall prevail. Q.E.D.

The alleged spread of democracy is greatly exaggerated. It involves counting on the plus side many countries whose adherence to democracy is skin-deep, merely formal, and almost certainly fleeting. Thus Thailand, to take far from the most egregious example, is listed in the democracy column one week; but, after one of the military coups that are part of the ritual of Thai politics, it is off the next. In much of Latin America there has been little change in political cultures that, over generations, have sustained routine swings between genuine dictatorship and faux democracy.

As for the claim that democracies are not bellicose, it is worth recalling that one of the first inventions of modern democracy was the *levée en masse*, which mobilized the entire male population of revolutionary France and made it available to Napoleon for a two-decade assault on the rest of Europe. In 1914 Britain, France, and Germany were as liberal and democratic as many, if not most, of the countries now accepted as functioning democracies. They fought the most terrible war in history. And, of course, most democracies, including the United States, have often been tempted to fight "splendid little wars" against nondemocracies.

Both the Global Village and Pax Democratica models rest on the central faith that the New World Order will see a decline in the efficacy, and therefore the use, of force. That belief has now been seriously undermined by the Gulf War itself, in which military power was spectacularly decisive while the much heralded new economic superpowers—Germany and Japan—were feeble and irrelevant. As a result, two other versions of the New World Order, which allow a role for force, have recently gained ground.

The Collective Security Model. On close examination, this model is a retread of a pre-1939 favorite. The prominence of the United Nations in the Gulf War and the fact that for once the Security Council functioned according to the manual immediately led to claims that the Cold War was at last over and that a system of collective security was achievable. In his address in February to the Economic Club of New York, the President put it plainly: "So, the New World Order, I think, foresees a revitalized peace-keeping function of the United Nations."

This claim ignores the extent to which the Gulf War was a special, probably unrepeatable, case. It provided a perfect villain, one who not only lacked any redeeming virtues but was, as it turned out, obligingly stupid. It involved clear and unambiguous aggression. The presence of oil gave it urgency. And Saudi Arabia provided a large, secure land base from which to conduct operations. Is there any other hot spot on Earth that offers such a helpful set of conditions for collective security? Surely not. And, of course, in a dispute in which a veto-possessing member of the Security Council is the transgressor, the UN will be as ineffectual as ever.

> THE MOST INTERDEPENDENT SOCIAL ORGANIZATION WE ENTER INTO IS THE FAMILY, AND IT IS IN FAMILIES THAT MOST MURDERS OCCUR.

The Pax Americana Model. Can the United States, as the one authentic, all-round superpower, impose order on a recalcitrant world? In the afterglow of a glorious victory, this version of a New World Order does not lack support. Indeed, there is more than a hint of it in George Bush's depiction of the United States as the country that does "the hard work of freedom" and his claim that America's intervention in the Gulf was setting down new "ground rules" for the post–Cold War era.

The irony of the triumph in the Gulf, however, is that it establishes conclusively the impossibility of a Pax Americana. Far from writing any new ground rules, the scale of the American effort—half a million troops, a huge air force, six aircraft carriers, a lead time of six months, not to mention the subordination of all other policy issues, domestic and foreign—ensured that it was not replicable on a regular basis. The Gulf War cannot serve as a precedent.

The post–Cold War world will certainly be different in some important ways: Power will be distributed differently; ideological rivalry will be less prominent; nuclear and biological weapons, and the missiles to deliver them, will be more widely dispersed. If people could use the term "New World Order" in a neutral, nonprescriptive way—perhaps without the capital letters—it might be useful as a term to acknowledge that there have been changes in the world. But, alas, they can't. With President Bush taking the lead, the term simply serves to foster illusion and encourage the reemergence of the utopian strain in American thinking on world affairs. It is better avoided.

IAN BURUMA *is foreign editor for* The Spectator *in London. His most recent book is entitled* God's Dust: A Modern Asian Journey, *published by Farrar, Straus and Giroux.*

A MORALITY

We have entered a New World Order, a marriage, if it works, of decency (democracy and human rights) and realpolitik. The Vietnam syndrome, so we are told by the President of the United States, is no more. The real issue in the matter of the New World Order, whether this is openly stated or not, is the legitimacy of U.S., or U.S.-led, intervention.

National Liberationists, isolationists, and enemies of "U.S. imperialism" have long argued that America should keep its hands off other nations under all circumstances. If there is any ordering to be done, it must be done by the United Nations. This position sounds fine in principle, but in practice the United Nations without the United States is toothless and cannot order much.

Champions of the so-called Third World have long assumed that American interests could not possibly coincide with those of poor, non-Western countries. Such champions, often journalists or academics with some expertise in these areas, like to emphasize the cultural ignorance and insensitivity with which Uncle Sam puts his muddy boots into faraway lands. Champion-experts tend, in these matters, to reflect the opinions of semi-Westernized Third World intellectuals, traumatized by the colonial past, who blame every misfortune on the United States. Pol Pot: Henry Kissinger's fault. Pinochet: a mere American puppet. Saddam Hussein: an American creation. The invasion of Kuwait: a CIA trick. And so on. There was some justification for this facile view when the Cold War was still hot and "our bastards" were often just that, but the good times for anti-communist dictators now appear to be over. Even so, the champion-experts have hardly changed their tone.

During the Gulf War, experts on the "Arab mind" warned that U.S. ignorance would cause catastrophe: The entire Arab world would rise against the West. I have also heard the argument that fighting Saddam was just a way of imposing "Western values" on an alien world. But if the New World Order means anything, it is that basic rights and freedom from tyranny have little to do with culture. No one—not Arabs, Chinese, or Tibetans—is culturally programmed to enjoy being bullied. Cultural differences do not excuse tyrannical rulers. This might seem an obvious point, but such was and still often is exactly the reasoning of the many people, from right to left, who justified the actions of Chairman Mao, among other Third World dictators. There were many arguments to be made for or against using military force against Saddam, but whether or not President Bush understood Arab culture was irrelevant.

NATIONAL INTERESTS ARE RELEVANT. IT IS PERFECTLY TRUE THAT WITHOUT OIL, THE WORLD MIGHT HAVE LET SADDAM HUSSEIN BE. BUT SO WHAT?

National interests, of course, *are* relevant. It is perfectly true that without oil, the world might have let Saddam Hussein be. But so what? Did that make the case against him less just? The idea that the United States can be looking after its own interests and be doing good at the same time is particularly painful and confusing to Third Worlders and National Liberationists, for it means they have lost the moral high ground. Henry Kissinger's doctrinaire realpolitik could be condemned as being immoral or, if you prefer, amoral. But Bush's New World Order has a moral basis, badly articulated, perhaps, but moral nonetheless.

This is, of course, not to say that his policies will always be right or that the New World Order is without its problems. One of the most obvious problems was plain to see in the Gulf from the moment Saddam's men marched into Kuwait. What was the United States to do? Punishing Saddam for gobbling up a sovereign state was an aim on which it was relatively easy to reach agreement. The sovereignty of borders is a principle upon which orderly international relations are based. Once you let go of that principle, people will be invading all over the place. But another, less openly stated, aim was to break the power of Saddam in his own country, because he is a danger to others and a tyrant to his people. There was a clear interest in pursuing this goal, and it was morally decent to boot, but it did mean infringing on the sovereignty of Iraq. So what about the principle of respecting national borders? There was no good answer to this, so the President had to, as it were, beat around the bush.

This same problem came up during the war-crimes trials after World War II. The Nazi leaders were punished for what they did *during* the war, after many borders had been crossed, but not for what they did *before* the war began to their own people, principally the Jews. Even in the extreme case of Nazi crimes, such trials would have meant interfering with a sovereign nation—a nation ruled by thugs, perhaps, but still a sovereign nation.

It is worth pondering whether the New World Order allows us to reconsider the principle of sacrosanct sovereignty. In practice, we have been rethinking it all along. Few liberals protested against sanctions aimed at the South African government, even though apartheid was an internal South African affair. And President Bush has been criticized, and rightly so, for not protesting more forcefully against the killings in Beijing, let alone Lhasa. But protesting is one thing. Should the United States and its allies not go much further than that? If freedom from tyranny is indeed a universal human right, should we not actively intervene when tyranny becomes intolerable? Should Pol Pot have been stopped by force? Or Idi Amin? Or Ne Win?

The answer is yes, in principle but not inevitably in practice. Neither the United States nor any other country can or should act as a permanent fire brigade, putting out every fire in the world. Nor does every dictator merit a war. It would be too expensive, in human life and in revenue, and it would not necessarily do any good. It could, on the contrary, make things worse. Because the New World Order has a moral basis doesn't mean that it should be a moral crusade.

To expect to impose democracy on others by force is a vain and dangerous illusion. But democracy can be encouraged where there is a demand for it—in China, in Burma, or in any country where this demand is squelched by force. If we have finally abandoned the idea that such aspirations are misguided yearnings for Western values, or that the sovereignty of nations is always of greater worth than the liberation of people (not The People), then the New World Order will have proved its value already.

RICHARD BARNET *is a co-founder of the Institute for Policy Studies, in Washington, D.C., and the author of twelve books on foreign policy. His most recent book is entitled* The Rockets' Red Glare: War, Politics and the American Presidency, *published by Simon & Schuster.*

AN ILLUSION

When Operation Desert Storm ended in the triumphal hundred-hour ground war, George Bush's mysterious slogan "New World Order" suddenly took on meaning. The United States is now the only global military superpower, and the new political arrangements in the Middle East, whether formally negotiated or not, will be in large measure a Pax Americana. The United States will be more assertive in pressing for an Israeli-Arab settlement, and, with the realignment of forces in the region, some progress may well be made. Saudi Arabia is now firmly in the American camp. Syria has been accorded the status of an honorary former terrorist state and is using its new financial support from coalition partners to build up its military forces. Iran is biding its time. Cheap oil is here to stay until the next crisis, and the quick and efficient destruction of much of Iraq and Kuwait may well lift the United States out of recession.

What sort of New World Order will be built on all this? The war in the Gulf has already changed the political culture of the United States. "By God, we've kicked the Vietnam syndrome once and for all," President Bush exulted at a White House appearance. The United States finally fought a big war against a plausible, if inflated, enemy; won decisively; and the public applauded. The Pentagon's reticence about fighting wars that risk estranging the military forces from the civil society has given way to justifiable pride in a war well fought, and to new confidence that the administration will stop the budget cuts and borrow enough money to finance the permanent preparation for an endless series of high-tech wars across the planet.

Last January the country was divided about the risks of the war and, to a lesser extent, the morality of resolving the crisis by killing tens of thousands of Iraqis who themselves are the victims of Saddam's crimes. The stunning victory has blown away all thought of risk, and, for all but a tiny minority, success has settled the moral questions, too. It will be easier now to convince the public that the escalating misery in the poor countries of Asia, Africa, and Latin America is essentially a continuing military problem.

Does this mean that the United States is now embarked on a worldwide military crusade for the New World Order? Is our top export now to be high-tech war, our slogan "Have smart bombs, will travel"? In his remarks to the Economic Club of New York, before the ground war began, President Bush suggested that American leadership in fighting the Gulf War would result in "vastly restored credibility" for the United States that could be translated into more "harmonious" relations with its major industrial competitors. In other words, the leverage over the allies that the United States enjoyed during the Cold War but lost when the Soviet Union dropped out of the global conflict can now be restored by the United States' becoming the policeman in strategic areas of the Third World. This notion of America's role in the world is reflected in high-level Pentagon statements about the missions of the armed forces published several months before Iraq invaded Kuwait. General A. M. Gray, commandant of the Marine Corps, wrote, three months before the invasion of Kuwait, that the United States must maintain "a credible military power projection capability with the flexibility to respond to conflicts across the spectrum of violence throughout the globe."

This shift in the political culture will have an effect on the U.S. budget. The "peace dividend" lies buried in the desert. But will the war that worked bring about a fundamental change in the U.S. role in the world? I think not. It is hard to think of sites for future wars that feature all the essential conditions that made the Gulf War, despite the numbers of troops and the financial cost, the most splendid of little wars: Saddam's brutal aggression against a small, defenseless country without even a shred of a plausible legal claim; a villain out of central casting, with nuclear ambitions and a weakness for poison gas, who at both the negotiating table and on the battlefield revealed an unerring instinct for his own jugular; the absence of Soviet opposition; a treeless battlefield ideal for high-tech slaughter; shared oil anxieties stronger than the economic rivalries dividing the United States, Japan, and Europe; countries rich enough to pay the warriors not only to fight a "free" war but also to rebuild what they destroyed.

The politically sophisticated generals who crafted the Gulf operation, having restored the reputation of the armed forces, are in no hurry to risk it again. They understand that other political crises will not offer such promising terrain and that long, inconclusive, and disappointing wars are just as dangerous to the health of the United States' military now as they were before President Bush exorcised the demons of Vietnam.

Nor are Germany and Japan, the principal beneficiaries and reluctant financiers of the

U.S. war effort, willing to support the United States in a crusade against evil regimes around the globe. Once the real economic costs, the disastrous environmental effects, and the long-term political fallout of the war are assessed, the United States' major industrial competitors are likely to be more restrained in supporting future crusades for world order orchestrated by this nation—even to the limited extent that they have cooperated in this one. The more the United States assumes the posture of the Lone Ranger and continues to treat the United Nations as a flag of convenience, the more guarded they will be.

For all the bravado in Washington about the dawn of the second American century, making war will not be the primary basis of national power in this new century. Having neglected its technological and industrial base, the United States is now extremely dependent on short-term foreign capital. If the United States, Europe, and Japan continue to move toward competitive trading blocs, such an economic world order cannot be policed by American military power.

The American role in the New World Order will ultimately be determined by economic constraints. The growing vulnerability of the U.S. economy, its dependence on foreign capital, its failure to invest in roads, bridges, schools, and civilian technology are now taking such a dra-matic toll on civil society that unless the investment priorities are radically changed, American influence will inevitably decline. The Soviet Union, it should be remembered, disappeared as a global political actor at the very moment when it was at the pinnacle of its military power. Despite the promilitary sentiment sweeping the United States, it may not be politically possible for an American president to lead the American people into the next century as the new Sparta: The United States is the only advanced industrial nation without national health insurance. It is number one in the percentage of the population behind bars. And it has a murder rate unequaled anywhere in the world that keeps statistics. As the President himself noted in his victory speech to Congress, during the one hundred hours of the ground war more Americans were killed by gunfire on our city streets than in the Kuwait-Iraq theater of operations. The afterglow of victory is not enough to restore the sinews of nationhood, and as these weaken so does the real power of the United States to influence the New World Order. For the crucial battles of the new century, our industrial competitors concentrate on their economic bases, while the United States, seemingly unable to understand the shifting foundations of national power, risks being caught in a time warp of an American century that is long gone. ∎

Article 7.2.   The Meaning of the New World Order: A Critique

James Petras takes exception to President Bush's gulf war initiative, arguing that it was designed to assure U.S. global supremacy. According to the author, the administration sought to militarize U.S. culture and society through a carefully orchestrated military blitz. The campaign reflected the administration's desire to reshape a new world order based on military supremacy over its market-based competitors and to protect and cultivate those governments whose support is essential to America's political and economic interests. The president's strategy, which is both flawed and risky, is certain to deepen political antagonisms and increase economic competition.

The Meaning of the New World Order: A Critique

By JAMES PETRAS

THE U.S. WAR in the Persian Gulf was an attempt to recreate Washington's role as world policeman, to re-subordinate Europe to U.S. power and to in-

JAMES PETRAS writes from Swarthmore, Pa.

timidate the third world into submission. It was an attempt to regain the position of global supremacy held by the United States at the end of World War II. In this sense George Bush was executing, in its most extreme form, the political vision of the Reagan period. The massive buildup of military power, the worldwide pressure on clients, allies and neutrals to collaborate, the vast economic expenditures, the unprecedented unleashing

From America, May 11, 1991, pp. 512-515. Reprinted with permission of America Press, Inc., 106 West 56th Street, New York, NY 10019. © 1991 All Rights Reserved.

of aerial bombardment, all speak to the momentous historical changes that underlie this war.

The preparation for the war demonstrated the enormous capacity and resources that Washington has at its disposal. It also reflected a deep-rooted sense of decline and fear of growing challenges to that global supremacy. The war was not about "oil" — and even less about "self-determination" (no country can match the U.S. record of violations of national integrity over the past two decades), but about creating the foundations for launching a new set of political, economic and social relations to sustain the United States as the dominant power in the world. That is the meaning of the Bush and Baker vision of a new world order.

Prior to the Gulf War there were numerous indications that the global decline of the United States was accelerating. In Eastern Europe and the Soviet Union the "ideological victory" over Stalinism also revealed the tremendous incapacity of the United States to provide economic resources to reshape these economies to its needs or even to subsidize new client regimes. Instead, most observers saw Germany as the dominant power in the region. In Western Europe the decline of NATO substantially weakened U.S. leverage over European governments and economic policy. European-centered military and security proposals paralleled tighter economic integration. At the policy level, declining influence became obvious in Washington's incapacity to impose its liberal agricultural and "services" (banking, finances, etc.) agenda during the Uruguay round of the GATT (General Agreement on Tariffs and Trade) meetings. The proximity of 1992's European union is seen as a strategic threat, closing off markets in Western Europe and challenging the American position elsewhere.

The cumulative gains of Japan and its virtual displacement of the United States as the major investor and trading partner in Asia—the most dynamic growth region in the world—are a clear signal of declining influence. In a world in which global power is increasingly determined by industrial and financial activities and market exchanges based on strong industrial states, Washington strategists must have recognized that the United States will be a sure loser.

The decline of U.S. global power is evident even in Latin America, where haphazard efforts have been made to preserve areas of traditional domination. Bush's "Enterprise for the Americas" proposal was more rhetoric than substance, more pillage of existing markets and resources than any strategic commitment to large-scale, long-term investments to expand productive capacity. The initial sums promised ($300 million) would cover Latin America's foreign debt payments for four days. More to the point, the continuing massive outflows of interest payments and profits from Latin America to the United States ($35 billion per year) and the incapacity of the United States to reconstruct the economies of small, reconquered nations (Grenada, Panama, Nicaragua) demonstrate the tremendous gap between U.S. power to dominate and U.S. incapacity to rebuild economically viable client states.

This global context of deteriorating power—power lost to capitalist competition and third-world challengers—would, if it continued over time, either force internal structural change in the United States or lead to the relegation of this country to a status of non-hegemony. The impending loss of global supremacy and the incapacity to take economic advantage of the openings in Eastern Europe, Russia, China and the rest of Asia is frustrating to U.S. policymakers. Blocked by economic weakness from seizing the new openings, Washington's frustration has increased because of the tremendous stockpile of advanced military weaponry at its disposal. The disjuncture between military and economic power in the new post-Cold War configuration has been acutely felt and was instrumental in launching the Gulf War. Of what use were guided missiles and stealth bombers in competing for influence in Western European markets? How were Pentagon budgets to compete with Deutschebank loans for influence in Eastern Europe or the Soviet Union? The contradiction is transparent: In the post-Cold War period (and even before that), the rules for achieving global power have been rooted in competition in the world market, while the United States is still geared toward projections of military power.

The U.S. war in the Gulf was in its deepest sense a means of changing the rules of global power: subordinating economic competitors into bankers of U.S. military conquests; converting economic resources from markets toward war subsidies; loosening European alliances in favor of U.S.-centered coalitions; trading third-world debt payments for military contingents under U.S. command.

THE Gulf War was in its broadest contours an effort to *reverse* world historical trends that are moving to relegate the United States to the status of a second-class power. It was meant to define a new military-centered global order in which markets, income and resource shares are defined not by technological-market power, but by political-military dominance. Under these rules Washington's comparative advantage in military power would insure U.S. global supremacy, and would undermine the capacity of competitors to mount an effective challenge to its position.

The Bush Administration's attempt to change the rules defining global power relations and economic conditions—internal and external—under which imperial revivalism takes place, will have a profound effect on U.S. society as well as on future relations with competitors. Launching a major war at a time of declining economic activity and deteriorating urban life means, unlike previous wars, this one absorbed scarce economic resources and further eroded social conditions. It undermined public services and increased financial instability. This imperialist war could not provide economic payoffs for labor, tying the working class to the war through higher wages and better jobs. This war exploited labor at home to support wealthy rentier clients in the Gulf: The international linkages were financed by appropriating internal resources.

THE ABSENCE of imperial payoffs for labor creates a serious political problem: How can the Bush Administration sustain a campaign for global hegemony that cannot rely on economic payoffs and spinoffs to labor and business to reinforce chauvinist ideological appeals? The answer lies in the militarization of U.S. culture and society through a mass propaganda blitz. Almost 24 hours a day during the war every major media outlet was engaged in a campaign to capture the hearts and minds of the American people. The war, as presented by the state and the media, was defined strictly according to the military censors, television and radio programs organized to focus on military strategies and rationales presented by military officials and strategists of war. News commentators selectively interviewed rank and file soldiers, giving the Pentagon a "back home" face. Bombings were described in terms of objects destroyed, according to technical formulas approved by military officials. The issues and prospects of the war were defined by the military and the chief policymakers. Congressional officials competed with the executive branch in embracing the new military metaphysics. Liberal columnists reinforced the same message: The merits of warfare techniques were debated rather than any critical aspects of the rentier classes and global power interests being served.

Nowhere was the massive destruction of Iraq, the terror bombing of the population, the enormous economic and human cost to the American people significantly and publicly debated. More important, the larger political-military issues of global U.S. power that underlay the war were totally obscured by rhetoric about liberating Kuwait, defending democracy, opposing Hussein. Vague references to a "new world order" effectively obscured the role that Washington foresaw for itself as the prime beneficiary and dominant force in this new order.

The "militarization" of American society serves to create a culture of citizen obedience to military authority and submissiveness to the imperatives of war. Mass campaigns are encouraged to support the soldiers as a way of blunting criticism of the war makers. This barrage even affected sectors of the anti-war opposition, with every call to end the war being balanced by "support" of our soldiers. This misplaced accommodation to state rhetoric thus replaces any effort to fight the economic system that fails to provide meaningful, productive work at home and lures young people into the military.

If the Gulf War was primarily about the United States reshaping a new world order anchored in military supremacy over its market-based competitors, it also involved the protection and cultivation of client regimes whose interests are linked to this global project. The Gulf oil monarchies recycle hundreds of billions of dollars of earnings to U.S. banks. Israel provides overt military support to the United States in the Mideast and clandestine arms and intelligence to U.S. client regimes. The U.S. defense of the authoritarian Kuwaiti regime and the autocratic Saudi monarchy is in part political payment for their economic support of U.S. policy in South Asia,

South Africa, Central America and elsewhere. More important, these states do not *compete* with the U.S. economy in global markets. They share the U.S. *parasitical* relation to the producer countries, north and south, east and west. While the United States extracts loans and debt payments, the sheiks receive ground rents.

Israel is in an analogous position; its economy is heavily based on arms sales, U.S. and, to a lesser degree, European grants and aid (public and private), land appropriated from the Arabs, professionals and skilled labor trained and educated at the expense of Communist societies and Western taxpayers. Like the United States, Israel lives off ideological appeals and military capacities that far outrun its economic-technical production. U.S. military definitions of the new world order resonate with Israeli comparative advantages—particularly as Israel seeks to carve out a role as a regional power. The Israeli military definition of politics has been refracted through its supporters among the leadership of major Jewish organizations in the United States. From the beginning of the Gulf conflict, these organizations seconded and encouraged every major escalation of the war and gave unconditional support to President Bush's policy. They were practically the only major ethno-religious organizations to adopt such an unequivocal position.

The chauvinist rhetoric pumped out by the mass media and the military rationale elaborated by the press for the educated classes tacitly recognized the growing gap between the classes paying for and fighting the war and the local and overseas promoters and benefactors. The militarization of cultural life can be temporarily successful only insofar as the reality principle can be avoided. As the costs mount at home and abroad, directly affecting the lives of millions of Americans, and as the unequal benefits and costs become increasingly transparent, a political backlash is likely to occur, pitting pro-war ideologies and the state apparatus against formidable opponents.

THE NEW world order that President Bush and Secretary of State Baker hope to fashion out of the Gulf War is also based on the notion of subordinating Europe and Japan to U.S. global ends. Throughout the war, the U.S. news media presented Japan and Germany as ungrateful oil importers benefiting from U.S. military activity without contributing their share of money and military forces. The war's morality aside, neither Germany nor Japan had any great interest in or commitment to a military confrontation in the Gulf: Their market positions insure their supply of petroleum. Neither country has an interest in diverting economic resources from technological development to a military buildup that has no positive impact on its economic expansion, particularly in international markets. Moreover, a war on behalf of monarchical clients of the United States would hardly enhance their influence.

Even during the war, U.S. supremacy over its allies was more appearance than substance. The economic contributions dribbled in (and in part took the form of credits and loans to bankrupt U.S. Mideast clients), and delivery lagged far behind promises. Washington's policy of "creating facts" — projecting power and then forcing the Europeans and Japanese to support U.S. positions—has temporarily pre-empted the formulation of the common

---

Vague references to a "new world order" effectively obscured the role that Washington foresaw for itself as the prime beneficiary and dominant force in this new order.

European position, and England has been able to reassert its primary loyalty to the U.S.-led military alliance over and against a common European policy. But this European "retreat" before American primacy has no structural basis: Washington has neither the economic capacity nor the military will to hold Europe and Japan under its tutelage. Even England's role in the Gulf is less a product of U.S. policy than a function of its own financial interests in the Gulf banks.

If Washington could not fully reassert its primacy in the midst of the war, how can it be expected to reestablish a framework for supremacy after the war, when the scramble for contracts, markets and oil will unleash all the expansionist appetites of Japan and Europe? To accomplish dominance, new rules will have to be established to enable the United States to pursue its vision of a new world order. In all likelihood such rules would resemble those of the neo-mercantilist world of the 18th century. The United States would presumably impose economic charges for its military services. The Seventh Fleet might serve as a kind of "toll collector," charging fees for oil shipments to Europe and Japan. Of course this is a farfetched idea, but so is the idea of establishing a new world order based on U.S. military supremacy over its powerful economic allies. The alternative is even less plausible: the use of military threats to coerce Germany and Japan into falling in line with the command structure of the United States, an idea hardly likely to carry much weight with the U.S. Treasury, in debt to Japanese banks, and U.S. multinationals dependent on European markets.

THE BUSH-BAKER notion of a new world order based on U.S. military power is really a transplant of the role and practice of "extractive capitalists" in the United States—the oil and raw material investors in the third world. Their view of the world is derived from their experiences in the third world, where they extend their economic interests through Pentagon and C.I.A. influence to establish favorable client regimes that then open up their countries to exploitation. In these extractive contexts, U.S. military power serves to consolidate hegemony over client states.

George Bush is largely a product of two important exponents of "extractive" thinking: Texas oil and the C.I.A. His effort to expand the practices and relations of extractive capitalism in the third world to a world scale is not only doomed to failure, but reflects the total ineptitude of U.S. strategic thinking today. Germany and Japan are not about to submit to U.S. dictates on trade policy as Mexico has done. Their banks finance us, not vice versa. Nor is the United States likely to find senior military officers in these countries eager to submit to their U.S. counterparts in efforts to undercut national industries.

The unreality of the new world order pursued by President Bush and Secretary Baker bespeaks limited vision— one that looks only at the ideological and military role of power and not the economic; one that looks only at U.S. success in third-world counter-insurgency and ignores U.S. failures in market competition; one that looks backward to a past era of U.S. dominance and ignores the present and future world of relatively equal competitors; one that celebrates ideological victories over Communism and ignores the hollowing out of urban capitalism in America. The blind spots are not minor; they are major determinants of global power, or strategic failures.

To pursue a global imperial vision that is so fundamentally flawed is to court disaster: To mount a grand army abroad is to further hollow out the American economy at home. Never has there been such a clear-cut case of a "zero-sum game." The new imperialism paradoxically exploits its own people in order to expand militarily abroad. The new world order is built on extracting economic surplus at home to strengthen rentier classes abroad; it deepens the social polarization between wage, salaried and small business classes on the one hand and the overseas extractive capitalists on the other. The new world order, insofar as it attempts to harness Japan and Germany to its "neo-mercantilist" vision, is certain to deepen political antagonisms and heighten economic competition. In the end, the Bush-Baker notion of a new world order is likely to crumble in the face of the powerful economic currents that will shape global economy in the real world and political resistance at home. ■

SELECTED BIBLIOGRAPHY—SECTION II

Aslund, Anders. *Gorbachev's Struggle for Economic Reform*. Ithaca, N.Y.: Cornell University Press, 1991.

Banac, Ivo. *The National Question in Yugoslavia*. Ithaca, N.Y.: Cornell University Press, 1988.

Bell, Coral. *The Reagan Paradox: U.S. Foreign Policy in the 1980's*. New Brunswick, N.J.: Rutgers University Press, 1990.

Bertsch, Gary K. *Reform and Revolution in Communist Systems: An Introduction*. New York: Macmillan, 1991.

Borneman, John. *East Meets West in the New Berlin*. New York: Basic Books, 1991.

Brewer, Thomas L. *American Foreign Policy: A Contemporary Introduction*. Englewood Cliffs, N.J.: 1986.

Carter, Jimmy. *Keeping Faith: Memoirs of a President*. New York: Bantam, 1982.

Clemens, Walter C., Jr. *Can Russia Change? The USSR Confronts Global Interdependence*. Boston: Unwin Hyman, 1990.

Crabb, Cecil V., Jr. *American Foreign Policy in the Nuclear Age*. New York: HarperCollins, 1988.

Davies, R.W. *Soviet History in the Gorbachev Revolution*. Bloomington, Ind.: Indiana University Press, 1989.

Doder, Dusko, and Louise Branson. *Gorbachev: Heretic in the Kremlin*. New York: Penguin Books, 1991.

Fuller, Graham. *The Democracy Trap: The Perils of the Post-Cold War World*. New York: Dutton, 1992.

Gaddis, John Lewis. *The Long Peace: Inquiries into the History of the Cold War*. New York: Oxford University Press, 1987.

Hazan, Baruch A. *Gorbachev and His Enemies: The Struggle for Perestroika*. Boulder, Colo: Westview Press, 1990.

Hyland, William G. *Mortal Rivals: Understanding the Pattern of Soviet-American Conflict*. New York: Random House, 1987.

Inglis, Fred. *Everyday Life and the Cold War*. New York: Basic Books, 1991.

Kegley, Charles W., Jr., and Eugene R. Wittkopf. *American Foreign Policy: Pattern and Process*. New York: St. Martin's, 1987.

Kwitny, Jonathan. *Endless Enemies: The Making of an Unfriendly World*. New York: Penguin Books, 1991.

Markusen, Ann, and Joel Yudken. *Dismantling the Cold War Economy*. New York: Basic Books, 1992.

Melanson, Richard A. *Reconstructing Consensus: American Foreign Policy since the Vietnam War*. New York: St. Martin's, 1991.

Michalak, Stanley, Jr. *Competing Conceptions of American Foreign Policy: Worldviews in Conflict*. New York: HarperCollins, 1992.

Morrison, John. *Boris Yeltsin: Russia's First President*. New York: Dutton, 1991.

Ninic, Miroslav. *Anatomy of Hostility: The U.S.-Soviet Rivalry in Perspective*. San Diego, Calif.: Harcourt Brace Jovanovich, 1989.

Nixon, Richard M. *RN: The Memoirs of Richard Nixon*. New York: Grosset and Dunlap, 1978.

Nogee, Joseph L., and Robert H. Donaldson. *Soviet Foreign Policy since World War II*. New York: Macmillan, 1992.

Oye, Kenneth A., Robert J. Lieber, and Donald Rothchild. *Eagle Resurgent? The Reagan Era in American Foreign Policy*. New York: HarperCollins, 1987.

Rourke, John T. *Making Foreign Policy: United States, Soviet Union, and China*. Pacific Grove, Calif.: Brooks/Cole, 1990.

Sodaro, Michael J. *Moscow, Germany, and the West: From Khrushchev to Gorbachev*. Ithaca, N.Y.: Cornell University Press, 1991.

Spanier, John. *American Foreign Policy since World War II*. Washington, D.C.: Congressional Quarterly Press, 1988.

Vance, Cyrus. *Hard Choices: Critical Years in America's Foreign Policy*. New York: Simon & Schuster, 1983.

Wiarda, Howard J. *Foreign Policy Without Illusion*. New York: HarperCollins, 1990.

Wood, David M. *Power and Policy in Western European Democracies*. New York: Macmillan, 1991.

PEACE, WAR, AND CRISIS

Revolution is a fact of life in the Third World, as well as in many parts of the industrialized world. It typically occurs as a result of popular dissatisfaction with the regime in power and the policies of the governing elite. Once the revolutionary leaders seize control of the government, they may, if they choose, institute the promised reforms that initially inspired their struggle, or they may simply choose to substitute one kind of tyranny for another—which is often the case.

Many nations owe their existence to revolutionary movements, among them the United States, France, Soviet Union, and People's Republic of China. Several years ago, Henry A. Kissinger, former secretary of state, coined the term "revolutionary state," which according to Kissinger poses a serious challenge to world order. Revolutionary states are not new nor are they always totalitarian. Indeed, in the late eighteenth century, France could be classified as a revolutionary state in aristocratic Europe.

Typically, revolutionary leaders challenge the injustices of the day, be they poverty, illiteracy, disease, or war. Their argument is relatively simple—that is, the poor are poor because they have been systematically exploited by the ruling class. Wars are waged, they maintain, to enhance national prestige, acquire new territories, or secure financial gains. Ultimately, only the privileged class benefits, while the masses die in the defense of a corrupt order. Their answer is equally simple: peace, freedom, and justice require the destruction of the established order in favor of a revolutionary regime. By definition, the revolutionary regime is dedicated to "permanent revolution," or the elimination of all vestiges of the old order.

Revolutions are generally motivated by ideological, cultural, and religious beliefs. According to Marxist ideology, revolution is the inevitable consequence of class conflict. In Marxist-Leninist thought, history is sequential—that is, states move from feudalism to capitalism to socialism and, ultimately, to communism. In the past, revolutions have been rationalized as instruments of social justice and attacked as vehicles of violence and immorality. In truth, they comprise both elements.

In recent decades, the world has witnessed the rise of "revolutionary liberators"—states that seek to free others or act as catalysts or supporters of revolutionary movements. According to political scientists Charles W. Kegley, Jr. and Eugene R. Wittkopf, this role conception is particularly common among those nations which themselves developed out of revolutionary circumstances. For instance, phases of China's and Algeria's post-World War II involvements are cogent examples of revolutionary liberators.

Revolutions are laden with dangers as well as opportunities. As often as not, they fail to produce many of the changes desired by the masses. Indeed, one order is simply replaced by another order, only to ignore its promises or to institute equally corrupt or far worse practices. Many experts would contend, for example, that the revolutionary movement that precipitated the fall of the Shah of Iran merely substituted one form of oppression for another.

In the case of the Third World, coups d'etat are also quite common. These are precipitated by religious, ethnic, and tribal rivalries, as well as social, political, and economic dissatisfaction with the government in power. Since World War II, more than two hundred coups d'etat have occurred, over one hundred of which have proved successful. They are an unfortunate fact in the developing world, where conditions are often ripe for such upheavals. Possible explanations include: (1) the concentration of power in an isolated elite (frequently the military); (2) the absence of democratic traditions; (3) widespread public apathy; and (4) the lack of any institutionalized mechanisms for succession. Typically, the leaders of a coup d'etat attempt to seize or murder top-level political and military leaders, capture control of government buildings and public utilities, and lay hold of the communications apparatus to stem the fears of the masses and win their acceptance of the new regime.

Coups d'etat pose a formidable threat to totalitarian governments, military oligarchies, and even democratic regimes, particularly in those nations that are plagued by widespread poverty and social injustice. Since these governments often rely on terror and coercion as a means of control, they face a precarious future in which dissidents or revolutionary groups may seek to topple them from power. Once a coup d'etat begins, these governments are quick to declare a national emergency, suspend the constitution, and impose martial law. In such cases, the government may attempt to place the military under civilian control or, at the very least, to curb its power once the crisis subsides.

In many instances, military governments tend to be rather conservative and reluctant to play a prominent role on the world stage. Claude E. Welch, Jr., an expert on the subject of civilian control of the military, contends that many Latin American military coups d'etat may have resulted from a "fairly benign international environment in which the military is confined to dull, repetitious garrison duty." Welch argues that military involvement in foreign conflicts might have succeeded in reducing their participation in domestic affairs, whereas excessive idleness may have encouraged internal plotting.

At times, governments that view themselves as prime targets of potential coups d'etat will solicit help from the major powers, hoping that such aid will reduce the likelihood of potential insurrection. Many Third World leaders, for example, depend on the United States and the Soviet Union to guarantee their personal safety, as well as maintain their rule. For example, if a coup d'etat were to arise in Saudi Arabia or other Persian Gulf nations, it is highly likely that the leaders of these nations would turn to the United States to help suppress the uprising. Obviously, the likelihood of a coup d'etat increases when local conflict and instability exist. These regimes must strive to promote order and stability as well as economic and social progress if they hope to minimize the possibilities of future coups d'etat.

For myriad reasons, the fragility of many Third World governments can be traced backed to colonialism and the practices that it instilled. Under colonialism, the major powers sought to establish and govern numerous territories and peoples, who they held in a dependent and inferior relationship. The term, colonialism, is often used interchangeably with imperialism, which is a conscious or unplanned state policy in which one nation attempts to dominate or control another. In reality, colonialism is a manifestation of imperialism.

Throughout history, colonialism has been motivated by economic gain, national prestige, social responsibility, political adventure, power politics, religious loyalties, and sheer avarice. Colonialism waxed strong until the late 1700s, at which point many colonies in the Western hemisphere rebelled, due to geographical distance, political dissatisfaction, economic exploitation, and national pride. However, in the late 1800s colonialism experienced a new resurgence in Europe, when various European powers turned their attention to Asia and Africa. By World War I, colonialism had begun to wane, a trend which was exacerbated by World War II and the establishment of the United Nations. In the end, colonialism collapsed, suggests political scientist Forest L. Grieves, as a result of war, world opinion, the influence of Western intellectual precepts, the nature of the nation-state system, and a buoyed sense of identity and nationalism.

Colonialism, like imperialism, has sparked a fierce intellectual debate, one that has been marked by polemics on both sides. In the main, colonialism bequeathed a legacy of economic and political exploitation. The colonial powers saw these territories as a prime opportunity to control investment and trade, regulate currency and production, and manipulate labor. In addition, colonialism satisfied their desire for power and national triumph and was a vehicle to achieve hegemony and influence.

Ultimately, colonialism collapsed, fueled in part by the cry of self-determination and the rise of numerous independence movements. These newly independent states were bolstered by the principles enunciated in the Declaration Regarding Non-Self Governing Territories of the United Nations Charter, which heightened their quest for nationhood. Indeed, by 1960, the number of new nation-states had more than doubled the membership of the United Nations.

Despite these developments, colonialism has reemerged, albeit in new forms. Although the former colonial powers no longer physically occupy or govern these developing states, they wield enormous influence in many Third World nations. This is made possible, contends Leon P. Baradat, a specialist in international relations, by the fact that the industrialized powers own large shares in the major industries of many developing countries. In addition, foreign aid, with its attendant political strings, has enticed them into economic relationships similar to colonialism. Finally, Third World independence has, in many cases, been undermined by the role of international corporations, which have injected themselves into the political affairs of the emerging states. These corporations frequently operate outside the legal system, unfettered by legal restraints, owing to their corporate structure and wealth. As Baradat notes, "The power relationship between the international corporations and the host countries is frequently so uneven that the developing nations find themselves needing the companies more than the companies need them." Clearly, the role of these corporations in Third World countries has often led to improper involvement in the domestic and international political affairs of the developing country, stimulating charges of oppression, exploitation, and neocolonialism.

Section III, "Peace, War, and Crisis," consists of five chapters. Chapter 8, "Africa," explores the future of South Africa, assessing the impact of apartheid and sanctions on the social, political, and economic fabric of that country. The author contends that South Africa stands at a critical juncture. It can either choose genuine negotiations or heightened conflict, either of which will determine the future of that country for decades to come. The second selection—a hard-hitting interview with Zairian President Mobutu Sese Seko—examines a plethora of controversial issues, including human rights abuses, political corruption, economic mismanagement, social neglect, and the cult of personality. The interview probes the thoughts and actions of this Third World strongman, whose pro-Western policies have been the subject of considerable controversy.

Chapter 9, "Asia," surveys the deteriorating political situation in India, which the author views as critical. Despite several major democratic reforms, the nation stands poised, argues the author, for a major conflagration—one that may well give birth to a new India that is finally free of bureaucratic intransigence, cultural divisiveness, intractable poverty, and large-scale violence and instability. In the second selection, the author analyzes the future of Hong Kong, as that Asian nation prepares itself for Chinese rule. Despite its present problems, maintains the author, Hong Kong has demonstrated a remarkable resiliency throughout its turbulent history, suggesting that, like previous crises, the population will weather the current storm, if only cooler heads prevail and the entrepreneurial class does not desert the country.

Chapter 10, "Europe," examines the plight of five hard-line Marxist-Leninist states, each of which has proven immune to the tides of reform that have swept the rest of the communist world. The author discusses the reasons for the lack of reform as well as proposes a possible U.S. strategy for transforming these societies. In this anti-reformist profile, he contends that the U.S. must use its influence to build powerful political and economic structures that will awaken the peoples of these communist regimes and provide them with new hope and direction. Ultimately, however, the impetus for reform must come from within these societies. No amount of outside encouragement or pressure will prove sufficient unless the peoples themselves are committed to change. The second article discusses the issue of German unification which, in spite of the initial euphoria, has produced any number of vexing problems. Today, Germany is struggling to develop a new national identity, a task of enormous proportions. Indeed, the psychological impact of unification is proving far more onerous than anticipated. As Germany struggles to solve its problems, it is certain to play a constructive international role, one that is commensurate with its vast economic power.

Chapter 11, "Latin America," assesses the plight of Nicaragua since 1990, when Barrios de Violeta Chamorro scored a triumphant victory over the Sandinistas and was inaugurated as president. Despite high expectations, many of President Chamorro's campaign promises have turned out to be little more than political rhetoric, owing to what the authors describe as a series of pacts with the outgoing Sandinista leadership—pacts, which the authors contend, have subverted democracy and inflicted new hardships on the Nicaraguan people. The second selection surveys the battered dreams and shattered hopes of the tiny Caribbean nation of Haiti, which finds itself struggling to overcome decades of oppression and exploitation. Specifically, the author focuses on Haiti's new president, Jean-Bertrand Aristide, a thirty-seven-year-old socialist priest who stunned the world by becoming that country's first democratically-elected president since the ouster of the brutal Duvalier family dictatorship in 1986. The author examines the prospects for change, concluding that Aristide stands an excellent chance of democratizing his country, if only he can seize control of the military while maintaining his support among the masses. Only time will tell.

Chapter 12, "Middle East," reviews the prospects for a Middle East peace settlement, noting that the gulf war has created a new window of opportunity. The author contends that the Bush administration must pursue the peace as eagerly as it pursued the war against Iraq. The time is ripe, he concludes, for American-initiated diplomacy, which is respectful of and cooperative with the United Nations, by exploiting as many opportunities as possible for peacemaking. The second article surveys the status of the Arab world, suggesting that while it is always foolhardy to make predictions about the Middle East, recent evidence suggests that unless efforts are undertaken to rescue these countries from economic paralysis, deteriorating security guarantees, and domestic unrest, it seems safe to conclude that the region is likely to face renewed turmoil in the future.

DISCUSSION QUESTIONS

1. In what sense, if any, has apartheid undermined South Africa's position in the international community?
2. Is the de Klerk government committed to the abolition of apartheid?
3. What major social, political, and economic problems will South Africa face in the future?
4. How difficult will it be for South Africa to build a multi-racial society?
5. What explains the tribal conflict that plagues South Africa?
6. What does the future of South Africa hold?
7. Why is one-party rule so common in Africa?
8. Is Zaire's human rights record cause for concern? Why, or why not?
9. Why is corruption so prevalent in the developing world?
10. Is President Mobutu any better or worse than other Third World leaders?
11. Why is the United States so reluctant to take action against the Mobutu regime?
12. Has democracy significantly improved the quality of life in India?
13. How has the Indian bureaucracy thwarted political reform?
14. Is India's diversity politically manageable? Why, or why not?
15. How will the death of Rajiv Gandhi affect India's future?
16. Are India's social, political, and economic problems solvable? If so, how?
17. Is there reason to be optimistic about the future of Hong Kong?
18. What will Chinese rule mean to the future of Hong Kong's free-enterprise culture?
19. Why are so many of Hong Kong's professional, technical, and managerial class leaving the country?
20. To what extent, if any, does Great Britain remain the key to Hong Kong's future?
21. What explains the lack of democratic reform in such communist states as Cuba, China, Vietnam, North Korea, and Albania?
22. Is it likely that the democratic tide will ultimately sweep away the remaining hard-line Marxist-Leninist regimes? Why, or why not?
23. Can the United States hasten the collapse of these hard-line communist governments? If so, how?
24. What major developments led to German unification?
25. In what sense, if any, is German unificatlon a mixed blessing?
26. Is unification likely to produce a new nationalism in Germany?
27. Does the world have anything to fear from a united Germany?
28. What explains President Violeta Chamorro's stunning victory in Nicaragua?
29. Why did the Nicaraguan people turn against the Sandinistas?
30. Has life changed for the better in Nicaragua? If so, how?
31. Why was President Chamorro forced to accede to many demands of the Sandinistas?
32. Has President Chamorro compromised the integrity of her government by agreeing to the demands of the Sandinistas? If so, how?
33. Is national reconciliation a reality in Nicaragua today?
34. What explains Haiti's dubious distinction as the poorest country in the Southern hemisphere?
35. Is it likely that Haiti's newly elected president, Jean-Bertrand Aristide, will be able to end or curb the influence of the military?
36. Why were the dreaded Tontons Macoute able to strike such fear in the hearts of most Haitians?
37. How likely is it that Aristide will prove successful in bringing democratic rule to Haiti?
38. Why do most Haitians view Aristide as Haiti's last chance?
39. What can or should be done to reinvigorate the Arab-Israeli peace process?
40. Has the gulf war made peace more likely in the Middle East? Why, or why not?
41. Which side, if any, is to blame for the lack of progress?
42. Are there signs, however faint, that either the Arabs or Israelis are prepared to make new concessions in the interest of peace?
43. Why is the Middle East such a violent and unstable region?
44. How has the debt problem affected the economies of most gulf states?
45. What explains the rising domestic discontent in the Arab world?
46. How would the destruction of Iraq affect the political map of the Middle East?

KEY TERMS

AFRICAN NATIONAL CONGRESS   An organization created in 1912 in the Union (now Republic) of South Africa by four Black lawyers, demanding full democratic rights, universal suffrage, and a multiracial society.

AFRIKANERS   South African Whites of Dutch-German-French descent, who constitute about 58 percent of the total White population, but only 9 percent of the total population of the nation.

APARTHEID   An Afrikaans word meaning "apartness" or "separateness," the policy of the government of South Africa that segregates the races according to law.

BERLIN WALL   A fortified barrier that separated West Berlin from East Berlin and East Germany from 1961 until 1989.

CAUDILLO   A military leader, in Spanish-speaking countries, who is for all intent and purposes a dictator.

CIVIL WAR   A conflict fought between an established government and dissident factions, or during an interregnum between groups contesting for power and control of the new government.

COLOREDS   South Africans who are officially identified as being of mixed racial ancestry, comprising about 9 percent of the population.

CONTRAS   A U.S.-government backed rebel army which sought to overthrow the leftist Sandinista government of Nicaragua.

CULTURAL REVOLUTION   A nationwide political movement led by Mao Zedong from 1966 to 1969, to purge Communist China of ideas and individuals who he identified as symbols of bourgeois or reactionary culture.

DIVESTITURE   The act of liquidating financial interests in South Africa.

INSURGENCY   A revolt or insurrection against an established government.

MILITARISM   The predominance of the armed forces in the administration or policy of the state.

MILITARY RULE   A regime established by military coup d'etat and later controlled by either active or retired officers of the armed forces.

MONARCHY   A state ruled by a king or an emperor, who is the sole and absolute authority.

NATIONALIZATION   The conversion of industry, agriculture, commerce, or public service, together with the means of production, from private to governmental ownership and control.

ONE-PARTY SYSTEM   A state organized around a single political party that seeks to represent the collective interests of the nation.

PALESTINE LIBERATION ORGANIZATION   An umbrella movement of eight guerrilla groups formed in 1964 in support of self-government for the Palestinians, which initially refused to recognize the existance of the state of Israel, but has since changed its position and expressed a willingness to negotiate the future of the occupied territories.

PEASANTS   Members of the class comprising small farmers and laborers on the land where they constitute the primary work force in agriculture.

POLITICAL CORRUPTION   The practice by government leaders or politicians of selling or exchanging rights, services, privileges, or entitlements for private gain.

PRESIDENTIALISM   A governmental system in which the president controls all institutions of state and is the chief political force in the country.

SANCTION   A coercive action adopted usually by several nations acting together against a state violating international law.

SANDINISTAS   Nicaraguan guerrilla forces that overthrew the government of Anastasio Somoza Debayle in 1979, only to be ousted from power in 1990 by Violeta Barrios de Chamorro in an internationally-supervised free election.

SULLIVAN PRINCIPLES   A set of guidelines proposed in 1977 by Reverend Leon Sullivan for American firms employing Black workers in South Africa.

TONTONS MACOUTES   The semisecret police force of Haiti established by President Francois Duvalier, which eventually consisted of 30,000 to 300,000 armed civilians from the lower social classes, which systematically terrorized the people and engaged in officially condoned spying, blackmail, extortion, torture, rape, and murder.

TRIBALISM   The organization, culture, or beliefs of a tribe.

Article 8.1.   The Destiny of South Africa

The article examines the future of South Africa which, the author maintains, faces serious racial, cultural, and economic problems. In his view, it will prove difficult to solve South Africa's socioeconomic problems, institute meaningful land reform, build a multi-racial society, and eliminate tribal conflict. With the dismantling of apartheid, South Africa now stands at the crossroads. The actions it takes may well determine its future for years to come. It can either pursue the path of heightened conflict or genuine negotiations. Given South Africa's past, the two approaches are equally likely.

The Destiny of South Africa

by Ralph Slovenko

What lies ahead for South Africa? What kind of country will the new South Africa be? The future of any country is shaped by its past, its population, its economy, and its role in international relations. What are the hard truths about South Africa? And what are the hard choices that lie ahead?

As everyone knows, apartheid—separation of races by law—has made South Africa the pariah of nations. It has damaged the country in moral, social and economic terms.

In his historic speech of February 2, 1990, President F.W. de Klerk declared an end to apartheid in all its forms, and unilaterally extended a hand of peace to the African National Congress (ANC), and other formerly banned organizations. He made it clear that, beyond the abolition of apartheid, his goal is to create a new constitution, through negotiations with every sector of society, establishing full democracy and justice in the country.

The new South Africa faces formidable socio-economic problems of wealth and poverty, and racial and cultural differences. There is no easy solution to the imbalance between the haves and the have-nots. For one thing, the whites have had a superior education and training and hence have superior skills. The majority of the population has been steeped in an underclass culture, and has been let down by an inferior education system. They are ill-equipped for urban life, and are unemployable. Likewise, the returning exiles, almost to a man, have no skills—still they will want to move into positions of control.

Educational problems of blacks are pandemic. Black students in 1991 failed high school graduation examinations at the highest rate in South Africa's history. Only 36 percent of the 233,000 black students who took the tests passed, compared with 42 percent the previous year, and of those, less than a quarter passed well enough to enter a university. The pass rate for whites was 97 percent; for Asians, 95 percent; and for those of mixed race, 79 percent.

Few developing countries in Africa have an established educational tradition in Western terms. Compusory education is largely unknown and the percentage of school-age children at school varies with country. In

1955 in South Africa there were only 35,000 black pupils at secondary school. By 1989 the number had increased to 1,346,403. More than five million black pupils (81 percent of all school-age children) are now at school in both primary and secondary schools in South Africa. The annual national budget for eduaction for blacks was increased by 27 percent since the late 1970s—a far greater growth rate than for any other state department. Of the total increase in educational expenditure last year, 64 percent was spent on black education. President de Klerk on February 2, 1990, announced a program of integrated schooling. The controversy is whether standards will be lowered, with quantity education replacing quality education.

Many of today's black teachers are products of an era that saw endless boycotts, and that climaxed in the adoption of the slogan Liberation Before Education. Although the slogan has since been renounced, it is still being acted upon by some people. During Nelson Mandela's U.S. tour, Winnie Mandela told American television viewers that black pupils regarded their schools as legitimate military targets, a view consistent with the armed struggle.

The link between revolutionary fervor and educational apathy has not gone unnoticed. The ANC declared 1991 the "Year of Mass Action for the Transfer of Power to the People." An ANC slogan declared There Is Nothing More Beautiful Than A People In Revolution. "That sort of language," wrote the *Economist* (January 19, 1991), "hardly encourages black children to stay at their desks." While Nelson Mandela has called for discipline and an end to the boycott of schools, he has found that ungovernability, once

---

Apartheid and sanctions have retarded and distorted South Africa's economy, and have prevented South Africa from achieving broad economic development.

---

taught, is very difficult to undo.

Mark Mathabane, who left South Africa and wrote the bestsellers *Kaffir Boy* and *Kaffir Boy in America*, says, "Things have happened in the name of black liberation which are very authoritarian. I wish people had the knowledge … to single that out, but unfortunately they haven't … and … are suffering the consequences. Whoever invented the phrase Liberation Before Education made a very calculated move…. Black education may not have been the optimum, but at least it was something."

Mathabane is sickened that even as socialism collapses in Eastern Europe and elsewhere, young South Africans can be led to believe that it is a system "worthy of emulation." Had they not been isolated from the world, he says, his countrymen "would have known what communism really means, what capitalism really means, and they would have also known that there are certain things which the liberation movement shouldn't do and for which it has to be held accountable."

LAND REFORM

South Africa's future will be affected by physical as well as by human capital. Land ownership is a major question. In its failed policy of separating population by race, the white-dominated govern-

ment uprooted millions of people. Property claims by dispossessed black landowners will now have to be seriously addressed. Access to land is going to be a key issue in negotiations. President de Klerk has assured the country's 60,000 white farmers that their title deeds are safe, as the government is not prepared to negotiate about their land.

On the one hand, the country cannot maintain the status quo. On the other, nationalization of land, to judge by examples of other countries, would be a disaster. Nelson Mandela says he is open to an alternative to nationalization. In its comments on the land issue, the ANC has stressed the need for "affirmative action."

Leon Louw, director of the Free Market Foundation of Southern Africa and coauthor of two best-sellers—*South Africa: The Solution* and *Let the People Govern*—says that with the repeal or amendment of land laws, prospective black farmers could procure loans, form consortiums, and buy up the farms of those inefficient white farmers who will go bankrupt without state support. Another way to help transfer white farms into black hands, he says, would be by the introducing of a land tax based on the soil's potential yield. This would encourage better farming and discourage underuse of land.

FOREIGN RELATIONS

South Africa's foreign relations will be tremendously affected by the abandonment of apartheid. On the African subcontinent, South Africa could play a pivotal role in scientific and technological development. Europe no longer feels implicated in Africa's predicament. Funding by the European Community (EC) for southern Africa declined in real terms by 30 percent last year. The United Kingdom is also divesting from the region. Chester Crocker, former U.S. assistant secretary of state for Africa, opines that instead of a polecat, South Africa can become a pole of growth, political tolerance, and openness, and a source of security for the entire subregion. It could offer to southern Africa (and perhaps beyond), its best chance to strengthen linkages with the advanced industrial nations of Europe. Still, doing business in Africa is fraught with peril, the reason the EC is pulling out. South Africa has several advantages over European interests in this context.

South Africa dwarfs the economies of its neighbors, and for all its flaws, its economy is a model of robustness and sophistication by comparison. Unfortunately, the history of apartheid and the legacy of cross-border raids has severely impeded normal relations. The resolution of South Africa's problems opens the way for closer contact. While there are fears in Africa that the South African economy will entrap its neighbors in a relationship of permanent dependency, one cannot but feel also a sense of optimism about the subcontinent, with South Africa as its hub, drawing on mutual ties for the benefit of all parties.

Developments in South Africa do not take place in a vacuum. Political changes in any country coincide with and are influenced by major trends in world politics. With the communism collapse in Eastern Europe, support for the ANC's "armed struggle" has faded: the reason the South African government could risk releasing Nelson Mandela. Other threats have also waned. Cuba has agreed to withdraw its forces from Angola. A settlement was reached in Namibia. South Africa has entered into direct relations with countries that until recently regarded it—and it, them—with

---

The animosities in South Africa are not so much racial as tribal.

---

outright hostility (the Soviet Union is one example). Yet, the status of South Africa in the United States and in the United Nations remains problematic, given that antiapartheid lobbies are deeply entrenched and have a life of their own.

A MULTI-RACIAL SOCIETY

South Africa has been damaged by more than 40 years of misrule, but even at its worst it was never totalitarian and never genocidal. Its critics typically focus on the low points, but one can see in any South African city large numbers of ordinary people of all races walking, shopping, selling and buying, and getting on with life. One would be hard put to find another place with such a mixture. South African writer Denis Beckett says, "To see the past as simply one long line of lunacy and tragedy is out of order. If South Africa's lunacies and tragedies are the most famous in the world, it is not because theirs were the world's worst but because they were the most visible." When South Africa legislated racial separation, it made *de jure* what is *de facto* in other countries. Apartheid—both the term and the system— was introduced in 1948; prior thereto, discrimination in South Africa tended to be sporadic and ad hoc.

By Western measures, South Africa has a free and vigorous press and an independent judiciary. Among its lawyers, many have defended politically unpopu-

---

lar clients and have spoken out boldly in support of racial equality and personal liberty. While franchise has been limited to the white population, elections have been fairly conducted. Bribery is not a way of life. Its scholarship ranks near or at the top in just about every field.

The usual image of South Africa, however, is a scenario of diabolical whites and martyred blacks. The image is frozen in the Soweto riots of 1976, like that presented in the film *A Dry White Season* and in the musical *Sarafina!* Audiences take it to be a depiction of day-to-day life in South Africa. In actuality, on June 16, 1976, several thousand black students in Soweto took to the streets to protest being taught half their subjects in Afrikaans ("the oppressors' language"), and burned books and destroyed school buildings, shops, and clinics.° Police confronted the protesters and opened fire. Four days of rioting followed. An official death toll of 176 was admitted, and at least 1,800 were injured. June 16 in South Africa is a day of nationwide mourning and protest, an unofficial holiday.

Not one of the recent films about South Africa shows the marked changes that have taken place in the country. For instance, segregation in public facilities has been done away with. More blacks attend the theater in Cape Town than do in Detroit, where blacks comprise more than 70 percent of the population. Sports are integrated. Racial laws have been repealed, as are laws against racial intermarriage (President de Klerk's 24-year-old son is engaged to a colored wom-

° Afrikaans-medium instruction allegedly was the justification for the riots but a Jewish social worker was the first victim caught and beaten to death in Soweto. He had, more than once, strongly and publicly urged that Afrikaans instruction should not be introduced. The true cause of the riots probably was the feeling at that time that "everything's going our way," following Portugal's withdrawal from Angola and Mozambique in 1974-75.

an), the pass laws, and the Jobs Reservation Act, which prevented black workers from advancing to management-level positions. Trade unions, once all white, are now multiracial and are highly politicized. Over 40 percent of all university students and one-third of all middle managers are black. There are more black graduates and more black women professionals in South Africa than in all the rest of Africa combined.

Visiting last year at the Imperial Hotel in Pietermaritzburg, the best hotel in the city, I found it was entirely occupied by blacks celebrating a wedding. A number of guests drove up in new Mercedes cars. More cars are owned by South African blacks than there are private cars in all of the Soviet Union. In fact, no white in South Africa would be as rude to a black as people in communist countries are to their own countrymen.

At the same time, it would be wrong to say that South Africa has nothing in common with the ravaged continent around it. As the *Economist* put it, "South Africa is as different from the countries of black Africa as it is similar to them." South Africa is a microcosm of the world: both a First World country and a Third World country. In the First World component, there are attractive cities, a well-developed transport and communication infrastructure, a first-class university system, strong medical and pharmaceutical industries, sophisticated financial networks, large engineering enterprises, high-level agriculture, and good entrepreneurial skills in much of the population. In the Third World component, which makes up 70 percent of the population and is growing fast, many South Africans are as poorly fed and educated as people elsewhere in Africa.

Among the internal pressures remaking South Africa is demography. The rate of black population increase in South Africa is many times that of the whites, developing a greater density of population in black homelands and, now, in urban areas as well. During the last 75 years South Africa's population has grown from six million (25 percent urbanized) to over 35 million (50 percent urbanized). In 1951 the country's population was 12.6 million consisting of 8.5 million blacks, 2.6 million whites, 1.1 million coloreds, and 366,000 Asians. Last year the population was 35.2 million consisting of 26 million blacks, 4.9 million whites, 3 million coloreds, and 913,000 Asians. By the year 2010, South Africa's black population is expected to reach 48.5 million; and more than two-thirds of them will be urbanized.

Owing to this demographic change, manufacturing is replacing mining and agriculture as the economic mainstay. The Afrikaner population has become bourgeois, and unskilled labor has become a burden on the country. For the interests it was originally designed to serve, apartheid became more and more irrational—and costly. The dynamic of the economy now depends on encouraging a professional black population and on drawing people into the industrial sector. By century's end, urban black population will be up from about 11 million to about 27 million and blacks will outnumber all other population groups by about three to one. In other words, the population balance that formerly determined the character of urban life in South Africa has already changed.

TRIBAL CONFLICT

The political problem in South Africa is extraordinarily difficult and complex. It is a country of minorities. The whites are a minority, as are the Asians. The black population is not, as is commonly believed, homogeneous—it consists of some nine tribes (Zulu, Xhosa, Ndebele, Swazi, South Sotho, North Sotho, Tswana, Tsonga, and Venda) that speak different languages and are often mutually hostile. After Winnie Mandela's conviction for kidnapping, Jesse Jackson and others protested that she was not tried by her peers—but who are her peers? The animosities in South Africa are not so much racial as tribal. (Unlike in Ireland and elsewhere, the animosities are not religious.) In many cases, members of one tribe will not work alongside members of another tribe. Also, the Asians feel threatened by the black population. In 1985 blacks burned Mohandas Gandhi's home. The University of Natal at Westville, once for Asians, is now integrated with blacks; conflict between the two groups frequently resulted in closures. Consequently, Asian families contemplate emigrating, but to where?

What will one man one vote in a unitary state bring? The fear is that, with power in prospect, communist-oriented ANC militants would intimidate people in all townships and, in every tribal territory. A kind of unity might be enforced, although areas of opposition from the numerous and powerful Zulus would remain to be crushed—or possibly fought in a civil war. That would be black rule, but not black majority rule.

There is no end in sight to the killings in the townships. More people died in South Africa in black-on-black violence this past year than in any other year this century—nearly 4,000, more than twice the previous highest number. The horrifying level of violence dwarfs even the dark days after the Soweto riots of June 1976 and the unrest era of the mid-1980s. The violence has been more intensive than any the country has known since the Boer War.

Many claim that negotiations over the new South Africa are the cause of the violence, with political rivals vying for a place at the negotiating table and everybody being terror-stricken at the prospect of one group dominating others. Chief Mangosuthu Buthelezi's Zulus are fighting Nelson Mandela's Xhosas—a power struggle continues between Buthelezi's Inkatha and Mandela's ANC. Rumor abounds that President de Klerk will bring both Mandela and Buthelezi into his cabinet.

Others blame the violence on the legacy of apartheid, and the homelands policy which accentuates tribal differences. Themba Molefe, a political reporter in Soweto, writes, "The violence is the result of the bitter pill of 300 years of black subjugation and 42 years of white minority rule and apartheid." Yet, without the white man's intervention, many African tribes would likely have wiped each other out.

The impoverished living conditions of blacks throughout Africa, as in South Africa, breed frustration and hostility, a condition exacerbated by international sanctions and divestment. There are calls for better housing, schools, and elimination of poverty, but there are also calls for continued sanctions which lower the capacity to meet these demands. There is a direct correlation between the levels of violence and unemployment—when unemployment goes up (currently at 44 percent), so does violence.

The current clash between black tribes in South Africa is the result of a combination of political conflict and material conditions that overlap and feed the issues of ethnic identity. Apartheid was a manifestation of tribalism, that is, the Afrikaner tribe's striving to secure its own survival and

the greatest possible share of resources. Tribal sentiments are kept alive by factors such as: the absence of an effective state that can protect the individual's life, property, and chances for advancement; the absence of a national system of social security; economic conditions that lead to internal competition for gainful employment and resources in general; and the social disruption caused by urbanization and intergroup competition.

The migration of rural black population into urban areas has been marked by escalating crime. Crime in the cities last year surpassed all records with a more than 30 percent increase over the previous year. Johannesburg and Cape Town have the highest crime rates in the world, and Cape Town is rated highest for murder among the world's 100 largest metropolitan areas. Cars are hijacked in broad daylight. Restaurants get held up. At Witwatersrand University in Johannesburg, the vice-chancellor had to rule that guns should not be carried on campus.

There's a sense of bitterness on all sides that law and order are breaking down. Certainly it is souring the political climate. Comparisons with Lebanon are being made. With uncertainty over the future, professionals are emigrating in large numbers. One survey found that in a single year 4,500 students (about a quarter of the country's annual output) left the country upon graduation, although fewer are leaving now than in the mid-1980s.

APARTHEID AND SANCTIONS

Even with the lifting of sanctions, investment will not readily return to South Africa. Investors will not invest where people are killing each other. "What we cannot do is attract new investments in an atmosphere of violence," Fi-

nance Minister Barend du Plessis warned recently. Without investments, the South African economy could spiral downward into chaos.

Apartheid and sanctions have retarded and distorted South Africa's economy, and have prevented South Africa from broad economic development. The gold mines, that generate half its exports, are gradually winding down, as shafts get deeper and the ore gets poorer; in the 1980s output fell by a tenth. Such an economy cannot support the huge expansion of welfare that black South Africans expect, nor can it create jobs for the 1,000 newcomers who join the labor force each day. (Grimly, the AIDS epidemic could change that by reducing population growth, but will bring soaring health bills and falling labor productivity in its turn.)

The economy's privatization offers promise. For years South Africa has had both a free-market and a state-run economy. In 1948, when the Afrikaners (white South Africans whose forebears came from Holland) obtained political power, they started an affirmative action program called *apartheid*, or separateness. Devastated by war with the British at the turn of the century, and hurting from the economic depression of the 1930s, the Afrikaners determined to improve their lot. Apartheid, as such was aimed, not at the blacks, but at the British. For the first half of the twentieth century, to talk of poverty in South Africa was to talk of white (Afrikaner) poverty. An electioneering pamphlet in 1943 declared that "the Afrikaner nation is the poorest element in the white population, and is even poorer than the Indians." It was this distress that Afrikaners set out to relieve with apartheid.

They nationalized most of the country's heavy industry and

created a huge civil service staffed with their own people. Under apartheid, the government provided employment to at least half of the Afrikaners. Apartheid laws were spurred not by industrialists, but predominantly by white workers and farmers. Economics professor Walter Williams, in his book *South Africa's War against Capitalism*, describes the history of apartheid as a glorification of centralized state power.

The Afrikaners saw the business community as an enemy, representing the destructive influence of British capital. In 1948, when the Afrikaners came to power, the ruling caucus consisted overwhelmingly of farmers, clergymen, teachers, and small-town professionals. Even in the 1960s, Prime Minister Verwoerd warned business to keep out of politics, a sentiment repeatedly echoed in the 1970s by Prime Minister Vorster. It was not until Harry Oppenheimer, chairman of the Anglo-American Corporation, sat down with a National Party prime minister in 1981 that there occurred the first formal meeting in 33 years between the private and public sectors. As a long-serving opposition member of Parliament, and as the elder statesman of the private sector, Oppenheimer reiterated that apartheid was an affront to human dignity and human rights, and that attempts to segregate rigidly according to race were incompatible with modern industrial society.

In 1948, "racial problem" in South Africa referred to the hostility of the Afrikaners for the English-speaking elite. The Afrikaners, living in poverty on their farms or seeking work in cities, were bitter and angry, an emotional legacy that has lingered. Until recently, Afrikaners forbade their sons and daughters to even socialize with the English. Afrikaner schoolboys made the national an-

them tolerable by altering the words: "God save our noble King,/Wash him in paraffin/And put fire on him." Afrikaners often compared the great trek northward by their ancestors in the nineteenth century to escape British rule with the Israelites' flight from Egypt.

On the highway from Johannesburg to Pretoria is the Voortrekker Monument, built to commemorate the deeds of the Boers, who rejected British rule and trekked away from their beloved Cape to found their own two republics. When the foundation stone was laid in 1938 to mark the centenary of the original trek, one hundred thousand people attended. As part of the celebration, a group of idealistic Afrikaners retraced by ox wagon the route of their ancestors. Thousands joined in. Afrikaners came together to pay tribute to their ancestors, an event celebrated annually.

As a part of their affirmative action program, the Afrikaners, on coming to power, devised new policies and made more intensive use of the existing instruments of colonial policy to alleviate their distress. Their program included racially specific wage preferences in favor of whites, severe restrictions against black laborers in competing for work and business, preferential quotas and set-asides for whites, a systematic expansion of government jobs, and much more. In an article in *Orbis* (March 1988), Nicholas Eberstadt described apartheid as "a vast and ambitious anti-poverty program: as the earliest, and to date the most audacious, of the affirmative action programs to be adopted in the postwar era by Western governments in the name of uplifting a group deemed to be disadvantaged."

The huge public sector built up under Afrikaner nationalism is in the process of being disman-

tled and privatized. "Pretoriastroika," as it is called, will not be simple, but as the country already has a large private sector, it will be easier to accomplish than the Soviet Union's "perestroika." Black nationalists, however, understandably suspicious, say that "Pretoriastroika" is asset-stripping, intended to perpetuate white control. They want to replace Afrikaners with blacks in state-run enterprises, as a way to uplift their lot. In a future South Africa, whites want a Bill of Rights that says, at a minimum, Thou Shalt Not Tamper With Private Property. The black nationalists say that, the vast inequities resulting from South Africa's long history of racial discrimination require the state to redistribute wealth. Black nationalism may raise an uglier head of domination and discrimination than white Afrikaner nationalism. This is the heart of the dilemma that faces the future of white South African politics.

In a swing of the pendulum, black affirmative action is to replace Afrikaner affirmative action, but in the end, "group rights"—as affirmative action may be called—will breed not harmony but new hostility. It is the lesson of South Africa, a lesson the United States is learning with its version of affirmative action. Problems of race are resolved not by race-based legislation, but by color-blind legislation (or no legislation). Race-based affirmative action programs, meant to compensate for past discrimination, instead create a host of new injustices. Eschel Rhoodie, a South African now living in the United States, in his book *Discrimination in the Constitutions of the World: A Study of the Groups Rights Problem*, writes, "Group rights recognition is by its nature divisive. The giving of special rights and privileges to an enclave of the larger society emphasizes differences and fosters discrimination."

There are two main movements in South Africa. One drives the demand for Africanization, authoritarianism, and a one-party state. Many blacks tend to equate apartheid with capitalism and insist on communal distribution schemes. The other movement in the direction of globalism, and favors personal choices, political pluralism, and free market flexibility.

One proposal gaining momentum, suggested by Leon Louw, is for a form of government modeled on the Swiss canton, or territorial, system. A small central government would remain, and cantons would compete in a "government market": Marxist cantons could exist alongside free-market ones and white-supremacist ones. People could vote with their feet and show their preferences by moving a few kilometers up or down the road.

A variety of political scenarios has been proposed and analyzed. Constitutional think tanks of the government envisage a two-chamber legislature with a lower House of Representatives elected by one-man, one-vote, on a common voters roll. Groups voluntarily formed around common principles such as language, culture, or religion—but not race—would be equally represented in an upper house, or senate, along with representatives of 10 geographic regions. Groups would exercise powers disproportionate to

their numbers through various mechanisms, including a requirement that the Senate approve all legislation—by a two-thirds majority—and through an "advice body" that would resolve deadlocks between the two houses, by a three-quarters majority. Only senators would serve on the advice body. One representative for every group would also serve in a multiparty cabinet, along with one representative for every region and seven members of the lower house.

Other features of the Constitution would include: (1) A Bill of Rights that would, by protecting individual rights, protect languages, religions and cultures as well as human rights. (2) Devolution of power to 10 autonomous regions (corresponding to the present economic regions) that would in turn devolve power to local councils. (3) Regions could differ in languages, education policies, public holidays and flags. (4) A 300-seat lower house based on one-man, one-vote, and proportional representation. Parties would need to win at least 3 percent of the vote to be represented.

(5) A cabinet of seven members elected from the lower house, one each from the 10 regions and one each from political parties. The idea would be to establish a Swiss-style grand coalition with shifting alliances on different issues. (6) A largely ceremonial head of state elected by the legislature, and a rotating executive prime minister chosen from each of the cabinet groups. (7) Legislation to be originated from either house with consensus being reached, as in the American system, by joint committees of both houses. (8) Changes in the constitution only by a two-thirds majority of both houses. (9) An independent high court to guard the Bill of Rights and the Constitution and to settle disputes between federal and regional governments. And (10) an economic system based on free-market principles.

The dismantling of apartheid has spurred interest in future-oriented studies about South Africa. The country is now at that crossroads where what is done now will influence the course of its history for years to come. The present moment is delicately poised between heightened conflict and genuine negotiations. The two processes are equally likely. ■

Ralph Slovenko is professor of law and psychiatry at Wayne State University in Detroit. He has made several lecture tours in South Africa.

Article 8.2.   Mobutu Sese Seko: "I Have a Clear Conscience"

In recent years, many political observers and human rights activists have singled out the African republic of Zaire for special criticism. They are deeply disturbed by persistent rumors of human rights abuses. Reports of such violations are both serious and unassailable. In 1988, amid mounting criticism of the Zairian government, the authors challenged its president, Mobutu Sese Seko, to a no-holds-barred interview, to which he agreed. The result was the longest and most far-reaching interview that Mobutu has ever granted. In the conversation that follows, Mobutu responds to questions on a wide range of topics, including charges of human rights violations, Zaire's one-party system, personal and state corruption, the country's deteriorating infrastructure, malnutrition and disease, economic deprivation and the pauperization of the masses, and the AIDS epidemic.

Mobutu Sese Seko:
"I Have a Clear Conscience"

By Jeffrey M. Elliot and Mervyn M. Dymally

Sitting astride Africa's mid-section and bordering nine other countries, Zaire has an importance that is both strategic and symbolic. Its size — roughly equal to the United States east of the Mississippi River — its rich natural resources and its firmly pro-Western policies have ensured continuous financial and political backing from western Europe and North America.

But enthusiasm for that support has recently been tempered by questions about the nature of Zaire's government. The conservative Washington, D.C.-based Heritage Foundation says Zaire "is one of America's most consistent allies in Africa" but calls President Mobutu Sese Seko a "corrupt Third World strongman."

Mounting criticism of continuing U.S. aid to Zaire recently prompted Representative Mervyn Dymally (D-CA.), who currently chairs the Congressional Black Caucus, and Dr. Jeffrey M. Elliot, a writer and political scientist from North Carolina Central University who advises Dymally on foreign affairs, to visit Zaire, where they spent ten days traveling with Mobutu. For the third installment in

our series on Zaire, we present the following excerpts from their conversations.

JEFFREY M. ELLIOT: According to Amnesty International, your government has, over the past two decades, either ordered, approved, or condoned myriad human rights violations, including detention without charge or trial, imprisonment of political opponents, torture and ill treatment of prisoners, extrajudicial executions, and illegal surveillance and extortion. How can you justify such flagrant abuses?

MOBUTU SESE SEKO: First, let me say, I appreciate your candor. I can say, however, without equivocation, that I have a clear conscience. Most political outsiders view human rights in the context of a multi-party system. They demand that I institute such a system, which I refuse to do. Africa's history and traditions will not permit a two-party system. Nowhere in this continent have there been two chiefs in one village: a majority chief and an opposition chief. Dating back to ancestral times, there has been only one chief. In the United States and Europe, it is commonly accepted that enlightenment emanates from the clash of ideas. In Africa, we follow an ancestral policy in which, when a problem arises,

we rally around the leader and work out a solution. Zaire is a shining example of this policy in action. For this reason, we have become the most stable country in Africa.

In Zaire, freedom of expression, which is guaranteed by the Constitution, is respected. During my tenure as president, I have struggled hard to restore peace, unity and security. My efforts are based on a firm belief in human rights. To demonstrate my commitment, and to quash the baseless charges against my country, I established a high-level department on human rights, which reports directly to me. You will not find a similar department anywhere in Africa. Moreover, I urged Amnesty International to return to Zaire. Their delegation spent eight days here this past November. They conducted a thorough investigation, during which time they spoke to everyone they requested to see. In the end, they left satisfied. Later, the Association of African Lawyers which, like Amnesty International, is deeply concerned with human rights issues, and whose current chairman is a Senegalese, requested my permission to establish a branch in Zaire. I immediately approved the request.

Let me ask you a question: How many of Africa's 50 independent states have a multi-party system? Of these 50, how many can boast a better record than ours? Zimbabwe, for example, experimented with a multi-party system, but was forced to abandon it and return to a one-party system. Ask Zimbabwe's socialist president, Robert Mugabe, why it failed. His answer should prove instructive.

When I took power in 1965, I inherited the Belgian system – a system that was totally corrupt. At the time, the Belgians had established Catholicism as the official state religion, relegating Protestantism, Kibanguism, and Islam to second-class status. That act was a direct assault on religious freedom. Although I am a devout Catholic, I abolished religious inequality and placed all religious denominations on an equal footing. I did so in order to serve freedom and justice.

MERVYN M. DYMALLY: But Amnesty International maintains that hundreds of political prisoners have been arrested, detained or imprisoned, often without ever being charged or tried. Do you dispute these accusations? If so, why do you think they persist?
MOBUTU: I wonder if a head of state should swear, but if anyone can cite the name of a single political prisoner, supported by hard fact, who is presently in any Zairian prison, I will immediately resign. As far as Amnesty International is concerned, I indicated that they were in Zaire last November at the invitation of the special department that oversees human rights and civil liberties. They left satisfied, and so am I. Without overstating the case, I am convinced that Amnesty International's attitude towards Zaire has changed markedly as a result of their investigation.

ELLIOT: Your opponents contend that the government does not respect the fundamental rights of workers. There is no freedom of association with respect to independent trade unions; collective bargaining agreements are not guaranteed; working conditions are abysmal; purchasing power has plummeted; and unemployment is at a record high. How can your government be described as anything but anti-worker? Don't these facts speak for themselves?
MOBUTU: They would if they were true, but they're not. In fact, they bear no resemblance to the truth. The truth is, my government recognizes fundamental worker rights, a fact acknowledged by our membership and participation in the International Labor Organization. The National Union of Zairian Workers (UNTZA), a federation of several earlier independent and Christian trade unions, is active on the international scene, affiliated with international labor organizations, and enjoys close relations with your AFL-CIO. Collective bargaining agreements – approximately 600 – are guaranteed. While working conditions may fall short of Western standards, they are much better in the organized sector represented by UNTZA than in the informal sector. No labor leaders are presently in detention, and several former leaders who have disagreed with union policies are now free and pursuing their personal interests.

DYMALLY: Despite several presidential amnesties to Zairian political exiles, reports persist that many of your critics have been subjected to detention and/or arrest. Are you prepared to welcome home all of your political opponents, both those in the United States and abroad, with the promise that they will not be harassed or imprisoned?
MOBUTU: Absolutely. In fact, tens of thousands of Zairians who fled the country during or after the rebellions of the 1960s and the Shaba events of 1977 and 1978 have already returned to their homeland. They know they are welcome – that Zaire belongs to them, not to President Mobutu. If you meet any of them in the United States or Europe, assure them that they have my word; that they may return home without fear. Those who are most qualified will certainly find jobs. That is a national priority, not simply mine.

Corruption

ELLIOT: According to top officials of the International Monetary Fund (IMF), Zaire is plagued by "uncontrollable corruption" and the "illegal outflow of wealth from the country." The IMF charges that money for improving farms, roads and agricultural projects has been diverted into personal use by government officials. In one speech, you yourself called bribery "the Zairian illness." If this is true, why hasn't your government punished the guilty parties and adopted strong measures to prevent future corruption?
MOBUTU: Your last quotation is inaccurate. I never stated that bribery is "the Zairian illness." I once condemned corruption, but I never described it as my country's illness. To be accurate, I stated – while expressing New Year's wishes to my officers – "We keep hearing about corruption, without knowing who is corrupt and who is corrupting."

At the time, I was specifically referring to you – the Americans and Europeans – who taught us the art of corrupting. When you come to Zaire to sell your products, you tell our officials, "It costs $800. But for you, I'll set aside $200 per piece. That would amount to one million dollars – all yours." That is corruption, and you introduced it. You are therefore unfit to educate us on public morals, since you have yet to address the same ethical concerns in your respective societies.

Corruption is not a Zairian problem; it is a world problem. Take the Lockheed case, for example, which involved high-ranking government officials in the United States, Germany, and Japan – and ultimately President Jimmy Carter. No, the sole purpose of these rumors is to spoil the good name of Zaire. If our critics were honest, they would point the finger at those nations which are most guilty of corruption. We all know which are the most corrupt nations in Africa. Unfortunately, for diplomatic reasons, I can't cite them.

> *If anyone can cite the name of a single political prisoner, supported by hard fact, who is presently in any Zairian prison, I will immediately resign.*

DYMALLY: Your critics argue, with strong conviction, that Zaire's security forces have, over the past two decades, engaged in wanton corruption. Doesn't this reflect a failure of leadership?

MOBUTU: Although some abuses and lack of discipline among low-level security personnel may occur from time to time, major efforts have been made since 1985 to improve security force conduct. For example, regular police roadblocks have virtually disappeared. While incidents of extortion are reported on occasion, the practice is not condoned by the government and the perpetrators are increasingly brought to justice. Practices introduced during the colonial period, when security forces under Belgian control employed harsh measures, are presently being corrected.

DYMALLY: Your critics contend that you are fabulously wealthy, with an estimated personal fortune of $5 billion, which includes 11 palaces in Zaire and numerous villas in various European countries. How did you accumulate such enormous wealth? Isn't your lifestyle incongruous with the abject poverty that plagues Zaire?

MOBUTU: Although this question has been raised – and answered – many times, I will respond to your inquiry with total frankness. My conscience is clear. I challenge the existence of these alleged international financial experts – who frequently choose to hide under the cloak of anonymity in order to spread false propaganda against me. Who are these financial experts? These reports emanate from the press. Why do they persist? Frankly speaking, some reporters have been manipulated by questionable interests. Who are these interests? In truth, I have been singled out for attack because I am a nationalist. Moreover, I am intransigent on the subject of nationalism. In 1967, for example, I nationalized the *Union Miniere*, today known as Gecamines, making it the exclusive property of the Zairian people. Ironically, from that date on I became the object of scorn and derision, as I was widely considered to have pilfered Gecamines' profits in order to enrich myself, even though its finances are closely monitored by company auditors. Yet, its balance sheet bears no budget titles suggesting my involvement in its financial operations. Let me repeat: Gecamines is the exclusive property of the Zairian people.

When I assumed power, my budget was called a "dotation"– a special presidential fund. However, unlike other presidential funds, mine is known and is subject to parliamentary approval. Every year I submit a budget proposal which must be approved by Parliament. At times, it has voted to disapprove various presidential requests. This year, without my requesting a raise, Zaire's elected representatives voted to increase the presidential fund, after assessing the uses to which it was put. Thus, my budget is officially known by the Parliament and the people.

In the past, when I went to Europe, I stayed in sundry hotels. However, my European friends repeatedly advised me, "Mr. President, your security is not assured when you reside in such hotels. We strongly urge you to purchase several homes, as your security is of the utmost importance. You should own your own homes, where you can guarantee your security. Look at such and such head of state. He has proper security. By the way, if Zaire can afford to spend so much on your security when you travel abroad, then buying homes should not prove exhorbitant." The very friends who gave me this advice are the same ones who disseminated the false rumors about the myriad castles and villas I am supposed to have. These are typical of the kinds of intrigues and conspiracies to which I have been subjected.

Clearly, I would be lying if I said I do not have a bank account in Europe; I do. I would also be lying if I said I do not have considerable money in my account; I do. Yes, I have a fair amount of money. However, I would estimate it to total less than $50 million. What is that after 22 years as head of state of such a big country?

As for my alleged fortune, do you recall the remark which a Belgian once made to one of his country's top-ranking officials? The man who made the remark has been my subordinate for over 20 years, first in the army, and now at the Presidency. He was asked a similar question about my finances, to which he replied: "From the way things are going, I am afraid for this man. He has a large family, with many children. If he dies, he will do so in misery. He has spent his money building chapels, temples, cathedrals, schools and clinics. Patients who could not be treated at home were flown to Europe or the United States. That is how he has spent his money."

Besides, of Africa's 50 independent countries, can you name one leader – just one – who can boast of having spent as much of his own money to benefit so many people? No, I have a clear conscience. I am an honest man. I have not pocketed one dollar of the people's money.

Finally, my so-called fortune has proven extremely beneficial to many African causes. An American journalist should be sent to Mozambique, so that that country's president, Joaquim Chissano, could tell him how helpful I have been to that nation's freedom fighters. The former president, Samora Machel, was likewise aware of my assistance. Thanks to my alleged fortune, I sent trucks, jeeps and officers to train Mozambique's army in Tanzania, while arms and ammunition were sent day and night via our pilots. On Mozambique's independence day, 3,000 Mozambique soldiers marched into that country through Tanzania, all of whom were clad in helmets, boots and uniforms supplied by Zaire.

The same alleged fortune has proved extremely helpful to the security of my neighbors and other African states. It enabled me to train five battalions of paratroopers – two for Burundi, one for Rwanda, one for Togo and one for Benin. It also enabled me to train 250 Mauritanian commando-paratroopers, as well as to help Chad score a crushing victory over Qaddafi. We trained five battalions in Zaire, and a sixth is presently being trained. All of this has been done without publicity, very much unlike France, the United States, Great Britain, Japan or Canada, who would typically follow up such good deeds with self-serving press releases.

Moreover, when Mauritania, Senegal, Mali, Cape Verde and Guinea were hit by a drought, for two years running I sent them checks drawn on the Bank of Zaire to help them to ease the crisis. This was done quietly and without fanfare. Similarly, when Sekou Toure's Guinea was hit by an earthquake, I sent a check for one million dollars to help them as a sister nation. They were the ones who made it public. Last year, when yet another African country, Cameroon, suffered a gas explosion, I sent them $200,000, as well as doctors and 20 soldiers who delivered tents and medicines worth over $200,000.

That is how I have used my alleged fortune – to strengthen the security of African countries and to lessen the plight of disaster victims. We have not done this because Zaire is rich; we are no richer than any other African nation. No, we want to teach our fellow African citizens the noble art of sharing.

During 22 years as head of state, I have never disclosed such inside information to anyone, for my mother taught me never to brag about my deeds of kindness to others. Because your question was so searching, I decided to be forthright and to open my mind to you, not for the pride of it, but in order to lay out the facts.

ELLIOT: Still, after over 20 years of your rule, the evidence reveals little improvement in the quality of life for the average Zairian. Indeed, the ordinary Zairian earns one-tenth of what he or she earned in 1965 before your government took power. It has been reported that half of the children die before the age of three, and one-third of those who survive past the age of three will die of malnutrition. Are you fighting a losing battle? Can the present situation be reversed? Is there reason for optimism?

MOBUTU: The statistics and criticisms you cite, which have been published by *The Washington Post*, come from the Belgian press. They stem from the kind of dishonesty and unfairness that you would expect to find, given our checkered historical relationship.

There is, however, a major difference between the People's Republic of Zaire, my fatherland, and many other African countries. Let's go back to 1960 to 1965, a period I know quite well. At the time, Zaire was in complete ruins, following the most destructive civil war ever fought in Africa. Schools, churches, ports, roads and ferries stood in ruin. When I took power in 1965, my priority was to launch a massive reconstruction effort, whereas other African nations, such as the Ivory Coast, Gabon and Morocco began by building on what the colonial powers had left behind. This is an important difference, both from a social and economic standpoint. I rebuilt schools, bridges and hospitals throughout the country. I also repaired damaged tracks and replaced both broken engines and railroad cars. The projects culminated in the construction of the Inga Dam and the conveyance of hydroelectric power, which spans a distance of over 2,000 kilometers, from Inga to Shaba. In addition, I opened a much-needed maritime company, the Zairian Maritime Company, as well as Air Zaire. Reconstruction took a long time.

Meanwhile, I still had to deal with the problem of terrorism. For nearly a year, I left the capital and assumed residence in Shaba province in order to conduct the war. These obstacles should be considered when assessing my record. The rehabilitation program, coupled with the war against terrorism, cost Zaire billions of dollars and plunged my nation into debt – one that now totals $5.1 billion.

My friend, when you criticize me, please do not cite the foreign press, for these articles originate from Belgium. I can produce copies of all of them from my home library. There is not a grain of truth in any of them, for their sole purpose is to spoil the good name of Zaire. I hold nothing against the Belgians, or Belgium, for that matter. I simply cannot harness my nationalistic pride. It is only natural for me, as an unabashed nationalist,

> *I would be lying if I said I do not have a bank account in Europe; I do. I would also be lying if I said I do not have considerable money in my account; I do. However, I would estimate it to total less than $50 million. What is that after 22 years as Head of State of such a big country?*

to resist any attempt by another country smaller than mine to interfere in our internal affairs, even if by a historical misfortune they once colonized us. I will never live to see that happen again. I place the interests of my country first; everything else comes after. I might sound like an unprogressive leader, but before criticizing Zaire, compare it with other African countries. In my view, we have made enormous progress.

ELLIOT: Granted that you have made considerable economic progress, most experts insist that the economy of Zaire remains fundamentally weak and vulnerable. Indeed, many observers contend that the Zairian people are deeply resentful of their economic plight – the "pauperization of the masses," as one analyst put it – but that they have been frightened into silence. Specifically, what measures have you initiated to improve the economic plight of the average Zairian?

MOBUTU: As you know, Zaire, like many other sub-Saharan African countries, has experienced slower economic growth and deteriorating terms of trade since it won its independence in 1960. However, we are among those few nations fortunate enough to have benefited from a prolonged period of civil stability and peace, which has provided our people with relative physical security for the past 20 years.

Since 1982, I have initiated several major economic reforms which have increased business confidence in Zaire's future and have had a positive impact on the overall standard of living. Owing to the elimination of exchange and price controls, parallel markets have virtually disappeared and profits now accrue to legitimate marketers and small farmers, thus encouraging more regular supplies to markets. As a result, the supply of both foreign and domestic goods in Zaire's markets has noticeably increased, eliminating the periodic shortages that used to occur.

Moreover, improved fiscal controls since 1983 insure that key industries like mining now receive the foreign exchange and local currency they need to operate and to maintain their productive capacity, thus providing continued employment for Zaire's industrial workforce. In addition, improved fiscal and monetary policies have reduced rates of inflation and currency depreciation, and have encouraged a modest resumption of business investment. Although there have been setbacks in the external environment, the reform program has survived and conserved its momentum, leading to realistic hopes of progress and real growth in the medium term.

Health Care

DYMALLY: Many experts argue that your government has done little to improve health care in the country. For example, isn't it true that your government has not built one new

hospital since 1965? They point out that in 1965, Zaire had at least two hospitals in every city. Today, less than 50% of these hospitals are functioning at 80% capacity. Of the five hospitals in Kinshasa, only two are accessible to the general public. Why does your government tolerate such a situation? Isn't this reason enough for action?

MOBUTU: First, I must take strong exception to the statistics you've cited. They're simply not accurate. I suspect you obtained them from *The Washington Post*, which, as I stated earlier, simply parrots whatever the Belgian press reports. These sources are completely unreliable.

Let's talk facts. At independence, Zaire had one of the most extensive infrastructures in Africa, with more than 400 hospitals. The current need is not to build new hospitals but to make the existing ones more functional. A few hospitals have been constructed, such as the one at Goma. With the help of foreign assistance, construction is nearing completion on a new hospital in Kinshasa.

During the pre-independence era, there were always two "hospitals" in each administrative zone – one for the Europeans and one for the Africans. This "double standard" was abolished and the expatriate clinics have been closed and/or converted into other service establishments, such as health centers. Today, there are several public hospitals in Kinshasa, including Mama Yemo, Kinoise, Kintambo, University Clinic, Ngaliema and Kimbanseke. My goal is to create 22 urban health zones and hospital centers, which will make health care more universally available.

As for the doctor-to-patient ratio, according to international sources, the ratio of patient-to-nurse-to-doctor has improved greatly since 1960.

The population-to-physician ratio improved from 79,620 to one in 1960 to 14,780 to one in 1980. The population-to-nurse ratio improved during the same period from 3,510 to one to 1,920 to one. These figures compare favorably to those of other sub-Saharan countries. This past year, Zaire graduated about 1,700 nurses; in 1988, the number is expected to increase to 2,400. Those are the facts.

DYMALLY: Like many other African nations, Zaire faces a serious AIDS epidemic. It has been reported that one out of seven women is infected with the disease. What steps, if any, have you taken to meet this crisis?

MOBUTU: Once again, your statistics are inaccurate. In fact, the AIDS virus is estimated to be present in approximately 6% to 8% of the urban population. Still, there is ample reason for concern. Although we have a lower incidence of AIDS than many of our neighbors, we have nevertheless vigorously addressed the AIDS problem. In this regard, we have initiated an aggressive information campaign aimed at educating the general population about the dangers of the disease. In a country of marginal literacy, this program have been innovative and creative in its approach, and has included: 500,000 leaflets warning of the dangers of the disease and the best ways to avoid it have been distributed; two episodes of the nation's most popular television show have addressed the AIDS problem, and several documentaries have been broadcast; a song about the dangers of AIDS by a widely

The population-to-physician ratio improved from 79,620 to one in 1960 to 14,780 to one in 1980. These figures compare favorably to those of other sub-Saharan countries.

popular singer has been recorded; newspaper and radio accounts of AIDS and question-and-answer columns and programs have been produced; churches and other organizations have been used to spread the word at services and special meetings; and 100,000 copies of a comic book has been published, which tells the story of a businessman who ignored warnings about promiscuity and caught the disease, passing it on to his family and friends.

In addition to these preventive measures, Zaire is presently collaborating with the international medical community, including the Pasteur Institute of Paris and the United States Centers for Disease Control, in an effort to find a cure for the disease.

Only recently, a team of Zairian and Egyptian doctors announced promising findings with a new drug known as MM1. During a six-month study of 39 AIDS patients, 12 of the 19 members of the test group survived and showed definite signs of improvement in their immunological responses, while all 20 of the control group died. A new study is presently underway, involving a larger group of patients, in order to verify the initial results to determine if MM1 is indeed a cure for this deadly disease.

ELLIOT: Many analysts charge that Zaire's socioeconomic infrastructure has broken down due to neglect by

came bigger and heavier and contributed to the rapid deterioration of fragile dirt roads, particularly during the rainy seasons. Starting in 1972, however, I created a National Roads Office that has been increasingly effective in improving road maintenance. Despite funding problems, this department has reopened some of the roads that were closed during the 12 years following independence, and is presently maintaining 30,000 to 40,000 kilometers a year.

Debt and Foreign Policy

ELLIOT: In order to resolve the debt crisis stemming from the $5.1 billion you said Zaire now owes, you signed an unprecedented agreement with the International Monetary Fund, which your critics contend will produce deepening poverty and misery among the Zairian people. Why did you agree to such stringent IMF demands? How long can Zaire hold out without the danger of civil disorders – or worse?

MOBUTU: First, I deserve credit for having limited Zaire's foreign debt to $5.1 billion, irrespective of our nation's wealth. Not long ago, I

Belgium, Canada and Japan. Thus, no one could claim that Zaire would be endangering the international banking system if it failed to repay its debts. For instance, we owed $40 million to Canada, but they chose to cancel it.

Let me discuss our agreements with the International Monetary Fund. These agreements were signed at the end of 1982. Up until 1986, Zaire had fully complied with the terms of the agreement with her international partners, including the World Bank and the IMF. In October, 1986, the Central Committee of our national party (the Popular Movement of the Revolution), met to evaluate the austerity measures imposed by our partners. It found that those measures had been extremely costly to Zaire.

The assessment showed that Zaire had, for four years (1983 to 1986), disbursed $1.9 billion toward the payment of our credits. Meanwhile, over the same period, we had received only one billion dollars in foreign assistance. In other words, Zaire had become a net exporter of $900 million of hard currency, as compared to what we had received. This upset many Central Committee members, who subsequently ordered

---

Two years ago, American military aid amounted to the equivalent of 21 jeeps and assorted spare parts for our aircraft.

---

the nation's leaders. Your once extensive road network is now covered with bush. Eighty-three percent of the people live without electricity and telephones, many in mud huts. Do you dispute these statistics? If not, why haven't you attempted to correct the situation?
MOBUTU: Despite the assumptions implicit in your question, the road system in Zaire has shown some improvement in recent years. Before 1960, the rural road network was maintained by forced labor under the Belgian colonial administration. During the civil disturbances from 1960 to 1965, bridges were blown up and roads mined, closing thousands of kilometers to vehicular traffic. At the same time, trucks be-

asked an eminent professor of international economics to evaluate the percentage and likely impact of this debt as compared to Zaire's known wealth. He concluded that it represented less than 2.5% of our national wealth. Clearly, $5.1 billion is modest when measured against the staggering debts of other African countries – for example, $8 billion, $12 billion, $19 billion, $26 billion, $40 billion. In addition, these nations owe their foreign debts to private international banks, while only 5% of Zaire's foreign debt is due private international banks. The remaining 95% results from financial assistance and government loans granted by friendly countries, including the United States, France, Great Britain,

U.S. Aid to Zaire

Military:

Fiscal Year
1984: $7 million
1985: $7 million
1986: $7 million
1987: $4 million
1988: $3 million

Economic (Development Assistance, Economic Support Fund, food aid):

Fiscal Year
1984: $40 million
1985: $54 million
1986: $62 million
1987: $56 million
1988: (approximately)
$55-$60 million

Source: U.S. Department of State

my government to discontinue the austerity program.

We are prepared to fulfill our commitments as best we can, but this must not involve austerity measures intended to make the Zairian people suffer. The Central Committee also placed a 20% limit on any payments from export earnings. That is, if we receive one billion dollars in export earnings, we should pay back no more than $200 million.

DYMALLY: Many African leaders, yourself included, have been extremely critical of American foreign policy, particularly as it concerns Africa. In your view, is the Reagan policy doomed to failure? If so, why?

MOBUTU: First, it is not my place to dictate United States foreign policy in Africa. However, present policy does not enhance the image of a great power like the United States. For example, recent statistics on American aid to Africa reveal that Egypt receives over one billion dollars, followed by Morocco and Tunisia, which receive hundreds of millions of dollars. Yet, famine and misery have exacted a heavy toll on several African countries south of the Sahara. How do you explain this disparity? How can you justify the billions of dollars given to North Africa, while many of the neediest countries receive next to nothing?

I don't mean to criticize your government's policy; I am merely pointing out certain facts. Unfortunately, the situation is not likely to improve, what with President Reagan's recent announcement that American aid to the Third World would be cut by 20%. The International Monetary Fund has, as you know, created a special fund estimated to total $11.5 billion over the next three years. This fund was intended to help ease the crisis in the developing world, especially Africa. The major participants in this partnership include the World Bank, the International Monetary Fund, France, Great Britain and Japan. The United States refused to participate. What explanation can you give for its refusal?

ELLIOT: As you know, Rep. Ronald V. Dellums (D-CA), has introduced legislation to withdraw military aid and put controls on economic aid to Zaire by the United States. How do you respond?

MOBUTU: Does Zaire, in fact, receive military aid from the United States? In my view, such legislation only complicates our present relationship. You know all too well that American military aid is, for the most part, negligible. Two years ago, it amounted to the equivalent of 21 jeeps and assorted spare parts for our aircraft. If that is the extent of your aid, how would we suffer if it were curtailed?

Since independence, Zaire has been a dependable ally of the United States. However, we are paying dearly for our friendship. Indeed, time after time, the United States has invented myriad excuses for denying us aid – human rights violations, South Africa, corruption, etc. These charges are completely unfounded.

In all sincerity, I believe that those African countries which are inclined toward a Marxist-Leninist ideology, with close ties to the Soviet Union and its Eastern Bloc allies, are treated far better than is Zaire, which has opted for close ties with the West. For us, it has been a virtual sea of troubles. I expressed this same view to Vice President Bush, when he visited Zaire. In reality, Zaire receives little if any aid from the United States. How are we repaid? With ingratitude and criticism. Bush himself acknowledged that America's strongest critics are always rewarded, while their faithful friends are always poorly treated.

Let me cite a case in point – namely, the August, 1975 OAU summit, which was held in Kampala under the auspices of Ugandan President Idi Amin. President Jaafar Numeiry of Sudan introduced a virulent motion aimed at the Western powers. Although I am not paid by these nations to defend their interests at the OAU, I strongly opposed Numeiry's motion, not wanting the OAU to be regarded as ideologically anti-West or at the disposition of the East. President Nu-

meiry again took the floor and lambasted me, stating, "He [Mobutu] can't speak up. He is a servant of the United States, a puppet of the West." This caused an uproar. The motion was then put to the floor for a vote. Almost everyone else followed my lead, and the motion was defeated. Two years later, President Numeiry chased out the Russians and his Eastern allies from Sudan and opened his doors to the United States. Since then, Sudan has been a yearly candidate for $100 million in American economic assistance.

In answering your question, I am making a great effort to choose my words carefully, for when I recall that trying incident, I am tempted to break all ties with your country. Numeiry insulted me, condemned you, and then reversed his stand, only to be rewarded with $100 million each year for additional aircraft, cannons, etc., while Zaire hasn't received a cartridge. At the same time, the United States has been fulminating a variety of problems in Zaire under the pretext of human rights violations, political corruption, South Africa and the like. If I have, against all odds, decided to remain a faithful friend to the United States, it is because in politics one must be courageous. Political courage cannot be defined as doting after a great power in the anticipation of future aid; what matters most to me are friendship and faith. That is the true meaning of courage.

ELLIOT: Isn't it true that Zaire has, at the urging of the CIA, allowed the Kamina Base to be used to provide covert American aid to Jonas Savimbi's rebels in Angola and that you have provided direct assistance to Savimbi?

MOBUTU: No. You know very well the geography of Africa. If you examine a map of Africa, you will discover that Angola stretches 2,600 kilometers along our southern frontier. This boundary line is controlled by the legitimate ruling government of Angola. Everyone knows that for aid to reach this land-locked country, it must pass through South Africa or some other country, but not Zaire. Any aid that we might provide would inevitably fail to reach Savimbi, who is well off to the south – indeed, less than 20 kilometers from Angola's southern border with South Africa.

Not long ago, I officially requested that the chairman of the Organization of African Unity (OAU) appoint several military experts to improve the surveillance system at Kamina Base. They would be paid by OAU member states – although Zaire would be prepared to shoulder all of the expenses – and would be charged with the responsibility to examine the contents of every aircraft that lands or takes off. Although this approach would run contrary to current military practice, it would go a long way toward monitoring any possible violations.

DYMALLY: The Organization of African Unity has, for many years, supported a boycott against Israel. Yet, Zaire was the first African country to renew diplomatic relations with Israel that were severed during the 1973 Middle East War. At the same time, you have openly criticized Israel before members of Congress and castigated Israel for its Palestinian policy. How do you explain this seeming contradiction?
MOBUTU: No contradiction exists. I view Israel as a friend, but this does not imply that I am slavishly obliged to endorse her policies. Even within Israel, where the government has hitherto enjoyed the complete backing of the people, voices of disapprobation regarding her West Bank policy can be heard. Thus, we are friends with Israel, but we have voiced strong opposition to those actions that we deem unjustifiable. Therefore, no contradiction exists. The United States supports Israel 100%. Yet, you recently criticized her West Bank policy, but are still friends. We view our relationship much the same way.

ELLIOT: In recent years, you have expressed strong opposition to Libyan President Muammar Qaddafi and his efforts to expand his sphere of influence. How serious is the Libyan threat in the region?
MOBUTU: First, my goal is not to

Mobutu Takes Charge

On June 30, 1960, the Belgian Congo became independent. Within weeks, army mutinies and the attempted seccession of Katanga - now Shaba – province combined with domestic political rivalries and foreign intervention to create what came to be known as the "Congo Crisis." (United Nations Secretary General Dag Hammerskjold was killed in a plane crash during an attempt to mediate that conflict.)

From the beginning, the then Joseph Desire Mobutu was a major player. Three months after independence he ousted President Joseph Kasavubu and Prime Minister Patrice Lumumba, who was later killed under mysterious circumstances. Mobutu returned the government to a civilian administration but remained powerful as head of the armed forces.

He seized control again in a coup on Novermber 24, 1965, and has ruled Zaire ever since.

oust Qaddafi as head of state. Rather, I oppose many of his policies aimed at his sister countries in Africa, including Zaire. His occupation of Chad, for example, is in direct violation of one of the major clauses of the OAU Charter, which prohibits the occupation of one African country by another. The Charter recommends that all disputes be settled through peaceful negotiations.

Obviously, Qaddafi has resorted to military occupation for the simple reason that Libya is far more powerful than Chad. While Zaire is also less powerful, it still condemns Libya, both verbally in international forums and through its unconditional support for an independent Chad. Our position is consistent with the OAU Charter, which calls for non-interference in the internal affairs of other countries.

In this regard, I decided to brave Qaddafi's threats by intervening in Chad. This may be called the "right of interference," since Zaire does not share a common boundary with Chad. We are merely close friends. I do not expect praise for my position; it is a question of justice. Unfortunately, I have become a target, and wherever I travel in Europe I am heavily guarded. We are aware of, and are closely monitoring, Zairian Libyan-trained terrorists seeking to destabilize our country. Regardless of the personal conse-

quences, I will not haul down my flag or retreat from Chad. Recently, we dispatched 3,000 paratroopers to Chad. Since that time, we have lost 22 of our best young men.

DYMALLY: Many critics have argued that consistency is not your most prominent trait. You speak of the need for African "authenticity" and for Africans to cast aside the bonds of "neocolonialism," yet Zaire is one of white-ruled South Africa's top African trading partners. How do you square this apparent inconsistency?
MOBUTU: Your question makes me laugh. But, please don't think that I am laughing at you. You are an American, a citizen of the United States. You are fully aware that your country enjoys diplomatic ties with South Africa, as evidenced by the existence in Washington and in Pretoria of your respective embassies. My situation is quite different. We are drawn together by one simple fact: the transportation of our minerals through the Southern Road to our land-locked country. That is the extent of our relations. By the way, are Western journalists unaware that all European countries have embassies in South Africa – that they engage in economic trade and military cooperation?

Don't forget, Zaire is hemmed in, and is required to use the Southern Road, which transports 25% to 30%

of our minerals. The national port simply cannot accomodate more than 40% of our imports or exports. The remaining 60% is transported by the Southern Road or the Tanzanian Road. Therefore, our relationship with South Africa is, strictly speaking, a matter of survival. Moreover, it is not a gift from the South African government; we are billed for using their railway.

Obviously, my policy has drawn sharp criticism. However, consider those other African nations that cannot survive without South Africa; nothing is said about them. Zaire is the only scapegoat. That is my response.

ELLIOT: As far as South Africa is concerned, do you support President Reagan's policy of "constructive engagement"? Do you favor stronger sanctions or direct military intervention in South Africa?
MOBUTU: Let's not go too far afield. If only the actions recommended by the United Nations were implemented to the letter, and with the full backing of the Western powers, we would not be where we are today. Clearly, the great powers are playing games in South Africa.

DYMALLY: According to your critics, you bear direct responsibility for the death of former Prime Minister Patrice Lumumba, who was arrested by your troops and flown to Katanga, where, it is believed, he was killed by Congolese or Katangese troops. Indeed, some observers maintain that you were part of a CIA plot to assassinate Lumumba. What role, if any, did you play in the collapse of the Lumumba government and the subsequent assassination of Lumumba himself?
MOBUTU: As a black leader in your country, you are obviously sensitive to the plight of Africa and its peoples. However, your interest in Zaire's internal affairs is consistent with your nation's treatment of African countries as a whole. It seems to me that you are here in search of a scapegoat, as reflected by your probing questions concerning human rights, Savimbi, South Africa and now Lumumba. In some ways,

I feel that I am on trial. In any event, let me respond.

First, I was not a high-ranking government official in 1961; I was in charge of the armed forces, not the Head of State. I don't wish to criticize my predecessor, President Kasavubu, but it was he who ordered Lumumba's arrest and his subsequent transfer to Lubumbashi in Shaba province, where he died.

When Lumumba was assassinated, I was in Kinshasa, carrying out my duties as chief of staff of the army. I was as surprised as anyone when the news of his death was reported. Since I wasn't there at the time, I don't know exactly what occurred. Neither do I know President Kasavubu's motives for transferring him to Shaba province. I don't know who assassinated Lumumba, and thus can't be of much help. To repeat: I wasn't the head of state; I was a soldier. I did not initiate policy; I merely executed orders from above. Besides, Lumumba's transfer was not within my jurisdiction. Nonetheless, I was, and remain, implicated in Lumumba's assassination because I was a member of the ruling government.

Let me try to shed some light on the actual sequence of events. In January, 1961, the period in which Lumumba was transferred and later murdered, the troops that were stationed in Shaba province, then known as Katanga province, were not under my command. This absolves me of the charge that "It was you, the army officers, who gave the orders." I had no control over the troops in Shaba, but was under orders from the government to suppress the secession. Thus, I held no position of power, either politically in Kinshasa or militarily in Katanga, to be held accountable for anything.

Why did I begin my answer with such a prologue? It appears that some people in your country would like to tie economic and military assistance to African countries to events such as this. Liberia is a case in point. As head of state, I shouldn't criticize another nation. However, you force me to give you an example. If you calculate American aid to Liberia, dating back to when Samuel Doe took power up

until 1987, you would find that it is double that of Zaire's. Why don't you question Doe on his predecessor's assassination? Liberia receives far more aid, but is not asked such questions; we receive virtually no aid, and can't live in peace. How can you compare Zaire's president, who did not murder his predecessor but merely removed him from power, to someone who brutally murdered his predecessor? [Note: Mobutu refers here to his overthrow of President Joseph Kasavubu in 1965.]

Until his death, for example, President Kasavubu enjoyed all of the privileges due an ex-president: a full salary, cars, etc. When he died, he was given full military honors at his funeral. Thus, how can you compare these two cases?

Today, you can still see the small home President Kasavubu left in Kinshasa, and in which his widow and family resided. In my view, it wasn't dignified for the wife of an ex-president, so I decided to erect a more spacious home for her and her family. All of Kasavubu's children, who survived him, studied in Europe at my expense. His eldest son, a veterinary surgeon, is presently working closely with me; his daughter is a member of the Central Committee; and his wife is earning a salary equivalent to a full cabinet minister. Where else can you find a similar situation in Africa? It would be instructive if you could meet and talk to Mrs. Kasavubu, so that you could learn the facts first-hand.

As for Lumumba, his son, a virulent critic of my government, and one who fomented rebellion in Europe, is slated to return to Zaire within a fortnight. Go to Cairo, where Mrs. Lumumba has taken up temporary residence, and ask her whether she has received help from President Mobutu, what favors I've done her. I would like you to act as an intermediary in securing her return home, either through the intervention of a journalist or a friend. I am prepared to finance the mission.

The widow of Liberia's former president, William Tolbert, is presently residing in New York. Ask her if I have been helpful to her and her son, a law student in New York, whenever I visit there. Ask her son whether I have provided him with financial assistance? Ask him how many times he has visited Zaire? Ask him how President Mobutu received him? These are facts that once a year, and when he did the event was celebrated for days on end, sometimes up to a week.

I am unable, however, to disappear for a year; I must be visible every day. The paramount chiefs of larly the paratroopers. As you know, I was a paratrooper myself. Among the military pilots, I am considered to be one of theirs. Since the army issues from the people, it is a reflection of their faith and confidence. My political survival is that simple.

Believe it or not there's no "cult of personality" in Zaire. It exists only in the minds of our critics.

---

shouldn't be overlooked, although, of course, I don't mean to blow my own trumpet.

ELLIOT: Your opponents insist that you are extremely egotistical. Indeed, a Zairian presidential hymn includes the words: "Today, we are going to admire the Guide Mobutu. If you see him, admire him. If everyone sees him, let them admire him. The country is called Zaire." Why have you so attempted to personalize Zairian politics? Aren't there dangers in establishing a government based on the cult of personality?

MOBUTU: Believe it or not, there is no "cult of personality" in Zaire. It exists only in the minds of our critics. Zaire is not France, Great Britain, Denmark or the United States. Zaire is Africa in miniature. The customs and traditions you have witnessed over the past week do not even represent a quarter of what is tribal, authentic Africa. Since becoming head of state, I have supported a policy of cultural revival, in the hope that Zairians will rediscover themselves and their heritage.

Ambassador [Nguz a] Karl-i-Bond, for example, comes from a tribe in Shaba province, which has dedicated a song to its paramount chief. The song is called "Ndjalelo", which means "Hail to the Chief." In that tribe, the chief appeared only that province decided to dedicate the song to me, stating, "He is more popular and more successful than was any emperor in our history." That is how I came to be honored with the song "Ndjalelo," which is now sung not only when I visit Shaba province, but whenever I salute the army.

This reverence has never been imposed on the people. It emanates from deep within them, and it is a demonstration of their personal loyalty. Yet, this treatment is far short of what our African traditions require of the people. Therefore, when the Zairian people pay tribute to me as their chief, they are simply following their authentic, indigenous traditions.

DYMALLY: Finally, at age 57, you have survived it all: coup attempts, invasions by Katanganese rebels, defections by your highest officials. To what do you attribute your longevity – your survival? What explains your remarkable durability?

MOBUTU: The answer is quite simple. My support over the past 22 years has come from the Zairian people – their loyalty and their love. Beyond that I can't say more. That relationship, viewed on a somewhat formal level, is one of complete loyalty. Although I am the boss, when I meet the troops, they regard me more or less as a comrade, particu-

I cannot judge myself, only the people can. For a country as large as Zaire, the leader must know his job, and must be accepted by the people. I know I am doing my job – that I am responding to the people's needs. Thus, I shouldn't brag about it. The people are the ultimate judge.

I've never had any illusions about the people's loyalty and faith, for there are clear signs and these signs do not mislead.

You might have heard rumors, for example, about my so-called illness and alleged death, which surfaced recently when I was out of the country. When I returned to Zaire and the people discovered that these rumors were baseless, I was accorded an unprecedented welcome by the Kinshasa population.

According to the media, of that city's 3 million inhabitants, 2.5 million men, women and children flooded the streets to give me a triumphant welcome. Neither me, nor a visiting statesman, had ever before received such a welcome. That is a clear sign – an unmistakable sign – of the people's affection. I will not belabor the point.

I have an idea. Let's drive to the university in my car, without a bodyguard, and without notice. I'll just bring my hat. Don't leave me for a second, so you won't think it was pre-planned. Let's try this experiment. It will reveal, most clearly, how I am viewed by the people. ∎

Article 9.1.   India: The Seed of Destruction

Anita Desai explores the current political situation in India which, in her view, is laden with uncertainty. At present, Indian politics are dictated to a large extent by the whims and caprices of that country's politicians and bureaucrats, who have proven themselves to be both unpredictable and impetuous. Plagued by illiteracy, disease, crime, and backwardness, the system is incapable of responding to the needs of the masses. The article reviews the triumphs and failures of the Nehru and Gandhi dynasties, concluding that the long-held dream of a single, unified nation remains unfulfilled. Today, India stands at the political precipice, facing a bloody and awful future—one that threatens to engulf the entire country. According to the author, it is unlikely that India will avoid the funeral pyre that lies in waiting. Out of the ashes, however, could emerge a new India, an India free of violence, division, and neglect.

India: The Seed of Destruction

Anita Desai

—New Delhi

In India, the line between the sacred and the secular is a thin and wavering one. Together, they weave a web, and the web is spun by its people who are also its captives. The gods do not reside in some towering cathedral or remote shrine; they establish themselves in kitchens, storerooms, offices, even vehicles. In a land where a bus or taxi driver hangs an oleograph of a deity on the dashboard and decorates it with garlands of fresh flowers, where merchants set an idol upon their cashboxes and shopkeepers do not begin their trade before lighting incense and intoning prayers to their chosen god, the presence of the divine is so pervasive as to become intimate and familiar, woven into the texture of everyday.

In the present time, in which the laws and whims of politicians and bureaucrats are as pervasive and powerful as those of the gods, not only must a minister be propitiated before he will issue a license, allot a house, or award a pension, but so must every clerk through whose hand the relevant file passes. A railway booking clerk alone can decide whether to allow you to travel or not, and even a postman is capable of holding back your mail or a plumber of keeping a drain blocked until he receives a favor. Such men become the earthly variants of the gods, as demanding of devotion and appeasement. Like the divine ones, who are subject to passions, whims, and caprices; they too are unpredictable, impetuous, and fickle, and must be courted and placated if one is to make one's passage through life: register a birth, admit a child to school or college, obtain a job, receive medical aid, a house, a pension. Each gathers about him his courtiers, and requires a bodyguard, to bolster and protect his power. Power is not possible without money, and money must be obtained by every means at hand. When every petty clerk and district official wields such authority over the lives caught in his little local web, imagine the might that resides at the center, on the throne of Delhi!

Democracy has not altered that system to any great degree. It calls for periodic elections, true, and asks each man and woman to make a decision and voice an opinion—but how is this put into practice? The strongman of the village, or locality, will choose his candidate for parliament—one who will naturally return the favor later—and announce his decision, threaten anyone who shows an inclination to go against it, and—to make certain he does not get away with it under cover of secret balloting—sends his henchmen to fire some shots over the heads of the queue waiting at the polling booth, scatter the people, and go in to stamp all the ballot papers themselves. Or sends them in the night before to wrest the ballot box from the election officers and stuff it with suitably stamped papers before anyone else has a chance. More effectively still, a recalcitrant voter or two may be gunned down as an example to others or, even better, an opposition candidate can be simply eliminated. Does the hero of the standard Bombay film not vanquish his opponents and win the heroine by wielding an AK-47 or a Kalashnikov?

This newfangled system of voting can be settled best by violence; violence alone proves a point dramatically and irrefutably. In the northern states of Bihar and Uttar Pradesh, synonymous in the minds of most Indians with backwardness, illiteracy, and crime, the police have either stood by and watched helplessly or actively colluded with the local strongmen. The passions that overtake a politician when an election is announced—and already when it merely appears as a speck upon the horizon—is the passion to acquire power, even if only a

shard of the power that glitters and tantalizes at the center, in Delhi. To achieve it, there are no lengths to which he will not go—don saffron robes and the prayer beads of a holy man if necessary, or tear down a mosque and build a temple if it will please the Hindu majority, or nominate film stars and cricketers in a bid for popular appeal. And, of course, spend stupendous sums of money.

It is not that the Indian voter, the man in the street, is more gullible or passive or easily threatened or seduced than people elsewhere. He may watch the election campaign open-mouthed as though it were a *tamasha* (show) or Bollywood (film made in Bombay) melodrama. But he is no longer a mere spectator and the government is no longer a distant, invisible Raj that does not concern him. Sitting in the village tea shop under that cliched banyan tree, or working on a building site or road repair works in a city to which he has gone to earn his living, he hears the promises made by politicians of *Rama-rajya* (the rule of Rama, the golden age), sees the promises held out by advertisements on television and cinema screens, of ease, comfort, pleasure. Yet he cannot reach out and grasp them. He finds himself as helpless as a fly caught in the web of the social system and of bureaucracy. His emotions on watching the power play of caste and class are no longer passive and fatalistic: one may still find docile fatalists among the older generation, but none among the younger. He wishes to express his opinion—and sees he must fight to have it heard. So much is at stake, and he is willing to fight. The politician may assume he is a god or a raja, but such assumptions are being questioned by the earthlings, the mortals. The politician must descend to earth and engage with him on the level on which he lives.

The Nehru family became synonymous with the Indian polity through

the generations—from Jawaharlal Nehru, who personified the wise, noble leader of the nation, through his daughter Indira Gandhi, with all the fire and electricity she created around herself, down to her son Rajiv Gandhi, who came to politics reluctantly but took to it as to the manner born. Between them they kept the Congress party in power almost all through India's independent history, and so it came to stand for continuity, and stability, and the Nehru family became as familiar as the Hindu pantheon to the populace of even the most distant village and hamlet to which the finer details of political activity had barely filtered. The inclination to see them as a dynasty is not inexplicable in a country that has been ruled by one dynasty or the other since the Aryans arrived in the second millennium BC. Nor is it entirely an Oriental aberration—Britain, with centuries of success with its parliamentary system, still retains its monarchy, as do a number of efficient Scandinavian countries, while America seemed to come close to a parallel with the Kennedy clan. What is extraordinary is that a family that has dominated the political scene for half a century has also convinced the people that it has done so democratically, and that it represents progress.

The conviction was established by Jawaharlal Nehru, a Cambridge-educated Socialist of the early Fabian school, who worshipped the rivers, forests, and mountains of India with an Aryan passion but also had a vision of India as a self-supporting industrial power and, during his lifetime, initiated the change from a traditionally rural and agricultural society to an urban, industrialized one. The vast steel plants at Rourkela and Bhilai, the mammoth Bhakra Dam, the space research and nuclear power program ("only for peaceful purposes," it is always quickly added), and the monolithic city of Chandigarh built by le Corbusier at the foot of the northern hills became symbols of this vision. But, like the monoliths of Egypt, they towered above the people without altering their lives in a sufficiently rapid and beneficial way.

When Indira Gandhi came to power—she was said to be "groomed" for it by her long and close relationship with her father—the people, with the new technology within their grasp, began pressing for faster progress and chafing at the restrictions placed upon their new ambitions by the rigid bureaucratic system devised to control all development through a central power. Her younger son, the ill-fated Sanjay whose career was cut short by his death in a plane crash, represented this impatient new ambitiousness in the manner in which he overrode all legal and constitutional norms in setting up an automobile plant in collaboration with Suzuki. The elder son Rajiv Gandhi's brief term in power between 1985 and 1989 saw the coming to bloom of the new commercialism in India, and the establishment of the new middle class—the small shopkeepers and petty traders of the past breaking into the new era of enterprise and entrepreneurship. The cities became filled with the rural poor desperate for a share in the new wealth, streets became noisy with the urgent little Maruti cars, marketplaces overflowed with goods, shoppers jostled to buy what they had seen advertised on television the night before—Wrangler jeans, Benetton shirts, track shoes, and Pepsi-Cola.

There were those who wondered at the young prime minister's insistence on the necessity of computers in a country where few schools or offices had electricity; others who thought he was trying to counter poverty with potato chips. Nevertheless, the movement swelled through the Eighties into a stampede. The aggressive and the unscrupulous pushed ahead, others fell under their feet and were trampled. Millions found themselves held back for lack of an education, technology, economic power, or out of the restrictions placed on them by the ancient traditions of a caste-bound and hierarchical society. A huge wave of resentment swelled even as cities flourished, skyscrapers rose into the sky, and streets resounded with traffic. Those left outside the orbit of prosperity became more visible, the contrast of their lives more shocking, for they still lived in slums or encampments of shacks with no water, health care, schools, or even food, small children being sent to work in order to stay alive, and every attempt made to improve their lot hijacked and subverted to benefit the middlemen along the way.

The two currents—one upwardly mobile, frenetic, and charged with ambition, the other seething with bitterness, frustration, and a hunger for a share in the profits—have been meeting and clashing with increasing violence through the Eighties: the air resounds with the clash, steel on steel.

The aggression and bullying of those who have, and the despair and rage of those who have not, affects the whole fiber of society and is reflected in their manners by increasingly brusque and explosive speech, vehement and threatening gestures, violent acts. To live in India today is to live in a constant state of tension, conscious of the explosive forces building up under a surface no longer calm and likely to erupt at any moment.

The riots in Delhi in the early 1980s when the youthful and impetuous Sanjay Gandhi tried to forcibly sterilize slum dwellers and remove them ("resettle them," he said) to camps outside the city, the devastating bloodiness of the military assault in 1984 on the Golden Temple in Amritsar where Sikh secessionists had entrenched themselves, the riots that followed the assassination of Indira Gandhi in which Sikhs were set upon and killed by Hindus, the riots in Ayodhya when members of Hindu revivalist parties broke through police cordons in an attempt to pull down a mosque and build a temple in its place, the riots by upper-caste Hindus in 1990 when V. P. Singh, briefly prime minister, declared his intention to increase the number of places reserved for the lower castes in educational and bureaucratic institutions, the increasingly militant demands for separate lands by Sikhs in Punjab and Muslims in Kashmir and the United Liberation Front of Assam...these have marked a decade of India's life with their fires and blood.

The web so intricately woven by political and religious threads, by the sacred and the secular, has no seemly pattern, no orderly design: it is tattered and frayed by assault and agitation. Other nations have gone through such periods of change—the Industrial Revolution of Europe is often cited as an example of what is happening in India now: it, too, was marked by injustice, rioting, and violence. But nowhere else was the situation so complicated by the religious, linguistic, cultural, and ethnic diversity of a people as in India, or subjected to the immpossible pressures of a population that has reached totally unmanageable proportions. One can find a parallel in the Soviet Union and in Yugoslavia of the growing demand by states with widely differing ethnic and cultural identities for control over their own administration, trade, industry, and educational policies; and in India too a mistake is being made in seeing these movements as secessionist and antinational instead of an inevitable movement toward federalism. That is the natural outcome of a period of centralization.

The dream of a single, unified nation persists, and it is not exclusively modern, independent India's. It was the dream of every invader who entered India through its high mountain passes on horseback and with sword in hand, from the eighth century onward, in-flamed with the passion to conquer the whole of the land. It lay behind the pious desire expressed by British imperialists "to unify India"—an illusion pursued by those who keep alive the fantasy of the "Raj." It is a dream that has proved stubbornly resistant to the realities of the time, with its demands and aspirations. In a country with such an immense and rich diversity of religion, language, culture, and race, one might think it a natural development to hand over authority to each cultural unit over its own way of life; held together by a federal system, but functioning independently on a much smaller, more manageable scale, it might finally become a dream that works.

Why can such a development not be brought about peacefully, through the parliamentary system of democracy? Is there something inherently wrong with the system, or is it India's interpretation of it that carries in it the seed of destruction? It is probably both.

The parliamentary system that was conducted with relative dignity and propriety under Nehru's leadership, failed to take into account the urgency of the problems at hand. Nor was he above a godlike, or raja-like, inclination to think of himself, the father of the nation, capable of making all the decisions for all the people. Had he not been lawfully elected by the people to speak and act for them? In Indira Gandhi's time, politicians wrested more power into their hands by breaking all legal niceties that were seen as restrictive or delaying, and so she could declare a state of emergency and seize extraordinary powers when she felt threatened. All down the line politicians began to grasp at power without waiting to win it. Of course they could not act in this manner indefinitely—Election Day was inevitably Judgment Day—and it was necessary to have the support of large enough numbers of people—"vote banks," they came to be called. So the politicians played one community against the other, one religion against another—Muslims against Hindus, Hindus against Sikhs: a dangerous game to play, bringing all their feudal instincts, and all their medieval statecraft into account.

Rajiv Gandhi, like his mother and grandfather before him, might have liked to "rule" India without having to involve the opinions and prejudices of all his unruly countrymen: it would have been neater, quieter, more orderly that way. He would have liked his liberalism, his lack of prejudices, and his commitment to modernization taken for granted. But even he had to woo the electorate, and by pleasing one group inevitably antagonized another: if you grant a favor to a low-caste sweeper, you enrage a high-caste landowner; if you appease a Muslim, you arouse the suspicion of a Hindu; if you grant additional benefits to an industrialist, you deprive a farmer; if you spend on defense, you neglect education and health care; if you build a dam, you destroy a forest.... The seeds he assiduously sowed came up as swords.

There are many who suspected Rajiv of having a hand in the killing of Sikhs after his mother's assassination by her Sikh bodyguards. There are Hindus in Kashmir who felt Muslims had been pampered and conditions created for a Muslim insurrection in the state; there are Muslims who suffered atrociously in the military reprisals against them. There are many supporters among the Tamils in the south for a Tamil state within Sri Lanka who hate him for having sent the Indian army to Sri Lanka to help it put down the movement for Tamil Eelam, and recently for forcing the resignation of the state government of Tamil Nadu that he suspected of harboring and encouraging the Liberation Tigers for Tamil Eelam (LTTE). During the election campaign this last month, the Hindu revivalist party of the Bharatiya Janata Party (BJP) had seen in Rajiv and the Congress its only serious rival and obstacle to success: since the Congress party is effectively the Gandhi party, without him it is crippled.

The elections are being held, a mere fourteen months after the last, because Rajiv had suddenly and unexpectedly withdrawn the support he had promised the minority government of Chandra Shekhar, thereby causing it to topple prematurely. Any one of these groups or communities or parties could have been party to his assassination. So many hatreds, so much bitterness and frustration exist—how can it not express itself, eventually, in violence? One's initial reaction to the news of his death—"Impossible!"—very quickly gave way to the admission that it had been not only possible but probable all along, and that it was only a matter of time before the drama arrived at its climax.

Even in Hindu mythology, the gods do not merely recline upon a pink cloud as they rule the universe; it is a part of their godliness to come down to earth and woo or vanquish the earthlings in courtship and battle, and blood will surely flow.

The climax has been reached, predictably bloody and awful, and a period of catharsis follows for India. Watching the funeral pyre flame and flicker, one could be forgiven for thinking one saw India upon that pyre, burning, out under a sun half-obscured by smoke and the dust of the open cremation field. Not in the sense that Rajiv Gandhi represented India and with his death it is extinguished, but in the sense that the fires that have been lit are likely to rage further and higher and engulf the entire country. Then, perhaps, a clearing will be made in which a new beginning will sprout.

Article 9.2.   Hongkong: The Case for Optimism

An optimistic assessment of Hong Kong's future, this article analyzes the problems and prospects of this affluent Asian country as it prepares for the transition from British to Chinese rule in 1997. Today, Hong Kong faces a host of unresolved issues, among them the fate of the Vietnamese "boat people," democracy, emigration, and inflation. Despite its present difficulties, many experts believe that Hong Kong will survive and flourish, even under Chinese rule, if only the doomsayers remain there to take advantage of the opportunities that will surely present themselves. After all, Hong Kong has survived typhoons, stock-market crashes, and enemy occupation. There is every reason to believe that it will survive the immediate crisis.

There is an ancient Chinese curse that says: 'May you live in interesting times.' The people of Hongkong have spent the last 150 years living under that curse. They have never lived in any other sort of times.

And today the curse is at its most pernicious with so many unresolved issues: the Vietnamese 'boat people', democracy, emigration, passports, inflation and the confidence crisis itself —issues which have succeeded in dividing the British and the people of Hongkong and China, creating a matrix of problems.

The Hongkong people could be seen to fall into two camps—the optimists and the pessimists. The optimists continue to hold great faith in Hongkong's future, believing that Hongkong is too economically valuable to China for the People's Republic ever to risk destroying its free-enterprise culture. The pessimists are fearful that sovereignty is too important an issue for China ever to condone 'one country, two systems'.

Let us be clear about what Hongkong could be. With Hongkong's tradition of enterprise and its continuing access to the world's largest emerging market, Hongkong could continue to be the business success story—the economic hub of the Far East. Or its economy could be destroyed through lack of business confidence and emigration. They say the difference between the optimist and the pessimist is that the optimist sees the doughnut, the pessimist sees the hole.

In discussing Hongkong's future, it is interesting to look back over the Colony's historic growth. Hongkong was inhabited from earliest times, although few people lived there until the nineteenth century. In 1841 the Treaty of Nanjing ceded Hongkong Island in perpetuity to the British. Two further treaty grants in 1860 and 1898 enlarged the territory, first through the freehold of Kowloon and Stonecutters Island and then by the leasehold of the New Territories.

Hongkong was an 'enterprise' culture long before Mrs Thatcher's Ministers popularised the concept. A gas company, electricity supply companies and tramways began and developed when Queen Victoria was on the throne. By the turn of the century, Hongkong's housing, sanitation and water conservation programmes were the envy of all Asia—and almost every other British colony. By the end of the century, Hongkong's revenues to Britain through shipping and trade were far in excess of Britain's other trading partners, most of which were ten times larger than Hongkong.

So Hongkong was 'booming' over a century ago in spite of the many setbacks the Hongkong people have suffered over the years. Fire, disease and typhoon all took their toll. The Taiping rebellion, the fall of the Manchu dynasty, the Japanese invasion of China and the Chinese civil war all brought sudden massive immigration. The Japanese occupation during the Second World War had reduced the population from 1.5m to 600,000 six years later. So Hongkong has experienced many ups and downs. Today Hongkong continues to thrive.

If there is one quality which characterises the people of Hongkong, it is resilience. That is why it is premature to pen Hongkong's obituary. Claims such as 'Hongkong is probably finished—it is like a gold town in the Yukon in the 1890s' do not present an accurate picture.[1]

When I first arrived in Hongkong 24 years ago many despaired of Hongkong's future. There were full-scale riots in progress. We witnessed an unnerving run on the banks—and in Hongkong the banks issue the currency and are not protected by a lender of the last resort. In 1967 we were in the middle of the Cultural Revolution; people were saying 'it's all over' and half the town was packing its baggage.

But the people of Hongkong, many of them refugees, are astonishingly resilient. They have an incredible instinct, not only for surviving but for prospering, too. Look at the industries Hongkong has been into and out of only to bounce back again. Maybe it is the refugee mentality that drives Hongkong forward—the search for security and a firm base.

When I arrived, those 24 years ago, everybody seemed to be making money from wigs and plastic flowers, and then it was camphor wood chests. That all went wrong somehow—the wigs disappeared overnight, like the bowler hats in London, and watches and consumer electronics were the rage, after that toys. Hongkong then progressed to shipping and was told that it was bigger than the Greeks. That all changed and somebody announced one day that Hongkong was the fourth largest finance centre in the world; banks were springing up all over the place. In 1970 Hongkong discovered the stock-market. Everybody was involved. It could take up to six months to have a shirt made because the tailors were preoccupied with their stock-market deals.

From a peak of 1770 the index fell to 152 and people were flinging themselves out of windows. Property boomed in the late 1970s and then dropped 60 per cent in 1983 almost overnight. So Hongkong has had its problems, but it has always scrambled back. Yet every time people said: 'This time it's different.

Even today, amidst all its real and imagined uncertainties, Hongkong is still:

● the eleventh largest trading economy on earth. It exports nearly one-third of what mighty Japan exports;
● the world's busiest container port;
● one of the world's largest financial centres;

From *The World Today*, June 1990, pp. 101-103, published by the Royal Institute of International Affairs, London.

● Asia's main destination for tourism;
● the world's largest exporter of watches and second largest exporter of garments and toys.

From the Star Ferry across Victoria Harbour, you can see the single building which manufactures 10 per cent of all the watches sold in the United States. Hongkong is also the most exciting city on earth. You only have to be there an hour to feel the energy of the place: 5,5m driver-ants going for their lives. Hongkong's average per capita income in 1989 was $11,000—Britain's was $12,000. At average growth levels—not recent booms, but the growth pattern over the last 20 years—its living standards will be higher than Britain's within three to four years. Statistically, by 1997 the average Hongkong family would be taking a cut in its living standards if it were to come and live in Chelsea, let alone in Chingford. Woodrow Wyatt, Lord Wyatt of Weeford, was right when he wrote recently of the 'sublime conceit of many British' who believe that the people of Hongkong long to settle in this country.

Yet one cannot deny that underneath the bustle today Hongkong is depressed, edgy and insecure as it moves closer to 1997. The essential ingredient of this insecurity is, of course, 'fear': fear that the freedoms of its inhabitants will be curtailed, fear of retribution if they do not conform and obey, and fear of the uncertainty of it all. Uncertainty is the greatest enemy of economic progress. One contributory factor to all this uncertainty is that Hongkong was not given an equal place at the negotiating table.

Initially Britain had a strong negotiating position. I do not think that the Chinese realised that Britain would be so accommodating on the value of the 'perpetuity' rights of Hongkong and Kowloon. Britain should have insisted that Hongkong participated in the discussions on its future.

But the British government did not. In consequence, two heavyweights, miles apart, deliberated and negotiated Hongkong's future and Hongkong has been left stranded between the two, victim of melting loyalties, wondering which side is going to let it down first. From the very beginning Hongkong should have been an equal party to the discussions, which would have enabled it to feel far more confident in presenting its own united view firmly. Instead, Hongkong has been stranded high and dry, left to ponder the underlying motives of the Chinese and the British.

The huge divergence of opinion in Hongkong itself on many issues finds expression in the diverse interpretations of the Chinese and British conduct. So we are sorely wronged people at the moment, experiencing great difficulty in communicating our position because we are simply not in the show. Moreover, this relegation of Hongkong to the sidelines has led to a lack of understanding between all three parties: China, Britain and Hongkong. That is very apparent in the democracy issue.

In some ways, we in Hongkong have a clearer understanding of China's motives than those of the British. It is clear to us that China can see the positive economic value of Hongkong. We do business with them to the tune of $40bn a year—we take 40 per cent of their exports, we provide them with two-thirds of their foreign investment, we employ 25m of their people. No landlord ever had a tenant paying that kind of rent.

It is depressing for Hongkong to think that its future may in some way depend on an internal struggle about the succession of Mrs Thatcher, or assessment of electoral benefits to be gained from articulating prejudice. It is a tragedy that the future of an economy, whose enterprise and vigour puts Britain to shame, may be determined by manoeuvres aimed at winning short-term political advantage.

Hongkong boasts an historic growth rate over the last 20 years in excess of 8 per cent compounded. Given Hongkong's success record and its direct access to one of the world's largest emerging markets, the 1984 Declaration between Britain and China should be the commercial deal of the century. Hongkong nurtures talent. Its health and education records are outstanding —life expectancy in Hongkong is two years longer than in Britain or the United States. It is clear that Hongkong can be one of the world's great economic powers. After 1997, as the engine-room driving the economy of the world's largest emerging market, its capacity for growth and prosperity should be unlimited. If it remains the focus of China's trade then there can be no doubt that it could become the economic hub of Asia.

It is depressing that in this environment we are watching the outflow of Hongkong's greatest asset—and Hongkong really only has one asset—its people. They are leaving because of present uncertainty, and because they want to get passports to give them the confidence to stay. So far, in order to get those passports they have been forced to relocate and spend perhaps three years or more in the host country offering passports. Usually they do not return and, even if they do, uncertainty is compounded by the fact of their leaving—at precisely the time when they are needed.

Let me stress once more that people do not leave Hongkong because they wish to live in another country. They move to acquire foreign residential qualification because, whatever their hopes and expectations, they have anxieties about what may happen after 1997. Events in Eastern Europe suggest we should not be fixed in our assessment of the nature of any Communist government in seven years. But one cannot be surprised that parents, middle managers, skilled young people and other key individuals want an insurance policy.

Emigration today is Hongkong's biggest problem. And it is an immediate problem: 19,000 people left the colony in 1986; 30,000 in 1987; 45,000 in 1988; and 55,000 are expected to leave this year. This rate of emigration feeds on itself—the more people leave, the more the process accelerates. Nobody likes to be the last. It is necessary to stop the haemorrhaging now. It is not much good theorising about the potential beyond 1997 if the economy is shot to pieces before we get there.

Hongkong's main concern is for the departure of professional, technical and managerial staff. Many are between 22 and 40. Most are degree-holders—they are essentially tomorrow's managers.

Let no one imagine that they want to move to Chingford, Thurrock or any of the other bastions of opposition to the British Nationality (Hongkong) Bill. Their desire and their determination is to remain in Hongkong. None of the 200 senior managers of my company who have foreign passports are leaving Hongkong. It is the 280 who do not hold that insurance policy who have applied to Canada, Singapore, Australia or the United States. This is not because they wish to live there, but because only by physically moving can they secure the right to an escape-hatch if things go wrong after 1997.

It will be encouraging if France, West Germany, Belgium and Luxembourg help provide 'passports to stay'. Singapore has already introduced such a scheme. It is desirable that other European Community and Commonwealth countries do all they can to help. There is a measure before the American Congress which would raise the immigrant quota from Hongkong to 20,000 per annum, and allow beneficiaries to defer settlement until 2002—time enough to take up the 'insurance policy' or, more likely, to regain confidence in the Territory's future and let that policy lapse.

But Britain is, and Britain remains, the key to the international equation. Not only is Britain Hongkong's colonial parent. Not only are its people British subjects, who fought for Britain in two world wars—and indeed in the Falklands. But Britain has a solemn, legal obligation under the Joint Declaration to 'maintain and preserve' the 'economic prosperity and social stability' of Hongkong until 30 June 1997.

It is to Mrs Thatcher's great credit that she has never questioned that obligation. In 1984 the people of Britain gave the people of Hongkong their word. Now is the time to honour it. It has been claimed that the provision of 50,000 passports is elitist. That might be arguable if this legislation sought—as Australia's and Canada's immigration policy unashamedly seeks—to poach the best and the brightest immigrant talent.

But the British Nationality (Hongkong) Bill is not an immigration policy. It is its precise opposite: an anti-emigration policy. It is designed to reinforce Hongkong's role as the economic star of the East. It is directed principally to Hongkong's future. But that is materially as well as morally important to Britain because billions of pounds' worth of British investment is tied up in the future of Hongkong. It is open to only one 'principled' objection: the number of passports on offer is not sufficient and should be increased to improve the chances of this anti-emigration policy working.

I have spoken of the resilience of the people of Hongkong, of how they have survived stock-market crashes, typhoons and enemy occupation. Would Hongkong survive the crisis of confidence that would follow if Britain—through no fault of Mrs Thatcher's or her government—ended up reneging on its obligations under the Joint Declaration? I have no doubt that it would. The people of Hongkong would battle back, as they have before, as they will again. But what a terrible legacy it would be to a community admired internationally for its drive and tenacity—a

community which has always loyally fought Britain's corner. What a sordid end to the closing chapter of the British Empire. It would represent—in the words of a recent *Sunday Times* editorial —'A colonial trust betrayed'.

I am an optimist about the future. Our group is investing $40bn in Hongkong over the next five years. Other companies have made similar commitments. I was in China recently and I see no reason to alter that view. I think the months ahead will be quieter. There will be a process of convergence through to 1997 rather than a sudden event on 30 June 1997—what is now called 'the through-train'.

But confidence is a delicate flower. It is not often outside wartime that one society, in this case Britain, has as much potential to affect a very different society, in this case Hongkong, for good or ill. Our communities have had a long and fruitful association. Hongkong has a legal system based on English common law. Its government is run on British lines, English is the official language. Its educational system is based on that of Britain. Its flag contains the Union Jack. The Queen's head appears on Hongkong stamps and coins.

If we can only get people to stay in Hongkong, to take advantage of the opportunities to grow and prosper, Britain will reap great benefits. It will be good for the West, good for Hongkong, and good for China. If, on the other hand, this country is perceived to be the society responsible for wrecking Hongkong's economy, for triggering a crisis of confidence, there will be great bitterness towards Britain.

Recently I was in China for the brilliantly successful launching of a space satellite. The satellite is owned jointly by British, Hongkong and Chinese interests. It will have the capacity to offer sophisticated communications to a market place of 2,5bn people. I can think of nothing more symbolic of what the future holds for Britain, China and Hongkong in Asia—if we take the right steps to secure Hongkong's future.

SIMON MURRAY

[1] See Keith Colquhoun's Note of the month, 'Hongkong—the despair and the hope', in the April 1990 issue of *The World Today*.

Article 10.1.   Reforming the Nonreforming Regimes

The author focuses on the future of five remaining hard-line communist states—Cuba, China, Vietnam, North Korea, and Albania—each of which is headed by a powerful political elite firmly committed to Marxist-Leninist philosophy and the suppression of democratic rights. Despite declining Soviet support for Cuba and Vietnam, for example, these governments came about as a result of internal wars waged by indigenous forces, which make them considerably different from the Soviet-imposed governments of Eastern Europe and, as such, more resistant to change. In the case of China, it is clear that the present government will do whatever is necessary to retain power. As for Albania and North Korea, they have been the most resistant to democratic pressures, owing to the veil of self-isolation between their peoples and the rest of the world. The author describes a possible U.S. strategy for promoting democratic reform in these countries, which is based on employing instruments of communications technology to penetrate these societies.

Reforming the Nonreforming Regimes

The ultimate impetus for political transformation will arise from within oppressed societies.

Robert L. Pfaltzgraff, Jr.

Robert L. Pfaltzgraff, Jr., is president of the Institute for Foreign Policy Analysis and Shelby Cullom Davis Professor of International Security Studies at the Fletcher School of Law and Diplomacy at Tufts University.

The remarkable revolution of 1989 swept away nearly all communist systems in Central Europe, only bypassing Albania, followed in February 1990 by the electoral defeat of the Sandinistas in Nicaragua. What remains is a group of disparate communist states including Cuba, China, Vietnam, North Korea, and Albania. These countries share the common fate of having governments based on political elites espousing Marxist-Leninist principles and imposing on their peoples a repressive political and economic system. As such, they appear increasingly to be anachronisms —out of step with the dramatic changes that are sweeping regions extending from the Western Hemisphere to Europe and the Asia-Pacific area.

Once seen as a vanguard of Soviet power posing a threat to U.S. interests in its own front yard, Fidel Castro's Cuba now seems more a relic of a failed political-economic experiment than a model for revolutionary change. China's domestic retreat back toward the communist political orthodoxy of its early decades in the aftermath of the Tiananmen Square massacre has served only to point up the widening gap separating its present leadership and nearly all other states of the Pacific Rim. Clearly, the rising tide represented by the revolutionary forces that have altered the international landscape from Managua to Bucharest has had an unequal impact on communist structures around the world.

Those communist regimes in Europe that have been replaced by democratic forces pressing for political pluralism and market economies shared the common fate of having been occupied by the Soviet Union and its communist cadres as a result of World War II. Once Mikhail Gorbachev made clear that Moscow was no longer able or willing to make Soviet military forces available to keep them in power—as had his predecessors in the case of Hungary in 1956 and Czechoslovakia in 1968—they fell like a house of cards. In retrospect, all these regimes lacked the political legitimacy, or popular acceptability, conferred by truly free elections providing periodic tests of accountability for their leaders.

Moreover, it had proven increasingly difficult over time to isolate the peoples of Eastern Europe behind the Iron Curtain that had been erected as a barrier to what the ruling communist elites regarded as political contamination from the outside world. By the time the East German communist regime fell in late 1989, nearly all East Germans had been able for years to receive West German television broadcasts. As a result, they had undoubtedly been exposed visually to West German political figures more constantly than to their own government elites and been shown by vivid contrast the drabness of their own existence. The pace of contacts from the West elsewhere in Central Europe had quickened as well as a result of the growing impact of information and communication technologies.

An assessment of those factors that appear decisively to have contributed to the fall of communist regimes in recent months is a necessary prerequisite to developing U.S. policy toward residual Marxist–Leninist-style states whose political systems, it is hoped, will be similarly transformed.

To the extent that the United States had a coherent and constant strategy, it was that of containment, whose purpose was to thwart the expansion of communism, whether directed from Moscow itself or through intermediaries such as Cuba. In the final analysis, it was a combination of factors, including (1) the dramatic contrasts between the vibrant societies of the West shielded by the military capabilities of the United States and its allies, together with (2) the patent economic failures of the Soviet Union, which led to a growing disillusionment with communism on a global scale, and (3) a new Soviet strategy, adopted by Gorbachev, that set in motion the events leading to the collapse of communist systems.

It would be logical to expect empires first to crumble at their periphery and only subsequently at the core as they reach the limits of their expansive capacity. Such is the pattern of imperial structures from the ancient world to the recent past. In this respect, the revolutionary changes in Central Europe stand in sharp contrast, for the communist empire has crumbled at or near its central point. By the same token, it is unlikely that communist systems, having disintegrated in Central Europe, could be sustained long by the Soviet Union at the much greater distance represented by Cuba. It follows that, in the case of Soviet-sponsored states such as Cuba and Vietnam, the willingness or ability of Moscow to support such regimes could be expected to diminish, leading to consequences as dramatic as those in Central Europe.

What is different

What is different about Cuba and Vietnam, however, is that, in contrast to the Soviet-imposed governments of Central Europe, these regimes came into existence as a result of internal wars fought by indigenous forces with Soviet support. Neither Cuba nor Vietnam has relied on Soviet military power to prevent the overthrow of their regime. Therefore, the present life-support system provided by the Soviet Union for client states such as Cuba and Vietnam lies principally in the economic realm. As long as they still possess vast military and internal security forces, such regimes are likely to prove more resistant than were their Central European counterparts to reformist pressures.

Much of this antireformist profile applies to China, to which the Bush administration has made numerous approaches in an effort to mitigate the consequences of the tragic events of Tiananmen Square for Sino-American relations. In contrast to an official U.S. policy providing for minimal contact with Cuba, Vietnam, and North Korea since the early 1970s, the United States had developed a thickening web of bilateral relationships with China. Until the Chinese crackdown in June 1989, the effects of policies toward China pursued by successive administrations had seemed to bear fruit. At a state-to-state level, the United States and China have shared a parallel interest in preventing the extension of Soviet hegemony.

Moreover, the increasing ties between China and the outside world were accompanied the 1980s by a remarkable rise economic growth rates, reac as high as 10 percent an China embraced refor nomic policies that in pecially in the agri tor, market pri thousands of C ent in were permitte while China foreign tr order to accelerate the modernization process. What the leadership of Deng Xiaoping failed to grasp, however, was that economic reform would lead inevitably to pressures for political change that could be prevented only by force of arms.

The lessons of Tiananmen Square clearly lie in the realization that, as long as it is both possible and necessary, the Chinese leadership will employ whatever means are deemed essential to assure that it remains in power. Chinese "sticks," in the form of repression against its recalcitrant population, will be far more important to the political elite's perceived need to assure that it remains in power than will be the proffered "carrots" of outside governments, including the United States. Indeed, the lack of responsiveness and increased obduracy of the Beijing authorities to the overtures of the Bush administration has seemed to grow in direct proportion to the demise of communist regimes elsewhere.

Without the action taken in ananmen Square, it must be soned in Beijing, the Chinese ership might have suffered me fate as Nicolae Ceauşes- Romania. Far from being st hurrah" of a ruling racy, China's antirefor- ies are those of a gov- hose premier, Li Peng, ars old. The Politburo r relatively young Deputy Premier the party head, ho strongly op- licies. Hence, it re to suggest assing of the r in a new purred by a adership. will d f 1989 ina's in

their power to prevent reform in the years ahead, having seen the consequences of such change in other socialist states.

Among the policies to be pursued for this purpose will be a marked reduction of contacts between the Chinese people and the outside world, especially students sent abroad for education. Those communist states—namely Albania and North Korea—that have been most immune to the tides of reform have been most successful in imposing a largely impermeable veil of self-isolation between their peoples and the outside world. To an extent unequaled elsewhere, both regimes have succeeded in maintaining a monopoly on sources of information and news. Both are largely untouched by the reformist forces that have swept other states.

Although Seoul, the dynamic capital of South Korea, with its rapidly growing economy based on high-tech industries and an increasingly open, pluralistic political system, lies geographically close to the Demilitarized Zone (DMZ) separating the two Koreas, otherwise it is light years away from the hermetically sealed dictatorship of the aging Kim Il Sung.

A U.S. strategy

Can one derive the elements of a strategy for the United States to pursue from a comparative survey of the remaining antireformist states? More fundamentally, to the extent that such regimes stand in isolation from the outside world, posing little or no threat to their neighbors, should the energies of the United States be directed toward effecting change of the magnitude seen elsewhere?

Whatever their common features, the importance to the

United States of these regimes differs. To the extent that their ability—by themselves or at the behest of the Soviet Union—to threaten vital interests of the United States has diminished, it follows that their importance to U.S. security has lessened. As such regimes become isolated from their outside base of support, their future rests inevitably on the durability of their military and internal security apparatus. Most vulnerable in this respect, it would appear, is Cuba. Castro's tangible links with Moscow may continue to weaken as Soviet priorities shift elsewhere, and he faces a population that has never been effectively isolated from the outside world. Whatever the impact of Radio and TV Marti and other such efforts, they are likely to be resisted by the Cuban government, with its still formidable military forces and internal security apparatus.

The proper focus of U.S. strategy lies in the consolidation of those vast changes that have destroyed repressive regimes at the core of the erstwhile Soviet empire—in Central Europe—rather than the diversion of major resources to the remaining communist states whose economic and political future appears to be bleak. Nevertheless, if only as a basis for allocating limited resources among greater or lesser priorities, the United States must develop a strategy toward nonreformist communist states.

The broad elements of such a strategy are to be found in an approach that includes an acceleration of the flow of information about the outside world from Cuba to East Asia and provides other support, to the extent politically feasible, for those reformist elements that exist in such countries.

In the case of China, the United States faces the difficult

task of maintaining correct state-to-state relations with a government that will probably become increasingly unpopular both at home and abroad. On the one hand, the United States has an enduring stake in a multilateral power balance that includes China, both in the Asia-Pacific area and at a global level. On the other hand, it faces a China whose domestic policies clearly do not accord with American values and whose foreign policy contains important elements—for example, the proliferation of missiles—that run counter to U.S. interests. This argues for a highly restrictive policy of U.S. technology transfers, combined with a greater effort to diminish the isolation of China's people from knowledge of the forces transforming the outside world.

In the four decades since the outbreak of the Korean War in 1950, North Korea has continued to pose a threat to the stability of the Korean peninsula. Periodic efforts on the part of South Korea to take steps toward reunification, dating from the early 1970s, have foundered. Meanwhile, North Korea has acquired its own armaments production capability as part of a persistent military buildup designed to provide the means to strike across the DMZ. Reportedly, North Korea is in the process of becoming a nuclear power. As North Korea obtains such capabilities, Soviet leverage over North Korea is likely to decline, despite the growing interest in the Pacific enunciated by Gorbachev. In this respect, North Korea can be expected to differ from East Germany.

At this time, North Korea combines the characteristics of increasing military independence and a tightly controlled population kept in isolation from the world beyond its largely sealed borders. Hence, compared, for example, even to Cuba, few opportunities are available to encourage its political transformation. The eventual succession of Kim Jong Il, the son of Kim Il Sung, would in all likelihood bring to power an equally repressive leadership. Therefore, the threat posed by North Korea may grow, rather than diminish, in the years ahead.

Such a prospect argues for the preservation of the security relationship between the United States and the Republic of Korea, together with efforts to probe whenever possible the limits of North Korean control of its population.

The world of the 1990s will feature the emergence of regional power centers—states with growing military and technological capabilities, including the means to produce atomic weapons, missile delivery systems, and other capabilities for high-intensity warfare. It is in such a broader context that nonreformist communist states, especially China and North Korea, as well as Cuba and Vietnam, should be considered. To the extent that the ability of Cuba and Vietnam to export military power within their respective regions is lessened, accompanied by a reduction in Soviet support, the threat that they pose to U.S. interests will thereby be diminished.

U.S. strategy toward the communist reform "refuseniks" should be designed as fully as possible to use our instruments of communications technology to penetrate closed societies. In all cases, our interest lies in the promotion of change leading to governments of the kind that have begun to be installed in most Central European countries and Nicaragua. Although the catalyst for such change can be strengthened from outside by policies beyond containment, the ultimate impetus for political transformation will arise from within oppressed societies, as events of recent months have so dramatically shown. As now in Europe and elsewhere, our task will then lie in assisting as fully as possible the formidable task of building political and economic structures capable of providing the freedom of choice sought by so many peoples and yet denied by nonreformist communist regimes.

Although German unification has been achieved, many problems still remain, chief of which are the staggering economic and social costs, which have created an atmosphere of increasing concern. While the merger produced a wave of initial enthusiasm, the Federal Republic now faces a host of domestic obstacles, which may influence Germany's future international position. The Federal Republic must reassess its international role while simultaneously tackling the domestic problems of unification. In the process, it must reevaluate its relationship with the United States; its role in Europe; and its growing ties to the Soviet Union. The question remains what direction German foreign policy will take in the wake of unification, as it struggles to develop a new identity and asserts its new leadership role.

THE ONE GERMANY

by Angela Stent

The division of Germany has ended. But the unification of Germany has only just begun. Between October 1989 and October 1990 what once seemed unattainable became a reality: the swift merger of the two Germanys with active support from the United States and remarkably little resistance from the Soviet Union. German national enthusiasm reached its climax during the first weeks after the opening of the Berlin Wall, as all Germans began to realize the full implications of the collapse of communism. However, by October 3, 1990, the formal reunification date, the harsh economic realities and mounting social costs of the merger were creating a more sober atmosphere across both parts of Germany. As the new German state consolidates itself, many domestic hurdles must be overcome. The way these problems are resolved will fundamentally influence Germany's international role. The Federal Republic of Germany's (FRG) allies—past, present, and future—have begun to see the potential for markedly different relations with the new German state over the next decade.

In 1991, the new Federal Republic must redefine its international role even as it tackles the domestic problems of unification. Germany faces a host of issues: its relationship with its chief ally—until now—the United States; its role in Europe, which will have a major influence on the future of the European Community

(EC); and the balance between these old commitments and its expanding ties to the Soviet Union. But the United States and other countries will also help shape Germany's new direction, giving it guidance as it reenters the international community as a fully sovereign member. Questions about Germany's evolving world role abound. Will Germany be willing and able to accept the new political responsibilities that come with economic might? Should Germany's partners encourage Germany to assume a more assertive world role? What stake will the new Germany have in a viable Soviet Union?

Understanding the problems Germany faces in the new decade demands first an examination of the past. Central to a look back is the question of what Germany's division achieved from the perspectives of the main protagonists: the United States, the Soviet Union, and the two German states. The division of Germany represents a classic example of muddling through and improvisation. The United States and the Soviet Union shared one goal in 1945: to prevent Germany from ever again threatening the world militarily. They disagreed, however, on how to achieve this goal.

From the U.S. standpoint, the division of Germany into occupation zones agreed at Yalta and Potsdam was intended as a temporary measure until a more satisfactory solution could be found. No master plan existed for creating a strong West Germany that would eventually become a major strategic asset to America. The deteriorating economic situation in the western

ANGELA STENT, *associate professor of government at Georgetown University, is writing a book on Soviet policy toward Europe.*

zones of Germany, the need for a coherent set of institutions to administer the economy, and the realization that the USSR would not accept this enterprise led to the unification of the American, British, and later French zones. As Soviet policy grew ever more confrontational, the United States became increasingly concerned about preventing further Soviet expansion. Only after the creation of the Federal Republic in 1949 and the consolidation of the U.S. policy of containing the Soviet Union did American views begin to anticipate a future West Germany as a bulwark against Soviet power.

Moscow, like Washington, initially was ambivalent about Germany's future role and had no blueprint. Soviet leader Joseph Stalin expected significant reparations from the western zones of Germany—which he never received—and believed that total Soviet control had to be imposed in his zone to guarantee German loyalty. He feared the establishment of a unified, pro-Western German state; hence his blockade of Berlin in 1948–49. Although Stalin did offer the West a united, neutral Germany in 1952, this proposal sought to prevent West Germany's entry into NATO rather than to create a single state in good faith. Only after Stalin's death did the USSR, like the United States, begin to view "its" Germany as a major political and strategic asset.

The psychological impact of uniting the two Germanys will be considerably greater than statistics suggest.

Neither the United States nor the Soviet Union, therefore, had a clear idea of what the two German states would become when they were created. Washington believed it was imperative to create a democratic, prosperous West Germany within a democratic Western Europe, ensuring it would remain peaceful; Moscow saw its first priority as taking what was left of East German industry and destroying its remaining democratic political forces. Subjugation would guarantee a compliant Germany. The two German states were objects of U.S., British, French, and Soviet policy rather than active participants in the post–World War II order.

Yet the division of Germany did more to support U.S. strategy in Europe than initially anticipated. Perceptions of Germany changed as the product of both the FRG's rapid development

into a democracy with a thriving market economy under Chancellor Konrad Adenauer and the changing international situation. A number of factors altered American perceptions: the founding of NATO in 1949, the outbreak of the Korean war in 1950, the creation of the European Coal and Steel Community in 1951, and then French Foreign Minister Robert Schuman's vision of European unity with a Franco-German axis at its core. Although the United States probably would have accepted German unity if the Soviet Union had agreed to any of the various Western proposals of the 1950s, Washington welcomed the establishment of a strong, pluralistic West German state. By the late 1960s, West Germany had become America's most important NATO partner. The need to guarantee the FRG's security vis-à-vis the Soviet Union became the principal rationale for a continued U.S. military and political presence on the Continent.

For the Soviet Union, the results of Germany's division were more mixed. Unlike U.S. policy toward Germany, which ignored the German Democratic Republic (GDR), Soviet policy was aimed at both Germanys. Moscow actively tried to stabilize the GDR and weaken the FRG's ties with the West.

Until 1961 East Germany took priority. After suppressing the 1953 uprising there, the Kremlin strengthened its commitment to the loyal but unpopular Stalinist Walter Ulbricht. The presence of Soviet troops supported the GDR government as it consolidated control and achieved what was regarded as its own "economic miracle." The construction of the Berlin Wall in 1961 finally stabilized the regime by effectively imprisoning the population. The GDR emerged as the Soviet Union's most important trading partner, and its army as a pillar of the Warsaw Pact. By 1969, East Germany had become a critical security asset for the Kremlin.

Soviet achievements toward the FRG proved rather meager in the 1950s and 1960s. The Kremlin failed to prevent the FRG from joining NATO. West Germany's refusal to recognize East Germany—or indeed any other East European country—along with its close ties to the United States were the major impediments to improved Moscow-Bonn relations. The division of Germany remained a major Soviet objective as long as the FRG remained a revisionist power refusing to recognize the postwar status quo. Ironically, the timing of Nikita Khrushchev's ouster as Soviet leader in October 1964 was dictated by his forthcoming visit to the FRG. He was accused, after his fall, of trying to "sell out" East Germany to West Germany. Said one of his opponents, then Soviet Presidium member Mikhail Suslov, close Soviet-GDR relations "are not for sale, even if all the gold in the world were offered for them."

During this era of reconstruction, the two Germanys developed very different stakes in the division. Amid occupation and the loss of sovereignty, Adenauer's Federal Republic maintained a constitutional commitment to reunification. This commitment, however, could not obscure the fact that West Germany benefited politically and economically from Germany's division. The chancellor himself, a Catholic Rhinelander, showed less interest in unification than in ties with the EC and especially with France. The opposition Social Democrats, initially the party of reunification, changed their position in 1960 as the issue lost domestic poignancy.

The GDR, by contrast, fared much worse from the separation. It lost much of its industry to the Soviet Union during the late Stalin years, and millions of its population fled to West Germany before the completion of the Berlin Wall. Arguably, the small elite around Ulbricht prospered, but the East Germans did significantly less well than their Western cousins. After 1961, East Germans were often said to be living in a "niche" society, making individual peace with their existential predicament. The events of 1989 revealed just how fragile and unsatisfying those niches were.

Détente and the Germanys

Détente changed both inter-German relations and the attitudes of the superpowers toward their respective German allies. New risks were suddenly introduced into the delicate German balance. The division of Germany became less total, the Berlin Wall more porous. The United States and the Soviet Union began to experience new frictions with the two Germanys as the FRG and the GDR normalized diplomatic relations and developed their own inter-German dialogue. Both superpowers and the two German states accepted the status quo of the division of Germany. Yet even though détente initially reinforced the separation of the two states, it ultimately led to unification because it undermined the East German system.

Adenauer was critical of President John Kennedy's tentative moves toward détente with the USSR after the Cuban Missile Crisis of 1962. But a decade later, the tables were reversed. In the 1970s American policymakers were worried that Moscow would play its "German card" and entice the FRG away from NATO with promises of closer inter-German ties. The United States grew uneasy about the pace of then Chancellor Willy Brandt's Ostpolitik—his policy of rapprochement with the Soviet Union and Eastern Europe—and his willingness to question the seriousness of the Soviet threat to West Germany. As U.S.-Soviet détente disintegrated at the end of the 1970s, Washington and Bonn openly disagreed over the state of East-West ties, with the FRG insisting on retaining the fruits of its own détente with the Soviets. The litany of U.S.-West German disputes that ensued—the neutron bomb, the Siberian gas pipeline, the deployment of Pershing and nuclear-armed cruise missiles—highlighted the development of FRG foreign-policy interests that were sometimes opposed by the United States.

Despite these new U.S.-FRG tensions, exacerbated by concerns over West Germany's trade surpluses with America, Washington and Bonn were able to hold on to the core of the relationship. Until shortly after the Wall fell, the United States saw no reason to question the centrality of its alliance with the Federal Republic, which justified and made possible its large, ongoing military presence in Europe.

The Soviet Union, by contrast, found it increasingly difficult to choreograph the triangular relationship between Bonn, East Berlin, and Moscow in the 1970s and 1980s. Ultimately, but too late, the Soviets realized that what had improved its ties to West Germany threatened its interests in East Germany. The Kremlin did not foresee the corrosive effect inter-German rapprochement would have on East German society. Détente between the two Germanys undermined whatever legitimacy the GDR system had by ending its international isolation, increasing contacts between the two populations, and bringing scenes of freedom and prosperity from West German television into East German homes.

The GDR remained an asset to the Soviets in foreign-policy terms until recently through its support of Soviet activities in Africa, the Middle East, and Latin America. East Germany also remained a loyal member of the Soviet bloc. However, as U.S.-Soviet relations hit a low point in the mid-1980s, the thinly disguised polemics between East Berlin and Moscow over the need to maintain inter-German détente signaled the end of GDR compliance. The Soviets finally succeeded in forcing party leader Erich

Honecker to cancel a scheduled trip to Bonn in 1984. But after 1985 the GDR became highly critical of changes in Soviet policy, with Honecker reproaching Moscow for straying from the true socialist path.

The GDR continued to be the Soviet Union's leading trading partner and its top supplier of advanced technology. However, the relationship increasingly drained Soviet energy resources as the USSR supplied cheap, soft-currency oil to the GDR and its other East European dependents, thereby forfeiting potential hard currency earnings. By 1985 it was debatable whether the GDR represented a net economic asset to the Soviet Union.

Mikhail Gorbachev already knew that the old-style socialist system was finished when he decided to stop propping up the increasingly vituperative Honecker amid antigovernment protests in 1989. However, until shortly before the first free East German elections in March 1990 the Soviets expected the continuation of two German states, one capitalist and one reformed communist. Gorbachev did not appreciate the extent of the GDR economy's weakness, nor how rapidly the East Germans would demand unification as their only hope for material salvation.

Over the two decades before unification, Soviet ties with the FRG improved but then deteriorated during the latter years of Leonid Brezhnev and the pre-Gorbachev interregnum. Soviet–West German ties ultimately proved more durable than Soviet–East German relations despite Moscow's failure to weaken the Federal Republic's ties with NATO. The economic hopes pinned to enhanced relations with West Germany never materialized because the Germans remained skeptical about potential economic and political payoffs. Nevertheless, when Gorbachev resumed cordial relations with Bonn in 1987, the favorable experience of *Ostpolitik*, as practiced by such German statesmen as Chancellors Willy Brandt and Helmut Schmidt and Foreign Minister Hans-Dietrich Genscher, was able to ensure a receptive response by the West German government and public.

At the beginning, West Germany's détente with the Soviet Union carried no great expectations. Brandt's *Ostpolitik* even reflected a sense of resignation. He accepted the postwar status quo and recognized East Germany. He also realized the revisionist *Ostpolitik* practiced by previous governments had failed to change the status quo. As Brandt explained in his memoirs, *People and Politics: The Years 1960–1975*:

I was well aware that, throughout its phases of historical development, Germany had never entirely corresponded to the "classic nation-state" . . . . I nevertheless remained convinced that the nation would live on. . . . Germany had always existed as a cultural nation, and it was as a "cultural nation" that it would retain its identity.

Through its rapprochement with the Soviet Union and Eastern Europe, the FRG rehabilitated itself internationally. West Germany's growing economic and political strength enabled it to play a key role in the Conference on Security and Cooperation in Europe (CSCE) process and to become a major force in East-West relations. *Ostpolitik* ultimately paid off, inasmuch as relations between the two German states radically improved after 1969.

After Brandt's resignation in 1974, the FRG engaged in a constant balancing act between its *West-* and *Ostpolitik*. West Germans depended on the United States for security, but on the Soviet Union for continued inter-German rapprochement. Tense U.S.-Soviet relations presented Bonn with unwelcome choices, though it ultimately accepted the major U.S. policy decisions. Generally content with its role as a major economic and political player in Europe, the FRG wanted no significant responsibilities outside Europe and consigned its ultimate defense to the United States.

Despite official West German commitment to unification and pursuit of closer ties with the GDR, the German political establishment did not believe unification would occur for decades. In 1988 Chancellor Helmut Kohl was asked, "Will you yourself experience unification?" He replied, "No, probably I will not live to see it." Indeed, before the Wall's breakdown—and even for some time afterward—few members of the political establishment seriously desired unification. The inter-German relationship—essentially East German humanitarian concessions in return for West German economic largesse—had seemingly stabilized the GDR and reinforced its separateness. West Germany had achieved an acceptable modus vivendi with the GDR regime that amounted to the management of partition.

In the early détente era, the GDR benefited internationally from the belated diplomatic recognition it secured from the FRG in 1972. East Germany's international stature and activities grew. However, increased international legitimacy did not translate into greater domestic legitimacy. Honecker's policy of *Abgrenzung*—insulating East German society from the perni-

131

cious effects of close contact with West Germany—failed miserably. Despite Honecker's increasing contempt for Gorbachev, he understood that Soviet troops were all that stood between the GDR leadership and political oblivion. But even as he grew increasingly out of touch with domestic realities, he must have calculated that the GDR was the linchpin of the Soviet security glacis in Europe. Thus, Honecker must have believed he could blackmail Moscow into preserving his power because without him communism in East Germany would disappear. Such thinking proved to be a fatal miscalculation.

The Soviet Union, facing a domestic economic crisis and widespread ethnic tensions, simply could not afford to underwrite the East German system. The division of Germany for which the Soviet Union had worked so hard no longer enhanced Soviet security. The GDR proved too expensive and rested on shaky political foundations. The 40-year-old edifice of the "first workers' and peasants' state on German soil" crumbled within two months. Its reason for a separate existence extinguished, the GDR quickly became extinct. Thus the Soviet Union ultimately helped create what had always been depicted as its worst postwar nightmare—a united, capitalist Germany in NATO.

The New Nationalism

What direction will German foreign policy take now that Germany is united and sovereign? The Kohl government has reassured the world that unification merely adds 16 million Germans and five new states to the Federal Republic and thus will have a limited impact on future policies. Some, however, both inside and outside Germany, worry aloud that unification will encourage the resurgence of historical ambitions and aggression that were only contained by division. Between these two extremes, some observers argue that Germany can adopt a new, responsible leadership role, though only through considerable effort. The new German challenge comprises four aspects: domestic post-unification developments and their impact on foreign policy; German-Soviet relations; Germany's role in the EC; and German-U.S. relations.

Although the GDR included one-third of prewar German territory and had only 16 million inhabitants, numbers alone offer a misleading view of unification. The psychological impact of uniting the two Germanys will be considerably greater than statistics suggest. For the first time

in 45 years, Germany is not an occupied country and has finally paid for its role in World War II. How will the new German national identity evolve, now that Germany is one again? The evidence from the Federal Republic is encouraging. Citizens there have internalized democratic, nonviolent, even antimilitarist, values. Those who fear a resurgent German militarism should remember that in the first half of the 1980s the United States was primarily concerned with an excess of pacifism and antinuclear sentiment in Germany. If the experience of postwar West Germany is any guide, the new German nationalism will not be aggressive, but rather directed toward peaceful, all-European goals. Certainly, all the treaties signed during unification stress Germany's historical responsibilities and its future peaceful world role.

The East German contribution to the new national identity is less certain. Before 1990 East Germans had an incomplete national consciousness. They never believed in a separate socialist German identity but they were also not West Germans. Instead, their local regions provided their sense of *Heimat*, or homeland. Therefore, East Germans have yet to develop a viable German identity. Moreover, East Germans possess a pronounced inferiority complex vis-à-vis their West German cousins, further complicating the process of integration. The East Germans face the challenge of developing a national identity that will assure they are fully integrated into the new Germany and are not second-class citizens. The overriding goal of the 1989 revolution was to oust the repressive government so the people could lead normal lives. Supporters of the overthrow did not seek to reestablish a mighty German state. Since the liberation from communism, right-wing, antiforeigner, anti-Semitic, and militaristic groups have formed in East Germany as they have in all East European countries; but their numbers remain small and the groups are unlikely to find much support in a united Germany unless a worldwide recession has a major impact on the German economy.

The economic problems of unification complicate the process of political integration. No one knows how much unification will cost; speculation puts the price at far more than anyone had originally envisioned: more than DM 775 billion (more than $500 billion). Unemployment is rising in the eastern part of Germany. The social dislocations are also considerable. Hard questions will persist in both parts of Germany about why unification had to happen so fast and whether it had to be so disruptive. But given

Germany's inherent economic strength, it will eventually overcome the current problems and expand its economic influence in both parts of Europe.

The addition of the GDR to the FRG should not, in the near future, have much direct impact on German foreign policy. West German policymakers will continue to make Germany's foreign policy, and East German leaders will have little influence on the new Germany's international posture. Moreover, foreign policy did not occupy an important place in the East German population's political consciousness. GDR foreign policy concentrated on supporting Soviet activities in the Warsaw Pact and the Third World. These policies tied East Germany to some of the least appealing regimes, and did not represent a major source of pride to East Germans. In fact, most East Germans are generally opposed to an activist German foreign policy, particularly if it involves military force.

Ultimately, the way Germans view their new world role will depend on how they come to terms with the past. The West Germans have, to a large extent, acknowledged and condemned their Nazi past. The acrimonious *Historikerstreit*—the debate in the FRG in 1985–88 over whether, among other things, the enormity of Stalin's crimes somehow diminishes the uniqueness and horror of Nazism—revealed how controversial some questions remain. But at least there has been debate. The East Germans have not fully examined or accepted their past; instead they were taught that West Germany was the sole inheritor of the Nazi state. Indeed, East Germans must grapple with two pasts: Nazi and communist. They must face these legacies simultaneously as they integrate into West Germany. They may be tempted to claim they were victims, placing all the blame on Hitler, Stalin, Ulbricht, and Honecker. But East Germans' refusal to acknowledge shared responsibility for these two dark pasts would not bode well for their future attitudes toward the outside world.

East Germans possess a pronounced inferiority complex vis-à-vis their West German cousins, further complicating the process of integration.

German-Soviet relations will be another key determinant of the new Germany's world view. Traditionally, Russia and Germany have carried on a love-hate relationship. From Peter the Great's invitation to Germans and other Europeans to build up Russia's economy and the nineteenth century rise to political prominence of the Baltic Germans to the Rapallo Treaty of 1922 and the Nazi-Soviet Pact of 1939, Germans and Russians have both admired and feared each other. Their common bonds run deep and, in modern history, periods of amity have outnumbered periods of enmity. Prussians in particular have always believed that their destiny was entwined with Russia's, though Western-oriented Germans like Adenauer and Kohl more often looked across the Rhine rather than the Elbe—until Kohl had the imperative of unification thrust on him. The Cold War therefore represents an aberration rather than the norm in a shared Russo-German destiny.

There are a variety of opinions in the Soviet Union on that country's future relationship with Germany. Some Soviets in recent months have reiterated a traditional theme: A new Rapallo represents the ideal vision of the future, a special Soviet-German relationship of mutual interest with Germany unfettered by entangling alliances. Key discussions about unification were consciously held in places with historical resonance: Brest (formerly Brest-Litovsk), Münster, and Moscow itself, where the Treaty on the Final Settlement with Respect to Germany was initialed in September 1990. When the Rapallo pact was completed, the Soviets and Germans were international outcasts. The secret military collaboration that preceded the treaty represented the only way Germany could rearm. In the 1990s some Soviets might well dream of a new Rapallo with Germany, but such an agreement would hold little attraction for the Germans. Germany will have no interest in exchanging its role in Europe and the Western alliance for an exclusive pact with the Soviets.

Nonetheless, Germany will play an important role in the Soviet Union's evolution in the foreseeable future. Both countries are counting on this influence. The USSR would like to restore the Russo-German economic relationship to its pre-1914 position. Germany traditionally acted as Russia's most important trading partner, with bilateral trade being largely complementary. Germany always provided more economically to Russia than vice versa. In 1913, for instance, 47 per cent of Russian imports were from Germany while Russian exports to Germany were 29 per cent of Russian exports. In 1989, the two Germanys together were the USSR's largest trading partner. In the near term, it is in Germany's interest to give considerable economic assistance to Moscow in order to stabilize Gorbachev's beleaguered government and ensure that the 380,000 Soviet troops withdraw from Germany without incident there or disruption in the USSR. The FRG has already agreed to pay the Soviets DM 12 billion (about $8 billion) to support, repatriate, and retrain Soviet soldiers. This sum will grow in the future. In the longer run, through trade and eventually direct investments, Germany will enlarge its economic presence in the Soviet Union. Yet Germany cannot save the Soviet economy; and if the Soviets' ambitious program for a transition to a market economy fails, all the German capital and expertise in the world will not be able to keep the Soviet economy afloat indefinitely.

If the Soviet economy does recover sufficiently, the USSR might well develop a relationship of economic dependence on Germany. This arrangement would suit Germany well, provided the FRG receives economic and perhaps political compensation. The economic payoffs might involve privileged access to Soviet raw materials. The political payoffs might come through cooperation with the Soviets in a refurbished all-European security arrangement that would remove any future Soviet threat to Germany.

The loss of East Germany might at first seem a damaging blow to Soviet security. But in the long run the USSR may benefit from German unification once it has redefined its security interests. Since the ring of loyal, communist buffer states no longer exists and Germany has no aggressive designs on the Soviet Union, Moscow is beginning to redefine security in terms of a multilateral all-European system. The Soviet Union sees Germany as its entree to Western Europe, both politically and economically. The Soviets hope to collaborate with Germans to institutionalize a security system that will eventually make NATO, like the Warsaw Pact, obsolete, thereby eliminating the growing asymmetry between a moribund Eastern pact and a healthy, though restless, Western alliance.

Germany's relationship with the USSR will also include cooperative arrangements for Eastern Europe. As Moscow struggles to find its way out of communism, it is losing the ability to exercise influence over the countries of its former empire. Indeed, Germany is poised to become the most important power in Eastern Europe. It will most likely be a major force in reconstructing Eastern Europe once the unification process is finished. But stabilizing these countries is also in the Soviet interest. However, what kind of role the USSR will be willing or able to play in Eastern Europe in the future remains unclear.

These scenarios are premised on the continued existence of the Soviet Union. The Germans, like most others outside the Soviet Union, want Gorbachev to remain in power and successfully complete his agenda. To this end, they will do everything possible to support his government. But ethnic, regional, and political fissures are widening within the Soviet Union, and Germans may be faced with a prospect that they fear: serious instability in the western regions of the USSR. Germany could work effectively with a future independent Russian Republic under the leadership of Boris Yeltsin, for example. But Germany would have difficulty coping with demands from ethnic Germans in the Soviet Union or Poland, or indeed with demands from independent Baltic states or the Ukraine if the USSR breaks up. Neither the Germans nor any other major power would welcome a reopening of sensitive questions involving ethnic German minorities and the boundaries of Central Europe.

The New German Identity

Once unification is successfully completed, Germany is poised to become the premier power in Europe—Eastern and Western. However, members of the EC are increasingly concerned that the preoccupation with the unification process and the added burdens of the Soviet Union and Eastern Europe may dilute Germany's enthusiasm for European integration. Until now, Germany has been an engine of integration. Before the revolutions of 1989, the single European market of 1992 was the major West European concern. Now the issue has faded from the public eye, partly because the demise of communism and the return of German unity have gripped attention. But the EC, and Germany's role in that organization, will significantly shape the new German identity. The addition of East Germany complicates the process because East Germans, unlike West Germans, lack a European consciousness. They remain more provincial and unaccustomed to being part of the EC. European integration will receive less domestic support in Germany as a whole until the 16 million eastern Germans develop a European identity. Moreover, some Germans may conclude that the economic and political demands of the EC must take second place to those of unification.

The problems and readjustments of unification may reinforce the sense that momentum toward closer European political union is slowing. The Persian Gulf crisis has revealed the difficulties of achieving political cooperation. It seems certain that during the trying process of unification the FRG cannot help but be less involved in Europe and more self-absorbed; this preoccupation may have a long-term effect on developments within the EC, including questions of expansion with new Central European members. The French and others increasingly ask whether Germany will be willing to quickly renounce its newly regained political and economic sovereignty to a supranational European entity.

Of all the basic factors in Germany's future outlook, the relationship with the United States appears to be the most predictable and the strongest. After all, Germany might not yet have been united had it not been for the Bush administration's immediate and unwavering support for unification and its pressure on the USSR to speed up the process. At the very least, the external aspects of unification would not have been so quickly resolved.

But the past 40 years of strong relations furnish no guarantee of future closeness. Unification may ultimately prove detrimental to U.S. security interests—possibly more detrimental than to Soviet interests—unless policymakers redefine U.S. interests. Both sides must devote hard thought to how their relationship might be restructured. The United States will no longer be the chief guarantor of German security in the post–Cold War, post-unification world. Once Soviet troops withdraw from Germany, pressure will grow in Germany (as well as in Washington) to remove most of the American troops. Moreover, as new security structures evolve in Europe, Germans may increasingly question their membership in NATO, particularly if the Social Democratic party were to enter office again. The psychological impact of unification and the restoration of sovereignty remains unknown. But Germans will inevitably reassess their dependence on the United States, formerly an integral part of Bonn's foreign policy. The United States, for its part, will have to rethink its reasons for stationing troops in Europe if the primary military mission and Soviet threat no longer exist.

Since World War II, U.S.-German ties have developed on a variety of levels and the basis for a continuing partnership will persist. But that geopolitical partnership will not continue unaltered in the new era. Reshaping U.S.-German relations will require a conscious effort. Otherwise, Germans may resent what they view as a continuing unequal relationship, and Americans may see the Germans as ungrateful erstwhile allies who turned their backs after Washington worked hard to ensure German unification. As it did in the immediate postwar situation, the United States knows what it does not want Germany to be but is unsure about what it wants Germany to become.

Perhaps the answer is to redirect the focus away from an exclusive U.S.–German relationship and develop a more multilateral American policy toward Western Europe as a whole. Until now, Washington has perceived its relationship with Germany primarily in bilateral terms. Although it encouraged the founding of the EC, partly as a means of anchoring West Germany peacefully in Europe, it has conceived of the U.S.–FRG relationship as the centerpiece of its European policy. This exclusive focus on Germany might prove harmful to U.S.–German relations in the future if the United States becomes disappointed by the lack of immediate tangible response from the Germans in light of the strong U.S. support for unification.

To avoid this possible disillusionment and its negative repercussions for U.S. policy, Washington should modify its policy of focusing separately on each European country and actively support the FRG's continued role in a more integrated Europe, even if that implies a reduced U.S. role. Moreover, as long as NATO is alive and well—and it may well last into the next century in some form—the United States should encourage the Europeanization of the alliance with a less dominant U.S. role.

In general, the most productive way to assist the transformation of U.S.-German relations is to encourage Germany's active membership in multilateral organizations in which the United States also participates. Indeed, both within and without Germany support remains strong for the concept of channeling German ambitions and energies through broader international frameworks. Kohl and Genscher of late have been stressing Germany's commitment to strengthen the CSCE process—and herein lies an opportunity for Washington. There is considerable skepticism in the United States about the CSCE's effectiveness as a security organization; but many East European countries view the CSCE as the most promising future security institution— short of the entire Warsaw Pact joining NATO. The United States should actively contribute to the reorganization of CSCE, which will ensure an important American role on the continent while it strengthens Germany's commitment to Europe. Other multilateral structures may either be created or redesigned, including a West European defense force; but all should serve to integrate Germany in a series of structures designed to assure Europe's peaceful future.

The most basic question is how the new Germany will adapt to its future leadership role. German ability to exercise appropriate, responsible leadership will depend both on domestic developments and on outside guidance. Germany has become an economic giant, but has consciously limited its own political engagements. With the support of other NATO members, the FRG has hidden behind its constitution to justify its unwillingness to project power overseas militarily or politically in cooperation with its allies. But as Kohl and his colleagues have realized in the Gulf crisis, Germany will now have to reconsider those constitutional provisions that prevent its playing a more assertive international role. As in the case of Japan, it is worth pondering whether it is wise to encourage Germany to become a world power again. No casual decision can be made on such an important subject. But realistically, the FRG will have to assume new responsibilities in a world with a considerably weakened Eastern Europe and Soviet Union.

If the past 40 years are any guide, Germany will be able to develop leadership qualities suitable to itself and its neighbors. Germany is surely capable of playing a constructive international political role commensurate with its economic might. The process of reasserting leadership will not be smooth and will require sensitivity from the Germans and cooperation from old and new allies. If the Federal Republic succeeds in forging this new identity, then the united Germany will become a great power with a major voice in shaping the twenty-first century.

Article 11.1.   As the World Turns

In this article, the authors survey the changing political scene in Nicaragua, insisting that little progress has been made since Violetta Barrios de Chamorro ascended to the presidency in 1990 following the defeat of Sandinista President Daniel Ortega. Despite promises of democracy and reform, President Chamorro entered into a series of pacts with her former communist foes, which have served to paralyze the new government and assure continued Sandinista influence. Although the new president would be quick to draw a distinction between national conciliation and pacts, disappointment reigns supreme throughout Nicaragua while the people bide their time until the next election, when they exact their retribution.

As THE WORLD TURNS

By Arturo Cruz Jr. and Consuelo Cruz Sequeira

Be it in a partisan tale told to a child by an ancient veteran or in the equally partisan meditations of the country's great protagonists, the history of Nicaragua is rendered as a labyrinthine account of the horrors inflicted on a virtuous majority by a fractious and immoral minority. Simple, perhaps atavistic, this is a powerful story. And, unfortunately, it contains a good deal of truth.

So Nicaraguans hope against hope for moments like that day in April 1990 when Doña Violeta Chamorro ascended to the presidency dressed in white—a white as pure as the immaculate conception. Meant to mark the beginning of a new history, her triumph, however, became merely the beginning of another labyrinthine year. One by one, as so often before in Nicaragua's history, the powerful—from the Ortegas to the Chamorros—adjusted to a changing reality, only to retain as much as possible of the old. The politics of democracy became the politics of pacts.

The swiftest adjustment was made by "the General of all the Nicaraguan Armies," who, shortly after Chamorro's victory, addressed his 3,000 officers, anxiously crammed in the Olaf Palme convention center awaiting instructions from their *jefe* on how to behave in the new Nicaragua. General Humberto Ortega, the Sandinista leader who kept his position as chief of the Nicaraguan

ARTURO CRUZ JR. is a visiting research fellow at the Hudson Institute. CONSUELO CRUZ SEQUEIRA is a doctoral candidate at MIT.

armed forces after the election, talked for hours. He argued that socialism was no longer a viable option; he lauded Antonio Lacayo, the son-in-law of the president-elect, and thus recognized the power behind the throne; and he dared criticize Cuba, even though he knew that the leaders of the Frente Sandinista still saw Fidel, the man they called "El Viejo," as a prophet.

Now Humberto asked his officers, "How many of you have studied in Cuba?" Almost all raised their hands. "And how many of you would like to live in Cuba?" The officers sat motionless, hands resting in their laps. Colonel Xavier Pichardo—the chief of the air force—listened quietly until the end, when the 3,000 men emerged from the hall and spilled like an olive-green river into the hallways. Immediately Pichardo sensed their perplexity. True enough, the officers admitted, no one wanted to live in Cuba; but like family secrets, certain things should remain unspoken. Besides, what would happen to them?

Led into such political temptation, Pichardo began to behave like a rooster. He hinted that the Frente Sandinista should forge an alliance not with Chamorro's son-in-law, but with Virgilio Godoy, the independent-minded vice president-elect. Humberto, however, shrewdly detected the potential rebellion in his colonel and summoned him to his office. The colonel obeyed, but was far from docile. "Prepare the helicopters for combat," he ordered his men before leaving to see Humberto, "and put the base at Punta Huete on alert."

From *The New Republic*, June 17, 1991, pp. 22-25. Reprinted by permission of *The New Republic*, © 1991, The New Republic, Inc.

By the time Pichardo reached Humberto's office, Humberto had already been informed about the colonel's preparations for combat. "What is wrong with you, Pichardo?" Humberto asked menacingly, confronting him with the evidence. The petty chief shrank before the caudillo, and laid all blame on his second-in-command, Lieutenant Colonel Oscar Cortés. "All right," Humberto replied, "if you are in fact innocent, then you will call your units, and tell them to disarm." Even as Pichardo called, Humberto dispatched one of his reliable colonels to take over Pichardo's bases. And a few days later, with the crisis controlled, Humberto brought the rebel before the Council of Colonels, which promptly discharged him for insubordination. And, in one of those moves characteristic of caudillos, Humberto spared the second-in-command, thus retaining an officer who, from then on, was both grateful to and fearful of his general.

Humberto had survived not only his brother Daniel's electoral defeat but also the first coup attempt by his own people. What's more, he managed to take away from Comandante Tomás Borge the internal security apparatus, which he merged with his army. Then he demobilized thousands of his own soldiers and officers; and in order to retain his four stars, he resigned, with profound relief, from the Frente Sandinista. In his view, the party was in a deep crisis, its 41 percent of the votes notwithstanding. A party without access to the public budget, Humberto reasoned, was just one more in a multiplicity of parties; and a party with a troubled ideology was likely to oscillate between paralysis and chaos. Also, there was the disgraceful spectacle of the piñata: the discrediting scramble among the Sandinista leaders immediately after their electoral defeat—for vehicles, houses, factories, industries, and farms that fell from within the ruptured state.

Humberto survived by calculating his moves precisely. Now it was time to support Chamorro, which he knew would increase the chance of aid from the Western democracies. He had reduced his army but still needed to feed and dress his remaining 28,000 soldiers, all of whom had grown accustomed to fine boots and meals. (To this day, Humberto's army absorbs 16 percent of the national budget, an exorbitant share even for prerevolutionary Nicaragua. In 1977 Somoza had a joint army and police force of 7,000 men, with three Sherman tanks and machine guns that had to be cooled down with splashes of water.)

Humberto's lucidity in the face of change contrasted with the disorientation of the other militants. They denounced politics and began to look for jobs—a new and trying experience for many—in order to pay for the essentials they had once received from the Sandinista state. The comandantes too responded as best they could. Luis Carrión Cruz announced he would study public policy at Harvard. Jaime Wheelock, the father of the agrarian reform, became the largest landowner in 170 years of national history. Tomás Borge remained in the fold, patiently betting on a resurgence of ideological faith. And Daniel Ortega took control of the syndicate of urban laborers and public employees, which he would launch against the Chamorro government during the first months of its administration.

In the meantime, Doña Violeta surrounded herself with relatives and turned over de facto power to her son-in-law, Lacayo, who entered into a close alliance with his brother-in-law, former contra leader Alfredo César. Almost spontaneously, the two relatives decided on a division of labor that reflected the ingrained habits of their political culture and of their individual talents and personalities. Lacayo, who had once studied to be a Jesuit, is earnest, industrious, frugal. A manic centralizer, he demands total obedience from his ministers and won't talk to his own vice ministers unless they request a formal appointment. As soon as he won power, Lacayo carefully selected for his Cabinet able technocrats: decent men who lacked public stature.

César was ideally suited to take control of the National Assembly, which in times of transition turns into a realm of high Machiavellian politics. César is the nation's finest power technician. Somehow he manages to work without exerting himself and always looks refreshed, as if he has just bathed in the cologne of success. César recoils not from ill-defined agreements but from clearly specified obligations; and, like Talleyrand, he would rather not commit word to paper, not even his own signature. César's team is one of craftsmen of mischief: they coat sinecures, hand-outs, and bribes in the idiom of compassion even as they shove competitors into oblivion and discard exhausted helpers.

From the start Lacayo and César identified Virgilio Godoy, their own vice president, as their "scorpion": an intimate who comes to be seen as a venomous creature strategically positioned on the collar of one's shirt. César, assigned the task of neutralizing the scorpion, turned to the gifted politico Fernando Zelay, whom everyone knows as "The Devil." The Devil, in turn, went to the Sandinistas in the National Assembly and made a pact to undermine the constitution in order to disempower the vice president. By the terms of the 1987 constitution, when the president is temporarily absent from the country, he or she is replaced by the vice president. So the Devil dreamed up the idea of redefining "temporary" to mean a minimum of thirty days, and as a result, whenever President Chamorro travels abroad for a few weeks, power is either not deposited in anyone or is left in the hands of her designated successor, likely to be a family member.

In this atmosphere of deal-making and rule-breaking, Daniel Ortega, the electoral loser, could not be expected simply to accept exclusion. If his brother Humberto could ensure himself a place at the banquet table, why not he? Daniel began to agitate for inclusion through his labor union. Between May and August Daniel's strikers sabotaged the government's bid to restore some sanity to the economy. The government was continuing the effort by the Frente Sandinista between 1988 and 1989 to fight inflation through a sharp cut in public spending and a rise in imports. But now Daniel managed to convey his message to César that he was to be taken seriously. At the end of October his syndicate and the government signed a pact in which they agreed to reduce the budget deficit "gradually"—meaning never.

At the end of October the ruling family prepared to shake another scorpion off its collar: Francisco Mayorga, the president of the Central Bank. Mayorga had erred as early as the presidential campaign, when in his bid for a high profile he even imitated Doña Violeta: he too dressed all in white; and he too invoked God at the drop of a hat. Once in his post, Mayorga refused to admit that he was simply an employee of the señores; that he had no right to aspire to prominence in the public theater, because even though he had earned a doctorate from Yale, he had been born not an aristocrat from Granada but a "respectable middle-classer" from León.

Mayorga was removed; and a few days afterward there was a wave of disturbances. This time it was the turn of the demobilized contra soldiers and the anti-Sandinista mayors to vent their discontent. By then the magnitude of the contra demobilization was clear: instead of the expected 7,000, more than 22,000 rebel soldiers had become civilians. Humberto became their champion, arguing that their demands for land must be met. "Franklyn," a prominent contra comandante, soon felt cozier with General Ortega than with President Chamorro's relatives. And Humberto, having forged this bond, now insisted that his demobbed troops also be given land. And, guided by his uncanny political acumen, he settled demobilized contras and Sandinistas in the same zone, each camp on either side of a road. Humberto was determined to become the maximum leader of a community of warriors.

Meanwhile the government also began to woo the demobilized contras, by naming two of their former comandantes as vice ministers. And the old contra chief Colonel Enrique Bermudez returned home to build a power base among the still-rankled contras in the north. Because his effort met with significant success, shortly before Easter he was shot in the head at close range. The deed was carried out with scientific precision. Not even the investigative authorities would admit to possession of the bullet, and the political cost of his death was almost nil. After all, Bermudez was not only the son of a humble woman who had earned her living pressing suits, he was also a former Somocista who dared obstruct the crafting of a magnificent structure of pacts by the elite.

Eating iguana and retreating to the beach are two Easter traditions in Nicaragua. At every traffic light, especially now that unemployment has reached 40 percent, the poor sell their reptilian merchandise. They approach the stopped air-conditioned vehicles and display the iguana close to the windows. So there he was, Comandante Borge, still not quite used to having to stop at traffic lights like an ordinary citizen, suddenly eye-to-eye with a frightened iguana. A homicidal rage overtook him. He gasped that he was being insulted, taunted, humiliated now that he was down. Out he jumped, ready to disfigure the innocent salesman. Fortunately, the comandante was restrained by his own bodyguards.

This spring, Lacayo too grew edgy. He knew he had to impose order on a country that, though naturally rich, simply did not produce. And he had to do so before meeting with the international creditors and potential donors who would decide if Nicaragua deserved their help. By then Nicaragua was $350 million in arrears with the World Bank and the Inter-American Development Bank, a debt it had to clear before it could borrow afresh. So just before Easter, Lacayo and his economic team, in front of their *presidenta*, announced a program based on fiscal discipline and a massive devaluation of the gold peso aimed at export promotion and internal price stability. The conference broke all rules of form: Lacayo and his team talked for more than three hours while Doña Violeta marveled placidly at the good tidings promised by her son-in-law, smiling as if she were witnessing his miracles already, gesturing proudly at the Cabinet when he spoke of projected increases in exports.

Lacayo's rhetoric was as populist as Daniel's, who, now that he was seated at the banquet table, allowed his unions to agitate in public for a 500 percent wage increase, but then called them in private and told them to sign a new pact with the government in which they agreed to a mere 300 percent. The truce was even put to paper, so that Lacayo might take it to Washington as proof of progress in the government's effort to satisfy the international financial institutions. But when Lacayo arrived in Washington, he was told that he would have to wait for a decision to be made at the Paris meeting of the World Bank consultative group, toward the end of May.

Lacayo returned to Nicaragua hopeful. At the end of Easter week, at San Juan del Sur, the resort of the elite—with its caravans of Toyota land-cruisers and satellite dishes imploring the night skies—the powerful reassured themselves: the money, they kept saying, was coming in May. Also at the end of Easter week, Comandante Wheelock, no longer content to be a mere landowner, began to agitate through his rural union against the restitution of expropriated farms, until he was brought into the pact. The pact is essential to government and Sandinista allies alike: like the traditional señores and caudillos, they believe it will bring stability when all it really brings is a perpetuation of self-indulgence.

Now a certain gravity has descended upon the country. The older generation complains about how before the Revolution five families used to sit at the banquet table, with plenty of morsels left for the people, whereas now ten families sit at the table—and few morsels fall for the rest. The younger generation, like the Sandinista rank-and-file, denounces a revolution that began in idealism and ended in the old politics of pacts and thievery. Urbanites say that in Nicaragua nothing works, not even "imports" that are such successes elsewhere. They tell you about a famous circus that came to Nicaragua with African lions and elephants but lost its huge tent to a tropical storm. And what about the Blue Angels airplane that took a nose-dive into Lake Managua? Anything would fail in this God-forsaken country, they swear, where a feather will sink to the bottom of a pond and lead will float like a feather.

In the countryside the mood is even graver. Disillusioned peons along the banks of the San Juan river await their "esteemed *patrón*"; the self-same autocratic *patrón* who so often mistreated them. In a village near the fortress of El Castillo, a state worker lauds the last Somoza—"a fair man who lived and let live." The politicos and chiefs, for their part, still assume that the outside world is like their family barrio: intimate, nosy, and concerned about their fate. And that Nicaragua is an intrinsically desirable object, much as it was when English pirates looted its cities. Doña Violeta herself cannot tell the difference between the absentee American senator and the page seated in his place to spare her the embarrassment of a half-empty Congress.

Like the señores and caudillos of the past, today's politicos and chiefs fail to draw a distinction between national conciliation and pacts. The former would represent an exercise in principled opposition, and an attempt to build real bonds of trust, even sympathy; the latter is a temporary and fearful activity, the pact's participants held in check by mutual sharing, but also sorely tempted to betray one another as the booty disappears. The funds from abroad will surely come, of course, and the booty has not yet disappeared. But Nicaragua is a "democratic" country now. And the rest of society is biding its time until the next elections, when it will surely take its revenge. ●

Article 11.2.   From Horror to Hope

While "Papa Doc" Duvalier subjugated the spiritual and political life of Haiti, the new president, Father Jean-Bertrand Aristide, a charismatic proponent of democracy and liberation theology, stunned his critics in the Haitian establishment by winning a landslide election. Promising an end to the Duvalier legacy of lawlessness that pervades Haitian society, Aristide vowed to deliver Haiti from the past and honor his commitment to establish a democratic rule of law for the first time in the nation's history. Since his election, President Aristide has demonstrated unexpected political acumen, diplomacy, and a conciliatory approach toward easing the sharp divisions in Haitian society. Still, there are signs that not all is well, as Aristide's detractors accuse him of ignoring new democratic institutions, surrounding himself with a handful of ideologues and sycophants, and personalizing the presidency. Despite these charges, the president remains immensely popular with the Haitian masses, who look to him as their last chance.

Throughout Port-au-Prince, Haitians were trying, for the first time in 30 years, to dig out of their own filth. From their wretched, unsanitary hovels, they came at twilight, pouring into the streets by the thousands. Most carried homemade brooms and rakes, others used their bare hands to assault the mountains of human refuse that had risen about them for so many decades, largely unnoticed and insignificant, until now.

Clouds of dust and smoke choked the city for the next week, as laughing, radiant Haitians swept and hauled and burned. Sidewalks gradually emerged where none had been seen for years. Rotten, blackish heaps of everything from orange rinds to moldering mattresses disappeared. The rusting hulks of old cars were carted away. A few people even attempted to skim the pestilent, open sewers. Chickens and pigs and goats scattered shrieking into the night; scrawny dogs chased them with delight; throbbing Creole music filled the air.

Lavalas. In Creole it means "flash flood." Now it's what Haitians call the grass-roots movement that elected Jean-Bertrand Aristide, a 37-year-old socialist priest, president last December, in the country's first free elections since the brutal Duvalier-family dictatorship fell in 1986. "Together, we are the *lavalas*," he told them. Together, they would wash all Haiti's nightmares away. No more, he swore to them, would Haiti belong to just a precious few. Now everyone would "sit around the table, instead of just a few, with the rest underneath, catching the crumbs." He won in a landslide.

Democracy sweeps through Latin America, everywhere flinging tyrants from power, and now, at last, Haiti, the poorest country in this hemisphere, also belongs. *Lavalas.* In the weeks before Aristide's February 7 inauguration, its magic was everywhere. Artists painted dazzling murals on city walls, mostly of Aristide's campaign symbol, the brilliantly feathered fighting cock. Others painted cheap plastic juice bottles red and blue, the colors of the Haitian flag, then strung them on electrical poles, makeshift ornaments fluttering with all the bright pride of neon. Even most of Haiti's beggars had temporarily disappeared. "Aristide, he tells us that we must work," said one little boy who wanted $1 but offered, in exchange, a crude but clever hand-carved bird.

Lavalas. It even has its own language. Throughout Haiti, people were crowing with more raw joy than the barnyard roosters. "*Rrrrrr uh rrrrr!*" squawked a laughing, ragged old man, Alex DeNir, standing in the shadows of what was once the eternally lighted Duvalier-family crypt, now a crushed pile of weedy rubble. He grabbed his armpits and, flapping his elbows wildly, crowed again, and again. Soon a crowd of at least 50 others drifted toward the sound, all crowing and flapping, and laughing, too.

For now, at least, it seemed that all of Haiti was laughing as it tried, in its own small way, to dress up for perhaps the greatest moment in its sad history. By inauguration day, the shantytowns of Haiti, home of 6 million of the poorest, most diseased, illiterate, brutalized and overlooked people on Earth, were as spotless and gay as human effort could make them. In those final hours, no one thoughtlessly tossed even a stray candy wrapper or cigarette butt into the gutters. Visitors were astonished, and even Haitians marveled at what they had wrought in honor of the young priest they affectionately call Titid. Little Aristide.

Expelled by his Salesian order two years ago for fomenting class warfare, his presidential victory still the object of stony Vatican silence, Aristide may next be stripped of his priesthood altogether. But now he sweeps through Haiti with the aura of a Messiah. "Hallelujah," a lilting, melancholy Haitian version of the classic Handel chorus, has virtually replaced the national anthem. "God has sent us Titid," explained one exuberant teen-ager, taxing his English. "So we clean, because we do not want that he must come and sit for us in the nasty."

Lavalas. After decades of docility at the point of army Uzis and vicious, paramilitary goons called Tontons Macoute, 34 years after a country doctor called Papa Doc set up the Duvalier tyranny in 1957, and two centuries after Haitian slaves, in one of the most heroic moments of black history, threw out the French to establish the world's first black republic, only to descend into ever worsening misery, now comes frail, myopic, homely little Jean-Bertrand Aristide, to see if he can do any better for Haiti himself.

By election day on December 16, Aristide had antagonized, alienated and alarmed every pocket of power and privilege in Haiti. From the fenced mansions in the hillside suburbs above Port-au-Prince to the downtown enclaves of big business and government sinecures, he was being called a demagogue, another Papa Doc, a closet Communist and, because he is given to what his friends call "nervous prostrations," maybe mentally unstable, too. They scoffed at his slum origins, his faded '60s rhetoric and even made fun of his appearance, his thick lips and drooping left eyelid. "I call it the E.T. syndrome," sniffed one millionaire. "He's so little and ugly, even I want to protect him." But few had the nerve to utter a word of this in public.

Because hand in hand with *lavalas*, January was also the month of terrifying *dechoukaj*—in Creole, the "uprooting." In reality, in the weeks leading up to February 7, it meant mob justice.

Dechoukaj. It began with real enough cause when, on the night of January 6, Roger Lafontant, former leader of Duvalier's infamous militia, the Tontons Macoutes—disgruntled because he had been disqualified as a presidential candidate himself—staged a short-lived coup. Lafontant had barely cleared the National Palace doors with his band of 16 cohorts before the conch shells were sounding all over Haiti, the same alert to danger that the slaves used centuries ago. By dawn, the streets swarmed with hundreds of thousands of enraged Haitians. The army moved in; Lafontant and company were jailed within 12 hours.

But the blood bath lasted two days. Eighty-seven Haitians died. The street in front of Lafontant's headquarters was littered with corpses, some of them Macoutes, others merely hapless idlers. They were chased down and shot or hacked to death in the streets. Or burned alive. For the first time, Haitians have picked up the South African habit of "necklacing" their victims with burning tires.

"It was something to see, to see how they ran, ran, ran, trying to escape. But the people caught them, and they went to see God," said a gas-station manager, laughing, and ashamed of himself for it. "It is not a happy laugh—it is bad to see Haitian killing Haitian, but. . . ." He began giggling helplessly again. "It's just that I never thought to see those big, tough guys, running, running, trying to get away like snakes." In a few instances, captured by news photographers, Haitians also ate pieces of the dead Macoutes. "When you hate someone so much, killing is not enough," said one young cannibal, maybe 20, standing in front of a burned-out hotel.

Dechoukaj. It was the same terror of the Duvalier days, only reversed. Now, as then, nobody was safe. Two weeks after the Lafontant coup, a rumor spread that yet another coup was in the making. Mobs swarmed again. By dawn, 17 more were dead—including two popular local musicians, both blind. They were necklaced, supposedly because the crowd thought they were celebrating Aristide's rumored downfall. As it turned out, they had been hired by a proud father, also murdered, to help celebrate his 18-year-old daughter's birthday.

In January, to have even served the Macoutes a beer or cashed their checks was enough to invite disaster. Hotels, supermarkets, private homes burned throughout the capital. Anybody even remotely associated with the old Duvalier regime either fled the country or sat in dread, wondering just how far the *dechoukaj* would spread. At times, Macoute seemed a virtually meaningless word, a catch-all phrase for anything disagreeable or suspect.

"I saved all my life to build this place," sobbed Nicador Victor,

For the First Time in Decades, Haiti Has a Popularly Elected President. Can He Steer His Country Away From Its Bloody Past?

'He suffers so for the people, just like Jesus,' said a woman in the market. It is not a comparison Aristide discourages.

54, a burly one-time New York City longshoreman, sitting amid the ruins of his business, a combination restaurant-whorehouse. Before burning the place, mobs had stripped it of refrigerators, beds, even stolen the hookers' clothes. "Sure, some Macoutes were customers, but I am not a political man; I ran a business. What was I supposed to do, ask them for IDs? Tell them to get out and get shot?"

And heaven help the Haitian actually known to have been a Tontons Macoute, Creole for "bogeyman." In reality, the Macoutes—estimated to number anywhere from 30,000 to 300,000, depending on whom you ask—were basically a band of hired thugs, with some seriously evil leaders and killers but, otherwise, just a loosely organized crowd of illiterate, armed, costumed country boys, hustling a buck and a macho identity. Most just liked strutting around the airport and hotels in their dark glasses, red bandannas and bell-bottom jeans, looking tough. (In a bid for respectability, Papa Doc's son, Jean-Claude, later forced the disappointed Macoutes into boring blue uniforms.)

"It was 15 years ago, and I joined because you had to. It was the only way to make money and to get a safe-conduct pass, to keep them from hurting me and my family," said a slender man of perhaps 40, sitting in his one-room hut with his wife and four children. Everybody was whispering. "I've moved [from his rural village to Port-au-Prince], and I don't think anybody here knows that I once wore the uniform. But I'm scared. If they find out," he said, trembling, "they will *dechouk* me, for sure. They will come with the cans of gas." A curtain of cheap beads across his door rattled in the breeze, and he jumped. "I never hurt anybody, I swear," he whimpered. "I only did what they told me. I was just a little Macoute."

Dechoukaj. Now the tables were turned. The people were in charge. Long displeased with the Roman Catholic Church's treatment of Aristide, mobs also took revenge on the Vatican's ambassador, Papal Nuncio Guiseppe Leanza. Before burning the luxurious hilltop nunciature to the ground, they stripped him for the amusement of the crowds, then nearly beat his protesting chief aide to death. Others went searching for the archbishop, Francois Wolff Ligonde, whose standing with Aristide supporters had hit rock bottom when he warned the populace, during a New Year's Day Mass, against embracing "a defrocked social bolshevism rejected by the countries of the East." But he escaped the country. Now Haiti has neither an archbishop nor a nuncio.

Through it all, Aristide refused to calm his people. Instead, in a radio address, he blamed the attacks at the nunciature on Macoutes, who were trying to derail the *lavalas*, and even further inflamed the population. "I understand your will to catch the big Macoutes so they will not massacre us tomorrow," he said. "That is legitimate. Watch that they don't commit bad acts and blame them on us. Watch them, catch them, stop them and prevent them from creating disorder."

"He is inciting people to riot! We have all the ingredients here for a new fascism. Human rights violations have been as severe in the last month as they were under Duvalier," exploded Jean-Jacques Honorat, head of the Haitian Center for Human Rights, one of the few willing to go public with his complaints. "As a Haitian, I am ashamed! We have political prisoners [Lafontant and others] who are being held incommunicado. Lawyers are afraid to defend them! Journalists are afraid to criticize. *Everybody* is afraid. . . . But even Papa Doc *didn't burn blind musicians alive!*" he finished, shouting.

But Honorat is only one idealist, and Jean-Bertrand Aristide is a priest fast making the transition to Third World politician. The power of the mobs, as he well knew, was all that stood between him and a successful coup, all that held the 7,000-man army in check, all that kept him alive. Already he had escaped at least three assassination attempts: In the bloodiest, a gang of killers stormed his church, Saint-Jean Bosco, during a mass in 1988 and massacred 12 of his congregation with Uzis and machetes, while soldiers stood by. Aristide reportedly remained frozen in his pulpit, praying aloud. until somebody snatched him to the safety of a locked courtyard, where he watched as his church went up in flames. Assassins were still trying, too. Only days before the election, hand grenades were thrown into a political rally he had departed only a few minutes earlier. That time, seven died.

Dechoukaj. It goes both ways. Five days before his inauguration, arsonists—presumably the "big Macoutes"—set fire to an orphanage Aristide had founded for 200 street children. Four youngsters were burned to death. Aristide came to the scene and cried. The small bodies, charred beyond recognition, were left on display at the morgue all day, so that Haitians might witness this latest, cruelest assault on Aristide, on their fledgling democracy, on themselves. Hundreds passed by, more rage than sorrow in their faces. The city braced for the *dechoukaj* that was sure to happen that night.

But no conch shells sounded, no bullets were fired, no buildings burned. Only five more days until the inauguration of

Titid. That night, the streets were eerily empty; even the taxi drivers were afraid to go out. The city was frightening in its silence. Next morning, Haitians returned to their sweeping. *Lavalas.*

Jean-Bertrand Aristide is one of them, a son of the slums himself, raised in a fatherless household, with one older sister, by a mother who was once a street vendor and part-time domestic. He grew up in and around the neighborhood of La Saline, a place on the road from the airport, where tourists can still see people bathing in sewers, grimy charcoal vendors laboring under inhuman loads and smoke rising from the huts of voodoo priests, first and last resort of those without the resources for modern medicine. In La Saline, there is no running water, only a few public water taps. Children suffering from that disease of terminal malnutrition called kwashiorkor, characterized by red hair and bloated bellies, are a routine sight here, 750 miles from Miami.

Nearly everyone, most of them refugees from the ruined rural countryside, is unemployed—eight out of 10 Haitians earn less than $150 a year. Hundreds line the curbsides, eking out a few pennies a day, selling everything from vegetables, rubber thongs and charcoal to smuggled cans of Carnation milk. Sometimes, one of Haiti's legendary artists will also appear, offering to sell some brilliant piece of his soul for whatever the buyer can please give.

Born in 1953, Aristide grew up during the cruelest days of President-for-Life Francois Duvalier's long reign. Throughout the '60s, Haitians were either exiled for the merest hint of dissent or, worse, taken away by soldiers and Macoutes to a yellow edifice on the edge of town, known as Fort Dimanche, a place from which uncounted thousands never returned. (Although campaign literature says only that Aristide's father was a peasant who died when Aristide was 3 months old, La Saline locals swear that the senior Aristide was a local shoemaker and street musician, shot at Fort Dimanche for criticizing Papa Doc, when his son was 5.)

During Aristide's childhood, Haitians were not even permitted to walk on the sidewalks in front of the National Palace, which rose like some ephemeral white fairy-tale castle amid the shantytowns of its impoverished subjects, who could only imagine what luxuries lay within, what opulence their leaders enjoyed. All they could see from afar were the glittering ballroom chandeliers beyond the tapestries and the Rolls-Royces descending from the hillside suburbs, discharging guests in elegant evening dress, golden military braid and clerical collars.

Aristide was 18 when Papa Doc died, bequeathing Haiti to his obese 19-year-old son, Jean-Claude (promptly nicknamed Baby Doc). But Haitians almost never saw their new President-for-Life. Baby Doc was reportedly so depressed by the misery in his streets, he rarely left the palace. When he did, he flung small change from his car windows to people groveling in the gutters. Meanwhile, his glamorous, chain-smoking mulatto wife, Michele, briefly attempted to play Evita to the poor, building one of the best-equipped hospitals in Haiti, which she named for herself.

By the time the Duvalier regime finally fell five years ago, with the royal couple escaping to France aboard a U.S. government jet in the wake of massive public demonstrations, Jean-Bertrand Aristide could take some credit. By then, he was among the most powerful voices for change in Haiti.

Aristide owes his escape from a dead-end life in large part to the Salesian Fathers, who took him into their huge school in La Saline at age 6 and educated him, sending him to high school and college in Haiti, where he earned a bachelor's degree in psychology. Then the Salesians sent him abroad for three years of advanced studies in Israel, England and Canada. By the time he returned to Haiti in 1982, when he was ordained, he was conversant in six foreign languages. Today, half the people in La Saline claim to recall the studious, smart, tiny boy. "Aristide was always the best student, very serious, very smart," says Salesian Father Cazo Nau, a one-time Boy Scout leader who best remembers Aristide as very diligent in earning his merit badges and "always a good person."

Aristide has been horrifying the Salesian Fathers, among the most conservative of orders to begin with, almost since the day of his ordination. What the Salesians had created, they soon discovered, was a headache that would not go away. Aristide had become a committed liberation theologian—one among that progressive breed of Latin priests who use their pulpits to preach social justice for the poor, blending Scripture with Marxist terminology. Assigned a parish near La Saline, Aristide was soon electrifying the poor, as much with his courage as with his message: Not only must the Duvaliers go, so must all those who had helped

'Justice. First, Haitians need justice, OK?' Aristide says, patiently. 'So I start by hearing the voice of everybody. This is the way to a government of democracy.'

maintain Haiti's cruel status quo, from the U.S. imperialists, complacent Catholic bishops and greedy elite to the killer army generals and Macoutes.

"Capitalism is a sin," he preached. "They use their capital to exploit the people. They use the army to kill those who are working for real democracy." He decried U.S. businessmen as "bloodsuckers" for exploiting Haiti's slave wages of $3 per day; the U.S. government—those "cold imperialists to the north"—could keep its foreign aid, if it continued to arrive in a form that was "destroying Haitian dignity and national productivity."

He attacked the Vatican for seducing the poor into passivity. He compared the Pope to the chief executive officer of a multinational corporation, "whose job is to ensure efficiency, continuity and profit while maintaining the status quo." He took special aim at Archbishop Ligonde, a distant relative of Michele Duvalier, for hobnobbing with the dictators over fine food and wine in the palace while presiding over what Aristide calls "the parish of the poor."

"The whole of Haiti is like a bicycle," he said in one sermon, "and the wheel is in our hands. Everyone wants us to turn right, but that would maintain the corruption. We must turn left. Does that mean we are communists? No. But we must have a society where we can respect the communists and all sorts of people, and not shoot them, although what we choose for ourselves is a socialist society. I think it is the only type of society where everybody can find justice and respect and food."

And, finally, Aristide advanced the notion of *dechoukaj.* He quoted Scripture in urging Haitians to defend themselves against the army and the Macoutes: "And he that hath no sword, let him sell his garment and buy one" (Luke 22:36). "Don't be fooled," he told his flock. "A machete is useful in almost any situation. Those rusty blades are long and sharp. They remind me of [Simon] Bolivar's sword."

The Salesians tried to transfer him out of the country. But each time they tried, Aristide's growing flock rebelled, once occupying the splendid pink and yellow cathedral in a week-long hunger strike. Aristide continued, with escalating passion and mounting nerve. A tremendous showman with a flair for theater, he kept a mannequin of a Macoute in his office, in sunglasses and red bandanna, that he sometimes berated for the TV cameras. He periodically held mock funerals for Duvalierist ministers and generals.

Before long, thanks mainly to the sloppiness of the henchmen who were trying to kill him, he had also come to be widely regarded as divine. Haiti is, after all, the land of voodoo, a place of walking spirits, of living sacrifices and zombies and possession, where evil and good co-exist without the judgmental stress of other religions. In voodoo, very little is impossible—and it remains at the spiritual heart of Haiti, despite the missionaries. It was the burning of Aristide's church and the massacre of his congregation that turned speculation into widespread faith that Aristide is possessed of supernatural powers.

"Their bullets cannot kill him. God protects him. Aristide can disappear whenever he wants," said Luisa Charlemaigne, a vegetable vendor. Even Aristide's fragile appearance and much discussed "nervous prostrations" only lend to the mystique. "He suffers so for the people, just like Jesus," said another woman in the market. It was not a comparison Aristide discouraged. Two months after the church burning—which, remarkably, the Vatican never publicly condemned—he emerged from seclusion, looking haggard, to remind his flock that "Jesus wasn't a priest either." By then, he was also referring to himself as the prophet of the people.

During the years following the Duvaliers' flight to France (looting the treasury of anywhere from $200 million to $800 million in the process), Aristide's anger toward the United States escalated, as he watched five U.S.-backed governments—three of them led by Duvalier's generals—perpetuate corruption, killings, sham elections, coups and mass misery. And nothing would change, Aristide preached furiously to his followers, because Washington was not interested in real democracy in Haiti—only in "the appearance of elections," in order to install yet one more puppet government to do its bidding.

"Revolution, not elections," he was exhorting Haitians, almost until the day he entered the race himself.

I n many respects, Haiti is still a slave revolution in progress. Its beginnings were glorious. In 1791, Haitian slaves rose in terrifying might against their French masters and, to the horror of the colonial world, won. After a vicious 13-year war, Napoleon Bonaparte was obliged to give up one of his richest possessions, a lush island bursting with sugar, coffee, spices, indigo and fruits, the envy of the Caribbean. "We have a false idea of the Negro," one of his retreating generals remarked. In 1804, Saint Domingue, on the western third of the island of Hispaniola, bordering the Dominican Republic, became Haiti, the world's first black republic. Haitians have been paying for it ever since.

For decades the fledgling nation was isolated from the world, partly through its own paranoia that the French would return,

but mainly because colonial powers, despising the precedent set by these rebellious slaves, refused to trade with Haiti. The French ultimately extracted about $150 million in reparations for lost plantations. The U.S. embargo lasted until 1862.

Shunned by the world, its leaders illiterate and unworldly, with no frame of political reference beyond that imposed by white kings and emperors and their own diverse African tribal customs, Haiti never developed a democratic tradition. A potpourri of different peoples ripped from all parts of Africa, communicating in the slaves' improvised, communal language of Creole, now flung together in search of instant national harmony, Haitians seemed doomed from the start. From the outset, violence marked the changing of Haitian regimes, as did the tendency of Haitian leaders, aping their colonial masters, to name themselves to lifetime positions. In all, Haiti has had nine emperors, governors and Presidents-for-Life.

Nor did Haiti ever overcome the racial hatreds that gave birth to the country in the first place. Even before the revolution, the mulattoes, lighter-skinned and finer-boned, half-breed descendants of the French and their slaves, were often granted privileges that black slaves were not, ranging from better food to French lessons. In later decades, mulattoes gradually took control of Haiti's civil service and professions, while blacks worked the fields and manned the army.

Today, the small mulatto minority, maybe 10% of the population, remains better educated, speaks French and owns most of the national wealth; 75% of the blacks are illiterate and speak Creole. In another class distinction, mulattoes tend to publicly deny any attraction to voodoo, while black Haitians, even those who are also nominally Catholics or Protestants, overwhelmingly rely on it just as they did 200 years ago.

Class resentments have always been a bonanza for ambitious Haitian politicians, mulatto and black alike. Francois Duvalier rose to power on the promise of restoring black nationalist pride. He also fed on the fierce anti-American sentiment that resulted from a 19-year U.S. occupation of the island, from 1915 to 1934. Fearing that the Germans might attempt to establish a Caribbean outpost during World War I, the Americans invaded Haiti and treated it as their own.

By then, Haiti had already slipped into such disrepair that American largesse was welcome in many respects. Hospitals, highways and communications systems were built. But the insult to the pride of the slave nation was so great, the Jim Crow attitudes of white Marines so offensive, that even today older Haitians cannot hide their remembered bitterness. But, to many, the single most damaging legacy of the American occupation was the newly equipped, efficient Haitian army the United States left in its wake—a military machine that has, in the decades since, virtually dictated who Haitian rulers will be.

Thanks to the army, Francois Duvalier was able to slam the doors once more on the outside world and run Haiti his way. When his corrupt, murderous regime finally became too notorious to ignore, President John F. Kennedy cut off U.S. aid in 1963. It was not restored until a decade later, when Jean-Claude took over. In theory, the young, supposedly dim-witted son would be more amenable to U.S. suggestions about how a civilized country should be run. The only difference turned out to one of form: Baby Doc didn't look at whites with such naked hate. But Fort Dimanche remained a busy place. Haiti's decline continued unabated.

Whatever statistic you pick, Haiti is at the bottom of the world charts. Malnutrition is still the leading cause of death, followed by such treatable diseases as tuberculosis. Infant mortality is one in four: the average life expectancy is 54.

Some 5% of the population owns 50% of the wealth. Meantime, the cost of living soars—a chicken now costs $10.

Haiti is a country where nothing works. Because corruption has been more rampant than ever, during the past five years of political upheaval, even basic services have gone ignored. Roads are crumbling, where they exist; such state-owned services as telephones barely work and Haitians are now lucky to get three or four hours of power a day, which, in turn, is driving small businesses into ruin. Water has been in pathetically short supply for years. Only 13% of the population has access to potable water.

In perhaps the saddest note of all, Haiti's urban problems are only compounded by the ruination of its once lush countryside. Impoverished peasants have cut down all the trees to provide charcoal fuel either for themselves or to sell in the city. As a result, the topsoil has been eroding for decades at a dramatic rate, clogging the dams, plugging the few irrigation ditches. Now only 30% of the country is arable. Much of the once tropical Haitian countryside looks like central Nevada.

Then, like some final blight from hell, came the AIDS panic of the early '80s, falsely stigmatizing Haiti as a source, costing the country all that it had left, its tourist trade and thousands of jobs. Completing the ever-descending picture, while dozens of foreign assembly plants are still based in Haiti, employing about 45,000 people at $3 a day, even some of those are now leaving the island. Long the world's biggest producer of major-league baseballs, Haiti recently lost Rawlings, one of its largest employers, to Costa Rica.

Since the Duvaliers were overthrown, it has been a revolving door at the National

Bella Stumbo is a Times staff writer.

Palace—five regimes in five years, all supposedly leading Haiti toward democratic elections. First came Gen. Henri Namphy, one of Duvalier's favorites. He proved as repressive as his boss, presiding over what turned out to be an election-day massacre in 1987, when 34 voters were shot at the polls, as soldiers reportedly stood by. Another election, early in 1988, was so crippled by voter fear and bribery that no one regarded the winner, a professor named Leslie Manigat, as legitimate. Manigat took himself so seriously that he attempted to purge the army, starting with the arrest of Gen. Namphy—who promptly put the misguided Manigat aboard the next plane to Santo Domingo, four months into his term.

It was during what Haitians call Namphy Two that Aristide's church was burned. This time, Namphy only lasted four months, before being deposed in a coup led by Gen. Prosper Avril. By then, many were wondering if there was a general in Haiti that the United States wouldn't trust—and, to the surprise of no one, within 18 months, Washington was obliged to fly Avril out of the country, too, after he began Duvalier's old trick of exiling critics. In March, 1990, the first civilian provisional government was appointed, headed by former Supreme Court Justice Ertha Pascal-Trouillot. By then, Haiti had sunk into such demoralized chaos that former Tontons Macoute chief Lafontant, who had fled into exile when the Duvaliers did, felt confident enough to return last summer.

After the army refused to enforce a warrant issued for his arrest, Lafontant declared himself a presidential candidate. The stage for his coup attempt was set when he was ruled ineligible under a highly controversial provision of the 1987 constitution, which says that until 1997 no person can seek office who is "well-known for having been by his excess zeal one of the architects" of the Duvalier dictatorship. That, bristled the Macoute, "was undemocratic."

As recently as last summer, Aristide was also assailing the constitution, as well as the scheduled elections, as just another U.S. sham. He told the people, entry into the race. When he did announce, he ascribed it to the will of God and the people: "If the people say I must run, then I must run. . . . When I know I am doing God's will, I am at peace," he said, adding, "I could sleep from now until election day and still win." He was right, too. The day after he announced, a million illiterate Haitians registered to vote—to mark their X in the box of the little fighting cock.

With about 700 United Nations poll watchers swarming through the island, nobody cheated, nobody died. Aristide won with 66% of the vote in a field of 11 candidates. Remarkably, most Western political analysts viewed it as an upset. Until election day, few were taking Aristide's candidacy seriously, predicting instead that Marc Bazin, a dignified former World Bank economist, widely regarded as the U.S. government's candidate, was certain, at least, to force a runoff.

"Bazin didn't win because he spent more time talking to us than the Haitians," said U.S. Embassy information officer Bruce Brown, disgustedly. "Face it, we can give advice and support, but we can't vote for them." His boss, Ambassador Alvin Adams, was more circumspect. "We are only interested in democracy for Haiti. . . . We will work with whoever is elected," said Adams.

"Without us, there wouldn't even have been an election," said Brown, exasperated. A young diplomat who last served in Manila, Brown finds the anti-American attitude of Aristide's people highly annoying. "They'll never let us forget that we supported Duvalier," he sighed. "Well, in my opinion, Duvalier was a logical consequence of Haitian history. Here it's only a matter of time until presidents get overthrown or assassinated. . . . So, we put up with Duvalier, just like we'll put up with Namphy, just like we'll put up with Aristide. . . . What do they think we're going to do—send in the Marines? This isn't Panama. Besides, who the hell wants Haiti? Castro? He's not crazy!"

In any case, Brown finished, all this tough talk won't last. "They'll like us well enough when budget time comes around."

F irst impressions of the small man sitting beyond the big, bare desk, adorned only by a wooden plaque honoring the black nationalist W.E.B. DuBois, is that he is either braced for attack or prepared to hear confession. He is wearing a gray suit and white shirt, slightly too large at the collar, accenting his smallness. His front tooth is chipped, his left eyelid droops oddly. His unflinching gaze is riveting.

For the next 45 minutes, he sits utterly still, hands clasped on the table in front of him, face grave, speaking so softly that the listener must strain, even from two feet away, to hear, and uttering not a single word that hasn't been considered. Despite his résumé's claim that he is fluent in eight languages, he speaks English with the simplicity of one who has just completed a Berlitz course.

"I love everybody. . . . I have to, otherwise I should not be able to feel free, to feel happy," he says. "When you love people . . . just because they are human, then you feel free, you feel happy. When you don't love people, you don't feel happy."

What about the Macoutes? Does he love them, too? His odd eyes flicker with mild annoyance. "Listen, I am a theologian, I am not a judge," he says. "So I cannot judge people. I ought not to judge people. Right now, what I have to do is build democracy; it's to respect our constitution, it's to welcome *every*body, to be together . . . building a society of justice. . . . It doesn't matter to me if some people don't understand that, or don't know who I am."

Does he expect the Pope to expel him? At this, his eyes smile briefly. "I don't want any kind of conflict with him," he says. "I have just to continue to do my job, the way I'm doing it. If I respect what I have to respect, then I feel at . . . peace." He clearly expects to stay a priest, and if not, as he told the people, he might just get married—"if the Haitian people give me a wife."

("They won't *dare* touch him," predicted his friend Smark Michele, Minister of Commerce and Industry, earlier, laughing. Already, said Michele, the Vatican has approached Aristide, asking him to quietly resign. "But Aristide threw the ball back in their court. He told them he will not oppose them—*if* they make their request public. So far, he hasn't heard another word.")

The public Aristide is now equally diplomatic about almost everything else. Of his relationship with the United States, he says, "We have very good relations, and I want to build a very beautiful future from this very good relation." He hoped that Vice President Dan Quayle would attend his inaugural. "It would make me very, very happy."

As for the army he has so long assailed, he no longer even dreams of a Haiti without one. "The constitution provides for an army, so it is not for me to say," he says. "It is for me to accept what the constitution says. My personal feeling is a constitutional feeling." He will not be baited. Not even into a smile.

The new president of Haiti is trying hard to make the leap from firebrand to statesman. It's such a different game now than last fall, when he was riding white horses into the countryside, driving the crowds wild with his teasing smiles and furious rhetoric. In time he may even master the art of political doublespeak. Meantime, he is compelling, even likable, in his determination. If he privately wonders what the hell he's gotten himself into, he hides it well.

What are his priorities? Where does he begin to fix his ruined nation? He studies his questioner. Aristide doesn't like mainstream American journalists. He sees them as little more than agents of the U.S. government—shallow mirrors of a privileged culture that will never understand that Haiti is not a place where sewage systems will ever be priority number one.

"Justice. First, Haitians need justice, OK?" he says, patiently. "So I start by hearing the voice of *everybody*. This is the way to a government of democracy. And, if you obey the constitution, of course you will get justice. If you respect human rights, of course you will get justice. If you respect the rules of democracy, you will of course get justice. And I think what we are doing is exactly that. You cannot

Haiti

govern a country without law . . . and once you do that, *everybody* will realize how their right is respected. . . . You just have to obey the constitution, to obey the law." For a man who formerly thought the constitution was a piece of junk, Aristide now loves it perhaps best of all.

Aristide's inauguration passed largely ignored by the world. Only three heads of state attended—from Venezuela, Jamaica and Belize. France sent its first lady. A delegation of 26 Cubans came, but not Fidel Castro. Former President Jimmy Carter came on his own, but, in what was widely regarded as just another in a long line of insults, the U.S. government sent a delegation headed by Health and Human Services Secretary Louis W. Sullivan, the Cabinet's only black.

But nothing could mar this day for Haiti. Here stands Titid, at last, taking the oath of office. "*Lavalas*," he says softly, teasingly, a faintly amused smile on his lips. "*Lah-vah-las*," he repeats, treating each syllable like a kiss of congratulations: Together, they have done it. They have won. The crowd outside the National Palace explodes in ecstasy. For the next half hour he plays with them, tells them stories, sets up riddles, leads them in question-answer chants familiar to every Haitian child. He tells them, as he always does, "I am in love with you."

Then, President Jean-Bertrand Aristide seized upon this moment, perhaps the single most powerful hour of his five-year term as president, to do what is both dangerous and virtually unprecedented: He publicly purged the army of six of its most feared generals, in the most humiliating fashion possible. Turning to Herard Abraham, the poised, U.S.-trained army commander-in-chief who sat at his side, he said, almost tenderly, "I love you, too, general"—and, in the next breath, politely but firmly read off the names of the six generals that he "suggested" Abraham should retire. Immediately.

Aristide also rejected his own $10,000 monthly salary as obscene, promising to donate it to the poor. He announced a travel ban on 100-plus top former officials until their financial records can be investigated. He also detained provisional president Ertha Pascal-Trouillot on suspicion of conspiracy in the Lafontant coup. (Earlier this month, she was jailed overnight, and then placed under house arrest.) He called on France to help recover the millions stolen by the Duvaliers.

Not least, he publicly called for the killing to stop, for the people to join hands "in a marriage with the army" to fight the Macoutes through the courts of law. He urged Haitians to treat soldiers as friends, thus putting the military on notice: For however long it may last, the army is now an institution under popular control. He finished by thanking several nations for their promises of aid—pointedly omitting the United States.

That night, this nation of slaves danced in its clean streets, celebrating its new beginning. Twenty-four hours after he was sworn in, Aristide went to Fort Dimanche, where human bones are still turning up in the desolate field and, as thousands of Haitians wept openly, planted a tree, turning the place into a museum of memories. Then he threw open the palace gates and invited hundreds of the poor inside for lunch. Nobody on Aristide's staff was able to explain how the guest list was compiled. The guests were among the oldest, sickest, most pitiful citizens of Port-au-Prince. Even by Haitian standards, these people stood out.

There were perhaps 300 of them, and they came, not in a joyful flood, but slowly, quietly, like people who sense some trap. No soldiers were there, no Uzis, but they were still afraid to be in this mysterious place. An old woman with a massive tumor on her neck wore a pair of shredded nylons. A blind man wore a wrinkled red tie over his filthy brown shirt. A young man with no legs shoved himself along, wearing a brand-new T-shirt with a rooster on it and the single word: *Lavalas*. Through the manicured gardens, past the marbled halls with their antiques and tapestries and ivory-tusked sofas they went, most keeping their eyes to the ground, careful not to depart from the pathways, as they made their way to that corner of the palace lawn where the president would be. And where the food was—hot bowls of a thick chicken noodle stew. They fell upon it with pathetic need.

Aristide speaks Creole, the language of the people, in public, but, now, in a stunning bit of theater, he lapsed into a few minutes of French, as he stood before the TV cameras, watching his starving subjects eat. He took aim at the heart of every rich Haitian household, so removed from this dirty, desperate scene: He spoke directly to their children. "Go to your parents tonight, as you sit at your nice dinner table," he said, "and ask them if they couldn't please share just a little bit of all that you have with the poor people of Haiti. And if they say yes, then give them a kiss, and say that it is from Titid."

Haiti has always been a place that bypasses the brain and strikes directly at the heart, and this was just another of those moments.

So little has changed. Haiti today, as in 1804, remains hostage to Western beneficence. Without massive aid, Aristide has no real hope of bringing his country into the 20th Century. Just how much help his nascent democracy will receive from such major donors as Canada, Germany and France remains in question. The United States announced that it would increase by about $30 million the $54 million it has annually funneled indirectly into Haiti for years. But terms and conditions are unclear.

Worse, although Aristide has promised to make the Haitian rich pay their fair share through tax reform and a crackdown on corruption, by the time he gets his government together, he may find that much of Haiti's wealth has disappeared. From the lovely, misty enclaves above Port-au-Prince, where the azure swimming pools are always full and dozens of servants flutter about, to the moss-laden plantation palaces of the interior, elegant aristocrats are predicting that Aristide won't last more than a year before being either overthrown or assassinated. At the same time, some have admittedly been busy, transferring assets abroad, just in case the priest gets serious about redistributing wealth.

"Just who is this young man, anyway?" asked a white-haired old lady, a Sorbonne-educated mulatto who owns a big chunk of Haiti but spends most of her year in Paris where she sometimes lunches with her friends, the Duvaliers. "Such a different class, you know? Well, I do wish him well. Those poor people have been living like animals for years. . . . I've always been struck at how hard Haitian women have to work, just carrying water to their families. Those buckets on their heads look so heavy." Once, she recalls, she even drilled a well for them on one of her ranches.

"He's another Papa Doc—he appeals to their primitive instincts. He's their new *houngan* [voodoo priest]. Even if he's sincere, those around him will be corrupted, just like all the rest," said another U.S.-educated landowner, as annoyed by American condescension as Aristide is, but for different reasons. "Those people," he said, gesturing vaguely toward the city below, "are ignorant. They can't even read. Haiti isn't ready for the democracy that you Americans insist on imposing everywhere you go."

February 7 had barely passed, at least temporarily quelling the threat of *dechoukaj*, before some leading politicians were also doing their best to undermine Aristide to the Western press. (Haitian journalists won't listen; they adore Aristide as much as the general public, at least for now.)

With ill-concealed satisfaction, Aristide's critics expressed their alarm that, mere days into his administration, the new president was already showing signs of becoming Haiti's latest black nationalist demagogue. They accused him of ignoring the nation's new democratic institutions, of arrogance, of surrounding himself with a handful of fawning yes-men.

Translated, this meant that Aristide was ignoring them—he had bypassed leaders of the various parties to pick, as his prime minister, Renee Preval, 47, an old friend in the revolutionary trenches and a local bakery owner. In naming his cabinet, he compounded the insult by picking doctors, spaghetti makers and notary publics—political novices whose views on how to govern a nation were as murky as Aristide's. "We don't know who the hell half these people *are*—much less what their programs are going to be—if they *have* any," summarized the ever-succinct Bruce Brown of the U.S. Embassy. Even now, no one has any real idea of what programs Aristide has in mind, what his economic and social policies may be. Few Aristide-watchers expect him to make any serious attempt to socialize Haiti. "He's not stupid," said one of his critics wryly. "After all, what's to socialize? If anything, he's going to have to privatize the state companies [telephone, power] he's got, if he wants them to work."

All of it, according to a typical American press account in the Washington Post, was "stirring concerns that [Aristide] plans a highly personal style of government that disregards political parties and other national institutions." Many of those whose "concerns" are "stirred" can be discovered on any given evening lounging about the terrace of the Hotel Grand Oloffson. A wonderfully decadent white gingerbread complex in the heart of Port-au-Prince, made famous by Graham Greene in his novel "The Comedians," the Olòffson continues to be the favored meeting place for those with preten-

They scoffed at Aristide's slum origins, even made fun of his appearance. 'He's so little and ugly, even I want to protect him,' sniffed one millionaire.

sions to power or status. Foreign journalists lurk on the balcony like birds of prey.

"I am the most popular leader, after Aristide, but he hasn't even called me! To me, this is unbelievable! All the people in the streets think Aristide has chosen me for prime minister, and he hasn't even *called* me," sputtered Louis Dejoie, one of the losing presidential candidates, a mulatto so Americanized he might pass for a Chicago ward healer. His father was Papa Doc's most important competition in 1957, and the Dejoie name remains extremely popular.

What the supposed U.S. candidate, Marc Bazin, had to say about Aristide was entirely off the record. Bazin clearly expects to become president yet. "I intend to remain quiet for a while," former president Leslie Manigat snapped, "until Haitians can see for themselves what they have done."

"U.S. policy-makers don't try to get the pulse of the people. They stay in Villa Creole [a luxury hotel above the city], which is why we now have an anti-American president," said newly elected Sen. Bernard Sansarique, a former Miami exile whose chief claim to fame was his bloody 1982 attempt to invade Duvalier's Haiti with a small band of exiles. He also aspires to become president.

"But they [the Americans] said I was *too* nationalistic," lamented Sansarique. Now, he predicted, the hammer and sickle may fly over Haiti within a year, since, as everyone knows, one of Aristide's chief economic advisers is Gerard Pierre-Charles, a well-known communist. As for Preval, the new prime minister, "from what I hear, he was just an errand boy, he was sent to buy Cokes, get ashtrays and make phone calls."

Always, it comes back to Aristide's inner circle. If Aristide fails, it will probably be, just as the Oloffson pundits say, because he has surrounded himself with such a mixed bag of advisers. They run the gamut from insufferable Marxist ideologues from New York City to earnest young organizers from the interior to those who privately suspect that Aristide is no ordinary mortal.

"This is a typical fight against imperialism," said Aristide's friend Antoine Izmery, a wealthy food importer of Lebanese descent who calls himself a Palestinian rebel. Irrepressibly colorful, Izmery financed more than half Aristide's $500,000 campaign. He is often held up by Aristide's critics as a mirror of things to come, mainly because he is hopelessly in love with the rhetoric of revolution.

Izmery is convinced, as many are, that the U.S. government was directly involved in the attempted Lafontant coup. "The [American] plan was to let Lafontant take over and kill Aristide, then they could fly Lafontant out of the country, like all the rest, and start over again!" he exclaimed. ("What nonsense," said ambassador Adams.)

"His relationship with the Haitian masses is almost uncanny. And his command of the Bible has always amazed me," said Patrick Elie, another confidante, a biochemist and now chief of staff to Prime Minister Preval, who confides that he is among those who wonder if Aristide might not possess supernatural powers. "I admit it, he has put a little crack in my scientific armor. You know [after one assassination try], some of those people involved just, well, they suddenly died—for no apparent medical cause."

In between the extremes are such charming, exuberant newcomers to politics as Smark Michele, 54, an affluent businessman whose father was shot for political dissent at Fort Dimanche. He flushes with emotion discussing it, sitting in his pretty house above the city. "At first I didn't like Aristide. I thought he was too uncompromising," said Michele, who met Aristide in 1986. "I finally learned that Aristide is *always right*. He can sound arrogant in his certainty, but in the end he always turns out to be right. He speaks eight languages! He's some sort of a genius! He's a miracle!"

Others of Aristide's inner circle are tough sophisticates like Fathers Antoine Adrien and William Smarth, who operate a school in the shantytown of San Martin. "Haiti is just a banana republic to your government," said Adrien, chuckling at how the election had backfired on Washington, burying its man, Bazin. "The U.S. is absolutely convinced that a small nation in its back yard should be docile. They cannot believe that the masses could give power to anyone, that the slaves would resist the will of Big Brother. [But] now we will prove the U.S. wrong. Our goal is a very modest one—to go from dire deprivation to decent poverty—and we don't want your billions. We can do a lot by ourselves."

Aristide's inner circle also includes some former Duvalierists, people such as Gladys Lauteur, a wealthy pharmacy owner and former cohort of Michele Duvalier. They thrived under the dictatorship, but now they see the light. "Aristide is a man of God; he is not going to take my home away. This talk of Marxism is nonsense," said Lauteur. "If you go with God, then you are right. He will govern with the Bible in one hand, the constitution in the other." And she bustled away, a plump mulatto with a silvery pony tail, in billowing skirts. Lauteur's home, a huge, open-air estate, locked away from the public behind not one but two gates, was something akin to a sorority house in the days preceding the inauguration, aflutter with a gaggle of sleek, cunning matrons.

"The private sector, the well-to-do, represent only 10% of the population. It's time for us to go with the majority, for our own interests, if nothing else," said Arlette Batiste, a coffee exporter. Elegant in a white linen suit, her hair in a tight French chignon, Batiste, whose family has thrived for generations under whatever regime was in power, wore an expression of mild amusement as she explained her shift with the political winds.

"We live the good life. The majority is living a worse life every day. Our situation will be less fragile if everyone lives better," she said. "I am here from self-interest, as every wealthy Haitian should be. This man is our last chance. Haiti is on the verge of revolution. I can't understand why the U.S. doesn't see that Aristide is what Haiti needs right now. We can either move with the public mood or be destroyed. After all," she added, smiling, "how can we put our best linen on the bed until we dust?"

I n the end, it may be Marjorie Michele, 27, a Brussels-educated psychologist, daughter of Smark Michele, who can tell us most about the enigmatic priest who now leads Haiti. She is, by her own description, the closest thing Haiti has today to a first lady.

"He's a very secret person, you'll never know exactly what's on his mind," she says over lunch. "And the man is ridiculous. For a psychologist, he has no idea how to take care of himself. He's killing himself. He doesn't eat, he doesn't sleep. . . . This is why I'm first lady. I run into his office, and I say, 'Please, I think now we should go eat.' When he stays [at her father's house], I go into his room and I turn off the light and I say, 'OK, now it's time to sleep. . . .' "

She became his friend, she says, right after the Salesians expelled him, an event that didn't simply anger him—"He was crushed. He felt so alone. He was so used to living in groups, with other priests. But, suddenly, he was left so alone. He told me, 'Now I'm sitting here in this room alone, with no family, except the poor people.' "

She smiles, lights a cigarette and, in French, orders the pigeon. The restaurant is another of those serene terraced Port-au-Prince enclaves, a world away from the misery outside. Michele is at home here, both poised and glamorous in three-inch earrings, her white cotton dress revealing cleavage.

During the inaugural she sat in the family box. She shows up at most of Aristide's press conferences. Just recently, a New York Haitian newspaper announced her engagement to the new president. She laughs, enjoying the gossip, but says, pointedly, "We are social friends. Political friends. With Aristide, if you don't fit into his priorities, you're out. And my priorities are also the poor people. I don't have a superiority complex; I want the people to be *like* me. So Aristide and I, we fit."

Politics besets the friendship. "He worries that we are not born to the same class. He tells me that. He has no problems with me, or any other social class. But when the people see him with me, they see the bourgeoisie. It's a very big problem for him. And if he has to sacrifice me for the people, he will. For example, if we have to have a civil war, the people's feelings are first. If I get killed, he accepts it. If 20,000 are going to die, it's fine for the movement. It is all that matters to him."

She agrees with Aristide's critics, that he's surrounded himself with yes-men. "All these people, Gladys, Renee, Adrien, William [Smarth], even my father, they will never push him very hard," she says, exasperated. "They fight behind the scenes, but in front of him, they're peaceful. They protect him. They say, 'Oh, no, we will not tell him this or that now, because he's so tired.' They are always pampering him, protecting him. I tell them to stop it. I am the first lady because I am the only one who will tell him the truth. I don't swallow anything from him. I tell him when he's full of it!"

She is also looking ahead, to the end of Aristide's five-year term. "I keep telling him, it is very important that he takes someone near to him now, to teach. Because in five years more, Haiti will need another Aristide. If Aristide died today, there is absolutely no one who can replace him. The people don't just like him, he is their *God*. I want Haitians to be their own god. He's human! Over my dead body will he be king." ▬

Article 12.1.   Remaking the Mideast

In this article, Richard W. Murphy, former U.S. Assistant Secretary of State for Near Eastern and South Asian Affairs, offers a post-war blueprint for peace in the Middle East, which calls for the removal of U.S. and other non-Arab forces from the region; an American willingness to pursue collective action primarily through the U.N. Security Council; an increased U.S. emphasis on inter-Arab relationships; a renewed American effort to advance the Arab-Israeli peace process; and U.S. action to control missiles and nuclear/chemical/biological warheads in the region. For the blueprint to succeed, President Bush must pursue the post-war regional agenda as vigorously as he pursued the gulf war. If he does, the present "window of opportunity" may well lead to a lasting peace.

REMAKING THE MIDEAST

For seven years Secretary Murphy negotiated with every Mideast leader. Here is his blueprint for seizing postwar momentum to build political stability.

—

By Richard W. Murphy

Richard W. Murphy ("Mideast: Strategies for Stability," WM October '90), is Senior Fellow for Middle East at the Council on Foreign Relations. He was US Assistant Secretary of State for Near Eastern and South Asian Affairs, 1983-89. His ambassadorial assignments included Saudi Arabia, Syria, Mauritania, and the Philippines.

THE AFTERMATH OF THE GULF WAR requires Washington to be more—not less—involved in the Mideast.

That dictum runs contrary to neo-isolationist arguments that the US fought the war in order to turn inward to domestic problems.

But there is no inherent reason that America has to become isolationist in order to tackle its backlog of domestic needs. To the contrary, the most cost-effective approach for the future is to capitalize on the great effort invested in the war by pursuing creative diplomacy in the Mideast without in any way undermining work on the domestic agenda.

To do otherwise is to repeat on the world scene what Americans so foolishly did on the domestic scene in the past decade: mortgage the future.

American, British, and French soldiers repeatedly told interviewers during the war that they would rather see the campaign through, despite

From *World Monitor*, April 1991, pp. 28-33. Reprinted by permission.

the risk, than find themselves or their younger brothers and sisters coming back a few years later to do the job again.

That same sentiment should apply now to suggestions that Washington turn inward and relax pressure for diplomatic settlements of the region's longstanding problems. That would be the diplomatic equivalent of asking younger brothers and sisters to face perhaps worse Middle Eastern problems later.

OPERATION DESERT REHAB

Political repair after war is always harder than physical repair.

We know Kuwait City and its nearby refineries —and eventually Baghdad and Iraq's power plants and bridges—can be rebuilt. The crush of American and European construction firms jockeying for Kuwaiti contracts is turning into Operation Desert Rehab (with Bechtel as its Schwarzkopf).

But political and economic repair is more complex by far. And going beyond mere repair to design new relationships among nations takes vision, hardheaded realism, and—paradoxically— both decisiveness and patience.

It's easy to coin slogans; harder to make them realities. "New World Order" reminds us of "New Deal," "Great Society," and glasnost. All started as political rallying cries without specific content.

President Bush and his advisers pursued the war with great concentration and vigor. No less an effort will be needed to win the peace. Secretary of State James Baker's first postwar tour to the governments of the area was a good start, and his description of it as a probing operation was well taken. He (and Washington) can't *dictate*, even in the wake of one of the most decisive war victories in history. But the Bush administration can and should follow up on the determination expressed by the president in making his March victory speech to Congress: that, in order to ensure lasting peace, all of its friends—the Arab members of the recent military coalition and Israel—must cooperate to change the diplomatic face of the area.

That means serious attempts to control (and reduce) arms, reinvigorate the Israeli-Arab peace process, deal with the Palestinian problem, and help devise a development program that will better distribute the wealth of the Gulf states throughout the region.

A reinvigorated American regional policy must accompany the political and military defeat of Saddam Hussein. Some US critics have continued to accuse the administration of risking soldiers' lives and devastating Iraq for cheap oil and for the benefit of the Kuwaiti ruling family. While high-tech US arms and decisive leadership have gained America considerable respect, many in the Arab community also believe that Western power is used in the region mainly to safeguard oil,
pro-Western Arab rulers,

and Israel. To these general suspicions must be added the particular bitterness among Palestinians over the defeat of Saddam and their continued suppression.

To deal with these charges, President Bush should spell out his long-term comprehensive plans for the Middle East. That should be possible soon after he turns his attention from the UN-centered negotiations on policing the postwar agreements forced on Iraq. By then he and Secretary Baker will have assessed the results of Baker's Mideastern tour and consulted with their European allies. (New security arrangements could be precedent-setting and relatively easy to devise.)

A suggested blueprint for White House action might include five sets of plans:

1. How peacekeeping forces should operate after the quick exit of US forces from the Gulf—to make sure that Iraq, Iran, and the Gulf states remain in peaceful balance.

2. How to strengthen the UN for refereeing regional disputes.

3. How the Arab members of the allied war coalition will now relate to other states in the region.

4. How to make use of the narrow window of time during which (a) both Israel and the Arab members of the coalition feel keenly indebted to Washington for defeating Saddam; and (b) the Arab coalition states that cut their financial aid for the PLO will still want to show new support for Palestinians in another manner.

5. How to control arms in the region—including intermediate-range missiles, existing stockpiles, and any future production of nuclear/chemical/biological weapons.

First (and in many ways easiest to accomplish): the exodus of US and other non-Arab forces from the region. Straddling the Iraqi-Kuwaiti border there should be a United Nations peacekeeping force as a tripwire in the event of any future Iraqi encroachment.

Saudi Arabia will probably want to bid farewell fairly quickly to coalition ground forces. The Saudis have always sought to project the image of a self-reliant country that relies on its own strength wherever possible, and will not tolerate the image of needing constant foreign protection.

The Saudis might, however, welcome some strengthening of their own forces and those of the five other members of the Gulf Cooperation Council (GCC) through the long-

 *n American commitment to use the UN may be of more lasting importance for future crisis management than the allies' extraordinary military achievements.*

term addition of Egyptian units. These would have the advantage of being both Arab and Muslim, two characteristics that the Saudis will likely insist upon in any quasi-permanent foreign military presence.

The United States may well want to leave much of the military equipment and supplies lifted to Saudi Arabia since last August and pre-position them for use against a future threat to regional peace. This precaution will probably be acceptable to Saudi Arabia and other member states of the GCC as long as the US custodial presence is limited.

President Bush's position has rightly been that US forces will not stay in the area one day longer than necessary. Some units can be quickly removed, and their return began immediately. Just how long Western forces will remain will depend upon how soon the Kuwaiti government has fully recovered its capacity to provide civil and policing services. It will also depend on how soon the UN-authorized peacekeeping force can be put in place to monitor Iraq's compliance with UN resolutions. But in any event, the bulk of American forces should be withdrawn in the next few months.

Washington should, as President Bush has indicated, maintain a naval presence at a level higher than the normal fleet of five to six ships that has patrolled the Gulf for the past 40 years.

The US should also quickly negotiate agreements with the GCC states to provide for future joint military exercises and access to local ports and airfields. These would be executive agreements not needing US Senate approval. It is unlikely that the Gulf states would ask for, or that the Senate would approve, more formal arrangements such as mutual defense treaties.

Second: the role of the UN. In his 1991 State of the Union message, President Bush called upon the international community to "fulfill the long-held promise of a new world order—where brutality will go unrewarded and aggression will meet collective resistance." Under this new order, *collective* action in handling a regional crisis is preferred to *unilateral US action*. Recent diplomatic and military cooperation at the UN and in the field has set a solid precedent for fulfilling that goal.

This is not to ignore the reality that there may well be future crises where only the US will have the political and military wherewithal to counter aggression effectively. An American commitment to pursuing decisive action primarily through the UN Security Council may be of more lasting importance for future crisis management than the allies' extraordinary military achievements in January and February and their new weapons systems.

Whether or not the Security Council can play so central a role in future crises depends largely upon the readiness of those with veto power to let it do so.

If the Gulf crisis is going to lead the Middle East into a more peaceful 21st century, there is no doubt that the United States must not just react to crises as in the past but play a direct and healing role in constructing new regional security and political arrangements.

Third: shifting inter-Arab relationships. The coalition, assembled in the course of the first few months after the invasion, was an unusually mixed bag of participants drawn together for different reasons and with differing objectives. The Gulf Cooperation Council states were united by fear that if Iraq absorbed Kuwait, then all of them could be subject to increased Iraqi intimidation. Egypt saw a threat in Baghdad's growing inclination to challenge Egyptian leadership in the Arab world. Syria's reaction was not conditioned on solidarity with Kuwait's royal Sabah family. Rather, the split between the two wings of the Baath Party (in Syria and Iraq) and the deeply rooted personal animosity between the Syrian and Iraqi presidents moved Hafez al-Assad to join the Western coalition.

Both Egypt and Syria also had reason to expect significant financial rewards from the Gulf oil states for having stood with them.

The convergence of interests of these governments, for whatever reason, has led to more intense and intimate communication and cooperation among Cairo, Damascus, and Riyadh. This cobbled-together alliance may outlast the fears that drove it together. And that could bode well for future Arab-Israeli negotiations.

Fourth: the indebtedness of Israel and the coalition Arabs to Washington for defeating Saddam Hussein —and the brief opportunity it affords to advance negotiations before the window closes. Israel has brooded since the invasion last August that the Gulf crisis might somehow end in "costing" Israel. The

Shamir government, while delighted with the coalition's elimination of Iraq as a strategic threat, anticipates a renewed American effort to advance the Arab-Israeli peace process. Flashes of that US determination appeared even during the period when Mr. Bush was frequently on the telephone to Mr. Shamir assuring him of their readiness to defend Israel against Scud attacks in return for Israel's sitting out the war. Israel now finds itself in an awkward position when it criticizes US arms sales to Gulf states.

The Israelis obviously are quite content with the close and supportive American posture toward Israel's security needs, yet they view the Bush administration's position regarding the peace process with increasing mistrust. Prime Minister Shamir believes that Washington distorted his 1989 initiative to launch both state-to-state Arab-Israeli negotiations and Israeli-Palestinian talks by overly focusing on the latter.

On the positive side, Israel has consistently stressed that it wants to open direct state-to-state talks with its Arab neighbors. The prime minister specifically endorsed talks on a nuclear and chemical weapons-free zone in the Middle East. It remains to be seen whether he will predicate such talks on prior political normalization.

Shamir has also said, unofficially, that he might be willing to change one crucial position: that Israel will not negotiate step-by-step confidence-building measures with Arab neighbors prior to their recognition of Israel. That is exactly the kind of change Messrs. Bush and Baker will want to pin down to get the peace process started.

The Palestinian problem will not improve with neglect. However, this may not be the moment to revisit the question of *who* best represents the Palestinians, given the setbacks suffered both by the PLO and Jordan's King Hussein for having backed Saddam Hussein. It could be a propitious time to encourage the king to sit with West Bank Palestinians to see whether a joint delegation for talks with Israel might be possible without debating whether or not they represent the PLO.

There certainly is little evidence that the Palestinians in the occupied territories would be ready any time soon to sit down alone with Israel. The frustrations that led to their supporting Saddam last summer and cheering the Scud attacks on Israel have created deeper bitterness and a sense of helplessness at his military defeat.

Jordan has lost from its strategy of depending on Baghdad as its defender against Israel. But, because King Hussein stood with Iraq, he should be able to enjoy the favor of the Palestinian community for some time to come. He is keenly aware that the Palestinian cause, if not the PLO leadership, will retain its power to stir Arab emotions. And he may seek a leadership role in any revived Arab-Israeli peace process.

Chairman Arafat of the PLO, like King Hus-sein, cast his lot with Saddam and deplored the campaign of the UN-approved coalition forces. This criticism prompted the Saudi and Kuwaiti leadership, the PLO's primary financial benefactors, to suspend longstanding assistance programs. (The subsequent assassination of Abu Iyad, Arafat's heir-apparent, was probably the direct result of his having irritated Baghdad. Abu Iyad had warned against the PLO's tilt as violating one of that organization's basic precepts—noninterference in inter-Arab conflicts.)

Whatever the postwar balance, the PLO will lose. Its leadership chose the wrong side, again.

The Palestinian problem will continue to haunt the Arab countries after the current crisis, whether or not Saddam is dethroned.

The Palestinian community will be forced to reevaluate its leaders. There are a number of younger PLO leaders and prominent Palestinians in the West Bank and Gaza who are willing to compromise and deal with the Israelis. Ironically, the three-year-old *intifada* seems to be spawning a new generation of Israeli leaders in the Likud Party, aptly nicknamed, "the Princes." These new younger leaders, looking to the future, have hinted that they might be more flexible in negotiating with the Palestinians after peace is arranged in the region. This may be only tactical maneuvering, but the US should prod further to see if any of these future leaders might be enticed to the negotiating table.

For their part the Arab coalition partners have been accused of abandoning the Palestinian people, as well as helping to destroy another Arab country.

To offset these accusations those leaders will be interested in showing the Palestinians some sign of tangible support. They not only will owe Washington one for conquering Iraq but also will feel they owe the Palestinians something on Arab political and humanitarian grounds.

Iraq's crushing defeat touched many issues that bedeviled previous efforts to get negotiations started. For example, Syria and Jordan have for years asserted they can negotiate with Israel only within an international framework. There is no recent evidence that Israeli hostility to all such frameworks has diminished.

Fifth: controlling missiles and nuclear/chemical/biological warheads in the region. As long as Israeli leaders fear being overrun by their Arab neighbors, they will not give up the deterrence of nuclear (and high-performance conventional) weapons. They will not yield up those weapons in return for guarantees of outside military protection.

And as long as Israel maintains its missiles, nuclear warheads, and superior air force, Arab governments will fear Israeli strikes and attempt to acquire similar weapons.

In the wake of the massive shakeup of the Gulf War, however, some opportunities may arise to break this impasse. Prime Minister Shamir's call

*he Middle East has eluded many well-intentioned efforts at peacemaking since World War II. And it could either catalyze the New World Order or destroy it.*

for a regional nuclear-free zone reflects this fresh line of thinking.

This war has shown clearly just how out of control the arms race has become in this passionately divided region. Former administrations paid little effective attention to this deadly and expensive competition. Washington often asserted that the United States was the only arms supplier that conscientiously weighed its arms sales against their effect on the regional arms balance. However, arguments cautioning against major sales were often put aside in the name of Cold War competition and the security of Israel. Sales to Israel have been and will probably continue to be measured against the guideline that Israel should maintain a qualitative edge over any potential combination of Arab armed forces.

With the easing of the Cold War this equation has changed. Moscow has rejected Syria's goal of gaining strategic parity with Israel. And the USSR will probably be hesitant to resupply Iraq at its former level. In addition, the regional actors seem readier to acknowledge economic necessity to redirect defense expenditures to civilian concerns. This creates a more promising atmosphere for an effort to reduce arms in the region than at any point in the past generation.

Unfortunately, the lack of formal relations between many of the participants will hinder the negotiating process. But the opportunity afforded by the end of the Gulf War should be quickly seized—to eliminate acquisition of weapons of mass destruction, slow down the sales of conventional weapons, and begin the long process of reducing levels of weaponry in all categories.

MANAGING CRITICS

Those who say this is an impossible task should be reminded that similar words were often spoken about reducing Soviet and NATO arms in Europe. And no one now needs to be reminded of what Scuds and chemical weapons mean to civilian populations. Unrealistic as it may sound, arms control

negotiations could spur fresh approaches to the more traditional issues of the peace process—land and peaceful relations.

Those who argue that the American position in the Middle East has been irrevocably damaged by this first Arab-American war rush to judgment. The Arab world has split along new fault lines. Although the present realignment, as represented by coalition members and their critics, may not prove long-lasting, it does give the international community a new political situation to work with. US political and military leadership of the coalition has won respect as well as outspoken resentment from Arab political leaders.

Islamic fundamentalists and Arab nationalists viewed American intervention as a revival of colonial manipulation of the Arab world and as an insult to Islam. They will be watching the next steps of American diplomacy through jaundiced eyes.

One way to manage such critics in advancing toward the goal of a more stable Middle East will be to exploit as many opportunities as possible for peacemaking, within the UN framework. Prior to the outbreak of war Washington found it possible and productive to work within the UN Security Council, and has returned to the Council to formalize cease-fire arrangements.

America's Gulf experience may not be a precise guide for handling future crises. Nonetheless, contrary to the contention of American neo-isolationists that the US should "stop trying to be the world's policeman," this postwar period—with its diminished Soviet threat—is the time for American-initiated diplomacy respectful of and cooperative with the UN.

The Middle East has eluded many previous well-intentioned efforts at peacemaking since World War II. And it could either catalyze the New World Order or destroy it. But if President Bush pursues the postwar regional agenda as vigorously as he pursued the war, what began life as a catchy slogan just might turn out to have marked a new start for us all. **WM**

In this article—written just prior to the gulf war—the author warns that the Middle East could well be headed toward further turmoil unless steps are taken to reverse the economic collapse, dissolving security arrangements, and rising domestic discontent which plague the region and which could give rise to a new era of military coups, interstate conflicts, and even Islamic revolutions. Although the United States did not precipitate the gulf crisis, it should move cautiously to avoid aggravating or escalating the tensions that exist. Further, any attempt to create a permanent U.S. presence in the gulf is likely to antagonize many Arab states, who would view it as yet another example of Yankee imperialism.

Revolution, Reform, or Regression?

Arab Political Options in the 1990 Gulf Crisis

Yahya Sadowski

An old Arab proverb about the romance of war goes: distant drums, sweet music. Most Washington pundits believe that the Bush administration will bring the Kuwait crisis to a close before the spring of 1991. Either Saddam Hussein's troops will bow to international pressure and walk out of Kuwait, or they will fold before an American military assault and be carried out on stretchers. After this victory America will sit back and enjoy "the new global order." But whatever transpires on Kuwaiti sands over the next few months, America will soon have to confront two painful facts. First, the Iraqi invasion of Kuwait is only one symptom of a much wider crisis in the Arab world. Second, this wider crisis is going to persist and fuel renewed instability in the region regardless of whether America claims a victory in Kuwait.

Yahya Sadowski, a research associate in the Brookings Foreign Policy Studies program, is the author of Political Vegetables: Businessman and Bureaucrat in the Development of Egyptian Agriculture *(forthcoming).*

From *The Brookings Review*, Winter 1990/91, pp. 17-21. Reprinted by permission.

To many Americans, the Middle East in the 1980s appeared to be an unstable and violent region. The U.S. press was filled with unsettling reports about civil wars in Lebanon and the Sudan and regional wars pitting Israel against Syria and Iraq against Iran. But the truth is, the 1980s was a period of relative stability in the region.

During the 1960s the Middle East was markedly less stable — as it may be again soon. Not only were the troubles in Lebanon, the Sudan, Israel, and Iran already evident, but they were compounded by a series of conflicts that have since disappeared. The oil-rich, underpopulated, and conservative monarchies of the Gulf were threatened by republican or Marxist insurgents in the Yemen, tribal rebellions in Oman, and underground Arab nationalist parties in Kuwait and Bahrain. The poor, overpopulated, Arab nationalist regimes in countries like Syria and Iraq were wracked by a seemingly endless series of military coups d'état. A regional power struggle, which Malcolm Kerr dubbed "the Arab cold war," aggravated these domestic disputes. The struggle pitted a coalition of Arab nationalist governments led by

Egypt against a rival coalition of pro-Western regimes led by Saudi Arabia.

In November 1967 King Feisal of Saudi Arabia and President Nasser of Egypt, both shocked by Israel's victory in the June war, met in Khartoum to call a truce and lay the foundations of a new Arab order. The Saudis and the other Gulf emirates began to offer billions of dollars of foreign aid to the poorer Arab nationalist regimes. In exchange, the nationalist regimes stopped supporting the insurgencies in the Arabian Peninsula and began to collaborate with the Gulf monarchies in dealing with non-Arab security threats like Iran and Israel. Military coups became less frequent because the poorer Arab states were able to buy a measure of popularity among their citizens by offering consumer subsidies, public employment programs, and lucrative state contracts.

That arrangement of buyoffs between and within Arab states, sometimes called the Arab state system, was criticized by both Leftists and Islamists, who claimed that it insulated the ruling elites from popular pressures, stifled social change, and fostered corruption. Their criticisms struck a chord, but most Arabs clung to the system because it provided peace, relative political stability, and a rising standard of living.

During the 1980s, however, the system became harder to sustain. The Middle East had an exceptionally fast growing population. Egypt's population, which had been 30 million in 1966, reached 50 million by 1988 and was projected to exceed 67 million by the year 2000. Jordan had the second-fastest growing population in the world (ranking just behind Kenya). The annual growth of population was higher than 3 percent in the Yemens, Sudan, Syria, Iraq, Saudi Arabia, and Kuwait.

Under the best of circumstances such growth would have taxed the local economies, but standards of living were rising too. People who had been content to eat pasta developed a taste for meat. Countries like Egypt and Iraq, which had been food self-sufficient in 1970, today import 80 percent of their basic foodstuffs. This growth of consumer demand might have been met by investing in local industrial and agricultural projects. But a large share of the petrodollar wealth was squandered by corrupt elites or spent cultivating political loyalty. The few productive ventures that did receive investment were hamstrung by economic policies (such as price controls and overvalued currencies) that inhibited the growth of internationally competitive enterprises. The only sectors of the economy that typically grew faster than population were commerce and government bureaucracy.

In 1982 and again in 1985, oil prices slipped badly. The total value of Arab oil exports, which had been $212 billion in 1982, fell to $95 billion by 1987. Petrodollar aid transferred among Arab states dropped correspondingly. At first the oil-poor, heavily populated states tried to compensate by borrowing abroad. Jordan built up $8 billion in foreign debt; Morocco, $20 billion; Algeria, $25 billion; Egypt, $50 billion; and Iraq, $80 billion. But within a few years most Arab states had reached the limits of their credit with foreign lenders.

By the late 1980s, it was no longer possible to sustain the expenses involved in propping up the Arab state system. Just servicing existing debts crippled the economies of the poorer states, draining their hard currency revenues. Even the richest Gulf states began to run budget deficits and dip into their cash reserves. Across the Arab world, right-wing monarchies and left-wing military dictatorships faced a crisis of rule. Whatever popularity these regimes had acquired in the struggle against colonial occupation had long since evaporated. The lavish state patronage that had allowed them to maintain their authority was sapped by a growing economic crisis. Increasingly, the mass of Arabs saw their rulers as ideologically bankrupt, politically corrupt, and socially alien.

The Arab state system was eroded and fragile. From 1987 onward, each of the Arab countries began to react — in different ways — to that new reality. Three different styles of reaction prevailed, according to the needs and assets of each country. Kuwait, Jordan, and Iraq exemplify the three types of reaction.

> *By the late 1980s, it was no longer possible to sustain the expenses involved in propping up the Arab state system. Just servicing debts crippled the economies of the poorer states, draining their hard currency revenues. Even the richest Gulf states began to run budget deficits and dip into their cash reserves.*

Kuwait: Getting Out

During the 1970s, the Kuwaitis had been among the more imaginative of the rich Gulf states. Rather than spend the bulk of their cash on public works and subsidies, they had set aside $100 billion in two huge reserve funds to finance the needs of future generations. Many of these funds were invested in stocks abroad: British Petroleum and Hoechst metals, to name a few. In the 1980s, the Kuwaitis discovered they were actually earning more from these investments than from oil exports.

That discovery suggested a way for Kuwait to deal with the crisis of the Arab state system. Kuwait's rulers dreamed of turning their country into a Middle Eastern analogue of South Korea: economically linked to the West and defended by American power.

Economically, the Kuwaitis decided to expand and consolidate their investments in the West. For this, they needed more cash fast. They drastically reduced the aid they dispensed to their foreign neighbors, rebuffing Jordanian requests for emergency economic assistance and notifying Iraq that they still expected repayment of more than $10 billion lent during the war with Iran. They increased their petroleum exports, exceeding their OPEC production quota and driving down the price of oil, in a frantic search for cash.

Politically, too, they began to contemplate closer ties with the West. They believed that Iraq, in the end, had failed to defend them from Iran. Instead they thought that America, through its agreement to reflag Kuwaiti tankers and its naval intervention in the Gulf, was the force that cowed Khomeini. They paid less attention to the Arab League and more to the Gulf Cooperation Council, a regional security alliance fostered by Saudi Arabia. They began to admire the Saudi "special relationship" with the United States.

The Kuwaitis, and other Gulf regimes, began to exit from the Arab state system. They began to rely more on an American security umbrella. In some ways, they were returning to the conditions of the 1960s, when Great Britain protected the Gulf states from their hungry neighbors.

The poorer Arab states were not happy about that development, and their resentment toward Kuwait and the rich states grew. They had no big cash assets; they faced an immediate economic crisis. Their choices were exemplified by Jordan.

Jordan: Economic Austerity

In 1988 conditions in Jordan were already desperate. The country needed $700 million in hard currency each year just to service its foreign debt and another $800 million to cover its trade deficit. Aid from Arab states, which had run $2 billion annually in the early 1980s, had dwindled to less than $200 million a year. The economy was slowing and the dinar was losing its value.

By early 1989 the Jordanian government no longer had enough money to keep repaying its debt. It was forced to turn to the Paris Club to arrange rescheduling. But the Paris Club would not act until the International Monetary Fund certified that the Jordanians were taking measures to strengthen their economy. So Jordan had to negotiate with the IMF, which insisted upon its usual austerity program: the currency had to be devalued, the budget cut, and consumer subsidies eliminated.

In April 1989 Jordan began to implement the austerity plan, announcing massive cuts in public spending and increases in the prices of cigarettes, gasoline, electricity, milk, and bread. The immediate result was a week of the worst rioting the kingdom had ever seen.

To halt the rioting, King Hussein sacked his prime minister and promised new elections. When the elections were held that fall, radical Islamist candidates won a clear plurality.

In most of the poorer Arab states, energetic Islamist movements wait in the wings. The oldest opponents of the Arab state system, they have developed an elaborate ideology that criticizes the ruling elites for their foreign ties, their corruption, and their injustice to their downtrodden subjects. They are experts at grassroots organizing, using mosques, medical clinics, and student organizations to propagate their program. They are not generally hidebound clerics like the Iranian ayatollahs, but young postmodernists who rejected Western culture after flirting with it. They are dedicated and effective.

The Islamists are a significant force in most Arab countries and are well positioned to exploit the anger aroused by economic adjustment programs. They prospered in Tunisia and Morocco after the bread riots of 1984, took power in the Sudan after the economic collapse of 1985, and swept the municipal elections in Algeria after the government adopted an economic austerity program in 1988.

Obviously economic adjustment is so dangerous a policy that Arab leaders have adopted it only when all other choices are closed. Some Arab states, like Egypt, Algeria, and Iraq, still have enough influence in regional affairs that they have been able to attempt a different strategy: to try to reconstruct the Arab state system. That is what Iraq has been attempting to do.

Saddam could have gotten most of the concessions he wanted from Kuwait through a few military maneuvers on its border and some hardball negotiations. But he knew that the process would be long and painful. He decided instead to gamble on resolving all these problems at once with a demonstration of his power: he invaded Kuwait.

Iraq: Rebuilding a Streamlined System

Despite its domestic oil resources, Baghdad needed as much economic help as any of the poorest Arab states. Iraq had spent more than $241 billion prosecuting war with Iran (more than it had earned from oil exports since they began in the 1930s) and needed billions more to repair the damage. It had already borrowed heavily, and repayments on foreign debt consumed more than $4 billion a year. Iraqi citizens, having tolerated austerity during the war, insisted on a tangible increase in their standard of living.

Saddam Hussein desperately wanted to keep the Arab state system alive. He told his richer neighbors he still deserved their aid because his army kept Iran at bay. He began to hint that he would use his military to challenge Israel, if only the other Arab states would continue to foot his bills.

At first he put his case across peaceably. He recruited Egypt, Jordan, and the Yemen to join him in forming an Arab Cooperation Council to lobby the rich Arab states for more aid. To lend credence to his campaign, he began to cultivate ties to the poorest groups of Arabs: Palestinians in the refugee camps, Mauritanians, the Sudanese.

But his entreaties went unanswered. The Kuwaitis and the United Arab Emirates continued overpumping oil, undercutting his revenues. The Saudis and Kuwaitis refused to forgive his debts. By May 1990 Saddam had changed his tone and suggested that if the Arab state system could not be held together voluntarily, he would hold it together by force.

Saddam could have gotten most of the concessions he wanted from Kuwait through a few military maneuvers on its border and some hardball negotiations. But he knew that the process would be long and painful and that it would be followed by slower negotiations with the Saudis, and even more laborious talks with the distant emirates. He decided instead to gamble on resolving all these problems at once with a demonstration of his power: he invaded Kuwait.

In one way, the Iraqi invasion of Kuwait eased the crisis of the Arab system: it doubled oil prices. But even in the richest Gulf states, the doubling of oil prices will not create the kind of funds that might be used to resurrect the old Arab state system. In real (inflation-adjusted) terms, the price of oil still stands below its 1980 level. Yet the price of security in the Arab World has risen dramatically.

Saudi Arabia, for example, may earn a $25 billion windfall from oil exports over the next year. But the prospect of a Gulf war has also scared off an anticipated $10 billion of foreign investment. The kingdom may already have spent $8 billion to $10 billion resettling 200,000 Kuwaiti refugees, bailing out local businesses distressed by the crisis, and defraying the costs of Asian workers fleeing the Gulf. It will also spend more than $10 billion supporting the American military deployment in the region.

Since the invasion, the Saudis have wrestled with the same security dilemma that confronted the Kuwaitis. Some figures inside the royal family think that the American deployment itself foreshadows the solution of their security problems. They are trying to entice Washington into making a long-term commitment to the kingdom, involving permanent bases, more advanced weapons for the Saudi armed forces, and a formal military alliance of the two countries. To make themselves a more attractive ally for America, they have toyed with the idea of creating quasi-democratic institutions.

But a permanent American presence in the Gulf frightens many in the region. The Iranians and Syrians have already announced that, over the long run, they consider American troops more of a threat than Iraq. Many Arabs would see such an alliance as an exercise in old-fashioned imperialism, with America allying itself with local despots to preserve its access to oil. Even conservative Saudis are worried about the local social changes that might be galvanized by an intimate relationship with America.

Thus other members of the Saudi royal family would rather limit the kingdom's American entanglements and rely instead on Arab allies for its security. They have been delighted that Egypt, Syria, and Morocco have contributed troops for their defense. They note that while America can deter formal armies from invading the kingdom, other Arab states can do more to protect it from subversion by tribal guerrillas, emigré dissidents, or military cabals.

Plenty of states are willing to supply *condotierre* for the Saudis. At the beginning of 1990 Egypt was immersed in a paralyzing economic crisis and was contemplating an IMF-dictated austerity program. Cairo's solidarity with Saudi Arabia in the Gulf crisis has earned it direct aid from the Gulf and forgiveness of $7.1 billion in American military debt, and revenues from its modest oil exports have risen. But that does not mean that Egypt will enjoy the kind of prosperity it had during the heyday of the Arab state system. Its increased revenues barely offset the costs the Gulf crisis has imposed on Egypt: the loss of billions of dollars in income from emigré workers in Iraq, tourist receipts, and Suez Canal tolls.

Many of the oil-poor Arab states have been hit much harder than Egypt. A million Yemeni workers, who supplied most of their country's hard currency, have been sent home from Saudi Arabia. Jordan has been devastated. Over the next year Amman is expected to lose $660 million in Iraqi debt repayments, $250 million in transit business, $230 million in tourist business, and $180 million in oil grants. The total bill is projected to be $2.1 billion — more than half the country's gross domestic product. Many observers fear King Hussein may lose his throne before Saddam Hussein loses his.

It is always dangerous to make any predictions about the Middle East. But in conditions of economic collapse, dissolving security arrangements, and rising domestic discontent, it seems a safe bet that the region is heading into an era of renewed turmoil. Coups, interstate feuds, and even Islamist revolutions seem likely prospects.

Potentially the most unstable state in the region is Iraq. We do not yet know how much damage the international embargo and the looming war may do to the country, but it is clear that Saddam Hussein has committed economic suicide. Baghdad has already lost its oil receipts for this year and swallowed the costs of another massive military mobilization. So long as Saddam is in power the country cannot expect rescheduling of its debts, much less new loans. And foreign firms, critical to Iraq's planned reconstruction, are unlikely to invest in a country where their employees might be made "guests by force" at any moment.

None of this bodes well for regional security. Traditionally, the Gulf states have played Iraq and Iran off against each other in a balance of power. If Iraq lapses into anarchy, who would offset the power of the Islamic Republic? If Saddam does survive, will he accept the mantle of Nasser and lead the oil-poor Arab states in another cold war against the Gulf monarchies?

The United States did not create the current crisis in the Arab World. Even if the Iraqis withdraw from Kuwait, the crisis will not be over. Yet whether or not we go to war in the Gulf will have an effect, tempering or aggravating the imbroglio. If we urge Arab to fight Arab, we may revive the Arab cold war. Every Iraqi our troops kill will provide fresh ammunition for the Islamist campaign to expunge Western influence in the region. If we demolish Iraq, we may clear the way for a resurgence of Iranian power. There is no elegant solution for the crisis of the Arab system. We had better start thinking seriously about how we are going to live with it. □

It is always dangerous to make any predictions about the Middle East. But in conditions of economic collapse, dissolving security arrangements, and rising domestic discontent, it seems a safe bet that the region is heading into an era of renewed turmoil. Coups, interstate feuds, and even Islamist revolutions seem likely prospects.

SELECTED BIBLIOGRAPHY—SECTION III

Bill, James A., and Robert Springborg. *Politics in the Middle East*. New York: HarperCollins, 1990.

Darnton, Robert. *Berlin Journal: 1989-1990*. New York: W.W. Norton, 1991.

Dinges, John. *Our Man in Panama: The Shrewd Rise and Brutal Fall of Manuel Noriega*. New York: Times Books, 1991.

Dragnich, Alex N., Jorgen S. Rasmussen, and Joel Moses. *Major European Governments*. Pacific Grove, Calif.: Brooks/Cole, 1991.

Elliot, Jeffrey M., and Mervyn M. Dymally. *Voices of Zaire: Rhetoric or Reality?* Washington, D.C.: Washington Institute Press, 1990.

Ferguson, James. *Papa Doc, Baby Doc: Haiti and the Duvaliers*. New York: Basil Blackwell, 1987.

Fisk, Robert. Pity the Nation: The Abduction of Lebanon. New York: Touchstone Books, 1990.

Friedman, Thomas L. *From Beirut to Jerusalem*. New York: Anchor Books, 1990.

Galtung, Johan. *Europe in the Making*. Bristol, Penn.: Crane Russak, 1992.

Gerner, Deborah J. *One Land, Two Peoples: The Conflict over Palestine*. Boulder, Colo.: Westview Press, 1991.

Goodwyn, Lawrence. *Breaking the Barrier: The Rise of Solidarity in Poland*. New York: Oxford University Press, 1991.

Hanrieder, Wolfram F. *Germany, America, Europe: Forty Years of German Foreign Policy*. New Haven, Conn.: Yale University Press. 1991.

Havel, Vaclav. *Disturbing the Peace*. New York: Vintage Books, 1990.

Heller, Mark A., and Sari Nusseibeh. *No Trumpets, No Drums: A Two-State Settlement of the Israeli-Palestinian Conflict*. New York: Hill and Wang, 1991.

Karsh, Efraim, and Inari Rautsi. *Saddam Hussein: A Political Biography*. New York: Free Press, 1991.

Mahler, Gregory S. *Israel: Government and Politics in a Maturing State*. San Diego, Calif.: Harcourt Brace Jovanovich, 1990.

Meer, Fatima. *Higher Than Hope: The Authorized Biography of Nelson Mandela*. New York: Harper & Row, 1990.

Mufson, Steven. *Fighting Years: Black Resistance and the Struggle for a New South Africa*. Boston: Beacon Press, 1990.

Peters, B. Guy. *European Politics Reconsidered*. New York: Holmes & Meier, 1991.

Peretz, Don. *Intifada: The Palestinian Uprising*. Boulder, Colo.: Westview Press, 1990.

Pye, Lucian W. *China: An Introduction*. New York: HarperCollins, 1991.

Reshetar, John S., Jr. *The Soviet Polity: Government and Politics in the USSR*. New York: HarperCollins, 1989.

Smith, Gordon B. *Soviet Politics: Struggling with Change*. New York: St. Martin's, 1991.

Urban, Michael E. *More Power to the Soviets: The Democratic Revolution in the USSR*. Brookfield, Vt.: Edward Elgar, 1990.

Walker, Thomas W. *Nicaragua: The Land of Sandino*. Boulder, Colo.: Westview Press, 1986.

Wiseman, John A. *Democracy in Black Africa: Survival and Revival*. New York: Paragon House, 1990.

Woods, Donald. *Biko*. New York: Henry Holt, 1991.

Yi Mu, and Mark V. Thompson. *Crisis at Tiananmen: Reform and Reality in Modern China*. San Francisco, Calif.: China Books, 1989.

THE BALANCE OF TERROR

These are perilous times, which is why every nation is preoccupied with the issue of national security. The dangers posed by conventional and nuclear weapons demand that every country possess the ability to strike back with deadly force if attacked. National security is a federal responsibility. Indeed, the preamble to the U.S. Constitution requires the federal government to "provide for the common defense." At America's founding, the framers were motivated by the need to protect the nation from conquest or political domination by hostile European powers that retained strongholds in North America. At the time, they could not possibly have appreciated the relationship between national security and economic independence. Nor could they have envisaged such twentieth century dangers as large-scale guerrilla war, global terrorism, and nuclear annihilation, which threaten not only the security of the United States, but that of the entire world.

Today, America faces a host of actual and potential threats, both short-term and long-term. Some of these are domestic: static growth, declining productivity, environmental degradation, racial conflict, family disintegration, educational deterioration, political apathy, urban neglect, and a national economy heavily dependent on the military budget. A variety of external threats to U.S. national security exist as well, among them: regional instability, international drug trafficking, economic competition, worldwide starvation, local wars, debt crisis, and nuclear war.

National security is an elusive concept—its meaning defies simple definition. Still, few experts would disagree that the development and deployment of nuclear weapons pose an ominous threat to humankind. Fortunately, these weapons have been used only twice in the past half-century, both times at the dawn of the nuclear age. To that extent, the "balance of terror" has probably prevented World War III. On the other hand, one can take little solace in this fact, as it has created a dangerous arms race, in which nuclear stockpiles of the two superpowers have steadily increased in numbers and devastation. Although total megatonnage has declined, the flight time for many of the weapons of the strategic arsenals of both sides has been reduced from hours to minutes.

Clearly, a conventional confrontation between the United States and Soviet Union could well escalate into a strategic nuclear war. Although the Cold War has ended, there still exists some degree of hostility and mistrust between the two superpowers, leaving open the possibility of miscalculation. Perhaps more ominous, nuclear proliferation continues unabated. More likely than nuclear war, however, is the possibility of a conventional confrontation—one directed at U.S. allies and friends. Although such an attack would not prove immediately catastrophic to the industrialized world, it would certainly undermine their position in the long run. Of immediate concern, though, is the predicament of the Third World, which is plagued by a litany of problems. Internal instability, coupled with regional conflicts, pose a serious threat to world peace and international order.

In the end, the United States must develop a national security policy that accurately reflects Soviet goals and behavior. In addition, it must come to grips with the realities of the U.S. economy and devise means to reduce U.S. dependence on other nations. It must also carefully reassess its nuclear doctrine as well as its political and military strategy for dealing with regional conflicts. As national defense expert Harold Brown maintains, the government must "foster a national security policy that is directed at assuring, insofar as possible, that the United States will be free to evolve internally in the direction of its own ideals."

During the past several decades, the United States, among various other countries, has significantly contributed to the arms race by selling billions of dollars worth of weapons to its allies and, in some cases, to its enemies. Foreign arms sales bolster the defense industry by providing a profitable outlet for goods produced originally in response to Department of Defense contracts and also aid the balance of trade figures of the United States. In addition, such sales may reduce the unit cost of certain weapons systems by increasing the number of items produced, may help maintain assembly lines that would otherwise remain idle, and may be used to advance U.S. foreign policy aims.

The major arms producers market their wares through trade fairs in Europe and elsewhere, and through presentations made directly to interested parties or governments. Arms sales to foreign nations has been a fact of life since the late nineteenth century, when arms dealers helped create the conditions that led to World War I. While such sales provide positive benefits to the U.S. economy (and to the economies of the Soviet Union, France, Great Britain, Germany, and China, among others), the arms dealers have much to answer for. By selling (or allowing the sale of) weapons and support technology to Third World countries, the United States (and the industrialized world) has directly or indirectly contributed to wars, skirmishes, and internal uprisings that otherwise could not exist or sustain themselves. It has also helped to maintain in power ruthless dictatorial regimes which ultimately may not share U.S. foreign policy aims. The recent trend in providing "first-line" equipment—weapons currently being used by the U.S. military as their primary systems, or newly developed weapons and technology not sponsored by or for the Department of Defense, where the U.S. company simply sells management and technical knowhow to the foreign user—has created a "brain drain" to profitable overseas markets.

Arms transfers also pose a serious challenge to world peace. The idea began with the Lend Lease Act of 1940, which transferred forty "obsolete" U.S. destroyers to Great Britain to help bolster its war against German submarines. These transfers are also made for "credits," which are either never repaid by the receiving country or for which goods may ultimately be traded. Arms transfers can be handled much more quickly than the purchase of new weapons from the defense industry and are often intended to fill urgent, temporary needs. The host country's inventory is then replenished by ordering replacements.

The arms transfer system is a peculiarity of modern defense strategy, used by both superpowers to strengthen their European pacts, to provide support for Third World allies, and often to generate short-term political gains. The transfer of first-line weapons systems to unstable nations has, however, resulted in several unfortunate long-term problems, including the loss of major military technology to the opposing superpower, or even the use of such weapons against allied states or the originating power. Such transfers, if used unwisely or precipitously, can also destabilize previously stable areas of the world, creating new sources of conflict between the superpowers. Arms transfers are supported heavily by the defense industry lobby, which benefits directly when depleted stockpiles must be replenished.

The arms race is attributable, in large measure, to the influence of the "military-industrial complex," a term coined by President Dwight Eisenhower in 1961. According to Eisenhower: "We have been compelled to create a permanent armaments industry of vast proportions. . . . This conjunction of an immense military establishment and a large arms industry is new in the American experience. The total influence—economic, political, and even spiritual—is felt in every city, every Statehouse, every office of the Federal government. . . . In the councils of government, we must guard against the acquisition of unwarranted influence, whether sought or unsought, by the military-industrial complex. The potential for the disastrous rise of misplaced power exists and will persist."

In brief, the theory posits that as new weapons go through a predictable sequence—research, development, testing, selection, production, and deployment—an interested constituency tends to emerge. This consists of the civilian contractors and their employees, the military leaders associated with the specific weapon, and the politicians in whose districts the weapon or its components will be produced or deployed. These parties exert enormous pressures for producing the weapon by rallying their constituencies. Once this process gains momentum, it is extremely difficult to stop the project.

The military-industrial complex plays a prominent role in the development and deployment of new weapons systems. Proponents of this view contend that the phrase should, in fact, read, the "military-industrial-governmental-scientific-labor complex." The theory, however, is not without its critics. For example, John Spanier argues that this view is riddled with contradictions. "On the one hand," notes Spanier, "it is suggested that American foreign policy is too interventionist, too involved, and too expensive, and that it distorts national priorities. . . . On the other hand, almost every group in the United States seems to have a cash interest in international tension, including the growers who supply flowers for battlefield monuments. If so, the nation must have an interest in the continuation of Cold War policies."

Spanier's critics disagree, insisting that the military-industrial complex undermines democratic institutions (e.g., political parties and legislatures) and civilian control of the military. Moreover, the military-industrial complex serves as an instrument of coercion, disguising its true motives with patriotic rhetoric, while impugning the motives of its opponents. By raising false fears and attacking their critics, the beneficiaries of the military-industrial complex distort national objectives and lure the American people into a false sense of security, not realizing that they have been deceived into supporting costly weapons systems in order to benefit the economic and political interests of the military-industrial complex.

In order to prevent war—and maintain political stability—most nations rely heavily on intelligence, or information collected by a government about other nations' capabilities and intentions. In the case of the United States, the Central Intelligence Agency is charged with this responsibility. Created by the National Security Act of 1947, it operates under the aegis of the National Security Council and the president. Its duties include research, espionage, and a wide range of functions covering overt (open) and covert (secret) activities. The CIA is headed by a civilian director, appointed by the president with Senate approval, who frequently participates in NSC meetings at the behest of the president.

At times, the Central Intelligence Agency has exceeded its congressional mandate, engaging in a variety of clandestine activities (e.g., political assassinations, coups and revolutions, and extensive surveillance of U.S. citizens). Although the Congress has established a watchdog select committee to oversee CIA operations, it has achieved mixed results. For example, no one outside the agency's most "classified" circles knows precisely the amount of its budget or how it is spent, how many agents it employs and in which areas, or the nature and extent of its activities in various countries. Indeed, outside the intelligence community, few know much about intelligence products or processes, which may explain, for example, why there are so few major pressure groups with either knowledge or sufficient power to influence the formulation of intelligence policy.

The Central Intelligence Agency remained, by and large, unchanged until the early and mid-1970s. Since then, the CIA has been the subject of increased public and private scrutiny, culminating in a series of shocking revelations of wrongdoing. As a result, the agency came to be viewed as a service function, an unfortunate but necessary evil. This resulted in major cutbacks in manpower, resources, and support personnel. In addition, numerous legal restrictions were imposed on the agency in the form of federal laws, presidential executive orders, and agency guidelines. These measures dramatically altered the nature of CIA activities, which were, for the most part, limited completely to official covert operations. A new emphasis was placed on relatively clean, risk-free data collection. Despite agency denials, there is ample evidence to suggest that the CIA was involved in covert operations in Nicaragua, El Salvador, and the Middle East. Under President Ronald Reagan, the CIA experienced a new resurgence, enjoying its largest buildup, both budgetary and personnel-wise, since the 1950s. In 1987, the CIA was rocked by charges that the agency played a leading role in the Iran-Contra affair, in which weapons were sold to the Iranians in exchange for release of U.S. hostages, with the profits being diverted to the Nicaraguan Contras, in direct defiance of the law.

Section IV, "The Balance of Terror," features four chapters. Chapter 13, "Intelligence and Security," concentrates on foreign intelligence. The first article reviews the history of the Central Intelligence Agency, with special emphasis on what the author sees as its principal shortcomings in recent years: international narcotics, terrorism, industrial espionage, and the proliferation of chemical weapons. Specifically, the article focuses on the CIA's recent failure to anticipate Iraq's invasion of Kuwait. In the second article, the author examines the status of the Soviet KGB, which is struggling to reshape its identity amid the present chaos in the USSR. He discusses several optimistic predictions about the future of the KGB, which forecasted the "emasculation" of the agency and redistribution of its powers to various republican security forces.

Chapter 14, "The Arms Race," describes the current arms race, in the wake of the U.S.-led defeat of Iraq. Despite the Bush administration's call for a "New World Order," the president has advocated increased arms sales to several Middle Eastern countries which, the author contends, is certain to inflame the situation and to escalate the arms race. The second selection addresses the same theme, but focuses on the Third World in general, and on Iraq in particular, and offers seven specific recommendations to curb arms sales. These include: reconvene the Conventional Arms Transfer Talks; call an international conference on nuclear and chemical disarmament in the Middle East; impose economic and trade sanctions against nations developing nuclear weapons; and reduce or restrict international aid to nations developing domestic arms industries.

Chapter 15, "The Nuclear Revolution," focuses on the principles of deterrence and non-proliferation, calling for a drastic and swift cut in U.S. and Soviet nuclear forces, as well as the adoption of measures to control the development of new weapons and their sale to Third World countries. These initiatives are all the more important, warn the authors, because of the current instability in the USSR and the "window of opportunity" that now exists to reduce the risk of nuclear war. The second article describes Iraq's pre-war nuclear program, suggesting that while Saddam Hussein's nuclear capability was vastly overstated, Iraq may still be able to design and build a bomb. However, for Iraq to pose a major threat to its enemies would require that it enlarge its own stock of highly enriched uranium, obtain materials secretively, and produce its own nuclear material. Although Iraq's "nuclear sites" were targeted for destruction during the U.S.-allied offensive, the result of the air attacks remains uncertain. At this point it is clear that Iraq will not be able to develop a nuclear capability without outside assistance.

Chapter 16, "National Defense Redefined," analyzes the impact of the gulf war on American power, suggesting that it will not only influence the way the nation thinks about military weapons but the institutions that employ them. Although the author applauds the success of the U.S.-led coalition, calling it "superb," he warns the nation not to ignore the uniqueness of the conflict, and to remember the importance of civilian control of the military. In the second selection, the author maintains that in spite of the need for industrial preparedness, American industry is woefully unprepared to support the nation and its allies without substantial lead time. For this reason, concludes the author, the United States must immediately develop strategic investment and trade policies that will ensure a strong military-industrial base.

DISCUSSION QUESTIONS

1. Why did the CIA fail to predict Iraq's invasion of Kuwait?
2. Is the CIA an unnecessary relic of the Cold War? Why, or why not?
3. Should the CIA be revamped to reflect current political realities?
4. In what ways, if any, does the KGB differ from the CIA?
5. Is it likely that the KGB will be eliminated? Why, or why not?
6. What explains the KGB's eagerness to reform itself?
7. Why has President Bush approved additional arms sales to many Middle Eastern nations?
8. How has the Bush administration attempted to boost exports for U.S. arms makers?
9. What are the major forms of U.S. arms transfers to foreign buyers?
10. Should stricter controls be put on U.S. arms sales? If so, what?
11. How did the U.S. attempt to deter possible Soviet military action during the Cold War?
12. Does the USSR still pose a military threat to the United States? Why, or why not?
13. Should the U.S. take the first steps in reducing its nuclear weapons?
14. What countries are most responsible for fueling the arms race?
15. Does Iraq pose a nuclear threat to the region? Why, or why not?
16. What, if anything, can be done to prevent Iraq from acquiring additional nuclear explosive materials from other countries?
17. In what sense, if any, will America's success in the gulf war influence its position in the world?
18. How has the gulf war affected the way most Americans think about military power?
19. To what extent, if any, did Iraq pose a formidable military threat to the coalition forces?
20. How likely is it that the U.S. military will be able to replay its success in the gulf war in a future conflict?
21. Does the Pentagon's success in the gulf war, and the praise that it subsequently received, threaten the principle of civilian control?
22. Is U.S. industry prepared to support the demands of the military in the event of a future war, or even a protracted low-level conflict?
23. What are the principal weaknesses in the industrial base of America's military system?
24. In what sense, if any, do military needs exert a powerful influence on the U.S. economy?

KEY TERMS

AEROSPACE AND DEFENSE INDUSTRY   That element of business with a dedicated financial interest in the awarding of defense contracts to the private sector, or in the producing of arms commercially for export to other countries.

ARMS RACE   The competition between nations to maintain their real or perceived military superiority.

ARMS SALE   The marketing of weapons and military technology, usually to overseas consumers.

ARMS TRANSFER   The donation or sale of weapons from existing inventory to a foreign military establishment.

COVERT OPERATIONS   Secret activities planned and executed so as to conceal the identity of, or permit plausible denial by, the sponsor.

FIRST STRIKE   The launching of an all-out nuclear attack without warning, ostensibly to destroy the enemy's ability to retaliate.

INTERCONTINENTAL BALLISTIC MISSILE   A land-based fixed or mobile rocket-propelled vehicle capable of delivering one or more warheads over intercontinental distances, which is defined as in excess of 5,500 kilometers.

MILITARY-INDUSTRIAL COMPLEX   An alleged informal alliance among the professional military, defense-corporation executives, and pro-defense members of Congress, whereby these groups use their power and influence to win support of increased defense spending, which, in turn, serves their economic and political objectives.

MILITARY PARITY   A perceived balance in the weapons and defense capabilities of two or more states.

MILITARY POWER   A nation's ability to safeguard its homeland, protect its interests, aid its allies, and achieve its objectives.

MOBILIZATION   Measures adopted by a country to prepare itself for war.

MUTUAL ASSURED DESTRUCTION   A theory of strategic deterrence, often referred to as "mutual suicide," whereby one nation seeks to deter a nuclear attack by possessing the capacity to retaliate in kind to an adversary's first strike.

NUCLEAR STOCKPILES   Nuclear weapons or warheads stored in strategic locations for deployment in the event of war.

NUCLEAR SUPERIORITY   The capacity, as defined by a nation's leaders, to inflict greater nuclear damage against an adversary than one's opponent can inflict.

NUCLEAR WAR   A hostile conflict waged with atomic and/or hydrogen bombs, in which one or more nations stand vulnerable to destruction.

NUCLEAR WARHEAD   That part of a missile, rocket, torpedo, projectile, or other weapon containing the nuclear or thermonuclear system.

RESEARCH AND DEVELOPMENT   The invention and construction of new weapons or weapons technology by the defense industry.

STRATEGIC NUCLEAR WEAPONS   Long-range weapons intended for nuclear attack against strategic sites or for active defense against such an attack.

THEATER NUCLEAR WEAPONS   Nuclear weapons designed to destroy military bases and support facilities.

TRIAD   The three components of the strategic nuclear forces of the United States, consisting of land-based intercontinental ballistic missiles, submarine-launched ballistic missiles, and manned bombers, which have recently been supplemented by air-launched cruise missiles.

Chapter 13

Intelligence and Security

Article 13.1.   Has the CIA Become an Anachronism?

With the gulf war now over, many experts have raised serious questions about the role of the Central Intelligence Agency in the conflict and its failure to anticipate Iraq's invasion of Kuwait. Clearly, the CIA failed to either predict or warn of the invasion even after many Westerners had left the country. Still, neither the agency nor the Bush administration has initiated a major review of the intelligence service in light of its performance. Instead, the CIA has fallen back on scare tactics, requests for more money, and scrambles to protect its bureaucratic flanks. This was not the first agency blunder in recent times. CIA ineptness is equally apparent in its war against international narcotics, terrorism, industrial sabotage, and the spread of chemical weapons. Past performance suggests the need for a revitalized intelligence service that reflects the requirements of an obviously new world.

NATIONAL AFFAIRS

Has the CIA Become an Anachronism?
by Roger Morris

Its failure to anticipate Iraq's invasion of Kuwait was the latest evidence that the Agency no longer is fulfilling the function it was created for.

SEVERAL days before the Iraqi invasion of Kuwait on Aug. 2, 1990, high-level officials of U.S. oil companies quietly began to slip out of Kuwait City. Other Americans living in the small Persian Gulf state sensed immediately that there was danger in the air, and several anxiously telephoned the U.S. Embassy. "No, no. You're just being silly," one American woman remembered the words of the Embassy officer. The U.S. government could assure its citizens in the area that there would be no Iraqi attack on Kuwait.

At the same time, we now know, U.S. diplomats in Baghdad—armed with identical assumptions—were assuring Saddam Hussein and his regime that Washington regarded the old Iraqi oil and frontier dispute with Kuwait as an "Arab-Arab" problem, and therefore would not "interfere" or take sides. Within days, the nervous Americans in Kuwait were trapped in front of rolling Iraqi tanks and some of the same U.S. officials in Baghdad, along with hundreds of others, had become pawns and hostages in the most deadly international confrontation of the post-Cold War era.

What they all had in common was the tragically inept and mistaken assessments of the Central Intelligence Agency—a CIA whose satellite photography could make out the epaulettes on Iraqi officers massed for the assault, yet whose ranking officials could not predict or prudently warn of the imminent invasion even after the savvy Western oilmen had packed their bags.

"The fact is that the U.S. Embassy in Kuwait was caught by surprise. . . . So was George Bush. So were the American people," Knight-Ridder columnist James McCartney wrote later of the Gulf crisis. "Once again, the Central Intelligence Agency, which was created to serve as both the President's and the nation's eyes and ears, had failed to foresee an international crisis."

Nor, McCartney might have added, was it likely to be the last CIA failure of such magnitude. For behind the blunder in the Persian Gulf was a seamy history—and some equally tangled politics—as our somewhat myopic spies search for a well-funded new mission in the very different world of the 1990s.

Of all the rusting relics of the Cold War, none lingers on with more resistance to its growing anachronism than the Central Intelligence Agency. Born in the crucible of the great postwar U.S.-Soviet rivalry and some of its worst expedients, often with no

Dr. Morris, a Santa Fe, N.M., freelance writer, was a senior staff member of the National Security Council in the Johnson and Nixon Administrations.

apparent vision save conflict and no abiding purpose except bureaucratic justification or aggrandizement, America's ministry of espionage should be facing some candid questions about its real mission and its practical and constitutional role in the international relations and security of a democratic society. Yet, there seems to be little evidence that either the CIA or the Bush Administration has begun to ponder a more relevant concept of an intelligence service in a radically changed world.

Not surprisingly, the CIA has resorted to the hoary, but dependable, politics of the past 45 years. It has trotted out suitably new, old, or simply hidden dangers, asked for more money, and scrambled to protect bureaucratic flanks.

Along with its 11 related institutions in the U.S. espionage community—including the Defense Intelligence Agency and the electronic eavesdroppers and codebreakers of the National Security Agency—the CIA dined well on the flush national security spending of the 1980s. Intelligence budgets tripled over the decade to reach nearly $30,000,000,000 in Fiscal Year 1990. Money for CIA operations and analyses has continued to grow throughout the past five years, even as Pentagon appropriations have peaked and declined.

To preserve and extend that expanding domain while much of its rationale disappears, the CIA has begun to advertise new perils of the postwar period—international narcotics, terrorism, industrial espionage, and even the spread of chemical weapons of the type that now threaten U.S. forces in the Middle East. In each field, however, the Agency's performance has been inept, if not worse.

From hostage-taking to airline bombing, U.S. intelligence on terrorist attacks has been notoriously flawed, and it was little better on the commerce and intrigue that built chemical warfare arsenals in the Middle East. As for policing the narcotics trade, the CIA itself stands shrouded in a long history of alleged, still unresolved, complicity with drug traffickers—from mountain tribesmen and corrupt colonels of Southeast Asia in the 1960s to Panama's Manuel Noriega and the contras of Central America in the 1980s.

As if aware of the vulnerability of these newer projects, CIA lobbyists have summoned an old ally in the budget wars—the Agency's major foreign counterpart and, in some disturbing ways, its mirror image, the Soviet K.G.B. Thus, the predictable speeches, leaks, and briefings in which CIA Director William H. Webster sees what he calls "more aggressive, more robust" Soviet intelligence efforts, lavishly funded and cunningly effective despite the veritable bankruptcy, political chaos, and disintegration within the U.S.S.R.

The Soviets somehow retain their secret police control in Eastern Europe even as the communist bloc crumbles, Webster told one audience in the winter of 1989-90. The now-acknowledged backwardness and disarray of their economy, he maintained, only means even greater KGB zeal in industrial and technological espionage.

Moreover, there are the imminent new U.S.-Soviet arms agreements, the intelligence demands of on-site monitoring and verification, the inspectors who are spies, and, thus, the spies to watch the inspectors. Nor can it all be done safely for a mere $10-15,000,000,000 more for new radar-imaging satellites, part of major investment in reconnaissance and listening posts already committed by Congress and the White House.

In its perennial rivalry with electronic intelligence, the CIA will require added "humint" (human-collected intelligence) and, thus, more manpower. As Webster told the National Press Club in November, 1989, his needs are "staggering." Peace, it turns out, is going to be even more expensive than the Cold War and, by all odds, a growth industry for the intelligence community.

It is symptomatic of our gagged dialogue on national security that there has been so little challenge from Congress or the media to this campaign, however transparent or contrived. As usual, hard edges of issues and money have been softened by settling on personalities—in this case, on the somewhat bland and dutiful Webster.

A U.S. Court of Appeals judge from St. Louis and FBI Director for nine years, Webster came to the Agency in 1987 to calm everyone after the swift exit and death of William Casey amid the Iran-contra affair—still another scandal in which the CIA was embroiled deeply, yet escaped virtually free of consequence. Webster was hardly a reformer. He had left behind at the FBI an unsavory record of surveillance of dissident groups as well as charges of racial discrimination. His anemic response to the Iran-contra affair was to dismiss a pair of lesser officials and demote or reprimand five others, moves widely interpreted in Washington as essential immunity for the Agency at large.

The new Director went on to oppose the creation of a quasi-independent CIA inspector general, legislation that became law late in 1989 despite Bush Administration opposition and, to date, the only potentially significant new oversight measure to emerge from the Iran-contra revelations. For his loyalty, Webster has been rewarded with fattening budgets and only occasional sniping of the sort reserved by the intelligence bureaucracy for exogenous directors. (In acid comparison with William "Wild Bill" Donovan, the legendary head of U.S. wartime intelligence and godfather of the CIA,

Agency veterans reportedly call the current Director "Mild Bill.")

Rather more ominous were the first accounts in the spring of 1990 by *Houston Post* reporter Pete Brewton of extensive ties between failed financial institutions and the CIA. More than 20 savings and loan institutions and at least two banks had Agency connections or relationships with organized crime figures who had links to the CIA.

Money laundering, looting of thrifts to finance forbidden covert actions, manipulations of markets, and Mafia alliances hover over the *Post* stories, and an inquiry by the House Select Committee on Intelligence revealed too-familiar, too-believable ghosts. It is all too consistent with the shady margin on which the Agency has operated for so long and which now threatens to mock Webster's hands-off management, if not his personal rectitude.

The CIA's dark past

The CIA has been at the core of America's Cold War Faustian bargain. At least 900 major projects and several thousand secondary actions occurred over more than four decades, often deliberate decisions to enlist or engage evil in the service of perceived good and to match in kind an enemy whose values we supposedly deplored.

It will not be necessary for scholars of the next century to seize upon the Agency's relatively rare renegade departures from presidential edict. The record of proposing, organizing, executing, rationalizing, and then concealing authorized policy will be enough for the most extraordinary chapter in the history of American foreign relations.

The proof, as they like to say at CIA Headquarters, is in results. Off only the briefest roll call—Iran, Guatemala, Indonesia, Zaire, Ecuador, Ethiopia, Chile, Somalia, Brazil, Angola, Libya, Nicaragua, Vietnam, El Salvador, Cambodia, Panama, Lebanon, Korea—some conclusions already are plain. Whatever the presumed alternative, most CIA interventions have consigned or left countries to repression and prolonged suffering. Despite billions in

secret subsidies from U.S. tax dollars, several of our most favored clients fell of their own savagery and corruption, leading to violently anti-American successor regimes. Many of our secret police proxies and proteges have displayed an amazingly consistent penchant for torture.

Yet, history may not judge so harshly, after all, the seedy bagmen or sleepy watch officers counting off the moments to a faraway *coup d'etat.* Far worse than any covert action, however wrong or misshapen, is an intelligence agency's intellectual dishonesty—the ideological, political, or bureaucratic corruption of the information that is the essence of the art. Except to deceive everyone else, it never must lie to itself willfully or by incompetence.

That the CIA has done exactly that so often, especially *vis-a-vis* the Soviet Union, the main object of its study, should raise the gravest doubts about its future role and funding. The Agency's bafflement at the process launched by *glasnost* and its ignorance of the volcanic forces so closely beneath the surface of Soviet society is only the latest and most spectacular failure.

There also is what one scholar has called "politics and guesswork"—the systematic overstatement of Soviet military expenditures since 1948, distorted estimates that, in the Cold War twilight of the past decade, came to look somehow moderate beside the wildly tendentious and budget-pumping analyses of the Defense Intelligence Agency.

Without a discourse of integrity, the CIA could not gauge the Soviet threat accurately or honestly inform U.S. policy in response. Now, with little sense at home or abroad of an authentic politics of the left, the CIA sees clearly neither the present nor the future of a new Soviet Union that still is the most important power in Europe or Asia.

Reconversion is as essential to the CIA as to so much of the bloated weapons industry it helped feed. In a Washington no longer in thrall to the old myths of ideology and power, most political intelligence could be vested in a revitalized foreign ministry and diplomatic service, where it belongs. Military intelligence, much too important and tempting to be left to the generals, should be shifted entirely to a broader new

National Security Agency with no stake in either the Pentagon budget or bureaucratic quarrels.

What would be left—with open budgets, openly arrived at—would be a truly new CIA for an obviously new world, a select and streamlined agency shorn of its operational folly and extra-constitutional means. That new agency would be dedicated unequivocally to analyses centered on socio-economic developments in the larger sweep. One might hope that these would create a new relevance in governmental decision-making—from development aid to control of arms- or drug-trafficking, from combating AIDS to fostering human rights. The peace dividend of that new CIA not only would be billions in savings and a more genuine national security, but also a fresh generation of talented and idealistic young officials for whom intelligence once again was a public service.

Like high priests railing at an end to exploitable superstition, the intelligence professionals certainly will call such plans heresy and impossible. If only they could tell us that the danger really were gone. Only then could we change this obese, tunnel-vision relic, slouching toward Capitol Hill for still more money and still more ominous briefings on a world already past.

However, the Persian Gulf crisis apparently has postponed any such reckoning. Ironically, despite its typical blindness at the outset of the crisis, the CIA has been wrapped again in its national security dressing, unquestioned, unappraised. Webster reluctantly, if dutifully, has gone before television interviewers to say discreetly as little as possible about such delicate matters, and the media—almost as if afraid to get the real answer—never have sullied the granted audience by substance. It has been one more demonstration that the Agency and its blunders live not by bureaucratic wiles alone, but by journalistic and public abdication as well.

Meanwhile, American forces in the Arabian desert are perilously dependent on their nation's intelligence, and their fate may hang on what the Agency chooses to see, or say, about a region where it already has been tragically wrong.

Article 13.2.   The KGB: Still a Potent Force

Despite optimistic claims predicting the emasculation of the Soviet KGB, recent events suggest that such claims may have been premature. Under its new chief, Vadim Bakatin, a shrewd politician, the KGB is likely to remain a pivotal force as the Soviet leadership struggles to retain power and prevent further chaos. Although the KGB will attempt to reshape its image and redefine its mission, the agency is already deftly creating a place for itself in the new Soviet order. At the same time, the appointment of

Bakatin, a close Gorbachev aide with reformist sympathies, signals the first step in a complete housecleaning and restoration of public support. Although it is likely that the KGB will be totally revamped, dismantling the agency will prove to be a difficult, if not impossible, undertaking.

The KGB: Still a potent force

In a disintegrating nation, the Committee for State Security may still hold the keys to power

Two long shadows disappeared from Lubyanka Square in central Moscow last week. One was the shaft of darkness cast by a 14-ton statue of Felix Dzerzhinsky, founder of the Soviet secret police, which was hauled away by jubilant demonstrators after the coup collapsed. The other was the shadow of fear cast across the U.S.S.R. for the last seven decades by the brooding Lubyanka building, KGB headquarters.

A chilling era of Soviet history is ending, perhaps even with the demise of the dreaded Committee for State Security. But an old Russian folk saying holds that "you can't scrub a black dog white," and although celebrants have scrawled "Freedom" and "Butchers Go" on Lubyanka's rough stone walls, reform may only mean replacing one secret police with another — or others — as the disintegration of the Soviet Union quickens. Under new chief Vadim Bakatin, a skilled politician, the KGB is likely to remain a vital key to consolidating and holding power amid the chaos.

Optimistic analysts were prompt to predict the emasculation of the KGB and distribution of its powers to various republican security agencies. It's also possible that the KGB could be split into domestic and foreign branches, giving it a structure similar to the CIA and FBI in the United States. "The KGB must be shorn of many of its functions," says Oleg Kalugin, a dissident ex-KGB general. "It must be killed as a state within the state."

That will not be easy.

"The KGB will seek to destroy its old image, perhaps even change its name," predicts Victor Yasmann, an analyst at Radio Free Europe/Radio Liberty. "But its people will stay." Yasmann argues that the KGB actually is skillfully crafting a place for itself in the new Soviet order, even if that requires abandoning its historic role as the "sword and shield" of the Bolshevik revolution.

Housecleaning. The KGB's first post-coup moves back this charge. The moment the putsch ended, the agency issued a statement insisting that "KGB servicemen have nothing in common with illegal actions by the group of adventurists." It banned Communist Party activity in the security service, a move it previously rejected. The appointment of Bakatin, a Gorbachev aide with a pro-reform reputation, to head the KGB is an important first step in cleaning house at Lubyanka and winning public respect for the KGB.

Another early move could shift control of many domestic KGB units to the republics. That would put 70 percent of the KGB's domestic network at the disposal of Boris Yeltsin and of his vision of Russia. Conservatives such as Supreme Soviet Deputy Victor Alksnis pointed to the quick closing of Communist Party buildings as proof that anti-Communist, anti-conservative purges already have begun.

Disassembling the KGB will be a massive undertaking. It reaches from Lubyanka into almost every aspect of Soviet life. At home, the KGB not only protects the country's borders and its leaders, it spies on Soviet citizens and has dossiers on everyone from journalists to high officials. Abroad, its First Chief Directorate agents carry on the world's largest espionage operation, operating out of Soviet embassies, trade missions, businesses and under cover as journalists, tourists and other travelers. Kalugin estimates that the KGB has more employees in Moscow alone than the Central Intelligence Agency and Federal Bureau of Investigation have together, worldwide. The agency attracts many of the Soviet Union's best and brightest with above-average pay and privileges such as better housing, a precious commodity in Soviet cities.

Ironically, under Gorbachev the KGB has become more powerful than ever. Former KGB chief Yuri Andropov was Gorbachev's political mentor and instilled in his protégé respect for the agency's capabilities. In 1985, then KGB chief Victor Chebrikov backed Gorbachev in his fight to become Communist Party general secretary.

In return, Gorbachev expanded the KGB's powers, giving it the leading role in fighting organized crime, which has burgeoned. This year, Gorbachev ignored reformers' warnings and accepted a new law codifying the KGB's sweeping powers in language so vague that it gave Lubyanka virtual carte blanche to define and enforce state security as it saw fit.

Beyond sheer size and tenacious bureaucratic survival smarts, the KGB has another powerful reason to resist reform: a past stained by the killing of at least 20 million people under Lenin and Stalin. Many of the officers who in more recent years persecuted dissidents and cultural figures, stifled religion and broke up democratic political rallies while ignoring legal niceties still hold senior posts in the agency. KGB professionals argue that they only followed orders, but they are horrified at the prospect of offices being ransacked and secret files revealed, as they were in Eastern Europe when Communist rule collapsed there.

Party villains. The KGB's eagerness to revamp itself may help explain the agency's ambiguous role in the failed putsch. Conventional wisdom holds that younger officers refused to carry out orders from the coup leadership. But the aftermath of the crisis suggests a more complex struggle at Lubyanka.

KGB AT A GLANCE

- *The KGB has 220,000 uniformed troops, more than the U.S. Marines. It has more tanks than the British Army.*
- *The KGB's domestic duties range from border patrol to fighting organized crime, environmental protection and guarding the Soviet leadership.*
- *The KGB and its forerunners, including Stalin's NKVD, have killed at least 20 million people since 1918.*
- *Where the Soviet Union has just the KGB, the United States has 20 separate intelligence agencies.*

Ex-KGB chief Vladimir Kryuchkov is billed as the junta's main villain, a reactionary who masterminded the coup. But Kryuchkov isn't just a conservative. He represents something else that the agency must bury if it is to survive: its Communist past. Kryuchkov was not a KGB professional but a Communist Party functionary grafted into the agency's leadership, a common practice.

KGB careerists always chafed under the leadership of party apparatchiks, but now communism has become an albatross around the agency's neck. Its elimination is vital if the KGB hopes to transform itself into a professional organization along Western lines.

The departure of Iron Felix leaves just one monument in the square outside Lubyanka: a rough-hewn boulder, commemorating the millions who perished in camps run by the KGB's forerunners. For now, the Soviet people seem to accept this as the appropriate memorial to the KGB's past—and a necessary warning about its future. ■

BY JEFF TRIMBLE

168

Chapter 14

The Arms Race

Article 14.1.   Re-Arm the World

Peter Montgomery claims that in spite of the Bush administration's stated opposition to a new arms race in the Middle East, the president has been quietly lobbying for additional arms sales around the globe to reinforce U.S. foreign policy goals, as well as to help American defense contractors, who have been hurt by recent cuts in the military budget. For example, the administration contends that Iraq's swift victory over Kuwait demonstrates all too clearly that Saudi Arabia and other Persian Gulf countries require additional weapons. Interestingly, during the 1980s fifty nations provided Iraq with over $50 billion worth of arms, while twenty-eight countries supplied weapons to both sides. Although the United States did not directly sell arms to Iraq, it did encourage others to do so, in an effort to halt weapons sales to Iran.

RE-ARM THE WORLD

The Bush administration may be talking a new world order, but it's hawking U.S. weapons like never before.

BY PETER MONTGOMERY

"It would be tragic," President Bush told Congress shortly after the lopsided U.S.-led defeat of Iraq, "if the nations of the Middle East and the Persian Gulf were now, in the wake of the war, to embark on a new arms race."

Secretary of State James Baker sounded a similar theme when he appeared before the House Foreign Affairs Committee in February. "The time has come to try to change the destructive pattern of military competition and proliferation in this region," he said, "and to reduce arms flows into an area that is already overmilitarized."

That's the new-world-order White House talking. But the business-as-usual White House has been pushing arms sales around the world to support U.S. foreign policy and help out American defense contractors at a time of U.S. budget cuts. The *Washington Post* reported in late April that the administration's new-order and business-as-usual partisans were nearing a compromise on limiting arms sales to the Middle East.

The administration's plan, yet to be released, reportedly would fall short of the moratorium requested by some foreign leaders and members of Congress. After the administration notified Congress earlier this year that it was considering increasing U.S. arms sales to the Middle East, some members began to balk.

"One day we promote the idea of Middle East arms control, the next day we step back," said Sen. Joseph Biden (D-Del.) in March. "One day we promote a postwar order based on security with fewer weapons, and the next day the State Department notifies Congress of its intent to sell 46 F-16s to Egypt, with billions more in arms sales in the pipeline for other Middle East countries."

The administration says Iraq's swift conquest of Kuwait shows that Saudi Arabia and other Persian Gulf nations need to boost their defenses. But there's another way to see it.

Critics point to recent congressional testimony by Rear Adm. Thomas Brooks, chief of Naval Intelligence. "Iraq today is the nightmare example of what can happen in an atmosphere of virtually uncontrolled weapons and technology proliferation," he said. "Both East and West armed Baghdad

Peter Montgomery is an associate editor. Interns Ian Fisk and Marshall King contributed research.

to the teeth and now we have to pay the price."

THE NIGHTMARE

"Western political leaders and Western businessmen must shoulder a large share of the blame for the present bloody mess in the Persian Gulf," said Rep. David Obey (D-Wis.) at a February speech to the Council on Foreign Relations. "Western governments and Western arms dealers and chemical manufacturers have miscalculated for decades by rationalizing that they could pump arms into the region on the grounds of regional balance or on the grounds that if they didn't do it someone else would."

Nowhere was that rationale more evident than in the long, bloody war between Iran and Iraq. During the 1980s, 50 countries supplied Iraq and Iran with more than $50 billion worth of weapons. Twenty-eight nations supplied *both* sides, according to James Adams, author of the 1990 book *Trading in Death*. Iraq bought 2,300 Soviet and Chinese tanks, 64 Mirage F-1 fighters with Exocet missiles from France, 2,650 armored vehicles from European nations and more than 500 Scud missiles from the Soviet Union. Bombs, mines, grenades and other weapons came from Portugal, Brazil and Chile. According to the Brookings Institution's Janne Nolan, "Iraq's missile program is a fully multinational enterprise, representing the combined efforts of Soviet, French, West German, Italian, Swiss, Austrian, East German, Egyp-

Thanks to the government's "Project Accelerate," most arms export licenses are now issued within ten days.

tian, Pakistani and Brazilian materiel, experts and engineers."

U.S. policymakers point to the fact that American arms aren't on that list. "*Our* weapons didn't create the gulf crisis," Undersecretary of State Reginald Bartholomew said during recent questioning by members of the Senate Foreign Relations Committee.

But that statement is disingenuous. Despite a declared policy of neutrality in the Iran-Iraq war, U.S. officials encouraged other countries to equip Saddam Hussein and led an international effort to stop arms sales to Iran. Then the Reagan administration broke its arms embargo to sell weapons to Iran in hopes of freeing American hostages in Lebanon. (The secret dealing with Iran may have started earlier — possibly during the 1980 Reagan campaign, according to former National Security Council staffer Gary Sick.)

To bolster Iraq's defense against Iran, the Reagan administration also took Hussein's regime off the State Department's "terrorist" list in 1982, a move that lifted many trade restrictions and cleared the way for U.S. exports that helped to build his war machine. (Similarly, in recent years U.S. firms have exported tens of millions of dollars' worth of high-tech shipments to Syria, whose presence on the terrorist list makes it ineligible for U.S. arms exports.) American trade with Iraq grew seven-fold from $571 million in 1983 to $3.6 billion in 1989, according to *U.S. News & World Report*.

Much of the equipment supplied by U.S. companies had the potential for both civilian and military uses; between 1985 and 1990, Iraq bought $1.5 billion worth of such "dual use" technology. Beginning in the mid-1980s, Commerce and State department officials who wanted to increase sales and influence in the region approved a number of exports over strenuous objections by Defense Department officials that there was a high probability that the equipment would be put to military use. The United States sent Iraq advanced computers, communications gear and other electronic equipment. One manufacturer warned the U.S. government that the specialized furnaces Iraq was seeking could be used to develop nuclear weapons. The Commerce Department gave him the go-ahead anyway.

When Rep. Howard Berman (D-Calif.) complained in 1984 about the sale of ostensibly non-military helicopters to Iraq, the State Department responded, "We believe that increased American penetration of the extremely competitive civilian aircraft market would serve the United States' interests by improving our balance of trade

and lessening unemployment in the aircraft industry."

Even though those same "civilian" helicopters were used in 1988 to spray Kurdish villagers with poison gas — killing thousands — the White House successfully fought House of Representatives approval of anti-Iraq sanctions that had passed unanimously in the Senate in September 1988.

Throughout the 1980s, while some members of Congress condemned Iraq's abominable human rights record, the White House and other members of Congress remained determined to do business with the Hussein regime. The government's stance gave American businesses a green light; more than 70 major corporations joined the U.S.-Iraq Business Forum, created in the mid-1980s by a former State Department official. "No matter what happens with political issues between the U.S. and Iraq," Saddam Hussein told a delegation of American businessmen in 1989, "your business interests will always be welcome."

The enthusiasm was mutual. Touting an international business fair held in Baghdad less than a year before Iraq's invasion of Kuwait, U.S. Ambassador to Iraq April Glaspie said, "We are pleased to announce that a record number of companies are participating, representing a wide range of America's most advanced technologies and demonstrating American confidence in Iraq's bright future. The American Embassy places the highest priority on promoting commerce and friendship between our two nations."

The Commerce Department has refused to release a list of companies that supplied Hussein. But some businesses on record as having exported technology to Iraq are using the government's actions to justify their sales. A spokesperson for Hewlett Packard, which sold Iraq advanced computers, told the *Los Angeles Times*, "We are not in the foreign policy business. When the guys in the black hats can change so quickly, we look to the federal government to help us decide who to sell to."

SELL HIGH AND LOW

During the boom years of the Reagan military buildup, American defense contractors could view exports as the icing on the highly profitable Pentagon cake. But the thawing of the Cold War, the end of the Reagan buildup and the prospect for smaller Pentagon budgets pointed to a leaner future for U.S. defense contractors as the 1980s drew to a close.

Tens of thousands of defense-related jobs have been lost each year since the late 1980s. The Pentagon's Defense Science Board and the private Center for Strategic and International Studies have warned of the dangers of letting the defense industrial base erode. Arms makers and policymakers alike began to seek relief by expanding overseas arms sales.

A similar scenario was playing out in other countries. Industrial nations were curbing defense spending, and the emerging Third World arms industry was falling on hard times with the end of the lucrative Iran-Iraq war. The result was fierce international competition.

The Bush administration has expressed concern that lagging U.S. demand would drive up the unit cost of many big-ticket items. "Indeed, the long-term survival of a number of important domestic arms programs is tied to foreign sales: M1A2 Abrams Battle Tank, Blackhawk helicopter, HAWK surface-to-air missile, Boeing 707 aircraft, to name a few," an administration report to Congress warned this year. "These programs represent skilled labor and jobs in the defense industry. Our military and political influence abroad and our own national security will be diminished if we fail to maintain support for these and other critical production programs into the 1990s."

For the U.S. government, arms sales have long been considered a foreign policy tool to support allies and draw countries into a U.S. sphere of influence. But the end of the Cold War has "eliminated the major rationale for U.S. security assistance," says Prof. Edward Laurance of the U.S. Naval Postgraduate School. A more pragmatic, bottom-line orientation has taken over U.S. policy.

"As old ideological motivations and strong U.S.-Soviet competition for geostrategic influence around the world wane, you find more and more that economics is providing the motivation and determining factor in arms sales," says Lora Lumpe, who edits a Federation of American Scientists newsletter on arms transfers.

The Bush administration has developed a number of ways to boost exports for U.S. arms makers.

American exporters had long griped about delays at the understaffed State Department Office of Munitions Control, which authorized export licenses for sales by American firms to foreign firms or governments. So in January 1990 the State Department created a new office to speed licensing and promote U.S. weapons exports. The Center for Defense Trade, says a State Department spokesperson, was created to help make sure that American firms "get a fair shake" in the international arms marketplace.

Within a year the center's staff jumped from 36 to 66. Center publications boast that thanks to "Project Accelerate" most export licenses are now issued within ten days and that the department is working to shrink the list of items that are prohibited for export.

"The prevailing view [within government agencies] is that it is time for the U.S. government to begin to actively help our industry overseas within the limits of our foreign policy and national security concerns," wrote center director Charles Duelfer last summer. "Those charged with assessing the national security equation are giving more weight to the positive value a defense export may have on the industrial base."

In addition, Duelfer said in February, when the State Department evaluates the performance of U.S. embassies, support for defense companies "is one of the things they'll be graded on."

Exporters got another boost last July, when Deputy Secretary of State Lawrence Eagleburger sent a classified memo to embassies ordering staff to be more helpful to defense firms. A recent *Legal Times* article on the export promotion activities of Eagleburger and National Security Adviser Brent Scowcroft reported that "ambassadors now open doors . . . and the State Department helps push sales."

"The difference between 1980 and 1990 is pretty close to a quantum leap," Fred Haynes, a vice president for planning at the LTV Corp, told *Legal Times*. "The most significant change is that defense exporters are receiving cooperative support from U.S. agencies and are no longer viewed as pariahs."

"Our role has been to stay with it and keep the pressure up," added another industry official. "This administration has been absolutely superb."

The most recent gesture to arms exporters came in March, when the administration announced a plan for the U.S. Export-Import Bank to provide up to $1 billion worth of loan guarantees for foreign purchases of American weapons. Since the late 1960s, the bank has been prohibited from financing military sales to developing countries, and it has had a policy of not financing any military exports since 1974. The proposed policy change, reportedly controversial within the administration, has been widely criticized, even by some industry officials who worry that it would divert loan financing from non-defense exports and lessen the Eximbank's political support.

But Congress set a precedent for such action last year. Sen. Christopher Dodd (D-Conn.) successfully pushed for an exception to the Eximbank's ban on financing defense sales to enable Turkey's purchase of helicopters built by Connecticut-based Sikorsky. Dodd also introduced an amendment to the Export Administration Control Act that would loosen the restrictions on Eximbank financing for arms deals. Dodd's measure, which he said "would allow the U.S. defense industry to compete for European and Japanese markets without one hand tied behind its back," is an example of the economically driven support for exports that is likely to characterize the arms debate in the '90s. Big defense company layoffs put even ardent arms control advocates in Congress in "a very sticky wicket," says one industry observer.

The industry wants to make sure Congress gets the point. One trade association, the American League for Exports and Security Assistance, recently hired the Ohio-based consulting firm Foresight International to assess how disapproval by Congress of a potential $23 billion arms package to Saudi Arabia would affect the U.S. economy. The study predicts hundreds of thousands of job losses and an initial $45 billion drain on the economy. For political convenience, the study breaks down economic and job loss estimates by state and congressional district. "It is imprudent to ignore economic con-

"You find more and more that economics is providing the motivation and determining factor in arms sales."

siderations in foreign policy decision making," writes co-author David Louscher.

That view was confirmed by the gulf war, some analysts say. The United States was able to pull off the massive military operation because of its strong economic and defense industrial capabilities. White House spokesperson Marlin Fitzwater told reporters the administration's Eximbank plan would help offset Pentagon budget cuts and give American companies the same kind of support foreign competitors get from their governments.

Fitzwater denied there was any inconsistency with Bush's stated aim of reducing the level of armaments in the region. "We're not talking about cutting off all arms sales," he said. "We're talking about balance and stability in the region. That requires a number of countries have military capability in order to maintain that balance, in order to achieve that stability."

WAR TOYS

U.S. manufacturers hope that the gulf war, which turned into a globally televised commercial for high-tech American weaponry, will help keep production lines humming.

"The military market . . . appears to be of very large order as many nations of the world are upgrading their armed forces to cope with regional insecurity," Don Fuqua, president of the Aerospace Industries Association, said in February. "We can expect the intensity level of international competition to escalate from fierce to furious."

There seems to be little doubt that the war is already boosting demand for some items — there's a global clamor for the Patriot missile. For some Third World nations that invested heavily in inexpensive, low-tech weaponry, the crushing of the vaunted Iraqi army was a lesson not to get caught with yesterday's weapons. Pakistan's prime minister said the war demonstrated the need to make his country "an impregnable fortress" and made it clear that it was "disastrous" to underestimate the im-

portance of scientific research and technological advances in war-making.

The "challenge of the technology," as the Pakistani prime minister put it, has new urgency in the wake of the war. Even though Iraq's Scud missile attacks were mostly unsuccessful and its expected poison gas attacks did not materialize, the specter of Third World countries possessing longer-range missile technology, and the potential in some cases for chemical or nuclear payloads, has refocused attention on technology proliferation.

Many Western export controls were designed to keep technology with military applications away from the Soviet bloc. European governments and American companies, responding to the declining threat from the Soviet Union, have been pushing for a relaxation of such controls.

Last July, a month before Iraq invaded Kuwait, the White House lifted export controls on over 30 types of U.S.-made equipment and materials, many of which have applications in nuclear weapon and ballistic missile production. Stephen Bryen, a deputy undersecretary of defense in the Reagan administration, points out that Iraq got most of its weaponry from the Soviet Union and says freer technology sales to Eastern European countries could hasten the arrival of advanced weaponry in the Third World. If the Soviets had had access to some of this technology a few years ago, he says, American troops fighting Soviet weapons in Iraq could have had a much harder time.

The Western nations' forum for restricting high-tech exports to the Soviet Union and its allies is the Coordinating Committee on Multilateral Export Controls (CoCom). Last November, Bush issued a presidential directive removing all items on CoCom's dual-use list from a list of prohibited exports by June 1 unless "significant U.S. national security interests would be jeopardized."

The Center for Defense Trade is working to meet that deadline. But it's aiming at a moving target, since CoCom is preparing to decontrol more items in mid-May. "The whole infrastructure for building modern weapons is going to be decontrolled," says Bryen, who headed the Pentagon's technology transfer division from 1981 to 1988.

Bryen and others hope the war will

slow down the planners. "There were a lot of big lessons in this war from the technology point of view that should have caused a serious rethinking in this administration," he says. For its part, the Bush administration announced in March that it was tightening U.S. export controls on technology and chemical "precursors" that could be used in the production of chemical weapons. The White House says the new regulations would also tighten access to key nuclear and ballistic missile technology. Controlling access to technology, though, may become even more difficult as the global economy becomes increasingly competitive.

The Brookings Institution's foreign policy studies director, John Steinbruner, wrote recently that CoCom nations should "abandon the increasingly ineffective strategy of controlling dual-use technology by denying it altogether and to require instead disclosure of its end use."

Others suggest that the United States is short-sighted in limiting its attention to the "big four" systems that are already subject to international controls — nuclear, chemical, biological and ballistic missile technologies. The U.S. military victory in the Gulf demonstrated that increasingly sophisticated conventional weapons — some of which are based on technologies now being decontrolled — could also have an enormous impact on regional military confrontations.

SWORDS AS PLOWSHARES

"Security assistance has long been an indispensable element in U.S. policy to build a more secure and peaceful world," says a Pentagon-State Department report explaining the administration's 1992 budget request for military assistance programs. "Arms transfers, judiciously used, can help to deter aggression; strengthen mutual security relationships; and foster internal and regional stability." Military assistance, say its supporters, gives the United States some influence over how its weapons are used, influence that disappears if the buyer shops elsewhere.

U.S. arms transfers take a variety of forms. Commercial sales to foreign buyers, subject to Center for Defense Trade approval, are one. Sales brokered by the government are another. As part of the $8 billion security assistance program, the U.S. government

SHOPPING LIST

Between 1981 and 1988 developing countries spent $345.6 billion to acquire:

▶ 37,000 surface-to-air missiles

▶ 20,000 artillery pieces

▶ 11,000 tanks and self-propelled howitzers

▶ 3,200 supersonic fighter planes

▶ 540 warships and submarines

gives foreign governments more than $4 billion a year to buy weapons. (This financing used to be in the form of loans provided by Uncle Sam, but the debt burden became so staggering to some countries that late in the Reagan administration the program was switched almost entirely to grants.) Outside official channels, a global network of private arms dealers buys and sells weaponry. Tens of millions of dollars' worth of U.S. weapons illegally flows overseas every year, according to government estimates.

U.S. intelligence failures and bad endings to alliances with dictators — in Iran, the Philippines, Panama and Nicaragua for example — make some experts nervous about the escalating destructive power of the weapons the United States and other countries are now pumping into the Middle East and around the globe.

In the Middle East the United States is selling highly destructive weapons to nations that are potential combatants. Massive sales of sophisticated weaponry to Saudi Arabia trigger demands to give Israel compensating firepower. The potential damage in another Arab-Israeli war could be devastating. In other regional conflicts, such as the tense Pakistan-India standoff, the massive military buildup on both sides means that if shooting starts, the results could be cataclysmic.

Arms sales and other forms of military assistance can also strengthen the military in countries where it is often an impediment to democratization and civil society. "One of the clearest correlations in the politics of Third World nations is the relationship between militarization and repression," wrote Notre Dame University Prof. George Lopez last year in the *Bulletin of the Atomic Scientists.* Washington analyst Ruth Leger Sivard has also noted this link. "In the ultimate mockery of 'defense,' " she says, "military power wedded to political control turns inward to terrorize the people it is intended to protect."

In response to congressional directives, the program for training foreign military officers in the United States has been expanded "to promote military professionalism" and "foster greater respect for . . . the principle of civilian control of the military," says an administration report to Congress.

While quick to cite Amnesty International reports on Iraq's human rights abuses in occupied Kuwait, the United States has long relegated human rights to the diplomatic back burner to justify arms sales for strategic purposes. Egypt, for example, has been the second largest recipient of U.S. military assistance since it signed the Camp David accords with Israel. But a 1990 Amnesty report stated, "The use of torture has become widespread to the point that it now appears to be a matter of policy by the security forces."

The notion of a moral dimension to arms exports briefly was factored into U.S. policy when the Carter administration tried to reduce arms sales and discouraged U.S. embassy personnel from assisting American arms suppliers. But the Reagan administration was quick to overturn that policy, emphasizing the value of security assistance and dramatically increasing American exports.

Opponents of arms transfers take heart from the fact that the war has at least stirred up some debate on the issue. In April five House Democrats — Dante Fascell (Fla.), Lee Hamilton (Ind.), Sam Gejdenson (Conn.), Richard Gephardt (Mo.) and David Obey (Wis.) — urged Bush not to "squander" the opportunity to seek regional arms controls in the Mideast. They asked for a temporary unilateral pause in arms sales to the region, arguing that it wouldn't affect the nations' security and could "bring supplier nations and regional states together to pursue a range of arms reduction and arms control proposals, including an arms moratorium." The White House opposes a moratorium, saying there are regional imbalances that must be addressed.

Proposals to cool down the global arms export race have also been float-ed by several foreign leaders. But such proposals face opposition from a wide variety of sources. Many Third World nations see the development of an indigenous arms industry as a major step toward long-term independence from the superpowers. They see hypocrisy in U.S. calls to control the spread of weapons and technology.

"It is fashionable among industrialized nations to deplore acquisition of high-technology weapons by developing nations," said one Indian analyst, "but this moralistic stand is akin to drug pushers shedding tears about the weaknesses of drug addicts."

In addition, weaponry's proven profit potential makes it likely that countries in need of cash will continue to sell. China has indicated that it has no plans to discontinue its missile sales. The government of Czechoslovakia, the only Warsaw Pact country to send troops to the coalition forces in Saudi Arabia, announced in March that it would resist U.S. pressures to forbid arms sales to Iran, saying that would be "economically stupid."

When British Prime Minister John Major tried and failed to get a promise from Soviet leader Mikhail Gorbachev not to rearm Iraq, a Soviet official responded that restraint "must be shown all around, not just on the part of a single seller or a single buyer." In 1988 the British concluded the largest arms deal ever, a long-term agreement that will send tens of billions of dollars' worth of advanced fighter planes and other equipment to Saudi Arabia.

The British-Saudi deal was reached after the U.S. Congress had refused to allow the sale of advanced fighters to Saudi Arabia; Margaret Thatcher then took a personal interest in sealing the agreement. The deal is cited as proof by U.S. arms manufacturers that unilateral restrictions will only undercut American companies and U.S. influence — not slow down the arming of the world.

But supporters of stiff controls on arms sales say the United States should take advantage of the rare opportunity presented by the extent of international cooperation against Iraq. Some unilateral restraint right now, they say, would strengthen U.S. credibility in efforts to reach some kind of control agreement among arms supplier nations.

So far, most of the proposals focus

on the Middle East. That may be short-sighted, given long-term trends in arms sales. Despite the ferocity of the Iran-Iraq war, arms sales to the Middle East region as a whole actually declined between 1983 and 1988. But other regions are picking up the slack. The world's most promising growth market is South Asia, where arms imports jumped more than 20 percent annually between 1983 and 1988, according to the U.S. Arms Control and Disarmament Agency.

In March the Canadian government called for a "world summit on the instruments of war and weapons of mass destruction" and said "a special responsibility for arms buildups resides with the major exporters and states leading in the development of weapons technology." At a meeting with Canadian Prime Minister Brian Mulroney in March, President Bush downplayed the Canadian proposal, saying that it "might have some merit, but it's a little early."

Bush might take a look at a speech made by then-Secretary of State George Shultz at a United Nations special session on disarmament in 1988. "Advanced weapons technology is spreading throughout the globe," Shultz said. "These are not simply East/West issues, they concern every state here represented. And we must all recognize that if we are not part of the solution, we are part of the problem."

♦

Article 14.2.   Fueling the Fire: How We Armed the Middle East

The author contends that if world leaders had agreed to President Carter's call for restraint of U.S. military sales to the Third World, it is quite possible that Iraq would never have become such a formidable threat to world peace and stability. The gulf war experience suggests that the United States should show restraint in agreeing to future arms sales to the Middle East, at least until there is some progress in the peace process. Instead, the Bush administration has proposed a new round of multi-billion-dollar weapons sales to pro-West nations in the region. The president's decision was met by considerable congressional criticism, which forced him to scale down his initial request. However, he subsequently incorporated the items removed from the list into another package scheduled for later consideration. According to one prominent publication, other major suppliers—including France and Britain—have stepped up their arms sales to the region such that 1991 should top all existing records for arms sales to the Middle East.

FUELING THE FIRE:
HOW WE ARMED THE MIDDLE EAST

By MICHAEL T. KLARE

From *The Bulletin of the Atomic Scientists*, vol 47, no 1. Copyright © 1991 by the Educational Foundation for Nuclear Science, 6042 S. Kimbark Avenue, Chicago, IL 60637 USA. A one-year subscription is $30.

Warning that "the virtually unrestrained spread of conventional weaponry threatens stability in every region of the world," President Jimmy Carter attempted in the mid-1970s to constrain U.S. military sales to the Third World and to negotiate a mutual curb on arms exports with the Soviets. These efforts failed. Carter's attempt to limit U.S. military sales collided with the use of arms transfers as an instrument of diplomacy—especially in the Middle East—and his overtures to Moscow were forestalled by a resurgence of Cold War tensions. Since then, no serious effort has been made to curb international arms trafficking, and sales to the Third World have skyrocketed. As Carter predicted, unrestrained commerce in conventional arms has fueled local arms races and inspired aggressive powers like Iraq to employ their bulging arsenals in unprovoked attacks on neighboring countries. If the present crisis in the Persian Gulf is to have any positive outcome, therefore, it should be to demonstrate the urgent need to curtail the global arms trade.

The arms-trade danger is underscored by the relative ease with which Saddam Hussein was able to assemble a massive arsenal of conventional weapons. Between 1981 and 1988, Iraq purchased an estimated $46.7 billion worth of arms and military equipment from foreign suppliers, the largest accumulation ever of modern weapons by a Third World country.[1] Included in this largesse were some 2,300 modern Soviet and Chinese tanks, 64 Mirage F-1 fighters armed with Exocet missiles, 2,650 armored personnel carriers, and 350 Scud-B surface-to-surface missiles.[2] These and other imported weapons enabled Baghdad to prevail in the Iran-Iraq War and subsequently fed Hussein's vision of Iraqi dominion over Kuwait and the western Gulf area.

U.S., French, and British troops now face the unappealing prospect of head-on conflict with Hussein's well-armed forces, but Western officials and arms suppliers are understandably reluctant to discuss their role in enlarging the Iraqi arsenal. Although direct U.S. arms sales to Iraq have been largely blocked since the late 1950s when Iraq became a client of the Soviet Union, Washington has on occasion permitted sales of military-related science and technology. Soviet leaders are also tight-lipped about Moscow's contributions to Hussein's military capabilities. But Iraq would not represent such a powerful threat to global peace and stability if

world leaders had agreed to the mutual restraints Jimmy Carter proposed in 1977.

On the basis of this experience, U.S. officials should be wary of transferring more arms to the Middle East—at least until some multilateral constraints are in place. Instead, the Bush administration has decided to proceed with a new round of multibillion-dollar sales to friendly nations in the region. In August, Bush authorized the transfer of 150 M-60A3 tanks, 24 F-15 aircraft, and 200 Stinger anti-aircraft missiles to Saudi Arabia (a $2.2 billion deal), and in September he approved a $21 billion package of tanks, aircraft, and missiles. The White House subsequently agreed to downsize the second package in order to allay congressional concerns, but the items removed from this sale are incorporated into another package scheduled for early 1991. Bush also agreed in principle to sell $1 billion worth of additional military hardware to Israel, and forgave a $7 billion Egyptian arms debt in order to allow new military sales to Cairo. Meanwhile, as *Aerospace Daily* reported in early September, other major suppliers—including France and Britain—have been flocking to the Middle East, looking for new military sales of their own, helping to insure that 1990 and 1991 will break all existing records for arms sales to the region.

In approving new arms exports, the administration maintains that the weapons will help deter further Iraqi aggression. But most of the weapons ordered in 1990 and 1991 will not be delivered until 1992, 1993, or thereafter—long after the present crisis in the Gulf has been resolved by one means or another. These new arms shipments will then be available for other military purposes, regardless of the administration's claims. The intended beneficiaries of these sales will continue to pursue their own political and military objectives—often risking armed combat with their neighbors in the process. The most likely outcome of fresh arms deliveries to the Middle East will thus be intensified regional tensions and a heightened risk of armed conflict.

This prospect dampens hope that the Persian Gulf crisis will help usher in a new era of peace and stability, as some in Washington suggested. "Out of these troubled times," George Bush told a joint session of Congress on September 12, "a new world order can emerge," one in which "the rule of law supplants the rule of the jungle, [and] nations recognize the shared responsibility for freedom and justice." While the Gulf crisis has engendered an extraordinary degree of international cooperation, it has not resulted in any talks on controlling the conventional arms trade. As long as contentious regional powers are able to obtain large quantities of sophisticated weapons, the prospects for averting future conflict are not promising.

Saddam Hussein has collected the most modern arsenal in the Third World— with help from the United States, the Soviet Union, the French, the British, the Germans, the Chinese . . .

Michael T. Klare is the five-college associate professor of peace and world security studies based at Hampshire College, Amherst, Massachusetts. He is the author of American Arms Supermarket *(1985).*

George Bush proposed $23 billion in sales to Saudi Arabia of weapons that could not possibly arrive in time for the current crisis in the Gulf.

The risk of escalating conflicts in volatile Third World areas has led nations to agree on the need to prevent sales of chemical and nuclear weapons and to curb the diffusion of ballistic missile delivery systems. Despite repeated crises, however, there are no such constraints on conventional weapons—especially on modern tanks and aircraft that can be used for aggressive military moves of the sort undertaken by Iraq. Are curbs on arms transfers possible?

"Reverse dependency"

Many countries offer some type of weapon for sale, but the trade in major combat systems is highly concentrated. According to the Congressional Research Service of the Library of Congress, in the 1980s the United States and Soviet Union accounted for three-fifths of all arms sales to the Third World, and five other nations—France, Great Britain, West Germany, Italy, and China—shared another 22 percent. These nations remain the source of most heavy weapons supplied to Middle Eastern countries, and it is their sales policies that must be addressed if the flow of combat gear is to be constrained.

Many factors—political, economic, and military—figure in these nations' arms export behavior. For the superpowers, economic considerations have generally played a secondary role to political and strategic considerations. Samuel Huntington suggested in 1987 that U.S. and Soviet involvement in the Third World reflects "the bipolar structure of world politics and the competitive relationship they have with each other." In their mutual quest for strategic advantage, each superpower has sought to expand its own perimeter of influence while "minimizing the power and influence of the other."[3] As part of this process, each side has used arms transfers to lure new allies into its own camp or to discourage existing allies from breaking away.

This use of arms transfers began in the Middle East in 1955, when President Gamal Abdel Nasser of Egypt turned to Moscow for the modern weapons the West had denied him. By giving Egypt advanced weapons, Moscow forged a *de facto* alliance with Cairo, and succeeded, for the first time, in leaping over the ring of hostile states organized by the United States to contain Soviet power in Eurasia. This feat prompted Washington to establish arms-supply relationships with other countries in the region, including Iran, Israel, Jordan, and Saudi Arabia. These moves, in turn, aroused anxiety among the more radical Arab regimes, leading Syria, and then Iraq, to forge military ties with the Soviet bloc. Egypt switched sides following the October War of 1973, but the Middle Eastern arms acquisition patterns established in the mid-to-late 1950s have remained essentially intact to this day.

In justifying U.S. arms transfers to the Middle East, U.S. leaders repeatedly asserted that supplier and recipient were bound by common opposition to communist expansionism. For their part, Soviet leaders stressed the common struggle against imperialism. However, the recipients' principal motive for acquiring arms was not the struggle between communism and imperialism, but rather a desire to offset the military might of their regional rivals or to deter attack by an antagonistic neighbor. As Stephen M. Walt suggested in his masterful study of Middle East alliance patterns, "The superpowers sought to balance each other, [while] their clients sought outside support to counter threats from other regional states."[4]

At first glance, this system has a certain logic: each party receives something it wants, and the various arms deliveries balance each other out. In reality, however, the system is fundamentally unstable. No recipient is content with balancing its rivals, but seeks a margin of advantage—either to allow for a preemptive strike (should that be deemed necessary), or to compensate for the other side's perceived advantages. Any major weapons delivery to one side automatically triggers a comparable but larger delivery to the other, prompting a new round of deliveries to the first party, and so on. The only break in this grim pattern occurs when one side or the other seeks to forestall an imminent shift in military advantage to the opposing side by launching a preemptive attack—as has occurred again and again in the Middle East.

This instability is mirrored in the relations between client and supplier. By agreeing to provide arms to a client, the supplier seeks a local ally for its ongoing struggle against the other superpower. Once the relationship has been forged, however, the recipient comes to expect continuing and even expanded arms deliveries in exchange for its continued loyalty to the supplier—and any reluctance on the part of the supplier will be condemned as evidence of inconstancy and unreliability. Such charges usually have the effect of prying additional or more advanced weapons out of the supplier's hands.

The result is "reverse dependency." The patron finds itself beholden to the good will of the client, and must satisfy the client's appetite for modern arms. As Walt points out, "A large [military] aid relationship may actually be a reflection of the client's ability to extort support from its patron, rather than being a sign of the patron's ability to control its client." For the Soviet Union, the principal beneficiaries of reverse dependency were Egypt (until 1973), Syria, and Iraq; for the United States, they were Iran (until 1978), Israel, and Saudi Arabia.

Carter, Iran, and CATT

It was the U.S. arms-supply relationship with Iran that first prompted U.S. policymakers to perceive a need for restraints. The relationship was initially forged in 1954, after the U.S. Central Intelligence Agency engineered the overthrow of Mohammed Mossadeq and installed Shah Mohammed Reza Pahlavi as virtual dictator. During the late 1950s and throughout the 1960s, Washington provided Iran with a steady, but not exorbitant, supply of munitions in order to balance Soviet military deliveries to neighboring Iraq. In the early 1970s, however, there was a sharp increase in U.S. arms deliveries as the Shah, with mounting oil revenues at his disposal, sought to greatly enhance Iran's overall military capabilities. Iran's desire for arms was complemented, moreover, by a U.S. desire to recover some of the petrodollars sent to the Middle East in the aftermath of the 1974 OPEC oil price increase, and to implement the so-called Nixon Doctrine, which called for Third World allies to shoulder more of the burden of regional defense against Soviet-backed insurgents and regimes.

Between 1972 and 1978, Teheran ordered $20 billion worth of advanced U.S. armaments—the largest arms export endeavor ever concluded with a Third World nation up to that point. For the first time, U.S. officials agreed to transfer front-line U.S. combat equipment, including F-14 aircraft, Spruance-class destroyers, and Phoenix air-to-air missiles. These sales were widely applauded by Defense Department officials and American arms makers. But Congress became concerned when the scale of the transactions were revealed and when it was disclosed that U.S. companies were using bribes to get Iranian officials to sign military orders. According to a 1976 Senate Foreign Relations Committee staff report, "U.S. arms sales to Iran were out of control" in the early 1970s, with senior administration officials routinely approving the Shah's extravagant arms purchases.

Suggesting that the United States had become "a kind of arms supermarket into which any customer can walk and pick up whatever he wants,"[5] Sen. Hubert H. Humphrey in 1975 sponsored legislation to give Congress veto power over major U.S. military sales. The resulting measure, later incorporated into Section 36(b) of the Arms Export Control Act of 1976, gives Congress some control over arms transactions, but unfavorable court decisions, and a waiver allowing the president to overrule congressional reservations when he concludes that critical national security issues are at stake—which Bush used to rush tanks and aircraft to Saudi Arabia in September—have diluted congressional power.

With Carter's election in 1976, the momentum shifted to the White House. On May 13, 1977, Carter formally adopted an "arms export restraint policy"—Presidential Directive No. 13 (PD-13)—which imposed an annual ceiling on the dollar value of U.S. arms sales to all non-NATO nations except Israel, Japan, South Korea, Australia, and New Zealand, and restricted the export of certain high-technology weapons to Third World countries. "I have concluded," Carter affirmed on May 19, "that the United States will henceforth view arms transfers as an exceptional foreign policy implement, to be used only in instances where it can be clearly demonstrated that the transfer contributes to our national security interests."[6]

The Carter policy also called for negotiations with other suppliers—including the Soviet Union—that might lead to the adoption of multilateral curbs on arms transfers. Carter made clear that the United States would adhere to self-imposed limits only so long as it appeared likely that other major suppliers would follow suit. "I am initiating this policy," Carter noted, "in the full understanding that actual reductions in the worldwide traffic in arms will require multilateral cooperation."

At Carter's urging, U.S. and Soviet representatives began the Conventional Arms Transfer Talks (CATT). Most observers expected little progress, and were surprised when the first few rounds of talks, held in Washington and Helsinki in December 1977 and May and July 1978, resulted in agreement on parameters of a regime to restrain conventional arms transfers. In October 1978, U.S. negotiator Leslie Gelb testified that "harmonized national guidelines" similar to those of the London Suppliers' Group (for nuclear technology) were "realistic possibilities."[7] But before further progress could be achieved, CATT fell prey to a souring international environment and to bureaucratic wrangling within the Carter administration that pitted Gelb against the president's hawkish security adviser, Zbigniew Brzezinski; no further talks were held after a fruitless negotiating session in December 1978.[8]

By late 1979, Carter's unilateral arms restraint policies and the CATT process had been essentially abandoned. The decline in presidential enthusiasm for these measures was prompted, to a considerable degree, by Iran's Islamic revolution and the Soviet invasion of Afghanistan—events that largely erased any public or congressional support for U.S. initiatives of this type. In a more fundamental way, however, the policy of restraint was doomed from the start by the administration's failure to question the politics of arms sales. Washington still viewed arms transfers as an effective tool for diplomacy—one of the few such tools available—and Carter was never able to significantly reduce the role of military sales in U.S. relations with such allies as

Egypt, Iran, Israel, Jordan, and Saudi Arabia.

The fate of Carter's initiatives became apparent early on. In February 1978, only nine months after PD-13 was signed, the White House approved a multibillion-dollar sale of advanced jet fighters to Egypt, Israel, and Saudi Arabia. The "aircraft sale of the century," as it was called at the time, had been in the works for several years, and its cancellation would have provoked howls of dismay from the nations involved, along with threats to shop elsewhere—threats Carter was not prepared to face. For much the same reason, Carter then approved a new $8 billion arms request from the Shah, despite Iran's internal unrest, which his advisers warned could result in chaos. Any hopes of keeping arms exports under the ceiling Carter had set were dashed in 1979, when, as part of the Camp David Accords, the United States agreed to provide billions of dollars worth of new arms to Israel and Egypt.

"Arms replace security pacts"

By the time Ronald Reagan became president in 1981, arms export restraint was no longer a major objective of U.S. foreign policy. Nonetheless, Reagan felt compelled to denounce his predecessor's initiatives and to promulgate a new, open-door approach to foreign military sales. In a May 1981 speech unveiling the new policy, Undersecretary of State James L. Buckley affirmed that "this Administration believes that arms transfers, judiciously applied, can complement and supplement our own defense efforts and serve as a vital and constructive instrument of our foreign policy."[9] Reagan quickly approved the sale of F-16 fighters to Pakistan, F-15s and AWACS radar patrol planes to Saudi Arabia, AH-1 Cobra helicopter gunships to Jordan, and similar items to other U.S. clients in the Middle East and Asia.

U.S. arms flowed to the Third World in record amounts. Capped by a $5 billion sale of F-15s and AWACS to Saudi Arabia, total U.S. military sales rose to $19.1 billion in fiscal 1981, an all-time record. Only the oil-induced recession of 1983–84, which greatly constricted the spending ability of would-be Third World arms buyers, prevented new records from being set in subsequent years. The recession notwithstanding, Washington continued to use arms sales to extend U.S. influence abroad and to counter similar efforts by the Soviet Union. "Arms sales are the hard currency of foreign affairs," an unidentified State Department official told *U.S. News and World Report* in 1983. "They replace the security pacts of the 1950s."[10]

What was true for Washington was true for Moscow. Lacking funds to offer economic assistance or capital investment, Soviet leaders employed the one foreign policy tool available to them in seeking influence abroad: arms transfers. According to the Congressional Research Service, Soviet arms transfers to the Third World from 1981 to 1988 amounted to a whopping $139 billion (in constant 1988 dollars), an amount that exceeds the U.S. total by a significant margin. The major recipients of Soviet arms in the 1980s were clustered in the Middle East and South Asia, with the largest deliveries going to Algeria, India, Iraq, Libya, Syria, and the two Yemens.

As in past years, both superpowers also sought to woo away each other's allies and clients, often using arms transfers in the process. The Soviet Union, for instance, has readily supplied Jordan and Kuwait with modern weapons when leaders of these countries encountered difficulty in obtaining high-tech systems from the West. The United States, for its part, has encouraged several long-standing Soviet allies, including India and Iraq, to diminish their military dependence on the Soviet Union. Consistent with this policy, the Reagan administration raised no objection to French sales of advanced missiles and aircraft to Iraq, or to Brazilian sales of multiple-launch rocket systems. In a further effort to pull Baghdad out of the Soviet orbit, Reagan (and later Bush) authorized the sale to Iraq of $1.5 billion worth of sophisticated U.S. scientific and technical equipment—much of which has apparently been used in the development of conventional, nuclear, and chemical weapons. Indeed, so eager was Washington to forge links with Iraq that Reagan and Bush continued to allow deliveries of such equipment even after it had become evident that this technology was being diverted for military purposes, and long after Iraq had used chemical weapons in attacks on Iran and its own Kurds.

As a result of these deeply entrenched arms-supply patterns, many Middle Eastern nations now possess arsenals comparable or superior to those found among the front-line states in NATO and the Warsaw Pact. But if the genesis of these arms-supply relationships was the early Cold War, it would seem logical for them to fade as the Cold War draws to a close. U.S. and Soviet leaders have lent some credence to this assumption. In an August 1990 letter to U.N. Secretary-General Javier Perez de Cuellar, Soviet Foreign Minister Eduard Shevardnadze wrote that "the Soviet Union considers that the inclusion on the U.N. agenda of the problems of restricting international sales and supplies of conventional weapons is a logical development of the trend toward the internationalization of the dialogue on most important questions of world politics."[11] President Bush and Secretary of State James Baker have made similar comments, noting that the control of conventional

Both superpowers have used arms transfers to woo away each other's allies and clients.

Curbs on arms transfers are essential to post–Cold War stability.

arms transfers should be considered along with efforts to curb the proliferation of nuclear arms, chemical weapons, and ballistic missiles.

Despite progress on the rhetorical front, however, the superpowers have taken no steps to curb their exports of conventional arms to the Third World. As noted above, the United States has announced record-breaking sales to Saudi Arabia, and sales of sophisticated arms to Egypt, Israel, Turkey, and the United Arab Emirates are in the offing. The Soviet Union continues to supply major equipment to India, Libya, and Syria, and was pouring arms into Iraq until the moment Saddam Hussein ordered the invasion of Kuwait.

Economic conditions have something to do with this. The Soviet Union is desperately in need of hard currency for its industrial rehabilitation, and weapons are among the few commodities it can successfully market abroad. Arms exports give U.S. weapons manufacturers an attractive "safety valve" at a time of declining military spending at home. But political factors remain a major determinant of the superpowers' arms transfer policies. Moscow and Washington once sought Third World allies in their struggle with one another; today they seek allies in order to better position themselves for global influence in an uncertain, polycentric era.

In the view of senior U.S. strategists, this era is likely to witness the emergence of regional powers, many of which will be armed with weapons of mass destruction, and some will be hostile to long-term U.S. interests. "The emergence of regional powers is rapidly changing the strategic landscape," President Bush noted in an address to the U.S. Coast Guard Academy in May 1989. "In the Middle East, in South Asia, in our own hemisphere, a growing number of nations are acquiring advanced and highly destructive capabilities," posing a significant threat to U.S. security. In this environment, any effort by the United States to protect its overseas interests through military means—as in Operation Desert Shield—will require the cooperation of friendly Third World powers. "Where American intervention seems necessary," the U.S. Commission on Integrated Long-Term Strategy affirmed in 1988, "it will generally require far more cooperation with Third World countries than has been required in the past."[12]

And cooperation is secured through arms transfers. In arguing for congressional approval of the administration's September 1990 emergency arms package for Saudi Arabia, Undersecretary of State for International Security Affairs Reginald Bartholomew told the House Foreign Affairs Committee that these sales are intended to "develop the interoperability that will allow the U.S. and other friendly forces to reinforce the Saudis more effectively should

that ever again be necessary," and to "help contribute to stronger and more stable post-crisis security arrangements."[13] In other words, arms sales are the essential glue for the "regional security structure" that Secretary of State James Baker told the House Foreign Affairs Committee on September 4 the administration wants to establish in the Middle East.

Whether the Soviet Union has similar intentions cannot be determined. It is clear that Soviet leaders want to maintain close ties with regional powers like Syria and India, and to establish new ties—cemented by arms transfers if necessary—with other powers in the region. Potential buyers are still able to play one suitor off against the other, obtaining favorable conditions for the acquisition of ever more capable weapons. Whatever impact the end of the Cold War may have in other areas, it has not diminished the intensity of local arms races—or the likelihood of regional conflict—in the Middle East.

Seven ways to curb arms

There is no escape from this pattern if the major powers continue to view arms exports as tools of convenience in their quest for political advantage, and if regional powers continue to rely on military means to resolve disputes with their neighbors. U.S. and Soviet leaders—and subsequently, the leaders of France, Britain, and China—must be convinced that a stable international order cannot be achieved in a world of uncontrolled arms transfers, and that curbs on arms are essential to post–Cold War stability. At the same time, Middle Eastern leaders must be persuaded that the best hope for long-term protection against dissension and bloodshed lies with a regional peace agreement that respects the national aspirations of unrepresented peoples, eliminates nuclear and chemical weapons, and limits the acquisition of offensively oriented conventional weapons.

These objectives may take years of effort, but intermediate goals could build momentum for more sweeping and long-lasting objectives. Seven measures could produce real improvements in global security:

■ **Reconvene the CATT talks.** As the only U.S.-Soviet negotiations ever undertaken in this field, the Conventional Arms Transfer Talks are a useful mechanism. At the original sessions, CATT negotiators reportedly reached agreement on many basic elements of nomenclature, scope, and applicability which could save months of future talks and consultations. Resuming CATT talks would also send a powerful signal to other suppliers and to recipients that the two superpowers had agreed on the need to constrain the arms traffic.

179

A U.S.-Soviet agreement to limit sales to $8–10 billion per year would be a start.

If the talks are resumed, the two sides should agree to set a mutual ceiling on arms transfers (perhaps $8–10 billion each per year) while pledging to negotiate lower levels in subsequent talks, after experience has been gained in implementation and verification. The superpowers should also agree to ban or restrict the sale of particularly inhumane and destabilizing weapons such as wide-area cluster bombs, fuel-air explosives, incendiary devices, shoulder-fired anti-aircraft missiles, and long-range bombers.

■ **Expand and enhance the MTCR.** The Missile Technology Control Regime, established in 1987 to restrict exports of ballistic missile technology, represents an important precedent for multilateral action. But it has critical defects: several countries that have played a vital role in the transfer of missiles and missile technology to areas of conflict are not signatories—notably Argentina, Brazil, China, and the Soviet Union. And the MTCR generally exempts technology used in developing missiles for space exploration, most of which can be converted to military use.

To be effective, the MTCR needs to be substantially strengthened. Including the Soviet Union should be the most immediate priority, particularly as Soviet officials have already met with their U.S. counterparts to discuss possible cooperation in this area, and an agreement would be consistent with policy statements issued by Soviet leadership. It would then be easier to persuade other holdouts to join. Restrictions on the transfer of sensitive technology, including space-related technology, should be tightened.

■ **Establish controls on other advanced military systems.** Instruments similar to the MTCR should be established for controlling the export of other destabilizing weapons, including cruise missiles, submarines, and deep-penetration strategic bombers.

■ **Convene an international conference on nuclear and chemical disarmament in the Middle East.** No lasting progress toward regional security can be made unless the nations of the Middle East agree to restrict possession of weapons of mass destruction and their means of delivery. A Middle East agreement will require progress in other areas, including boundary disputes. But the history of East-West negotiations demonstrates that progress on arms control will not occur unless countries talk to one another, and preliminary negotiations can often result in the adoption of confidence-building measures that help set the stage for political accommodation.

When the crisis in the Gulf is resolved, efforts should be made to convene a U.N.-sponsored regional conference on nuclear and chemical disarmament, which might also provide the impetus for adopting confidence-building measures

The transfer of military technology to states developing nuclear or chemical weapons should be barred.

tailored to the Middle East. These could include international inspection and monitoring of nuclear and chemical facilities; establishing "hot lines" for communication between hostile nations in a crisis; and mutual promises to sign and abide by the Nuclear Non-Proliferation Treaty and the proposed Chemical Weapons Convention. A U.N. conference could also develop into an ongoing negotiating process, as did the Conference on Security and Cooperation in Europe.

■ **Impose economic and trade sanctions against nations developing nuclear weapons.** The U.N. trade embargo has prevented the transfer of materials and technology to Iraq's weapons development and production facilities, including its nuclear and chemical installations. These sanctions should be maintained until Baghdad agrees to dismantle its nuclear and chemical weapons facilities under international inspection. When the current crisis is over, the United Nations should develop an array of trade and economic sanctions to apply against nations that persist in developing such weapons after international norms are established. Sanctions could be limited to a ban on transfers of military technology in the case of states that agree to participate in regional negotiations, or entail more stringent measures if states refuse to participate in such a process.

■ **Reduce or restrict international aid to nations developing domestic arms industries.** Many of the more affluent Third World countries are developing elaborate military-industrial complexes modeled on those found in the major military powers of the industrialized "North." These complexes contribute to the worldwide diffusion of conventional weapons, and, in the case of Iran and Iraq, help to sustain regional wars of great duration and ferocity. Most of these countries receive significant technical and economic assistance from the North that enables them to divert scarce national resources to pet military projects. In the future, such assistance—whether provided by individual governments or by multilateral agencies like the World Bank—should be denied to states that divert an excessive share of their national income to military-industrial purposes.

■ **Establish an international clearinghouse for intelligence on clandestine arms technology transfers.** Iraq's apparent success in acquiring sophisticated arms-making technologies through black market arms channels highlights the need to collect and process intelligence on clandestine arms operations. A clearinghouse could track suspicious "front" operations in target countries and inform police and military authorities of any apparent wrongdoing. Such a mechanism might draw on the staff and experience of COCOM (the Co-ordinating Committee for East-West Trade Policy), the Western agency established to intercept transfers of high-technology goods to the Soviet bloc.

In the absence of controls, the arms trade will continue to operate as in the past, and there will be a continuing series of regional crises and conflicts. But these seven measures could significantly improve the global security environment and set the stage for a comprehensive solution to the Middle East's outstanding security concerns.

Presidents Bush and Gorbachev have spoken glowingly of the new world order they hope to construct on the ruins of the Cold War system. But a new order cannot be built on the premises that have guided international behavior in the past. Obsolete practices will have to be abandoned, particularly the practice of supplying implements of war in return for political promises and favors. Only when munitions are eschewed as an instrument of statecraft and diplomacy will a more peaceful order be possible. ■

1. Richard F. Grimmett, *Trends in Conventional Arms Transfers to the Third World by Major Supplier, 1981-1988* (Washington, D.C.: Congressional Research Service, Library of Congress, 1989), p. 51.

2. Stockholm International Peace Research Institute, *SIPRI Yearbook 1990* (Oxford and New York: Oxford University Press, 1990), and earlier editions.

3. Samuel P. Huntington, "Patterns of Intervention: America and the Soviets in the Third World," *The National Interest* (Spring 1987), pp. 19–20; for a discussion of supplier and recipient motives, see Andrew J. Pierre, *The Global Politics of Arms Sales* (Princeton: Princeton University Press, 1982).

4. Stephen M. Walt, *The Origins of Alliances* (Ithaca, N.Y.: Cornell University Press, 1987), pp. 50–103.

5. Quoted in *New York Times*, Oct. 19, 1975.

6. U.S. Congress, House Committee on Foreign Affairs, *Changing Perspectives on U.S. Arms Transfer Policy*, Report by the Congressional Research Service, 97th Cong., 1st sess., 1981.

7. U.S. Congress, House Committee on Armed Services, *Indian Ocean Arms Limitations and Multilateral Cooperation on Restraining Conventional Arms Transfers*, Hearings, 95th Cong., 2d sess., 1978, p. 17.

8. See Jo L. Husbands and Anne Hessing Cahn, "The Conventional Arms Transfer Talks," in Thomas Ohlson, ed., *Arms Transfer Limitations and Third World Security* (Oxford: Oxford University Press, 1988), pp. 110–25.

9. James L. Buckley, address, Aerospace Industries Association meeting, Williamsburg, Va., May 21, 1981 (U.S. State Department transcript).

10. Quoted in *Wall Street Journal*, June 19, 1983.

11. *Izvestiya*, Aug, 16, 1990 (translated in *Foreign Broadcast Information Service-Sov-90-159*, Aug. 16, 1990, p. 6).

12. U.S. Commission on Integrated Long-Term Strategy, *Discriminate Deterrence* (Washington, D.C.: U.S. Government Printing Office, 1988), p. 10.

13. Testimony, October 3, 1990 (State Department text).

Article 15.1.   The Nuclear Threat: A Proposal

During the Cold War, American foreign policy was motivated by two major objectives: first, to deter a possible Soviet nuclear attack, particularly against Western Europe and, second, to prevent the spread of nuclear weapons. Today, the United States faces a new threat—namely, that an unstable Soviet Union may lose control of its nuclear arsenal. The gulf war demonstrates, according to the authors, that the superpowers must redouble their efforts to halt the proliferation of nuclear weapons, lest they fall into the hands of leaders such as Saddam Hussein or Muammar Qaddafi. In this regard, the authors propose an immediate and massive reduction in U.S. and Soviet nuclear weapons. This would force both nations to renew their efforts to halt the spread of nuclear, chemical, and biological warheads, and advanced delivery systems. Ultimately, global security will depend upon eliminating the threat of nuclear war. The United States must take the first steps in that direction, which will demand strong, effective presidential leadership.

The Nuclear Threat: A Proposal

Hans A. Bethe, Kurt Gottfried, and Robert S. McNamara

1.

For decades the United States and its allies have maintained nuclear forces designed for one overriding objective: to deter Soviet military action, particularly an attack against Western Europe. In addition, the United States has sought to prevent the proliferation of nuclear weapons, but this goal was never considered as important as the first.

Now the crumbling of Soviet power and the war in the Gulf have shattered the assumptions that underlie Western nuclear policies. An entirely new danger has arisen: that a disintegrating Soviet Union might lose control over its immense nuclear arsenal. Among the causes of the war in the Gulf, moreover, was the fear that Saddam Hussein would acquire nuclear weapons capable of hitting distant targets and drawing the Great Powers into a nuclear conflict. New policies controlling nuclear weapons must be adopted to reduce as quickly as possible risks of both kinds.

The crucial first step, we shall argue, would be a very deep and swift cut in US and Soviet nuclear forces, which should be reduced from their present total of approximately 50,000 warheads to something on the order of two thousand. To do so would, at one stroke, force the US and the USSR to adopt far less dangerous nuclear strategies and strengthen the global effort to halt the spread of nuclear weapons.

These changes in nuclear policy would be a major step toward a world in which relations among nations would be based on the rule of law, supported by a system of collective security, with the United Nations and regional organizations able to resolve conflicts and keep the peace.

That the peaceful period between the collapse of the Berlin Wall and the arrival of tanks in Kuwait and Vilnius was so brief should dispel any illusions that such a goal is within easy reach. Nevertheless, at least it is clear that no regime in Moscow will be able to recreate the threat of the cold war years. This brutal century, in our view, has taught some lessons that should be applied as we plan for the next: that war between major industrialized states can no longer be perceived as the continuation of politics by other means; that long-term security depends on cooperation, especially with former enemies, as the success of Western policy toward Germany after 1945 demonstrates; and that a more peaceful and civilized international life will depend on the emergence of institutions with the resources and authority to encourage cooperation and to mediate conflict.

Deciding the role of nuclear weapons in a new system of international security is the easier part of the problem. Whether or not one believes that the numbers and disposition of the US and Soviet nuclear forces were appropriate before 1989, it should be clear they are incompatible with the new political realities. Compared to conventional forces, moreover, nuclear forces are designed to be used in extreme and highly unlikely circumstances; they have little impact on domestic life, and no connection with day-to-day international affairs. Presumably these facts explain why it is a matter of indifference to most people that the world's inventory of tens of thousands of nuclear warheads remains virtually intact, even though of all the results of the cold war it is the one that poses the gravest danger to survival.

The danger of nuclear war has not vanished along with the Soviet conventional threat. Soviet instability, regional conflicts in the Middle East and elsewhere, and other, unforeseeable, situations present a continuing risk of nuclear destruction that is unacceptable. To reduce this risk, the United States must seize the initiative and exploit the opportunities created by new geopolitical relationships. Our proposals suggest both the immediate strategic objectives called for by today's situation and workable policies for pursuing them.

2.

America's nuclear policy originated, to a considerable extent, in order to counter three factors: (1) the large conventional armies that the Soviet Union maintained in the center of Europe after 1945, (2) the belligerent character of Soviet military doctrine, and (3) the Soviets' geographic advantages in a European war. In the early phases of the cold war, the US policy of building large nuclear forces, tactical as well as strategic, was to a substantial degree intended to offset the imbalance in conventional arms. Under the policy of "flexible response," tactical nuclear weapons were to be used if NATO's conventional defense forces were in danger of collapse. The missiles and bombers with nuclear warheads that made up the US strategic forces were also to provide "extended" deterrence, i.e., in addition to their primary mission of deterring a strategic attack on the United States, they were intended to deter an attack by Soviet conventional forces on Western Europe as well. The war plans, targets, weapons, and command organization of US strategic forces long reflected these two requirements.

By the late 1960s the Soviet Union had, in effect, achieved parity with the United States in strategic weapons, and it went on to acquire strategic forces that are, if less flexible and sophisticated, at least as powerful as those of the US. In recent years, the emphasis of the arms race has been on "modernization" of both Soviet and US arsenals by improving their versatility and accuracy. These goals are still being pursued by the US and the USSR. They have not been much affected by the geopolitical earthquake of 1989.

The expensive and dangerous process of modernization could continue in isolation from other relations between the US and the USSR because the military goals that each side has tried to meet in recent decades have been largely set by its opponent's strategic capacities. While there are significant differences between the two strategic forces, both base their war plans on "worst-case" assessments—i.e., they assume the other side would mount the most powerful and effective attack of which it was capable. They largely fail to ask what political motives could plausibly impel the other side to take so desperate a gamble.

This concentration on the adversary's nuclear forces has an insidious inner logic. Each side has sought to protect itself by acquiring the means to swiftly disrupt the other's strategic forces and its command systems, with the result that both strategic forces and command systems are more vulnerable than ever. For example, in addition to targeting Soviet missiles the US is now developing warheads designed to penetrate the deep underground command centers built for Soviet leaders. The Soviet ICBM force has long had similar objectives. No wonder that senior officials in both Moscow and Washington have made it known that they place great emphasis on the ability to launch missiles promptly on being warned of an attack. Both governments have made heavy investments to this end.

3.

The present size and composition of both sides' strategic forces are not only expensive anachronisms but pose a latent threat that can no longer be justified, even by the criteria that once led many to accept the risk of nuclear war as an inescapable evil. Each of the military commands must be able to ensure that weapons will be launched if, and only if, legitimate orders from civilian authorities have been issued. But they must fulfill this responsibility knowing that the command systems themselves, as well as the bombers and land-based missiles, are vulnerable to missiles that take from fifteen to thirty minutes to strike their targets after being launched. As a consequence, in a nuclear crisis each side's survival depends on the ability of the command systems on both sides to function without gross error, and, above all, to correctly assess information warning of attack, while being under pressure to do all this in a matter of minutes.

Such requirements become all the more menacing when we realize that modern command organizations are extremely complex combinations of hardware, software, procedures, and human beings that have an astonishing tendency to fail disastrously as the result of what the Yale sociologist Charles Perrow calls "normal accidents." Chernobyl and a number of tragedies on Soviet submarines, ships, and pipelines show that Soviet organizations are especially prone to normal accidents, and we ourselves are hardly immune to them. The Western press has often asked whether warring factions in the Soviet Union might acquire nuclear weapons, and Soviet officials have implied that they have taken steps to eliminate such a risk, a kind of reassurance that can only heighten such concerns.

From a Western perspective, however, the risk that Soviet nuclear weapons will become embroiled in civil war is overshadowed by the risk that the chaotic breakup of the Soviet government could cause the officials who run the Soviet nuclear command system to take actions that would have catastrophic results, especially if the breakup were to occur during an international crisis that threatens Soviet security. Should such circumstances arise, it is not inconceivable that a mixture of misperceptions, confusion, and panic could somehow lead to an unauthorized or inadvertent launch of Soviet missiles. No doubt there is only a small probability that such a chain of events will occur; but the scale of the ensuing tragedy would be so great that, as with other paths to nuclear catastrophe, every effort must be made to eliminate the risk.

In short, the existing strategic forces serve neither the interests of the United States nor the Soviet Union. The only remaining justification for the enormous size of each state's strategic forces is the other's strategic forces. Both sides should be willing, therefore, to move rapidly to far smaller nuclear arsenals. The US must take the initiative. It remains possible that a Soviet regime bent on making trouble for the West could come to power, and should that happen it would be best if the USSR were not so prodigiously armed with nuclear weapons.

4.

The principal objectives of the new US nuclear policy should be, first, a rapid and deep cut of Soviet strategic forces so as to decrease greatly the vulnerability to destruction of the remaining US forces; and second, creating conditions that would give the greatest possible support to the effort to control the spread of nuclear, chemical, and biological warheads, and sophisticated means for their delivery.

After the START reductions have been carried out, the US will still have roughly nine thousand deployed strategic warheads and the Soviets about eight thousand. Each will also have many thousands of strategic warheads that they will be forbidden to deploy but that they need not destroy as well as thousands of tactical nuclear warheads. In addition, China, Britain, and France together can be expected to then have over 1,500 fission and thermonuclear warheads, while the "undeclared" nuclear powers (including Israel and India, and probably Pakistan and South Africa) would have a very much smaller number. This, by any measure, will still be an unacceptably dangerous nuclear armory. If the goals we advocate are to be achieved, negotiations much more ambitious than those now underway are needed. These could not succeed unless the American and Soviet governments first recognized that their separate interests would be best served by abandoning the strategies that have shaped their forces in the past.

This shift would replace today's strategies for fighting a nuclear war with a strategy of minimum deterrence, a policy that would result in nuclear forces that are models of common sense compared to those now held by both sides. This is so because minimum deterrence would explicitly discard the basic goals that advocates of war fighting strategies have vainly pursued: the ability to retaliate immediately and decisively by destroying a major portion of the enemy's strategic forces so as to limit damage to oneself and to compel the opponent to refrain from further escalation. Logical as these objectives may be in the abstract, in reality their pursuit has only amplified vulnerability on both sides and fueled the arms race. Furthermore, minimum deterrence would not have the deterrence of conventional attacks as one of its purposes. Indeed, the credibility of this aspect of nuclear strategy was always questionable, and its rationale has now been eliminated by the collapse of Soviet power in Central and Eastern Europe. Finally, minimum deterrence would not seek weapons specifically designed to eliminate the Soviet leadership. For such a minimum strategy, the ability to stop any nuclear combat as quickly as possible—which puts a premium on the survival of leaders—would be more important than any other.

Under a policy of minimum deterrence, the forces and their command systems on both sides would be able to survive to the extent that they could guarantee retaliation even after absorbing a surprise attack. Military commanders would be able to defer recommending a nuclear response until they had taken the time to evaluate the nature and purpose of the attack. Stability in a crisis would be greatly enhanced because the existing pressures to launch nuclear weapons when warned of an incoming attack, or when under attack, would be eliminated.

Minimum deterrence would (1) ensure that the side that mounted a nuclear attack would suffer swift destruction on a scale that would exceed anything that has been wrought in wars in the past and would be unacceptable by any standards to a rational opponent; but (2) it would not threaten the destruction of the opponent's strategic forces or the very survival of civilization. In contrast, current strategies call for almost simultaneous attack on a vast range of military and industrial targets—some five thousand of them—while "withholding" sufficient strategic forces to gain the upper hand in "peace" negotiations. The ceiling on future forces should be defined by the two main characteristics of minimum deterrence we have just mentioned. As for the floor, it should be high enough to make clandestine cheating unproductive and technical breakthroughs futile, and also sufficient to make it difficult for either side to gain a significant advantage by a crash rearmament program should US–Soviet relations turn sour.

The size and composition of the minimum deterrence forces must be determined by a complex process of analysis and negotiation, in which the hardest bargaining would probably not take place between the US and the USSR but would almost certainly go on within the American body politic, among the US allies, and within the Soviet Union. But it seems evident to us that a total inventory some twenty times smaller than each side has today should be sufficient for minimum deterrence—that is, on the order of one thousand tactical and strategic nuclear warheads apiece. This is not meant to imply that global security will forever require such inventories, for the destructive power of these "small" arsenals would still be tens of thousands times larger than that of the Hiroshima bomb. Further reductions should therefore be sought after experience has established that deep cuts of the size we suggest, along with stringent barriers to proliferation, have been able to create a reliable system of nuclear arms control and disarmament.

5.

The bilateral treaty agreements that American diplomacy should now seek from the Soviet Union fall into two groups: one group should reduce sharply the possibility of a nuclear confrontation between the two countries; the other should reduce the ability and desire of other countries to acquire nuclear weapons.

The composition of a nuclear force that would assure minimum deterrence have been much discussed. We believe there is wide potential agreement on what weapons should be included. As we have said, a ceiling on warheads should be established that is about 5 percent of current levels. A combination of submarine, air, and land-based delivery systems, with constraints on multiple warheads, would render futile a "counterforce" attack designed to eliminate the other side's nuclear weapons. Tactical nuclear weapons should be eliminated from a region extending from the Atlantic to the Urals and from naval vessels as well. There should be verifiable means of ensuring that undesirable kinds of weapons "modernization" not take place. To that end, antisatellite weapons should be banned and ceilings imposed on missile flight tests to slow down innovation and to prevent the deployment of nuclear weapons specifically designed to attack command centers. The Anti-Ballistic Missile (ABM) Treaty would have to remain in effect in order to give both sides confidence that a sudden deployment of strategic defenses could not neutralize the minimum deterrent.

As for nonproliferation of nuclear weapons, an international agreement would have to include the following measures if it were to be effective: ceasing production of fissile materials for weapons; monitoring of all nuclear weapons production facilities along the lines initiated by the INF and START accords; verification of the destruction of warheads; and a sharp reduction in the number and yield of underground tests, with a commitment to subsequently ban all such tests. All but the last of these measures would be necessary to provide confidence that the US and the USSR were adhering to the reductions they would have independently agreed on. But they all are, in addition, highly important for blocking proliferation.

The proposals we have made here would take decades to negotiate were the pace to be that of past arms control talks. But global security would be greatly improved were such measures put into effect promptly. Both sides should consider taking steps toward arms control that could precede formal agreements. Such steps must be reversible should relations with the Soviets become contentious, and they should be conditioned on reciprocal action by the USSR.[1]

We have hardly mentioned the other "declared" nuclear powers, Britain, China, and France. Since all three target their nuclear weapons on the Soviet Union, at some point they must participate in nuclear arms control if the reductions we propose are to occur; and

[1]Such measures could include a moratorium on production of fissile materials (all US facilities are now shut down because of malfunctions);
(*continued on next page*)

they should in any case be concerned to strengthen efforts toward nonproliferation. That they are unlikely to join in at the outset of US–Soviet efforts to reduce nuclear weapons is no excuse for the US or the Soviets to postpone that process. The nuclear superpowers have a long way to go before they could plausibly blame any reluctance to reduce their own forces on the smaller nuclear powers.

6.

Nuclear proliferation has been less rapid than was originally feared, in part because Washington and Moscow have cooperated to discourage other countries from acquiring weapons, even when their bilateral relations were far from amicable. Nevertheless, current trends are disquieting. A number of states are apparently close to attaining an "undeclared" nuclear capacity, or may already have it. Furthermore, the Soviet domestic crisis may encourage highly qualified nuclear experts to sell their services on the world market. This could have serious consequences because sophisticated know-how is more valuable for constructing nuclear weapons than purloined devices or plans. Long-term security therefore demands much stronger efforts to stop proliferation. If this is to occur, the nuclear superpowers must demonstrate that they not only preach nuclear abstinence but are dramatically reducing their own nuclear addiction. The policies we propose would make this change of attitude unmistakable.

Demands for nonproliferation have always been handicapped by the double standard inherent in the post-Hiroshima world. That double standard is reflected in the Non-Proliferation Treaty first signed in 1968. The declared nuclear powers that have signed a moratorium on antisatellite (ASAT) flight tests (the Soviets already maintain such a moratorium, while Congress is unlikely to continue funding the ASAT program); a reduction in the number of flight tests of new missiles; a sharp cut in the number and yield of underground tests (the Soviets have had to curtail their testing because of pressure from environmentalists); and the removal of all NATO and Soviet tactical weapons from Europe (which would enlarge on NATO's proposal restricted to nuclear artillery). The administration should also recommit itself to the traditional interpretation of the ABM Treaty which bans the testing of space-based ABM systems.

it—Britain, the US, and USSR—are free to build weapons, whereas other nations that have not signed it (e.g., India and Pakistan) would, if they did so, have to adhere to a stringent code of abstention. This double standard cannot be eradicated, but it could and must become less flagrant. The nuclear powers, starting with the US and the USSR, should therefore not only cut back their nuclear forces, but revise as well their attitudes toward international monitoring of their nuclear weapons programs.

With the INF and START treaties, the US and USSR recognized that verification requires the parties to monitor some of each other's sensitive activities. The verification of the new bilateral US–Soviet agreements we are advocating would require additional monitoring of testing, production, destruction, and disposal of nuclear weapons. The US and the USSR should offer to have a substantial portion of this monitoring performed by an international agency. Were the nuclear superpowers to set this example, the other three countries that have declared themselves as nuclear powers would come under pressure to follow suit. All permanent members of the UN Security Council would then have committed themselves to international monitoring.

Verifying a more stringent system for controlling nuclear weapons presents difficult technical and political problems. Safeguards against the diversion for military purposes of fissile materials from civilian activities are the responsibility of the International Atomic Energy Agency in Vienna. But the IAEA may only inspect "declared" facilities, and has no authority to investigate other sites even if they are suspect. Nor can the IAEA monitor the military activities of the declared nuclear powers. It is questionable whether the IAEA should be adapted to perform these tasks, for that could undermine its ability to perform its current mission.

A new international institution with its own means for space surveillance may thus be needed for monitoring proliferation of weapons of mass destruction. Responsibility for directing the global nonproliferation program should then be turned over to the UN Security Council.

The Comprehensive Test Ban Treaty (CTBT)—which has not so far been endorsed by any of the declared

nuclear powers except the USSR—is often seen as indispensable to nonproliferation of nuclear weapons. This is not so: the Non-Proliferation Treaty will survive even if a Comprehensive Test Ban Treaty is not signed, and a test ban could not stop proliferation by itself since weapons development could still go forward without testing. Nevertheless, by signing the CTBT the nuclear powers would be proclaiming that they have given a high priority to nonproliferation, and we strongly support a comprehensive test ban for this and other reasons. The technical and political issues involved lead us to suggest that the US propose a treaty that would, for a few years, set a limit of at most fifteen kilotons for each test (as compared to the current 150 kiloton limit) with a low annual ceiling (of perhaps five) on the number of tests; the treaty should specify that after the interim period, a comprehensive test ban will come into effect.[2]

Truly deep cuts in Soviet and American nuclear weapons and comprehensive bilateral agreements along the lines we have described would, for the first time, fulfill the commitment of the nuclear superpowers to "the cessation of the nuclear arms race and to undertake effective measures in the direction of nuclear disarmament" which they accepted when the nonproliferation treaty went into force in 1970.

These steps by the US and USSR, together with nuclear arms reductions by the other nuclear powers, and a strengthened system to stop proliferation, would greatly increase the obstacles to "going nuclear." They would provide a new basis for both domestic and international opposition to the spread of nuclear weapons, and also complement current efforts to constrain the spread of chemical and biological weapons and of ballistic missiles. But it would be naive to presume that all nonnuclear states would thereafter refrain from seeking nuclear weapons if the nuclear

[2]A technically advanced country may not consider testing indispensable in developing its first fission weapon. But testing will surely be necessary if it wants to acquire thermonuclear weapons because they are much more complicated; testing would also be important for developing compact warheads for ballistic missiles. As for US opposition to the Comprehensive Test Ban Treaty, the military has always maintained that stockpile reliability requires testing despite the

powers—which include most of the world's strongest states—were to claim that their own security requires "small" nuclear arsenals as large as those we have described here. The barrier to proliferation of weapons of mass destruction can be maintained for the long term only if the international community creates increasingly credible and enforceable guarantees against aggression for all states, accompanied by further substantial cuts in the number of warheads held by the nuclear powers.

7.

America's existing strategic forces were planned to deal with threats that differ fundamentally from today's two primary sources of nuclear danger—an unstable Soviet Union armed to the teeth with nuclear weapons, and a world moving toward greater proliferation of such weapons. The United States must therefore put forward new policies that address the dangers that now exist, rather than those of yesterday.

If a shift toward a policy along the lines we have proposed took place, enormous benefits would follow, for the administration, for the Western alliance, and the world at large—benefits in resources saved, and above all, in true security for the living and the unborn. No government other than that of the United States is in a position to take the first steps in this direction, and no one but the President himself can effectively provide the leadership required. Continuing with outdated policies now would come to be seen as a deep failure on the part of the US even if the dangers that exist do not lead to tragedy. For the first time in four decades the opportunity has arisen to dramatically reduce the risk of nuclear war. It must be seized. □

contrary advice of many of its technical experts. Indeed, the bulk of the testing program is devoted to modernization. However, recent examination of some existing warheads has shown that it would be desirable to redesign their chemical high-explosives triggers to make them more secure against accidental (nonnuclear) detonation (*Nuclear Weapons Safety*, Committee on Armed Services, House of Representatives, December 1990). Our proposal would allow sufficient testing for this purpose.

Article 15.2. Iraq and the Bomb: Were They Even Close?

In this article, the authors assess Iraq's nuclear "potential," both as it was understood and existed prior to the gulf war. Despite President Bush's contention that Iraq possessed a nuclear capability, the authors insist that, at the time, Iraq was many years away from producing usable nuclear weapons. According to the authors, Iraq's nuclear potential was so "primitive" that it posed little if any threat. This does not negate President Bush's strong case against Iraq, but it does call into question whether Iraq's nuclear program made it essential that the U.S.-led coalition destroy that nation's nuclear capability before it was unleashed against its enemies.

IRAQ AND THE BOMB:
WERE THEY EVEN CLOSE?

By DAVID ALBRIGHT and MARK HIBBS

Whatever reasons there may be for the Gulf War, "Iraq's nuclear program isn't one of them."

Just two hours after U.S. warplanes began attacking Iraq on January 16, President Bush went on national television to report the goals of the assault. "As I report to you, air attacks are under way against military targets in Iraq. We are determined to knock out Saddam Hussein's nuclear bomb potential," the president said, before ticking off other objectives.

The prominence Bush gave to Iraq's nuclear "potential" repeated a theme that the administration began pushing vigorously last November as a rationale for the use of military force against that country. But after a months-long

David Albright is a senior scientist at Friends of the Earth in Washington, D.C. Mark Hibbs is European editor of Nuclear Fuel *and* Nucleonics Week, *in Bonn, Germany.*

investigation of the requirements any country would need to build nuclear weapons, and an assessment of Iraq's ability to meet those requirements, we conclude that Saddam Hussein was many years away from developing usable nuclear weapons.

Indeed, the Iraqi nuclear bomb-making capability was so primitive that the international sanctions put in place after the August 2 invasion may have had more substantive effect than the tons of bombs dropped by U.S. and allied planes five months later. "There may be good reasons to go to war with Iraq," one U.S. government official said before January 16, "but Iraq's nuclear program isn't one of them."

The timely boycott

Immediately after Saddam Hussein invaded Kuwait last August, the German Foreign Office issued an internal memo to its export control officials. The document ordered an end to a training program three German firms had been conducting for Iraqi engineers, "in the light of newest evidence of German involvement in the nuclear weapons field in Iraq, and threatening political complications [arising from] such a suspicion."

The training program was part of a concerted Iraqi effort to overcome what Western experts believe was its nuclear Achilles heel, lack of skilled personnel. The three firms—one of which was Interatom GmbH, which supplied staff from its advanced reactor department—had been training the engineers for nearly a year before the export control office was informed of the full scope of the training program. The Iraqis were on the staff of a Baghdad organization known as Industrial Project Company (IPC), which the Mossad, Israel's intelligence agency, believes is at the pinnacle of Iraq's entire military procurement effort.

Although Interatom officials told German export authorities that the transfer of nuclear know-how was forbidden, customs agents emphasized that IPC staff expressed a keen desire to get specific and extensive nuclear-related information. IPC is also behind a company called Al Fao General Establishment, in Baghdad. According to U.S. and Israeli intelligence reports, Al Fao has been active in procuring missile technology for Iraq. A U.S. government expert said that Al Fao wanted laboratory equipment from Interatom which could be used as a clean room for manufacturing missile guidance systems, or centrifuge components needed to enrich uranium for use in nuclear weapons. A work room, German investigators said, was the first dual-use (civilian-military) export to Iraq which was stopped after Kuwait was overrun.

From *The Bulletin of the Atomic Scientists*, vol 47, no 3. Copyright © 1991 by the Educational Foundation for Nuclear Science, 6042 S. Kimbark Avenue, Chicago, IL 60637 USA. A one-year subscription is $30.

Last July, President Saddam Hussein of Iraq said on French television, "We do not have nuclear weapons, but we would see no problem in a Western nation helping us to develop nuclear arms to help compensate for those owned by Israel." But because Iraq's quest still depended heavily on foreign help, as these incidents illustrate, the U.N. boycott imposed after the invasion may have been the most effective way to delay Iraq's quest for the bomb. The embargo stopped several significant technology transfers which might have advanced Saddam Hussein's drive to make nuclear explosive material. Based on numerous interviews with U.S., European, and Israeli government officials and a December 1990 conversation with a former German centrifuge expert who met with Iraqi centrifuge designers in Baghdad two years ago, we conclude that even before war broke out Iraq was five to ten years or more from having the ability to make the highly enriched uranium it would need for a nuclear arsenal.

Last Thanksgiving Day, President George Bush told U.S. troops in Saudi Arabia that "those who would measure the timetable for Saddam's atomic program in years may be seriously underestimating . . . the gravity of the threat." But that warning and others were based on sketchy information and improbable assumptions (see the following article). Most evidence supported the view that Iraq remained far from possessing the infrastructure needed to produce nuclear weapons, and worst-case assessments such as the president's seriously overstated the risk that Iraq would soon detonate a nuclear explosive.

It is true that Iraq had more than one path to possessing nuclear weapons. The first method was to seize the small amount of highly enriched uranium in its possession, which was under international inspection, and fabricate it into a single nuclear weapon. Another was to acquire more fissile material clandestinely from other nations.

The surest route to a nuclear arsenal, however, depends on developing the indigenous capability to produce nuclear explosive material and fabricate it into deliverable nuclear weapons. Iraq appeared committed to do this, even though it signed the Nuclear Non-Proliferation Treaty. According to intelligence collected by Western governments in 1990, Saddam Hussein got serious about acquiring technology and equipment for nuclear weapons in 1987. Two different organizations were involved in the procurement and development tasks for his clandestine nuclear program: The first, Al Qaqaa State Establishment, located in Iskandariya near Baghdad, was thought to be in charge of developing the non-nuclear components for a nuclear weapon, German intelligence

documents say. The second, Nassr State Enterprise in Taji, also near Baghdad, was said to be responsible for Iraq's uranium enrichment effort. Independently of these organizations, IPC agents in Europe actively sought weapon and uranium enrichment technology and equipment as well.

The quest for a workable weapon

The biggest immediate concern was that Iraq would construct one nuclear explosive out of a small amount of highly enriched uranium which remained in its civilian nuclear program. This material was committed to peaceful uses and inspected every six months by the International Atomic Energy Agency (IAEA), which last checked in November and found the material intact. But the possibility existed that Iraq would snatch the material between inspections and use it in a bomb. Even now it is impossible to say where this material might be.

A nuclear weapon, even a crude one, has thousands of parts. Los Alamos National Laboratory has produced a secret document detailing what is needed to make a nuclear weapon and where to buy it; the document is 500 pages long.[1] For a country such as Iraq, which has little electronic, chemical, or metallurgical manufacturing capability, constructing a nuclear weapon is a formidable task.

An Iraqi nuclear explosive device would have to be a fission device (as opposed to a thermonuclear, or hydrogen, bomb), presumably based on an implosion design. Such designs, one of which was the basis for the bomb dropped on Nagasaki, are well known. Figure 1 is a rudimentary schematic of one such device. An implosion bomb contains a mass of nuclear material—in this case, highly enriched uranium—in its center. The conventional high explosives around the central mass detonate simultaneously, imploding and compressing the fissile material to a supercritical mass. At that instant, neutrons must be injected into the material to initiate the chain reaction and explosion. An alternative fission bomb design, the "gun" type, was used to destroy Hiroshima. But because it requires more fissile material, Iraq was unlikely to pursue that design.

Many aspects of the design and development of an implosion fission device present special problems:

■ **The fissile material.** Iraq might not have enough highly enriched uranium for a "crude" nuclear device, that is, one containing just slightly less fissile material than necessary to achieve criticality when the device is assembled. To make a crude implosion device using weapon-grade uranium (enriched to over 90 percent uranium 235), one would have to start out with at

Making the bomb: the shopping list

■ **Fissile material.** The central core of a nuclear device (page 17) is composed of **plutonium** or **highly enriched uranium.** Each is capable of a self-sustaining explosive chain reaction (fission). Plutonium is produced in nuclear reactors and separated from the irradiated fuel in remotely operated chemical processing plants.

Iraq's status: trying. Iraq has no plutonium that we know of, and since Israel bombed the Osiraq reactor in 1981, Iraq has no reactor large enough to produce significant quantities of plutonium. Highly enriched uranium is produced in isotope separation plants, and Iraq is trying to develop such a plant using **gas centrifuge technology.**

■ **Tamper/reflector.** A core-tamping material such as natural uranium, beryllium, or tungsten surrounds the fissile material in a nuclear weapon, holding it together longer while it fissions, and reflecting neutrons back into the core to speed the fission rate.

Iraq's status: capable. Designing the tamper and obtaining dense material, such as natural uranium, is relatively easy.

■ **High explosives.** Conventional (non-nuclear) high explosives surround the tamper and fissile material. Detonating the high explosives creates a shock wave focused on the core, compressing the material so that it "goes supercritical," that is, achieves a self-sustaining explosive chain reaction. The most familiar designs depend on carefully **shaped charges** containing both slow- and fast-burning explosives.

Iraq's status: unknown.

■ **Fuzing system.** The fuzing system of a nuclear explosive device is the collection of electronic components that set off the conventional high explosives. The sophisticated devices on which the system depends must operate reliably within a fraction of a microsecond. A relatively simple design would include a **detonation capacitor** and a high-speed switch, or **krytron,** for each detonator.

Iraq's status: unknown. Iraq has claimed that it can make detonation capacitors. Iraqi agents have been caught trying to purchase more sophisticated detonation capacitors and have expressed interest in acquiring krytrons.

■ **Neutron source.** When the fissile material is compressed, neutrons must also be injected to start the chain reaction. Neutrons can be produced either through special **beryllium-polonium sources** or sophisticated **timed neutron generators.**

Iraq's status: probably capable. Iraq has acquired neutron generators for oil exploration, but these are probably not suitable for use in a nuclear explosive.

Beryllium-polonium sources would be easier to produce.

■ **Conversion and fabrication.** Nuclear materials are usually converted into metal then fabricated into bomb components.

Iraq's status: capable. Iraq's supply of safeguarded highly enriched uranium would need to be separated from unused reactor fuel before it could be used in a nuclear explosive. This is a fairly simple operation. The International Atomic Energy Agency estimates that a country could convert the material into metal and fabricate bomb components in as little as one to three weeks.

■ **Theoretical calculations.** The extensive calculations needed to design and construct a nuclear weapon cover the dynamic behavior and explosive power of a nuclear detonation: the physical and chemical properties of materials at extremely high temperatures and pressures, fluid dynamics of highly deformable materials in the presence of chemical and nuclear energy release, the processes of nuclear fission, the maintenance of a chain reaction, and the prediction of nuclear yield.

Iraq's status: capable. Extensive calculations are required, but not necessarily sophisticated computing capabilities.

■ **Implosion package testing.** Testing the implosion system—the symmetry of the shock waves and force of compression—requires a steady supply of surrogate core materials (such as natural uranium), detonation circuits, and conventional explosive charges. Special testing equipment to determine compressions achieved in the nuclear core includes flash X-ray machines, high-speed cameras, radioisotope sources placed at the center of test material and used with radiation detection equipment, and electrical conducting pins located at various depths within the core.

Iraq's status: unknown. Some U.S. officials doubt that Iraq is capable of conducting the number of tests needed.

■ **Weaponization.** A nuclear explosive device must be made into bombs or warheads for aircraft or missiles.

Iraq's status: limited capability. Making a bomb to be carried by an attack aircraft is relatively easy, but making a missile warhead may be impossible without full-scale nuclear tests or extensive outside help. Iraq could conceivably deliver a nuclear device by a ground vehicle or a ship.

—D.A., M.H.

The most challenging task in making the bomb is producing fissile material.

least 15 kilograms. This assumes that the design would incorporate a thick reflector/tamper and that little fissile material would be lost in processing—although such losses can under many circumstances reach 10–20 percent. But Iraq has only 12.3 kilograms of 93 percent enriched uranium, some of which might fuel the Tammuz II research reactor at Tuwaitha Nuclear Research Center near Baghdad. The material was intended for the 40-megawatt Osiraq reactor, destroyed by Israel in 1981 just before it was scheduled to begin operating.

Iraq also has about 10 kilograms of 80 percent enriched uranium at the 5-megawatt IRT-5000 reactor supplied by the Soviet Union. Up to two-thirds of the enriched uranium has been irradiated in the reactor and would require remotely operated chemical processing to extract the highly enriched uranium, a step that would have been difficult for Iraq to accomplish quickly, even before the bombing of Tuwaitha. The unirradiated highly enriched uranium, however, could be added to the 93 percent material, possibly providing Iraq with just enough material for a crude bomb.

According to Theodore Taylor, a former nuclear weapon designer, the smaller the quantity of fissile material, the more difficult it is to compress, requiring a more sophisticated high-explosive implosion system and more precisely machined bomb components in the core. He added: "The minimum amount of material necessary to make a militarily significant bomb is in principle unanswerable. But in practice, there are well-defined quantities of nuclear material that have been used in various devices, but these quantities are secret."

■ **Calculations and experimentation.** Before a nuclear device could be assembled, the designers would have to complete certain steps in order to have confidence that it would work. They would have to perform theoretical calculations, then a significant number of experiments, including non-nuclear explosions, to confirm the theoretical calculations. These would require a steady supply of electronic components, conventional explosive charges, and fabricated nuclear components, probably made from natural uranium.

Carson Mark, former head of the Theoretical Division at Los Alamos National Laboratory, thinks Iraq would have needed at least a year of hard work to make one nuclear explosive device out of about 12 kilograms of weapon-grade uranium. Most of this time would be spent developing confidence that the device would work. Mark said that accomplishing this goal would require an appreciable commitment of resources and skilled personnel, including physicists, chemists, metallurgists, electrical engineers, and persons capable of precision machining. Even then, he said, the designers would probably be unable to predict the device's nuclear yield.

A U.S. government official said in December that he would be surprised if Iraq had been able to conduct the large numbers of implosion tests necessary to develop confidence in a nuclear design. He said that it took the Pakistanis several years to master an implosion system, even though they were working from a proven design provided by an "external source." Press reports have often identified China as the source of Pakistan's weapons design.

■ **Electronics and high explosives.** Building a more sophisticated design places a premium on acquiring advanced electronics and high-explosive capabilities from industrialized nations, which Iraq was aggressively pursuing. In the last five years the U.S. government approved the sale to Iraq of $1.5 billion worth of computers, electronic equipment, and machine tools which could be used in its nuclear, chemical, and ballistic missile programs.[2]

Iraq was caught last March trying to smuggle military-standard and -specification detonation capacitors from CSI Technologies of San Marcos, California. The capacitors' many applications include nuclear weapons as well as conventional warheads and military laser systems.[3] An implosion system can use this type of detonation capacitor, which stores large amounts of electrical energy, with a high-speed electronic switch, called a "krytron." This assembly can supply within a fraction of a microsecond a burst of electrical energy to the detonator or blasting cap which sets off the conventional high explosives. Following an 18-month undercover investigation by the U.S. Customs Service in collaboration with the British government, five persons were arrested in London and the capacitors they were carrying—they had been given dummies instead of real ones—were confiscated.

Customs officials identified the end-users for the capacitors as the Al Qaqaa State Establishment, the top-secret facility involved in developing missiles and explosives for Iraq's Ministry of Industry and Military Industrialization. German intelligence believes that Al Qaqaa, which has experience with modern conventional high-explosive and high-speed measurement technologies, was given responsibility to develop the non-nuclear components of a nuclear explosive device. Three scientists from Al Qaqaa attended a 1989 symposium at Portland, Oregon, on detonation physics, hosted by Lawrence Livermore National Laboratory. According to a U.S. customs agent involved in the capacitor case, these scientists inquired about krytrons at the conference.

Soon after the March arrests, Saddam Hussein asserted that his Ministry of Industry and Military Industrialization had succeeded in producing similar capacitors. While this claim cannot be verified, in 1989 Iraq was able to buy about 150 lower-quality capacitors from Maxwell Electronics, a California-based firm. The head of that company speculated that Iraq may have upgraded these capacitors.[4]

William Higinbotham, who headed the electronics group at Los Alamos during the Manhattan Project thinks that is possible. "It is not a question of know-how, which is now widespread," he said in a December interview, "but a matter of whether Iraq has the highly devel-

At a 1989 symposium in Portland, Oregon, Iraqi scientists inquired about krytrons.

The embargo was, and may still be, the best way to keep Iraq from making a bomb.

oped skills and trained operating personnel necessary to make these types of capacitors and high-speed switches." He believes, however, that Iraq could easily have taken six months or longer to make them, even if they had blueprints.

■ **Neutron source.** To initiate the chain reaction in the highly enriched uranium after it is sufficiently compressed, neutrons must be injected into the material. One type of initiator, located at the very center of the device, could be made from alternating spheres of polonium 210 and beryllium, separated by a thin layer of material able to shield the beryllium from the alpha particles produced by the radioactive decay of polonium 210. When the shock wave from the high explosives hit the initiator, it would crush the beryllium and polonium together, producing copious numbers of neutrons. Polonium 210, a decay product of uranium 238, is relatively easy to obtain in sufficient quantities for a nuclear explosive device.

Another type of initiator would be a timed neutron generator, located outside the high explosives, which would inject neutrons into the core at the right moment. One common type is a vacuum tube that produces neutrons by accelerating deuterium into a tritium target. Iraq acquired neutron generators of this type, used in oil exploration. But, according to Higinbotham, this particular kind of generator is probably unsuitable for nuclear explosives, which require extremely precise timing.

None of these problems presents an insurmountable obstacle to a determined and well-funded research, development, and procurement effort. Eventually, Iraq will probably be able to design a deliverable nuclear weapon, if it is still determined to do so. But an effective embargo could still inhibit its ability to obtain high-technology components that would make the task easier.

Because the status of Iraq's program to design and make nuclear explosives is not well known, speculation ranges widely on how long it would take Iraq to make a single weapon. Direct confirmation of the relevant activities is lacking, as is information about all the types of helpful equipment and technology Iraq obtained before the embargo.

In a National Intelligence Estimate completed last fall, the U.S. intelligence community estimated that Iraq could build a nuclear explosive device in "six months to a year, and probably longer."[5] This estimate assumed that Iraq would mount a crash program to build an explosive out of its safeguarded material, and that it possessed advanced bomb-making technology. Even so, the assessment noted that the device would have a low nuclear yield, would be too bulky to deliver by missile or even by aircraft, and might not detonate.

A recent German intelligence assessment concluded that Iraq would need considerable help from abroad to complete a successful nuclear weapons program. That assessment pointed out that, up to now, there are no indications of direct foreign assistance to Iraq in the development of nuclear weapons.

The quest for an arsenal

Although Iraq may still be able to design and build a bomb, building a sizable arsenal that would present a meaningful threat to its enemies is a challenge of a much higher order, because it depends on acquiring additional nuclear explosive materials. Iraq has three main ways to do this:

■ **Enlarge its own safeguarded stock.** If the embargo remains after the war on shipments of safeguarded highly enriched uranium, Iraq will be unable to acquire more highly enriched fuel for its IRT-5000 reactor—if it can be operated after the bombing of Tuwaitha. It would therefore have to use the 80 percent enriched fuel it has in stock, further reducing its inventory of weapon-usable material.

If the embargo is lifted, the Soviets may resume their sales of highly enriched fuel to Iraq. An alternative would be to supply lower-enriched fuels that could not be used in

---

Making the bomb: producing fissile material

■ **Uranium mining.** Uranium is a common, naturally occurring element found worldwide.

Iraq's status: doubtful. U.S. government officials with access to intelligence information do not believe press reports claiming that Iraq has been mining uranium. They say U.S. intelligence agencies have looked in vain for such operations.

■ **Yellowcake production.** Yellowcake is a uranium oxide refined from uranium ore, but can also be refined from phosphates.

Iraq's status: capable. Iraq was producing yellowcake in its phosphate operation at Al Qaim near the Syrian border. Iraq has also accumulated several hundred metric tons of yellowcake from foreign sources since the late 1970s.

■ **Conversion.** Uranium hexafluoride is produced from yellowcake and fluorine.

Iraq's status: currently incapable. There is no evidence that Iraq has ever had a uranium hexafluoride plant.

■ **Enrichment.** The fraction of uranium 235 in uranium hexafluoride is increased by various processes, including gaseous diffusion and gas centrifuges.

Iraq's status: early stage of effort to develop gas centrifuges.
—D.A., M.H.

The most challenging task is building an enrichment plant.

weapons, but this may present problems. France once tried to substitute low-enriched uranium fuels for the highly enriched fuels that were to run the Osiraq reactor, but Saddam Hussein objected. Furthermore, the Soviets probably have not yet developed the kind of low-enriched fuel the reactor would require. To do this they could expect help from Western countries, including the United States, which have successfully converted many of the world's research reactors from highly enriched uranium to 20 percent enriched uranium fuels.

■ **Obtain materials clandestinely.** A possible clandestine source of both highly enriched uranium and plutonium is civilian or military nuclear programs in other parts of the world. The civilian plutonium programs in Europe and Japan handle large quantities of nuclear explosive materials, making them targets for theft or diversion.

In the early 1980s, senior Iraqi military figures were interested in buying more than 30 kilograms of plutonium from an Italian arms smuggling ring that claimed to have such material for sale. The deal fell through when the smugglers were unable to produce any plutonium.[6] As the amounts of plutonium in international and national commerce increase, security will need to tighten to prevent these materials from being stolen.

■ **Produce its own material.** To assure its supply of nuclear material, Iraq would have to develop the ability to produce such material. The bombing of the Osiraq reactor closed off one potential plutonium route to the bomb. According to a U.S. official, Iraq might still have been pursuing a plutonium route to the bomb before the war, but this was secondary. Instead, Iraq was concentrating its efforts on the difficult task of making highly enriched uranium.

The embargo was, and may continue to be, the most effective way to prevent Iraq from succeeding in this effort. The actions of German export officials, followed by the economic embargo cutting off access to foreign technology, had already hampered Iraq's uranium enrichment program before war broke out.

Iraq's enrichment program

For several years Iraq had been pursuing the development of gas centrifuges, which use rapidly spinning rotors to separate the more desirable uranium 235 isotope from the more plentiful uranium 238 isotope [see sidebars, pages 21, 22, 23]. Any country intent on mastering the gas centrifuge process must go through several time-consuming steps before it can expect to build a pilot plant containing a few thousand relatively unsophisticated machines —the minimum number necessary to produce

Making the bomb: the enrichment plant

Uranium hexafluoride ("hex") is received at the enrichment plant in cylinders (below, left). The cylinders are heated to vaporize the hex in **autoclaves,** and the vapor feed is piped to the **centrifuge cascade** (bottom), where it is enriched: the amount of fissionable uranium 235 is increased in proportion to nonfissionable uranium 238. The enriched product is removed from the cascade and piped to cold traps or **desublimers** (right), where it is condensed and put into cylinders. The depleted uranium (tails) is also condensed and stored (center).

Iraq's status: According to *Nuclear Fuel*, Iraq tried unsuccessfully to acquire desublimer technology, either for enrichment or missile purposes, from German firms that provided this technology to Urenco. But most of its effort has been directed toward developing centrifuge technology. —*D.A., M.H.*

The most challenging tasks are making centrifuges and successfully operating a cascade.

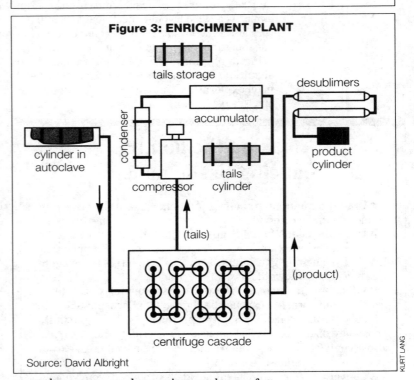

Figure 3: ENRICHMENT PLANT

tails storage

desublimers

condenser

accumulator

cylinder in autoclave

compressor

tails cylinder

product cylinder

(tails)

(product)

centrifuge cascade

Source: David Albright

KURT LANG

enough weapon-grade uranium each year for one nuclear explosive.

First Iraq would have to develop and test the gas centrifuge itself, illustrated in figure 3. And since each centrifuge can enrich uranium only slightly, engineers would have to learn how to connect centrifuges together by pipes into "cascades" that cumulatively produce significant quantities of enriched uranium.

Bruno Stemmler, a former centrifuge expert at the German firm MAN Technologien GmbH, met secretly with Iraqi centrifuge design engi-

Making the bomb: the gas centrifuge

A gas centrifuge normally consists of thin-walled cylinders with diameters of 75–400 millimeters, held in a vacuum and spun at very high peripheral speeds—on the order of 300 meters per second. To achieve these speeds, the rotating components must be manufactured from specialized materials and machined very precisely to minimize imbalances.

In addition to the **rotor assembly** (page 23), some of the major **non-rotating components** of a gas centrifuge are the following:

■ **Magnetic suspension bearings.** This top bearing contains two ring magnets, which couple. The upper magnet is suspended within a housing containing oil as a damping medium; the other is fitted to the top cap of the rotor assembly. Designing and making a top bearing requires knowledge of high-speed dynamics. The highest-intensity magnets are made of samarium cobalt.

Iraq's status: possesses parts. Inwako GmbH, in Bonn, sent Iraq about 100 ring magnets made out of aluminum, nickel, and cobalt.

■ **Bottom bearings.** The bottom bearing, a pivot or cup assembly mounted on an oil damper combined with a needle attached to the bottom cap of the rotor assembly, is much more difficult to manufacture than the top bearing.

Iraq's status: researching, probably having difficulty. According to one Western enrichment expert, the bottom bearing "is a problem." Bruno Stemmler concurs.

■ **Molecular pumps.** A molecular pump, which has internally machined grooves, prevents uranium hexafluoride that leaks through the top bearing from entering the vacuum area between the rotor tube and the outer casing.

Iraq's status: researching.

■ **Outer casing.** The rotor spins in a vacuum-tight casing, to minimize drag on the rotating components. Since the rotor may break, the casing must be strong enough to contain the debris so that the system's vacuum is not breached.

Iraq's status: may possess.

■ **Motors and inverters.** Ring-shaped stators (hysteresis motors), designed to operate in a vacuum, spin the rotor at high speeds. Inverters (also known as frequency changers or converters) power the motor.

Iraq's status: may possess. Centrifuge stators are relatively easy to obtain. Although simple inverters suitable for one centrifuge test stand are widely available, inverters suitable for use in cascades are not.

■ **Scoops.** Small tubes located at the ends of the central post extract enriched and depleted uranium hexafluoride. They are typically manufactured from aluminum alloys, brass, or stainless steels.

Iraq's status: unknown. The exact design and placement of the scoops within the rotor assembly can be difficult.

—D.A., M.H.

The most challenging centrifuge technologies are the rotor assembly and bottom bearing.

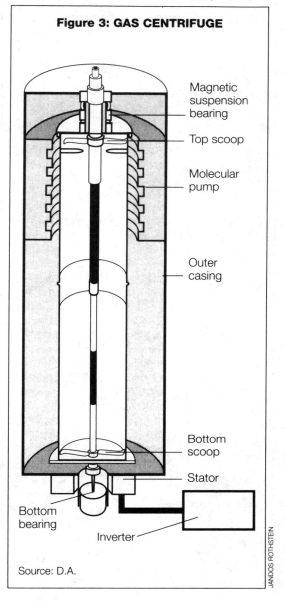

Figure 3: GAS CENTRIFUGE

- Magnetic suspension bearing
- Top scoop
- Molecular pump
- Outer casing
- Bottom scoop
- Stator
- Bottom bearing
- Inverter

Source: D.A.

JANDOS ROTHSTEIN

neers in 1988. Stemmler said in a December 1990 interview that Iraq appeared to be at an early stage in the development of the centrifuge itself. He described a visit to a secret laboratory on the southeast edge of Baghdad, still under construction, in which he was shown a bench centrifuge apparatus, or a "test stand." He said that the building had only one test stand, and he saw no testing equipment such as would be used to check the rotor bearings or the balancing of the rotor. He saw no inlets or outlets in the casing other than for the vacuum system, implying that uranium hexafluoride was not being used, and thus that the apparatus was unable to enrich uranium. Stemmler said he helped Iraqi experts solve problems in the test stand's vacuum system and was asked where the Iraqis could obtain more vacuum equipment. He concluded that the test stand could only be used for elementary mechanical tests of the rotor.

Stemmler estimated that Iraq would need five years of testing and many additional test stands

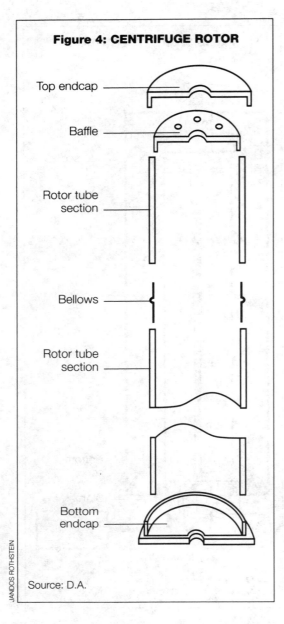

Top endcap

Baffle

Rotor tube section

Bellows

Rotor tube section

Bottom endcap

JANDOS ROTHSTEIN

Source: D.A.

to get an operating centrifuge, and at least another year or two of testing with uranium hexafluoride to get a machine operating at a capacity of roughly one "separative work unit" (a standard measure) per year. He said that he met with up to 15 excellent Iraqi centrifuge design engineers, but he did not think that Iraq had enough technical support personnel or facilities to back up the complex testing program needed to develop gas centrifuges. According to an official at Urenco, Europe's commercial enrichment consortium, several dozen technicians are needed to provide support to each test stand, as it goes from initial tests to "hot" testing using uranium hexafluoride.

But other evidence makes it clear that Iraq tried, with limited success, to acquire technologies and components for the entire enrichment

Making the bomb: the rotor assembly

■ **Materials.** Centrifuge rotor components (a thin cylinder, or a number of connected cylinders, fitted with internal baffles and disc-shaped endcaps) are made out of high-strength materials such as **maraging steel** or **high-strength aluminum.**

Iraq's status: probably possesses. Some mystery surrounds Iraq's source of maraging steel or other nuclear-grade metals, or the quantities it has acquired. It bought some grade 250 maraging steel through the German Export-Union GmbH, a trading firm, but it is only marginally usable in rotors, compared to grade 300 and above.

■ **Rotor tubes.** The tubes can be shaped on a **flow-forming machine,** which cold-presses preformed cylinders ("preforms") into thin-walled cylinders. Automated machines can produce about 100 rotor tubes a day; non-automated ones can do eight a day. Alternatively, metal sheets can be cold-rolled and welded into a cylinder using electron beam welding.

Iraq's status: questionable. Iraq acquired three flow-forming machines from the West German firm H&H Metalform GmbH. Iraq ordered maraging steel preforms from the Swiss firm Schmiedemeccanica, but the order was not filled because of the international embargo.

■ **Endcaps.** The top and bottom endcaps, each with a hole, are welded to the rotor tube to contain the uranium hexafluoride. The top cap would typically support part of the upper bearing, and the bottom cap would carry the rotating element of the motor and part of the bottom bearing.

Iraq's status: nearly obtained. Last July German and Swiss customs officials seized shipments bound for Iraq containing 250 top caps and 250 bottom caps forged by Schmiedemeccanica, and **spin-forming machines,** which can shape endcaps, from the Swiss firm Schäublin. Investigators also found 30–40 blanks for endcaps on the premises of Schäublin. The blanks, supplied by Schmiedemeccanica, were to be used to test machine tools built by Schäublin for Iraq. All were made out of grade 350 maraging steel of unknown origin.

■ **Bellows.** Rotor tubes are connected by bellows to reduce vibration in advanced centrifuges.

Iraq's status: probably does not need. Iraq is known to have acquired the G1 centrifuge design, which has only one rotor tube and is less advanced. It has a separative capacity of less than two separative work units a year. By contrast, the G2 centrifuge which Pakistan is said to have acquired from Urenco has two rotor tubes connected by a bellows and a separative capacity close to five separative work units a year.

■ **Baffles.** The baffle isolates the chamber of the rotor in which the slightly enriched uranium hexafluoride is extracted from the centrifuge. In some cases it causes the gas to circulate within the rotor tube, increasing the centrifuge's separative capacity.

Iraq's status: nearly obtained. Also confiscated last July were 250 baffles made out of grade 350 maraging steel.

—D.A., M.H.

program, including the manufacture of centrifuges. More than a year after an undercover

Iraq's "nuclear complex"

Confusing reports in the early days of the war suggested that Iraq had extensive nuclear weapons facilities, and Pentagon secrecy about bombing targets added to the confusion. But Iraq's nuclear weapons research and related activities are almost certainly carried out at only a few sites, and the major ones are largely devoted to other activities. Here is what we know about sites that may be related to nuclear weapons:

■ **Tuwaitha.** This complex of nuclear facilities located south of Baghdad is the main nuclear site, with two small research reactors: the French-supplied 0.5 megawatt Tammuz II and the Soviet-supplied 5.0 megawatt IRT-5000. Neither is able to produce significant amounts of plutonium—but the highly enriched fuel for them, and for the destroyed Osiraq reactor at the site, might be diverted for bomb use. This fuel was at Tuwaitha in November but could have been moved before the reactors were bombed in January.

Also at the site are three "hot cells" provided by Italy and one associated with the Soviet IRT-5000. These could separate highly enriched uranium from fresh fuel. There is also a facility to fabricate natural-uranium and low-enriched-uranium fuel, not related to weapons.

Tuwaitha is suspected of conducting weapon-related uranium enrichment research and development activities, although there is no direct evidence of this.

■ **Taji.** This large heavy-industry complex about 10 miles north of Baghdad is involved in military and armaments production and has metallurgical processes from smelting to producing final forms. It is not known to be capable of producing maraging steel or other high-strength materials useful in centrifuges and missiles. According to German intelligence, however, Nassr State Enterprise at Taji is responsible for the program to develop and manufacture centrifuges.

■ **Factory 10.** This artillery factory northwest of Baghdad is suspected of manufacturing centrifuge components.

■ **Nuclear lab.** German centrifuge expert Bruno Stemmler saw a uranium centrifuge test apparatus at a facility on the southeast edge of Baghdad in late 1988. The laboratory was under construction at the time.

■ **Al Qaqaa State Establishment.** This top-secret weapons research, development, and production facility of the Ministry of Industry and Military Industrialization is in Iskandariya, about 30 miles south of Baghdad. It is involved in modern explosive and high-speed measurement technologies and was the intended destination of detonation capacitors Iraq tried to import in 1990. German intelligence believes that Al Qaqaa was developing non-nuclear components of nuclear weapons.

■ **Al Qaim Phosphate Plant.** At this plant north of the Euphrates near the Syrian border, uranium is extracted from phosphates and converted into yellowcake. The plant capacity is probably small. Reports persist of a uranium hexafluoride conversion plant here, but there is no direct evidence of this.

—D.A., M.H.

investigation failed to substantiate allegations, the German government still believes that German centrifuge design officials who had been involved in Urenco's enrichment effort in Germany tried to recruit other centrifuge experts to work for Iraq. Iraq also was given blueprints for several German centrifuge designs. Stemmler said that Iraqi engineers showed him designs for the G1-type centrifuge, which Germans developed in the 1960s and early 1970s, with a separative capacity of less than two separative work units.

A Nassr State Enterprise official, Safa Al Haboobi, was appointed director of Technology Development Group (TDG), an Iraqi procurement firm based in London. Intelligence sources say that through Haboobi, TDG acquired an 18 percent share of the firm Schmiedemeccanica AG, in Biasca, Switzerland. Intelligence sources say Schmiedemeccanica, which manufactured centrifuge endcaps and baffles for Iraq, also agreed last year to supply preformed maraging steel cylinders ("preforms") to Iraq for centrifuge rotors. According to a U.S. nuclear proliferation expert, the order was not filled before the U.N. embargo started. Before 1988 the German firm H&H Metalform Ltd. sold Iraq flow-forming machines, which could shape the preforms into thin centrifuge rotor tubes or outer missile casings.

The U.S. official also said that Iraq ordered spin-forming machines, which can shape centrifuge endcaps, from another Swiss firm, Schäublin. But the machines were confiscated in July 1990, before they could be shipped to Iraq. The same official said that Iraq acquired seven machine tools, which he described as simple computer-controlled lathes.

Iraq also ordered about 50 metric tons of low-grade maraging steel from the German firm Export-Union GmbH. The material is only marginally usable for centrifuge rotors, but it could be used for missile applications. According to a company official, only a "test shipment" of 3-millimeter steel sheets actually went to Iraq, although the original order included maraging steel rings with a diameter of about 800 millimeters, used in the manufacture of missile casings.

On December 16 the London *Sunday Times* claimed that Iraq had a cascade operating at Tuwaitha, the location of Iraq's known nuclear facilities, which are inspected by the IAEA. Stemmler called this assertion ridiculous. He said that developing a cascade would be "far, far more difficult" than balancing a rotor in a single centrifuge. Iraq would need large quantities of uranium hexafluoride, computerized control equipment to maintain precise pressures and temperatures throughout the cascade, autoclaves for inserting uranium hexafluoride into the cascade, and desublimers for withdrawing it (see figure 2). Although Stemmler thought that Iraq would have little trouble obtaining a power supply (frequency inverter) for a single rotor assembly, getting the power supply for an entire cascade would prove "extraordinarily difficult."

A Western enrichment expert said that the biggest obstacle to operating a cascade is developing equipment that will run for years without failing. "Infant mortality," the crashing of a centrifuge during startup, is a major problem that must be addressed in the development stage, since the failure of one centrifuge can cause the entire cascade to fail. The expert said that Iraq would probably concentrate on building one reliable centrifuge, then test and prove a cascade of 10 centrifuges before moving on to cascades of 100–150 machines.

The *Sunday Times* also claimed that Iraq was mass-producing centrifuge components at a facility code-named Factory 10, located northwest of Baghdad. Stemmler and a colleague, Walter Busse, visited the factory in 1988. Both said that they saw no evidence that Iraq was manufacturing centrifuge components at the facility, although Stemmler said he saw what might have been a single outer casing of a centrifuge.

How long?

To gauge the amount of time Iraq might have needed to build a pilot enrichment plant, it is useful to consider Brazil's unsafeguarded enrichment program, which has benefitted from a more sophisticated industrial and nuclear infrastructure than Iraq's. Brazil decided to develop centrifuges in the late 1970s and still has not reached its goal of 1,000 operating centrifuges. In September 1982, Brazil succeeded in producing slightly enriched uranium in its own centrifuges. In 1984 it operated its first cascade of nine machines. In 1988 Brazil inaugurated a new gas centrifuge enrichment plant at Ipero, in the state of São Paulo, with 50–100 machines.

Brazil now plans to expand the Ipero plant to about 1,000 machines, each with a capacity of about two separative work units per year. About 1,600 people, including about 800 engineers, are working on the enrichment program at Ipero and an experimental center on the campus of São Paulo University. About 40 Brazilian companies are under direct contract to the enrichment program, working on steel, alloys, welding, vacuum technology, and synthetic materials. Another 160 companies are indirectly linked to the program.

After all this effort, and assuming it operates 1,000 machines, Brazil would still need about two to three years to produce enough weapon-grade uranium for one crude nuclear explosive. It seems safe to assume that what has taken Brazil over a decade would have taken Iraq at least that long.

Meantime, Iraq's "nuclear sites" were prime targets in the early raids by U.S. and allied warplanes. But the effect of air attack on the Iraqi weapons program, such as it was, is highly questionable. The research reactors at Tuwaitha, which may have been destroyed, were unconnected to the bomb program. The highly enriched uranium fuel left over from the Osiraq reactor, or not yet irradiated in the IRT-5000, could easily have been moved before war broke out—as could any key pieces of laboratory equipment. Nuclear scientists and engineers have presumably stayed out of harm's way. The war may put a damper on any future program by damaging Iraq's industrial capacity, but the nuclear effort was at such an early stage that there was little to destroy. If Iraq is determined to pursue nuclear weapons after the war, outside help will still be the key to its success. ■

The nuclear effort was at such an early stage that there was little to destroy.

1. Bob Davis, "After Years of Secrecy, Nuclear Arms Plants Show Off Technology," *Wall Street Journal*, Dec. 4, 1990, p. A1.
2. Stuart Auerbach, "American Sales to Iraq Totaled $1.5 Billion," *Washington Post*, Nov. 1, 1990, p. C1.
3. U.S. Customs Service, "News: Customs Uncovers Illegal Scheme to Export Nuclear Devices to Iraq," news release, March 29, 1990.
4. Paul Lewis, "Iraq Says It Made an Atom Trigger," *New York Times*, May 9, 1990.
5. Michael Wines, "Hard Data Lacking on Iraqi Nuclear Threat?" *New York Times*, Nov. 30, 1990.
6. Leonard S. Spector and Jacqueline R. Smith, *Nuclear Ambitions* (Boulder, Colo.: Westview, 1990), pp. 40–41.

Chapter 16

National Defense Redefined

Article 16.1. After the Battle

The author maintains that America's military success in the gulf demonstrates, beyond any doubt, that the United States will be a preeminent force in the world for decades to come. The gulf war will not only influence the way in which officials view American arms but the institutions responsible for them. Like previous wars, the gulf conflict should encourage a critical examination of the nation's performance on the battlefield. Although the Pentagon performed exceedingly well, the fact remains that Iraq proved to be "a wolf in wolf's clothing"—an evil but incompetent foe, who lacked nuclear weapons, modern surface-to-surface missiles equipped with chemical weapons, advanced conventional submarines, or space-based intelligence gathering systems. Although it is unlikely that America will face a similar enemy in the future, it is important that the nation clearly understand why Desert Storm succeeded so well, and the United States should seek to draw lessons from it. The gulf victory produced new confidence in and respect for the military, but civilian leaders cannot and should not delegate their constitutional responsibility to make policy to the military. It would be a mistake to do so, as the military is poorly equipped to perform such a role. The principle of civilian control must guide and shape the direction of all future conflicts.

AFTER THE BATTLE

By Eliot A. Cohen

"Battles are the principal milestones in secular history," Winston Churchill once wrote. "Modern opinion resents this uninspiring truth. . . . But great battles, won or lost, change the entire course of events, create new standards of values, new moods, new atmospheres, in armies and in nations, to which all must conform." The spectacular success of American arms in the Persian Gulf will shape us as a power in international politics for decades to come. It will affect not only the way we think about the military power this nation possesses, but the institutions that create it.

Every major American war has resulted in reform of the military and a transformation of its purposes. In this century the Spanish-American War gave birth to a strategic commitment in the West Pacific and a modern general staff system in the Army. World War I marked the beginnings of American naval supremacy and the creation of our first workable interservice planning system. World War II led to the creation of an independent Air Force and the Department of Defense. Korea bred a military of unprecedented size per-

manently positioned, in large numbers, overseas. Vietnam ended a more than thirty-year-old system of peacetime conscription, and forged an Army heavily dependent on reserve forces. The Persian Gulf war will leave its marks as well.

Perhaps the greatest test of our strategic maturity will be our willingness to view critically our performance in this rout. Victory has a way of excusing a multitude of sins. Advocates of every weapon, every personnel policy, and every command arrangement will reach for the rhetorical support of an argument that begins, "Desert Storm proved . . ." We must inoculate ourselves against such arguments until the facts are in and yet also be open to the possibility that this conflict marks a change in the nature of warfare in the same way the introduction of the tank and aircraft did in the 1920s and 1930s.

Soviet marshals have warned their leaders since the early 1980s of a "revolution in military affairs" brought about by new information technologies as well as long-range propulsion and accuracy. They may be right. If so we need a comprehensive investigation to find out what the nature of this revolution is. A multivolume

From *The New Republic*, April 1, 1991, pp. 19-26. Reprinted by permission of *The New Republic*, © 1991, The New Republic, Inc.

history of the war and its lessons—conducted in cooperation with, but outside of the Pentagon—is a critical first step in making this happen.

The Pentagon conceived and conducted this war splendidly. Yet we shouldn't forget its peculiarities. The United States had the fortune to have as an opponent a wolf in wolf's clothing—an unambiguously villainous yet maladroit enemy. Had Saddam Hussein taken advantage of any number of openings between August 2 and January 16, he could have made it difficult if not impossible to wage war against him thereafter. The United States fought in a theater ideally suited to our military strengths, an empty desert. Saddam's forces failed to make us fight a house-to-house battle in Kuwait City, where our reluctance to cause civilian casualties and the nature of urban warfare could have made the battle much bloodier. We had half a year to mass and train troops, and to prepare elaborate plans to attack. Had Saddam's men continued to roll south in early August we would have had to fight our way into parts of Saudi Arabia, not just Kuwait. We also had the luxury of one of the best port, road, and air base networks in the world, including military facilities built by our engineers, and the support of a wealthy and cooperative host nation.

Furthermore, the war with Iraq took place at a peculiar strategic and technological moment. We could bring to bear the weight of our cold war-rich armed forces without fear of Soviet opposition in the theater or aggression elsewhere. We attacked an opponent who did not yet have nuclear weapons, modern surface-to-surface missiles equipped with chemical weapons, advanced conventional submarines, or space-based intelligence gathering systems. It detracts nothing from the valor and skill of American soldiers to say that in retrospect this war looks like the battle of Omdurman in 1898, when an Anglo-Egyptian force numbering some 25,000 smashed a dervish force more than twice as large. In that battle Sir Herbert Kitchener's forces took fewer than fifty dead and slew some 10,000 of the enemy: roughly the casualty ratio here. A year later, however, the British met a "Third World" opponent—the Boers—who knew how to handle modern military technology, and the result was very different. It is unlikely that we will find ourselves in that position anytime soon, but the tale is a cautionary one. We need to understand in detail why Desert Storm succeeded so well, and to what extent we can draw lessons from it.

A transformation of American strategy was under way in any case, because of the end of the cold war and the collapse of the Soviet Union as a conventional (though not as a nuclear) military power. For forty years our national security establishment has had the strategic assumptions of the cold war hard-wired into its organizations and habits of mind, and this makes our adjustment to change slow and difficult. From now on our strategic position will certainly be good—we are the only superpower, as the saying goes—but our environment will be uncertain. As Samuel Huntington puts it, the world will likely "lack the clarity and stability of the cold war and be a more junglelike world of multiple dangers, hidden traps, unpleasant surprises, and moral ambiguities." It will be a world not of "good guys and bad guys," but of "gray guys." Religious and ethnic passions, economic dislocation brought on by the decay of the world trading order and demographic pressures, the loss of a steady bipolar world order—all these shifts suggest that the United States will need to rethink, in a fundamental way, the kind of military that it wants.

We have been in this position before. In 1938 George C. Marshall, then assistant chief of staff of the Army, addressed the Air Corps Tactical School:

> With us, geographical location and the international situation make it literally impossible to find definite answers for such questions as: Who will be our enemy in the next war; in what theater of operations will that war be fought; and, what will be our national objective at the time?

Marshall thought the solution straightforward: "a conservatively balanced force" to protect the United States while it mobilized to meet any challenge that might emerge. And this strategy is very much that proposed by the Bush administration and envisaged under the new command array proposed in recent congressional testimony by the chairman of the Joint Chiefs of Staff, General Colin Powell. It differs only in that it would keep a large standing military establishment and rely less on rapid mobilization than during the interwar period, although more than it has during the cold war. Just as Marshall wanted to keep the embryonic Army Air Forces from thinking they would have an unduly large or independent role in the conduct of future wars, the Pentagon wants to trim all of our forces over the next five years, cutting the Navy less, the Army more. The basic elements of American deployment would remain unchanged, including large forces stationed in Europe and the Pacific.

After the Persian Gulf war, the case will be made that the new model armed forces could, with an effort, replay Desert Storm, and that will be its major justification. But it is not self-evident that we will want forces to replay Desert Storm. And the smaller defense budgets that we now plan may leave us without the wherewithal for prolonged large-scale deployments.

The new defense budget debate will focus, as such debates usually have, on the aggregate size of the different services and on the question of what equipment (and how much of it) to buy for them. These customary questions, however, may not be the important ones. It's just as important, for instance, to ask about the nature of a force so dependent on reservists. The Army sent some of its armored and mechanized divisions to the Persian Gulf without the brigades from the National Guard that should have made up a third of its combat punch. After weeks of special training one brigade had its commanding officer relieved, another had scores of soldiers going absent without leave. Neither was ready for high-intensity combat. The reserves also may face a recruiting and retention crisis after the war if reservists and their families feel that the emotional and financial hardships of one war are enough.

Some of the most important issues are not directly budget-related at all. Foremost among these are the new command arrangements that the Pentagon reportedly wants. In a move that originated with General Powell, we may soon begin one of our largest postwar military overhauls. Currently our forces are trained and administered by the armed services and then assigned to a command that controls them in war; the services make the tools, as it were, and the command decides how to use them. Most of the commands are geographic entities, such as Central Command, which has responsibility for the Persian Gulf region and Indian Ocean; some commands, however, are functional, such as Strategic Air Command, which controls intercontinental ballistic missiles and most of our long-range heavy bombers. Each command is headed by a commander in chief (known in military jargon as a "CINC"), and the power of these generals has grown steadily over time, to include participation in the creation of defense budgets. Powell's new plan—not yet formally unveiled—would sharply reduce the number of operational commands, creating four war-fighting organizations (the Atlantic, Pacific, Contingency, and Strategic Commands) and supporting organizations, dealing with space, transportation, mobilization, and research and development. The Pentagon prefers, at the moment, to speak of this new structure in terms of "forces" rather than "commands," but for simplicity's sake, I'll use the more familiar term.

The four new operational commands would be as follows. The Atlantic Command would absorb today's Atlantic, European, and Central Commands. Before the war, the Pentagon assumed that we would keep two Army divisions and three or four tactical fighter wings—100,000 men or more—in Europe. The Pacific Command would continue, with only slightly reduced forward deployed forces in Korea and Japan. The Contingency Command would include the Army's airborne, air assault, and light infantry divisions, and one mechanized division, as well as special operations forces and some Marines and air forces. The Strategic Command would consist of offensive nuclear forces and, perhaps, defenses bred of the Strategic Defense Initiative.

At first blush, this seems like a sensible structure, and yet closer inspection suggests difficulties if the plan takes effect and the United States ends up with a force

Check, Please

The Defense Department began its current round of budget cuts by ostentatiously trimming the January 1990 Annual Report of the Secretary of Defense, saving no less than $121,800. This flashy parsimony produced a feeble document that did nothing to explain how the Pentagon planned to cope with the end of the cold war.

The new budget proposals are considerably more serious. Last year the Pentagon was ready to accept a budget decline of 2 percent a year in constant dollars. It's now projecting a sharper decline, amounting to 11 percent this year, 1 percent in 1992, and nearly 3 percent a year in 1993, 1994, and 1995. By 1995 the Pentagon will spend barely 3.5 percent of the gross national product—the smallest such proportion since before World War II.

And all this is quite aside from the direct costs of Desert Storm and the indirect costs of veteran benefits. The reluctance of the administration to issue pink slips to those who have just won battle ribbons may mean

that personnel budgets will remain high, even while overall spending continues to decline.

Current plans would take the Army down from twenty-eight divisions to eighteen, a reduction of about 35 percent; the Navy would go from 545 ships to 451, a reduction of around 17 percent; the Air Force would lose ten of its thirty-six tactical fighter wings, a reduction of about 28 percent. These proportions would be reflected in manpower cuts, which again would hit the Army hardest (31 percent), the Navy and the Marine Corps least (roughly 13 percent each), and the Air Force somewhere in the middle (28 percent).

In a speech on the day that Iraq invaded Kuwait, President Bush called for a defense budget that would devote more attention to research and development, rapid deployment, readiness, and mobilization. But it is hard to see how the United States can do all this. The attempt to preserve the bulk of our cold war forces to build greater air and sea lift, to restore the large stocks of ammunition and spare parts expended in the war with Iraq, and still press the develop-

ment of new military technologies may prove more than the budget can handle. And in fact, the 1992 budget will cut spending on basic military research and development by more than 3 percent in real terms.

One solution might be the adoption of a formula for constant defense spending at a level of, say, 4 percent of gross national product per year. Although well below the cold war average (which went as high as 10 percent), this would enable us to keep sizable forces while investing in the technological edge that seemed to serve us well in the Gulf. A defense budget is a form of national insurance and merits the kind of regular investment that prudent individuals make.

After the cold war we no longer can know with certainty where new threats will emerge, much less size our forces precisely to match those threats. In the absence of a reliable enemy we need a way to ensure some kind of predictability for defense planners, and to provide for our security in what is still a dangerous world.

E.A.C.

structure dominated by super-CINCs in charge of these four military baronies. These officers, by virtue of their small number, high visibility, and extensive authority, would become extremely powerful, further crowding out the chiefs of staff of the armed services, who have already had their authority slashed in recent years. It is the normal tendency of theater commanders in chief to worry about the immediate problems before them; this can come at the expense of long-range calculations about the shape of the services, long-run investments, or fundamental changes in ways of doing business. Yet ahead looms a time when long-range calculations should dominate short-term requirements.

The construction of three of the commands appears problematic. The vast geographic scope of the Atlantic Command means that either it will need a huge headquarters staff or it will operate with subordinate commands duplicating the functions of the three current unified commands it would absorb. In the first case the command would be ponderous; in the second, it would simply add an unnecessary layer of organization. The logic of having a Contingency Command serve as an operational command, rather than as a holding pool for the geographic command, is unclear. Presumably the Atlantic and Pacific Commands would be primed to react quickly to events in their areas of responsibility, and would have the kinds of regional expertise required for military operations. Why, in that case, have a large command for military intervention? As for the Strategic Command, its operations would be complicated by the fact that many of the forces that we might use to deliver nuclear weapons should be available for conventional missions as well. With suitable modifications, all of our long-range bombers, such as the B-52, the B-1, and the B-2, could be used to conduct the kind of strategic bombing campaign that served us well in Desert Storm.

It is not clear, under the new scheme, how Caribbean and Latin American conflicts would be handled. Today they would be controlled by Southern Command, which has a kind of regional expertise that a Contingency Command might not have. The treatment of space may pose additional difficulties. The United States now makes extraordinary use of space to collect image and signal intelligence, to maintain high-volume communications, and to allow precision navigation by air, sea, and land forces. In the Gulf war we faced no attempts to blind or disable our satellites, and our enemy had no access to space for its own purposes. In the not-so-distant future this may change, and the United States may need the ability to engage in military operations in space to achieve the kind of leverage it had in the war with Iraq. In short, rather than being a medium through which military action is supported, space may become a crucial first theater of military operations.

Finally the four-command system appears to be predicated on retaining relatively large forces overseas, leaving aside those that may be required in the Persian Gulf after the conclusion of Desert Storm. Yet will the United States really wish, or even be able, to maintain 100,000 men in continental Europe to defend countries that made minimal commitments to a war waged, in part, to protect their oil? All of the trends are away from large-scale basing of American forces overseas (in the Philippines, for example), and even where host nations do not wish to be rid of the Americans it may be hard to keep ground forces abroad effective. In Germany today U.S. Army forces cannot maneuver freely over farmland the way they did only a couple of years ago.

The new command plan, if that is what it is (and the Pentagon has been coy about calling it such), merits consideration, but its organizational, matériel, and strategic repercussions are too extensive to be accepted without debate. Some reorganization—perhaps an even more dramatic one—is in order. When it comes it must take into account two broad considerations. First, we need to ask what kind of armed forces we want. "Conservatively balanced" forces may not be workable, and a more lopsided organization (Air Force and Navy heavy) may be called for. More important than budget share, however, will be the culture and temperament of the services. The armored and mechanized components of the Army, for example, will need to begin thinking less like a continental force and more like an expeditionary corps such as the Marines. The Air Force, which until now associated "strategic" bombing with nuclear warfare, will take away from the Gulf a new mission—strategic conventional bombing. The services may all have to rethink their approach to planning. Rather than focusing on a set piece global conflict with the Soviet Union, they'll need the kind of free thinking that the resource-poor but schooling-rich armed forces excelled at during the interwar period.

Part of the problem will lie in the application of technology that does not neatly fit current force structures or ways of doing business. Throughout the 1970s and 1980s large parts of the military establishment opposed the long-range cruise missiles that appear to have performed so well in the Gulf. Arms control agreements have left the United States in the odd position of renouncing the kinds of medium-range surface-to-surface and ground-launched cruise missiles that are weapons of choice for countries like Iraq. In the future our newfound enthusiasm for conventional arms control may deprive us of weapons that would be particularly useful in conflicts like the one we've just finished.

Then there's our system of high command. Over the last ten years we have seen a profound but little noticed transformation of the American military establishment that led to, and gained impetus from, the Goldwater-Nichols Act of 1986. During World War II and thereafter the United States had a system based on a Joint Chiefs of Staff, the uniformed heads of the armed services with an independent chairman, who could offer collective and individual advice to the president. Critics described it, correctly, as a system that often produced pablum rather than clear counsel. Goldwater-Nichols transformed our high command, bringing us, in effect, to a general-in-chief system backed by a joint general staff. In theory the chairman of the Joint Chiefs is not in the chain of command, which runs from the president through the secretary of defense to the theater commands. In practice, however, he is. The chairman controls the large Joint Staff, outranks all other officers, and is the principal military adviser to the president. He is obligated to consult with other members of the JCS only "as he considers appropriate," and is not always required to inform the president or secretary of defense of divergent views about military matters among the JCS. He is responsible for strategic planning, net assessments (hitherto a civilian preserve), contingency planning, and offering budget proposals different from those of the services. His latent power is immense.

The current chairman has used that power to the maximum. General Powell combines political shrewdness and force of personality with the will to exert his powers fully. As a result, he has authority unparalleled in our military history and has exercised it to great effect. One may greatly admire his tenure, however, while worrying about its legacy. A chairman of the Joint Chiefs now has not only legal authority but unprecedented prestige and political power. In Powell's hands, that is fine, but he is clearly the best chairman we have had in two decades. It is not comforting to imagine what a George McClellan or a Douglas MacArthur would do with the power.

Goldwater-Nichols has, furthermore, made the military doctrine of "jointness"—the integrated use of all armed services—an orthodoxy, to be challenged only at hazard to one's career. Jointness is, on the whole, welcome, but like all doctrines it can go too far. The initial plans for Desert Storm, for instance, only envisaged the use of air power to support a land offensive into Kuwait. Air Force planners came up with a more imaginative campaign plan—one that applied air power to targets throughout Iraq, including Baath and secret police headquarters—and sold it to the theater commander. Although tactically joint (it used naval aviation, for example), the air campaign was strategically independent, in the manner of the great air offensives of World War II. And it worked.

It will be a more serious problem if a doctrine of jointness distorts the restructuring of our armed forces. Goldwater-Nichols, for example, mandates that the Joint Staff be composed equally of officers from the three departments (the Marine Corps being included in the Navy), and it is a fair guess that the chairman's new command plan will allocate senior commands in roughly equal numbers to the three departments. Such allocations of bureaucratic influence should, however, correspond more to strategic reality (what kinds of forces we need and want) than to some abstract idea of fairness. And sometimes jointness may not serve our strategic purposes or tactical efficiency at all. Such would be the case if an Air Force officer, for example, hundreds or even thousands of miles from an action, were to control the sorties of a Navy carrier operating independently or a submariner were to direct a counterinsurgency campaign. Professional soldiers are rarely omnicompetent, and the complexity of each branch of warfare has only increased over time.

One happy consequence of the Gulf war is a new confidence of civilians in the military. And it is wonderful to see bonds not only of affection but of respect restored between civilians and soldiers. There is, however, one subtle if manageable danger in all this: civilian leaders may lose confidence in their right and forget their responsibility to determine the shape of military organizations and to probe and query military commanders about their war plans. In these areas (unlike those of military acquisition, where civilian control has been more assertive, if uneven) civilian leaders may yield too much to soldiers, who may, in turn, expect excessive deference to their views. As one great war minister put it, "The more developed the professional sense of an army, the more sensitive and touchy it is to anything which hurts, or seems to hurt, its interests and prerogatives."

The Bush administration's assertions that the generals ran this war probably conceal a more complicated reality. They may also convey the incorrect impression that civilian control of the military in wartime is merely a matter of setting broad objectives and getting out of the way. Our experience in previous successful wars suggests otherwise—and, alas, we cannot assume that we have finished with conflict. If we come to believe that we can make war by aphorism—"only use invincible force," "turn the war over to the military," "set simple objectives"—we will find ourselves baffled by other conflicts into which we will surely stumble. The Iraq war was brilliantly planned and fought, and our armed forces' skill and courage has surely bought us a more favorable, if not necessarily a tranquil, world order. But it is no more likely today than it was on August 1, 1990, that we have fought our last war, and we must think about our defense with that fact uneasily in mind. ●

In this article, the author examines the issue of industrial preparedness, noting that the U.S. Defense Department has initiated a major review in response to recent changes in the nation's military circumstances. These developments have made all the more urgent the need for strategic investment and trade policies. Evidence reveals that in the event of a protracted low-level conflict, American industry would find it difficult, if not impossible, to satisfy the basic military needs of the United States and its allies without significant lead time. It is essential, warns the author, that the U.S. initiate steps now to strengthen the nation's military-industrial base, rather than waiting for an emergency. Despite this need, some critics have raised strong objections to a strategic trade policy, most of which he discounts. Still, the author acknowledges that public concern is justified, particularly in cases where some would substitute government decisions for those of the market.

A DEFENSE INDUSTRIAL STRATEGY?

I. YES, PREPAREDNESS REQUIRES IT

MACKUBIN T. OWENS

Mr. Owens is a professor of defense economics at the Naval War College. From "Expand the Military-Industrial Complex? Yes—Preparedness Requires It" by Mackubin T. Owens, Orbis, Fall 1989, pages 539-548:

The Department of Defense is now emphasizing industrial preparedness not because of a hidden desire to aid inefficient industries, nor because of grand ambitions to interfere with the U.S. economy. Rather, the Pentagon's concern for industrial preparedness is the result of changes in America's military circumstances. These have created a demonstrable need for strategic investment and trade policies. While such policies must be limited and protected by stringent safeguards to prevent abuse, they must be enacted, and enacted as soon as possible.

Military exercises and war games reveal that in the event of war or even a protracted low-level conflict, American industry would be hard-pressed to support the military needs of the United States and its allies without substantial lead time. Some would argue that military needs already exert a significant influence on the U.S. economy, to the detriment of other sectors; and that further steps to direct trade and investment in the interest of national security, such as those proposed in two recent

Pentagon publications, are unnecessary during peacetime. But if American conventional forces are to provide a credible deterrent (and not just a trip-wire for nuclear weapons), it is irresponsible to wait for an emergency before undertaking the many steps necessary to improve the country's military-industrial base.

BACKGROUND

In the late 1940s, the conventional wisdom in the United States was that the postwar era would be characterized by a protracted conflict between the United States and the Soviet Union. The policy of containment, with its emphasis on meeting the Soviets everywhere at all times, reflected this viewpoint, as did other aspects of American foreign policy. Even while the U.S. military enjoyed a nuclear monopoly in the late 1940s, it recognized that opposing the expansionist tendencies of the Soviet Union would require strong conventional forces, including a peacetime draft and the maintenance of an industrial base capable of supporting such forces. The outbreak of the

Mackubin T. Owens, "Expand the Military-Industrial Complex? Yes—Preparedness Requires It" from *Orbis: A Journal of World Affairs*, Fall 1989, pp. 539-548, published by the Foreign Policy Research Institute; as it appeared in *Current*, March/April 1990, pp. 28-33. Format reprinted with permission of the Helen Dwight Reid Educational Foundation. Format published by Heldref Publications, 1319 18th Street, N.W., Washington, D.C. 20036-1802. Copyright 1990.

Korean War then confirmed these expectations.

The Korean War prompted passage of the Defense Production Act, which gave the United States, as President Harry Truman put it, the ability "to throw our great industrial strength onto the scales of war quickly and efficiently." Advocates of containment considered this mobilization capability an important component of the deterrence strategy, as well as a fallback in case of war. The Soviets had seen America's "arsenal of democracy" for themselves during World War II; policy makers hoped that maintaining this mobilization capability would convince the Soviets that, in the event of war, any early Soviet successes would be overwhelmed by the industrial might of the United States.

Although containment continued to serve as official U.S. strategy after the Korean War, its foundations were gradually undermined by the doctrine of massive retaliation and a belief that nuclear weapons had made protracted war a thing of the past. If this was the case, then the need for a mobilization capability was also undermined. So long as nuclear weapons deterred war, it was said, the peacetime capacity to produce a small but constant quantity of expensive, highly capable weapons would suffice. If deterrence failed, mobilization capacity would be superfluous. This led to the "force-in-being" approach to planning, adopted by the Air Force in 1955, which postulated that the next war would be total nuclear war, fought only with weapons available at its outset.

The adoption of a flexible response strategy in 1962 produced little change. In principle, this new strategy obligated the United States to be prepared for the full spectrum of conflict, from what is now called low-intensity conflict through conventional war up to global nuclear war. In practice, however, conventional fighting capabilities remained focused on limited wars, such as the one in Vietnam, and on other contingencies short of an East-West global war. Accordingly, flexible response had an effect on mobilization similar to that of massive retaliation. In a limited war, U.S. industry could capably support the military without resorting to extraordinary measures. A global conflict would be brief, win or lose, rendering industrial preparedness virtually irrelevant.

United States strategic theory began to change once more in the late 1970s. Soviet advances in nuclear weaponry rendered the U.S. nuclear deterrent far less credible. It made little sense for the United States to threaten to escalate a conventional conflict up to the nuclear level when its opponent had at least parity, and in some cases superiority, on most

rungs of the "escalation ladder." With this in mind, analysts began to speak of the need to improve America's ability to fight a conventional but large-scale war. That ability, in turn, would depend upon a strong military-industrial base.

In short, weaknesses in the industrial base of America's military system were deemed acceptable until quite recently. So long as the United States enjoyed nuclear superiority, that edge was thought able to deter large-scale conventional wars. Only the end of U.S. nuclear superiority forced policy makers to question their assumptions and to recognize the increased possibility of large-scale conventional warfare. This awareness prompted the recognition that the U.S. industrial base might not be able to support American forces in such circumstances. That, in turn, has spurred the Department of Defense to take an unprecedented interest in questions of trade and investment.

AMERICA'S MILITARY-INDUSTRIAL BASE

The U.S. military-industrial base consists of three levels. *Basic industrial capacity* comprises the foundation industries that produce raw goods necessary for both civilian and military output: metals, chemicals, and energy. *Subtier industries* produce the components and parts that are put together to create final products. *End-product industries* include those dedicated exclusively to military production, the "defense industries" plus that part of the civilian sector that can be converted to military production.

What the U.S. military requires of this industrial base is to maintain a technological edge over potential adversaries; then, in time of war, to meet the needs of national security in a timely and economical manner. At minimum, this means efficient peacetime production, support for the military's existing force structure and war reserve, and surge capacity (rapidly expanded production within the existing industrial plant). In the event of a major conventional war, U.S. industry would also have to be mobilized (a structured, systematic increase in production rates over one to two years). Mobilization requires a major expansion of industrial capacity; circumstances may require not only that wartime losses be replaced, but also that support be provided for significantly enlarged forces.

At present, U.S. industry cannot meet the minimum requirement, much less mobilize in response to a global crisis. Problems exist at all three levels. With regard to *basic industrial capacity,* structural changes in the U.S. economy and increased foreign competitiveness have caused much traditional heavy industry to move overseas. While this de-indus-

INCAPACITY

trialization is probably the American economy's most highly publicized problem, it is in fact the least troubling. The shift of heavy industry to countries such as Japan, South Korea, and Taiwan reflects the workings of comparative advantage, and so reinforces economic efficiency. This international division of labor means that the remaining American producers of such products as steel are more efficient. Excessive attention to the changing structure of America's heavy industry obscures a critical point: in time of crisis, the United States would have access to an alliance-wide industrial base. While this global industrial base has obvious vulnerabilities, for a maritime nation the advantages of exploiting an international division of labor far outweigh the costs.

Problems at the level of *sub-tier industries* are much more severe. Resources have been diverted from military production because of the sustained growth of the U.S. economy since 1983, leading to heightened civilian demands, and declining real military budgets after 1985. This combination has resulted in increased lead times, rising costs, and bottlenecks. In some cases, the military depends on a unique producer—who may not wish to do business with the U.S. government. The army's attempt in the 1970s to surge tank production was frustrated because the lone producer of tank castings could not meet the increased demand. In 1988, the sole producer of aerospace-grade continuous filament rayon yarn, a material critical to space and strategic missile systems, announced that it was closing and filing for bankruptcy.

Sub-tier production has also been affected by increased foreign competitiveness; much of the U.S. productive capacity has shifted overseas—especially in such areas as electronics, machine tools, fasteners, and precision optics. Although the alliance industrial base partially offsets that shift, the erosion of the traditional U.S. edge in technology remains a legitimate concern. American planners seek to offset the Soviets' numerical superiority with technological superiority. In this critical area, a balance must exist between cooperation with allies and the need to avoid over-dependence on foreign sources for critical technologies during a crisis.

A different set of problems exists at the *end-product* level, where the free market hardly exists. Because the federal government is the sole buyer, the market is monopsonistic. Washington also imposes the regulations under which the sellers must operate. This relationship between supplier and consumer tends to build their mutual interest and to de-emphasize their concern with price. Industries serving the military face many barriers to entry, including overly exact specifications, purchases of small quantities, annual procurements, high uncertainty of project funding, long gestation periods, a likelihood of low profits, and the highly specialized nature of military research and development. Other barriers to entry reinforce inefficiencies and make it difficult to match the lower cost practices of the commercial sector. These include government sponsorship of research and development, high overhead, specialized capital equipment and labor, and military specifications. Such problems are exacerbated by stop-and-go funding, excessive government regulations, and inflexible contracting and acquisition policies.

A recent study shows the decline in firms *DECLINE* willing to do business with the Department of Defense. In 1982, more than 118,000 firms provided manufactured goods to the military; in 1987, fewer than 40,000 remained. Some of the 80,000 went out of business, including about 20,000 small firms. Most, however, simply gave up on the Pentagon and sought out other customers. This is remarkable because, using constant fiscal year (FY) 1989 dollars, the military procurement budget grew from $54.9 billion in 1982 to $87.0 billion five years later. Of course, not every company's capacity is completely lost to the military-industrial base. In time of emergency or war, many would be available for military production, though in a less timely manner. Still, the movement of firms away from military production has exacerbated the structural distortions that characterize the U.S. military industry.

Even greater shortcomings affect the U.S. ability to surge production in times of emergency. Indeed, the lead times and the unit costs of producing weapon systems, resulting from such distortions in the peacetime acquisition process as the extension of programs (increasing the time over which a system will be produced in order to reduce expenditures during a particular fiscal year), stop-and-go funding by Congress, and constant tinkering with military specifications, have increased so dramatically that one can question the whole concept of surge capacity in the production of weapons platforms such as tanks and aircraft. Accordingly, the Department of Defense has focused its attempts to improve surge capacity in the area of sustainability items (spare parts and munitions), especially precision guided munitions, short-range missiles, and other ordnance. While improvements have been made, major deficiencies remain. For example, surging ammunition production would be tethered by a number of sub-tier constraints, leading to possible bottlenecks. Rolling mill and metal-forming firms are already operating at high levels of capacity. In the absence of action before an emergency, it would be difficult to shift some of this capacity to ammunition production. Similar problems would constrain the ability of sub-tier firms to produce ammonium perchlorate. Finally, many guidance systems and explosives are produced overseas.

CURRENT CIRCUMSTANCES

To understand the current problem, several points need to be established. First, the international division of labor is an irreversible fact. Strengthening the U.S. industrial base, therefore, does not mean seeking economic self-sufficiency, much less autarky. Even if this were a good idea, it is not affordable. Fortunately, the loss of U.S. industries to the international division of labor does not necessarily mean that their output is unavailable to the United States, even in time of war. An alliance military-industrial base exists, making it unnecessary to replicate the U.S. industrial base of the 1940s and 1950s, characterized by basic heavy industry. Making use of this alliance base, of course, places a premium on cooperation with the allies. As Robert Costello, former under secretary of defense for acquisition, has said about co-development of the FSX fighter with Japan: "We have to be tied to the Japanese in very direct ways because they have some things that we do not." It also points to the importance of strong naval forces; the navy protects those allies that provide critical materiel as well as the sea lanes of communications to them. But, while disruptions are always possible, overseas suppliers are by and large very reliable, and exercises and war games indicate that U.S. naval power is sufficient to serve its protective function.

Of course, an alliance industrial base has its limits. Vulnerabilities arising from interdiction of trade constrain the global base. But there are also political problems that arise in any alliance. For instance, as Edward Olsen has pointed out, a given country may not mind if its military alliance with the United States involves mutual economic dependence. But how pleased will that ally be if such an alliance involves U.S. economic dependence on a third state? Japan, for example, produces high-technology components for the U.S. military, and thereby accepts a partial U.S. dependency— but how would the Japanese feel about having the U.S. dependent on a third state for a critical part of the military-industrial base? In addition, economic interdependence grants an ally in disagreement with a particular policy the means to put economic pressure on the United States.

THE MARKET'S LIMITS   Second, the market alone cannot meet all the requirements of national security, primarily

for the structural reasons discussed above. This issue was argued at length at the beginning of the Reagan administration, as part of the debate between the Pentagon and the Office of Management and Budget (OMB). The former proposed an "Action Plan for Improvement of Industrial Readiness," calling for expanded use of Title III of the Defense Production Act, as amended. Specifically, the Defense Department wanted Congress to amend the Act to reinstate DOD's authority to borrow directly from the Treasury, as had been the case before 1974. OMB argued that the marketplace, stimulated by the military build-up, by reductions in tax rates, and by changes in depreciation schedules, would improve the military-industrial base without any help from the government. The result was a compromise between the Pentagon and OMB, weighted more favorably toward the latter's position. Unfortunately, the compromise did not have the intended effect, for the increase in expenditures did nothing to change industry structure, the crux of the matter. More spending only served to conceal industry problems, and, in the long run, to make matters worse.

Finally, caution is required with regard to the Soviet Union, even in an era of reduced tensions. In the early 1980s, the Soviets sharply increased military investment, as a percentage of their gross national product, over what was already a very high level. Combined with an increased stockpiling effort, that added investment has actually improved the ability of the Soviet command economy to meet the demands of protracted war. Thus, Moscow still has the potential, should its interests warrant, to increase military output and that is what, with all its problems, the Soviet economy does best. Even if East-West negotiations should lead to a shift away from a U.S. defense based on forward deployment and high levels of operational readiness, industrial preparedness remains a hedge against a return to business as usual by the Soviets.

FORMULATING POLICY

What should be done to improve industrial preparedness? The answer depends on one's perspective. Those who focus on the advantages of free trade tend to conclude that the U.S. government may have done too much already, and would reduce its role further. On the other side, those who mistrust the market would nationalize defense industries, or at least subject major segments of U.S. industry to the vagaries of government planning. But the most prudent approach to improving the military-industrial base lies between these poles, in the development of strategic policies.

Strategic trade and investment policies

allocate resources during peacetime to enhance national security in the event of an emergency. These policies acknowledge that the free market normally does not direct resources into the military sector during peacetime, and that waiting until emergency strikes is too late.

Strategic trade policy ensures that the United States does not become overly dependent on foreign suppliers—as might occur were the international division of labor to operate freely—and that it does not lose its technology base. One may disagree over the proper balance between economic efficiency and requirements of trade restrictions in the interest of national security, but national security does have a legitimate claim on the formulation of trade policy.

Strategic investment policy channels, in peacetime, economic assets into areas underfunded by the free market. It involves government allocation of resources into military-oriented research and development and the purchase of items with long lead times (such as tank and aircraft engines, and specialized machine tools). It also directs resources into advanced manufacturing technology, such as flexible manufacturing systems, which are computerized production assemblies (machine tools, a material handling system, a computer control system) that can be programmed to manufacture a variety of products, making it easy to shift from civilian to military production.

A prudent approach to industrial preparedness must include several elements. The U.S. government should:

SOLUTION *Establish a forum* to address emergency preparedness and mobilization, then connect these requirements to strategic investment and trade policy. At present, no single group accomplishes this goal. The Reagan administration made major advances by reversing the trend that had moved coordination of emergency preparedness out of the White House (the Office of Emergency Preparedness was abolished in 1973). In 1981, President Ronald Reagan created the Emergency Mobilization Preparedness Board (EMPB) and later folded its functions into the National Security Council. In 1988, Reagan further signaled presidential concern about emergency preparedness by issuing Executive Order 12656, which assigned responsibilities to Federal departments and agencies and strengthened the role of the National Security Council as the "principal forum for consideration of national security emergency preparedness policy."

Implement the Graduated Mobilization Response Plan, released by President Reagan in 1988. The plan gives the president options for gradually increasing U.S. military-industrial preparedness in response to increasing international tension. Because of the perception that mobilization is provocative (recalling World War I), it has often been treated as a measure of last resort. But if mobilization does not occur until the emergency is in full swing, it may be too late. The Graduated Mobilization Response Plan allows the president to take carefully weighted, incremental steps toward an improved state of preparedness, avoiding the extremes of provocation and inaction.

For instance, he can direct an increase in the purchase of long lead-time items or strategic minerals; direct certain industries to surge production to support requirements for existing forces; enhance production capacity by letting contracts to expand physical plant or by opening "cold" standby production lines; and review standby legal authorities. Such steps, taken before a crisis develops into a full-scale conflict, would signal U.S. resolve and could help defuse the emergency. At a minimum, steps taken under this plan would reduce lead times.

Use Title III of the Defense Production Act to carry out the strategic investment policy to ensure that the government can fulfill all phases of the GMR Plan. Investment should be limited to those cases where ordinary market mechanisms cannot meet national military needs, such as the advanced manufacturing technologies private corporations are unwilling or unable, due to structural distortions within the military-industrial base, to employ. Several programs already exist to invest government funds along these lines, including the Industrial Modernization Incentives Program (which provides incentives to contractors to make capital investments that improve productivity), the Manufacturing Technology Program (which invests in advanced production technologies), and the Semiconductor Manufacturing Technology Program, known as Sematech.

Build surge capacity into the acquisition process; push so-called surge funding, in effect requiring a contractor to pay for his own surge capacity as part of a contract with DOD.

Improve government-industry cooperation. The first step is to establish forums for cooperation such as a Manufacturing Advisory Council and a Defense Manufacturing Board. Next, antitrust policies should be relaxed, especially those that impede cooperative research and development. Joint ventures between government, industry, and the military should be permitted, even encouraged. This will speed conversion of industrial capacity to wartime requirements.

CONCLUSION

While some of the fears expressed by opponents of strategic trade policy are misguided, their instincts are not. Government intervention in the economy on behalf of national security must be done carefully, for it is fraught with dangers.

Not least is the danger that national security may become a Trojan horse. Writings of the left, such as Robert Reich and Ira Magaziner in *Minding America's Business,* have for some time advocated an industrial policy that seeks to substitute government decisions for those of the market. This approach has often been discredited, and never more dramatically than during the 1980s, when planners (even Japanese planners) could not predict future trends, much less individual winners. Free-market economists, who have to battle with these left-wing partisans of industrial policy, are wary of having to battle also with an industrial policy of the right, introduced as an adjunct to national security.

This is understandable. Already, domestic producers hide behind the banner of national security to achieve protection against more efficient foreign competitiors (as in the case of some electronics components, or, previously, steel). Usually these producers can count on the support of members of Congress, who see protection of domestic jobs as an irresistible political issue. Moreover, even some economists (notably Jacques Gansler) explicitly advocate military-industrial preparedness as the leading edge of a wider industrial policy.

But legitimate concerns about industrial policy do not undo the serious problems in the American economy that hamper the government's ability to provide for the common defense. The U.S. government in general and the Department of Defense in particular have important, if limited, roles to play in alleviating those problems.

SELECTED BIBLIOGRAPHY—SECTION IV

Adams, Gordon. *The Politics of Defense Contracting: The Iron Triangle.* New Brunswick, N.J.: Transaction Books, 1981.

Bamford, James. *The Puzzle Palace: A Report on America's Most Secret Agency.* New York: Penguin Books, 1983.

Clarke, Duncan L. *American Defense and Foreign Policy Institutions: Toward a Solid Foundation.* New York: Harper & Row, 1989.

Dellums, Ronald V. *Defense Sense: The Search for a Rational Military Policy.* Cambridge, Mass.: Ballinger, 1983.

Dyson, Freeman. *Weapons and Hope.* New York: Harper & Row, 1984.

Fallows, James. *National Defense.* New York: Random House, 1981.

Gansler, Jacques S. *The Defense Industry.* Cambridge, Mass.: MIT Press, 1980.

Goodman, Allan E., and Bruce D. Berkowitz. *Task Force Report on Covert Action.* Washington, D.C.: Brookings Institution, 1991.

Glynn, Patrick. *Arms Races, Arms Control, and the History of the Cold War.* New York: New Republic Book, 1992.

Harris, John B. *Nuclear Weapons and the Threat of Nuclear War.* San Diego, Calif.: Harcourt Brace Jovanovich, 1986.

Harwell, Mark A. *Nuclear Winter.* New York: Springer-Verlag, 1984.

Hertsgaard, Mark. *Nuclear, Inc.: The Men and Money Behind Nuclear Energy.* New York: Pantheon Books, 1983.

Johnson, Loch K. *America's Secret Power: The CIA in a Democratic Society.* New York: Oxford University Press, 1989.

Kaplan, Stephen S. *Diplomacy of Power.* Washington, D.C.: Brookings Institution, 1981.

Kull, Steven. *Nuclear Reality and the Inner Conflicts of Defense Policymakers.* New York: Basic Books, 1990.

Landau, Saul. *The Dangerous Doctrine: National Security and U.S. Foreign Policy.* Boulder, Colo: Westview Press, 1988.

Lifton, Robert Jay, and Richard Falk. *The Political and Psychological Case Against Nuclearism.* New York: Basic Books, 1991.

Persico, Joseph E. *Casey: From the OSS to the CIA.* New York: Penguin Books, 1990.

Pierre, Andrew J. *The Global Politics of Arms Sales*. Princeton, N.J.: Princeton University Press, 1982.

Richelson, Jeffrey T. *The U.S. Intelligence Community*. Cambridge, Mass.: Ballinger, 1989.

Rubin, Barry. *Secrets of State: The State Department and the Struggle over U.S. Foreign Policy*. New York: Oxford University Press, 1985.

Russett, Bruce. *What Price Vigilance?* New Haven, Conn.: Yale University Press, 1970.

Treverton, Gregory F. *The Limits of Intervention in the Post-War World*. New York: Twentieth Century Fund, 1989.

Yarmolinsky, Adam. *The Military Establishment: Its Impact on American Society*. New York: Harper & Row, 1971.

THE PATH TO PEACE

Collective security provides for global defense based on a pledge by all or most nations to support united action against any member that illegally violates the peace. It is based on the twin principles of deterrence and conjunctive action—that is, if deterrence fails, then the member-states will coalesce, employing military action, to defeat the aggressor. However, collective security is only applicable to the system itself; its purpose is to protect its members from other insiders. To be effective, collective security obligates the members to support each other, thus ensuring order and predictability. It also promotes the peaceful resolution of disputes, since the use of force is strictly prohibited. No consideration is paid to the reasons for using force, the issues behind the conflict, or the consequences of defeat for one side or the other.

Collective security was first articulated, at least on the international level, by President Woodrow Wilson following World War I, when he proposed a League of Nations. Indeed, the principle itself was embodied in Article 16 of the League's Covenant, which states: "Should any Member of the League resort to war in disregard of its covenants . . . it shall, ipso facto, be deemed to have committed an act of war against the other Members of the League." Unfortunately, the League proved ineffectual because of structural failings and ideological divisions. Although the major powers endorsed the principle of collective security, their actions were motivated by a desire to preserve the balance of power against specific foes. The small states were equally culpable, in that they showed little direct interest in collective security.

The failure of the League of Nations underscores the difficulties inherent in any system of collective security. In part, the problem derives from a lack of consensus over what constitutes "aggression." The classic definition—that is, the "violation of territorial integrity and political independence"—has proven inadequate. In addition, institutions such as the League of Nations or, for that matter, the United Nations, have found it difficult, if not impossible, to compel unified action. Although common action is not essential, collective security cannot succeed unless the major powers cooperate in action against an aggressor. In the past, states have been reluctant to act against a powerful neighbor, a close ally or friend, or the perceived victim of a conflict. For example, Albania refused to oppose Italy, its powerful protector, in 1935, while the Soviet Union would not condemn North Korea, an ideological ally in 1950. Like the League of Nations, the United Nations has been plagued by similar problems. According to its charter, the Security Council may ask all members to invoke sanctions against aggressor states under Chapter VII. When the council is deadlocked, the General Assembly is empowered to authorize collective action. However, any of the five permanent members (the United States, France, Soviet Union, Great Britain, or People's Republic of China) may block collective action by exercising its veto.

In its quest to resolve disputes and maintain peace, the international community has created a number of global structures to promote national security, economic development, and social intercourse. These international organizations seek to develop and implement policy among states, and do not exist independently from them. There are two main types of international organizations: those structures composed of governments (e.g., North Atlantic Treaty Organization) and those composed of private individuals and groups (e.g., Rosicrucian Order). The number of both types has risen sharply since World War II. Approximately 90 percent of present international organizations (2,400) are nongovernmental, while the remaining 10 percent (300) are governmental and far more influential.

International organizations, argue political scientists Walter S. Jones and Steven J. Rosen, can be divided into global and nonglobal organizations. Global organizations may be multipurpose (e.g., United Nations) or single-purpose or function, of which there are numerous types. These include: economic (e.g., Economic and Social Council); security (e.g., Security Council); anti-imperial (e.g., Trusteeship Council); nutrition (e.g., Food and Agricultural Organization); transportation—sea and air (e.g., International Maritime Organization and International Civil Aviation Organization); communications— mail and telegraph (e.g., Universal Postal Union and International Telecommunication Union); and judicial (e.g., International Court of Justice). Subglobal organizations may be classified into intrabloc, regional, and integrating organizations. These, too, fall into several categories. Intrabloc includes economic (e.g., International Monetary Fund) and security (e.g., North Atlantic Treaty Organization) organizations. Regional comprises economic (e.g., European Economic Community), security (e.g., Rio Treaty), and sociocultural and economic (e.g., Bogota Pact) organizations. Integrating encompasses economic (e.g., European Coal and Steel Community) and judicial (e.g., European Court of Human Rights) organizations.

Clearly, nations have influenced these international organizations to advance their own foreign policy interests and objectives. During the Cold War, most countries viewed these organizations as important institutional forums in which to pursue their goals and to resolve their differences. Moreover, these organizations are highly adaptive and quite capable of adjusting to meet changing political realities. Although one should not expect too much or, for that matter, too little, from these organizations, they wield considerable influence on the international stage. This is particularly true of organizations such as the United Nations, which are highly prized by Third World countries. Although the United Nations lacks authority and autonomy, it has shaped the actions of many states.

The most important international organization is the United Nations, which was founded in 1945 to establish norms of international conduct to outlaw war, provide for the peaceful settlement of international disputes, regulate armaments, govern trust territories, and encourage international cooperation in dealing with economic and social problems. The United Nations' modern roots date back to the Conferences at Munster and Osnabruck that produced the Peace of Westphalia (1648) and inaugurated the nation-state system; the Congress of Vienna (1815), which convened to explore the problems of post-Napoleonic Europe; and the Concert of Europe (1815-1914), at which the great powers of Europe assembled—over a hundred-year period—to resolve their differences "in concert."

In 1945, the United Nations, which succeeded the League of Nations, was spearheaded by the governments of the United States, France, Soviet Union, Great Britain, and People's Republic of China. The United Nations, which now totals more than 160 members, spanning six official working languages (Chinese, English, French, Russian, Spanish, and Arabic), is permanently based in New York. It is headed by a secretary-general, who oversees a staff of more than 6,000 specialists (recruited worldwide). Structurally, it retains many features of the League of Nations, and includes the General Assembly (a forum in which all members are represented), the Security Council (the primary organ responsible for the preservation of peace and security), and the Economic and Social Council (a central clearinghouse and administrative body that coordinates such policy areas as health, education, and human rights).

The United Nations, unlike the League of Nations, is better suited to the maintenance of collective security, in that it possesses more elaborate and ambitious provisions for sanctions and confers upon the Security Council the authority to identify the aggressor, require members to engage in nonmilitary coercion, and order its military forces wherever necessary, under the direction of the council. Still, as political scientist James L. Ray points out, its effectiveness remains largely untested, although the recent gulf war gives renewed hope to those who believe in its potential. Despite its several successes, the United Nations has, in many cases, failed to marshal the military forces necessary to the achievement of peace. Moreover, since every permanent member of the Security Council enjoys the right to veto actions of the council, it is virtually impossible to impose sanctions against one of the major powers.

Although the United Nations boasts a proud record of accomplishment (e.g., in agricultural development, international finance, world health, and educational, scientific, and cultural affairs), it has been beset by myriad problems, which are, by and large, the product of the nature of the organization and international political realities. According to political scientist Forest L. Grieves, these include: (1) (1) the myth of sovereign equality and membership problems; (2) parliamentary diplomacy, bloc voting, and the veto; (3) administrative isolation, internationality, and the political role of the secretary-general; (4) inadequate finances, spiraling budgets, disputes over assessments, and inflationary woes; (5) program coordination, overlapping jurisdictions, bureaucratic empire-building, and political wrangling; and (6) collective security, peacekeeping, international compliance, and ideological divisions.

In the end, the United Nations can only act where the major powers have important and immediate foreign-policy interests. Further, it can act in other areas only so long as it has at least tacit major power support. Despite its shortcomings, the United Nations continues to enjoy widespread international backing, providing a much-needed forum for debate, discussion, interaction, and, at times, action.

The fifth section, "The Path to Peace," includes three chapters. Chapter 17, "Arms Control and

Disarmament," describes the START Treaty negotiations, suggesting that, like the SALT I and SALT II Treaties, the process of winning ratification is highly political. The author maintains that, in spite of the Soviet admission that it does not believe a nuclear war is winable, the possibility of a nuclear war still remains. The second selection examines the impact of defense cuts on the Soviet economy. Although it is difficult to determine the true extent of Soviet military spending, it is clear that that nation must embark on an "economic conversion." The Soviets have already taken the first steps toward rescuing their economy by cutting weapons production and troop deployments. Still, the benefits from such measures, at least in the short-term, are likely to be minimal, owing to the huge costs associated with conversion.

Chapter 18, "The Limits of United Nations Action," assesses the changing role of the United Nations. The first article reviews U.N. procedures for settling international disputes, presents several case studies, including the recent gulf war, discusses U.N. decision making, examines the role of politics in the U.N., and analyzes the limits of U.N. action in the post-Cold War order. In the second selection, the author critiques the performance of the United Nations since its establishment, concluding that it is highly unlikely that in future world conflicts the U.N. can repeat the isolated successes of the Korean War and the gulf conflict. He advocates drastic changes in the criteria for membership, the structure of the organization, and its methods of operation.

Chapter 19, "Regional Security Organizations," considers the future of the North Atlantic Treaty Organization, in the context of the new U.S.-Soviet relationship. The author maintains that recent events underscore the need to reduce its combat force and to perhaps expand its geographic scope or devise a new framework to deal with future threats. The second selection analyzes U.S. security policy in Southeast Asia, examining the future of American bases in the Philippines, Singapore's offer to host a small U.S. naval and air presence, and the outcome of the Cambodian conflict. The author describes the changing U.S. military, political, and economic role in the region, arguing that American calls for burden-sharing, combined with a reduction in military tensions, has hastened an examination of U.S. relations with ASEAN. It has also forced ASEAN states to consider a new security posture.

DISCUSSION QUESTIONS

1. To what extent, if any, was the fate of the SALT I and SALT II Treaties dictated by political considerations?
2. Is the START Treaty, as suggested, a major improvement over previous arms control treaties? If so, how?
3. What major arms control initiatives remain to be negotiated?
4. Is the "window of vulnerability" idea a dead issue in future arms control discussions?
5. Does arms control significantly reduce the chances of war?
6. Will the "peace dividend" necessarily result in an increase in U.S. domestic spending?
7. Is it likely that the "peace dividend" will produce an upsurge in the Soviet economy?
8. Why do defense factories, both in the United States and Soviet Union, have so little incentive to switch to civilian production?
9. How has the gulf war affected the future of the United Nations?
10. Is the United Nations capable of maintaining international peace and security?
11. What should be done to make the United Nations more effective?
12. Has the United Nations outlived its usefulness? Why, or why not?
13. Is NATO still necessary, in light of recent changes in Eastern Europe?
14. How, if at all, should NATO's mission be redefined?
15. Is an alliance of Western democracies still necessary? Why, or why not?
16. Should NATO be pared down in terms of its size and structure?
17. How would Europe be different without the superpower alliances?
18. Is the United States justified in demanding greater burden-sharing on the part of its ASEAN allies? Why, or why not?
19. What should the United States do to force ASEAN states to open their markets to American products?

KEY TERMS

ARMS CONTROL   Measures taken unilaterally or through agreement to reduce the dangers of war through partial disarmament, security arrangements to prevent nuclear war, and the stabilization of force levels.

ASSOCIATION OF SOUTHEAST ASIAN NATIONS   A regional cooperative organization, established in 1967, to promote economic development and technical assistance among its members, which include: Indonesia, Malaysia, Philippines, Singapore, Thailand, and Brunei.

COLLECTIVE SECURITY   A system of states that band together, usually by treaty, to renounce the use of force and pledge to take common action against any state that illegally breaches the peace.

DISARMAMENT   The eradication of arms, either in their entirety or by specific group.

INTERNATIONAL ORGANIZATIONS   Institutional structures established on a global level to promote cooperation among members in social, economic, security, or related fields.

MILITARY SPENDING   The total defense expenditure for personnel costs, weapons procurement, maintenance and operations, research and development, and military construction.

NONPROLIFERATION   The limitation of nuclear weapons to those states that already possess them.

NORTH ATLANTIC TREATY ORGANIZATION   A regional military alliance, created in 1949, for the collective defense of North America and Western Europe.

PEACE DIVIDEND   Economic savings resulting from reductions in military and defense spending.

REGIONALISM   The concept that states situated in geographical proximity or sharing common goals can mutually cooperate through a limited-membership organization to solve political, military, and practical problems.

SALT I TREATY   A series of arms control talks between the United States and the Soviet Union that resulted in the Anti-Ballistic Missile Treaty and the Interim Agreement.

SALT II TREATY   A series of discussions involving the United States and Soviet Union that led to an arms control treaty that was never ratified, due to what its critics felt were too many loopholes.

START TREATY   An arms control agreement between the United States and Soviet Union designed to reduce nuclear weapons.

TREATY   A contractual agreement between two or more states that establishes, explains, or alters their mutual duties and obligations.

UNITED NATIONS   An international organization, established in 1945, to foster world peace and global understanding.

UNITED NATIONS DISPUTE SETTLEMENT PROCEDURES   Tools and methods employed by organs of the United Nations to resolve international crises and settle interstate conflicts.

UNITED NATIONS EMERGENCY FORCE   A special United Nations peacekeeping force, established in 1955, to prevent local disputes from erupting into armed conflict.

UNITED NATIONS GENERAL ASSEMBLY   The primary forum within the United Nations for the discussion of international problems.

UNITED NATIONS SECURITY COUNCIL   The principal peacekeeping organ of the United Nations.

WARSAW PACT   A regional military alliance, now extant, created by the Soviet Union and its Eastern bloc allies in 1955 to provide a united military command.

WORLD GOVERNMENT   A single supreme global political authority to promote peace and reduce conflict.

Chapter 17

Arms Control and Disarmament

Article 17.1.   STARTing Over

Adam Garfinkle contends that the adoption of the START Treaty was assured in late 1989, when the Soviets dropped their opposition to the Strategic Defense Initiative. In the author's view, START represents a major step forward, in that it is the first nuclear arms agreement to reduce nuclear weapons, a goal which was unrealized by the SALT I and SALT II Treaties. In the past, public debate has centered around the issue of strategic nuclear deterrence. Experts were divided over the significance of the existing ballistic counterforce imbalance, which is what gave rise to the "window of opportunity" thesis. In arguing the merits of START, Garfinkle concludes that, in the end, both its supporters and opponents must answer two fundamental questions: Does a reduced likelihood of war, presumably owing to the benefits of START, compensate for a reduced ability to wage a war in the event that deterrence fails? And does a reduction in relative capabilities lead to a better or worse redefinition of America's strategic doctrine?

STARTing Over

—Adam Garfinkle

EVER SINCE THE Soviet concession on SDI at Jackson Hole, Wyoming in mid-September 1989, expectations for a reasonably quick completion of a START Treaty have run very high. Judging from the pace of negotiations so far in 1990, these expectations are justified. In all likelihood, sometime this year the Bush administration will set a completed treaty before the Senate for ratification.

This rapid progress has struck most people as a wonderfully good thing and it is not hard to see why. START would be the first strategic nuclear arms agreement to reduce nuclear weapons, an achievement ardently promised but left unrequited in both SALT I and SALT II Treaties. START would also be seen as adding critical momentum to the improving state of relations between the superpowers—an appearance of no small polit-

ical importance to both Gorbachev and Bush.

But a closer look raises other possibilities. Even if completing an agreement turns out to be relatively easy, securing ratification may not be. Intoxicating as the present U.S.-Soviet mood may be, it cannot divert scrutiny from anything as critical as a major agreement on strategic weapons. The START ratification process will not resemble the casual cakewalk over the INF Treaty in early 1988. To the contrary, the administration is headed into a political hornet's nest of debate about strategic doctrine and programs. Indeed, despite vast changes in the last decade, START's ratification may resemble nothing so much as the SALT II ratification process of 1979.

Here We Go Again?

IT IS NOW standard political wisdom that SALT II was sacrificed on the altar of Washington politics. Attacks from both the Left and Right on the treaty, and related disputes over other issues such as the

Adam Garfinkle is coordinator of the Political Studies Program at the Foreign Policy Research Institute and contributing editor of the institute's journal, *ORBIS*.

size and composition of the defense budget, were too much for a weak Carter administration to parry. The result was a debacle. The Senate refused to ratify SALT II, and to avoid political embarrassment during the year before a presidential election, President Carter removed the treaty from consideration, using the Soviet invasion of Afghanistan as a pretext.

But politics alone did not kill SALT II. The main reason that SALT II was not ratified is that between the time negotiations began in earnest in 1974 and the time they concluded in 1979, a sea change had occurred in U.S. strategic doctrinal thinking and in U.S. views of the concordance (or lack thereof) between U.S. and Soviet conceptions of arms control and strategic liability. Had SALT II been ready for the Senate in 1975, or even 1977, it would have passed easily. But by 1979, new technological developments pertaining mainly to counterforce ballistic accuracies and new intelligence about how the Soviet Union was deploying that technology convinced a majority of observers that key U.S. assumptions about the very nature of strategic stability were no longer valid.

Specifically, Soviet deployments beyond numerical parity that had been thought to compensate for general American technological superiority were now seen instead as components of a war-winning first strike counterforce doctrine. If that were so, then post-SALT I expectations—that after the achievement of rough parity, the arms race would find a natural equipoise—were unwarranted. Also put in doubt was the assumption that Soviet accession to the ABM Treaty reflected a strategic viewpoint consanguine with that of the United States. Instead, the belief gained ground that Soviet interest in the ABM Treaty had more to do with limiting U.S. technological momentum and with guaranteeing a free ride for new Soviet counterforce systems.

This huge conceptual shift doomed SALT II. The Carter administration, whose own views on these issues were diverse, could not argue for the treaty with one voice. Officials were thus caught between the floors, so to speak, as the doctrinal debate evolved, and the deal went down.

Much has changed over the last ten years, but some things have not. In 1979, U.S. foreign and security policies were in deep malaise, while an aggressive Soviet geopolitical offensive and arms build-up proceeded unabated. In 1990, Western fortunes are waxing and it is the Soviet empire that finds itself in deep trouble. This shift gives rise to at least two ironies about the politics of arms control.

First, while improved U.S.-Soviet relations have opened up a host of opportunities for arms control, the reasons for pursuing them are both different and diminished. The new U.S.-Soviet detente, built as it is on Soviet weaknesses, has made arms control politically less important in the United States. In the popular mind, the Soviets are less a threat than a defeated basket case deserving of U.S. political advice and economic charity. The popular impulse, therefore, is to ask: Why split hairs counting warheads when peace is breaking out all over? So while agreements may be easier to get, we have less need of them politically than we have had for some decades.

Second, the conceptual divide about deterrence, strategic doctrine, and arms control that shaped the SALT II debate will return, but in a new form. Adherents of minimal deterrence who believe that only a few weapons are needed to deter one's opponents can now seize upon the calm of the early 1990s to argue that even if Soviet strategic doctrine once called for aggressive preemptive counterforce strikes, it does so no longer. Instead of "the empire isn't evil," we now hear "the empire isn't *still* evil." Such advocates will insist that Soviet doctrine is now reformulated as a "defensive strategy" in fact as well as in theory; that continuing Soviet counterforce deployments would cease if only ours did; and that the strategic balance itself has become virtually irrelevant.

One might have thought that we would have learned our strategic lessons by now, and that these old arguments would have been settled at last by experience and common sense. But some things never change. Democracies have short memories and American democracy, in particular, when allowed by normal times to be itself, has an almost unlimited appetite for circumscribing its military forces and commitments. The irony is that in seemingly calmer times, vigilance is undermined and exactly the kinds of "soft" positions that got us into trouble in the first place can return. And so, the doves are back, arguing for a general demobilization of deterrent U.S. military power. Such thinking followed virtually every other war the United States has fought; why should the end of the Cold War be different?

This is not to suggest that the Soviet Union itself remains unchanged. When the Soviets say that they *no longer* think a nuclear war can be won, they probably mean it. But the Soviet military has not abandoned counterforce for purposes of damage limitation. Damage limitation does not require the mix and size of forces that a war-winning strategy requires, and that is good. But the strategic balance has not become irrelevant; a nuclear war has not become impossible; nuclear weapons still cast political shadows; and deterrence has not somehow become self-regulating.

Prelude to Cacophony

ONE WAY OF thinking about the coming debate is to examine the travails of a certain infamous phrase: "the window of vulnerability." The phrase works like a catalyst: dropped into any argument about strategic affairs and arms control, it soon separates any intellectual mixture into its basic axiomatic assumptions. The notion also serves as a kind of transparent palimpsest; through it one can trace the evolution and debasing of a variety of arguments and the partisan designs of their advocates.

Since at least the mid–1970s, Americans concerned with arms control have been divided about basic premises concerning strategic nuclear deterrence. At the heart of this disagreement lies the disputed significance of the ballistic counterforce imbalance, depending in turn on disputes about Soviet strategic doctrine and policy. The imbalance is what gave rise to the "window of vulnerability" thesis itself. Even to refer to it is to conjure the strategic divide that separates one school of American strategic thinkers from another.

In plain English, the difference comes down to whether it is more effective to deter war by credibly threatening to destroy Soviet cities and people no matter what they do or when they do it; or whether it is more effective to confront the Soviets with the prospect that their relative military situation would be far worse after a nuclear exchange than before it. The former approach only requires that the United States have enough fairly accurate, but survivable, weapons systems capable of targeting enough Soviet cities to inflict "unacceptable damage," however that may be defined. The latter one requires a substantially larger number of survivable systems capable of accurate attacks against a range of Soviet military assets.

These doctrinal questions remain unsettled, and politics will again shape the arms control debate. For those who adhere to the more minimal view of deterrence, SALT II was defensible from a military perspective. For those who believe deterrence rests on more exacting strategic capabilities, SALT II was either a bad deal or a meaningless one. This dispute still matters. Those who liked SALT II will like START even if it leaves the relative Soviet advantage in prompt hard-target ballistic systems unchanged, or even if it enhances it. Those who opposed SALT II, other things being more or less equal, will also oppose START if it does not redress the counterforce imbalance.

As before, doctrinal disagreement will mix with peripheral but emotional arguments about the size of the defense budget and the level and types of strategic modernization to be sought. Clearly, if the administration cannot find a way to pull enough liberal Democrats behind its preferred modernization program and is forced to settle for less, it will lose conservatives when it comes time to count votes for START. And the collapse of communism notwithstanding, it still only takes a third of the Senate plus one to spoil the party.

Your "Window" or Mine?

IN ORDER to argue that the strategic balance is essentially irrelevant, many Democrats will insist that the counterforce imbalance is a bogeyman from bygone days. What vocabulary will they choose? They will claim that the "window of vulnerability" has been closed, and that President Bush's own adviser on national security, General Brent Scowcroft, was himself the one who closed it in April 1983 with the Scowcroft Commission report.

The assertion that the Scowcroft Commission closed the "window of vulnerability" in 1983 is one we are bound to hear repeatedly as soon as the treaty is completed and the White House begins to circle the wagons for the ratification debate. Indeed, this notion has become an indelible part of the Common Knowledge, but, like many other aspects of the Common Knowledge, it is quite wrong.

What treaty opponents said in 1979 was that SALT II would countenance the theoretical vulnerability of the *land-based* leg of the U.S. strategic triad. In its original formulation, the "window of vulnerability" never meant that the vulnerability of U.S. land-based missiles was tantamount to the literal vulnerability of the entire U.S. strategic force. But because the land-based force was the only leg of the triad capable of a counterforce response to a Soviet first-strike, its vulnerability was deemed crisis-unstable (such is the jargon), unhealthy for the credibility of extended deterrence, and therefore worth worrying about.

The original "window of vulnerability" idea was thus part of a serious debate about the dynamics of the then-new mutual counterforce strategic world. What were the implications of counterforce inequality—even amid overall rough numerical parity—on crisis dynamics? Would a superpower with a counterforce advantage be inclined toward great risk-taking at lower levels of violence? SALT II opponents had no monopoly of wisdom on these questions, and doubtless some of the fears they expressed ten years ago were exaggerated. Nevertheless, the problems encapsulated by the phrase "window of vulnerability" were real and so difficult that we are discussing them still.

Clearly, the "window of vulnerability" was shorthand for one approach to the bedeviling issues of stability in a counterforce imbalanced world, *not* a simple-minded notion that the Soviet Union would initiate a nuclear war "out of the blue" just because Minuteman was theoretically vulnerable. Opponents of SALT II never claimed that nuclear war was at hand because of the proposed treaty or for any other reason; such fearsome tactics instead became a staple of the Left and the nuclear freeze movement. SALT II was not undone, as some latter day pundits would have it, by a band of hysterical Cold Warriors whose views had not changed since the days of the 1948 Berlin crisis. On the contrary, it was the views of proponents of finite deterrence that were stuck in the rut, ignoring the implications of the on-going revolution in strategic technology.

The core argument over SALT II, revolving around the "window of vulnerability," was a serious one, but a funny thing did happen to the "window" on the way to the Reagan administration. President Reagan, as is well known, lacked a solid grasp of such esoteric matters; his strengths lay in other domains. One of them was political savvy, so when he came upon the evocative notion of a "window of vulnerability" through his advisers in the 1980 campaign, he took it with him into the presidential election season. As often happens with complex ideas spun out into a partisan environment, nuance gave way to the requisites of polemics. The "window of vulnerability" exited the campaign a simple-minded caricature. Suddenly, the vulnerability of Minuteman was tantamount to decisive Soviet military superiority as construed in the flattest and most primitive sense of the phrase.

Once this had happened, the "window of vulnerability" became easy prey for those who wanted to discount the very real problem it had originally described and who wanted to frustrate the Reagan administration's plans for modernizing U.S. land-based strategic forces. This explains how much of the erroneous Common Knowledge on this matter came about. It also helps to explain the strange notions about what the Scowcroft Commission did and did not do to the famed "window." As a result, the partisan battle over the "window of vulnerability" as a piece of strategic vocabulary was waged continuously between 1980 and April 1983, and when the Scowcroft Commission report was issued, it set off a stampede into print by those committed observers who were determined to make the report mean what they wanted it to mean. In the process, the truth was trampled still further.

The Scowcroft Commission report affirmed the vulnerability of the land-based leg of the strategic triad, and it did say early on that the vulnerability of U.S. land-based forces was not the same as the vulnerability of the entire U.S. strategic triad. But, as noted earlier, this was hardly news, for SALT II's opponents had never made such claims. Nevertheless, a lot of people, seeing what they wanted to see, threw down the report and picked up their pens. To give one of many examples of what happened next, the senior editors of the *New Republic* wrote in May 1983 that the report

. . . should be satisfying to certain critics of the Administration's strategic thinking as it should be embarrassing to the Administration. Some of the Administration's most fundamental strategic axioms—which the president has put to good political use, in the form of such slogans as "the window of vulnerability"—do not survive the Scowcroft Commission's scrutiny. . . . The vulnerability of America's land-based forces, in other words, is not the vulnerability of America. Or, to put it differently, we, without a first-strike force, are deterring them, and they, with a first-strike force, are deterred.

The scribblers did not read far enough. The Scowcroft Commission *supported* the fundamental strategic axioms of the Reagan administration; it affirmed rather eloquently the "window of vulnerability" argument as it existed in pre-Reagan 1979. If the window were really closed, why would the commission have insisted that the United Stated develop a mobile missile? Even though it is more than seven years old, it is worth quoting the report at some length because so many people seem never actually to have read it:

Effective deterrence of any Soviet temptation to threaten or launch a massive conventional or a limited nuclear war. . . requires us to have a comparable ability to destroy Soviet military targets. . . . A one-sided strategic condition in which the Soviet Union could effectively destroy the whole range of strategic targets in the United States, but we could not effectively destroy a similar range of targets in the Soviet Union, would be extremely unstable over the long run. Such a situation could tempt the Soviets, in a crisis, to feel they could successfully threaten or even undertake conventional or limited nuclear aggression in the hope that the United States would lack a fully effective response. A one-sided condition of this sort would clearly not serve the cause of peace.

In the report's conclusions, the critical issue of extended deterrence was addressed:

The serious imbalance between the Soviet's massive ability to destroy hardened land-based military targets with their ballistic missile force and our lack of such a capability must be redressed promptly. Our ability to assure our allies that we have the capability and will to stand with them, with whatever forces are necessary. . . is in question as long as this imbalance exists. . . . [W]e must have a credible capacity for controlled, prompt, limited attack on hard targets ourselves. . . . Consequently, in the interest of the alliance as a whole, we cannot safely permit a situation to continue wherein the Soviets have the capability promptly to destroy a range of hardened military targets and we do not.

Now, that is exactly what Paul Nitze and Eugene Rostow and Alexander Haig and Senators Henry Jackson and John Tower meant by a "window of vulnerability" during the SALT II hearings, as even a cursory review of their testimonies and statements from 1978 to 1979 makes plain. The Scowcroft Commission never closed the "window of vulnerability"—it only closed the ill-constructed shutters affixed by the Great Communicator, who was, in this instance at least, a "window of vulnerability" in his own right.

Closing the Window of Vulnerability

THE ORIGINAL "window of vulnerability" is still open, at least judging by the usual numbers and ratios. For all the Reagan administration's huffing and puffing, the ratio of Soviet to U.S. counterforce warheads actually *grew* over the eight years of Reagan's tenure. While the United States has fumbled around for more than ten years trying to bring to full operational capacity a new ICBM, arguing inconclusively between deploying a mobile MIRVed MX or a single-warheaded Midgetman, the Soviet Union—poverty, glasnost, perestroika, wild-eyed Lithuanians, and all—has designed, developed, and deployed *both* the SS–25 and SS–24. In addition, it has deployed what Moscow calls a modified version of the monstrous SS–18, but which is in fact qualitatively improved to the point that it is in essence a third new Soviet ICBM.

These three additions contribute considerably to the already daunting Soviet strategic advantage. Even with the 50 percent reduction in heavy ICBMs required by START, the Soviets will be able to maintain, indeed improve in relative terms, their prompt hard-target capabilities. Increased mobility, combined with improvements in missile guidance, will result in a more accurate, survivable, and dangerous Soviet strategic force. This effort is not born of absent-mindedness. On the contrary, now that the Soviet security perimeter in Eastern Europe has collapsed, and given the enormous expense of conventional forces, nuclear weapons are more important to the Soviet sense of security and superpower status than ever before. Soviet doctrinal adjustments notwithstanding, this continuing build-up simply must not go without an answer, and START, no matter how benign it might (or might not) be in other ways, cannot substitute for one.

Reducing warheads by half, even down to numerically equal levels, would not thereby create equal capabilities and equal risks that are conducive to deterrence. The mix of weapons would remain significantly different between the two powers, yielding different operational capabilities favoring the Soviet Union. There would also be two other related and important asymmetries. One is that if war begins, the Soviets will start it; the other is that, overall, the number of targets inside the Soviet Union is larger and better defended that ours. If available U.S. retaliatory warheads diminish dramatically relative to the Soviet target set—which includes some 3,000 buried and hardened command posts—we will find ourselves unable to do what our strategic integrated operating plan (SIOP) would have us do. We must then confront two questions: Does a reduced likelihood of war, thanks to the presumed political benefits of START, compensate for a reduced ability to prosecute war should deterrence fail? And does a diminution in relative capabilities drive us for better or worse to a redefinition of our strategic doctrine? These are crucial questions, and no ratification debate will be able—or should be allowed—to avoid them.

Arms control cannot substitute for military competition; it is rather *a part* of military competition. If the Bush administration tries to ignore these questions, those who led the attack on SALT II will lead an attack on START. The administration must find a way to modernize and reconfigure U.S. strategic forces effectively within a START-constrained context, or it will be undercut from the Right, perhaps decisively so.

If the administration does tend to business, however, it will face even stronger attacks from the Left. These will be easier to manage, but to do so, General Scowcroft and his associates will need to invest in a couple of cases of Windex to restore the "window of vulnerability" to its pristine condition circa April 1983.

Article 17.2. Is the Soviet Union Prepared for Peace?

The Soviet Empire has collapsed, and its economy is in a shambles. President Gorbachev has said on myriad occasions that little progress will be made until the Soviet Union and the United States end the arms race, which is draining the resources of both nations. Despite Gorbachev's assertions, Moscow has yet to drastically reduce its military expenditures, in spite of the projected savings. Although Soviet officials recognize the eventual economic gains of disarmament, they realize that any short-term benefits will be offset by the long-term costs associated with destroying existing weapons systems, verifying arms agreements, demobilizing and housing soldiers, and reorienting the Soviet economy toward domestic purposes. At present, the Soviets are preoccupied with their own internal problems. However, conversion to a peace-time economy will, in the long run, strengthen the Soviet economy, as well as encourage other countries to more seriously consider alternatives to the arms race.

IS THE SOVIET UNION PREPARED FOR PEACE?

Cuts in military spending could help save the nation's economy, but the transition to a peacetime footing may not be as easy as it seems.

BY MICHAEL G. RENNER

Five years into Mikhail Gorbachev's top-down transformation of the U.S.S.R., Soviet citizens' expectations of better living standards are skyrocketing past the capacity of an economy that could barely keep up with less extravagant desires. Store shelves remain bare, serious social needs are going unmet, and tempers are rising. The reasons for the malaise of the Soviet economy are numerous, but among the most significant is the lingering burden of excessive military spending.

President Gorbachev has stated repeatedly that ending the arms race with the United States is a prerequisite to invigorating the Soviet economy. At the 28th Communist Party Congress held in early July, Foreign Minister Eduard Shevardnadze claimed that "in the current five-year period, the sum-total peaceful dividend...can make 240 billion to 250 billion rubles." At official exchange rates, this would be equivalent to $380 to $400 billion, clearly a significant infusion of resources. Yet, so far, the fruits of Gorbachev's disarmament initiatives are not apparent.

Moscow faces a dilemma: While the eventual economic gains of disarmament promise to be sizable, they will no doubt be diminished in the near-term by costs associated with destroying military hardware, verifying arms treaties, demobilizing and housing soldiers, and reorienting military enterprises toward civilian objectives and retraining employees for that purpose. According to Valentin Smyslov, a high-ranking official with *Gosplan,* the state planning agency, the retooling of factories alone may cost some 40 billion rubles ($64 billion) over the next five years.

The Superpower Burden

The political liberalization under Gorbachev has spawned a fierce debate over the burden of heavy military spending. However, determining the extent of this burden is difficult, even in the heady days of *glasnost.* Soviet leaders say they spent 77.3 billion rubles (about $120 billion) on the military in 1989. But certain items—foreign military aid, military space programs, and parts of the defense research and development budgets—almost certainly are excluded from this figure. Additionally, the contribution of labor, machinery, and materials to arms production probably is undervalued to a considerable degree.

Because uncertainty surrounds the size of both the military budget and the total Soviet economy, verifying the relative burden

From *World Watch,* September/October 1990, pp. 11-19. WorldWatch Institute, Washington, D.C. 20036. Reprinted by permission.

217

of defense spending seems an impossible task. If the officially stated numbers are correct, then military outlays absorb about 9 percent of the gross national product (GNP). Estimates by the U.S. Central Intelligence Agency run in the 15 to 17 percent range, but economist Oleg Bogomolev, a member of the Congress of People's Deputies, asserts the real burden is as high as 20 to 25 percent of GNP (the world average is about 6 percent.)

A more telling picture of military spending might emerge by measuring the share of goods and services devoted to military purposes. Unfortunately, complete up-to-date figures are not available. David Holloway of the University of Edinburgh estimated in the early 1980s that one-fifth of the Soviet Union's total industrial output was absorbed by the arms sector, including two-thirds of the aircraft and shipbuilding industries. This is a much higher share than in other industrialized countries. A little over 6 percent of total U.S. economic output went to the military in 1989, although the military portion came to 53 percent in aircraft manufacturing and virtually 100 percent in shipbuilding.

Although the true extent of military spending in the Soviet Union is not clear, it is readily apparent that the country's leaders must shift resources from guns to butter, a process known as economic conversion. Along with the enormous shortage of quality consumer goods, numerous other pressing needs in Soviet society underline the need for such a policy. There is a serious housing shortage. One-third of all schools have no running water, and the Soviet Union has infant mortality and life expectancy rates closer to those of the Third World than the West.

Spending on environmental protection—currently at 1.3 percent of GNP, according to *The Economist* in London—is a pressing need but remains clearly insufficient. By the government's own reckoning some $56 billion will be needed to prevent the complete disappearance of the Aral Sea. Some scientists think double that amount, or roughly the equivalent of one year's military expenditures, will be required. Dealing with the effects of the Chernobyl nuclear accident, meanwhile, is now estimated to cost as much as $46 billion, and perhaps more.

These, of course, are just the two most publicized of the Soviet Union's many ecological disasters.

The easing of Cold War tensions has allowed the Soviets to take the first steps toward rescuing their economy; cutting weapons production and troop deployments will help rein in military spending. According to official statements, by 1991 total military spending will be 14 percent below 1988 levels. Prime Minister Nikolai Ryzhkov has said he expects the military budget to be trimmed by a third to a half by 1997.

Part of the savings derives from the withdrawal from Afghanistan. Unilateral force reductions in Europe amounting to 500,000 troops and 10,000 tanks will free up additional resources. The 1987 Intermediate-Range Nuclear Forces (INF) Treaty with the United States yielded a comparatively small net savings of $480 million, though that sum is large enough to build 30,000 to 40,000 apartments.

The remainder of projected savings in the military budget will come from a 19.5 percent reduction in arms production. Statements by various officials disagree somewhat about the specifics, but it appears that during the first half of the 1990s, tank production is to be cut by 50 percent, aircraft by 12 percent, helicopters by 25 or perhaps even 60 percent, and ammunition by 20 to 30 percent.

Although channeling these savings into civilian use would do wonders for the cash-short Soviet economy, much hard work remains before any gains will come. Military hardware needs to be adapted for peaceful purposes where possible; demobilized soldiers must be reintegrated into society; and, most important, military production facilities must be retooled for civilian use. In addition, supply-related and financial arrangements among individual factories (and the ministries to which they belong) need to be recast. These difficult steps, central to the process of economic conversion, have only just begun.

As it embarks on the conversion process, the Soviet Union joins China as the only other major power to do so in the post-World War II era China headed down this road a decade ago (see "Swords Into Consumer Goods," *World Watch*, July/August 1989).

Military Recycling

Options for adapting military hardware to civilian applications are often limited. In some cases, pieces of equipment might be refashioned and reused, in others, valuable components, such as engines, electronics equipment, or precious metals, might be salvaged and recycled. Of 10,000 battle tanks that are being withdrawn unilaterally, half are to be destroyed, some used for training purposes, and the rest converted to bulldozers and other equipment for civilian purposes. Meanwhile, Kranlod—an Odessa-based joint venture with West Germany—has begun to transform several hundred launchers for the SS-20 missiles banned by the INF accord into self-propelled hoisting cranes.

Unilateral military cutbacks turned some military equipment into surplus. Supplies worth a half-billion rubles, including motor vehicles, ships, transistors, and navigational equipment, were put up for sale to the public in 1989. Some 60 military transport planes, roughly 10 percent of the total fleet, have been made available for civilian tasks.

Unfortunately, most military hardware simply has no use in the civilian world. Scrapping missiles, tanks, and warplanes will save on maintenance and operating costs, but the expense associated with their destruction, treaty verification measures, and, in many cases, environmental cleanups takes a substantial bite out of any savings. In any event, the cost to society of building these weapons in the first place cannot be fully recouped.

Reintegrating Soldiers

Moscow's decision to demobilize 500,000 troops has led to some transitional problems. Conscripted soldiers generally return to their civilian jobs without much difficulty, but problems arise in reintegrating officers into civilian society, primarily because they need jobs and housing. By the end of the year, some 100,000 officers and 50,000 *praporshchiki* (non-commissioned officers) will have been discharged—primarily those of advanced age, judged incompetent or unmotivated, and those serving as reserve officers.

A number of measures have been taken to smooth the transition of demobilized soldiers to civilian life, including the provision of higher pensions. The Ministry of Defense and *Goskomtrud* (the State Committee for

Early Soviet attempts at conversion produced washing machines that cost twice as much as civilian models and television sets that exploded and caught fire.

Labor) have also established a joint retraining program; in conjunction with local authorities, they are responsible for job placement. It is too early to tell, however, whether these programs are working as intended.

Perhaps the most critical aspect of successfully decommissioning officers is finding housing. According to Alexei Izyumov of the Institute of the U.S.A. and Canada in Moscow, more than 20,000 officers' families had no permanent homes even before the current troop cuts, and the Defense Ministry will be able to provide no more than 7,500 apartments during 1990-91. The housing shortage is particularly acute in Moscow and other large cities in the European part of the Soviet Union, where most discharged officers wish to return.

These problems will soon balloon. Gorbachev has already agreed to reduce Soviet troops stationed in Europe from the current level of 565,000 to 195,000. Soviet forces are in the process of pulling out of Czechoslovakia and Hungary. They still remain in Poland and East Germany. But with the Warsaw Pact disintegrating rapidly, Moscow may have no troops left in Eastern Europe by the turn of the century. East Germany used to foot the bill for the 360,000 Soviet soldiers stationed there, and West Germany agreed to shoulder that burden, at over $700 million a year. But once these troops return home over the next four years, Moscow will have to pay for their upkeep.

If the soldiers are successfully reintegrated

into Soviet society, they can be a boon to an economy characterized by continuous labor shortages. If the effort fails, however, there could be serious political implications. In January 1960, for example, then-Premier Nikita Khrushchev announced a troop reduction of 1.2 million soldiers, coming on top of an earlier demobilization. Yet the policy was implemented with little preparation or regard for those affected. The military's dissatisfaction with the entire undertaking was an important factor in Khrushchev's downfall in 1964. The Gorbachev leadership is well aware that misgivings within the armed forces, of which there are already indications, could lead the military to oppose additional reductions.

Missiles into Baby Carriages

The most crucial element of conversion concerns the retooling of factories that produce war matériel. Successful retooling involves several steps: identifying alternative civilian products, conducting engineering studies to determine the feasibility of producing these goods, retraining employees and refashioning machinery where needed, organizing adequate supplies of energy and materials, and preparing marketing studies.

The factories that once produced missiles now proscribed by the INF accord have shifted part of their capacity to civilian production. The Votkinsk machine tool plant in the Udmurt Autonomous Republic, the Petropavlovsk facility in Kazakhstan, and a third factory in Volgograd are now manufacturing metal-cutting machines, drilling rigs and other oil industry equipment, washing machines, bicycles, and even baby carriages. Several missile design laboratories have also been reoriented toward civilian work, including the development of a rocket to carry meteorological equipment into orbit.

At Votkinsk, some 5 percent of the total number of skilled workers were retrained. Due to high production targets, the changeover to civilian output occurred without loss of employment. While the facility had already been involved in civilian production to some degree, the adjustment would have been smoother if conversion planning had been done in advance. To compensate for a drop in the plant's profits (and thus in its fund for wages and fringe benefits), the gov-

ernment allocated extra money during the transition period of 1988-90.

Retooling for Peace

The Soviet military sector has a long history of producing both military and civilian goods. The civilian share of military industry enterprises' output has doubled to about 40 percent between 1965 and today (see Table 1). Although official Soviet statements are contradictory, it appears that the defense industry now produces nearly 8 percent of all Soviet consumer goods. In 1989, some 345 military plants and 200 defense-related scientific research institutes and design bureaus were involved to varying degrees in civilian production.

According to plans approved by the Council of Ministers, the Kremlin cabinet answerable to Gorbachev, the portion of defense industries' output devoted to civilian purposes is to rise from the current 40 percent to 50 percent in 1991 and more than 60 percent by 1995. Put differently, the country's overall production of civilian goods is to rise by 5 percent through these measures. For 1990, a rather paltry sum of $6.4 billion has been budgeted to facilitate the changeover.

The additional civilian output of military enterprises will be targeted primarily toward the food-processing industry. Nearly half

Table1.

Share of Total Output of Selected Civilian Goods Produced by Military Industry Enterprises, 1965-1988				
	1965	**1975**	**1985**	**1988**
			(percent)	
TVs, Radios, VCRs, Cameras	100	100	100	100
Sewing Machines	na	na	100[1]	100
Tape Recorders	95	95	95	98
Vacuum Cleaners	49	46	75[1]	77
Washing Machines	41	32	27	69
Motorcycles & Scooters	73	68	63	61
Tramcars	72	65	60[2]	na
Refrigerators	48	48	48[2]	na
Bicycles	44	39	40	45
Watches	12	11	19	22
Tractors	13	14	15	na
Metal-cutting Machine Tools	14[3]	14	13	na
Passenger Cars	11[3]	10	12	na

[1] 1987 [2] 1980 [3] 1970

Sources: Julian M. Cooper, *The Scale of Output of Civilian Products by Enterprises of the Soviet Defence Industry*, CREES Discussion Paper, University of Birmingham, 1988 (for 1965-1985 data); John Tedstrom, *Is the Contribution of the Defense Complex to Civilian Production Growing?*, Report on the USSR, June 16, 1989 (for 1987-1988 data).

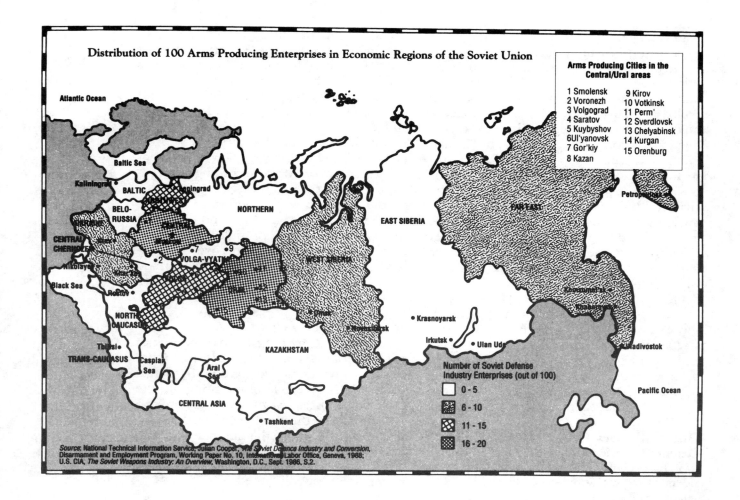

Distribution of 100 Arms Producing Enterprises in Economic Regions of the Soviet Union

Arms Producing Cities in the Central/Ural areas

1 Smolensk
2 Voronezh
3 Volgograd
4 Saratov
5 Kuybyshov
6 Ul'yanovsk
7 Gor'kiy
8 Kazan
9 Kirov
10 Votkinsk
11 Perm'
12 Sverdlovsk
13 Chelyabinsk
14 Kurgan
15 Orenburg

Number of Soviet Defense Industry Enterprises (out of 100)

☐ 0 - 5
▨ 6 - 10
▩ 11 - 15
▦ 16 - 20

Source: National Technical Information Service; Julian Cooper, *The Soviet Defence Industry and Conversion,* Disarmament and Employment Program, Working Paper No. 10, International Labor Office, Geneva, 1988; U.S. CIA, *The Soviet Weapons Industry: An Overview,* Washington, D.C., Sept. 1986, S.2.

the $59 billion of planned new equipment deliveries to the food industry under the investment plan for 1988-95 is to be provided by defense industry enterprises. The military sector has also been directed to produce $11 to $13 billion worth of goods for light industry, as well as to increase the output of construction materials, medical equipment, and plumbing supplies.

No More Lethal TVs

If previous experience is any guide, however, simply increasing the civilian share of military industries, without proper reorientation, is likely to spawn price and quality problems. Earlier Soviet attempts at conversion produced washing machines that cost twice as much as civilian models and television sets that exploded and caught fire. Similar problems exist today.

So far, the items selected for production have not always been well-matched with the factories targeted for conversion. Of 585

consumer goods scheduled to be manufactured in 1988-89 by all military factories, only 126 were successfully produced. The target for 1989-90 was scaled down to 126 products, but by the end of 1989 only 23 of these were actually being produced.

Part of the explanation is that the conversion endeavor is proceeding hastily, more improvised than properly planned and prepared. There are efforts at the factory level and attempts to direct the process from above, with the latter tending to neglect local conditions and capabilities in deciding what alternative products individual military enterprises should produce.

Defense industries, for their part, are accustomed to working with little regard for the costs involved, a practice that if simply transferred to the civilian sector could have disastrous results. Soviet observers agree that the civilian goods produced by military firms are often too expensive for their customers. As long as these factories remain in the orbit of the defense bureaucracy, some critics charge, they will never accord priority to civilian needs and principles.

Despite these dangers, the Soviet leadership has decided to enlist the services of the military industry (with its superior access to skilled labor, materials, equipment, and technologies) in its campaign to boost the production of consumer goods. The civilian industry is seen as too backward and hamstrung to realize the hoped-for rapid improvement in living standards. Thus, the civilian Ministry of Machine-Building for the Light and Food Industries was disbanded in 1988 and many of its 260 enterprises transferred to defense ministries. While it is uncertain whether this quick-fix approach will yield the expected results, there is a definite danger that it will backfire.

A debate is currently under way between those who want to keep the military sector as a separate "economy within the economy" and retain the capability to switch back to defense production, and those who favor its breakup. The outcome is crucial to the nature of Soviet economic conversion.

Out of Military Orbit?
Defense factories still have little incentive to switch to civilian production. Many engineers, along with blue-collar workers, see civilian production as clearly secondary in priority, temporary in nature, or imposed on them. As an inducement for defense factories to produce more civilian goods, the Council of Ministers decreed in September 1988 that factories could retain profits from above-quota production of consumer goods during 1989 and 1990.

Perhaps more important than ideological preference is the fact that wages, as well as housing, child care, and other social benefits available to military industry employees and their families are closely linked to the fortunes of defense factories. At least in some cases, profit margins and wages have dropped as factories have moved from military to civilian production. Unless the situation is remedied, it may sow the seeds of resentment, and possibly resistance to conversion. On the other hand, military enterprises may seek to compensate for lower profits by charging higher prices for their civilian products, endangering the success of this transformation.

At the same time, however, Alexei Izyumov argues that remaining in the military orbit is becoming less attractive for leaders of military-industry enterprises, especially now that the defense establishment is being put on a self-financing basis. Some seem prepared to accept the loss of privileges in return for greater independence from the constraints and pitfalls of rigid centralized planning.

Likewise, the military sector has lost a good deal of its earlier attraction for the non-managerial work force, according to Izyumov. During the past few years, virtually all of the superior wage and fringe benefits have evaporated for the rank and file, while the negative aspects of military industry employment—rigid discipline, overtime, unhealthy conditions, strict quality control, and limitations on travel abroad—have remained in place.

Wanted: Military *Glasnost*
Many Soviet analysts agree that the lack of military *glasnost* is a serious obstacle to successful conversion. According to Sergei Blagovolin, an economist writing in the magazine *Moscow News*, there are still no reliable data on the number of military enterprises, their location, the number of people employed, worker skills, the quantity and characteristics of the equipment, and the raw materials and supplies used.

---

*O*f *585 consumer goods scheduled to be manufactured in 1988-89 by Soviet military factories, only 126 were successfully produced.*

A sample of 100 arms-producing enterprises, assembled by Julian Cooper of the University of Birmingham in Great Britain, sheds some light on the regional distribution of military factories. He shows that the overwhelming majority of these enterprises are located within the Russian republic—

particularly in the Urals, in the central economic region around Moscow, in the Volga region, and around Leningrad (see Figure 1, which shows the distribution of factories in Cooper's sample by republic and, within the Russian Republic, by economic region). But much more far-reaching and detailed information is needed to assess both the problems and the potential of conversion.

The potentially most serious impediment to conversion is the lack of any adequate system to account for the enormous resources devoted to military purposes. As Paddy Ashdown, a member of the British Parliament, put it recently: "The army simply said what it wanted and industry supplied it. There were no overall budget limits, no effective costings system, and only the most rudimentary methods of cost control."

The revitalization of the Soviet economy depends crucially on a successful conversion of defense industries. But that success is in turn inextricably linked to the fate of Gorbachev's *perestroika*. Only with a meaningful set of costs and prices, rather than an arbitrary and unaccountable bureaucratic system, can a realistic conversion program be created. Reliable indicators are needed to assess the military's real drain on the economy and the possibilities for converting defense industries to civilian uses. Without such information, it may be impossible to decide whether to convert a given facility or close it and start from scratch, or to determine the success of any conversion undertaking.

To date, Soviet conversion has proceeded on an ad hoc basis. For example, the government's decision in early 1989 to slash the volume of arms production came out of the blue, leaving military factory managers with neither sufficient orders nor an alternative plan. There has been no overall integration of measures to promote greater civilian production.

To move beyond this haphazard stage, a National Commission to Promote Conversion has been formed—with representatives from *Gosplan*, the military-related ministries, the Academy of Sciences, and various universities—to design a proper long-term program. In addition, a draft economic conversion law has been submitted to the Supreme Soviet that, among other things, would provide a two-year allowance and a job information system for military workers who lose their jobs.

Although current conversion plans are directed from the top, there is growing public discussion and appreciation of the concept, and Soviet conversion proponents are seeking to share their insights with their counterparts abroad.

Gorbachev's Appeal

President Gorbachev's foreign and military policies have so far yielded far more political than economic dividends. While the domestic benefits of trimming the Soviet military apparatus will materialize only in the medium- or perhaps even the long-term, the country needs to mobilize considerable funds now to smooth the social and economic effects of disarmament.

The success of conversion depends on more than technical factors, as crucial as they may be. Just as important is the constellation of political concerns. Gorbachev needs to convince the military leadership that his unilateral military concessions are yielding

---

Soldiers successfully reintegrated into Soviet society could be a boon to an economy characterized by continuous labor shortages.

---

returns that make the gamble worthwhile. In other words, he needs tangible evidence that less military spending and fewer weapons do not translate into less security. And he needs to transform guns into butter fast, or else the rising tide of unmet expectations may drown his entire undertaking.

As open debate has increasingly replaced old taboos, the Soviets have become preoccupied with internal matters. But while the fate of Soviet conversion is of obvious domestic relevance, there is an important international dimension as well. The Soviet case is important because the country is a global leader in arms production. It demonstrates that conversion is a realistic option, even in a world that has barely begun to consider alternatives to the arms race seriously. If the West follows suit with its own demilitarization and conversion measures, the arms race may at long last be transformed into a "peace race." ●

Michael G. Renner, a senior researcher at the Worldwatch Institute, specializes in disarmament issues. He is the author of Worldwatch Paper 96, Swords Into Plowshares: Converting to a Peace Economy.

Chapter **18**

The Limits of United Nations Action

Article 18.1.   The U.N. in a New World Order

This article surveys the changing role of the United Nations, concluding that recent international developments have underscored the importance of the U.N. in a new world order. Clearly, the gulf war demonstrated that the United Nations has become increasingly effective in guaranteeing the security of countries through collective measures. For example, in responding to the Iraqi invasion of Kuwait, the Security Council showed itself capable of taking swift, decisive action. Although U.N. calls for sanctions were not adequately tested, the mere fact that it could even agree on such sanctions—and take steps to enforce them—evidences its new resolve. Moreover, by approving the use of force, the Security Council eventually secured compliance with all of its major resolutions. The United Nations has demonstrated that it possesses the power not just to preserve the status quo but to improve situations for the better. This realization should strengthen its ability to deter future conflicts, thereby making actual enforcement or peacekeeping less necessary. Still, it should not be assumed that the United Nations will automatically be able to play a similar role in future conflicts, as that will depend upon maintaining some kind of shared interests on the part of the five permanent members of the Security Council.

Bruce Russett
James S. Sutterlin

THE U.N. IN A NEW WORLD ORDER

The new world order envisioned by Presidents Bush and Gorbachev would be founded on the rule of law and on the principle of collective security. That principle necessarily entails the possibility of military enforcement measures by the United Nations. Twice in its history the Security Council has authorized such action. The first instance was in the Korean War in 1950; the second was in the Persian Gulf in 1990. More occasions are likely to follow.

The U.N. Charter gives the Security Council the authority "to maintain or restore international peace and security," and to enforce the will of the council on a state that has broken the peace. Use of military force by the council for these purposes was foreseen by the founders of the United Nations. Indeed it was seen almost half a century ago as an essential element in the world order that the United Nations was intended to

Bruce Russett is Dean Acheson Professor of International Relations and Political Science at Yale University. James S. Sutterlin, former Director of the Executive Office of the U.N. Secretary General, is a Fellow at Yale's International Security Programs.

establish. Should the need arise, countries would be protected from aggression by forces provided to the Security Council by member states, serving as a U.N. army at the council's will. Military forces, however, have not been available to the council on this basis and improvisation has therefore been required. The action taken by the Security Council in response to the Iraqi invasion of Kuwait amounted to just that—an improvisation to permit enforcement of the council's will without the specific means provided in the charter for that purpose.

Military force has much more frequently been used by the United Nations for the purpose of peacekeeping, something not foreseen in the charter at all. This improvisation was first devised in haste to facilitate an end to the 1956 hostilities in the Middle East. Since that beginning, which amply demonstrated the value of the technique, U.N. use of military and civilian personnel provided by member states for peacekeeping has become a well-established practice now supported by all the major powers.

The use of military force by the United Nations for both of these purposes—enforcement and peacekeeping—is surely essential to a world order in which international security is heavily dependent on the Security Council. The experience of the Gulf War and of the more distant past offers important lessons and raises trenchant questions as to how this can most effectively be done in the gulf (as action moves from military victory to the maintenance of peace in the region) and wherever else peace may be endangered.

II

Since the Suez crisis of 1956, the United Nations has developed a notable elasticity in using peacekeeping forces, to the point that it is now difficult to formulate a precise definition—or the limits—of what peacekeeping functions may be. The original role of standing between hostile forces has been expanded to encompass, among other functions, the maintenance of security or stability within a given area (as in southern Lebanon), the monitoring of elections (Namibia, Haiti), the provision of humanitarian assistance (Cyprus) and the disarmament of insurgents (Nicaragua). This flexibility greatly increases the value of peacekeeping forces as an instrument available to the Security Council in dealing with potential or existing conflicts. For example, the permanent members of the Security Council have recently developed a plan to bring peace to Cambodia that would use peacekeeping forces—both military and civilian—for broad purposes of pacification, stabilization and administration.

Three limitations on the use of peacekeeping have been consistently honored: (1) peacekeeping has been interpreted, as originally articulated by U.N. Secretary General Dag Hammarskjöld, as a provisional measure under the U.N. Charter, that is, as a measure undertaken without prejudice to the rights, claims or positions of the parties concerned; (2) peacekeeping operations have been undertaken only with the consent of all the parties concerned; (3) peacekeeping forces may use arms only in self-defense. Again in accordance with the original decision by Hammarskjöld, U.S. and Soviet troops have never been included in peacekeeping forces.

In domestic conflicts the consent of all the parties is likely to remain a compelling requirement. It was clearly shown in non-U.N. peacekeeping undertakings, in Lebanon in 1983–84 and more recently in Liberia, that without the consent of the parties grave risks are involved and the results can be disastrous. This may not, however, be the case in interstate conflicts. When peacekeeping forces are deployed between hostile forces after a truce or ceasefire has been achieved, an essential purpose is to deter a renewal of hostilities. In this sense deterrence is already an accepted function of peacekeeping. Yet in interstate conflicts a situation could well arise in which peacekeeping forces are needed for deterrence purposes but the consent of one of the parties is not obtainable. This should not, a priori, preclude a Security Council decision to deploy them if the other characteristic limitations are maintained.

The situation in the gulf could present the council with precisely such a need, as a long-term settlement of hostilities is sought. Some sort of convincing deterrent force will be needed to prevent renewed threats against Kuwait and, conceivably, to monitor any demilitarized zones that may be established. For the near term, further military adventures are unlikely. But in the long run, neither Iraqi motives and potential for revenge nor the ambitions of one or more of its neighbors can be ignored. Whatever misgivings some parties may have about the U.S.-led gulf operation, they have excellent reasons to converge on some sort of substantial U.N. presence in the gulf in the future. The emergence of the United Nations as an important institution for promoting international security can moderate any revival of Soviet-American tensions that might stem from disagreements regarding the gulf or other regions.

U.S. and Soviet forces could be usefully included in such an operation to ensure, through its size and composition, maximum credibility. But to be acceptable to the majority of U.N. members such a force must retain an indisputable U.N. identity and must not be dominated by one member state. In other border disputes—of which many exist—a comparable need for deterrence may arise, preferably under circumstances that would permit deployment of peacekeeping forces before hostilities actually occur. Indeed, if at the request of Kuwait a peacekeeping force had been deployed on its border with Iraq in August 1990, the Gulf War might have been avoided.

It is worth emphasizing that nothing in the charter prohibits the Security Council from deploying peacekeeping forces without the consent of all the parties, or from including troop contingents from the permanent members of the council in such forces where the need for deterrence arises. (U.S. and

Soviet military personnel already serve in U.N. military observer missions.) Such action would still fall under the definition of a provisional measure to be taken by the council "to prevent an aggravation of the situation" before deciding on enforcement action as foreseen in Articles 41 and 42 of the U.N. Charter. The provision of troops by member states for such deterrence operations would remain voluntary, as in other peacekeeping missions, with financing determined on an ad hoc basis by the council, either through assessment of all members or through payment of the cost by the countries requesting the deployment, as could be the case in a situation like the gulf where wealthy states are involved as parties.

The command structure need be no different from other peacekeeping operations: a commander of the U.N. force is appointed by the secretary general after the peacekeeping operation has been authorized by the Security Council for a defined mission. Troop contingents provided by member states serve under their national officers—a battalion commander, for example—who in turn receives orders from the U.N. force commander. The U.N. force commander reports to the secretary general from whom he receives operational guidance. The secretary general reports to the Security Council and obtains its concurrence if any change in the mission of the peacekeeping force is contemplated.

One can question whether it will be logistically feasible for the United Nations to mount, and maintain over a period of time, peacekeeping operations of sufficient size to provide a credible deterrent. It can only be said that where the need for peacekeeping has been evident, as in Namibia, the magnitude of required support has not inhibited action.

A good number of countries might well oppose in principle the idea of deploying peacekeeping forces without the consent of all the parties concerned, fearing that it would open the way to action contrary to their own national interests. Unlike the United States and the other four permanent members of the Security Council, they would not enjoy the protection of the veto. When a similar idea was put forward some years ago, in the course of confidential consultations in the Security Council on how its effectiveness might be enhanced, there was little response. The Gulf War has served, however, to heighten interest in effective deterrence using multilateral means not under the domination of one or several U.N. members. There is certainly now a broad recognition that adequate means of deterrence will be essential to a peaceful world order.

III

The second broad purpose for the Security Council's use of military force falls largely under the heading of compellence, or coercion, rather than simply deterrence. In the context of the Security Council such action is best understood as enforcement action. Use of "air, sea or land forces" for enforcement is specifically foreseen in Chapter VII, Articles 39–46 of the U.N. Charter, in which all members undertake to make available to the Security Council "on its call and in accordance with a special agreement or agreements, armed forces, assistance and facilities, including rights of passage, necessary for the purpose of maintaining international peace and security."

Since no such special agreements have been concluded, no standing multilateral force has been available to the Security Council. Therefore the Security Council authorized the use of ad hoc forces to restore international peace in Korea and the Persian Gulf. When the North Korean attacks on South Korea were formally brought to the Security Council's attention, the council's resolution of July 7, 1950—adopted in the temporary absence of the Soviet Union—called on member states to assist South Korea in resisting the North Korean aggression. It recommended "that all members providing military forces and other assistance pursuant to the aforesaid Security Council resolutions make such forces and other assistance available to a unified command under the United States." It requested further that the United States designate the commander of such forces. The same resolution authorized use of the U.N. flag.

Thus in the case of Korea the Security Council requested one member state to lead a combined effort on behalf of the United Nations to resist aggression. Notwithstanding his designation as commander of U.N. forces in Korea, General Douglas MacArthur, the commander named by the United States, never reported directly to the Security Council. (Routine, unclassified status reports were provided by the United States.) Neither the Military Staff Committee—a body composed of military representatives of the five permanent members intended to advise the council on military matters—nor the council itself had any role in directing military operations of the unified command. The General Assembly did, however, establish a three-nation ceasefire committee that sought a formula to end the war, and the secretary general suggested the procedure of direct talks between the military commanders that was ultimately followed and through which an armistice was achieved.

The advantages offered by this procedure were:
—Expeditious action to resist aggression. Only the United States had troops deployed in South Korea capable of taking quick military action.
—The unambiguous command structure needed for large-scale field operations.
—A practical way to meet the responsibilities of the United Nations under the charter in the absence of a multilateral force under the Security Council for which the necessary agreements with member states had not been reached.
—Validation of the concept of collective security, since states acted jointly in response to Security Council (and subsequently General Assembly) decisions.

The disadvantages of this procedure (which became more evident in the course of time) were:

—The United Nations lacked control or influence over the course of military action or the precise purposes for which it was exercised (e.g., to repel and punish aggression, to reunify the country).

—The military operation became identified with the policy of the nation leading the effort rather than with the United Nations.

—Divisive forces within the United Nations were encouraged by the dominant role of one member state pursuing goals not universally shared.

—Opportunities were afforded the aggressor to identify the struggle with one country, the United States, rather than with the international community as a whole.

All of these disadvantages were intensified in the Korean case by the bitter disagreements that prevailed at the time between the Soviet Union and the United States. Under conditions of harmony among the permanent members of the Security Council, these various disadvantages could have considerably less force.

In the Persian Gulf crisis the Security Council authorized, albeit in oblique language, the use of force for enforcement in another interstate conflict. After imposing a comprehensive embargo in order to bring about Iraqi withdrawal from Kuwait and the restoration of its legitimate government, the council called upon "those member states cooperating with the government of Kuwait which are deploying maritime forces to the area to use such measures commensurate to the specific circumstances as may be necessary under the authority of the Security Council . . . to ensure strict implementation" of the provisions laid down in the resolution relating to economic sanctions. Then, in Resolution 678 of November 29, 1990, the Security Council authorized "member states cooperating with the government of Kuwait . . . to use all necessary means to uphold and implement Security Council Resolution 660 and all subsequent relevant resolutions and to restore international peace and security in the area." All states were requested to provide appropriate support for "the actions undertaken."

This action, with specific reference to Chapter VII of the charter, constituted a new approach to implementation of the collective security concept. As in the earlier enforcement action in Korea, when there was no reference to Chapter VII, a basis for the council to mobilize a U.N. force for military enforcement action did not exist. Therefore the council again turned to member states to act in its behalf through such measures as might be necessary. But this time no unified command was established, and the use of the U.N. flag was not authorized.

The gulf action became possible because the permanent members of the Security Council cooperated on a matter of peace and security in the way originally foreseen when the

United Nations was founded. Representatives of the United States and the Soviet Union have repeatedly suggested that such action is an important element in a new world order; that is, a world in which nations will be secure because of the capacity of the United Nations to guarantee their security through collective measures. This fundamental goal of the United Nations is unquestionably brought closer through the sustained cooperation and a notably increased commonality of interests among the major powers, evident not only in the Gulf War but also in other conflicts such as Cambodia and Angola. Two questions nonetheless warrant careful examination: Is the approach that was taken to enforce the council's decisions with regard to the Iraq-Kuwait crisis necessarily a viable model for implementing collective security in the future? Is there a realistic alternative that would offer greater advantages?

IV

With regard to the first question, it is clear that the Security Council, in deciding on action to counter the Iraqi aggression, prescribed action for all member states. While it authorized individual states to take "the necessary action," it requested "all states to provide appropriate support for the actions undertaken." Thus all states were called on to assist in defending one state, Kuwait, from aggression. Actions to be taken for this purpose would seem clearly to constitute "effective collective measures for the prevention and removal of threats to the peace, and for the suppression of acts of aggression" as foreseen in Article 1 of the charter.

But the procedure adopted is not without its difficulties. The Security Council has no means of controlling when, how or in what degree the collective measures are applied. In the gulf case, the states concerned were only requested "to keep the council regularly informed"; some measures taken might not have had majority support in the Security Council or the General Assembly. The state that is in command may have from the outset an interpretation of U.N. goals different from that of other Security Council members, or its aims may become more expansive in the course of the operation. The latter happened in Korea with the U.S. decision to cross the 38th parallel and try to reunify the country by force. It would have been the case in the gulf had the United States pursued military action beyond the Kuwaiti theater of operations.

If the measures taken cease to have the endorsement of the majority of the Security Council, can they still be considered collective measures taken in the council's behalf? This problem is inherent in a procedure in which action is taken on behalf of the council but without any council control over the nature, timing or extent of the action. The major danger is that the entire undertaking will be identified with the country or countries actually involved in military action rather than with the United Nations. In any case, many U.N. members will not view the military action as an appropriate application of collective security if the action appears to conflict with the Security Council's goals.

The gulf operation and the terms for ending military action against Iraq offer a case in point. None of the 12 Security Council resolutions called for eliminating Iraq's war-making capability or deposing Saddam Hussein. But the former clearly became a goal of some coalition members, and the latter was widely suspected. President Bush and the coalition partners felt free to give their own interpretation to the Security Council resolutions. Those members, including the Soviet Union, that interpreted the resolutions more narrowly may be reluctant next time to give such unconstrained authority to member states acting on the council's behalf. In any operation, if the Security Council has asserted no control over the military action authorized, will it be possible for it to assert control over the terms of peace?

Such questions indicate the problems that can arise when a procedure such as that developed for the Gulf War is followed. Moreover the approach adopted in the gulf case is not likely to be viable unless vital interests of one or more major military powers are at risk. For example, the United States might not be interested in deploying substantial forces, even if authorized to do so by the Security Council, to deter or repel an Egyptian attack on Libya.

v

There are alternative procedures that might in the future be followed by the Security Council, ones that would offer the prospect of effective enforcement action without the disadvantages and problems associated with according responsibility to individual member states.

One would be a variant of the procedure followed in Korea. National forces could be brought together in ad hoc fashion under a unified U.N. command, with the commander designated by whichever happened to be the major troop-contributing country. The problems that arose in the Korean case could conceivably be alleviated if the unified commander were required to consult with the Security Council, or with some form of military authority appointed by the council, on the mission of the military operation and the basic strategy to be followed in achieving it. The country supplying the major troop contingent can be expected to resist such a procedure as inhibiting unacceptably the freedom of action of the commander and subjecting its forces to perilous uncertainties. But if favorable relations among the permanent members of the Security Council persist, such a consultative, though not command, procedure might be feasible. It would have the distinct advantage of maintaining a close U.N. identification with all action taken and of giving the Security Council some influence, if not control, over any military action.

232

The other alternative is the procedure defined in Articles 42 and 43 of the U.N. Charter, according to which all members of the United Nations undertake "to make available to the Security Council on its call in accordance with a special agreement or agreements, armed forces, facilities and assistance." In the Korean War, the "uniting for peace" resolution of 1950 recommended that each member maintain within its armed forces earmarked units so trained that they could promptly be made available for service "as a United Nations unit or units."

The hostile relations between the United States and the Soviet Union were long perceived as the major obstacle to implementing such provisions. If after the Gulf War the two countries remain in accord on using the United Nations, that obstacle may be lifted. The willingness of member states to commit themselves in advance to provide troops and facilities at the request of the Security Council for enforcement purposes has never been tested. It can be argued that such commitment is inherent in U.N. membership, a condition for which is acceptance of the obligations contained in the charter and ability and willingness to carry out those obligations. For such a commitment to be reliable, however, it must be embodied in agreements between the Security Council and those member states prepared to assume the obligations. Such commitments will not be undertaken lightly.

The subject was discussed in detail in 1945 in the U.S. Senate when the U.N. Charter was under consideration. John Foster Dulles, a member of the U.S. delegation to the San Francisco conference at which the charter was signed, told the Senate Foreign Relations Committee that an agreement with the United Nations on the provision of troops should be regarded as a treaty requiring approval of a two-thirds majority of the Senate. The recorded comments of the senators indicate wide agreement with that interpretation. It was also discussed whether the president would need to obtain the consent of Congress to provide troops, when called upon by the United Nations after completion of an agreement. No consensus emerged on the question, but one senator suggested at the time that the size of the force requested could be decisive. Two or three thousand troops for "police action" would not need congressional approval, whereas a battle force would.

Soviet representatives have recently expressed a positive view of a U.N. agreement on the provision of troops for enforcement purposes, but they have emphasized that in no case could the troops be provided without the specific approval of the Soviet parliament.

Once agreements on the provision of troops were completed with a fair portion of member states, the Security Council would have the capacity to call into being a multilateral force (land, sea and air) under a U.N. commander "to maintain or restore international peace and security." In military operations the commander would presumably have full tactical authority but would operate under the guidance of the Security Council or a body established by the council to serve this purpose. Subsequent understandings would be required on command, intelligence, logistics and other more or less centralized functions. The Military Staff Committee could, as foreseen 46 years ago, "advise and assist the Security Council on all questions relating to military requirements." It could do this without acquiring any command authority, which would be inadvisable since it functions on the basis of consensus.

In some ways a U.N. force of this type would be quite similar to a peacekeeping force, since it would be made up of troops provided by member states and would have a U.N. commander. It would differ markedly, however, in mission, armament, composition and command.

A U.N. force of this nature would not entail the problems and disadvantages that the other identified approaches could present. Identification with the United Nations from initiation to end of any operation would be assured, and control could be clearly in the hands of the Security Council. The likelihood of sustained support among U.N. members for the action undertaken would be strong. Yet in this approach, too, likely problems can be identified.

First of all, it is not clear how many states will be willing to conclude the agreements foreseen in the U.N. Charter—or how long this will take. It can only be said that international circumstances, especially in the wake of the Gulf War, appear more favorable than at any time since 1945. It is also questionable whether a force as large and elaborately equipped as one needed to maintain peace in the gulf, for example, could have been organized quickly on this basis. Any very large operation is bound to depend heavily on a major contingent from one or more of the principal military powers; the larger and more sophisticated the contingent provided, the less likely the contributing country will be willing to place it under non-national command.

Organization and deployment of a multilateral force by the Security Council would likely require more time than if action were delegated to one or more member states, especially if a large-scale operation were foreseen. To shorten the lead time, the secretary general might be given authority, not subject to the veto, to send an unarmed observer corps to any international border at any time. According to Article 99 of the U.N. Charter, the secretary general "may bring to the attention of the Security Council any matter which in his opinion may threaten the maintenance of international peace and security." To do so he needs to be informed. An authorization to send observers without specific consent of the parties raises difficulties, but it would allow the Security Council to be forewarned and to make quick preparations if an enforcement action were required. The very presence of observers can have a deterrent effect, possibly avoiding the need for subsequent enforcement.

Then, too, there is a very basic question as to whether a military action can be successfully carried out under multilateral strategic command, or as successfully as under national command. Administrative aspects of managing the use of force by the Security Council have received little attention. Save for peacekeeping and the peculiar conditions permitting the Korean operation, the prospects of using U.N. forces were nil during the Cold War. Nonetheless important multinational dimensions characterized U.S. military plans during the Korean War, in the U.S. commitment to NATO and notably in the Persian Gulf.

The force of the NATO and Korea precedents must not be exaggerated. In both instances there was virtual consensus on the nature of the military threat, decades-long experience of close cooperation and, in Europe, a high degree of cultural and political homogeneity—far more than likely in most future U.N.-sanctioned operations. If the United States should put its forces under another state's commander, one would have to expect a relatively much smaller contribution of U.S. troops and financing than in the gulf operations. By its treaty commitments and geographic deployment, however, the United States stood a great chance of being involved in any military operations in Europe and Korea. Any U.N. enforcement action would have to be authorized by the Security Council and would thus be subject to U.S. veto. This fact should reassure Congress.

One question inherent in any big multilateral action concerns the level at which integration of command of multinational forces would occur. The distinction in U.S. military terminology between command and operational control (OPCON) is useful in this respect. Command applies to such matters as discipline, pay, morale and logistics; most of these (perhaps not logistics) would be carried out at the level of the national military contingents. OPCON is likely to be different. If U.S. troops were involved there would probably have to be, under an overall U.N. commander from some country, a U.S. "component commander" operating with substantial independence. OPCON can be decentralized by confining each member's forces to a specific sector, physically dividing up the ground, as has been done in most U.N. peacekeeping operations.

Some other functions may be even harder to divide than OPCON. Intelligence gathering, for example, will be dominated by states with vast technological capacities for overhead and electronic surveillance. In the gulf operation other coalition members presumably accepted U.S. control of intelligence, but if there were substantial Soviet participation the Soviets would likely not accept it. Secure communications would be required among participating forces in the field, either through sharing encryption (politically very sensitive) or cumbersome procedures for transmission and delivery. It is likely that some states will be unable or unwilling to provide adequate logistical support for their troops, and that those with the motivation and ability to do so will have to provide for others. Some U.N. "headquarters" personnel and facilities will be required for these functions, probably drawing on the experience and capabilities of the secretary general's staff.

The problem of financing such military actions demands careful attention. The history of financing past peacekeeping efforts by voluntary contribution is, to say the least, not encouraging. The gulf operation was heavily dependent on the willingness and ability of the most deeply involved states— the United States, Saudi Arabia and Kuwait—to pay most of the immediate costs, and in turn their willingness depended upon their ability to control the means and ends of military operations. A future operation that less directly engaged the interests of such states would have to rely on broader support, probably through an assessment of all member governments. Reasonably complete and prompt payment of those assessments would have to be assured.

Such problems may be equally severe for the peacetime maintenance of standing earmarked forces. Unless any additional costs incurred can be covered by the United Nations, Third World states may be unable to participate. Certain central (non-state-specific) services, such as administration, intelligence, command and control, perhaps logistics and transport, must be prepared and institutionalized in advance. Provision in the regular budget of the United Nations might cover such ongoing costs of multilateral readiness, with special assessments made to cover the cost of any enforcement actions undertaken.

VI

The credibility of U.N. action to repel aggression and restore international peace and security, as foreseen in the U.N. Charter, has been profoundly affected by the response to the Iraqi invasion of Kuwait. The Security Council showed itself capable of taking decisive action. Its ability to impose comprehensive sanctions and see them enforced was clearly demonstrated, even though the ultimate effectiveness of the sanctions was not adequately tested. By authorizing the use of military force the council gained compliance with all of its relevant resolutions. The Security Council has shown that it has the capacity to initiate collective measures essential for the maintenance of peace in a new world order.

This development can enhance the United Nations' ability not just to restore the status quo as it existed prior to a breach of the peace, but also to change the parameters of the global order to something more favorable than existed under the prior status quo. In this it may even go beyond the vision of the U.N. founders. Furthermore knowledge that the United Nations has such a capability will also enhance its ability to deter breaches of the peace, and so make actual enforcement or later peacekeeping less necessary. Collective security may suppress incipient acts of aggression as well as defeat or punish those that do emerge.

Nevertheless it should not be assumed that any U.N. role in enforcement during the 1990s will be automatic. It will require a deliberate political judgment that can only be made by members of the Security Council acting collectively, and will depend on some continuing commonality of interests among the five permanent members of the council—the United States and the Soviet Union in particular. The effectiveness of the United Nations in dealing with international security problems, whether by enforcement measures, peacekeeping or mediation, will always be sensitive to the nature of relations between these two superpowers. A United Nations whose credibility in dealing with aggression and threats to peace has been restored, however, can serve to moderate any revival of tension between them by lessening the need for, or likelihood of, unilateral intervention in regional crises.

The manner in which the gulf military action was executed by the United States and its coalition partners will likely limit the willingness of council members to follow a similar procedure in the future—a procedure that leaves council members little control over the course of military operations and over the conclusion of hostilities. Neither the United States nor any other country will be ready to act under all circumstances to preserve or restore peace. Nor will other states always be ready to endorse unilateral actions. Some states may not wish to contribute to an operation, and the council may not always wish to depend disproportionately on a particular state's contribution.

Some U.N. capacity to carry out these functions on a permanent basis will therefore be desirable. For this reason, as well as others previously mentioned, the Security Council should be able to mobilize a force to serve under U.N. command for enforcement purposes. That capacity may be virtually indispensable in an emergent world order. The chance to achieve it should not be missed.

Although the gulf war revealed the strengths of the United Nations at its best, the aftermath of the
conflict shows why it is time, argues Brian Crozier, to reevaluate the role of the United Nations.
According to the author, the U.N. peacekeeping role has only "worked" in special cases—for example,
the Korean war. No reason exists to believe that future crises will parallel the unique circumstances of
either the Iraqi invasion or the Korean war. In his view, the United Nations is destined to fail, owing to
its archaic structure, rules and procedures, and methods of operation. Simply put, the author argues that
any peacekeeping mission must, by its very definition, exclude aggressor nations. In addition, terrorist
states must also be precluded from membership. As a practical matter, it would be extremely difficult to
expel such nations from membership. The answer, at least for the immediate future, would be to
reorganize the United Nations so that it better resembles an Association of Free Nations. This would
entail several categories of membership (full, associate, and candidate) combined with an inner council
that would also exclude "predator nations," leaving the inner council free to act without threat of
a hostile veto.

CLOSING TIME FOR THE U.N.?

BRIAN CROZIER

THE GULF WAR showed what the United Nations can do if skillfully handled. The aftermath of the battle showed what the UN can't do, and why the time is ripe for a fundamental change. Such as putting something else in its place.

Having done his Hannibal act, with stunning success, General Norman Schwarzkopf wanted to win the war as well as the latter-day battle of Cannae. The issues are clear enough. Do the Allies merely defeat Hitler in battle? Or do they push on, as agreed at Yalta, and oblige him to take his own life in the Berlin bunker? Does the United States help the Hungarians in 1956, or does it encourage them to rise, then sit by while the Red Army massacres them?

In other words, do we "liberate" Kuwait, then sit and watch while Saddam Hussein's forces massacre the Kurds? Or do we rid the world of an evil and bloodstained tyrant?

Mr. Crozier, an NR *contributing editor, is
the author of* The Gorbachev Phenomenon.

Understandably, President Bush wanted UN sanction for armed action against Saddam's regime. He obtained it, with great skill and perseverance ["Handling the United Nations," April 1]. Bush knew he could get a Security Council consensus for the liberation of Kuwait. He also knew that he couldn't hope for Big Five assent to a combined action to bring down the Iraqi dictator. China, with memories of the Tiananmen and Tibet suppressions still very much alive, would have vetoed any such move. So would the Soviet Union, in the wake of armed repression in Tbilisi and with unrest in Lithuania and elsewhere.

In major crises, the UN has "worked" in its peacekeeping role only in anomalous circumstances. In 1950, the Security Council united for action when the Korean War began, because the Soviet Union was boycotting it. This time, it united for action because Mikhail Gorbachev had been awarded the Nobel Peace Prize and is in the market for Western money. Even so, he tried for a peace of non-humiliation for the man the Soviets had helped so much: Saddam Hussein.

Flawed from Birth

THERE IS absolutely no guarantee that in future conflicts the UN will repeat the isolated successes of 1950 and 1990. In fact, the UN is a legalistic absurdity, deeply flawed from birth.

The accident of history that made the USSR the West's glorious ally also made it a permanent member of the UN Security Council, with power of veto over actions of which it disapproved. Furthermore, since the UN was the creation of the victorious Allies, the emerging major democracies, Germany and Japan, were automatically excluded from the role to which their economic power and military potential have long entitled them.

There were other *ab initio* flaws. One of the five permanent members was to be China, but the assumption that it would be Nationalist China was dashed by Mao Tse-tung's victory over Chiang Kai-shek. The Nixon–Kissinger initiative of 1972 rectified the anomaly without curing the fault.

The argument, sometimes heard, that at least the UN General Assem-

From *National Review*, May 13, 1991, pp. 44–45. © 1991 by National Review Inc., 150 East 35th Street, New York, NY 10016.
Reprinted by permission.

bly provides a platform where the disputatious may let off steam invites an answer: steam at that price comes too expensive, easily undersold by the steam New Yorkers can readily buy from Con Ed.

In 1969, writing in the shocked aftermath of Brezhnev's occupation of Czechoslovakia (which, incidentally, I had forecast), I first proposed a working alternative to the United Nations. I called it the Association of Nations. Today, in the light of the collapse of Communism in Eastern Europe, I offer a revival of the idea, with a small change of name: the Association of Free Nations (AFN).

In this context, "small" does not mean "minor." What is needed is an international body with an inner council of states that are free in the American, British, or German sense, with freely elected assemblies, freedom of speech, free economies, and the rule of law (the adverb "relatively" being understood in each stipulation). Not a military alliance, but a body concerned primarily to consider international crises of aggression and armed conflict, and take concerted action.

To write in these terms is not to be starry-eyed about our democracies, all of which are imperfect, each in its own way. But one major point shines out: democracies, it seems, don't go to war against each other. War between those traditional enemies, France and Germany, seems unthinkable so long as each is a democracy. And democratic Japan is hardly likely to do another Pearl Harbor.

An international body dedicated to the maintenance of peace must, by definition, exclude the predatory states. So what about the greatest predator of all: the Soviet Union?

To pose the question is to invite the reservation: wait and see. Wait and see whether the Soviet Union survives its current crisis, whether it turns itself into a kind of United States of Eurasia, whether Lenin's party (and Gorbachev's) stays in the Kremlin or yields to an elected alternative. Wait and see whether Moscow continues to keep a Communist regime in power in Afghanistan and to aid a Communist regime in Angola. So many waits, so many sees.

Initially, then, the AFN's inner council would exclude the USSR; it would consist of the U.S., Japan, Germany, France, Britain, Italy, and (possibly) Spain: free nations with economic substance and actual or potential military muscle. Free and nonpredatory countries such as Canada, Australia, Benelux, and the Scandinavians would automatically qualify for full membership.

Associate membership would be open to countries that are not free and democratic, but do not attack their neighbors. On this basis, even a very unfree country, such as Saudi Arabia, could be admitted. There would be marginal cases, such as South Africa and Argentina. South Africa: not yet a democracy but heading that way. Nonpredatory? In my view its involvements of some time ago in Namibia and Angola were ultimately defensive. Argentina? Quite recently democratic, but an invader not many years ago. *Candidate* membership could cover such marginal cases.

Apart from the Soviet Union, the biggest marginal case of all would be China. Countries that export terrorism, such as Libya and Syria, would be out in the cold, qualifying not for membership but for remedial action by

the AFN. Totally disqualified would be Iraq, Cuba, and probably Vietnam.

Discarding the existing UN would be tricky but by no means impossible. As the Charter stands, it is not open to any nation or group of nations to dissolve the United Nations. There is, however, nothing to prevent any nation from abrogating its membership. Expelling predatory states would cause unnecessary problems. It would be far simpler for the putative members of the AFN Council to quit, along with those qualifying for full membership. The associate and candidate members would soon follow, leaving the unvirtuous to ponder the merits of aggression and isolation.

The Balance Sheet

AM I SERIOUS? What a frivolous question! The benefits of an Association of Free Nations would be immense, the drawbacks minimal. At times of crisis, the inner council would be free to act, in most cases without fear of a hostile veto, since those likely to cause crises would be out in the cold. Predator nations would be isolated, and the pressure on them to mend their ways would increase. The old UN would be consigned to where it has long belonged: that mythical place that Khrushchev and other Communists used to call the garbage heap of history.

What I am proposing is a challenge to Western statesmanship. And there, I suppose, I have struck a snag. Statesmanship, just now, is in short supply. □

Chapter 19

Regional Security Organizations

Article 19.1.   A New Role for NATO

Jed C. Snyder argues that as a result of recent changes in U.S.-Soviet relations, the rigid bipolar security requirements of the past, which were designed to protect Europe in the event of Soviet aggression, have been significantly changed. During the Cold War, the West's chief concern was the security of Europe, which was defined in the context of East-West relations. As a result of the revolutions in Eastern Europe in 1989, the political map of the region has been permanently changed, marking the end of at least a phase of the Cold War. Despite recent developments, the issue of Soviet withdrawal from Eastern Europe is far from resolved. NATO was created for one express purpose: to deter Soviet aggression in Europe. It is unlikely that Europe will remain the focus for future superpower conflicts. For this reason, the author recommends reducing NATO's force to perhaps 225,000. In addition, the core members of NATO should consider either expanding NATO's geographical scope— which could be extremely dangerous—or developing a new framework capable of meeting new threats. The time has come, concludes the author, to build a post-NATO world.

A New Role for NATO

by Jed C. Snyder

Old alliances never die, they just become anachronisms. It is difficult to imagine NATO Secretary-General Manfred Woerner uttering this MacArthuresque farewell to the NATO generals and bureaucrats in Brussels. Yet, it is likely that he and other observers of the great transatlantic security experiment have begun to wonder privately whether the alliance as we have known it for more than four decades is, indeed, in the twilight of its existence.

The events of the last two years suggest that the postwar system of international relations is at least in transition, if not in the midst of an upheaval. The principal (if unwitting) agent of change, Mikhail Gorbachev, has altered the terms of reference for U.S.-Soviet relations, which has functioned as the scaffolding for the contemporary structure of global interstate relationships. In the rigid bipolar security environment dominated by the competing European alliances of the United States and the Soviet Union, the state of superpower relations tended to act as a barometer for European security. Since the first Berlin crisis of 1948, superpower attention has been focused (at times almost exclusively) on the possibility of East-West conflict in Europe, where U.S. and Soviet interests most clearly intersected.

Europe has been the nucleus of both Soviet and American power, from which radiated a series of bilateral and multilateral security commitments and a global network of supporting military installations. For better or worse, judgments about the temperature of the East-West rivalry in Europe affected nearly all of the other military, economic, and diplomatic intercourse that has distinguished the modern state system. For Washington and Moscow, Europe was the center of the universe.

It is assumed by the vast majority of scholars and pundits that the level of superpower competition in Europe and globally can be expected to decline dramatically over the next decade and, therefore, the structure supporting this competition will likely be transformed and reshaped to fit an as yet undefined "new world order." The starting point for this revolution in security affairs will be Europe, where it is expected that the system of alli-

> **The issue of Soviet withdrawal from Eastern Europe is far from settled, despite Soviet pledges to complete the process by 1994.**

ances created to regulate superpower competition will wither as the raison d'être for bloc politics disappears.

EUROPE'S TRANSFORMATION

Europe surely has been transformed as a result of the revolutions of 1989. One can no longer speak credibly of a Europe divided along an East-West frontier. The fall of the Berlin Wall and the reunification of Germany, the collapse of Soviet-sponsored and -supported authoritarian power in every Eastern European state, and the formal dissolution on March 31, 1991, of the Warsaw Pact have marked the end of at least a *phase* of the Cold War. Soviet forces in Czechoslovakia, eastern Germany, Poland, and Hungary—which enforced a peacetime alliance with Moscow's satellites—will (absent Soviet recidivism) have been removed over the next several years.

The remaining two Warsaw Treaty Organization states, Romania and Bulgaria, could hardly be counted upon now to provide political or logistical support to Moscow in the unlikely event that it was requested in a crisis. In sum, Moscow can no longer depend upon political or military support from its system of forced alliance, without which a sustained military campaign

against the nations of Western Europe seems highly improbable. More importantly, it is difficult today to identify a circumstance whereby the Kremlin leadership would feel compelled for strategic reasons to deploy forces to Western Europe.

The issue of Soviet withdrawal from Eastern Europe is far from settled, however, despite Soviet pledges to complete the process by 1994. Serious obstacles have already delayed the timetable for the departure of Soviet forces. Decades of political oppression by the Kremlin have come back to haunt Moscow as the former satellites insist on a series of compensating measures for the Soviet occupation. Poland, for example, initially insisted that the Soviets pay high tariffs before it would allow the passage of hundreds of trainloads of troops and equipment through the country. The Soviets, in turn, expected "compensation" from the Polish government for some of the occupation costs it had incurred. While many of these demands represented little more than desperate posturing, they vividly illustrated the power of the status quo even among the Eastern European nations.

Poland is a special case, as its government is concerned that a reunified Germany could slip into past patterns of behavior. While these concerns are surely exaggerated, many Poles are not persuaded that a unified Germany will not eventually seek to reclaim portions of Poland (Silesia and Pomerania, for example) that were annexed from Germany as part of the settlement after World War II. These areas, east of the Oder-Neisse rivers, are inhabited by several hundred thousand ethnic Germans who might prefer to see their regions returned to the Fatherland. The potential for a prolonged dispute between Poland and Germany over

the Oder-Neisse border could inflame nationalist sentiments of other ethnic Germans living in Hungary and Romania.

The Polish case is perhaps the most dramatic example of how distasteful and artificial many Europeans regarded the Yalta and Potsdam formulas for a postwar Europe. Ironically, the Cold War presence of one million Soviet and non-Soviet Warsaw Pact troops in Eastern Europe masked the seriousness of these nationalist and ethnic questions. The liberated governments of Eastern Europe may face strong nationalistic pressures from their populations to redraw current boundaries to reflect ethnic realities. Such pressures could create incendiary political upheaval—even civil war—as appears to be likely in Yugoslavia, for instance, where a weak federal government and collective presidency have failed to quell nationalist disputes. Serbian nationalism is actively opposed by Slovenes and Croatians, who are determined to prevent the Yugoslav federation from dissolving or falling under Serbian domination.

In sum, the Cold War-generated geographic labels of "East" versus "West" will cease to be useful strategic terms. One can no longer regard territory east of the Elbe River as "Eastern" vis-à-vis the West. Czechs, Poles, Hungarians, and East Germans regard themselves as Central or East-Central Europeans. This will clearly affect the way in which NATO defines its mission in the future. The Soviet Union will no longer have a grouping of aligned states acting as a buffer between itself and NATO. Most importantly, it will no longer be able to look to East Germany as its key military ally in Europe.

The dominant scenario for which Western and Soviet defense specialists have planned—

a massive and lightning strike by Soviet forces supported by the Warsaw Pact allies across the plains of Germany—for all practical purposes has been erased from the computers in Washington, Moscow, and Brussels. At the very least, planned conventional force (CFE) reductions will significantly increase the warning time available to NATO in the unlikely event of an attack.

It is unclear what conflict scenarios—if any—will replace the great Fulda Gap war games. NATO, it seems, is in search of a new threat.

Since the Soviet Union has

■

U.S. negotiators at both the CFE and START talks confirm the heightened presence and influence of the military at the bargaining table.

■

been the West's principal security preoccupation in the postwar period, its internal health must be considered an important factor in assessing the probabilities of future Soviet threats to Western interests.

UNCERTAIN SOVIET FUTURE

Nearly six years of initiatives designed to reform the Soviet economy (and most probably, as a consequence, to reorient Soviet society itself) have failed. There is a great debate among Western academics as to the reason for this failure. The arguments are complex and will not be repeated here. It is clear that whereas perestroika has not improved the standard of living in the USSR (it has, in fact, contributed to a further economic decline), it has awakened centrifugal political movements among the Russian and non-Russian populations of the USSR that are likely to present the greatest challenge to the integrity of the Soviet internal empire.

Although extraordinary internal problems are likely to preoccupy Soviet leaders for at least the next several years, it is at least plausible to suggest that opportunities for foreign adventurism will remain attractive. This is particularly the case considering how important it will be for Gorbachev to define a continuing role for the Soviet military. With the loss of Eastern Europe and the withdrawal of several hundred thousand soldiers back to the USSR, Gorbachev faces a dilemma. He must choose to (a) disband a large portion of the army and air force and risk adding significantly to an already growing and volatile unemployment crisis; (b) redeploy them abroad to another region; or (c) seek an expanded internal security role for them. The first and third choices are unattractive, but the second is not even plausible, absent an unlikely request by a friendly government for Soviet military assistance.

The military clearly understands Gorbachev's dilemma and therefore is seeking a new role for itself in Soviet society. Soviet military leaders have already moved to stall arms control initiatives that would erode further what influence remains for the military in Kremlin decision making. The last-minute decision by Soviet conventional force negotiators to redesignate several divisions of Soviet forces—in a transparent effort to exclude them from CFE reductions—is a desperate effort to maintain a larger peacetime army. The fact that these efforts were not vetoed by the civilian leadership suggests that Gorbachev cannot yet ignore the military as a force in Soviet politics. The visit to Washington in May (with Gorbachev's blessing) of the chief of the Soviet General Staff to discuss "outstanding arms control issues" was unprecedented and confirmed a continuing (perhaps increasingly) important role for the military in a wide range of defense and foreign policy issues.

U.S. negotiators at both the CFE and START talks confirm the heightened presence and influence of the military at the bargaining table, to the point that the military must now ratify new Soviet proposals offered by civilian negotiators.

While it is unclear whether the military could move independently of Soviet civilian authority and control, the continuing presence of more than 30,000 nuclear weapons (some of which are certainly still pointed at Western Europe) suggests that Soviet military pressure on the NATO allies cannot be ruled out completely.

GERMANY'S ROLE

Germany's reunification and the end of occupation rights for the four World War II allies created what is potentially the most powerful nation in Europe, by almost any measure. West Germany's population of nearly 65 million was second in Europe only to the Soviet Union. Its armed forces were the largest in Western Europe (the second largest in NATO Europe, exceeded only by Turkey). Its gross domestic product of nearly $1.3 trillion was significantly ahead of its nearest competitor, France, and its trade surplus was larger than Japan's by some $3 billion.

Despite these attributes of European superpower status,

Germany did not seek and therefore has not acquired any significant measure of political authority among the European nations. While one could argue that its Cold War status as a divided country severely limited opportunities to expand Germany's influence, the ghosts of the past are likely to haunt Germans and act as a brake on pursuing any delusions of grandeur.

For the past several decades, German security policy was essentially a function of American policy. German deference was institutionalized within the NATO structure and U.S. leadership in the alliance. Concern about the potentially expansionist tendencies of Soviet power left the Germans with little choice in the matter.

Just as West German leaders were obliged to accept American dominance in security matters, so, too, was Bonn forced to cater to European (particularly French) sensitivities about a resurgent German nation. As a result, successive Bonn administrations (both Social Democratic and Christian Democratic) grudgingly supported European integration through membership in the European Community, where it predictably was unable to take a leading political role despite the impressive power of German industry and the increasing influence of the Deutschmark on European currencies.

The great challenge for Germany over the next two decades will be to balance its desire for a leadership role in Europe against the ingrained suspicion of its European partners that German leadership could become hegemonic.

France, which is experiencing a Gaullist renaissance, will represent the most formidable obstacle to Germany's aspirations. The French are realizing that the two eventualities about

■

The Persian Gulf War created another obstacle to a continued presence of a large U.S. combat force in Europe—the perennial concern over burden sharing among the NATO allies.

■

which they have been most concerned—American withdrawal from Europe and German reunification—are occurring simultaneously. As one senior French defense ministry official admitted to the author privately, "This is our greatest nightmare come true."

France had discounted the possibility of German reunification, principally because the majority of French academics and officials assumed that Moscow would not permit it to occur and because the speed of the revolutions in Eastern Europe took them by surprise. The French strategy was to support German reunification—but only within the context of a united Europe, hoping thereby to blunt the increased German influence and power that could come with reunification. This explains the timing of French President François Mitterrand's efforts in 1989 and 1990 to pressure other European leaders to accelerate the 1992 European integration plan. He wanted to calibrate the EC-92 schedule with the unexpectedly rapid reunification timetable.

France is also concerned about Germany's natural proclivities toward close relations with the Soviet Union. While Mitter-

rand has spoken sympathetically about Gorbachev's courageous reforms, he is wary of a German-Soviet axis in Europe, particularly if it develops in the absence of a substantial U.S. military presence on the Continent. In that regard, the French are alarmed by increasingly large loans to the Soviet Union by German banking consortia, backed by the Bonn government. In addition, the French were somewhat critical of German willingness to finance much of the cost of Soviet withdrawal from East Germany, reported to exceed $15 billion. Here, however, the French are ambivalent. If a considerable amount of German capital is diverted toward financing perestroika and the rebuilding of eastern Germany, less will be available for markets in Europe and abroad. This could weaken Germany's considerable financial clout, perhaps increasing the relative weight of French financial influence.

Certainly, the costs of reunification will be substantially more than conservative Christian Democratic (CDU) Chancellor Helmut Kohl had promised during the 1990 election campaign. This has seriously imperiled the viability of his already fragile coalition government, which recently lost a key regional election. This electoral loss removed Kohl's working majority in the upper house of the German parliament, the Bundesrat. In sum, the financial difficulties that the Kohl government is encountering (chiefly as a result of reunification problems) could topple the CDU-led coalition, bringing the Social Democrats (SPD) into power. Considering the political proximity of the SPD to Soviet foreign policy, the French strategy could backfire, bringing a more Soviet-oriented regime to power in Bonn.

The Europeans' urge to integrate their economies, currencies, and ultimately their defense capabilities is likely to be delayed as competing concerns that sovereignty will be diluted in the process grow. Margaret Thatcher represented an extreme form of the alarm created by the expectation that national control of national interests will wither under a truly integrated supra-European structure. The image of economic (and perhaps, ultimately, foreign) policy made for all of Europe by anonymous bureaucrats in Brussels who are not impressed by the arguments of nationalism alarms those who see Europe catering to its weakest members rather than its strongest.

A least-common-denominator approach is the likely result in a genuinely integrated and centrally controlled economic alliance where a broad range of economies must be accommodated. Nevertheless, the increasingly powerful argument offered within European financial circles that Europe simply cannot compete with an increasingly protectionist United States and a simultaneous challenge by Asia (led by Japan) is a sound concern that is likely to eclipse the Thatcherite fears.

AFTER U.S. WITHDRAWAL

With the signing of the Treaty of Paris in November 1990 and the expectation that an agreement reducing conventional armed forces in Europe through the CFE Treaty will be ratified and implemented, European security policy will enter a new phase. That phase will be characterized most critically by the removal of all Soviet combat forces from Eastern Europe and the withdrawal of a significant percentage of U.S. combat power from Western Europe. Although CFE requires that the Soviets re-

move a much larger force than the allies, the USSR will still possess a very formidable capability in its western military districts, which could be redeployed into NATO territory in a crisis. Moreover, as U.S. Under Secretary of Defense for Policy Paul Wolfowitz testified before Congress last year, the Soviets continue "to outproduce all of NATO by 2 to 1 in tanks and 10 to 1 in artillery."

It is difficult to accurately estimate the post-CFE U.S. military force in Europe because a number of factors have intervened that call the validity of the CFE totals into question. The most prominent of these is the deployment of U.S. forces to the Persian Gulf during the Desert Storm operation. The centerpiece of U.S. combat capability was the Seventh Corps (three of the heaviest divisions in the Army's inventory), redeployed from western Germany to Saudi Arabia. With this redeployment, fully 50 percent of U.S. combat capability was removed from Central Europe. Only the U.S. Fifth Corps remains in Germany to perform a deterrent mission. While a final decision has reportedly not been made yet, it is doubtful that the Seventh Corps will return to Germany in full strength.

The Persian Gulf War created another obstacle to a continued presence of a large U.S. combat force in Europe—the perennial concern over burden sharing among the NATO allies. Although the British provided 40,000 troops to Desert Storm and the French contributed 10,000, allied willingness to share the burden of defending the Gulf was shamefully small— both in forces and funds. Germany was the only NATO member that pledged a substantial financial contribution to Gulf operations—and only after extraordinary pressure from Washington.

By comparison, the U.S. commitment exceeded 540,000 personnel, roughly 20 percent of the total U.S. active duty force, including one-third of active Army units and half of the Marine Corps. The author's discussions with Pentagon officials confirmed that U.S. forces contributed nearly 70 percent of the ground units, 65 percent of the naval forces, and more than 50 percent of the air forces for the Desert Storm operation. Considering comparatively higher European (and Japanese) dependence on Persian Gulf oil, the U.S. presence was disproportionate.

While Kuwait is clearly beyond the area of responsibility defined in the NATO Charter, the Persian Gulf region is just as clearly vital to the health (although not the integrity) of the alliance, particularly of the European members. The debate about whether and how the alliance members ought to regard "out of area" regions like the Gulf is not new. That debate, however, had occurred within the context of a still-impressive and immediate Soviet threat to Western Europe. The allies could argue (until recently with some credibility) that they could not be expected to commit resources to the security of the Middle East as well as to Europe. (Cynics would remind the allies that they have been reluctant even to commit resources to *Europe's* defense).

Many observers (including this one) felt that the Bush administration should have insisted on larger combat and financial roles for the allies in the Gulf operation, including Japan. This was not just another burden-sharing crisis. Rather, Iraq's invasion of Kuwait represented an unprecedented challenge to regional security in a vital and volatile theater where the United States and the Soviet Union have enduring (and conflicting) strategic interests.

Saddam Hussein's aggression signals the type of future challenges to the international security environment that can be expected from Third World states that feel unconstrained by the rules that prevailed during the Cold War. The Western industrialized nations cannot afford to ignore these "out-of-area" threats simply because they do not fall neatly within the parameters of a treaty drafted nearly five decades ago, when the nature of the threats to Western security were very different from what they are today. Whether NATO is the proper forum to address such threats, however, is a legitimate topic for debate.

NATO was created for one explicit purpose: deterring Soviet aggression *in Europe*. In that sense, alliance strategy has focused exclusively on East-West (that is, NATO-Warsaw Pact) conflict. Europe is now, for a variety of reasons, less likely to be the locus for conflict involving the superpowers, although it would be imprudent to *rule out* the possibility that, for example, a European crisis could quickly deteriorate, ultimately involving Soviet and allied forces. As a hedge against this possibility (and to guard against tempting Soviet recidivism), a reduced in-theater, multilateral, allied combat force of perhaps 225,000 (one-third of which—one armored corps—would be contributed by the United States) should be retained in Europe.

At the same time, the core members of the alliance (the United States, Great Britain, Germany, France, and Italy)

■

An alliance of Western democracies should exist only if a compelling rationale for its continued existence can be identified.

■

must seriously consider either expanding NATO's geographic scope (which is likely to create irreparable political damage to an already weakened structure) or establishing a new framework designed to meet new threats.

This new framework could be established as an allied command outside of the NATO framework (to avoid the hopelessly fractious debates within the NATO Council that would no doubt accompany an out-of-area crisis) that is committed to contingencies arising outside of the NATO Treaty area. This Allied Contingency Force (ACF), which I originally proposed in 1987, would be similar in concept to NATO's Ace Mobile Force (AMF), elements of which were sent to Turkey during the Desert Storm operation.

Unlike the AMF, however, the ACF would be independent of NATO authority and would draw its strength from those NATO powers that have strong interests in deterring future imitators of Hussein. To be credible, the ACF's minimal size would be on the order of two to three brigades (8,000-10,000 troops). Authority to deploy the force would rest with the nations contributing to it.

Unless a serious effort is made to establish a longer term, *non-NATO approach* to emerging *non-European security concerns* (including innovative military frameworks like the ACF), then alliance members will repeatedly find themselves in the unsustainable position of reacting to events after the fact, rather than anticipating them.

In conclusion, an alliance of Western democracies should exist only if a compelling rationale for its continued existence can be identified and if its members are willing to contribute *proportionately* to the costs of maintaining a deterrent. There is nothing magical about either NATO's current structure or its size. There are alternative structures and strategies to those that have served well for decades but have become threadbare over time.

The challenges of the "new world order" cannot be enumerated with any precision, but the uncertainties likely to face the West in the emerging security environment are serious and will require that some military force remain in Europe, albeit with a significantly reduced American component, while the allies construct new frameworks for new security challenges. It is time that candid discussions begin between alliance governments about how to build a post-NATO world.■

Jed C. Snyder is president of the Washington Strategy Seminar and a consultant to the Office of the Secretary of Defense. He is coeditor (with Patrick Cronin) of Crisis and Conflict Evolution in Eastern Europe, *which summarizes a 1990 conference on Eastern Europe's transformation.*

Sheldon W. Simon assesses the role of the United States in Southeast Asia. The author contends that America's Asian policy is in a state of transition, reflecting the twin issues of military relaxation and economic strains. Increasingly, many Asian nations, such as South Korea and the Philippines, have come to view the U.S. air and naval presence as incompatible with their own nationalist aspirations. At the same time, many ASEAN nations view the United States as a major source of regional security. These nations are highly dependent on U.S. markets, which they see as essential to their economic well-being. Still, the United States has warned its ASEAN allies that the existing chronic trade imbalances must inevitably lead to substantial defense reductions.

United States Security Policy and ASEAN

By Sheldon W. Simon
Professor of Political Science, Arizona State University

W HAT happens if peace breaks out?" is a question applicable not only in Europe but in the Asian Pacific area as well. While superpower détente has become increasingly prominent in the late 1980's, its implications for United States diplomacy in Asia are complex. United States foreign policy in the Pacific followed two tracks during the years of Ronald Reagan's presidency. The dominant cold war track emphasized the importance of maintaining a strong navy and a strong air force along the Asian-Pacific rim to balance their growing Soviet counterparts and to reassure allies like Japan, South Korea, the Philippines and Thailand.

An increasingly important secondary track, however, seemed to conflict with the first. As United States budget and balance of payments deficits ballooned, Washington began pressing friends and allies to open their markets to American products and to raise the value of their currencies. These economic pressures have strained United States political-strategic relations with Asian nations, calling into question Washington's long-term ability to sustain a cold war posture through the 1990's.

As the decade closed, these strains were exacerbated by the détente process itself, which challenged the need for maintaining United States military dominance if the Soviet threat were declining. The confluence of economic strains and military

relaxation portends troubled times for the Asian policy of President George Bush.

In effect, the Asian policy of the United States is in a period of transition. Alliances and the maintenance of an air and naval presence still contribute to stability; at the same time, however, they have become an economic burden to the United States and an affront to nationalist sensitivities in countries like South Korea and the Philippines. Nationalist pressures in an era of superpower détente, combined with the monetary costs of maintaining forward deployed forces, will inexorably lead to the reduction of United States forces in Southeast Asia over the next decade. If the size of Soviet deployments in Vietnam wanes, members of the Association of South East Asian Nations (ASEAN)[1] will view American ships and aircraft as increasingly irrelevant to their real security concerns: ethnic unrest, religious tensions and class-based turmoil over the distribution of the fruits of economic development.[2]

The movement toward democracy in Southeast Asia, leading to governments susceptible to popular pressure and shifting coalitions, will make United States policy more complicated on a daily basis. At the same time, there is consensus within ASEAN that only the United States is an acceptable provider of regional security. It is the only major power whose political motives are regarded as benign and whose open markets remain essential for regional prosperity. A United States commitment to Southeast Asian stability and development continues to form the basis of United States policy, even though the contribution Washington makes to regional economic goals is now shared with other donors, notably the countries of northeast Asia—Japan,

---

[1] The Association of South East Asian Nations (ASEAN) consists of Thailand, Malaysia, Singapore, Indonesia, the Philippines and Brunei.

[2] For a readable overview of the dilemmas facing the Bush administration's global policy, see Stanley Hoffmann, "What Should We Do in the World?" The Atlantic, October, 1989, pp. 84–96.

From Current History, March 1990, p. 97. Reprinted with permission from Current History magazine. © 1990 Current History, Inc.

South Korea and Taiwan. All three became major investors in ASEAN during the late 1980's.

As the United States reduces its military competition with the Soviet Union, it is simultaneously increasing economic pressure on allies like Thailand and the Philippines to open their own markets to United States products in order to correct trade imbalances. United States officials have warned their Pacific allies that chronic trade imbalances must lead to defense budget cuts.[3] For example, the United States ambassador to Singapore has insisted that countries under the United States protective umbrella "should absorb more of the costs of that protection." Concern that Washington may press Japan to assume maritime security responsibilities in Southeast Asia may well be energizing recent efforts by Singapore, Malaysia and Indonesia to acquire new missile-armed aircraft and warships to protect adjacent South China Sea waters increasingly on their own.[4]

The ASEAN states are also aware of the decline of Soviet deployments in the South China Sea–Indian Ocean theater in recent years; they know that the Soviet Union is retiring ships more rapidly from the Pacific Fleet than it is commissioning new units. To ASEAN audiences, Soviet officials stress the fact that their naval presence is designed primarily to protect their own important sea lanes to the Soviet Far East, essential for Siberian development. No threat is intended, therefore, by the Soviet navy's operations in Southeast Asia.[5]

In a reduced external-threat environment, combined with American pressures for burden-sharing, United States relations with ASEAN may best be assessed by examining the policies dealing with three major current regional concerns. They include the future of the Philippine bases, which will affect the ability of the United States Navy and Air Force to maintain a permanent Southeast Asian presence; the future of Indochina, pending a Cambodian settlement and the prospect for a new ASEAN-Indochinese political-economic relationship; and the possibility of greater ASEAN defense collaboration as well as ASEAN's role in a larger Pacific Basin economic arrangement. The outcome of these issues could well determine Southeast Asian security in the 1990's.

THE PHILIPPINE BASES

The future of the Southeast Asian bases encompasses both United States facilities at Clark Air Base and Subic Bay Naval Station in the Philippines and Soviet facilities at Cam Ranh Bay and Danang in Vietnam.[6] Their disposition in the 1990's will affect the security policies of all Southeast Asian actors. The termination or even the diminution of forces at the bases would mean that the littoral states would become increasingly responsible for regional defense.

Philippine defense officials admit that their armed forces could not provide for external security were the Americans to leave abruptly.[7] Other ASEAN members also fear that a precipitous United States withdrawal could bring Japanese, Chinese or even Indian naval forces into the region with unpredictable results. On the other hand, even staunch Filipino advocates of the bases agree that their years are numbered and that the facilities should be phased out by the turn of the century.[8] Achieving a gradual phaseout, however, is politically difficult.

Under the new Philippine constitution, the bases can be extended after 1991 only by treaty (not by executive agreement). Already, a decisive bloc of 11 Filipino senators have gone on record opposing renewal, a bloc large enough to prevent the ratification of any lease extension. Hoping to thwart the Senate preemption of the Philippine negotiating position (on which the prospect of considerable United States foreign aid depends), President Corazon Aquino has called for a national referendum on the bases. Assuming that Filipino voters support a lease renewal, public opinion could pressure the senators to drop their opposition.[9]

Because most Filipinos perceive the bases as rele-

[3] Remarks by then Assistant Secretary of State-designate for East Asia and the Pacific Richard Armitage, cited by Michael Richardson, "The ASEAN Scene: Differences Mount as Tension Eases," *Pacific Defence Reporter*, June, 1989, p. 15.

[4] Ibid., pp. 15 and 18. Also see the address by Secretary of State James Baker to the Asia Society, June 26, 1989, in which he calls for a new Pacific partnership with Japan that will be "based on a global sharing of responsibilities," United States Department of State, *Current Policy*, No. 1185, p. 3.

[5] Statements by Commander in Chief of the Soviet Pacific Fleet Admiral Gennady A. Kvatov, as reported in Robert Horiguchi, "Eyewitness with the Pacific Fleet," *Pacific Defence Reporter*, August, 1989, pp. 8–9.

[6] Space limitations preclude a lengthy analysis of the domestic and international issues involved in the bases renewal question. Excellent reviews may be found in William Berry, *U.S. Bases in the Philippines: The Evolution of the Special Relationship* (Boulder: Westview Press, 1989), and Fred Greene, ed., *The Philippine Bases: Negotiating for the Future* (New York: Council on Foreign Relations, 1988).

[7] Statement by Defense Secretary Fidel Ramos as reported in *The Manila Chronicle*, August 22, 1989, in Foreign Broadcast Information Service, *East Asia Daily Report* (cited as FBIS), August 23, 1989, pp. 80–81.

[8] Thai, Singaporean and Malaysian leaders all prefer a continued United States presence in the Philippines. See, for example, both *Bangkok Post* and *Far Eastern Economic Review* (*FEER*) of August 24, 1989, p. 14. Defense Secretary Ramos has called for a one-time extension of the agreement to 1998, *Agence France-Presse* (Hong Kong), August 24, 1989, in FBIS, August 25, 1989, p. 38.

[9] *The Asian Wall Street Journal Weekly* (*AWSJ*), August 28, 1989, and Quezon City GMA7 Radio-Television Arts Network, October 16, 1989, in FBIS, October 17, 1989, pp. 42–43.

vant only to Asia-Pacific defense needs of the United States (and not to their own defense), their continuation is justified as a device to generate United States aid and investment. Manila insists, for example, that any new treaty address all funding provisions explicitly. However, no treaty can bind the United States Congress in advance on appropriations, because the House of Representatives must initiate all financing bills. Moreover, the United States has already raised its assistance package for the Philippines from $180 million in the 1983 bases review to an annual figure of $481 million from 1988 to 1991. This sum is independent of an additional $200 million that the United States has promised for each of the next five years under the Multilateral Assistance Initiative.[10] Given American fiscal constraints, it is unlikely that the United States Congress will be willing to raise the annual figure for the Philippines much beyond its current level.

Paradoxically, a five- or ten-year phaseout could actually accelerate a United States decision to leave the Philippines. Instead of investing further in bases it has agreed to leave, Washington would use its resources for future base sites and related alternatives, probably accelerating the withdrawal schedule from Clark and Subic Bay.[11]

An additional Philippine roadblock lies in the path of a successful lease extension. Article II of the Philippine constitution appears to prohibit nuclear weapons on Philippine territory "consistent with the national interest." Should this provision be interpreted to require that the United States reveal the presence of nuclear warheads on its ships and aircraft, Washington would almost certainly leave the bases.

As the negotiations for renewal begin in early 1990, Manila's talking points seem to focus on the issues of joint use by the Philippine armed forces and an increase in United States imports and investments. If the bases are to be renewed, then the United States must demonstrate sensitivity to the moderates among Philippine nationalists. Washington stresses that the bases are the country's second largest employer, providing jobs for almost 80,000 Filipinos, and that they contribute $1 billion to the economy annually, approximately five percent of gross national product (GNP).[12]

The United States will also be asked to give the Philippines a greater voice in military operations from the bases in Southeast Asia while simultaneously helping to build the Philippine navy and air force so that they, too, can deploy from the bases for external defense.

The politically risky connection between the bases and Philippine nationalism was dramatically illustrated in the December, 1989, sixth and bloodiest coup attempt by military elements against Aquino's government. In the first days, an air attack against Malacanang Palace (the President's quarters) led to Aquino's request for United States military assistance. The Bush administration obliged by sending F-4's from Clark Airfield to fly cover over the Philippine air base from which the mutineers had flown. No fire was exchanged; but the tactic achieved its desired effect by keeping Philippine planes on the ground during the fighting.

While the United States Air Force action was a bold demonstration of Washington's commitment to the Philippine government and to the democratic process in that country, political costs related directly to the bases negotiations. First, the intervention of United States forces in an internal Philippine political situation was probably in violation of Philippine-United States defense arrangements, which prohibit United States involvement in domestic affairs. Second, the United States effort to help President Aquino put down the coup made her vulnerable to nationalist allegations that her government is a lackey of the Americans.

Ironically, these developments could negatively affect the future of the bases. To refute the nationalists' argument, the Philippine government might attempt to attach so many conditions to United States use of the bases that their operational utility will disappear. It is worth noting that if military considerations alone had driven United States policy, Washington might well have decided to let the coup play out without United States interference. If the plotters had won and installed a military-backed regime, renewal of the bases agreement would probably have been much easier. To its credit, the Bush administration acted in a broader political-strategic framework rather than a narrow military one.

THE SINGAPORE GAMBIT

In recent years, Philippine officials like Foreign Minister Raul Manglapus have urged other ASEAN states to share the burden of United States bases. In August, 1989, Singapore became the first ASEAN member to accept the challenge, setting off

[10]A good discussion of these problems is found in Gregory P. Corning, "The Philippine Bases and U.S. Pacific Strategy" (a paper prepared for the annual meeting of the International Studies Association Section on Security Studies, Whittier, California, November 9–11, 1989), pp. 17 and 20.

[11]This argument was made by Larry Niksch of the Congressional Research Service in a paper to the Defense Intelligence College—U.S. Pacific Command Symposium, Honolulu, February 27–March 1, 1989, titled "U.S. Bases: Why They Are Important—How To Keep Them."

[12]*Philippine Daily Globe*, October 25, 1989, in FBIS, October 25, 1989, pp. 40–41.

a heated debate in ASEAN councils over the association's preferred regional security future. This debate reveals the persistence of disagreement on the role of outside powers as ASEAN's protectors.

By offering to host a modest United States naval and air presence—just when Australian and New Zealand forces left Malaysia and Singapore—Singapore's Prime Minister Lee Kwan Yew reaffirmed his belief that the United States military has maintained the balance of power for all the Pacific and has provided the stable security environment within which the region's members could concentrate on export-led economic growth. According to Lee, these achievements should not be lightly dismissed in an emotional wave of nationalism.[13]

Although ASEAN solidarity was ultimately restored with respect to the Singapore offer when officials clarified the fact that the facilities would provide for only a token presence of United States air and naval forces, the controversy demonstrated that neither Singapore nor Thailand had yet come to accept regional neutralization as Southeast Asia's preferred security posture.

For Indonesia and Malaysia (for whom the creation of a Zone of Peace, Freedom and Neutrality (ZOPFAN) for Southeast Asia had been declared policy since the early 1970's), the existence of United States bases in both the Philippines and Singapore would appear to be a regression from the goal of excluding the armed forces of all external powers. A United States air base in Singapore would be particularly sensitive, because aircraft leaving or landing on that island automatically overfly Indonesian or Malaysian airspace. More subtly, Indonesian and Malaysian leaders interpreted Singapore's offer as a way to align with the United States less out of concern about the Soviet Union than to protect Singapore from any future threats from its immediate Malay neighbors.[14] Moreover, two ASEAN locations for the nuclear-weapon-equipped United States Navy would make a mockery of the association's 1987 call for the creation of a Southeast Asian nuclear-weapon-free zone.

Indonesia was particularly exercised that Singapore's offer would derail Jakarta's plans to become the dominant security actor in the region and the coordinator of ASEAN defense planning.[15] Jusuf

Wanandi, director of Jakarta's Center for Strategic and International Studies, summed up Indonesia's dilemma by stating that his country wanted the United States to maintain a military presence in Southeast Asia but could not endorse long-term foreign bases in that region. Looking ahead, Wanandi foresaw the prospect of a joint United States-Japanese naval task force in Southeast Asia by the turn of the century as the American burden-sharing policy takes hold.[16]

By late 1989, the Singapore bases controversy had apparently been resolved. Singapore's offer had been redefined so that it merely formalized current practice, in which the United States Navy uses repair and bunkering facilities and the United States Air Force flies from Singapore in joint exercises.[17] Thus, ASEAN could state that there was no new bases arrangement in the region and no setback for ZOPFAN.

INDOCHINA'S FUTURE

The key to Indochina's future relationship with ASEAN will appear in the political resolution of the Cambodian imbroglio. Vietnam's decade-long occupation of Cambodia (1979–1989) constituted the last vestige of the cold war in Southeast Asia, in which a Soviet client confronted an array of Western-oriented opponents grouped around ASEAN. Unlike the first two Indochina wars, however, the United States declined to commit significant resources to this struggle, deferring instead to both ASEAN and China.

However, Washington's lack of initiative has left unresolved a central policy conflict between ASEAN and China: the latter has been in no hurry to end the Cambodian war, seeing it as an opportunity to punish Vietnam for defying China's strategic interests and to insure that Hanoi remains economically anemic. ASEAN, on the other hand, has no hidden agenda against Vietnam. Once Vietnamese forces are verifiably out of Cambodia and a coalition regime incorporating at least some of Prince Norodom Sihanouk's resistance forces is established in Phnom Penh, the ASEAN states are prepared to normalize relations with Vietnam, to encourage international assistance for its recon-

[13] *The Straits Times* (Singapore), August 5, 1989, in FBIS, August 8, 1989, pp. 33–34.

[14] "Whistling Up a Storm," *FEER*, August 21, 1989, pp. 9–10; *Bernama* (Kuala Lumpur), August 28, 1989, in FBIS, August 29, 1989, pp. 45–46.

[15] See the editorial in *Jakarta Post*, August 8, 1989, in FBIS, August 11, 1989, p. 35.

[16] Author's interview, Los Angeles, September 9, 1989.

[17] *Bernama*, October 20, 1989, in FBIS, October 20, 1989, p. 36.

Sheldon W. Simon is a faculty associate of the Center for Asian Studies at Arizona State University (Tempe). A specialist on Asian security, his most recent book is *The Future of Asian-Pacific Security Collaboration* (Lexington, Mass.: Lexington Books, 1988). Research for this article was partially supported by travel grants from The Earhart Foundation (Ann Arbor) and the United States Information Agency.

struction, and even to consider some kind of formal relationship with Indochina.

The ASEAN orientation is epitomized by Thai Prime Minister Chatichai Choonhavan's plan to transform Indochina from a battlefield into a marketplace. Thai businessmen see Indochina both as a new source of raw materials and as a location for investment in labor-intensive manufacturing, once Cambodia's future is resolved. Although some détente developed in the late 1980's between China and Vietnam, permitting unofficial cross-border trade between the two neighbors, China has not endorsed Chatichai's vision for a prosperous Indochina; this suggests that ASEAN and Chinese strategies will continue to diverge.

The failure of the Paris talks in the summer of 1989 to arrange a comprehensive settlement in Cambodia illustrated that neither Hanoi's client government led by Hun Sen nor the Khmer Rouge believed that it was necessary to compromise.[18] Each believed that it could ultimately prevail on the battlefield as long as the resistance had external sources of support through Thailand and as long as Hun Sen was sustained by the Soviet Union and Vietnam. United States intelligence sources claimed that the Soviet Union had doubled its military aid to Phnom Penh in 1989 over 1988 levels, including 100 T-54 tanks, armored vehicles, heavy artillery and 16 MiG-21 fighters.[19]

As fighting continues in Cambodia, United States policy and ASEAN preferences appear to be on separate paths, with Washington once again leaning more toward China's polarized vision of Southeast Asia than toward ASEAN's syncretic views. Thailand has indicated that it is prepared to tolerate a Cambodia under Vietnamese political influence so long as there are no Vietnamese forces there. Chatichai believes that over time Thailand's economic influence would more than compensate for Hanoi's relationship to the Phnom Penh government.[20] The United States insists, however, that only a comprehensive settlement based on Prince Sihanouk's demands for an interim four-part coalition government, including the Khmer Rouge (pending internationally supervised elections), will warrant United States diplomatic recognition of Vietnam.

United States policy toward Cambodia in 1989 was not a model of consistency, however, possibly reflecting differences within the Bush administration over such issues as the legitimacy of a Khmer Rouge role, whether Prince Sihanouk remains the best hope for a non-Communist Cambodia, and a residual desire to continue punishing Vietnam. High-level officials have variously stated that the United States will refuse to consider Khmer Rouge participation in a successor Cambodian government or that the Khmer Rouge should be included since Prince Sihanouk believes it is the only way to contain the Khmer Rouge before elections.[21]

The United States has not acknowledged that the only rule provided to Cambodia over the past decade is that of the Heng Samrin-Hun Sen regime. Insofar as administration and social services exist, they were created and implemented by the regime placed in power and subsidized by Hanoi and Moscow in 1979. The resistance has nothing to take its place. This reality would seem to undermine the American plan that the resistance should replace the Hun Sen government. Only a coalition that incorporates the latter is a meaningful alternative to the status quo. In fact, this preference was articulated by both United States Secretary of State James Baker and United States Vice President Dan Quayle in their addresses respectively to the ASEAN summit in July and, two weeks earlier, to the Heritage Foundation in Washington, D.C.

Yet by the fall of 1989, the Bush administration had resumed its earlier pro-China position in support of a Khmer Rouge role in an interim coalition government, refusing to deal with Hun Sen. Only active Vietnamese pressure on its ally to agree to a coalition government and subsequent elections supervised by the United Nations would lead to normalization of United States relations with both Hanoi and Phnom Penh.[22] By imposing these new conditions for normalization, the United States maintains an international embargo on trade, aid and investment, thus further punishing Hanoi— apparently the continuation of America's post-Vietnam war legacy. Any new movement toward a compromise coalition will apparently develop only after the Khmer contenders test each other further on the battlefield.

FUTURE REGIONAL SECURITY

If superpower détente translates into a reduction of forward deployed forces in Southeast Asia during

[18]A good review of the diplomatic and political positions of all Cambodian participants is found in Douglas Pike, "The Cambodian Peace Process: Summer of 1989," *Asian Survey*, September, 1989, pp. 842–852.

[19]This analysis was made by *FEER* correspondent Nayan Chanda in a presentation to the Asia Society, Los Angeles, September 8, 1989. Also see Paul Lewis, "Soviets Said to Double Cambodia Aid," *The New York Times*, October 6, 1989.

[20]Mutthia Alagappa, "Malaysia's View of Cambodia," a presentation made to the Asia Society, Los Angeles, September 8, 1989.

[21]These contradictory views were expressed by Secretary Baker at the July ASEAN summit and later by Assistant Secretary of State for East Asia and the Pacific Richard Solomon in an address to the Asia Society, Los Angeles, September 8, 1989.

the 1990's, are the ASEAN states considering an alternative security posture? Although a formal ASEAN defense arrangement is unlikely, the association's membership has developed norms and a structure for the management of disputes sufficiently successful that military budgets have been restrained. Moreover, through annual meetings with the world's major economic powers as dialogue partners, ASEAN has advanced its members' mutual interests in a global setting.

Militarily, two developments can be anticipated for the 1990's: a movement toward regional arms control and confidence-building measures (including the normalization of relations between ASEAN and Indochina); and efforts to effect higher forms of military cooperation within ASEAN. In 1989, Malaysian, Indonesian and Singaporean officials discussed prospects for ASEAN-wide maritime defense, including trilateral exercises. The establishment of a Thai-Chinese arms stockpile also points toward innovative security arrangements as a reduced United States presence seems probable, despite Malaysian and Indonesian objections to China as a long-term security threat.

However, the possibility of a United States exit from Southeast Asia apparently exacerbates the differences among ASEAN states' regional security views. Indonesia sees a great power withdrawal as the best opportunity to become the region's primary maritime power. Thailand, in contrast, believes that a relationship with China remains essential to balance Vietnam. Malaysia and Singapore seem to be leaning toward Indonesia if Indonesia agrees to develop a cooperative defense arrangement for the Malacca Straits. The Philippines is too weak militarily and economically to make a regional defense contribution.[23]

Other clouds on the ASEAN-United States horizon cover economic relations. The United States is either the first or the second largest trading partner with every ASEAN state except Brunei. All, except Brunei, are in trade surplus with the United States; and all have benefited in the past decade from America's open market and insatiable appetite for foreign products. As Washington tries to put its economic house in order, however, efforts to expand United States overseas markets are regarded in Southeast Asia as attacks on ASEAN's economic growth. Pressures on Singapore, Malaysia and Thailand to revalue their currencies and remove restrictions on the entry of foreign goods as well as the need for local legislation to protect American intellectual property rights (patents and copyrights, particularly for computer software and pharmaceuticals) have led to charges that the United States is undermining its friends' prosperity.[24]

THE PACIFIC POLITICAL ECONOMY

In an effort to transcend bilateral economic frictions and to develop a Pacific-wide forum to respond to the 1992 creation of a single European market, three major Pacific economic powers (the United States, Japan and Australia) convened the first ever East Asian-Pacific consultative conference in Canberra in early November, 1989. This unprecedented Pacific Rim conclave brought the United States, Canada, Japan, South Korea, Australia, New Zealand and the ASEAN states together, although it excluded Hong Kong, China and Taiwan for the time being because of the political sensitivity of their situations subsequent to China's crushing of the pro-democracy movement in Tiananmen Square in June, 1989.

The Pacific Rim gathering had its origin in a 1988 proposal by then Secretary of the Treasury James Baker, who believed that such a group would ensure a strong United States role in the Pacific, providing a counterweight to Japanese dominance. The group would also establish a formal link between the industrialized Group of Seven and Asia's newly industrializing countries (NIC's).[25]

ASEAN agreed to the initiative with reservations. The association did not want to see its own annual post-summit meetings with the industrial countries diluted in a larger organization. Malaysia, the Philippines and Indonesia were particularly wary, while Singapore and Thailand saw the enlarged economic consultative mechanism more positively, as an opportunity to discuss regionwide trade and investment expansion. Kuala Lumpur warned that the meeting "shouldn't degenerate into a forum where the richer countries say everyone must do this or that." Washington indicated it would like the Asia-Pacific group to take common stands on trade issues in such multilateral negotiations as the Uruguay round—the current round of UNCTAD (the United Nations Conference on Trade and Development).[26]

The Canberra meeting led to a number of agreements, including the creation of working groups to explore ways of increasing regional trade (already

[22]Robert Pear, "U.S. Is Reassessing Indochina Policy," *The New York Times*, September 24, 1989. See also the report of United States presidential envoy General John Vessey's remarks in Bangkok in the *Bangkok Post*, November 1, 1989.

[23]These prospects are discussed by Donald E. Weatherbee, *ASEAN After Cambodia: Reordering Southeast Asia* (New York: The Asia Society, June, 1989), pp. 17–24.

[24]Karen Elliott House, "Mahathir Charges U.S. Is Trying To Hold Back Asian Growth," *The Asian Wall Street Journal Weekly* (*AWSJ*), November 6, 1989.

[25]"Baker Proposes 'Pan-Pacific' Alliance," *AWSJ*, July 3, 1989.

one-third of total world trade, or more than $200 billion in 1988), investment and technology transfer between rich and poor countries, and trade in services like telecommunications. New data systems will be devised to map these flows, which some officials foresee as eventually turning into a policy clearinghouse similar to the Paris-based Organization for Economic Cooperation and Development (OECD).[27]

In deference to ASEAN, the Asia-Pacific group agreed not to create a permanent secretariat and to convene every other meeting in an ASEAN state. (The next is scheduled for Singapore in mid-1990.)

[26]*Bangkok Post,* September 6, 1989; "Asia-Pacific Parley in Canberra Hoping to Lay the Groundwork for Cooperation," *AWSJ,* November 6, 1989.

[27]Jacqueline Rees, "First Step Taken," *FEER,* November 16, 1989, pp. 10–13.

[28]Charles Smith, "The Backroom Boys," *FEER,* November 16, 1989, p. 12.

Among the issues of particular interest to ASEAN were the further opening of the Japanese market to add Japan to the United States as engines of growth for Southeast Asia and new investment and technology transfers to ASEAN to broaden its industrial base.[28]

While ASEAN apparently welcomes the new Asia-Pacific group's plans to promote more pan-Pacific trade and investment, that welcome is tempered by Indonesia's concern that, just as the great powers may be leaving the region militarily, a new economic obstacle to Jakarta's regional prominence has appeared. To reassure Indonesia, other ASEAN states have tempered their enthusiasm for the Asia-Pacific conference, even though their own development may lie in the success of conference plans. The challenge to ASEAN solidarity in the 1990's may emanate as much from the global economic order as from regional military changes. ■

SELECTED BIBLIOGRAPHY—SECTION V

Baehr, Peter R., and Leon Gordenker. *The United Nations: Reality and Ideal.* New York: Praeger Publishers, 1984.

Barash, David P. *The Arms Race and Nuclear War.* Belmont, Mass.: Wadsworth, 1987.

Blacker, Coit D. *Reluctant Warriors: The United States, the Soviet Union, and Arms Control.* New York: W.H. Freeman, 1987.

Boyd, Gavin. *Regionalism and Global Security.* Lexington, Mass.: D.C. Heath, 1984.

Bretton, Henry L. *International Relations in the Nuclear Age.* Albany: State University of New York Press, 1986.

Brown, Harold. *Thinking About National Security: Defense and Foreign Policy in a Dangerous World.* Boulder, Colo: Westview Press. 1983.

Brown, Seyom. *The Causes and Prevention of War.* New York: St. Martin's, 1987.

Craig, Paul P., and John A. Jungerman. *Nuclear Arms Race: Technology and Society.* New York: McGraw-Hill, 1986.

Franck, Thomas M. *Nation Against Nation: What Happened to the U.N. Dream and What the U.S. Can Do About It.* New York: Oxford University Press, 1985.

Frank, Jerome D. *Sanity and Survival in the Nuclear Age: Psychological Aspects of War and Peace.* New York: Random House, 1982.

Halperin, Morton H. *Nuclear Fallacy: Dispelling the Myth of Nuclear Strategy.* Cambridge, Mass.: Ballinger, 1987.

Jervis, Robert. *The Illogic of American Nuclear Strategy.* Ithaca, N.Y.: Cornell University Press, 1984.

Lall, Arthur S. *Multilateral Negotiation and Mediation.* New York: Pergamon Press, 1985.

Levine, Herbert M., and David Carlton. *The Nuclear Arms Race Debated.* New York: McGraw-Hill, 1986.

Markey, Ed., and Douglas C. Waller. *Nuclear Peril: The Politics of Proliferation.* Cambridge, Mass.: Ballinger, 1982.

Moynihan, Daniel Patrick. *A Dangerous Place.* New York: Berkley Books, 1980.

Mueller, John. *Retreat From Doomsday: The Obsolescence of Major War.* New York: Basic Books, 1990.

Myrdal, Ava. *The Game of Disarmament.* New York: Pantheon Books, 1982.

Peterson, M.J. *The General Assembly in World Politics.* Winchester, Mass.: Allen & Unwin, 1986.

Riggs, Robert E., and Jack C. Plano. *The United Nations: International Organization and World Politics.* Chicago: Dorsey Press, 1988.

Snow, Donald M. *National Security: Enduring Problems of U.S. Defense Policy*. New York: St. Martin's, 1987.

Spector, Leonard S. *Nuclear Proliferation Today*. New York: Vintage Books, 1984.

Sweet, William. *The Nuclear Age: Atomic Energy, Proliferation, and the Arms Race*. Washington, D.C.: Congressional Quarterly Press, 1988.

Talbott, Strobe. *Deadly Gambits*. New York: Knopf, 1984.

Wilson, Andrew. *The Disarmer's Handbook of Military Technology and Organization*. New York: Penguin Books, 1983.

THE ECONOMIC CHALLENGE

In August 1982, Mexico's unexpected announcement that it could not repay its debt shook the world's financial system to its very foundation. Since that time, Western banks and governments have staved off the crisis by imposing their own "solution" on the developing world. Indeed, debt-induced austerity has resulted in a severe economic decline in much of the Third World, bringing with it a host of political and social problems. Today, Third-World debt amounts to around $1 trillion, about half of which is in Latin America. Latin American countries are presently exporting capital to the United States in the amount of some $30 billion a year as a result of the debt. In fact, many U.S. banks have Third-World loans greater than their capital base, meaning that non-payment would threaten the banks' survival.

In the early 1960s, President John F. Kennedy inaugurated his widely-praised Alliance for Progress, which was predicated on agrarian reform, social development, tax reform, and a more equitable distribution of national income. The Alliance was backed by a $20 billion investment to be made over a period of ten to fifteen years. Thirty years have since passed, and there have been few agrarian reforms, save for one exception: the one in Peru, which was carried out by the military government. There have been few agrarian reforms anywhere else, little evidence of tax reform, and scant progress in terms of income redistribution. Since then, Latin America's population has doubled, social problems have multiplied, shantytowns have escalated, and unemployment has soared. In addition, Latin America faces a staggering economic crisis. Unless measures are adopted to ease the situation, they will be forced to pay $40 billion a year for the next ten years—$400,000 billion—in ten years—in interest alone. This would represent twice as much money, every year, as President Kennedy proposed in aid over a far longer period.

The problem is compounded by a deterioration in the terms of trade, the flight of capital, high interest rates, and runaway inflation in Latin America. This crisis—if left unchecked— threatens to stem the tide of democratic openings in Latin America and create considerable social upheaval. In many cases, these nations are incapable of imposing greater sacrifices and restrictions, as has already been shown in three countries. In the Dominican Republic—a relatively stable nation—immediately following the implementation of the first of the International Monetary Fund's strictures—a spontaneous rebellion occurred, in which the army and police were summoned to quash the demonstration. More than fifty people were killed, with hundreds more wounded. In Panama, initiatves aimed at balancing the budget brought hundreds of thousands of people into the streets. And in Bolivia—which has been virtually paralyzed by the debt crisis—inflation soared to over 2,300 percent in 1986.

The newly democratic governments of Argentina, Uruguay, and Brazil—which enjoy widespread popular support—cannot expect to survive if the army and the police are called to fire upon the people. Indeed, many experts believe that if the lendor nations insist on collecting the debt, if they implement the IMF proposed measures and a solution is not found for the economic crisis, there will be widespread revolutionary outbreaks throughout Latin America.

Who is to blame for the problem? One could make the case that the banks are to blame, that the Third World governments are to blame, that the elites of the Third World are to blame, and that the OPEC countries are to blame. Clearly, there is more than enough blame to go around. Rather than fixing blame, which is a difficult if not an impossible task, it would be more helpful to ask who are the big winners in the debt game. The answer is quite clear: The banks are the biggest winners. Although they would like to be clear of the loans, they are still collecting something on what were bad loans, what should have been clear losses. Other winners are the private individuals and government officials of Third World countries who amassed extensive estates or huge bank accounts outside of their own country as a result of profits made from these loans.

There are also clear losers as well. The poor and middle classes of Latin American countries have witnessed twenty years of growth and development stripped away, as their governments have taken the recessionary steps the international structure requires of them. Their access to services, such as education and health care, has being diminished, and there is evidence that malnutrition and infant mortality are increasing.

It is estimated, for example, that at least two-thirds of Latin America's debt was contracted with U.S. sources. Several Latin American leaders contend that these loans were negotiated illegitimately and that they have no moral responsibility to repay their foreign debts. In some instances, their argument is persuasive. For example, traditionally, debtors used to appeal to the banks to borrow money. In recent years, that practice has been reversed. The banks amassed huge sums: among other things, they profited enormously from the large financial surpluses of the oil-producing countries during the oil-price boom. As a result, the banks negotiated massive loans, and lent staggering sums to many impoverished Latin American nations.

Nearly twenty-five years ago, Latin America had practically no debt. Today, that debt amounts to over $400 billion. How was the money spent? Clearly, part of it was spent on weapons. In Argentina, for example, tens of billions went for military expenditures. The same was true of Chile and other countries. Another part was embezzled, stolen, or wound up in foreign banks, frequently in Switzerland and the United States. Another part was returned to the United States and Europe as a result of the flight of capital. Whenever there was talk of devaluation, the privileged elite, out of mistrust, would simply change their money for dollars and deposit it in U.S.banks. Another part was squandered on unnecessary projects. Another part was used by some countries to pay for the high price of fuel. And, finally, another part was spent on economic programs.

Critics contend that these nations have a moral responsibility to repay their debts. However, when one talks about the Third World, one is talking about the people: the workers, the farmers, the students, the middle class—that is, the doctors, engineers, teachers, and other professionals—and other social sectors. Those opposed to repayment ask: What benefit did these people receive from the $400 billion that was spent on weapons, deposited in U.S. banks, misspent, or embezzled? What did they derive from the overvaluation of the dollar or the interest spread? The answer: practically nothing.

For these reasons, many Latin American leaders argue that repayment of the debt is an economic impossibility, a political impossibility. These leaders maintain that it would be much more moral to cancel the debt, which would benefit billions of people—in Latin America, Africa, and Asia. What is truly immoral, they contend, is to force the people to go hungry, to live in poverty, while spending billions of dollars on weapons of mass destruction.

Obviously, the creditor nations do not concur with this analysis. Indeed, in March 1987, forty-four nations assembled to discuss the debt crisis in Latin America. At this conference, financial representatives from these nations debated a proposal which, its critics maintain, would give the United States veto power over how billions of dollars in new loans to Latin America would be parcelled out. The debate focused on a U.S. proposal to exclude debtors from decisions on loans granted by the Inter-American Development Bank, which channels about $3 billion a year in loans throughout Latin America and the Caribbean. These loans help support small and medium-scale projects affecting the environment, energy, agriculture, transportation, and health.

Despite the urgency of the crisis, many industrialized nations have shown little interest in resolving the problem or attempting to mitigate its consequences. Up to now—with some notable exceptions—the United States and other industrialized nations have endeavored to either postpone the problem or tackle it through separate discussions with the various affected countries, making some concessions, such as rescheduling the debt, granting extensions for paying the capital, and proposing new formulas that fail to solve the problem, but offer only brief, spasmodic breathers that simply prolong the agony.

Clearly, Latin America faces numerous other economic problems: depressed prices, the flight of capital, excessive interest, the overvaluation of the dollar, protectionism, and dumping. These problems deprive the region of twice the resources they remit for what could be considered normal interest on loans. If the debt problem is not solved and these other problems remain, they will have won only a brief respite.

Over the years, various proposals have been advanced to confront the debt problem. In the end, there are five general approaches: (1) muddling through; (2) redefinition of assets; (3) sharing the cost; (4) linkage to domestic performance; and (5) repudiation. Option one suggests that the system has functioned, more or less well, since the 1982 Mexican debt crisis. Policymakers should draw on this experience, with or without augmented financial flows. According to the second approach, loans could be sold to a new international bank at a discount, and that bank would then be the collecting agency, insulating present lender banks from the illiquidity problems of debtors. The third approach would share the current adjustment costs among the banks, the debtors, and the beneficiaries of capital flight. The fourth approach would tie the debtor's payments to government performance and the ability to pay. It would

256

address the solvency and liquidity problems while providing some incentives to the debtor countries. The fifth approach, repudiation, is the most controversial, as it would be seen by many as a direct assault on the international banking system. Cuban President Fidel Castro advocated this approach several years ago.

Most experts believe—for good reason, that the best answer would invole a combination of cost sharing and linkage to domestic performance. This would be, they contend, the most effective and fairest approach. The present system, argues economics professor Kenneth P. Jameson, is simply "pyramiding added debt on top of the existing debt. As such, it is neither fair nor realistic." In reality, these debts will, in all likelihood, go unpaid. At the same time, their cost to the poor is staggering. A combination of lower interest rates, combined with linkage to the actual abilities of a debtor country to pay in terms of its exports, would confront both the liquidity and solvency problems at a more reasonable cost to the debtor countries.

Section VI, "The Economic Challenge," encompasses three chapters. Chapter 20, "The North-South Gap," examines the plight of the Third World, noting how difficult it is to define the term with any precision. Although the term is often used to connote poverty, inequality, waste, misrule, and powerlessness, it has come to include many countries, such as Hong Kong, Taiwan, Saudi Arabia, and Brazil, which possess more advanced economies. The author also predicts that the Third World will become increasingly less relevant to the industrialized democracies as they begin to focus their attention and aid dollars on the newly liberated nations of Eastern Europe. The second selection describes the problem of chronic malnutrition in the developing world, explaining that one out of every five people worldwide suffer from hunger. The author contends that most of the deaths associated with malnutrition are unnecessary, as the world produces more than enough food to feed the entire population. He cites ten reasons for the problem, among them: the expansion of export agriculture and commercial farming; government policies and aid programs that increase dependency; Third World debt; ethnic and religious oppression; and militarism and war.

Chapter 21, "Easing the Debt Crisis," analyzes the debt crisis in the Third World. The first selection explains why the bank loans came about in the first place, how most of them were used, and why they suddenly dried up in the 1980s. It also highlights the role played by the International Monetary Fund and the World Bank in the developing world, and concludes by discussing several of the proposed options to relieve the debt and allow these nations a modicum of development in the 1990s. In the second selection, the author advises the international monetary community to move cautiously in agreeing to debt reduction, as genuine progress is impossible without meaningful economic reform. He singles out the Brady Plan, which has provided positive relief for several borrowing countries, as they struggle to reduce their debts and institute the necessary safeguards.

Chapter 22, "The Changing World Economy," describes the economic failures of socialism in Eastern Europe, cautioning European workers to beware of proposals that demand "capitalistic austerity." The author rejects the view that American capitalism is the key to their future, arguing that the U.S. model is partially responsible for the myriad social problems that confront America, including homelessness, the drug epidemic, unemployment, inadequate health care, environmental pollution, and the savings and loan scandal, among others. In his view, the people of Eastern Europe should look to their own traditions rather than emulating the "Western cult of selfishness." The second article surveys the current rift between the United States and Japan. The author maintains that the resurgence of Japanese nationalism and self-confidence, coupled with an increasingly contentious American attitude toward Japan, has produced the deepest split since World War II, with the result that past economic and geopolitical ties can no longer be assumed.

DISCUSSION QUESTIONS

1. Is the term Third World useful in describing the developing world? Why, or why not?
2. Why is the developing world riddled with so many problems?
3. Who is to blame for the situation in the Third World?
4. Is the fate of the developing world likely to become less revelant to the industrialized world in the future?
5. What are the prospects for the future of the Third World?
6. How severe is the problem of malnutrition in the developing world?
7. What are the principal causes of Third World hunger and poverty?

8. Do international aid programs increase dependency in the developing world?
9. How do war and military spending contribute to the problems of Third World hunger and poverty?
10. What major factors contributed to the debt crisis?
11. Who is to blame for the debt crisis in the Third World?
12. Why is the debt crisis such a serious problem?
13. How has debt-induced austerity affected the Third World?
14. Is debt-swapping a viable answer to the problem?
15. How would debt cancellation affect the international economic system?
16. What is the long-term solution to the debt crisis?
17. To what extent was socialism responsible for the economic woes of Eastern Europe?
18. Is capitalism the answer to the economic problems of Eastern Europe?
19. What are the principal failings of American capitalism?
20. Is socialism incompatible with democratic government? Why, or why not?
21. What economic model stands the best chance of success in Eastern Europe?
22. Why have U.S.-Japanese relations deteriorated in recent years?
23. What explains Japan's extraordinary economic success in the post-World War II era?
24. Why is the U.S. trade deficit with Japan so large?
25. Is Japan guilty of unfair trade practices? If so, how?
26. What, if anything, should the U.S. do to retaliate against Japan?
27. Is the U.S. to blame for its own economic misfortunes? If so, how?

KEY TERMS

AGENCY FOR INTERNATIONAL DEVELOPMENT   A U.S. agency formed in 1961 to administer assistance programs to less-developed countries by making loans and arranging technical assistance.

BAKER PLAN   A growth-oriented, market-based solution to the debt crisis, it was proposed by former Secretary of States James Baker in 1985 to promote structural reform and eliminate inefficiency in fifteen "middle income" nations.

BALANCE OF PAYMENTS   An accounting of a nation's economic transactions with foreign countries over a fixed period of time, usually one year.

BRADY PLAN   A debt-reduction measure, introduced by Secretary of the Treasury Nicholas Brady in 1989, calling upon banks to either reduce interest or provide new loans to help less-developed countries solve their financial dilemmas.

BRETTON WOODS AGREEMENT   An international monetary system established in 1944 at a world conference, which led to the creation of the International Monetary Fund and the World Bank.

COMMERCIAL BANK   A state or national bank, owned by stockholders, that accepts demand deposits, approves commercial and industrial loans, and provides other banking services for the public.

DEBT CANCELLATION   A decision made by a debtor nation to either unilaterally or with the approval of the lendor not repay a loan.

DEBT FOR BOND SWAP   Exchange of an old debt owed by a less developed country for bonds issued by the national government in the debtor country.

DEBT RESCHEDULING   The process of negotiating new loans to offset existing obligations, either by extending maturities, deferring principal payments, or reducing interest rates, where the alternative is default.

DEBT SERVICE   The cash outlay required to meet principal and interest payments on a loan.

DEBTOR NATION   A country that is behind in interest or principal payments on debts owed to either bank lenders or international development agencies, such as the World Bank.

DEFAULT   Failure to comply with a contractual obligation, such as repayment of a loan by the debtor nation.

EXTERNAL DEBT   Total amount of bank debt owed by debtor nations to foreign lenders and creditor banks.

FREE TRADE   The flow of trade based on supply and demand, free from governmental regulations and controls.

GROSS NATIONAL PRODUCT   The sum market value of all consumer goods and services produced in a year, it is the primary indicator of the status of the economy.

GROUP OF SEVEN   An international body composed of the finance ministers of the leading industrial democracies who meet to coordinate economic and monetary policy.

INFLATION   An economic condition precipitated by rapid rises in prices and wages, resulting in diminished purchasing power and a lower rate of savings.

INTERNATIONAL MONETARY FUND   A specialized agency, created in 1944, to promote monetary stability in the world community, focusing on the payment of external debts owed by nations with balance of payments deficits.

LESS DEVELOPED COUNTRIES   Those less advanced nations, usually in the Third World, characterized by a low national income, a high rate of population growth and unemployment, and dependence on commodity exports.

MULTINATIONAL CORPORATION   Business enterprises owning subsidiary companies operating across international boundaries and in multiple markets.

NEW INTERNATIONAL ECONOMIC ORDER   A demand made by the less-developed countries for a more equitable distribution of the world's wealth, owing to what they view as past and present exploitation.

PROTECTIONISM   A law providing for a tariff on imported goods, aimed at protecting domestic producers from foreign competition.

RECESSION   A downswing in a country's economy, as measured by a decline in aggregate economic activity.

TARIFF   A tax on imports or exports imposed either to raise revenue or to protect domestic producers from foreign competition.

TRADE DEFICIT   Excess of imports over exports (deficit) or of exports over imports (surplus), resulting in a negative or positive balance of trade.

WORLD BANK   An international lending organization, founded in 1944, that provides developing nations with long-term, low-interest credit for industrial purposes when private financing is unavailable.

Chapter 20

The North-South Gap

Article 20.1.   The Rise and Fall of the Third World

In this article, the author suggests that the end of the East-West rivalry has rendered the concept of the Third World irrelevant, thereby necessitating a new term to describe the developing world. The concept itself originated in the Cold War era, a product of the superpowers' struggle for global preeminence. The term Third World has become increasingly ambiguous in recent decades. Although the "Third World" has become synonymous with poverty and powerlessness, it has traditionally included such diverse states as India, Bangladesh, China, Haiti, Singapore, Saudi Arabia, Zaire, Taiwan, El Salvador, and Hong Kong. With the end of the Cold War—and the battle for world supremacy—it is likely that the fate of Third World peoples will become even less relevant in the future. Indeed, the shift of the First World's attention to Eastern Europe suggests that the welfare of the developing world is of marginal concern to the industrial democracies. For these reasons, the Third World must begin to assume greater responsibility for their own destinies. Regardless of who is to blame for their predicament, the fact remains that the future of the developing countries will depend, more and more, on their own individual and collective actions.

The Rise and Fall Of the Third World

A concept whose time has passed

THE GLOBE AND MAIL

By John Cruickshank

It is not that the idea of the Third World lacks content— we are talking about the developing nations, three-quarters of all humanity living on two-thirds of the surface of the Earth. But the collapse of the global struggle between East and West that produced our modern vision of humanity divided into three worlds is rapidly rendering old ideas meaningless. If we cannot find new ways of talking about what we once called the Third World, we may stop thinking about it altogether, and that would have tragic consequences.

The concept of the Third World was a typical product of the cold-war era, a bit of ideological geography that reflected an obsession with the superpowers and lack of interest in the more populous, less powerful nations. We in the industrialized democracies of Europe and North America, along with Japan, Australia, and New Zealand, were designated the First World. Our deadly enemies of that era—the Soviets and their East European allies— were the Second World. All of the others, the 3.5 billion people living in the buffer zone between the great global rivals and in the developing Marxist states such as China, Cuba, and Vietnam were, by default, the Third World.

In fact, the idea of the Third World became less and less precise throughout the cold-war period. Although "Third World" is used as a shorthand term for poverty and powerlessness, the Third World has traditionally included the oil-soaked Persian Gulf states and China, a nuclear power. The term "Third World" has also become synonymous with misrule, inequality, and waste. But South Korea, Taiwan, Singapore, and Hong Kong have developed powerful economies and more egalitarian societies, by dint of decades of discipline, sacrifice, and often illiberal politics. Countries such as Brazil and India sustain sophisticated industrial economies in the midst of poverty. Successive

From the independent "Globe and Mail" of Toronto.

From *World Press Review*, February 1991, pp. 28-29. Reprinted by permission of The Globe & Mail, Toronto.

Argentine governments, on the other hand, have permitted the collapse of an advanced economy.

It is possible that the fate of the peoples who make up the Third World will become even less relevant to the emerging international structures and forces of the new era. Certainly, Third World nations have lost much of the leverage that they could exercise as ideological partners of the powerful in the cold war. World Bank figures indicate that this is not an insubstantial concern: "In 1988," says the bank's *World Development Report 1990*, "about 41 percent of external assistance was directed to middle-and high-income countries, largely for political reasons." Aid to Israel in 1988, on a per-capita basis, for example, was more than 250 times greater than aid to Nigeria, despite the relative affluence of Israel and the crushing poverty of Nigeria.

The shift of the industrialized democracies' attention (and aid dollars) to Eastern Europe also suggests that the future of the Third World is becoming of even more marginal concern to the rich and powerful nations. The newsmagazine *Far Eastern Economic Review* of Hong Kong notes that the Third World failed to share in the 1980s boom in direct foreign investment: In 1988, three-quarters of the $140 billion of this investment circulated within a select group of industrialized nations—the U.S., Britain, West Germany, and France—even though they account for only 45 percent of total world commerce.

Louis Emmerij, president of the Organization for Economic Cooperation and Development's Paris-based Development Center, has expressed fears that some countries are on the verge of "falling off the edge of the world." Yet, according to United Nations statistics:
•Life expectancy has risen from 40 to 60 years in the Third World.
•Child death rates have been reduced by half everywhere but in sub-Saharan Africa.
•The proportion of children in primary school has doubled, and the proportion going on to secondary school has quadrupled. Literacy rates have more than doubled.
•During a period in which Third World population doubled, food production tripled.
•The proportion of families in the developing world that practice family planning has increased from 9 percent in the 1960s to 45 percent today.
•Developing countries increased their share of world industrial output fourfold, from 5 percent to 20 percent.
•Although immunization of infants against measles, tetanus, whooping cough, diphtheria, tuberculosis, and polio used to be nearly non-existent in the Third World, more than 70 percent of children born this year will be immunized.

Moreover, since World War II, nations such as South Korea, Taiwan, and Singapore have dramatically illustrated that countries can escape Third World conditions. They are not the only models. In a single generation, Indonesia has achieved a huge leap forward. In 1970, almost 60 percent of the population lived in poverty; today, less than 20 percent do. Although Brazil has been far more successful at achieving economic growth than in eradicating poverty during the past 30 years, the portion of its population living in deep need has fallen from 50 percent to 21 percent.

World Bank analysts suggest that there is a critical path to be followed out of the Third World. According to the bank's most recent report, "Rapid and politically sustainable progress on poverty has been achieved by pursuing a strategy that has two equally important elements. The first element is to promote the productive use of the poor's most abundant asset—labor. It calls for policies that harness market incentives, social and political institutions, infrastructure, and technology to that end. The second is to provide basic social services to the poor. Primary health care, family planning, nutrition, and primary education are especially important."

Tragically, many Third World nations have slashed social services in response to the debt crisis. First World analysts charge that Third World countries are seeking savings in the wrong places. Third World leaders reply that they are forced to make structural adjustments to their economies on the backs of the poor—especially through reduced government spending—because the rich countries are refusing them vital aid. Even the World Bank notes that if a 10-percent reduction in military spending by the North Atlantic Treaty Organization were directed to the poor, it would double global aid.

But the question of what ought to be done tends to get transformed in international debates into who is to blame for the continuing poverty of much of the Third World. Many First World analysts say that the Third World must begin to shoulder responsibilities for its own failures. They point to:
•The surge in military spending: Third World arms imports averaged $22 billion annually during the 1980s.
•The larcenous and tyrannical character of the elites of many Third World countries. The flight of capital out of the Third World to the First World has contributed to the debt crisis.
•The inability of some Third World governments to overcome internal divisions and their failure to govern wisely.

Third World leaders reply that the First World indulges in oppressive trade practices that keep Third World products from the market. Further, they charge that unjust monetarist policies transfer the failings of First World economies to Third World borrowers and crush them with debt-servicing costs.

The prospects for the future of the nations of the Third World are decidedly mixed. As a group, the sub-Saharan African countries appear to be facing another decade of very slow progress. The extraordinary victory of democracy in Latin America in the 1980s, despite very tough economic conditions, probably indicates better days ahead. As governments become more responsive to all of their citizens, their public-policy decisions tend to improve. In South and East Asia—where about half of the billion people on Earth who survive on less than $400 a year now live—the prospects for the 1990s are improving.

Over the short term, it seems likely that the developing, and the deteriorating, nations of the Third World will be of less interest and concern than ever to the industrialized nations. Yet, over the long term, that will inevitably be reversed. We are moving into an era of ever greater, and perhaps ever more involuntary, interdependence. ∎

Today, more Third World people go to bed hungry at night than ever before. Nearly 950 million people are "chronically malnourished"—or one in five worldwide—while 15 million children die annually of malnutrition. The vast majority of these hunger-related deaths occur in the Third World: Africa, Asia, Latin America, and the Caribbean. Sadly, most of these deaths could be averted, as the world produces more than enough food to feed the planet. Surprisingly, more than one-half of this bounty is grown in the developing world, where the need is the most urgent. Unfortunately, little of this food reaches the needy, owing to the expansion of export agriculture and commercial farming, government policies and aid programs that increase dependency, Third World debt, IMF-sponsored economic austerity, militarization and war, farming practices that damage the environment, and ethnic and religious oppression, among other factors.

WHY THE THIRD WORLD GOES HUNGRY

SELLING CHEAP & BUYING DEAR

KATHY McAFEE

More of the world's people are hungry today than ever before. The World Bank has estimated that as many as 950 million people are "chronically malnourished": too hungry to lead active, productive lives. That's nearly one person in five worldwide. According to United Nations figures, more than 15 million children die each year of malnutrition and related sickness. Most of these hunger-related deaths, whether of children or adults, occur in Asia, Africa, Latin America, and the Caribbean—the global South, or third world. It has been calculated that food deprivation causes as many deaths in a year as would a Hiroshima-size atomic bomb dropped somewhere in the third world every two or three days.

Most of these deaths are needless. More than enough food is grown to feed everyone on earth. The World Resources Institute reports that if all the food produced were distributed equitably throughout the world, it could provide an adequate diet for nearly six billion people—one billion more than now live on the planet. More than half this bounty is grown in the third world. The UN Food and Agricultural Organization has documented that food production during the past twenty-five years has outpaced population growth in every major region except Africa south of the Sahara desert. But those who need this food—and who do most of the work of producing it—are often not the ones who consume it.

Some analysts, including Lester Brown and John Young of the Worldwatch Institute, warn that global population growth may soon begin to exceed the rate of increase of world food production—this as the result of erosion, deforestation, and other consequences of policies and practices that undermine the planet's capacity for producing food and fresh water. Their predictions may prove true, but that does not mean we can solve the problem of hunger by limiting population growth. Famine exists now, when there is food enough to feed the world. Unless we understand why today's surplus does not reach the needy, and until we do something about it, we will not be able to avert more widespread starvation in any future context of scarcity. Moreover, as explained below (point No. 7), the same factors that lead to hunger also serve to degrade the environment in many places.

Hunger makes news during severe regional famines, when cameras portray hundreds of thousands sinking toward death. But if the existence of chronic hunger in a world of abundance is rarely acknowledged, its root causes are even less understood. News media report emergency food shipments, foreign aid grants,

KATHY McAFEE, *senior writer and researcher for Oxfam America, has written extensively on international debt, causes of poverty, and alternative development models and processes emerging from the global South. Her book on debt and development in the Caribbean,* Storm Warning, *will be published in early 1991.*

From *Commonweal*, June 15, 1990, pp. 380-385. Commonweal Foundation © 1990.

private and governmental loans from the developed countries, leading us to assume that by these measures the rich countries are sustaining the battered economies of the third world. The opposite is closer to the truth. In the movement of wealth around the world, far more flows *out of* impoverished countries of Africa, Asia, and Latin America and *into* the richer economies of Europe, North America, and Japan. Every year since 1986, according to an estimate by the Overseas Development Council, at least $43 billion in net financial resources has been transferred from the global South to the North. The estimate is conservative; others put the South's net loss higher.

The measurable portion of this hemorrhage is made up in large part of debt payments. UNICEF reports that in 1988 would-be developing countries had to channel $178 billion to Northern nations to meet their debt bills. The total external debt of the third world is a crushing $1.2 trillion. In 1987, low- and middle-income governments paid out $102 billion in interest alone—3.4 times the total development assistance from all aid-giving nations. Other components of the measurable flow are the profits claimed by foreign owners of third-world businesses, and the deposits by the South's elite in Northern banks.

Other resources flow unseen, like underground rivers, in the same direction; they are harder to calculate, but very real. The mineral and agricultural products transferred out of Latin America, Asia, and Africa are vital to the global economy, but the prices paid for them do not begin to reflect their practical usefulness, or the profits they make possible for shippers, processors, and speculative commodity traders in the North. So also with the value added to garments, gadgets, and other goods assembled in export processing zones of the third world; workers there earn a small fraction of the wages paid to those doing comparable factory work in the North.

Still more unseen wealth is drained from the third world by illegal or semilegal means. Corporations disguise the removal of profits through the shady accounting practices of transfer pricing; individuals add to capital flight by smuggling out hard currency into foreign bank accounts. Tremendous sums are accumulated in the North at the expense of the South through the international drug trade. Andean peasants, many of whom can no longer find an adequate income alternative to growing coca leaves, receive a tiny fraction of the immense wealth gathered by the cocaine industry bosses, who use banks and corporate fronts in the U.S., Europe, and the Caribbean to launder their earnings.

Cumulatively, these massive transfers of wealth from the impoverished third world to the comparatively affluent industrialized nations constitute the most important underlying cause of third-world poverty and hunger. The poor of the third world are being integrated into a global economy in which allocation of food is determined by market criteria. It is a skewed system, as different as could be from the free and competitive model imagined by Adam Smith. In the only markets to which poor people of the third world have access, they have no control over trading terms, interest rates, investment choices, or the other rules of the game. Increasingly, those with greater control edge out those with less. The consequence is that millions of farmers are being deprived of resources they need to raise food for themselves and their communities: land, water, tools, draft animals, credit, traditional knowledge, and structures of community cohesion and support.

ll this is happening in a variety of ways.

1. *The expansion of export agriculture and commercial farming.* Wealthy countries have imported products like coffee, tea, and chocolate from the third world since the days of colonialism. Imports of such tropical products are still increasing; growing still faster are imports of foods like canned fish and meat, fresh fruits and vegetables, and fibers such as cotton—all products that can be produced in temperate climates but that can be raised and harvested more cheaply (or during winter) in the third world. The rich countries are also increasing their purchases of crops such as soybeans from Brazil, peanuts from West Africa, cassava from Thailand—foods that could nourish hungry people in the countries where they are grown, but are fed instead to livestock in rich countries.

Little of the money earned by these sales goes to the primary producers. In the fertile lowlands of Central America, for instance, peasants once grew crops that provided a nutritious diet: corn, beans, melons, squash, tomatoes, and chilis. Today, cattle ranches and plantations growing export crops such as sugar, coffee, cotton, and bananas cover much of this land.

The very profitability of third-world commercial crops has hurt rather than helped the poor. It has contributed to increased prices and rents for land, and to higher costs for irrigation equipment, fertilizers, and pesticides. Subsistence farmers who cannot afford these increased costs are being displaced by commercial growers. Half the farmers in the third world have access to less than 2.5 acres, often not enough to support a family. One-third of all rural third-world households have no access to land at all. Many peasants who have lost their farms now work as laborers on the same land they once owned, often earning too little to buy enough staples for an adequate diet. Other farmers, displaced by tractors and threshing machines, can find no work at all in rural areas, and must seek jobs in the third world's swelling cities, or abroad.

2. *Government policies and aid programs that increase dependency.* In many parts of the third world, land, wealth, and political power are concentrated in the hands of an elite. Efforts by farmers to resist displacement from their land, to gain access to land through land reform or, when that fails, through land occupations, are frequently met with repression that precipitates an escalating cycle of violence. Even where the poor have broader access to land, many governments provide farm loans, irrigation, seeds, and technical assistance for cash crops, but not for subsistence farming or local and regional marketing of food crops.

Few large-scale international aid projects are designed to promote local food production, and those that are food-related often result in increased dependency. Farming methods developed in Europe and the U.S. favor the relatively few landowners who can afford fertilizers, pesticides, machinery, and fuel. Over the past three decades, moreover, the bulk of development aid has not been for farming to meet local needs but for projects like large dams, ports, and power plants, or for export crops. Much of this aid money ends up in the bank accounts of contractors and consultants from the donor nations. Often, the aid is in the form of loans, but most of these expensive projects have failed to generate enough income to pay off the loans.

3. *Structures of dependency.* Although many third-world countries became politically independent during the three decades following World War II, most remained economically subordinate. They had inherited political and economic structures established to facilitate the transfer of raw materials to the colonial powers or other industrialized countries. For example: Roads, railroads, and communications lines, where they exist, generally link interior areas to port cities, but do not run between cities and towns, or even between countries in the interior of Southern continents. The goods removed via these routes were, and still are, processed and manufactured into finished goods in the nations of the global North, or in refineries and factories owned by foreign corporations. Thus, the phases of production which add the most value to—and raise the prices of—most goods that are traded internationally take place outside the territories and economies of the South. The prices of unprocessed commodity exports—crops and minerals—have been declining; most are at a forty-five-year low. Meanwhile, these same countries must purchase finished goods—trucks, steel, factory-made consumer goods—from the industrialized countries, at constantly rising prices.

4. *Third-world debt.* During the 1960s and 1970s, Western banks and governments encouraged third-world countries to borrow billions of dollars to make up the difference between their export incomes and their import expenses. The theory was that foreign financial fueling would enable Southern countries to "take off" on their own toward industrialization. Economic growth, it was said, would generate the funds needed to repay the loans.

It didn't happen. Because of the inequities built into global systems of production and trade, the third world continued to sell cheap and buy dear. Typically, countries which borrowed once soon had to borrow again. In 1973 and again in 1978, rising oil prices contributed to a massive increase in third-world debt. Non-oil-producing countries in the South had to double or triple their borrowing just to keep their economies going at pre-1970 levels. Then—also in the late 1970s—third-world debt bills rose sharply in response to a dramatic increase in interest rates. Many commercial bank loans to Southern countries were made at "floating" interest rates. When those interest rates rise, debt bills mushroom. A 1-percent increase in interest rates automatically adds $700 million to Mexico's annual debt bill. The World Bank calculated that interest rates affecting third-world borrowers rose 30 percent in just two years (1980-1982).

As interest rates soared, debtor nations were pressed by banks and international lending agencies to take on new loans just to keep up the interest payments on their previous loans. By 1983, 79 cents of each new dollar borrowed by Latin American nations was used solely to pay interest on past loans. Two-thirds of Latin America's export earnings were being consumed by debt payments.

Under pressure from their creditors, most indebted countries have increased the volume of their exports to make up for the lower prices they receive for them. Throughout the South, governments invite investors to fell more forests, mine more mountains, plow up pastures, drain wetlands, and replace staple foods with export crops. But worldwide competition among exporters of grains, other foods, minerals, and fibers has resulted in even lower prices for these commodities, and thus in lower incomes for many farmers (including some in the United States), and a decline rather than an increase in the earnings from exports by third-world nations.

5. *IMF-sponsored economic austerity.* As a consequence of their debts, many countries of the South have become subject to the economic stewardship of the International Monetary Fund (IMF) and the World Bank. Both institutions were established by the victorious industrialized nations in the aftermath of World War II. The purpose of the IMF, as established in its charter, is to promote the continuation and expansion of international trade according to "free market" principles. In line with this mandate, the IMF extends loans at close-to-market interest rates to countries faced with balance-of-trade and payments deficits. These loans are intended as short- to medium-term measures to tide countries over until they can balance their books by bringing expenditures into line with earnings.

It is customary to think of IMF's mission as a form of aid from the North to the South. More accurately, the IMF serves the international financial system and reinforces the system's underlying power relations. Thus, in practice, the IMF acts as a sort of "economic policeman" on behalf of commercial banks, Northern governments, and other international lending agencies. Indebted countries that are unable or unwilling to take IMF loans, repay them on schedule, and adopt economic policy changes acceptable to the Fund are often unable to obtain longer-term development loans, or even short-term credit to import desperately needed food, fuel, medicines, and spare parts for machinery.

IMF practices do not address the causes of third-world poverty, and IMF loans have done little to reduce overall debts. More often, they have contributed to increased debts as borrowing countries have been forced to take on loans from other sources to meet strictly enforced IMF repayment schedules and IMF-required targets for economic growth. Meanwhile, IMF austerity programs aimed at bringing about "stabilization" have severely weakened many third-world economies. As a condition of loans, the IMF requires recipient countries to adopt policies to increase their export earnings and simultaneously to reduce government spending on social services and most other programs not geared toward increasing exports. This means cuts in education, health care, nutrition programs, agricultural extension services, and environmental monitoring. Often it entails reduction or elimination of subsidies many Southern governments have used to keep food prices affordable for the poor of their nations, and thereby to keep a lid on social unrest. Many IMF programs call for devaluation of the borrowing country's currency as well. This makes the devaluing country's exports cheaper—and, in theory, more competitive—on global markets, and discourages imports by making them more expensive for the borrowing country.

But these same measures also lead to immediate and often drastic increases in the prices of food, transportation, and basic consumer goods. By making credit and imported inputs impossibly expensive while opening local markets to foreign competition, they frequently put local farms and factories out of business, adding to massive unemployment. By reducing social services, they increase the pressures on women and others who care for children, the elderly, and the infirm. In brief, IMF policies serve to shift the burden of debt repayment onto those least able to bear it, and thus to deplete the human capital on which development depends.

6. *World Bank failures.* The World Bank has come to play an even more important role than the IMF in directing the development policies of Southern governments. The Bank makes longer-term loans, sometimes at lower interest rates, intended to promote economic growth and trade through private enterprise. World Bank loans are increasingly geared toward export production, both in agriculture and in low-wage industries. Before the 1980s, most World Bank loans funded the construction of roads, ports, dams, power plants, and large-scale agricultural export projects. During the past decade, Bank priorities shifted. Today, about a quarter of the Bank's loans to the South are "sectoral adjustment" or "structural adjustment" loans. These loans finance economic reprogramming that alters not only the external trade policies but also the internal economic priorities of indebted countries.

tructural and sectorial adjustment programs redirect resources away from domestic needs. They require impoverished countries to reduce taxes on the wealthy, increase taxation of the working majority, sell land and other public assets to private owners, devalue their currencies further, raise still higher the prices of transportation and many food items, keep wages low, and offer tax breaks and cheap factory space and services to foreign manufacturers.

Structural adjustment programs rest on the theory that countries adopting them will be able to work their way out of debt through economic growth that will generate income to finance development and pay off debts, and, not incidentally, prevent banks in the rich countries from collapsing. In reality, largely as a consequence of structural adjustment and related export-promotion policies, more resources—food, minerals, labor power, and money—are flowing out of the third world to the wealthiest countries than ever before. Capital for local development is not accumulating but dwindling.

Structural adjustment programs are not working, even on their own terms. Their failure to promote sustainable growth and equitable development has been publicly recognized by a wide range of institutions and observers, including the UN's Economic Commission on Africa, the *New York Times*, and the U.S. Catholic Conference's administrative board in its statement on third-world debt (September, 1989). Even the World Bank's own chief economist stated in March that the bank intends to reduce its structural adjustment lending. (Its export emphasis, however, is unlikely to change.)

7. *Farming practices that damage the environment.* The pressure to increase export crops production and the lack of other ways of earning income compel growing numbers of farmers to adopt agricultural practices that undermine the long-term productivity of the land. The greatly increased use of chemical fertilizers often depletes the soil. Excessive employment of pesticides creates toxic hazards for present and future generations.

Peasants displaced from high-quality farmlands by commercial producers often have no choice but to try to raise food or cash crops on land not suitable for continuous farming. Cultivation of steep hillsides results in soil erosion. On the dry plains of Africa's Sahel, soil plowed to plant cotton and peanuts is quickly turned to dust by desert winds. In Amazonia and other moist tropical regions, thin rainforest soils that are too frequently replanted quickly lose their fertility. The same thing happens when good farm land is overcultivated, without fallow years and without replacement of organic matter removed from the soil. Under such conditions, the harder farmers work over the years, the less they get for their labor. Few would choose to farm such unfriendly fields if they had other ways to survive.

The incentive to conserve dwindles as the distance increases between those who produce food and those who control food-producing resources. Decision-makers in bank and aid agency board rooms seldom confront the consequences of their actions, which alter the lives and landscapes of millions. Neither do most reporters and financial analysts who cover these matters. Yet Northern pressure on Southern governments to produce quick cash for debt repayment virtually insures that third-world lands will not be developed or preserved in the interest of the majority.

8. *Militarization and war.* World-wide military spending has doubled over the past twenty years to more than $800 billion yearly. The amount spent every minute could feed two thousand malnourished children for a year. From 1977 to 1987 the third world's share of the global arms budget increased from 9 percent to 16 percent, draining resources that could be used to combat poverty and hunger. UNICEF has reported that third-world countries spent $145 billion in 1988 on weapons and armies.

There have been more than 130 wars since 1945, nearly all of them in the third world. These "conventional" wars have killed about 25 million people, made millions more into permanent refugees, and caused incalculable damage to third-world economies and environments. Third-world militarization is a result as well as a cause of increasing hunger: many third-world governments have come to power in the wake of food riots or other forms of mass protest against falling living standards. Enforcement of adjustment programs that multiply human misery will require increased coercion, repression, and military intervention.

9. *Ethnic and religious oppression.* Conquest and exploitation of some peoples by others, long a part of human history, acquired a new dimension in the colonial era. European powers carved what we now call the third world into colonies, creating states that did not correspond to existing political boundaries, dividing linguistic and cultural groups across arbitrary borders, and giving certain ethnic and religious groups new or greater power over others.

Where there is hunger today in the third world, all do not hunger equally. Members of oppressed castes, tribal groups, and religions often have less access to food-producing resources and government assistance, and are more likely to have to go without food. Indigenous people in Latin America and minority ethnic groups in Africa and Asia are among those who suffer most as policies to speed debt payments increase the pressure on their lands.

10. *Discrimination against women.* Although in many parts of the South women are the main food producers, more women than men suffer from malnutrition. Though women head one out of three third-world households, and perform an estimated two-thirds of all hours worked, it is women and girls who starve most often. Four times as many malnourished children are female than male, and their mortality rate is 40 percent higher than that of boys. In many societies in times of plenty, men and boys eat first; in times of famine, women and girls may not eat at all. Nutritional anemia affects about half of all third-world women of child-bearing age, draining their strength and lessening their resistance to disease.

The effect of modernization in many rural third-world areas has been to worsen the situation of women. Commercialization of agriculture in societies where men hold land titles and money means less control by women over family resources and food distribution. Mechanization of plowing and harvesting often means a loss of income for women, since agricultural loans and technology are often made available only to men. Efforts to accumulate quick cash for debt repayments accelerate these processes.

Thus the causes of world hunger are at once multiple and unitary; that is to say, systemic. They are deeply rooted and well protected; though needless hunger is a scandal, it is a hidden one, and ending it is not seen by the elites of North or South as serving their interests.

Yet there is cause for hope: North and South, a great many Davids are confronting their respective Goliaths, and, to an extent, they are learning to collaborate across borders toward achievement of common goals: to reduce hunger, eliminate its causes, bring about sustainable, broad-based development, and achieve a more just distribution of the world's resources. Linkages are most evident in the partnerships between nongovernment organizations engaged in self-help projects in the third world and private agencies in the North that provide these projects with modest funding and people-to-people publicity and support. Examples in the U.S. include Oxfam America, Food First, the American Friends Service Committee, Grassroots International, the Unitarian Universalist Service Committee, Catholic Relief Services, Food for the Poor, and Global Exchange.

Compared with the mega-projects financed by the World Bank or U.S. AID, these projects are small in scale: a women's cooperative processing local fruit, a community poultry-rearing project, an old cargo boat renovated to carry crops to market, to list some carried out by project partners of Oxfam America. Other projects are adopting new methods of conservation and reviving old ones, building small-scale irrigation works and better food storage facilities, organizing production and marketing co-ops, expanding women's income-generating activities: weaving, dairying, farming. They are developing literacy and skills-training programs, and making use of radio, popular theater, and creative new forms of research, education, and communication to enhance their understanding of the causes of poverty and the means of improving their lives.

The importance of such projects is partly that they provide a testing ground for development models—at their best, they embody or prefigure elements of an alternative and achievable definition of development—and partly that they are conceived and carried out by the aid beneficiaries themselves. In the process, participants strengthen their technical and leadership skills, confidence, the ability to identify problems and plan solutions.

In the context of an overall drain of resources out of the global South, even successful local projects cannot engender development by themselves. Understanding of this reality is spreading, however, and in consequence grassroots and nongovernment organizations in Asia, Africa, Latin America, and the Caribbean have begun to form regional and international organizations such as the Malaysia-based Third World Network and the women's organization, DAWN, with offices in Mexico, India, and Brazil. These, along with local, national, and regional organizations of farmers, women, workers, indigenous and minority peoples, certain scholars, and some government officials, have begun to formulate experience-based alternatives to the failing debt-financed, export-dominated model of development. Central to the goals being articulated with increasing clarity and unanimity by progressive third-world NGOs is increased food production for local and regional needs. They also hope to promote more South-South trade, closer agro-industry links, more use of local materials and skills, more control by Southern nations over the prices of their exports, greater involvement and consultation of farmers and others affected by development schemes; in a phrase, more workable and more genuinely democratic development. Needless to say, relief from the debt burden is a prior condition of progress.

For that reason, and because the "aid" policies of national governments in the North and the international lending agencies constitute the major obstacles to third-world development, local and regional groups in the South are asking citizens of wealthier nations for support. They are asking not for charity in the form of food shipments, but for change. Northern policies that require Southern governments to negotiate structural adjustment programs one by one and that enforce a strategy of exports-at-any-cost rule out alternative strategies based on self-reliance and regional cooperation. Insistence on drastic reduction of public services for the sake of meeting debt schedules saps human capital. Such policies, third-world groups contend, harm the long-term interests of the majority of citizens in the North as well as the South. Farmers who cannot sell their crops, workers who cannot earn a living wage, the growing numbers with no land or job at all cannot be good customers for Northern products. Governments that respond to the unrest of their impoverished peoples with military violence cannot be reliable allies.

As already noted, development and development education

agencies in the U.S. are responding to this call by entering into new relationships with third-world groups that replace almsgiving with partnership. In addition, some environmental organizations, such as the Environmental Defense Fund, are coming to recognize that saving the natural environment is impossible if it entails destroying the livelihoods of the people who inhabit rain forests and other threatened areas. Religiously motivated lobbying groups—in particular, Bread for the World—carry out extensive research on the causes of hunger and the impact of U.S. policies. Church-based organizations, under the multi-denominational umbrella of Interfaith Action for Economic Justice, are paying attention to alternative development proposals from the third world. So also are public policy organizations such as Development GAP and Policy Alternatives for the Caribbean and Central America (PACCA). And, across the country, citizens are forging links among towns, churches, and trade unions in Southern Africa and Central America and their U.S. counterparts. By supporting efforts like these, we can help the people of the South to overcome hunger and develop along their own chosen pathways. We can also help to avert ecological disasters of great consequence, and to prevent replacement of the East-West cold war by a devastating global struggle between the North and the South.

Chapter **21**

Easing the Debt Crisis

Article 21.1.   It Won't Go Away Alone

The $1.2 trillion Third World debt crisis continues to attract international attention, owing to the seriousness of the situation. Despite popular thinking, the problem did not result from excessive Third World borrowing. Unfortunately, much of the money disappeared through capital flight, borrowed funds were used for unproductive consumer goods or military expenditures, a good deal was used to finance huge government deficits, and the money frequently was invested in high-cost import substitution industries. Although the severity of the crisis has lessened in recent years, the debt crisis still remains a serious problem. It can only be solved by a comprehensive approach that seeks to strengthen the international financial system. This will require the cooperation of all parties, including the debtors, private creditors, creditor governments, international agencies, and perhaps even new participants, such as the insurance industry. Clearly, any solution will demand bold, aggressive, dynamic leadership, which could come from a creditor nation, the IMF, or the World Bank—or, hopefully, all three.

It Won't Go Away Alone

Christopher Korth

Christopher Korth is professor of economics at the University of South Carolina.

One of the most serious international economic and political problems today is the enormous amount of foreign debt owed by Third World countries. The burden of the debt problem, of course, varies significantly in different less developed countries (LDCs).

Some of these countries have indeed been able to avoid or overcome serious debt problems, thus creating a new category of new industrialized nations. Most of the success stories are in Asia—for example, Taiwan and South Korea. (Indeed, Taiwan has become a major capital exporter, and its government's international reserves are in excess of $70 billion.) However, most Third World countries are heavily burdened by their international debt.

Other LDCs, because of their extreme poverty and very poor credit prospects, share the dubious distinction of never having been able to borrow freely in the international private money and capital markets. Lenders, such as commercial banks and investors in the bond markets, have never found the prospects of returns attractive enough to make loans to these countries. As a result, these countries, "the poorest of the poor," have only been able to borrow from the governments of the wealthy countries and from international agencies, such as the International Development Association of the World Bank Group. Fortunately for those countries, loans from these official agencies are generally made on "concessionary" terms, with fixed, low-interest rates. Included in

This article appeared in the February, 1989 issue and is reprinted with permission from *The World & I,* a publication of *The Washington Times Corporation,* copyright © 1989.

this group of the very poorest are such countries as Chad and Mali in Africa, Suriname and Guyana in Latin America, and Bangladesh and Burma in Asia.

Middle-income LDCs

Most of the current concern about the welfare of the Third World countries tends to focus on the middle-income LDCs. Among these are most of the largest LDCs, including those countries that had been widely considered the most promising in the Third World—Mexico, Brazil, Argentina, Venezuela, the Philippines, Indonesia, and Nigeria.

It is this last group, the middle-income Third World countries, whose international financial status has deteriorated most markedly. They have been the subject of greatest concern in recent years. This will focus primarily on this group.

The 1960s and early 1970s: The watershed to the international debt crisis was the oil-price hike in December 1973. Prior to that time, both the magnitude of the debt problem and the relations between the major lenders, regulators, and borrowing countries were very different than they are today.

By recent standards, the borrowing needs of most developing countries, and their total international debts, were relatively small. Most of the international loans to *all* developing countries came from foreign governments and international agencies (such as the International Monetary Fund, the World Bank, and the Inter-American Development Bank), and from trade credits from suppliers. The LDCs were generally unable to borrow from commercial banks or in the bond markets. Even the Brazils and the Mexicos generally could not borrow from commercial banks.

In addition to having more limited international funding needs, the developing countries also benefited from economic conditions in the late 1960s and early 1970s. This made their international debts easier to service—both interest and principal. Interest rates were low. Exports from many developing countries were strong. Also, the prices of most of the major commodity exports from the LDCs were high (for example, between 1965 and 1975, the prices of major commodities rose more than 80 percent). As a result of these favorable conditions, serious financial problems at the time were infrequent: The debt burden was generally manageable.

The late 1970s and the 1980s: The 1970s saw ambitious economic expansion in many developing countries. That caused a sharp increase in their imports. There was also rapid inflation in most industrialized countries, causing the prices of manufactured products being imported by the LDCs to rise at the same time that the volume of imports was increasing. Although commodity prices (not only of oil, but of most primary products) remained strong through the end of the 1970s, the prolonged recession in the industrial world during the early 1980s sub-stantially weakened most of those prices. A result of this combination of factors was a sharp deterioration in the balance of trade in most developing countries.

This was also a period in which most governments greatly increased their budget deficits. In many countries, subsidies on basic products (both domestically produced and imported) rose sharply —especially on food and fuel. Rising interest rates on foreign debts exacerbated the problem, which further aggravated the funding problems of these countries.

The role of commercial banks

As was noted above, before 1973, the role of commercial banks in lending to LDCs was small. For example, as recently as 1968, commercial banks had provided less than 6 percent of all the international funding needs for Latin America. Beginning in 1972, however, that relative importance grew rapidly. By 1973, the international banking share of all funding needs for Latin America had grown to 44 percent. The stage had been set for banks' critical role in helping alleviate the oil crisis that was to come in 1974.

After 1973, the OPEC governments, having received huge increases in revenues from their oil-price increases, deposited most of the funds in the international banks. Seeking profitable ways to invest such receipts, the banks proved only too willing to service the borrowing requirements of the developing countries. For example, in Latin America (the region most attractive to commercial banks), the banks' share of the region's international funding reached 70 percent in 1979, compared with 7 percent in 1968.

Major defaults among the developing countries were generally averted until the early 1980s. This was often less because of successful debt management by the borrowers than because the lenders loaned the borrowers the money to make payments on their loans.

Additional time was gained as a result of two developments for which neither the countries nor banks can take much credit: the drops in the price of oil and in interest rates. Although the steep decline in oil prices has hurt such oil-exporting countries as Indonesia, Mexico, and Nigeria (and the banks that had loaned to them), the lower interest rates have helped most LDCs.

Bad loans, borrowers, or creditors?

The current international debt situation (or the credit situation, as seen from the perspective of the lenders) is extremely grave. The villains in this scenario are numerous, and they exist on both the borrowing and lending sides. Heroes are few. The United States, still an economic superpower, is the largest debtor nation in the world. Although calls consistently come from Western Europe and Japan attempting to push Washington to get its economic house in order, in reality it is an awkward situation.

There can be little doubt that when the oil crisis arose in 1973-74, many borrowing countries (e.g., Brazil) did little to make economic adjustments to reduce the sharply increased import burden. As a result, their international debts rose rapidly. Other countries, once they were able to tap the international banks, borrowed for nonproductive, often frivolous reasons (e.g., an expensive Nigerian sports complex), and in some cases actually to finance fraudulent projects to benefit dishonest government officials.

For their part, commercial banks and other commercial lenders were Pollyannish in their optimism that countries could and would honor their international obligations. Banks competed aggressively to lend larger and larger sums. They scrambled to be the lead managers of large syndicated credits, and in the process dragged in smaller, less experienced banks. Unfortunately, the lenders did not exercise prudence in evaluating the creditworthiness of borrowers.

Were the loans bad? Many of them, yes. Were the borrowers bad? A few, yes, but many more were simply foolish. Were the bankers bad? Perhaps a few, but even more were foolish.

Lenders have been very slow to adjust to the credit burden that hangs over their heads. For too long, they deceived themselves, as well as bank regulators, into thinking that if they could only hang on, the crisis would pass. They were living in a dreamworld and, as we have seen, they were lucky.

However, although it took them a long time to react meaningfully, banks have in general made much more of an adjustment than have the borrowers. The results are generally beneficial for the individual banks and the credit system, as well. However, although some of the adjustments have also brought benefits for some of the borrowers, some of the other adjustments do not bode well for the less developed countries.

Although there has not been any systematic, comprehensive program undertaken by the international commercial banks to confront the threat of the debt overhang, most major banks have made noticeable individual adjustments. Their actions have served to reduce the seriousness of the international threat to the banks. However, the threat is still there, and many of the banks are removing themselves as much as possible from any new financial ties with the developing world.

Many international banks have enjoyed high profits during the past few years. As interest rates have declined, so has the cost of the banks' funding—and even more rapidly than have the rates charged to borrowers. Some banks have used this opportunity to reduce the amount of LDC credits on their balance sheets by taking a "hit" against profits or capital by writing down all or part of their exposure in certain countries or to certain borrowers.

Many banks have also increased their capital, which can be accomplished by keeping more retained earnings (when profits are high) or, even better, increasing loan-loss reserves—with pretax money.

The increase of capital can also be realized by issuing either stock or bonds. A larger capital base and loan-loss reserve reduce the banks' exposure to the threat of default on their LDC loans.

Selling and swapping loans: During the past several years, a secondary market in LDC loans has developed. Some of the discounts on LDC credits are very substantial. If a country has the resources, swaps could be a very wise investment—a chance to retire part of its debt at bargain prices. Bolivia was able to buy half of its international debt from its creditors at an average price of only twelve cents on the dollar.

However, many more LDC loans are being swapped or exchanged by the lenders than are being sold. Billions of dollars of such transactions have occurred every year for the past several years. In some cases, these "loan conversions" have involved debt for debt exchange. With these loan swaps (and also loan sales), the total amount of the borrower's debts generally remain unchanged—only the owner of those credits changes.

An increasingly popular form of loan conversion involves exchanging debt for equity. Swaps of loans for equity generally involve the debtor government as a party to the agreement and generally lead to a reduction of the borrower's total debts.

In addition to adjustments in assets and equity, there has also been a strong shift among the major international banks in policies, priorities, and even financial activities. These adjustments have helped buffer most of the banks against the threats from their LDC debt portfolios.

One change has been a strong shift away from a willingness by banks to lend to LDCs. They have already suffered large losses by excessive exposure to the LDCs. Still, huge potential losses remain. The threat leads to much worry and additional work for the bankers—and closer scrutiny by boards of directors and regulators.

At the same time, banks are being drawn to other markets in response to deregulation and competition from other types of financial institutions that threaten to erode banks' markets. In the United States, the advent of interstate banking, the rapid increase in competition from nonbanks (savings and loans associations, credit unions, nonbank credit cards, brokerage houses, and even retailers, such as Sears with its Discover card), the shift of traditional customers to direct funding in the money and capital markets (thus bypassing the commercial banks), and the progressive dismantling of the restrictions on investment banking are offering both opportunity and threat.

All of these developments pull bankers' attention away from the developing countries. So do the domestic problem areas of commercial banks: oil and natural gas, real estate, and agriculture. This shift of focus and the increased interest in nonlending activities (e.g., advisory services, such as mergers and acquisitions, and the underwriting of Eurobonds) that bring fees without adding assets (i.e., loans) to the books is not a passing fancy. It is a fundamental change in commercial banking, meaning that debtor countries are going to have increasing difficulty in finding commercial (private-sector) sources of financing.

Although the acuteness of the threat has declined, the international financial system remains allergic to further serious economic shocks—whether from rising oil prices, rising interest rates, default by a major borrower, or any of a variety of other potentially system-disrupting crises. Recovery remains tenuous, and the inaccessibility of the developing countries to the private financial markets remains a serious problem.

This is a potentially explosive situation. Both humanitarianism and the self-interest of the industrial countries dictate that serious efforts must be undertaken to ameliorate those conditions. However, without access to the private financial markets, there will not likely be sufficient funding for most of the countries.

What is needed is a comprehensive response to this dual threat. Short-term, ad hoc responses are wholly inadequate, yet they have been offered since the debt crisis began.

A comprehensive response to the debt problem must attack both dimensions of the situation—the threat of the overhang to debtors and creditors as well as the problem of access to future funding by the developing countries. The bottom line for the accomplishment of these two objectives is the protection and buttressing of the international financial system. Failing that, neither objective is attainable.

Solution of these problems requires the participation and cooperation of many groups: the debtors, the private creditors, the creditor governments, the international agencies, and perhaps even new participants (such as the insurance industry).

Hampering the task of resolving the crisis has been the reticence of any leader to initiate the process of comprehensive reform. Perhaps what is needed is another Bretton Woods conference bringing all the major parties together. The catalyst might be a major creditor government. It might be a major creditor bank. It could even be a critical debtor.

The most likely candidates for the role are the IMF and the World Bank. They will be critical in the success of any outcome, and both have the credibility and resources to get the process moving.*

---

* A more comprehensive discussion of the history and current status of Third World debt, and of the author's recommendations can be found in his article, "The Vulnerability of the International Financial System," in *Rekindling Development: Multinational Corporations and Third World Debt*, Lee A. Tavis, ed. (South Bend, Indiana: University of Notre Dame Press, 1988), 169–204.

M. Peter McPherson examines the status of the debt crisis, concluding that, unless the debtor nations institute significant reforms, any debt reduction measures will be doomed to failure. Since 1989, numerous proposals have been advanced to ease the plight of Third World nations, which have found it exceedingly difficult to meet their obligations. One such measure, the Brady Plan—which called for debt reduction, voluntarily worked out between the creditors and less developed countries—has met with some success. Under this plan, the banks would either reduce interest payments or provide new loans to assist the debtor nations. At the time it was proposed, many banks raised strong objections, fearing that it would merely compound the problem. Eventually, the banks entered into an agreement with Mexico, which proved so successful that additional agreements were negotiated with several other developing countries, including the Philippines, Costa Rica, and Venezuela. In retrospect, suggests the author, debt reduction discussions may have served to reduce the discipline of some debtors. This suggests that the next round of negotiations will certainly be more difficult and complex. At the same time, it is important to note that while some Third World countries have exercised great responsibility, others have acted with less than good faith. Distinctions must be drawn.

Go Slowly on
DEBT RELIEF FOR
THIRD-WORLD
NATIONS

"Without reform, debt reduction is wasted."

by M. Peter McPherson

EARLY in 1989, a stalemate had developed between private banks and many troubled debtor countries. The latter owed billions of dollars, and both parties were dissatisfied with the situation. The Brady Plan, despite all its problems, has broken the impasse. Introduced by Secretary of the Treasury Nicholas Brady in March, 1989, it called for reduction of debt, voluntarily worked out between creditors and the less developed countries (LDC's). The banks either would reduce interest or pro-

Mr. McPherson is executive vice president, Bank of America, San Francisco, Calif.

vide new loans to help these nations find their way out of their enormous financial dilemmas.

Banks had real difficulty in dealing with the situation at the time. They knew that the quality of the LDC debt was deteriorating, but they did not have the tools usually available to deal with distressed debtors. With a commercial debtor, banks can ask changes in the way it is doing business, take more collateral, and request changes in leadership. Obviously, these approaches are not generally available with a sovereign debtor. Many had concluded by the spring of 1989 that the primary recourse for them was to withhold new funds. Each new loan

negotiation became harder to complete.

Debtor nations obviously had serious problems, too. Some had made progress—*e.g.*, lower ratios of debt to GNP. However, the uncertainty surrounding the debt problem and related economic concerns were exacting a substantial cost. For example, real interest rates in Mexico were much higher because of the unsettled situation. Also, many debtor country leaders argued that economic reform was getting very hard to impose on populations with no solution in sight. The threat of moratorium was everywhere, though thoughtful leaders saw that Peru's taking such a path had been a disaster for that country.

In short, both the lending institutions and debtor countries had severe problems that the process of the time didn't address. What was needed was a Chapter 11-type procedure tailored to the needs of sovereign nations. The Brady Plan, broad in concept, was to be tested and developed as conditions demanded. It encouraged banks to provide relief by use of enhancement monies from the World Bank/International Monetary Fund (IMF) for the purpose of buying zero bonds to back up principal and for limited interest guarantees. It also required that there be serious reform efforts in place. The Brady Plan provided a more-or-less orderly process for debt to be adjusted and for the borrowing countries to reform their economies.

The Brady Plan got off to a bit of a difficult start. Many banks at first thought it was driven by U.S. foreign policy considerations, rather than economic realities. Also, domestic politics of some nations produced calls for relief beyond real need. Since the Brady concept was new, it took everyone—lending institutions and debtor countries—time to come to grips with the idea.

Eventually, the banks and Mexico settled upon an agreement that probably is worth about $1,500,000,000 of reduced cash flow a year to Mexico and will eliminate the problem for the next generation. This will occur because the U.S. Treasury zero bonds that back up the converted debt will pay it off in 30 years. Moreover, real domestic interest rates in Mexico dropped 20% with the announcement of the plan, saving the country billions.

After Mexico, the bankers were able to put together agreements with the Philippines and Costa Rica. Each of these agreements was different, but, in each case, the country had a clear need plus a track record of economic reform.

The Bank of America chairs the Bank Advisory Committee for Costa Rica. Under the terms of the agreement, at least 60% of the commercial bank debt was eliminated and it is reasonable to expect that, over the next five to seven years, virtually all of it will be expunged through a debt-for-equity program. The agreement with Costa Rica probably is unique in the amount of debt reduced, but it shows the capacity of the banks and a debtor nation to work through a problem. For example, non-traditional exports in Costa Rica now exceed coffee exports because of exchange rate devaluations and a more open economy.

The banks also have a Venezuelan arrangement in principle and expect to finalize the full agreement in a reasonable time. This includes some additional options too technical to detail here, but reflective of the continued adjustments they are making. The Venezuelan agreement adds a major country to the Brady Plan with a serious economic reform program in place.

Economic reform is the key

Economic reform is an essential component of a Brady Plan agreement. Without reform, debt reduction is wasted. Sound economic policy is the foundation for economic expansion. Chile and Mexico clearly are benefiting from reform. It is the overriding consideration when we think about growth in most of these debtor countries, so it must be a critical factor when we structure relief. Resources, including those released by such reduction, only can back up economic reforms. If resources alone were the answer, the oil revenue inflows to Nigeria and Mexico in the 1970's certainly would have solved the growth problem. Also, non-payment by Brazil and Argentina in recent times clearly has not contributed to a solution in those countries.

The Brady Plan agreements negotiated to date involved permanent debt relief on the basis that countries had undertaken reforms and have lived with these programs for a time. Accordingly, banks had reason to believe that the borrowing nations were in a better position after an agreement to pay back the remaining debt. The international financial institutions have agreed to provide substantial resources to support Brady Plans in part because of reform track records. Tough as these agreements were to put together, they may have been easier conceptually than future pacts will be. The next negotiations apparently are going to be with countries that have relatively new and untested reform programs. Brazil, Argentina, and Poland all fall into this category.

There also may not be enough up-front monies for zero bonds and interest guarantees for some nations wishing to enter into agreements. Banks generally feel they should not provide permanent debt relief unless the IMF, World Bank, or others are willing to advance the financing for the zero bonds and the guarantees that make the agreement work. In other words, money provided by the IMF and the World Bank over a period of years and conditioned upon continued economic performance of the countries is not comparable to immediate and permanent relief asked of the banks.

In addition, the arrearages are becoming a major problem in negotiating deals. It is clear that some nations need relief, but the reduction discussions may have contributed to a deterioration of discipline of some debtors. Some amount of problems probably was unavoidable and a risk that, I am sure, Secretary Brady took reluctantly. Nevertheless, that gamble must be understood and countered. To that end, the IMF and World Bank have an important role in persuading countries to pay all they reasonably can. Such payments will be the foundation for a future relationship between debtor countries and the international financial community. As such, they are in the interest of those nations. The World Bank and IMF leadership surely understand this problem because they, too, are creditors and they should not forget that arrearage can become habit-forming. In brief, negotiations should and will go forward, but all parties will have to be imaginative to work through these difficulties.

Even if we get the debt problem more or less under control, much else must be done to achieve growth. For example, the private sector needs to be engaged again in lending to developing countries. There simply is not enough bilateral or multilateral donor money to provide the capital that is necessary to build modern economies. This is not going to be easy for most nations, though a sound economy and a history of good-faith dealing with creditors will be key factors in obtaining further loans. The private sector will extend some short-term trade credits to worthy borrowers in reasonably stable countries and may be willing to extend longer-term credit for viable projects where there is collateral such as minerals or oil exports. In addition, loans generally will be available where multinational companies provide a home office guarantee.

Nevertheless, there will be finance needs that can not attract the necessary equity and loans. These require attention now. Nations can help themselves, and some are taking steps. For example, economies must be open to foreign investment, and profits from them must be able to be taken out of the country. Chile has shown the importance of debt/equity deals in both reducing what it owes and attracting investment. Also, the World Bank and other donors probably need to review the way they use guarantees and other tools to leverage more private-sector funding. Clearly, this is a major difficulty, and traditional solutions do not appear to be sufficient.

The Brady Plan has made an important contribution, but the next series of negotiations present different and very tough issues. Still, we must work on ways to increase the financing for countries that really are reforming.

Article 22.1.   Capitalism Isn't All It's Cracked Up to Be

Despite the failures of socialism, the author rejects the assumption that capitalism holds the key to the future of Eastern Europe. He dismisses the myth that socialism is synonymous with failure, oppression, and poverty, while capitalism can be equated with success, freedom, and economic well-being. In too many cases, capitalism has resulted in closed factories, wage reductions, forced strikes, scab labororers, tax breaks for the wealthy, and cutbacks in essential services for the poor and working class. In their zeal to reform their economies, many Eastern European leaders have turned to the West for advice. Its answer: capitalist austerity, combined with individual sacrifice. Although Eastern Europe wants to be more like the United States, it would be well advised to study the problems that beset America's cities: drugs, crime, homelessness, and unemployment, among others. The failure of Eastern Europe is a political failure, the result of an apathetic, dictatorial, undisciplined system, which invested more in weapons than it did in people.

Eastern European Workers, Beware!

CAPITALISM

ISN'T ALL IT'S CRACKED UP TO BE

The economic failures of socialism do not prove that capitalism has succeeded.

by Cornelius Lehane

THE CHEST-THUMPING, hooray-for-us reaction of the U.S. press and various other flag wavers of free enter-

---

Mr. Lehane, assistant professor of English, Rockland County Community College, Suffern, N.Y., has worked actively in the U.S. labor movement.

---

prise to the phenomenal political and economic changes now taking place in Eastern Europe has been so one-dimensional as to be misleading, and so self-righteous as to be actually embarrassing. The overriding assumption seems to be that the people of Eastern Europe, so long oppressed by communism, finally have realized what the dumbest American knew all along: socialism means failure,

oppression, and poverty; capitalism, on the other hand, means success, freedom, and economic well-being.

For my generation, growing up in the U.S. in the 1950s, communists were the epitome of cruelty and violence. They enslaved nations, murdered nuns, and built iron curtains. In short, they were the enemy of freedom and truth. All things were justified in the name of fighting communism, including suspending civil liberties, firing tenured professors, blacklisting actors and writers, demanding loyalty oaths from union leaders, and jailing people for practices heretofore protected under the Bill of Rights.

All that is over now. Communism is finished, we are told by the TV anchors. Not only that, it's beginning to look like we were wrong about the communists all along. Far from murderous marauders, they turn out to be a bunch of old softies afraid to make the tough economic decisions and unable to discipline a lazy labor force that has been sitting around all these years not doing any work and living off government handouts in the form of subsidies for factories, housing, and food; free health care, pensions, and education; as well as laws protecting them from being laid off.

The rulers of Eastern Europe lacked the courage of the wimpiest of American bosses. Our economic rulers have closed factories, cut pay, and forced workers out on strike, then replaced them with scabs willing to do the job for less than half the going rate. They have destroyed entire cities with the flourish of a single pen (*i.e.*, Flint, Mich., and Gary, Ind.). They fight continuously for tax cuts for the rich and cutbacks in services for the poor and wage earners.

Lately, the rulers of Eastern Europe have smartened up and come to us for advice. Our recommendation is clear—a dose of good old capitalistic austerity. You have inflation?—just cure it with a depression. Already in Poland, thousands of formerly gainfully employed workers are out of a job. They believe their sacrifice will make Poland better for their children.

Eastern Europe wants to be more like America, where, in 1988, 20% of children under the age of 18 were living in poverty; where, according to the Washington, D.C.-based Economic Policy Institute, 31.5% of the population is working at poverty level wages; where, between 1979 and 1988, the top five percent of wage earners experienced a 9.6% gain in real income, while the bottom 20% suffered a 12.5% decline; where, between 1977 and 1987, the average family income of the poorest 10% of Americans fell 10.5%, while that of the wealthiest one percent rose 74.2%.

In addition to the entrepreneurial spirit, what the West exports is not freedom, but greed. In Rockland County, N.Y., where I work, no affordable housing has been built in recent years, nor is any on the horizon for the immediate future. Housing also has been a perennial problem in the socialist world. The reason there, however, is that they simply don't have

the money. (Some theorists suggest that the entire rearrangement of socialist nations is taking place precisely because they don't have capital and need to make themselves more attractive to the West to borrow some.)

In suburban America, it's the what's-in-it-for-me phenomenon that creates the problem. "If I can build a house and make $100,000 off it, I'd be stupid to put the same time and energy into one that I'd only make $5,000 off of." In New York City, tenants are forced out so owners can convert their apartment buildings into luxury condos. (In my old Upper West Side neighborhood, decent housing is affordable only for families with an income in the $150,000-a-year range.) Tenants in East Berlin may experience the same sort of phenomenon when the West German landlords take over their buildings. That's the other side of the profit motive everyone is so excited about exporting. In contrast, the old socialist morality of the U.S.S.R. was perhaps unrealistic, but certainly kinder and gentler, requiring that no one pay more than 10% of their income for housing.

The arrogant, I-told-you-so American economists now dancing on the grave of the Soviet communism they knew all along wouldn't succeed have yet to explain the growth of the U.S.S.R. into a world economic superpower during the first three-quarters of the 20th century. This occurred despite the absence of any economic base as late as 1920 and the destruction of their economic base during World War II. They fail to explain why the Soviet economy grew at *twice* the rate of the U.S.'s during the 1950s and continued to increase at a healthy pace into the 1970s, before beginning to decline.

It is obvious to all, it seems, that communism doesn't work, and that's the only explanation we need. Every band plays the same tune: stick to capitalism; capitalism won. It may not be the ideal system, but it's the only one that works. So what if we've created a drug epidemic we can't solve and a crime wave which does not abate, no matter how many prisons we build. So what if reliance on the market brought us face to face with a war over oil in the deserts of the Middle East.

By following in our footsteps, the people of Eastern Europe will be able to buy 400 different kinds of candy, but not find affordable day care. They will purchase new automobiles on time and subscribe to credit cards, then lose them when the steel mills shut down. They'll be able to live in luxurious suburbs with swimming pools until their version of Wall Street goes bust. They may eat prepackaged dinners cooked in a microwave and watch color television, but won't be

able to provide care for their elderly parents or afford to send them to a private nursing home. Their kids will drink juice from convenient throw-away cartons, then run out of landfill space in which to discard them.

I'm no economist and certainly not an expert on how one should structure an economy. I do have my own sense of priorities, though. A society requires good schools, adequate health care, clean air and water, enough housing for everyone, safe streets, and a myriad of other social needs that should be taken care of before we lose any sleep over Ivana Trump's divorce settlement. These necessities aren't being taken care of very well in the U.S.

What kind of ideas are we exporting?

Before we pat ourselves on the back for having beaten the communists, we ought to take a good look at the kind of ideas we are exporting: housing for the rich before schools for the poor; luxury cars before clean air and adequate mass transit; expensive medication and medical procedures for the elderly rich before preventive medicine; and corporate profits before job security or retraining.

In New York, 83% of the schools are in need of major repair, and it has a higher infant mortality rate than many underdeveloped countries. The streets of Manhattan are filled with more beggars than Bombay. Drugs are infecting an entire generation. Bridges, on the brink of collapse, have to be closed. Water mains explode weekly. Seymour Melman, a Columbia University industrial engineering professor, estimates that the cost of repairing the U.S. infrastructure could reach five trillion dollars. Instead of spending money to fix any of this, we build luxury apartment buildings, open trendy restaurants, and pour billions into the defense industry as we continue to act as the world's policeman.

The National Commission on Children reports that nearly 500,000 American youngsters are affected by malnutrition and 100,000 are homeless. Yet, this does not suggest to us that we have systemic poverty and a housing shortage of epic proportions. That almost 50% of African-American children live below the poverty level does not tell us that our society has failed dismally in its attempts to provide equal opportunity for all. Our steel mills have closed, our cars are produced overseas, and manufacturing jobs in the hundreds of thousands have disappeared. Obviously, something is wrong with the U.S.'s sagging economy and declining morality.

Is this the plan the workers of Eastern Europe want to embrace—the poor get poorer and the rich get richer? I suggest the steelworkers of Krakow consider the former steelworkers of western Pennsylvania, 61% of whom, according to a recent Gallup Poll, are making an average of $7.18 an hour less than they earned in 1980. Most of them also are without health insurance and pension benefits.

The realization is dawning on the Polish people that a system which throws them out of work and deprives their children of food to enable "entrepreneurs" in Warsaw to wear imported jeans, drive BMWs, and build luxury apartment buildings may require a second look. The railroad workers struck in the summer of 1989 and others are chomping at the bit. The Paris Club (17 Western nations to whom Poland owes money) have insisted on strict austerity measures if that nation is to postpone making payments on a $40,000,000,000 debt it can not possibly afford. The economic measures taken in Poland, under the auspices of Solidarity, have lowered the inflation rate significantly, stabilized the zloty against foreign currency, and created a trade surplus with the West.

When the other shoe dropped, however, they found a 40% drop in real wages for Polish workers and an unemployment rate zooming from one to eight percent in less than a year and heading higher. In the old days, bread cost the equivalent of a penny a loaf. When it arrived in the stores, it immediately was bought up and the shelves often were empty. Shortages were the bane of socialism. Now, even when there is food on the shelves, the prices are so high that most people can't afford to buy it.

An American capitalist's investment plan for the Gdansk shipyard is a case in point. Saving the birthplace of Solidarity required losing the patient. The plan called for slashing the workforce in half, freezing wages (this at a time of rapidly rising prices), and a no-strike guarantee for five years. The shipyard workers rejected this particular capitalist poison pill. Consequently, the Solidarity government, still preaching capitalism, continues it as a state-run operation.

The pre-revolution Solidarity membership of 10,000,000 has plummeted to around 2,000,000. Its approval ratings in the polls has dropped from 78% to 47%. This is not surprising, considering that unions are supposed to protect its members from those attempting to balance economies on the backs of workers.

The Soviet Union furiously is debating how quickly it should rush into the market economy. Not surprisingly, the workers there have been skeptical, given the Polish experience, and actually put up a fuss at the 1990 May Day celebration in Moscow, demanding safeguards and job security. They immediately were taken to task by William F. Buckley, Jr., who, in his syndicated column, championed unemployment and poverty as an important and necessary part of the capitalist package.

We can not deny that the economies of Eastern Europe are in dismal shape, brought down, at least in part, by the weight of their own bureaucracies. Central planning overwhelmingly has been rejected in democratic elections by the workers of Poland, Hungary, and Czechoslovakia. Those of East Germany have surrendered to the prosperous capitalism of West Germany.

This does not mean that socialism is dead, however, or that it even is the primary cause of all the economic difficulties of Eastern Europe. It certainly does not signify that the economic failures of socialism prove that capitalism has succeeded.

One of the biggest problems for the Soviet Union is the amount of money that country squandered on military expenditures, especially the ill-advised war in Afghanistan. All this expenditure on the military was money not available for upgrading the economic infrastructure.

When the smoke clears and the mirrors are removed, it's obvious that the U.S. has similar problems to the Soviet Union. Basically, America too must recover from the insanity of the arms race. The U.S. military-industrial complex employs 6,-500,000 civilian and military personnel. What will happen to them if peace breaks out permanently? The unexpectedly brief war in the Persian Gulf did nothing to improve our economy or solve our long-range problems. We have 135,000 factories, laboratories, and bases that, sooner or later, we'll have to begin dismantling. Many are wards of the Pentagon and function outside of the marketplace under a system of planning and pricing not all that dissimilar to the one they're trying to junk in Eastern Europe.

So much of our productive energy has gone into military research and development and production, particularly under the Reagan Administration, when military spending increased by as much as 50% in some years, that we seriously have weakened our industrial base. From 1894 until 1971, the U.S. annually produced a trade surplus. The concept of a trade deficit was unheard of. Now, it is heard of to the tune of $110,000,000,000 in 1989, and if we deducted military related exports, the sound would be deafening.

The economic recovery and expansion of the 1980s is illusory when debt is factored in. The U.S. was the world's largest creditor nation in 1980, with a surplus of $106,-000,000,000. By 1989, as the world's largest debtor nation, America owed $620,000,-000,000. Which means the nation is doing just fine until someone calls in the notes.

What we have as the legacy of our years of economic expansion is a large debt on top of a badly eroded industrial base. Does this sound familiar? Just ask a Pole.

Socialism resulted from the abuses, oppression, and exploitation of capitalism. People who have forgotten that—whether in the East or the West—must remember. Capitalism put little children to work in factories and fields (and still does), provided no relief from unemployment or poverty, and allocated health care only for those who could pay for it. (In the U.S., there still is qualitatively different health care for people with money and those without.) It provided no relief for old age and often did not provide food and shelter.

The fruits of socialism

To those East Europeans who argue that capitalism has redressed these grievances, I suggest that the relative well-being of their West European fellow-workers did not arrive in a gift package from the capitalists. Rather, it is the fruit of decades of struggle by workers' parties and militant trade unions, most of them led by communists and socialists.

Another phenomenon that the American press seems not to have noticed is that the profound changes taking place in Eastern Europe are occurring because the hated communists had the humility to admit when they were wrong and the courage to try new approaches. The people of Eastern Europe—communist and non-communist—are hashing out their differences and creating new societies.

The horn-blowers of democracy refuse to acknowledge the flowering of real democracy, a true people's movement in Eastern Europe. Why has so little been made of this? Have the "enslaved" ever thrown off the yoke so easily?

If capitalism returns to Eastern Europe, the workers will find that, if they ever want to convert back to socialism, it will not be accomplished with demonstrations and negotiations, but by the same brutal and bloody process we've seen in Latin America, Asia, and Africa. I remember the guns and dogs and tear gas that greeted those in America who had the temerity to disagree with the established order during the 1960s and I wonder why we don't stand back watching this European process of social change with hushed reverence. Instead, we holler from the rooftops, "We told you so," gloat over our own tenuous prosperity, and continue in our fathomless arrogance to think that we have the handle on everything.

An interesting piece of news from Hungary told how the democratization of the society was to include the dismantling of the Communist Party cells in the factories. Typically, the article did not explain why this was done, only suggested that these groups were seen as a threat to the new order. As someone who has spent a good part of his life as a union organizer and who knows how hard it is to get organizations set up in the workplace to begin with, I wonder why these groups need to be dismantled. The army certainly, even perhaps the militia, could prove a threat, but why the workers' organizations?

They would do it, it seems to me, for the same reasons bosses keep trying to break up unions here. The workers then would be less able to resist layoffs and speed-ups or complain about unsafe conditions and unfair treatment. Are the workers of Eastern Europe now the enemies of the new progress? If so, they must wonder about the nature of this progress.

Some of the less talked-about proposals being considered in the socialist world include the zero hours plan in East Germany whereby laid-off employees or those on short hours receive full pay until they find other jobs. The assumption of this kind of thinking is that workers need to eat and have a place to live, even if they do get laid off. It's something that, in kinder times, has been proposed in the U.S., though I'm sure no politician would dare mention the idea now. Mikhail Gorbachev is walking a middle road, trying to pacify the working people by promising no meteoric price increases or massive layoffs, while offering retraining and job placement for those displaced by the closing of factories. The Soviet Union has taken measures to involve more people in decision-making at all economic and political levels. Gorbachev has promised democracy on the shop floor. He suggested that workers elect their managers and take part in the decision-making of the plants. He even has proposed a referendum on the most important economic question of the day—ownership of private property.

Our political pundits now claim the Soviet Union is going too far toward democracy. The American press backs the *privilegentsia,* the Soviet Union's counterpart to our MBAs, professionals, stock manipulators, and junk bond salesmen. These people have seen a chance to make a buck—an opportunity for a plush condo and a BMW. They want the free market immediately. Like their counterparts in the U.S., they care nothing about the health of society as a whole. They just want to get theirs first. That mentality is dangerous to the process of change taking place in Eastern Europe. It also has dominated the American belief system for too long and has become dangerous here as well.

That seems to be the kind of political and economic change for which we are cheering. Perhaps the people of Eastern Europe should look to their own traditions in developing new economies, rather than get too caught up in the Western cult of selfishness. At the same time, perhaps we might look to the East and discover that job retraining is better than layoffs; that subsidized food is better than some eating well and others going hungry; and that society has a responsibility for the lame as well as the fleet-of-foot.

Article 22.2.   The Big Split

Carla Rapoport contends that a new Japan has emerged in the wake of the gulf war. No longer content to sit idly by in the face of Japanese-bashing in the United States, that nation is bristling with a new sense of arrogance and self-confidence. This has led to a major rift between the two nations, one that is likely to deepen and spawn new problems in the future. Angered by American criticism, Tokyo is talking back. Instead of condeming its trade practices, the Japanese believe that America should concentrate on improving its own economy. During the Cold War, Japan was dependent on the United States, both strategically and economically. That is no longer the case. Today, Japan is alive and well. Its economic success has rekindled a new sense of nationalism, which some observers have wrongly translated as anti-Americanism. The Japanese are unwilling to make further trade and defense concessions to the United States. Most believe that the time has come to exert Japan's independence, even if it means antagonizing America.

DOMO ARIGATO—Thank You, America—read placards on the big truck leading a march through central Tokyo this spring. But unlike most demonstrations, this one wasn't snarling traffic. Behind the truck was just one lonely marcher.

While Americans reacted to victory in the Gulf with unbridled pride, most Japanese saw the whole episode as *orokana senso*— that foolish war. Far from being ashamed of their checkbook approach to the Gulf, Japanese are bristling with arrogance and self-confidence. Japan's new mood, pitted against a souring American attitude toward Japan, has produced the deepest split between the two countries since World War II. The economic and geopolitical ties between the world's two wealthiest nations can no longer be taken for granted.

The U.S. trade deficit with Japan, though slowly decreasing, is still staggering. More Americans than ever believe that Japan's trading practices are restrictive at home and predatory abroad. Japanese think that America should get its own economy in shape instead of trying to tell Japan what to do. Americans have doubts that Japan can be counted on in the next crisis.

The results? Despite the cordial meeting between George Bush and Japanese Prime Minister Toshiki Kaifu in California in April, these developments are certain to cause political trouble at home for both of them. Here are some things to look for:

■ There will be increasingly bitter trade fights and at least some stirrings in Congress for retaliation, especially if deficit improvement flattens out.

■ The Democrats are bound to make U.S.-Japan trade a campaign issue in the 1992 presidential election.

■ The American-Japanese security alliance, in which bases in Japan have been a crucial part of U.S. global military power, will come under increasing strain.

■ Japan's growing strength in key high-tech industries will result in further penetration of markets worldwide.

OK, you say, you've seen this movie before and you know how it ends. Japan promises increased market access, and American industry promises to try harder, right? We decide that we need each other militarily and economically, right? Throughout the great trade battles, from textiles in the 1970s to baseball bats, beef, and supercomputers in the 1980s, that's the way it's been.

This rift looks more serious. Since 1945 the U.S. and Japan have been knitted together at the hip, strategically and economically. During the Cold War, the U.S. felt it needed a strong military presence in northern Asia to counter the Chinese Communists and the Soviet Union. Japan welcomed the American security umbrella. Economically, Japan needed access to the huge U.S. market, plus American technology, to keep growing. After initial postwar feelings that anything made in Japan was shoddy, Americans came to love Japanese goods for their value and high quality.

Now the Asian part of the Cold War is about to dissolve in Gorbymania. The Soviet leader's precedent-setting April trip to Tokyo is expected to lay groundwork for an end to the dispute over four Japanese islands held by the Soviets since the end of World War II. In exchange, Moscow is counting on bil-

lions in loans and credits.

U.S. policymakers want to keep America's 12 bases (two Army, three Navy, six Air Force, and a Marine air station) in Japan, with the Japanese providing a rising share of the cost, on grounds that accidents like the rise of a Saddam Hussein could happen in Asia too. But with the Soviet threat eliminated, many Japanese are uninterested in paying for U.S. troops they think are no longer needed.

THEN, CONSIDER trade. Japan's dependence on the U.S. has shrunk dramatically. Since 1986, exports from Japan to the U.S. have edged up only slightly while those to Europe and Asia have soared. Trade with the U.S. last year accounted for 27% of Japan's worldwide trade, down from 33% in 1986. This year the figure could be around 25%, and for the first time in 15 years Japan will export more to Asia than to the U.S. If anything, America has become more dependent on Japan these days, not the other way around. The Commerce Department says the Pentagon will have to rely on the Japanese for semiconductors and other high-tech equipment for its smart weapons of the future. In consumer electronics, Americans have plenty of choice—among the Japanese brands that dominate shelves.

Want proof of Japan's new sense of independence? If you can read Japanese, glance at a recent study of U.S.-Japan relations com-

REPORTER ASSOCIATE *Suneel Ratan*

missioned by Japan's Foreign Ministry and written by the International Institute for Global Peace, a Tokyo research organization with strong government ties. The report states: "It is apparent that the U.S. economy is not recovering and its capacity to manage its foreign strategy is declining—for example, its inability to bear the full costs of the Gulf war. The American people and policymakers seem to refuse to acknowledge the country's decline and need for improvement . . . If the entire U.S. political system is not reformed, the illogical, inefficient budget procedure is likely to continue."

The study says that Japan's rise as an economic superpower has reawakened Japanese nationalism in the form of anti-Americanism. "There is a growing feeling that further [trade] concessions to the U.S. are unnecessary." During the Gulf war, nationalism erupted as pacifism, especially among Japan's younger generation. The report points out that the "backlash" was not directed at leaders of the multinational forces in general, but "specifically at the U.S." The Foreign Ministry study concluded that all this spells trouble for Japan-U.S. security treaties.

Anti-Americanism? Surely, as the Japanese grew richer, traveled abroad more, and absorbed more Hollywood movies, they would want what Americans want—bigger homes, two cars, consumer credit to the max, and more leisure. Japan's role in World War II must make young Japanese, like young Germans, anxious to atone for their parents' nationalistic mistakes, right?

It's not happening. Most Japanese are working and saving as hard as ever. As for guilt, forget it. Says Hiroshi Kume, Japan's popular late-night anchor for TV Asahi: "We just don't think like you. We might dress in jeans, but we are still samurai, wearing swords. For us, Japan equals the earth. Going to England is like going to Mars. The U.S. is Jupiter. I've met junior-high kids who don't even know we fought a war against the Americans. Parents don't want to talk about it and schools don't teach it."

In comic books and on television, Americans have become the butt of jokes. The standard Touch-Tone telephone, called the "push phone" in Japan after its push buttons, is now known as the Bush Phone. Pick

it up, and it asks for money. Comedian Tokoro Joji draws laughs with this hardly humorous line: "Japan lends money to America so its people can maintain living standards three times higher than ours."

For years Japanese defended their aggressive trade policies by pleading poverty; the old we're-just-a-small-country-with-no-natural-resources line, usually accompanied by a deferential bow. A few still use it, but most Japanese unabashedly believe that their own robust economy will lead the world's development from now on. Japan is the world's largest donor of aid; eight of the world's ten biggest banks are Japanese; the country's huge industrial companies are rich and getting richer; what's more, city streets are still safe at night. The Japanese have so much of the world's advanced technology that even Western weapons makers are dependent on them. Well-respected economists in Tokyo now issue reports claiming that Japan, with half the population of the U.S., will have a larger GNP by the end of this decade.

Some Americans agree. William Spencer, CEO of Sematech, the government-backed semiconductor research consortium in Texas, says, in all seriousness, "Today's technology is not being driven by the Strategic Defense Initiative. It's being driven by Sony Camcorders." Japanese technology has become so important that IBM, Apple, Compaq, and Tandy are now *defending* Japan's electronics exporters against charges by smaller U.S. competitors that the Japanese are dumping flat-panel displays. The U.S. giants claim that American suppliers cannot meet the demand for this crucial computer component.

ON THE WEST COAST, Japanese banks kept the flagging real estate market alive most of last year. They continued lending after most U.S. institutions had all but stopped in the wake of the S&L crisis. Says Jack Rodman, a Los Angeles real estate consultant: "Developers are holding their breath, waiting for Japanese banks to turn on the taps again." In the job-hungry South, expect only raves about the Japanese. Says Tennessee Governor Ned McWherter: "[Japan] is what our future is all about."

A lot of other Americans, though, view Japan's power with growing uneasiness. In March, Jerry Jasinowski, president of the 12,500-member National Association of Manufacturers, wrote to President Bush seeking a "reassessment" of America's relationship with Japan. Jasinowski, whose organization represents 85% of U.S. manufac-

turing output, didn't spell out precisely what he wanted Bush to do. But such a reassessment might well open a discussion of those Administration taboos, managed trade and industrial policy, the Japanese versions of which Jasinowski apparently envies. Japan's goals, he wrote, appear to be more "intensely national and more thoroughly coordinated and pursued than our own." In a CNN interview later, he added, "In some cases we ought to do what the Japanese have done."

Polls reflect a hardening attitude toward Japan and, lately, Japanese products. A nationwide survey last fall by the Chicago Council on Foreign Relations showed that 60% of those polled consider that Japan's economic strength will be a "critical threat" to the "vital interests of the U.S." over the next ten years. In a poll taken since the Gulf war by Gordon S. Black/*USA Today*, 31% said they would be "less likely" to buy Japanese products than before. Says Mark Foster, former special counsel to the U.S. embassy in Tokyo and now a consultant to American companies trying to crack the Japanese market: "All across the country, people I talk to are looking at the Japanese as free-riders."

Even the Bush Administration, which has been extremely measured toward Japan, has begun to lose patience. Secretary of Agriculture Edward Madigan sent an emotional letter to Tokyo after Japanese officials threatened to arrest American farmers for trying to display packets of U.S. rice at a food exhibition. "There are more than two million farmers in America," he wrote. "Should they band together against buying Japanese products?" In March the Administration released its annual report on worldwide trade barriers. The tone was a lot calmer than Madigan's, but the longest section was devoted to Japan, including lengthy descriptions of such nontariff barriers as Japan's refusal to accept clinical testing data on U.S. pharmaceuticals on grounds that Japanese are physically different. More testing makes it more expensive for U.S. drug companies to crack the Japanese market.

Washington has soft-pedaled criticism of Japan through the years primarily because security arrangements have been deemed more important than trade. Push the Japanese too hard on imports, went the argument, and the U.S. might lose its important strategic bases. Nor has that view disappeared with the end of the Cold War. The Soviet threat has been replaced among some defense thinkers by the Great Vacuum threat. James Auer, head of U.S.-Japan

Studies at Vanderbilt University and a former assistant to the Secretary of Defense, sums it up: "The biggest threat in the Pacific is no longer communism but the potential breakup of the U.S.-Japan alliance. If the U.S. were not there, it would leave a vacuum that the Soviets or the Chinese or the Japanese might be tempted or even forced to fill."

Still, the notion of the primacy of security is fading. In a letter to President Bush this spring, Senator Max Baucus, Democrat of Montana and chairman of the Senate subcommittee on international trade, wrote, "No other bilateral issue [with Japan] is more important than trade." He urged a sweeping review of America's Japan policy, similar to the one on U.S. policy toward the Soviet Union that the CIA performed when Bush was director.

AT FIRST GLANCE, this shift in U.S. attitudes toward Japan seems odd. The trade deficit finally is moving in the right direction. From the peak of $57 billion in 1987, the gap narrowed to $41 billion last year. Japan's current account surplus with all its trading partners fell from 4.4% of GNP to 1.2%.

For many American companies, business in Japan has never been better. Coca-Cola earns more there than from its U.S. soft-drink business. Procter & Gamble is diapering Japanese babies from Okinawa to Hokkaido. Motorola is cleaning up in the cellular phone market. Apple computers are popping up in Japanese schools and offices. Investment banks like Salomon Brothers and Morgan Stanley are making serious money in Japan.

The problem is that no matter how fast U.S. companies expand in Japan, Japanese companies are expanding faster worldwide. And America's trade profile with Japan is beginning to look like that of a Third World country. The U.S. is gaining in exports of raw materials and food while Japan is gaining in high-tech, high-value-added manufactured goods.

At the same time Japan's share of high-tech markets worldwide is surging while the U.S. share is declining. Further, while U.S. exports to Japan have increased substantially in the past five years, the growth of exports from Europe and Asia to Japan has handily outstripped U.S. growth.

It has been six years since the yen doubled in value following the meeting of central bankers at the Plaza hotel in New York. The currency shift was supposed to solve the trade problem by making U.S. goods cheaper in Japanese markets. Japan's imports *have* gone up dramatically, but the main beneficiaries have been neighboring Asian countries that sell cheap consumer goods and Europeans who have exploited a new Japanese appetite for French wines, Italian suits, and BMWs.

And while the U.S. trade deficit has declined, its proportion of Japan's total surplus went *up*—from 62% in 1986 to 75%. America's electronics industry is the largest in the world (though Japan's may surpass it in 1991). Yet the U.S. electronics deficit with Japan rose from $17.5 billion in 1985 to $18.2 billion last year.

In data-processing and office automation equipment, a sector Americans pioneered, U.S. world market share has plunged from 50.8% in 1984 to 32.1% in 1989, while Japan's has surged from 14.4% to 32.4%. Japan's share of the world electronics market jumped from 21.7% to 31.2% between 1985 and 1989, while the U.S. share dropped from 64.5% to 50.5%.

In addition, the strong yen allowed Japanese companies to pick up U.S. real estate and American companies at half price. The cost of imported raw materials, like oil and steel, plummeted because of Japan's superstrong currency. Not only did the muscular yen not hurt Japanese businesses, but moreover the growth cycle that began in late 1986 is soon to become the longest in the postwar period, expanding the economy by 25% so far.

ON THE EVE of his latest trade mission to Japan, Commerce Secretary Robert Mosbacher complained that "Japan is an exporting superpower and an importing also-ran." Peter Petri, a Brandeis economist on sabbatical in Japan, explains: "The U.S. doesn't make cheap consumer goods anymore, and our luxury goods aren't rich enough for the Japanese. We're left with what we always sold—airplanes, sophisticated office equipment—things the Japanese couldn't make."

Japan's import tables bear out Petri's point. While imports from the U.S. climbed 76% between 1986 and 1990, imports from the countries of the European Community soared 133%. Sales from

France to Japan have gone up nearly 300%, and from Germany 144%. Imports from China more than doubled, turning a trade deficit into a $6 billion surplus. Imports from Southeast Asia rose 83% and from South Korea 106%.

Even if Japan takes more action to open its markets, the U.S. will not significantly benefit. To the Japanese, this fact seems obvious. Says Makoto Kuroda, a former top trade official who is a managing director of Mitsubishi Corp.: "America is not in a position to supply Japan, if we are leading in major industries."

This hurts many U.S. companies. Consider semiconductors. After years of rancorous trade fights that led to a Japanese commitment to increase imports but little action, American producers are finally making progress in the Japanese market. But Rod Canion, president of Compaq, and Jerry Junkins, CEO of Texas Instruments, recently told Congress that the improvement is coming too late. While the U.S. semiconductor industry has now begun to hold its own, it has, they claim, "gone from dominance to fighting for parity" (see Technology). Since 1980 the U.S. share of the world chip market has fallen from 57% to 40%, while Japan's share has risen from 27% to 47%.

Don't blame us, say more and more Japanese. Most revealing is a report titled *Japan, the U.S., and Global Responsibilities*, signed by 68 members of the Japan Forum on International Relations, including academics, writers, and the CEOs of Hitachi, NKK, Shimizu Corp., Nippon Life Insurance, Seiko Epson, and Yasuda Trust. At the end it states that the U.S. must abandon its preoccupation with the bilateral trade imbalance: "The U.S. should stop regarding each new tack in its efforts to resolve the trade imbalance as a panacea."

Looking at the matter coldly, the Japanese are right. While Americans earnestly push for a level playing field, the Japanese know that such a field doesn't exist. While the U.S. doggedly fights each trade battle, claiming victories in beef, oranges, and supercomputers, Japan's aggressive approach to trade doesn't change. When the U.S. finally got Japan to buy supercomputers last year after a seven-year fight, Japanese companies had learned how to make the machines themselves and had already taken 95% of the big public-sector market. Quotas came off beef and oranges last month but tariffs went up, so prices in the stores were unchanged or in some cases higher.

This doesn't mean the Japanese are cheating. They are simply playing by different rules. Economic policy drives Japanese society. As Mosbacher puts it, "It's difficult to know where the government ends and the private sector begins." Says Glen Fukushima, a former U.S. trade official now with AT&T Japan: "When tariffs and barriers come off, the Japanese are ready." Former U.S. trade negotiator Clyde Prestowitz Jr., now president of the Economic Strategy Institute in Washington, explains: "In the U.S., policies are canted toward the consumer. In Japan they are canted toward the producers."

Take a close look at the Japanese auto industry, touted by many American economists as the best example of Japan's wide-open competitiveness. Eleven makers slugging it out, right? In fact, only three of the smaller manufacturers—Mazda, Honda, and Suzuki—are independents, each sticking to a distinct area of expertise.

All the other automakers have strong links to one or two other manufacturers through stock ownership. Toyota is the leading shareholder of Hino, Japan's largest truck producer, and Daihatsu, another maker of minicars. Nissan owns 40% of Nissan Diesel Motor. Fuji Heavy Industries, maker of Subaru, would have been bankrupt long ago if Nissan and the Industrial Bank of Japan hadn't bailed it out. Bureaucrats tightly monitor overall production in all industries, and though there have been notable exceptions (they couldn't persuade motorcycle maker Honda to stay out of the car business), they have usually been able to curtail new facilities that might create overcapacity.

To get a feel for how this works, pretend that Teddy Roosevelt and the trustbusters never existed. Imagine that General Motors held stakes in all its parts makers, plus stakes in Bethlehem Steel, its biggest distributors, Prudential Life Insurance, Chase Manhattan, and Merrill Lynch. Imagine that it told all those companies that it would never sell the shares as long as they gave preferential treatment to GM wherever possible. Imagine the meeting GM would hold once a month with the CEOs of all those companies. Now you are getting the idea of a Japanese *keiretsu,* or industrial group.

Further, imagine senior managers from seven or eight of those groups sitting down with a bureaucrat at the Commerce Department. Says the government man: "Memory chips (or amorphous metals or whatever) are going to be crucial to all industries for the next decade. Here are the tax incentives and loans you can get if you decide to get involved in this business." The government keeps an eye on every important move the companies make, but it has also eliminated most of the risk. By making the business under discussion a top national priority, the government guarantees that markets will exist and no company will fail.

Is this collusion? Kinichi Kadono, a board member at Toshiba, doesn't think so. Looking back on Japan's move into high-power memory chips 15 years ago, he says, "The government acted as a trigger to get companies involved, but our investment since then has been huge." Is it fair? He answers with a touch of poor-little-Japan: "I was a teenager after World War II. You can't imagine the poverty and weakness we felt. Even with help from the government, we still thought we were helpless. The government played a big role here, but was it bad? I don't think so."

Though Tokyo's official attitude remains conciliatory on U.S. trade initiatives, Washington's efforts may now be beside the point. Japan's huge capital spending program, which was backed by the super-low interest rates and cheap capital costs of the late 1980s, has yet to bear fruit. Says Jeffrey Garten, a managing director of Blackstone Group, a New York investment bank that deals heavily with Japan: "The wave of Japanese exports that will come from that investment will likely dwarf anything we've seen so far."

Trade battles will become more acute, nonetheless. Expect computers to be next, and then watch for something called dual-use components. These are electronic devices that can go into a toaster or a Patriot missile. While Japan does not export arms, it does export dual-use electronics by the shipload. And it is this fact that brings trade with Japan back into the security arena. Says Andrew Grove, CEO of Intel: "All that high-tech stuff you saw in the Gulf war was based on U.S. technology developed in the 1970s. We controlled it then. Today, for the most part, we don't." After his fourth trip to Japan, Senator Jeff Bingaman, a New Mexico Democrat, wrote Deputy Secretary of Defense Donald Atwood: "A comparison of U.S. and Japanese efforts in critical technologies, particularly dual-use technologies, clearly shows adverse trends for the U.S."

JAPANESE EXECUTIVES take for granted that an important shift in the balance of power between the U.S. and Japan has taken place. Says Mitsubishi's Kuroda, an affable man who genuinely likes Americans: "The important thing is to make sure relations between Japan and the U.S. are good, and you'll have no problem buying Japanese chips. If your companies are not competitive, your government should help them. America should have the guts to tackle its problems."

Many Japanese in high places think it's only a matter of time before Japan stops giving in on U.S. demands for more trade concessions and more money for U.S. bases in Japan. They believe Japan should begin planning for an independent role on the world stage as befits its economic power and responsibilities. Says Shohei Kurihara, a former top government official who is now executive vice president of Toyota: "The strategic alliance [with the U.S.] is less important today." Adds Kume, the TV newscaster: "The military alliance makes me feel that World War II hasn't really ended."

Popular magazine articles have also taken up the topic, with titles like "Is America Japan's Military Policeman?" Outspoken Diet member Shintaro Ishihara, author with Sony Chairman Akio Morita of the popular book *The Japan That Can Say No*, is already campaigning for the U.S. to give back an air base to be used as a third Tokyo airport. Toyota's Kurihara is saying no in his own way. Though import promotion is an official government policy, he says the company can't find an American car to recommend to its dealers.

Japanese politicians are gradually beginning to realize that saying no to America means Japan will have to accept more responsibility for its own defense. A willingness to go it alone is growing among younger members of the Diet. The danger, says Koji Kakizawa, a Diet member who is director of the ruling Liberal Democrat Party's National Defense Division, is that Japan will turn isolationist and not cooperate with the U.S. on defense matters at all. As for trade, the Ministry of International Trade and Industry (MITI) is preparing its own list of what it says are U.S. unfair trade practices—including quotas on sugar and other agricultural products—that it plans to present to Washington this year.

The ground ahead of the U.S. and Japan on the trade and defense fronts will be the rockiest since the war. But each side can act now to make the damage as light as possible. Japan would do well continuing to stimulate its economy to keep imports and aid programs growing. Surely the ban on rice imports should be lifted, if only to show good faith to American negotiators.

On the U.S. side, a growing number of members of Congress and academics are looking at some kind of organized government support for targeted high-tech industries. Says Prestowitz: "The U.S. is becoming more dependent on foreign technology. The response of so many Japanese during the Gulf war showed that sometimes even allies may not see their national interest as coinciding with ours. Maybe we need a technology policy."

Such rumblings are even coming from inside the Administration. Managed trade, which would limit imports, is a nonstarter.

But government aid to industries that make dual-use products is under consideration. Says a senior Administration trade official: "My personal view is that we haven't given these [industries] the attention they deserve. I'd focus on areas like semiconductors, real basic stuff."

VOICES FOR SUCH MOVES come from Japan too. "If U.S. politicians made a strong stand and ordered American manufacturers to catch up to Japan, then the U.S. would easily catch up and surpass us," says Ishihara. Adds Toshiharu Miyano, president of Miyano Machinery, a machine tool maker: "America must become more protectionist. Save the domestic manufacturing sector."

Ishihara and Miyano obviously have scant knowledge of the realities of American politics. Still, their comments, however naive, highlight the difference in thinking between Japanese and Americans. The Japanese would never leave something so precious as their industrial base to the brutalities of market forces. Bureaucrats and legislators guard industry like protective hens. Americans have always backed away from such thinking as unnecessary—and anticompetitive—coddling.

America's adversarial business climate grew out of years of combat between crusading governments and big companies. Remember the suit filed on the last day of the Johnson Administration, seeking to break up IBM because it was too powerful? The suit was eventually dropped, but similar action against AT&T did lead to a sundering of the telephone giant. Can anyone imagine a Japanese government pursuing such goals? Clyde Prestowitz, for one, thinks change is due. Says he: "When John D. Rockefeller knocked out competitors by undercharging, we said it was bad. Today, when foreign competitors undersell domestic manufacturers, that ought to be bad too, but we say it's good for the consumer."

As the U.S. considers its responses to Japan's growing economic challenges, it will also have to take a hard look at the strategic relationship. The two sides should unwind their relationship only slowly. Japan spends about $30 billion a year on defense. As the Soviet threat recedes, Japan can provide more of its own defense and still join in arms reduction programs.

What the U.S. must accept in dealing with both trade and defense issues is that the terms of the relationship have changed fundamentally. This is not just another squall that will end with pledges of more concessions in Japan and more patience in Washington. The new self-assurance of the Japanese is a fact. It only seems to have blown up overnight. It has been building for years, along with Japan's economic power. The question now is whether both sides can accept each other as they are, and build a new relationship on that understanding. ∎

SELECTED BIBLIOGRAPHY—SECTION VI

Berger, Peter L. *The Capitalist Revolution: Fifty Propositions About Prosperity, Equality, and Liberty.* New York: Basic Books, 1988.

Bergner, Jeffrey T. *The New Superpowers: Germany, Japan, the U.S., and the New World Order.* New York: St. Martin's, 1991.

Blake, David H., and Robert S. Walters. *The Politics of Global Economic Relations.* Englewood Cliffs, N.J.: Prentice-Hall, 1987.

Bowles, Samuel, and Herbert Gintis. *Democracy and Capitalism: Property, Community, and the Contradictions of Modern Social Thought.* New York: Basic Books, 1987.

Branford, Sue, and Bernardo Kucinski. *The Debt Squads: The U.S., the Banks, and Latin America.* London: Zed Books, 1990.

Cetron, Marvin, and Owen Davies. *Crystal Globe: The Haves and Have-Nots of the New World Order.* New York: St. Martin's, 1991.

Congdon, Tim. *The Debt Threat: The Dangers of High Real Interest Rates for the World Economy.* New York: Basil Blackwell, 1988.

Frieden, Jeffry A., and David A. Lake. *International Political Economy: Perspectives on Global Policy and Wealth.* New York: St. Martin's, 1991.

George, Susan. *A Fate Worse Than Debt: The World Financial Crisis and the Poor*. New York: Grove Press, 1988.

Haus, Leah A. *Globalizing the GATT: The Soviet Union, East Central Europe, and the International Trading System*. Washington, D.C.: Brookings Institution, 1991.

Holstein, William J. *The Japanese Power Game: What It Means for America*. New York: Plume Books, 1991.

Korner, Peter, Gero Maass, Thomas Siebold, and Rainer Tetzlaff. *The IMF and the Debt Crisis: A Guide to the Third World's Dilemmas*. London: Zed Books, 1987.

Lewis, Paul H. *The Crisis of Argentine Capitalism*. Chapel Hill: University of North Carolina Press, 1990.

Lindblom, Charles E. *Politics and Markets: The World's Political-Economic Systems*. New York: Basic Books, 1980.

Lissakers, Karen. *Banks, Borrowers, and the Establishment: A Revisionist Account of the International Debt Crisis*. New York: Basic Books, 1991.

Marichal, Carlos. *A Century of Debt Crises in Latin America: From Independence to the Great Depression*. Princeton: Princeton University Press, 1989.

Nossiter, Bernard D. *The Global Struggle for More: Third World Conflicts with Rich Nations*. New York: Harper & Row, 1987.

Pirages, Dennis O. *Global Technopolitics: The International Politics of Technology and Resources*. Pacific Grove, Calif.: Brooks/Cole, 1989.

Prestowitz, Clyde V., Jr. *Trading Places: How We Are Giving Our Future to Japan and How to Reclaim It*. New York: Basic Books, 1991.

Reischauer, Edwin O. *The Japanese Today: Change and Continuity*. Cambridge, Mass.: Harvard University Press, 1988.

Riddick, Jackie. *The Dance of the Millions: Latin America and the Debt Crisis*. London: Latin America Bureau, 1988.

Schatan, Jacobo. *World Debt: Who is to Pay?*. London: Zed Books, 1987.

Spero, Joan Edelman. *The Politics of International Economic Relations*. New York: St. Martin's, 1985.

Thomas, Clive Y. *The Poor and the Powerless: Economic Policy and Change in the Caribbean*. New York: Monthly Review Press, 1988.

Todaro, Michael. *Economic Development in the Third World*. New York: Longman, 1989.

A WORLD IN FERMENT

It is amply clear that the world faces a host of difficult and complicated problems—none more important than overpopulation. Today, the world's population exceeds 5.2 billion people, growing by nearly 90 million each year. Experts predict that it will top 6 billion by the year 2000, and reach 10 billion by 2025. More than 90 percent of the projected increase between now and the year 2025 will occur in the Third World countries of Asia, Africa, and Latin America. Indeed, at present growth rates, these nations would double in population in thirty-one years.

Unfortunately, those countries that boast the highest birth rates are those which are least able to feed, clothe, and shelter their people. Hunger, poverty, illiteracy, and disease are rampant in the developing world. The speed of growth has made it exceedingly difficult for Third World governments to provide adequate services, let alone solve the myriad other problems that they face. Clearly, the combination of poverty and population growth has increased the level of deprivation to the point that it has dramatically slowed social progress.

Still, there is reason for optimism. Between 1960 and 1987, eight countries in East Asia and Latin America lowered their fertility rates by more than 50 percent. Progress in this regard can be attributed to the wide availability of contraceptives, public education emphasizing responsible parenthood, broad-based social and economic development, and government commitment to population stabilization.

Likewise, the world faces a serious environmental crisis. The problems are many and varied: soil erosion and desertification, deforestation and species loss, air and water pollution, acid precipitation and ozone layer depletion, and the greenhouse effect and climate change. Despite progress in some areas, many countries lack the ability to monitor change, to project long-term trends, and to anticipate the impact of current decision-making in such areas as population size, resource allocation, and environmental quality. It is imperative that every nation develop foresight capability if it is to anticipate problems while they are still manageable.

In their quest to develop and modernize, many nations have ignored the serious challenges posed by environmental pollution. At present, the world is pouring vast amounts of contaminants into the atmosphere, posing hazards to human health, harming the environment, and possibly altering the earth's climate. These pollutants can also cause cancer, genetic defects, and respiratory disease, as well as damage forests, crops, lakes, streams, coastal waters, and buildings. In addition, they threaten crop yields and marine food chains, and produce significant climate change. In doing so, they could alter weather patterns, worsen storms, destoy natural systems, and disrupt agriculture.

If the planet is to survive, it is vital to achieve widespread use of the least polluting energy sources on a global scale. This is a massive but essential task. Nations must develop initiatives to improve energy efficiency, limit fossil fuels, expand renewable energy sources, reverse deforestation, curtail emissions of sulfur dioxide and nitrogen oxides, eliminate chlorofluorcarbons, and foster sustainable agriculture.

Other problems also abound, few more critical than the violation of human rights. In recent decades, the international community has become increasingly aware of and concerned about the extent and severity of human rights violations, both in the developed and Third World. These abuses—which take myriad forms—are instituted in order to isolate or eliminate actual or potential political opponents and/or popularly organized opposition groups who may pose a threat to the ruler or regime.

Since 1975, for example, Third World governments have either ordered or condoned the political killings of hundreds of thousands of people by the army and police, regular security forces, special units, and "death squads" sanctioned by official authorities. Typically, these killings occur outside the legal or judicial process; the victims are denied all constitutional protections. Political dissidents are frequently abducted and illegally detained or tortured before they are murdered.

At times, the killings are orchestrated at the highest levels of government. In other cases, the government either refuses to investigate the murders or adopt concrete measures to prevent further killings. When murders are revealed, the governments usually deny that they occurred, blame their political opponents, or insist that the killings were the result of violent confrontations with government forces or of attempts by the victims to escape from official custody.

In addition to political killings, many Third World governments also systematically violate their citizens' basic civil liberties, including freedom of speech, press, religion, assembly, and petition. Some governmental authorities routinely abrogate the constitutional rights of political dissidents, individuals who pose a threat to their regimes. Typical targets include opposition politicians, government officials, judges, lawyers, military officers, labor union activists, religious leaders, journalists, teachers, and students.

Government opponents who escape imprisonment are nevertheless frequently subjected to intimidation, harassment, and violence. Many are forced to adopt disguises, travel secretly, and seek living quarters free of government surveillance. In many cases, opposition leaders are also obliged to abandon their families, give up their careers, live in poverty, and survive as outlaws in their own land. In these instances, the government hopes to isolate the dissidents, discredit their reputations, and destroy their followings.

In many developing countries, particularly those ruled by force, government officials employ even harsher measures, including kidnapping, torture, blackmail, and death threats. Other dissidents are denied the right to speak, write, organize, travel, and work. In many places, the courts exist in name only; they merely rubber-stamp the actions of high-level officials, who exert political pressure on judges to legitimize their conduct. Judges who do not acquiesce may be replaced, punished, or killed.

In parts of the Third World, rights to life, liberty, and property exist only on paper—to be abridged at will by government officials. Freedom is permitted only to the extent that it serves the objectives of the government. Despots fear democratic rule, for it encourages popular participation that could ultimately bring down the government. This explains in part why many Third World governments are quick to silence opposition newspapers, suspend political parties, close churches, and impose martial law.

Still other problems confront the world community. Terrorism, for example, looms increasingly important. As many experts have suggested, it is a difficult term to define, in part because it encompasses such a vast array of behaviors: rebellion, street battles, civil strife, insurrection, rural guerrilla war, coups d'etat, and a plethora of other acts and actions. It is also difficult to define because it involves a wider clash over ideologies and political objectives.

Over the past two decades, the world has witnessed several kinds of terrorism, but none more threatening than state-sponsored terrorism. It may involve direct financial aid to a terorrist group, training in weaponry, explosives, methods of assassination, para-military tactics, and intelligence. According to top officials, these skills are taught or have been taught at secret camps in Syria, Syrian-controlled eastern Lebanon, Libya, Iran, Nicaragua, and elsewhere. These countries support or condone terrorism because they derive clear political and ideological benefits from such actions.

Today, Iran is the leading supporter of terrorism, which it proudly espouses as a vehicle for spreading Islamic fundamentalism and counteracting Western influence. It has been heavily involved in Lebanon and supported Shiite terrorist bombings of the U.S. Embassy and the Marine barracks in Beirut, as well as an attack on the U.S. Embassy in Kuwait.

Other governments have also supported terrorist activities. For example, North Korea provides training, funds, and weapons to foreign terrorist groups, including selling large quantities of arms to Iran, and maintains ties with Japanese terrorist groups. North Yeman has supplied training and safe haven for Palestinian groups since the late 1960s. Syria has supported some of the most treacherous Palestinian terrorist groups, such as that of Abu Nidal, to further the political agenda of President Hafez Assad. It has also directed terrorism against Western targets, Egypt, Jordan, and the Arab states as a means of jettisoning a Middle East peace settlement.

Section VII, "A World in Ferment," is composed of seven chapters. Chapter 23, "The Population Explosion," examines current world population trends. The author argues that the growth rate is increasing dramatically in the Third World, and with it the need to develop strategies that will enable those governments to provide essential programs and services. In her view, this will require a significant increase in family planning and social spending. The second article also discusses the problem of overpopulation but focuses on the importance of good sex education and unlimited access to contraception and abortion. Acutely aware of the political implications of her recommendations, she suggests that there appears to be an emerging political consensus that recognizes the need to curb the world's fertility through the voluntary reduction of population growth and the promotion of family planning.

Chapter 24, "Poverty and Deprivation," analyzes the issue of world hunger, noting that, in spite of all the relief efforts, government assistance, and private volunteer help, nearly one-third of the population goes to bed hungry at night. The problem is especially acute in the developing world, which is plagued by widespread hunger, malnutrition, and starvation. The answer, contends the author, rests with the industrialized countries, which must combine forces to wage an all-out assault on the problem. In his view, hunger is a political problem—one that demands a global solution. It is essential to forge new cooperative relationships to assure the equitable distribution of available food. In the second selection, the author suggests that, like the rest of the world, Africa is confronted with an AIDS epidemic that could, if left unchecked, destroy decades of progress in such areas as health care and economic development. Apart from the present research that is underway, the international community must focus its attention on the deplorable state of Third World health systems, providing significantly increased support for development assistance.

Chapter 25, "The Environmental Crisis," advocates a "no regrets" environmental policy, arguing that the world community can learn much from America's environmental achievements. According to the author, the United States has demonstrated unprecedented resolve in addressing environmental challenges over the last two decades. Most of the improvements have occurred in the field of public health, though progress has also been made in the areas of environmental protection and air quality. Still, serious problems persist which, in his view, can best be solved through an economic incentives approach. In the second article, the author assesses the ecological impact of the gulf war, concluding that it ranks as one of the most environmentally destructive conflicts ever. After describing the specifics of the problem, he assesses the ecological consequences, both in the short- and long-term, insisting that the international community must develop improved mechanisms to address the environmental damage arising from armed conflicts, as well as redouble its effort to resolve disputes through peaceful means.

Chapter 26, "Energy and National Security," analyzes President Bush's energy strategy, which places major emphasis on the need for additional oil and nuclear power. The author maintains that Bush's strategy is both ill-advised and short-sighted. He cites a Department of Energy call to "streamline" the licensing process, which he maintains would exclude the public. Presently, a hearing is required both when a construction permit is issued and when the reactor is completed and about to go on line. The president favors eliminating the second hearing, as well as allowing nonutility producers to sell huge amounts of electricity, free of state regulation. This would allow them to build their own reactors and then market the power without having to secure the approval of local public utility commissions. The second article examines the impact of the gulf war on oil prices. He challenges the argument of "energy security," which holds that the best way to assure the continued flow of oil is to make major foreign policy concessions to the oil kingdoms. He concludes that appeasing Arab interests would not, in fact, make U.S. oil imports more stable and that, if anything, the oil cartel is far more responsive to markets than to politics. It would be irrational, he insists, to exchange political concessions for oil deliveries.

Chapter 27, "Human Rights and Democratic Rule," discusses the global democratic revolution, reviewing the reasons for the demise of communism and many Third World dictatorships. In reviewing these developments, the author presents several reasons for the replacement of authoritarian rule by democratic government, among them lost wars, economic crises, promises of reform, and international communications. He also describes the political consequences of revolution and the obstacles to democratization, noting that recent developments have made the world safer than at any time in the past half century. In the second selection, the author explores the issue of human rights, arguing that while, in principle, human rights should be free from politics, in reality it is a highly political issue. After reviewing America's recent past in promoting human rights, the author describes the hypocrisy of the Left in condemning human rights abuses in Nicaragua, El Salvador, and Guatemala—whose govern-ments they oppose—while failing to denounce similar abuses by Black African governments, Cuba, and the Soviet Union—whose governments they either support or refuse to criticize. This lack of evenhandedness, concludes the author, demonstrates a failure of principle.

Chapter 28, "The Rise of Terrorism," concentrates on the issue of terrorism. The author identifies ten options, which he calls "pro-legal or pro-active," that are often raised in the debate over terrorism. In his view, the problem can best be solved by selecting one option or a combination of options that will most deter the terrorists while minimizing the damage to democratic values. The world community should continue to oppose state-sponsored terrorism and prevent those nations from acquiring nuclear weapons. Clearly, this will require global controls and inspection procedures. The second selection explores the issue of political assassination, discussing the law as it relates to assassination, the question of humanitarian intervention, and the role of assassination in wartime. Specifically, the author focuses on the case of Saddam Hussein, maintaining that there are only two ways to eliminate him: to kill him by accident, or to deliberately target him for assassination. He concludes that those closest to Saddam stand the best chance of removing him, and that it would be both difficult and unwise for the United States to attempt to do so itself.

Chapter 29, "The International Drug War," analyzes the rise of narco-terrorism, focusing on the Medellin Cartel in Colombia. The author explains the history of the Colombian cocaine connection, the rise of the drug barrons, the violence and terrorism that the drug cartel has used, the anti-drug efforts of the U.S. and Colombian governments, the drug cartel's counterattack, and the need for international cooperation to curb the power of the drug lords. Although some progress has been made, both in terms of cooperation and interdiction, the problem will remain until the demand for drugs in the United States is significantly reduced or eliminated. In the second selection, the author discusses the drug war in Peru, noting that America's appetite for cocaine is clearly evident in the Huallaga Valley, where more than 65 percent of the coca leaf refined into U.S.-bound cocaine is grown. In order to win the war on drugs, American officials have forged an alliance with the Peruvian military. However, many top U.S. officials oppose financing the Andean military, fearing that it would involve the U.S. in a bloody civil war in Peru with the Shining Path, a Maoist guerrilla movement which has formed an alliance with the coca growers, providing protection in exchange for a cut of the profits.

DISCUSSION QUESTIONS

1. What accounts for the prediction that no less than 95 percent of the projected global population growth will occur in the Third World over the next thirty-five years?
2. Is it likely that the developing world will be able to provide the level of services required to keep pace with the anticipated population increase?
3. What explains the decline in food self-sufficiency in the Third World?
4. In what ways has the combination of poverty and population growth affected the environment in the developing world?
5. What can be done, if anything, to reduce overall rates of population growth in the Third World?
6. Why is family planning such a controversial issue in many developing countries?
7. Who, if anyone, is to blame for the problem of overpopulation?
8. Why is hunger and malnutrition so prevalent in the Third World?
9. How do the internal policies of developing countries contribute to the problem of hunger?
10. Is there an answer to the problem of world hunger? If so, what?
11. Why is it so difficult to document the extent of the AIDS epidemic in Africa?
12. What is likely to happen in the Third World if the AIDS problem is not brought under control?
13. Why is the overall rate of transmission of AIDS likely to remain greater in the developing world than in industrialized countries?
14. Is the Third World capable of responding effectively to the AIDS epidemic?
15. In what sense, if any, will the global underclass likely bear a disproportionate share of AIDS misery?
16. Is global warming as serious a problem as believed? Why, or why not?
17. Has the Bush administration demonstrated leadership in responding to the problem of global warming?
18. What impact will the continuing destruction of the earth's rain forests have on the world's environment?
19. Why will it be so difficult to save the rain forests and the endangered species of the world?
20. Will the economic incentives approach prove effective in combatting pollution?
21. In what ways has the gulf war proven ecologically destructive to the region?
22. What environmental lessons should be learned from the gulf conflict?
23. Why has the international community been so slow to respond to the environmental aspects of the gulf war?
24. What are the major features of President Bush's energy strategy?
25. Is nuclear power a viable answer to America's energy needs? Why, or why not?
26. How, if at all, would "streamlining" the licensing process for new nuclear power plants affect the public interest?

27. Is nuclear power a safe and clean form of energy? Why, or why not?
28. Why did the pundits err in predicting a dramatic rise in oil prices once fighting broke out in the gulf?
29. Is the West too dependent on foreign oil? If so, why?
30. Should the United States change its policy toward Israel to prevent the Arabs from using their oil weapon?
31. Is the Organization of Petroleum Exporting Countries more responsive to markets or politics?
32. What explains the democratic revolution that is sweeping the world?
33. Why have so many communist and dictatorial regimes collapsed in recent years?
34. Does the demise of authoritarian or totalitarian governments guarantee the success of democracy? Why, or why not?
35. How is the current democratic revolution likely to affect the prospects for an enduring peace?
36. To what extent has the United States sought to promote human rights internationally?
37. Why has the Bush administration been slow to comdemn human rights violations on the part of many right-wing governments?
38. Does the Left have a double standard when it comes to human rights?
39. Is assassination an appropriate and effective tactic to combat terrorism?
40. To what extent, if any, has the media encouraged terrorist incidents?
41. What can be done to prevent international terrorism?
42. Is improved intelligence an effective antidote to terrorism?
43. What explains the rise of narco-terrorism over the past decade?
44. Is the Colombian government winning the war against the Medellin Cartel?
45. Will the recent crackdown on the Medellin Cartel significantly curb the problem of drug trafficking?
46. What can be done to reduce the demand for drugs in the United States?
47. Is the war against drugs winnable? If so, how?
48. Why has the United States been so reluctant to intervene in the drug problem in Peru?
49. Should the United States finance Peru's military to fight drugs?
50. What, if anything, can be done to dissuade Peru's farmers from growing coca?
51. Does coca-leaf refining pose a serious environmental hazard? If so, what?

KEY TERMS

ACQUIRED IMMUNODEFICIENCY SYNDROME   A disease in which the body's immune system breaks down, leading eventually to death.

ALTERNATIVE FUELS   Fuels other than those derived from fossil fuels (oil, gas, and coal), including methanol, ethanol, liquid hydrogen, and electricity obtained from sunlight.

AMNESTY INTERNATIONAL   A human rights organization, founded in 1961, to aid political prisoners and others detained for reasons of conscience.

COCAINE   An alkaloid from the coca leaf, it is taken for its euphoriant effect by chewing the leaf, as snuff, or by intravenous injection.

DEFORESTATION   The cutting down or burning of forests which, in turn, can lead to desertification and erosion.

DEPARTMENT OF ENERGY   A department created in 1977 that exercises primary responsibility for the administration, policies, and programs in the field of energy.

DRUG ENFORCEMENT ADMINISTRATION   An agency established to investigate violations of all federal drug trafficking laws, as well as regulate the legal manufacture of drugs and other controlled substances.

ECOLOGY   The study of living things and their links to the environment and one another.

ECOSYSTEM   A system of ecological relationships in a local environment, including relationships between organisms, and between the organisms and the environment itself.

ENVIRONMENTAL PROTECTION AGENCY   An agency created in 1970 to administer federal programs aimed at controlling pollution and safeguarding the nation's environment.

EXTRADITION   Return by one country to another of a person accused of a crime.

FAMILY PLANNING   The practice of regulation of family size by careful use of contraception, sterilization and, on occasion, induced abortion.

GREENHOUSE EFFECT   The absorption and retention of the sun's radiation in the earth's atmosphere resulting in an increase in the temperature of the earth's surface.

HAZARDOUS WASTE   Chemicals and metals left over from industrial processes which can contaminate the air, soil, surface water, or groundwater, as well as harm people and ecosystems.

HUMAN RIGHTS   Basic rights of individuals, regardless of nationality.

MALNUTRITION   Inadequate nutrition, especially in children, which may involve all parts of the diet, or may be the result of protein or vitamin deficiencies.

NARCO-TERRORISM   The violent blending of illicit drug trade and political intimidation.

NUCLEAR ENERGY   The energy liberated by a nuclear reaction (fission or fusion) or by spontaneous radioactivity.

NUCLEAR POWER PLANT   Any device or assembly that converts nuclear energy into useful power.

NUCLEAR REACTOR   A mechanism fueled by fissionable materials that gives off neutrons, thereby inducing heat.

NUCLEAR REGULATORY COMMISSION   An independent agency established in 1975 to regulate the commercial atomic power plant industry.

ORGANIZATION OF PETROLEUM EXPORTING COUNTRIES   A producer cartel whose goal is collectively to fix the levels production and the price of crude oil on the world market.

POLLUTION   Substances that contaminate the environment and upset ecosystems.

TERRORISM   Violence, fear, and intimidation directed toward private citizens, public property, and political enemies by an individual or a group to achieve a desired end.

WORLD HEALTH ORGANIZATION   A specialized agency of the United Nations, it advises countries on how to develop health services, combat epidemics, and promote health education and standards of nutrition and sanitation.

ZERO POPULATION GROWTH   The close approximation in numbers of births and deaths needed to stabilize a country's population and prevent annual increases.

Chapter 23

The Population Explosion

Article 23.1. World Population Continues to Rise

In this article, Nafis Sadik, executive director of the United Nations Population Fund, reviews current trends in world population and offers several suggestions for curbing population growth rates. She contends that the world population is growing at an accelerating rate, outpacing its ability to provide such essential services as food, clothing, shelter, and health care. The choices we make over the next ten years, she argues, may well determine the kind of world our children will inherit in the future. To lessen the problem, she advocates a shift to cleaner technologies, energy efficiency, and resource conservation by all countries; a direct and all-out attack on poverty; and reductions in overall rates of population, especially in those nations with the highest rates of growth.

World Population Continues to RISE

BY NAFIS SADIK

The executive director of the United Nations Population Fund outlines the current world population trends and suggests strategies for curbing population growth rates.

The 1990s will be a critical decade. The choices of the next 10 years will decide the speed of population growth for much of the next century; they will decide whether world population triples or merely doubles before it finally stops growing; they will decide whether the pace of damage to the environment speeds up or slows down.

The world's population, now 5.3 billion, is increasing by three people every second — about a

From *The Futurist*, March/April 1991, pp. 9-14. Reprinted, with permission, from *The Futurist*, published by the World Future Society, 4916 Saint Elmo Avenue, Bethesd, Maryland 20814.

quarter of a million every day. Between 90 and 100 million people — roughly equivalent to the population of Eastern Europe or Central America — will be added every year during the 1990s; a billion people — a whole extra China — over the decade.

No less than 95% of the global population growth over the next 35 years will be in the developing countries of Africa, Asia, and Latin America.

It has been more than 20 years since the population growth rate of developing countries reached its peak in 1965-70. But it will be during only the last five years of this century that the additions to total numbers in developing countries will reach their maximum. This 35-year lag is a powerful demonstration of the steamroller momentum of population growth.

Racing to provide services to fast-growing populations is like running up the down escalator: You have to run very fast indeed to maintain upward motion. So far, all the effort put into social programs has not been quite enough to move upward in numerical terms. The absolute total of human deprivation has actually increased, and unless there is a massive increase in family planning and other social spending, the future will be no better.

Population Trends

Southern Asia, with almost a quarter of the current total world population, will account for 31% of the total increase between now and the end of the century; Africa, with 12% of the world's population today, will account for 23% of the increase. By contrast, eastern Asia, which has another 25% of the current world population, will account for only 17% of the total increase. Similarly, the developed countries — Europe (including the Soviet Union), North America, and Japan, which represent 23% of the current world population — will account for only 6% of the increase. The remaining 15% of the world's population, living in developing countries, will produce 23% of the increase.

By and large, the increases will be in the poorest countries — those by definition least equipped to meet the needs of the new arrivals and invest in the future.

Because of the world's skewed growth patterns, the balance of numbers will shift radically. In 1950, Europe and North America constituted 22% of the world's population. In 2025, they will make up less than 9%. Africa, only 9% of the world population in 1950, will account for just under a fifth of the 2025 total. India will overtake China as the world's most populous country by the year 2030.

Toward the end of the twenty-first century, a number of countries seem set to face severe problems if populations grow as projected. Nigeria could have some 500 million citizens — as many as the whole African continent had around 1982. This would represent more than 10 people for every hectare of arable land. Modern France, with better soils and less erosion, has only three people per hectare. Bangladesh's 116 million inhabitants would grow to 324 million, with density on its arable land more than twice as high as in the Netherlands today. This does not take into account any land that may be lost to sea-level rises caused by global warming.

It should be emphasized that these are not the most-pessimistic projections. On the contrary, they assume steadily declining fertility during most of the next 100 years.

Food

Between 1979-81 and 1986-87, cereal production per person actually declined in 51 developing countries and rose in only 43. The total number of malnourished people increased from 460 million to 512 million and is projected to exceed 532 million by the end of the century.

Developing countries as a whole have suffered a serious decline in food self-sufficiency. Their cereal imports in 1969-71 were only 20 million tons. By 1983-85, they had risen to 69 million tons and are projected to total 112 million tons by the end of the century. These def-

icits have so far been met by corresponding surpluses in the industrialized countries — of which the overwhelming bulk comes from North America.

World food security now depends shakily on the performance of North American farmers. Following the drought-hit U.S. harvest of 1988, world cereal stocks dropped from 451 million tons in 1986-87 to only 290 million tons in 1989, down from a safe 24% of annual consumption to the danger level of 17%.

Poverty

The world produces enough food to feed everyone today — yet malnutrition affects as many as 500 million people. The problem is poverty and the ability to earn a livelihood. The total numbers of the poor have grown over the past two decades to around one billion now.

Absolute poverty has shown a dogged tendency to rise in numerical terms. The poorest fifth of the population still dispose of only 4% of the world's wealth, while the richest dispose of 58%. Economic recession, rising debt burdens, and mistaken priorities have reduced social spending in many countries.

But population growth at over 2% annually has also slowed social progress. So much additional investment has been required to increase the quantity of health, education, and other services to meet the needs of increased populations that the quality of service has suffered.

In many sectors, the proportion of deprived people has declined. But this is a reduced proportion of a higher total population swelled by rapid growth. As a result, the total numbers of deprived people have grown.

The growth of incomes may be affected by population growth. On a regional basis, there is an inverse relationship between population growth and growth of per capita income. There is a lag of 15–20 years between the peak of population growth and the peak growth in the labor force. Already there are severe problems in absorbing new entrants to the labor force in regions such as Africa or South Asia. Yet, in numerical terms, the highest rates of labor-force growth in developing countries lie ahead, in the years 2010–2020.

The labor force in developing countries will grow from around 1.76 billion today to more than 3.1 billion in 2025. Every year, 38 million new jobs will be needed, without counting jobs required to wipe out existing underemployment, estimated at 40% in many developing countries. Complicating the issue will be the spread of new, labor-saving technologies.

The land still provides the livelihood of almost 60% of the population of developing countries. But most of the best and most-accessible land is already in use, and what is left is either less fertile or harder to clear and work. The area available per person actually declined at the rate of 1.9% a year during the 1980s.

Urban and Education Issues

In recent decades, urban growth in developing countries has been even more rapid than overall population growth. Town populations are expanding at 3.6% a year — four and a half times faster than in industrialized countries and 60% faster than rural areas. Rural migrants swell the total, but an increasing share of this growth now comes from natural growth within the cities themselves.

The speed of growth has outpaced the ability of local and national government to provide adequate services. The number of urban households without safe water increased from 138 million in 1970 to 215 million in 1988. Over the same period, households without adequate sanitation ballooned from 98 million to 340 million.

The total number of children out of school grew from 284 million in 1970 to 293 million in 1985 and is projected to rise further to 315 million by the end of the century. Also between 1970 and 1985: The total number of illiterates rose from 742 million to 889 million, and the total number of people without safe sanitation increased from about a billion to 1.75 billion.

Eating Away at the Earth

These increasing numbers are eating away at the earth itself. The combination of fast population growth and poverty in developing countries has begun to make permanent changes to the environment. During the 1990s, these changes will reach critical levels. They include continued urban growth, degradation of land and water resources, massive deforestation, and buildup of greenhouse gases.

Many of these changes are now inevitable because they were not foreseen early enough, or because action was not taken to forestall them. Our options in the present generation are narrower because of the decisions of our predecessors. Our range of choice, as individuals or as nations, is narrower, and the choices are harder.

The 1990s will decide whether the choices for our children narrow yet further — or open up. We know more about population — and interactions among population, resources, and the environment — than any previous generation. We have the basis for action. Failure to use it decisively will ensure only that the problems become much more severe and much more intractable, the choices harder and their price higher.

At the start of the 1990s, the choice must be to act decisively to slow population growth, attack poverty, and protect the environment. The alternative is to hand on to our children a poisoned inheritance.

Danger Signals

Just a few years ago, in 1984, it seemed as if the rate of population growth was slowing everywhere except Africa and parts of South Asia. The world's population seemed set to stabilize at around 10.2 billion toward the end of the next century.

Today, the situation looks less promising. Progress in reducing birth rates has been slower than expected. According to the latest U.N. projections, the world has overshot the marker points of the 1984 "most likely" medium projection and is now on course for an

eventual total that will be closer to 11 billion than to 10 billion.

In 15 countries — 13 of them in Africa — birthrates actually rose between 1960-65 and 1980-85. In another 23 nations, the birthrate fell by less than 2%.

If fertility reductions continue to be slower than projected, the mark could be missed yet again. In that case, the world could be headed toward an eventual total of up to 14 billion people.

Why should we be worried about this? At present, the human race numbers "only" 5.3 billion, of which about a billion live in poverty. Can the earth meet even modest aspirations for the "bottom billion," let alone those of the better-off and their descendants, without irreparable damage to its life-support systems?

Already, our impact has been sufficient to degrade the soils of millions of hectares, to threaten the rain forests and the thousands of species they harbor, to thin the ozone layer, and to initiate a global warming whose full consequences cannot yet be calculated. The impact has greatly increased since 1950.

By far the largest share of resources used, and waste created, is currently the responsibility of the "top billion" people, those in industrialized countries. These are the countries overwhelmingly responsible for damage to the ozone layer and acidification, as well as for roughly two-thirds of global warming.

However, in developing countries, the combination of poverty and population growth among the "bottom billion" is damaging the environment in several of the most sensitive areas, notably through deforestation and land degradation. Deforestation is a prime cause of increased levels of carbon dioxide, one of the principal greenhouse gases responsible for global warming. Rice paddies and domestic cattle — food suppliers for 2 billion people in developing countries — are also major producers of methane, another of the greenhouse gases.

Developing countries are also doing their best to increase their share of industrial production and consumption. Their share of industrial pollution is rising and will continue to rise.

At any level of development, larger numbers of people consume more resources and produce more waste. The quality of human life is inseparable from the quality of the environment. It is increasingly clear that both are inseparable from the question of human numbers and concentrations.

A Case for Change

Redressing the balance demands action in three major areas:

1. A shift to cleaner technologies, energy efficiency, and resource conservation by all countries is necessary, especially for the richer quarter of the world's population.

Carbon-dioxide emissions will be hardest to bring under control. If the atmospheric concentration of carbon dioxide is to be stabilized, cuts of 50% to 80% in emissions may be required by the middle of the next century. These will be difficult to achieve even with the most-concentrated efforts.

Four major lines of action will produce the greatest impact, especially if they are pursued in parallel. The first is improved efficiency in energy use. The second is a shift from fossil fuels, which currently account for 78% of the world's energy use, to renewable sources such as wind, geothermal, and solar thermal. The third is halting deforestation. The fourth is slowing population growth.

There are no technological solutions in sight for methane emissions from irrigated fields and livestock. They have both expanded in response to growing rural populations and to meet expanding world demands for cereals and meat. The irrigated area has grown by about 1.9% a year since 1970, slightly faster than world population. Livestock and irrigation will both continue to expand in line with populations in developing countries. Reducing population growth is the only viable strategy to reduce the growth in methane emissions from these sources.

2. A direct and all-out attack on poverty itself will be required.

3. Reductions are needed in overall rates of population growth. Reducing population growth, especially in the countries with the highest rates of growth, will be a crucial part of any strategy of sustainable development.

Reducing the rate of population growth will help extend the options for future generations: It will be easier to provide higher quality and universal education, health care, shelter, and an adequate diet; to invest in employment and economic development; and to limit the overall level of environmental damage.

What Needs to Be Done?

Immediate action to widen options and improve the quality of life, especially for women, will do much to secure population goals. It will also widen the options and improve the quality of life of future generations.

Education is often the means to a new vision of options. It encourages a sense of control over personal destiny and the possibility of choices beyond accepted tradition. For women, it offers a view of sources of status beyond childbearing. Because of this, education — especially for girls — has a strong impact on the health of the family and on its chosen size.

Women assume the burden of childcare along with their other tasks. They are in charge of nutrition, hygiene, food, and water. As a result, the effect of women's education on child survival is very marked.

Education's impact on fertility and use of family planning is equally strong. Women with seven or more years of education tend to marry an average of almost four years later than those who have had none.

Yet, there remains a great deal to be done in women's education, even to bring it level with men's. Women make up almost two-thirds of the illiterate adults in developing countries. The importance of literacy programs for adult women goes far beyond reading and writ-

ing: It also allows access to practical information on such matters as preventive health care and family planning, which are often part of the programs themselves.

Sustained improvements in health care give people a sense of control over their lives. With adequate health care, parents develop the sense that they have some choice over their children's survival. Parents' feeling of control over their lives is extended by modern family planning; they can protect the health of both mother and child by preventing or postponing childbirth. Preventive measures that the family itself can apply assist the process.

Support for Family-Planning Efforts

Political support from the highest levels in the state is essential in making family planning both widely available and widely used. Political backing helps to legitimize family planning, to desensitize it, and to place it in the forum of public debate. It helps win over traditional leaders or counter their hostility. It also helps to ensure that funding and staffing for family planning are stable and protected against damaging budget cuts or the competing demands of rival departments.

Support must extend far beyond the national leadership before programs take off. It may be necessary to involve a wide range of religious and traditional leaders in discussions before introducing population policies and programs on a wide scale. If these leaders feel that they have been sidestepped, their opposition may become entrenched. If they are consulted and involved, on the other hand, they may often turn into allies. In Indonesia, for example, Muslim religious leaders were consulted at national and local levels; they not only withdrew their opposition, but have added their voices to the government's call for family planning.

Four main barriers block the way to easy access to family planning. The most obvious is geographical: How long do people have to travel to get supplies, and how long do

Research must continue for the ideal method of contraception: cheap, totally effective, risk-free, reversible, without undesirable side effects, and simple enough for use without medical provision or supervision.

No such method is yet on the horizon. But research continues to push forward the frontiers, under conditions that have become more and more difficult.

The business of developing new contraceptives has changed radically. Tighter controls on testing and rising risks of costly lawsuits have made drug companies wary. The leading role has been assumed by the World Health Organization (WHO) and by nonprofit organizations such as the Population Council and Family Health International. But real spending on contraceptive research and development has not increased.

Some promising new candidates have been developed. Norplant, already approved for use in several countries, is probably closest to wide dissemination. It consists of six tiny rods containing the progestin hormone levonorgestrol. These are implanted under the skin of a woman's inside arm. Norplant, particularly suitable for women who have completed their families, prevents pregnancies for five years before it needs replacing. A two-rod version providing protection for three years is being developed. Norplant is highly effective, and unlike the injectable Depo-Provera, its contraceptive effect ends soon after it is removed. The drawback for some situations is that it requires a physician to insert and remove. The cost, at $2.80 per year of protection, is more than the pill at $1.95, but less than Depo-Provera at $4 per year.

Other long-acting hormonal methods may be introduced during the 1990s. They include biodegradable implants, providing 18 months of protection, and injectable microspheres lasting between one and six months. Vaginal rings containing levonorgestrol, which can be inserted and removed by the woman, are also being tested. And the Population Council is researching a male contraceptive vaccine.

— **Nafis Sadik**

they have to wait for service when they get there?

The second barrier is financial: While many surveys show that people are willing to pay moderate amounts for family-planning supplies, most poor people have a fairly low price threshold. Costs of more than 1% of income are likely to prove a deterrent.

Culture and communication are a third barrier: opposition from the peer group, husband, or mother-in-law; shyness about discussing contraception or undergoing gynecological examination; language difficulties; or unsympathetic clinic staff.

A fourth barrier is the methods available: There is no such thing as the perfect contraceptive. Most people who need one can find a method suited to their needs — if one is available. However, if high contraception use is to be achieved, suitable services must be not only available, but accessible to all who need them.

Suitable services mean high-quality services. In the long run, the quantity of continuing users will depend on the quality of the service.

Service providers do not need to be highly educated, but they should be sympathetic, well informed, and committed to their work. The service must be reliable, so that users can count on supplies when they need them. Good counseling is one of the most important aspects of quality. Family planning is loaded with emotional, social, and sometimes religious values. It is vulnerable to poor information, rumor, and outright superstition. Along with reliable supplies and a good system for referral in problem cases, good counseling can make a big difference to continuation rates.

Two other channels are useful in broadening the base and increasing the appeal of family planning: community-based distribution and social marketing.

Community-based distribution (CBD) programs use members of the community — housewives, leaders, or members of local groups — to distribute contraceptives. Older married mothers who are themselves contraceptive users have proved the best candidates. Maturity, tact, perseverance, and enthusiasm are essential requirements for the good distributor.

After many years of relying only on clinic and health workers to deliver services, family-planning programs are discovering the uses of the marketplace. The private sector provides contraceptives to more than half the users in many developing countries.

Social-marketing programs reduce the cost to the user and increase sales by subsidizing supplies. These two aspects — the integration of suppliers with regular health services through training and the subsidization of supplies — are felt to combine the ease of access of the market with the sense of social responsibility of service programs.

The potential of community-based distribution and social marketing has not been exploited in most countries. Out of 93 countries studied for one survey, only 37 had a CBD or social-marketing project. There is clearly a considerable potential for expansion as an essential complement to integrated health services.

The technology of contraception is usually thought of in terms of safety and reliability. But it should also be seen as another important aspect of improving access and choice in family-planning programs.

Currently, the most popular method worldwide is sterilization, with around 119 million women and 45 million men in 1987. Next in popularity was the intrauterine device (IUD), with 84 million users, followed by the pill, with 67 million. The pattern of use differs considerably from one country to another and between developing countries and developed. Sterilization is by far the most common method in developing countries, with 45% of users, though only one-quarter of these were male. The IUD comes next in popularity, with 23%. In the North, sterilization accounts for only 14% of users and IUDs for 8%.

Users balance all the advantages and disadvantages they are aware of before deciding on a method — or no method. If they do not like the available alternatives, they will simply drop out and use no method at all, or revert to less reliable traditional methods. One recent study in East Java found that,

among women who were not given the method they preferred, 85% had discontinued use within one year. Where women were given the method they wanted, the dropout rate was only 25%.

Diversity, then, is the key to providing options. Diverse channels of distribution create the widest possible access to contraception. Diverse technology offers the widest possible choice of methods. The combination maximizes use.

Developing Human Resources

Investment in human resources provides a firm base for rapid economic development and could have a significant impact on the environmental crisis. It is essential for global security. But in the past, it has often commanded a lower priority than industry, agriculture, or military expenditure.

It is time for a new scale of priorities: There is no other sphere of development where investment can make such a large contribution both to the options and to the quality of life, both in the present and in the future. Whatever the future returns, investment is needed now.

About the Author

Nafis Sadik is executive director of the United Nations Population Fund, 220 East 42nd Street, New York, New York 10017. This article is adapted from the Fund's *The State of World Population 1990*.

Article 23.2. Population: Red-Hot Realities for a Finite Planet

The author outlines the realities of overpopulation as an environmental issue, noting that population control is a political issue, one that is likely to antagonize a variety of special interest groups, ranging from anti-abortionists to radical feminists to minority groups, all of whom regard population control as either a threat to their interests or numbers. Regardless of the opposition, concludes the author, it is vital to reduce family size to below replacement level, which will require a massive international commitment to birth control and social change. At the same time, the author detects a shift in popular thinking, which finds increasing political support for the voluntary reduction of population growth and the promotion of family planning.

TALKING ABOUT OVERPOPULATION LEADS YOU RIGHT ACROSS A BED OF COALS — RED-HOT REALITIES LIKE SEX, DEATH, WEALTH, POVERTY, POWER, AND MORALITY. THERE ARE NO EASY ANSWERS. BUT HAVING COME THIS FAR WITH A MAGAZINE LIKE **GARBAGE**, YOU MUST BE WILLING TO CONSIDER SOME OF THE CAUSES AND EFFECTS OF ENVIRONMENTAL PROBLEMS. ARGUMENTS RAGE ABOUT MAXIMUM SUSTAINABLE NUMBERS, BUT IT'S A TRUISM THAT THE MORE OF US THERE ARE ON A FINITE PLANET, THE LESS RAW MATERIAL AND ROOM TO MOVE (OR TIME TO PLAN).

TAKING STEPS TO CURB POPULATION GROWTH COURTS CONFLICT WITH A SPECTACULAR ARRAY OF SPECIAL-INTEREST GROUPS, FROM ANTI-ABORTIONISTS TO A HANDFUL OF RADICAL FEMINISTS WHO REGARD GESTATIONAL PROCESSES AS SACROSANCT. OTHERS WHO TAKE A DIM VIEW OF POPULATION CONTROL ARE MEMBERS OF MINORITY GROUPS AND NATIVE PEOPLES, WHO HAVE GOOD REASON TO WORRY THAT LIMITING THEIR NUMBERS COULD LEAD TO THEIR EXTINCTION.

BY STEPHANIE MILLS

At first glance, it may be hard to see how overpopulation could be your problem — the effects of overpopulation are seldom evident as such. But population is a factor (although not the only one) in every problem associated with urbanization and industrialization — growth. Complicating our understanding further, there are dramatic regional differences in population growth-rates, and in per-capita resource-consumption rates, which means that the population problem is manifested differently in different parts of the world. In the developed world, overpopulation makes itself noticeable by compounding the consequences of excess: pollution, solid-waste disposal, automotive congestion, urban sprawl. In the developing world, the struggle for subsistence — from the land or sea — intensifies with every generation: Increasing numbers of subsistence farmers are driven onto lands that are unsuitable for farming; women are driven further afield in the quest for firewood; and fishery after fishery collapses from contamination and overexploitation. And, according to Zero Population Growth, for the past 25 years the rate of increase in atmospheric CO_2 — the greenhouse gas — has matched the rate of population growth almost exactly. So even in the wilderness you encounter adverse environmental effects, such as acid rain, which have been amplified and multiplied by overpopulation.

Once you grasp the implications of rapid population growth, it becomes difficult not to be strident about it. I know. I broke into the ecology biz back in 1969, announcing in my college commencement address something that seemed to be only common sense: People like myself, who thought that population was becoming an overwhelming problem, ought to do something about it, and not have children.

So I haven't. It seemed simple enough to me. The only thing that's going to reverse overpopulation is reducing family size to below replacement level. All that requires is birth control ... and rather a lot of social change.

THE AMAZING MATING MACHINE

But the time and room for debate are shrinking. World population stands at 5.4 billion now, and is expected to double in 39 years, according to the Population Reference Bureau.

Consider our history: In 35,000 B.C., according to best estimates, our species numbered 3 million. Livelihood was earned by hunting and gathering — very low-tech and sustainable. By 8,000 B.C., gar-dening had been invented, and our numbers increased to 8 million. With the arrival of the Bronze Age 4,000 years later, the human population reached 86 million. By the beginning of the Common Era, the numbers had increased to 300 million. At the dawn of the Renaissance 1,400 years later, there were 336 million people in the world. Steady growth that was alarming only if you happened to be an aboriginal occupant of a "new world," standing in the path of some empire's expansion. But in recent centuries, the growth has been compounding itself with shocking effect.

"In 1830, 1 billion people inhabited the Earth," writes Population Institute President Werner Fornos, in *Technology Review*. "A century passed before the population reached 2 billion. Thirty years later, in 1960, it hit 3 billion; 15 years later, 4 billion; and by 1986 — only 11 years later — 5 billion ... the 6 billion mark could be reached in 1995."

How did this runaway phenomenon come about? The basic constraints on the growth of any population of organisms are food supply, disease, and predation. Using our unique tool- and language-making gifts, we human beings have cleverly (if not wisely) evaded these constraints.

Since the days when there were only a few million of us, there have been quantum changes. Early on, we shifted from a nomadic to an agricultural civilization, increasing our food supplies and our ability to store food. This great change also marked the beginning of serious deforestation and the buildup of salt in irrigated lands. More recently, we tapped into the finite and never-to-be-repeated bonus of fossil fuels, which helped power the industrialization of agriculture and spurred urbanization. Disease control and greater food security decreased infant mortality.

This change in death rates is extremely significant. While human reproductive potential is fairly constant, the question of whether you live to exercise it is not. When the annual birth-rate exceeds the death rate, the population grows. So when family size exceeds two children, population growth follows. Every minute now, 180 people are born and 100 die, for a net gain of about 11,000 souls per hour.

EXPONENTIAL GROWTH

Population growth works like compound interest. If a couple has four children (the average number a woman bears today is 3.5), they've replaced themselves twice in one generation. If each of the children follows suit, there will be 16 grandchildren, then 64 great-grandchildren. In four generations, this Adam and Eve have multiplied

From *Garbage*, May/June 1991, pp. 46-51.

themselves better than 200 times. (How many showed up at *your* last family reunion?)

Mother Nature doesn't exhibit much tolerance for such growth patterns. In *Population Biology*, Thomas C. Emmel writes: "Exponential growth is abruptly terminated when the carrying capacity of the environment is surpassed and environmental resistance becomes effective more or less suddenly. Such growth curves are characteristic of rapidly reproducing and maturing annual plants, seasonal insect flushes, and man's population growth in recent years, but in general, they are very short-lived phenomena for obvious reasons."

There is a French riddle that illustrates exponential growth. Here's how it appeared in the 1972 classic, *Limits to Growth*:

"Suppose you own a pond on which a water lily is growing. The lily plant doubles in size each day. If the lily were allowed to grow unchecked, it would completely cover the pond in 30 days, choking off the other forms of life in the water. For a long time, the lily plant seems small, and so you decide not to worry about cutting it back until it covers half the pond. On what day will that be?

On the 29th day, of course. You have one day to save the pond."

THE MORE
THE MERRIER?

Well, things are getting pretty thick around the old lily pond, but we're still in denial about the necessity to limit our numbers. You can probably find some reasons in your own personal experience. How could all those perfectly human impulses — to bring forth and love children, to do like mom and dad did (or better) — be anything but good? The prospects of another baby to enjoy and another person to share the work and carry on the family name are compelling to parents, especially in agrarian societies. That can make zero population growth a tough sell in the developing world.

One screeching brake on our developing a useful approach to the population problem is theological. The dominant religions of the West reflect the premise that *homo sapiens* is the most important critter on the planet — God made man in His own image, after all — and this is reflected in the Biblical injunction to "be fruitful and multiply, and replenish the earth, and subdue it." These days there is a lively discussion over the accuracy of that King James translation, but valid or not, generations have read it as a manifest destiny.

Another impediment to perceiving and acting on overpopulation has been conventional economics, which activist and author Hazel Henderson has called "a form of brain damage." For the most part, economists have been so enraptured by growth, and the magic of markets, that they've been blind to growth's downside. The problem with economics is that it only values the things it can count. Much of what constitutes quality of life can't be measured or counted, and so is omitted from the definition of a successful economic system.

For example, economist Julian Simon, whose work has served as a rationalization for recent U.S. population non-policy, maintains that population growth generates its own solutions. An increased number of humans means not only increased inventiveness, but also additional demand, which will drive a search for substitutes for depleted resources, clean air, and fresh water. Even if this worked, however, the resource for which there is no substitute is biodiversity. Dr. Simon's cheery optimism is bad news for other species.

WHO'S TO BLAME FOR
OVERPOPULATION?

Even among those who agree overpopulation is a problem, there are strong disagreements. Within the environmental and social-change movements, population debate from the mid-'70s onward drifted into a polarity of contending world views, which I will call the Darwinists and the Marxists. Each defines the problem differently. (My apologies to scholars and devotees of these great thinkers, for employing the names as shorthand.)

To Darwinists, or "biological determinists," as they are sometimes known, the arrival of population equilibrium is an inevitability. The only question is whether it will come about through a decrease in birth rates or an increase in death rates from famine, pandemic disease, and war. Some Darwinists, like Earth First! co-founder Dave Foreman, have inferred that starvation and fatal diseases still have their rightful place in human ecology. It's a pretty unpopular view, but it does point out that our reluctance to employ birth control is far exceeded by our reluctance to give up death control.

Darwinists see planet Earth as an ecosystem, and our species as just one among millions, interdependent with all, and subject to the laws of nature. The detachment in this evolutionary view can tip over into an insensitivity to the tragedies of individual lives, and an obtuseness about politics. For one thing, human beings have all the votes on this issue, and it's all too human to place one's individual needs and desires before the good of the whole. For another, although *homo sapiens* is all one species, disregarding the inequality of means among people falsifies the picture.

The "Marxist" sector views the problem as one of power — who's got it and who doesn't. They conclude that social oppression and economic imperialism are the essential causes of all great ills. The belief that scarcity is socially caused and socially curable has led analysts from this camp to regard any proposal to limit human numbers as an evasion of the real issue — revolutionizing social and economic arrangements.

Besides these people, there are

the feminists, whose claim to an opinion on overpopulation is perhaps the most secure, because it is women's bodies and women's lives that determine — and are mostly determined by — reproduction. In all this discussion, it is important to remember that childbearing and nurturing have been women's lot, while policy-making has been the domain of men. Women are well aware that childbearing is one of the greatest causes of female mortality, and that generous spacing between births is healthier for all concerned, whether families are rich or poor. Consequently, mothers may have a slightly different take on the advantages of population growth than do merchants, bishops, generals, or kings.

"Overpopulation is just a symptom of a basic human-rights problem," says Hazel Henderson. The general idea is that if women were fully compensated participants in the economic life of their communities, and thus emboldened to control their fertility; and if men assumed equal responsibility for household duties and the nurture of their offspring, smaller families and greater prosperity might well ensue. As it stands now, sexism is such a pervasive force in the world that a preference for male babies even drives Chinese couples into violations of their country's stringent one-child-per-family policy. And in most of Asia, North Africa, and Latin America the death rate for young women is higher than that of men as a consequence of neglect.

CARRYING CAPACITY: RECOGNIZING LIMITS

So — suppose we admit there's a complex interplay of social, cultural, and biological factors driving overpopulation. And that — thanks to the intervention of medicine, technology, and trade — the consequences of population growth aren't always obvious. That complexity means that *any* action taken by individuals, communities, nations, and the community of nations will likely offend *someone*. Nonetheless, on a finite planet, maximizing human reproduction clearly comes at great ecological cost, and a considerable cost in human suffering. What would be a positive goal for humanity in all of this?

We need to determine an optimum human carrying-capacity for Spaceship Earth, then limit our numbers to that. Then we must get on with the colossal tasks of sustainable development in the third and fourth world, and sustainable de-development in the first. The number-crunching for this modest project began in earnest nearly 20 years ago.

The aforementioned *Limits to Growth* was the report of a global modelling study that explored Earth's human-carrying capacity. Using systems analysis, computer projections, and a veritable world of data, the authors played out numerous scenarios for the human future, based on different trends in food production, resources, population, industrial output, and pollution. Assuming no change in present patterns, the authors predicted a crash in both population and industrial capacity by the next century. That was the bad news. The good news was that the Earth could sustain indefinitely a population of 6 billion at a European standard of comfort. We're due to hit that 6 billion mark in four years, however.

Besides the sheer number of us, our environmental impact has also to do with the choices that we, industry, and government make about resource consump-

tion and waste disposal; about land use and transportation; about energy generation and conservation. Decisions about all those things can magnify or modify the impact of the increased human numbers.

Ecologists Paul and Anne Ehrlich, in their recent book, *The Population Explosion*, suggest the following equation for thinking about some of these interactions: Impact equals Population X Affluence X Technology, or I=PAT. Understood that way, there's no single culprit. I=PAT helps explain why population is not just a problem of the developing countries. Although countries like the U.S. and Japan have relatively low populations, this is counteracted by the abundance of affluence and technology. According to the Ehrlich equation, the environmental impact of a baby born in the U.S. will be 35 times that of an Indian baby, and 280 times that of a Haitian child. Therefore it makes both practical and moral sense for people on the affluent side of the equation to reduce their impacts on the environment by reducing waste and, ultimately, consumption, as well as by reducing family size.

OVERPOPULATION: WHY IS IT HARD TO TALK ABOUT?

Of course, if there is to be such a thing as family planning, let alone population control, there will have to be good sex education and unlimited access to contraception and abortion (because no contraceptive method is 100-percent effective).

I notice that now I feel rather nervous making that assertion, which was commonplace during the '70s. It's a measure of the chill and fear that the anti-abortion movement has imposed on the discourse. I am not, I confess, very eager to confront their unreason and occasional violence.

Their lobby has had disastrous effects: a 42-percent reduction in domestic family-planning funds; an increased incidence of teenage motherhood; a thwarted introduction to the U.S. of RU 486, a promising abortifacient drug widely used in France; and the reversal of our international population policy. A 1985 amendment to the Foreign Assistance Act eliminated U.S. funding to the United Nations Fund for Population Activities (UNFPA) and severely reduced our support of the International Planned Parenthood Federation (IPPF) on the grounds that they supported programs that condoned abortion. The funding cutoff hit UNFPA and IPPF at a time when the vast majority of countries in the developing world had subscribed to the voluntary reduction of population growth and the promotion of family planning, and were ready for help.

Few are immune to the fear. As a Congressman and U.S. Ambassador to the UN, George Bush spoke of the need to curb the world's fertility. But he's wimped out now, giving Senator Albert Gore cause to note that "An objective observer would have to conclude that Bush probably changed his mind on this question because he is politically scared of a tiny minority within the right-to-life movement." Perhaps not all terrorists live offshore.

Suppose we can muster the political backbone to weather the controversy, to preserve reproductive rights, and to support international family planning (a big if, but suppose). The promising news is that, despite overpopulation being a touchy subject for polite conversation, among the thinkers who confront it the old polarity seems to be shifting. A consensus seems to have emerged. Thus we find that Paul and Anne Ehrlich, the premier population-bombers of our time, have become very explicit in their advocacy of solutions that are embedded in a larger social context. The Ehrlichs maintain that the essentials of reduced fertility are "adequate nutrition, proper sanitation, basic health care, education of women, and equal rights for women."

It's hard to imagine a principled and humane person disagreeing with this approach (although Marxists and Darwinists might differ on significant details of population-control programs — say, incentives and punishments around family size). Coming up with the understanding, will, and wealth to act on the problem may seem impossible, however. The price tag for bringing about a stable population of 8 billion in the year 2050 would be about $300 billion, writes Chicago bioregionalist Beatrice Briggs, in the magazine *Conscious Choice*.

"While this is a staggering sum," she continues, "it is useful to consider that in the U.S. *each year* we spend $2 billion on firearms and hunting equipment, $4 billion on athletic footwear, $118 billion on advertising, and $300 billion on defense." If that doesn't put the price of population control in perspective, just try to imagine the necessities imposed by decently accommodating twice the Earth's current population, 39 years hence. 🗑

Stephanie Mills has been a prolific writer and speaker on issues of population and bioregionalism for two decades. She is the author of Whatever Happened to Ecology, *and the editor of* In Praise of Nature. *She lives in Maple City, Michigan.*

Chapter 24

Poverty and Deprivation

Article 24.1.   World Hunger Amidst Plenty

In this article, John W. Helmuth maintains that the problem of world hunger and malnutrition is likely to worsen in the years ahead unless concrete steps are taken to address the problem from an international perspective, one that will require coordinated monetary and fiscal policies. Hunger is a global problem, and global solutions must be found. Like other issues, it is also a political problem, requiring cooperation among nations. The author endorses the eight broad recommendations for policy change approved at the 1988 World Food Conference, which include the need for developed countries to stimulate economic growth in the Third World; continue, accelerate, and make income transfers more explicit; develop improved policy harmonization in trade, exchange rates, and monetary and fiscal areas; increase the capacity for environmental assessment; and restructure the developing world's debt.

WORLD HUNGER AMIDST PLENTY

"If progress is to be made toward alleviating hunger and malnutrition, agricultural, trade, and food-distribution policies have to be approached from an international perspective and coordinated with monetary and fiscal policies."

by John W. Helmuth

EVERY three days, the same number of people die of starvation as were killed by the Hiroshima atomic bomb. Approximately 40,000 children die each day from starvation. Fifteen million people are dying each year from starvation, malnutrition, and hunger-related diseases. The numbers are staggering, incomprehensible.

Estimates of the total number of hungry in the world vary, depending on the criter-

Dr. Helmuth, associate professor of economics and assistant administrator, Center for Agricultural and Rural Development, Iowa State University, Ames, served as executive coordinator of the 1988 World Food Conference.

ia used to define the term. The World Bank estimates that, in 1980, there were 680,000,000 people, worldwide, who did not receive enough calories to prevent stunted growth and serious health risks. Most of the chronically malnourished are children. In 1980, 1,500,000,000 people did not receive enough calories to lead an active working life. Fifty percent (730,-000,000) of these were living in developing countries, 40% (590,000,000) in low-income countries, and 10% (140,000,000) in middle-income countries.

The problem of hunger and malnutrition is not confined to developing nations. In the U.S., over 19,000,000 people were receiving food stamps as of May, 1987, and an average of 15-18,000,000 were re-

ceiving donated U.S. Department of Agriculture surplus commodities monthly.

Regardless of which numbers are used, or which measure is applied, the conclusion is inescapable—we live in a world stalked by the age-old specter of starvation. One-third of the Earth's population does not receive enough food to maintain an active working life, the economic loss is staggering, and the amount of human pain and suffering is incalculable. With all the relief efforts, government assistance, and private volunteer organizations combined, we are still in the dark ages in the battle against hunger.

The dreadful irony is that, during most of the 1980's, there was enough food to feed the hungry. Before the 1988 drought, food surpluses were five times larger than were needed for this purpose. Unfortunately, during 1975-86, non-emergency food aid to developing countries remained static at 7-9,000,000 tons per year. More than double that amount is needed. Now, the UN estimates world cereal stocks will fall by 80,000,000 tons as a result of the North American drought.

In 1900, the world population was almost 1,000,000,000. It took only until the 1920's for that population to double. By 1950, there were 2,500,000,000 people on Earth. That number doubled to 5,000,000,000 in 1987. Six billion are predicted by 2000; 8,000,000,000 by 2025. It is estimated that more than 90% of the world's population growth occurring between now and the year 2025 will take place in the Third World—those very countries already plagued by hunger, malnutrition, and starvation.

One billion more people are being fed today than in the early 1970's, but the number of hungry people continues to increase. The 1988 drought is a vivid reminder that we must not relax if we are to make progress. Droughts and pest infestations are a constant menace to our food supply, but a more serious long-term threat may result from the continuing misuse of agricultural land. The World Food Council estimates that erosion, salinization, and desertification potentially could reduce the land area available for food production by 500,000,000 hectares in Asia, Africa, and Latin America.

Much of the world's ability to produce more than enough food is a result of the new high-yielding varieties of wheat and rice that were the vanguard of the Green Revolution of the 1970's. Now, however, most of the increases possible because of these new varieties have been realized. Future productivity gains may be much harder to accomplish and have to be achieved in much harsher environments on much less productive, marginal soils.

There are economic reasons behind the disparity between food availability in developed and developing countries. It is due in part to faster demand growth in developing countries (resulting from higher population growth rates) compared to supply growth; greater vulnerability of developing countries to drought, pests, and other natural disasters; a lack of the necessary food production and distribution infrastructure in developing countries; the economic policies of individual countries; the reduced purchasing power of developing countries due to adverse exchange rate shifts; worsening debt problems; and the slow economic growth of developing nations. Trade barriers by some countries compound the problems. These factors highlight the increasing difficulty develop-

ing nations face in trying to provide food for their populations.

Protectionist trade policies, in particular, have been shown to have detrimental impacts on their economic growth. Developed nations adopting more protectionist policies tend to experience lower economic growth rates in both the industrial and agricultural sectors. Developing nations adopting such policies tend to harm their long-run food production prospects. The free trade economies adjusted better to the economic shocks of the 1970's than did protectionist economies. Furthermore, the World Bank indicates that the adoption of new technology has been faster in less protectionist countries than in protectionist, developing countries.

The protectionist policies of certain countries not only have led to a decline in trade, but also to a national income loss. Developed nations engaging in high levels of agricultural intervention, such as the European Community and Japan, are experiencing significant domestic efficiency and real income losses, compared to the U.S. and Canada. The World Bank estimates that Europe and Japan incurred real income losses of about $24,000,000,000 and $27,000,000,000, respectively, in 1980-82 because of agricultural intervention in the grains, meat, dairy products, and sugar markets. The higher rates of protection for processed agricultural products in developed countries result in fewer exports by developing countries of value-added products that can generate needed foreign exchange. This protectionism on the part of developed countries blocks the process of industrial development in the less developed countries.

In addition to the adverse effects of protectionist policies, the governments of the U.S., Japan, and Europe annually are spending approximately $100,000,000,000 to provide income support to their farmers. In a period of growing surpluses, these agricultural subsidies are becoming more and more difficult to justify.

The macroeconomic policies of developed nations in the 1950's and 1960's resulted in a period of relative economic stability. Major changes in monetary policy during the 1970's, however, resulted in widely fluctuating interest and exchange rates. The economic shocks of the last two decades have resulted in significant deterioration in the terms of trade for most developing countries, persistently high interest rates, and reduced access to development loans. The financial capability of developing nations to deal with these problems has worsened significantly since 1980. In that year, 98 developing nations had a net financial inflow of $39,600,000,000, resulting from new development loans minus debt repayment. In 1984, the net inflow to developing nations had become a net outflow, which reached a negative $24,000,000,000 in 1986.

Developing nations are being forced to repay debts from previous years, are not obtaining new loans, and do not have the resources to cope with the food needs of their populations. During the 1970's, when developing countries had a net financial inflow, they were able to increase their average imports of food per person by almost seven percent per year. From 1980 to 1986, as their net financial inflow turned to a net financial outflow, average imports of food per person declined by three percent per year.

The internal policies of developing countries often add to the problem. Land-use policies, market intervention, and the heavy taxation of agriculture often stifle the agricultural development necessary for improved food availability.

The world food system

Research by the Food and Agriculture Program of the International Institute for Applied Systems Analysis (IIASA) has concluded that the problem of hunger amidst plenty stems from a malfunctioning of the world food system. While the economic, trade, and agricultural policies of individual countries may seem rational in the light of national goals toward food self-sufficiency and a viable domestic agricultural sector, taken together as a world food system, such policies are a failure. Nations pursuing their individual goals do not operate necessarily in the best interest of the world food system as a whole or of the world's hungry populations.

IIASA's economic models demonstrate that, while markets are an efficient way to allocate resources, they do not ensure a desirable distribution of income. The world food system is driven by markets that determine consumer food prices, and these markets adjust to changing circumstances in ways that leave the poor hungry because of a sheer lack of income. They can not earn needed income because they lack the productive resources of capital, tillable land, and marketable skills.

There is widespread recognition that the world faces a crisis in food production and distribution. The decade of the 1980's has been characterized by declining agricultural exports, increasing protectionism and trade tensions, agricultural prices dropping to the lowest real levels since the 1930's, and a pervasive economic crisis among farmers throughout the world. Government programs in developed countries have exacerbated the problems of low prices and surplus production, added billions of dollars to government expenditures, and continued to stifle the necessary development in food deficit countries.

There is no doubt that we face a crisis. What can be done? In 1974, the United Nations World Food Conference resolved that, by 1980, no child should go to bed hungry and no family should fear for tomorrow's food. The world has fallen far short of the lofty goal of that resolution.

Solutions to the problem are not easy to find. Direct food aid to the hungry is not a long-run solution, because it tends to reduce incentives for local food production. While direct food aid is vital as a short-run solution to crisis situations, more comprehensive solutions are needed that deal with the world food system as a whole and address the complicated interaction of the monetary, fiscal, agricultural, and trade policies of various nations.

The 1974 World Food Conference was a beginning. It expanded on efforts that had been under way for a number of years to document and quantify the nature and extent of the problem. The Rome Conference drew attention to world hunger and malnutrition and searched for ways to increase production to meet perceived shortages in the 1970's.

We face a different set of problems in the 1980's. The food shortages of the 1970's gave way to the surpluses of the 1980's and a period of nationalistic internalization—during which individual policies have been designed to help individual nations, but have harmed the poor nations.

Other conferences have struggled with the problem. A 1976 World Food Conference in Ames, Iowa, strived to broaden and intensify the involvement of scientists and educators and searched for ways to alleviate hunger and food shortages through interdisciplinary cooperation.

In April, 1988, the newly formed International Policy Council on Agriculture and Trade hosted a World Food Conference in Brussels, Belgium, that emphasized the need for agricultural policy change and highlighted the importance of trade policy reform, particularly between the U.S. and the European Community.

The most recent World Food Conference, hosted by Iowa State University, the Iowa Congressional delegation, and Iowa Gov. Terry Branstad was held in Des Moines in early June, 1988. With a theme of "Hunger in the Midst of Plenty: A World Policy Dilemma," the goal was to bring together world leaders from private industry, government, and academia to promote cooperation and the coordination of worldwide economic and agricultural policies through the exchange of ideas and information. More than 430 participants

from 33 countries struggled with the general state of disarray in the production and distribution systems for food and other agricultural commodities.

Topics discussed included the glut in world markets of many major agricultural products; the widespread evidence of hunger and malnutrition; the enormous costs of agricultural production subsidies, which the national treasuries of many countries no longer can withstand; and trade patterns that continue to be distorted by government subsidies and protectionist policies.

The conference recognized that the symptoms of disarray stem from uncoordinated and *ad hoc* national economic policies, which are at the heart of the problems facing the world's food production and distribution systems. If progress is to be made toward alleviating hunger and malnutrition, agricultural, trade, and food-distribution policies have to be approached from an international perspective and coordinated with monetary and fiscal policies.

Hunger is a global problem, and global solutions must be found. In 1974, the problem was perceived as a technical one—how to produce enough food for the growing world population. Today, the problem is a political one—how to achieve cooperation among nations to equitably distribute the food that is available.

Recommendations

Eight broad recommendations for policy change were advanced by the 1988 World Food Conference:
● Developed countries should place increased emphasis on policies to stimulate economic growth in developing countries.
● Policy reform proposals explicitly should recognize impacts on poor and disenfranchised populations.
● Policy reform to make income transfers more explicit should be continued and accelerated.
● Policy harmonization should be emphasized in trade, exchange rate, monetary, and fiscal areas. A multilateral organization to develop a code for fiscal policy should be considered.
● Increased capacity for environmental assessment should be developed to help ensure sustainability. Assessments should be required of groups proposing policy change.
● A systematic means of restructuring Third World debt should be created.
● More realistic approaches to policy change should be developed, widely sharing the results of analysis, broadening participation, and directly addressing prob-

lems of adjustment, compensation, and changes in political and economic structure.
● Developed country donor organizations should broaden the set of nations in which they have programs and should target their efforts better.

There was consensus that income must be increased in developing countries and freer international trade policies need to be adopted. Freer trade can contribute to improvements in production efficiency and to a lower-cost world food supply. However, freer trade is not a simple solution. Policies encouraging it have differing impacts. Freer trade must be accompanied by compensation and adjustment policies that protect those who may be disenfranchised by changes in policy.

Perhaps the boldest recommendation to come from the 1988 World Food Conference was for a Marshall Plan for the 1990's and beyond. Envisioned as a jointly funded effort by major developed nations, this plan represents a significant long-run commitment to Third World development. It calls for pledges of institutional reform to stimulate economic growth in developing countries and bold and practical steps to resolve the Third World debt problem. Presently, less than one-half of one percent of the total world gross national product is devoted to economic development assistance, while approximately six percent goes for military expenditures.

The conclusion of the conference was that there needs to be a shift in priorities. Third World countries must have assistance in developing their entire infrastructures—education, health care, highways, harbors, and marketing and distribution systems—as well as their agricultural and industrial sectors.

Only through long-term, sustainable economic growth can the problem of starvation possibly be solved. When Third World nations are able to produce and sell the products efficiently for which they have a comparative advantage, they then will have command of the resources necessary to feed their populations. When economic development reaches this point, the investment of developed nations in economic assistance is returned many-fold.

The problem of world hunger is too big, too pervasive, and too permanent for any one country to solve alone. Its solution must be made the highest priority of all governments—of all humankind. That priority then must result in real, tangible, long-run action. All nations must work together against the common enemy. Only then will we stand a chance of knowing a world without hunger.

The AIDS epidemic has reached crisis proportions in the Third World, threatening to erode decades of improvement in health care and economic development. As many experts have noted, it is extremely difficult to calculate the scope of the problem. This is no less true in the developing world, where many governments lack the diagnostic equipment and funds necessary to document the extent of the problem. As a result, many AIDS cases go undiagnosed. The problem is particularly acute in some African cities, where the infection rate is more than 100 times higher than in the U.S. overall. According to the World Health Organization, over two million Africans carry the virus, making it the hardest hit continent. AIDS is also a problem in Latin America and the Caribbean, though less so than in Africa, with almost every country reporting at least some cases. To date, Asia has been the least hard hit, with the highest number of cases being reported by Japan. Still, there is ample reason for concern, as the AIDS virus could spread quickly in some countries in Asia, owing to an increase in prostitution and intravenous drug use associated with tourism. AIDS is an international disease. It knows no borders. It is imperative, warns the author, that the international community develop new approaches to global collaboration and cooperation. If not, this disease will reek havoc, both in the industrialized world and Third World.

AIDS: NEW THREAT TO THE THIRD WORLD

A Deadly Virus Could Unravel Decades of Development

BY LORI HEISE

Historically, epidemics have been as profound an agent for societal change as wars. The smallpox virus that Cortez loosed upon the Aztecs was largely responsible for Spain's conquest of this mighty empire. The plague that ravaged 14th-century Europe ruptured the bonds of feudalism, upsetting the power balance between peasant and lord.

Today a new disease, acquired immunodeficiency syndrome (AIDS), threatens to have an impact of equal measure in parts of the Third World. Unless brought under control, AIDS could undermine decades of progress toward improved health and sustained economic development.

AIDS kills by disabling the body's immune system, making its victim easy prey for certain opportunistic cancers and infections. Like

---

This piece draws heavily on the pioneering research of the Panos Institute and their publication, AIDS in the Third World.

syphilis—another disease endemic in much of the world—AIDS is transmitted through blood and body fluids during sexual intercourse. To a lesser but significant extent, it is also transmitted through blood transfusions, the sharing or reusing of contaminated needles, and from mother to child during pregnancy or birth.

Unlike syphilis, there is no known cure for AIDS. Once individuals become infected with the AIDS virus (known as the human immunodeficiency virus, or HIV), they remain at risk of developing the disease even though they may be symptom-free for years. Symptomless carriers are the invisible infectors who unwittingly fuel the AIDS epidemic.

Researchers estimate that for each reported AIDS case, 50 to 100 people may be infected with the virus. Present studies on the U.S. population suggest that of those infected, roughly 25 to 50 percent will develop full-blown AIDS within five years, and probably more will do so as time goes on. It is unclear,

From *World Watch*, January/February 1988, pp. 19-27. WorldWatch Institute, Washington, D.C. 20036. Reprinted by permission.

however, whether the disease will follow a similar course in developing countries.

By 1986, only five years after the virus was first identified, the World Health Organization (WHO) estimated that between 5 and 10 million people worldwide were HIV carriers. So rapidly is the infection spreading that by 1990 WHO projects 50 to 100 million people may be infected. If only 30 percent of these carriers develop AIDS within five years, 15 to 30 million people could be dead or dying of AIDS by 1995.

Assessing the scope of AIDS in developing countries is particularly difficult. Many Third World governments—given competing priorities and limited resources—lack the diagnostic equipment and funds necessary for AIDS surveillance. Others fear that acknowledging AIDS cases could jeopardize the tourist revenues and foreign investment upon which their economies depend.

Likewise, where only 30 to 35 percent of people are reached by modern health services, as is the situation in most African countries, many AIDS cases go undiagnosed. Consequently WHO statistics, which rely on voluntary government reporting, significantly underestimate the true impact of AIDS in the developing world.

African countries, for example, had reported a total of 6,635 AIDS cases to WHO as of November 25, 1987; the United States had reported 45,436. Yet blood surveys measuring exposure to the virus confirm that HIV is more prevalent in urban areas of certain African countries than it is in the United States.

Studies from several African cities have documented a 2 to 20 percent rate of HIV infection among healthy adults, with women being exposed as often as men. This compares to a figure of 0.15 percent among U.S. military volunteers—the best comparable nationwide figure for Americans in the same age-groups—and a figure of 2.9 percent for volunteers from New York, New Jersey and Pennsylvania.

Thus the infection rate in some African cities is about 100 times higher than in the United States as a whole, and five times higher than in the New York region. And AIDS in Africa is no longer confined to the cities. In some rural areas, especially near main roads, from two to five percent of healthy adults and of pregnant women now test HIV positive.

Together these studies lead WHO to estimate that two million or more Africans carry

---

the virus, making Africa the hardest hit continent in the world.

Yet no continent has escaped unscathed. Latin America and the Caribbean have reported a total of 5,366 cases with almost every country reporting some exposure. Haiti alone has 912. Bermuda and French Guiana have the highest infection rates in the world, roughly six times the U.S. level of 172 cases per million population. And Brazil reports 2,013 cases, although health officials fear that up to 400,000 Brazilians may already be infected with the virus.

To date, Asia has been the least affected, with the highest number of cases—43—being reported by Japan. There is concern, however, that AIDS could spread quickly in this region because of the prevalence in some countries of intravenous drug use and the prostitution associated with tourism.

AIDS Spreads in the Third World

Unlike the industrial world where AIDS is primarily communicated through homosexual intercourse and the sharing of needles between drug addicts, an estimated three-fourths of AIDS transmission in Africa occurs through heterosexual contact. The remaining transmission occurs from mother to child during pregnancy or birth, and through exchange of infected blood during transfusions or reuse of needles by health care providers.

It is thought that homosexual transmission

predominates in the industrial world because the virus first infected the male homosexual population. Here it stayed until women began to contract the disease through intravenous drug use and bisexual men. As more and more women contract the virus, the role of heterosexual transmission in the industrial world is expected to rise.

Nonetheless, the overall rate of transmission is likely to remain greater in the Third World than in industrial countries because of certain realities of life there.

For example, researchers believe that the genital sores that commonly accompany other sexually transmitted diseases (STDs) increase chances of infection. Sadly, STDs are far more endemic in the Third World than in industrial countries and treatment is less accessible. During the early 1980s, the rate of gonorrhea per 100,000 people in Kampala, Uganda was 10,000, in Nairobi 7,000, and in India 5,000. By contrast, the rate in Atlanta, Georgia was 2,510 and in London, only 310.

Many Third World governments also do not have the equipment or the money necessary to test blood before transfusions, a form of HIV transmission largely eliminated in the United States and Europe. The United States spends $80 to 100 million a year ($6 to 8 per unit of blood) to protect its citizens from a relatively small risk of contracting HIV from transfusions. In Africa today the risk to blood recipients may be as high as one in ten, yet in many areas blood is still not screened.

Unfortunately, conditions also conspire to make transfusions more common in tropical Africa than in industrialized nations. Severe anemias, long delays between obstetric or other bleeding and arrival at hospital, and many serious road accidents make the amount of blood needed by African hospitals as much as three times greater than that required by general hospitals in the industrial world.

Developing countries desperately need a quick, inexpensive blood test for HIV that is not sensitive to heat. There is hope that a test newly developed by Du Pont may be available for distribution this year.

In addition, underdevelopment promotes many forms of behavior that increase risks for transmission of the virus. For example, lack of economic opportunity in rural areas, political insecurity, famine, and war operate to increase the number of sexual partners of developing world citizens by displacing persons and separating families.

Likewise, medical overuse of transfusions in the absence of other remedies and the reuse of unsterile needles are practices of underdeveloped or overtaxed health care systems that encourage the spread of AIDS.

Unhygienic conditions resulting from poverty may intensify the impact of AIDS in many developing countries. It has been proposed that Third World peoples—indeed poor people in general—may be more susceptible to AIDS because of prior and repeated exposures to other infections that overtax their immune systems.

Evidence suggests that chronic exposure to viral and parasitic infections (which are endemic in the Third World) leads to certain immunologic abnormalities that could increase susceptibility to HIV infection and to expression of the full-blown disease. More research is needed to confirm this relationship, but it is becoming increasingly clear that individuals differ in their proneness to AIDS. Poverty, and the infections it breeds, may be one reason.

Indeed, the poor in developing countries—more at risk and less able to protect themselves from HIV infection—will likely be disproportionately affected by AIDS, just as poor, urban

---

Unless

brought under control, AIDS could undermine decades of progress toward improved health and sustained economic development.

---

blacks and Hispanics are in the United States.

As Jon Tinker, president of the Panos Institute, observes: The global underclass, those who live in rural and urban shantytowns, who cannot afford condoms and are not reached by family planning advice, who cannot read and therefore are least likely to be reached by educational campaigns, who have little or no access to health clinics, who may have to sell their own blood to buy food—this global underclass will likely bear a disproportionate share of AIDS's misery.

In Africa, certain demographic and genetic characteristics may combine with poverty to make AIDS particularly difficult to control. Forty percent of the continent's population is in its sexually active years, a higher percentage than anywhere in the world. The proportion of African children moving from prepuberty into the years of sexual activity is likewise greater. Moreover, researchers have found a genetic trait that appears to facilitate AIDS transmission among its carriers; the frequency of this trait is three times higher in central Africa than in Europe.

In other developing regions, prevention campaigns will have to contend with "traditional" healers who administer folk remedies without medical supervision or properly sterilized equipment. Health authorities estimate, for example, that Haiti alone has between 10,000 and 15,000 "piquristes" (injectionists) who could potentially spread AIDS through reuse of needles.

A Matter of Triage

AIDS strains the ability of even the most organized and wealthy countries to respond effectively. But circumstances in the Third World conspire to make an effective response to AIDS especially complicated.

Developing nations, for example, have even fewer options for treating the disease than countries in the West. Industrial world physicians largely respond by treating the secondary diseases, such as pneumocystis carinii pneumonia, that accompany AIDS. It's an expensive ordeal that often involves long hospital stays. The only drug currently available to attack HIV infection directly—azidothymidine (AZT)—costs $10 to 20 a day and requires multiple blood transfusions, effectively eliminating it as an option for Third World patients.

Instead, the treatment for AIDS in Kashenye, Tanzania, is necessarily crude: "a few days in bed, some aspirin, and then home to die." With only one doctor for every 32,110 people, one hospital bed for every 900 people, and an abundance of patients with illnesses that can be cured, Tanzania must practice triage.

And in Zaire, providing treatment for 10 AIDS patients comparable to that delivered in the United States would cost more than the entire budget of Mama Yemo, the nation's largest hospital. Yet physicians at Mama Yemo diagnose up to 15 new AIDS cases each day.

Researchers do not anticipate a vaccine for AIDS within the next five years, so prevention in the near term will have to rely on protecting the blood supply and on changing behavior to restrict the spread of the disease. While changing behavior is difficult in any setting, once again the Third World will confront special challenges.

People must first be educated on the causes of the disease and how to prevent it. However, carrying out mass education in the Third World, is particularly difficult. First, education is expensive. President Ronald Reagan has requested $247.5 million in 1988 for AIDS education and information in the United States. Health budgets in the Third Word cannot begin to achieve a comparable level of funding.

Second, fewer avenues of communication are available for reaching audiences. Many people in the Third World are illiterate and few have access to television. Although radio is widely available, it is most effective when used in conjunction with other communication

---

T*he global underclass will likely bear a disproportionate share of AIDS's misery.*

---

channels. And even radio must contend with the Third World's many tongues: India alone has 16 major languages.

Nonetheless, the changing conduct of the San Francisco gay community demonstrates that high-risk behavior—even sexual behavior—can be modified through education. It is on this hope that many Third World countries hang their future.

Indeed, some developing countries are moving energetically to control AIDS. Rwanda and Brazil already have government-run education campaigns, and the leaflets produced by the Kenya Red Cross, which counsel "Spread facts not fear," are some of the best in the world.

Uganda's slogan, "Love Carefully," appears on posters in the nation's 22 languages, while radio announcers encourage Ugandans to practice "zero grazing." President Kaunda of Zambia, whose son died of AIDS, has given notable leadership. And prostitutes in Nairobi are now more likely to ask their clients to use condoms.

AIDS and the Multiplier Effect

Improving Third World health standards has been a major focus of development efforts for decades. But for struggling health systems, AIDS poses a multiple challenge that could undermine hard-won health gains and threaten ongoing public health initiatives.

AIDS is an added drain on health care budgets already stretched too thin. In 1982, Haiti had $2.60 to spend on health care per citizen; the Central African Republic had $2.90. Rwanda's budget of $1.60 per person would not even buy a bottle of aspirin in the industrial world.

Yet these countries face epidemics of frightening proportions. In Africa alone, malaria claims one million lives each year. Worldwide, over 1.5 million people die of measles. And across the globe, five million children succumb to chronic diarrhea. With health burdens like these, diverting funds for the treatment or prevention of AIDS becomes a question of trading lives for lives.

Not only does AIDS compete with other diseases for limited health budgets, HIV actually magnifies the problem of existing diseases. The virus weakens the immune system of its hosts, leaving carriers more susceptible to renewed attacks from microbes that may be lying dormant.

For example, individuals contracting tuberculosis (TB) often remain carriers of the TB bacteria even after their immune system conquers outward signs of the disease. Once suppressed, the individual's immune system may be overrun by a fresh attack of the TB bacteria, leading to the active and contagious form of TB. Thus an epidemic of tuberculosis may be initiated in an otherwise healthy population by an HIV carrier who has no symptoms of AIDS.

Evidence suggests that HIV is already having this multiplier effect on preexisting diseases. Tuberculosis is increasing in the United States, where until the mid-1970s its incidence had been declining. TB is also on the rise in Africa, where there is good reason to believe that HIV is the cause. In a study of TB patients tested in Kinshasa, Zaire, 40 percent were found to be HIV-positive. By contrast, only six to eight percent of healthy adults in the Zaire capital tested positive.

Doctors also wonder whether HIV may be activating latent syphilis infections through the virus's depressive effect on the immune system. There are an increasing number of cases where healthy people—previously treated for syphilis—are developing late-stage neurosyphilis after infection with HIV.

Physicians hypothesize that low levels of the bacteria that cause syphilis may be "hiding" in the body's central nervous system even after treatment with antibiotics (the syphilis bacterium can cross the blood-brain barrier,whereas most antibiotics cannot). By suppressing immune function, HIV infection may allow the syphilis virus to attack anew.

Women and Children First

It is in the area of maternal and child health that AIDS poses the most direct threat to development gains. In the last 20 years there has been a revolution in the way development organizations have approached Third World health. Shedding the West's preoccupation with hospitals and high-technology medicine, development organizations began to emphasize "primary health care" rather than "curative care."

Primary care stresses prevention of disease by encouraging immunization, oral rehydration therapy, nutritional education, and breast-feeding. Together with increased female literacy, education in hygiene, and improved access to clean water and family planning, primary health care strategies have inaugurated a "child survival revolution" that has cut infant deaths in the Third World from 20 percent of live births in 1960 to 12 percent today.

These gains, while impressive, are precarious: AIDS stands to undermine decades of struggle for mother and child health. When an HIV-positive woman becomes pregnant, evidence suggests that she becomes more likely to develop full-blown AIDS in the next few years.

A mother also has roughly a 30 to 50 percent chance of passing the infection to her child either in utero, during birth, or possibly through breast-feeding. Once infected, newborns experience an accelerated course of the disease; half will die before their second birthday.

AIDS may soon be a significant factor in the mother/child survival quotient. In some African cities—such as Kinshasa and Kampala— 8 to 14 percent of women attending prenatal clinics in 1986 were infected with the virus. Up to half the children born to these women may be doomed from birth. Another portion may die from neglect when their mothers succumb to AIDS.

In Zambia, medical officials predicted that they would have 6,000 "AIDS babies" in 1987. The United States, with more than 37 times Zambia's population, has had less than 600 since reporting began.

Also alarming is the threat AIDS could pose to beneficial interventions that today are saving the lives of millions of children each year. Immunization programs, for example, are the life preservers of one million Third World children each year. Immunization, however, has the potential to communicate AIDS if unsterile needles are used. There is no evidence that this is happening with immunization programs, but studies do indicate that HIV is being transmitted through other medical injections (for example, antibiotics and penicillin).

One study of infants aged one to 24 months showed that HIV-positive children born of uninfected mothers had received significantly more medical injections than children who were not infected with HIV. Another study confirmed that African mothers strongly believed that medication by injection was more effective than pills taken by mouth. These attitudes, along with the high incidence of childhood diseases requiring medication, account for the large number of injections received by African children.

Unfortunately, for financial and practical reasons, health workers often reuse syringes without proper sterilization, setting the stage for spread of HIV from child to child.

The study of infants did not, however, show a relationship between immunization and HIV infection. This lack of association probably reflects the wider use of properly sterilized equipment in immunization programs, the absence of traditional healers in vaccination programs, and the relatively small number of vaccinations received per child (less than one percent of all injections administered in the developing world).

Even though immunization programs are most likely safe, they run the risk of being shunned by mothers who, through experience with medical injections, fear HIV contamination from needles. Health workers already note this happening in Brazil. Ironically, unless greater vigilance is applied in medical injection programs, AIDS could undermine immunization indirectly through guilt by association.

Likewise, more research is needed to establish any relationship that may exist between breast-feeding and HIV transmission. Researchers have isolated the virus in breast milk and there have been between one and five cases of newborns apparently contracting AIDS through their mother's milk. World Health Organization experts doubt that breast milk is a significant route of HIV transmission, but evidence to confirm this belief is urgently needed.

Without such evidence, multinational companies and governments promoting infant formula have a ready-made selling point. It could set child health back decades if mothers again began substituting milk powder for breast milk out of fear of AIDS.

Because of contaminated water, overdiluting, and the absence of antibodies found in breast milk, bottle-fed babies in poor Third World communities are twice as likely to die as breast-fed babies.

AIDS Undermines Economies

As the development community contemplates Third World debt, AIDS is quietly changing the face of economics in the developing world. Because the disease attacks men and women in their prime, it has the potential to sabotage the future sustainability of entire economies.

Unlike other illnesses that cull the weakest members of the population—the sick, the old, and the very young—AIDS eliminates the productive segment of the population. Approximately 90 percent of those with AIDS in industrial and developing countries alike are between 20 and 49 years of age.

The consequences of a fatal epidemic focused on this group will be immense. Children will be left without parents. And with little automation or mechanization to fall back on, societies will be without work forces. Zambia alone, with a population of under seven million, could have 700,000 people dead or dying of AIDS in the next decade.

Many of those lost will be the most educated and highly skilled of Zambia's first post-independence generation. Indeed, one study in the country's copper belt confirms that AIDS is already eroding the cornerstone of the Zambian economy: 68 percent of the men testing HIV positive in this region were the skilled laborers upon whom the mining industry depends.

The loss of such workers will have economic impacts that reverberate throughout society. Researchers at the Harvard Institute of International Development are attempting to quantify these impacts by modeling the indirect economic costs of AIDS in central Africa.

According to their projections, by 1995 the annual loss to Zaire's economy due to premature deaths from AIDS will be eight percent of the country's gross national product (GNP), or $350 million if measured against Zaire's 1984 GNP.

Not only does AIDS compete with other diseases for limited health budgets, HIV actually magnifies the problems of existing diseases like TB.

Even though this figure does not include direct treatment costs or losses due to illness, it is still more than the $314 million Zaire received from all sources of development assistance in 1984.

Other countries will experience similar losses, and collectively the economic growth rate of the seven countries of the African AIDS belt—Tanzania, Uganda, Central African Republic, Burundi, Rwanda, Zambia and Zaire—will slow as people divert savings from investment to treatment. By 1990, the Harvard team projects the loss from AIDS due to economic slowing will be $980 million in this region.

These economic losses come at a time when Third World nations—especially African countries—are already laboring under severe economic hardship. Personal income is declining sharply, debt is mounting, and foreign aid is being cut back.

Against this backdrop, AIDS threatens to further complicate balance-of-payment problems. Foreign exchange will be lost as governments seek to import items necessary to combat the epidemic; tourist dollars will decline in response to travelers' fears; export revenues will fall as skilled labor becomes more scarce.

There is even evidence that AIDS may be scaring off foreign investors who are seeking to avoid the high medical costs associated with the disease. (In Africa, companies traditionally assume the cost of most medical benefits.)

These macroeconomic worries translate into a horrible reality for individuals. The true costs of AIDS are both economic and personal. Nowhere is this clearer than in the observations of correspondent Robert Bazell, who recently confronted the human dimensions of this frightening disease.

"A few months ago," Bazell recalls, "the town of Kytera in the Rakai district of southern Uganda was a busy center of commerce. Now it is almost deserted. Most of the merchants have either died of AIDS or fled from it. Most of those walking the dirt streets are children, orphans with both parents dead of AIDS.

"In the tiny houses and mud huts in the surrounding farm area it is unusual to find a home where AIDS has not struck...In the six years I have been reporting about AIDS," Bazell concludes, "I never imagined it could become so horrible."

What will be the economic impact of this reality? We can count up the direct costs and calculate the indirect cost of lost wages from disability and death. But what of the psychological toll on those left behind? What is the productive potential of a generation numbed by grief? Economic tally sheets cannot capture the potential lost when a society's members no longer feel in control of their destiny, when people no longer dream.

The International Response

Meeting the global challenge of AIDS will require unprecedented cooperation among nations. Unfortunately, parochial interests, along with overwhelming denial of the problem by some governments, have slowed the international mobilization against AIDS.

Also operative has been the persistent view that AIDS is someone else's problem: homosexuals, drug addicts, Haitians, Africans. It is only now, with AIDS threatening to infiltrate the Western mainstream, that resources have been loosed to combat the disease.

This egocentrism has allowed the virus to spread unchecked, making its ultimate control even more difficult. AIDS must be viewed as everyone's problem if an untold loss of human life is to be avoided.

Because of its experience with eradicating smallpox and its international character, WHO is best positioned to spearhead a global attack on AIDS. After an embarrassingly slow start, WHO formed the Special Programme on AIDS (SPA) on February 1, 1987, finally bringing the agency's organizational response in line with its professed view that AIDS was an epidemic of "unprecedented urgency."

AIDS will

...put our global conscience to the test.

Since that time, WHO's AIDS program has grown rapidly, largely due to the determined leadership of Jonathan Mann, an epidemiologist on loan from the Centers for Disease Control in Atlanta. Starting with a secretary and a $500,000 budget, Mann has built the AIDS program into one of the agency's largest and most active, with a $37 million budget and staff of more than 65.

The Special Programme on AIDS acts primarily as a coordinating body for research and as a resource for governments trying to develop a national AIDS control plan. WHO provides technical assistance and serves as a middleman in the international funding of Third World AIDS strategies. WHO/SPA also tracks the spread of the disease; sponsors AIDS-related research, such as studies on sexual behavior in various cultures; and organizes technical conferences on topics like AIDS and breastfeeding.

As of November 1987, WHO health teams had visited 77 countries. Sixty-four countries had developed short-term strategies for coping with AIDS, and 27 had developed more mature five-year plans. Despite limited resources, African nations like Uganda and Zambia already have five-year plans. Interestingly, the United States does not.

Central to WHO's strategy for combatting AIDS is the integration of AIDS prevention activities into existing family planning programs and other national health care structures. This approach allows AIDS activities to draw on the strengths and experience of existing programs without creating new institutions that would compete for funding.

Moreover, existing maternal and child health programs, family planning centers, and STD clinics are uniquely well situated to combat AIDS because of their relationship with sexually active individuals and their experience dealing with delicate issues of reproductive health.

Unfortunately, the growing pandemic of AIDS coincides with a dramatic withdrawal of U.S. support for international family planning—a move largely orchestrated to undermine organizations that do not explicitly reject abortion.

Most significantly, the United States no longer contributes to the United Nations Fund for Population Activities or the International Planned Parenthood Federation. An estimated 340 million couples in 65 nations are affected by this retreat. The added threat of AIDS makes it even more imperative that the U.S. no longer play politics with this vital form of development assistance.

The AIDS pandemic also coincides with a period of decreasing support for WHO and its sister organization, the Pan American Health Organization (PAHO). The United States has contributed modestly to WHO's AIDS program, providing $2 million in fiscal year 1986 and $5 million in 1987. But cutbacks in the United States' contribution to the general WHO budget put the Agency's special AIDS effort in jeopardy.

As of January 1, 1988, the United States was at least $82.6 million in arrears in its treaty-obligated contributions to WHO and at least $14 million behind in its obligations to PAHO. Lack of funds from the United States—which normally provides 25 percent of the WHO budget—has resulted in across-the-board cuts in WHO programs. As the Overseas Development Council observes, "WHO's AIDS Program can only function effectively if the broader organization receives adequate support from all member nations."

Besides being a humanitarian duty, it is in the interest of the industrial world to assist developing countries with AIDS prevention to avoid the far greater remedial costs of responding to AIDS-induced crises and to protect three decades of investment in development progress.

The Common Enemy

In his classic novel *The Plague*, Albert Camus writes of an Algerian town's fight against Europe's Black Death. His message: While life goes on in the face of overwhelming death, all issues come to be discussed in the context of the plague. Recalling this message, Washington, D.C. Public Health Commissioner Reed Tuckson maintains that "when the history books are written, AIDS will define this era."

Does Tuckson overstate AIDS's potential effect? In terms of numbers and demographics, the answer may be yes. There are other preventable causes of disability and death that surpass the toll of AIDS: five million children die annually from diarrhea; cigarette smoking claims 2.5 million lives worldwide.

But numbers alone may not be a fair measure of impact. Unlike most diseases, AIDS is always fatal; there is no cure and no vaccine. Carriers may go for years without symptoms, evoking the paranoia and fear that accompanies uncertainty. And AIDS deals with the most intimate of human activities, the most powerful of human emotions. Collectively, these factors give AIDS a psychological charge that is unmatched by any other disease.

Moreover, AIDS reverses the natural order. Aging parents bury their adult children. Mothers die, watched by their infants. Indeed a nation gripped by AIDS faces a psychology not unlike wartime, when the young go off to die.

Significantly, this is one psychology that the industrial and the developing world will share. For once we have a common enemy: HIV. This means that people normally distant from Third World realities might for the first time see a problem of the developing countries as their own.

Whether through empathy or fear that unchecked infection will become the next illegal immigrant, people in industrial countries may prove more willing to tackle AIDS in the Third World than they have been to battle diarrhea or illiteracy. Indeed, by focusing attention on the desperate state of Third World health systems, AIDS may galvanize increased support for development assistance.

The added economic burden of AIDS may also force societies to reexamine their notion of health care. With treatment on average costing from $50,000 to $150,000 per patient, heroic measures to prolong life may give way to helping people "die with dignity." Already, costs threaten to make AIDS treatment a luxury of the rich unless national priorities change to pay the bills of the poor.

Potential cures and vaccines for AIDS also raise the specter of life for the "haves" and

---

*I*ronically,
AIDS could undermine immunization indirectly through guilt by association.

---

death for the "have nots." What if scientists develop a solution to AIDS that works for industrial nations but is either impractical or too costly for the developing world? Will the West consider further AIDS research a priority? Or will AIDS become like schistosomiasis and other "Third World" diseases that can be ignored because Americans and Europeans are not dying?

It is the power to arouse such questions that gives AIDS its exceptional character. And it is the quality of our response that may define our humanity. As Jonathan Mann, director of WHO's Special Programme on AIDS, points out, "AIDS will...put our global conscience to the test."

Fortunately, for now the interests of the industrial and the developing world align. AIDS is one of the few diseases that does not belong just to the "First World" or the "Third World." This convergence of interests provides fresh opportunities to forge new paths for collaboration, new models for international cooperation. The global challenge of AIDS is simply expressed: If one country has AIDS, the world has AIDS.

Lori Heise is a researcher at the Worldwatch Institute working on health issues in developing countries. She is a co-author of State of the World 1988.

Chapter **25**

The Environmental Crisis

Article 25.1.   A "No Regrets" Environmental Policy

C. Boyden Gray and David B. Rivkin, Jr. maintain that unilateral action is incapable of solving long-term global environmental problems, such as marine pollution, rain forest destruction, and the decline of biodiversity. This fact is illustrated by the difficulties in reaching international agreement in the area of global climate change. Although world environmental challenges loom large, many lessons can be learned from the the United States, which has made impressive gains in this area. This is evident in the vast number of existing environmental laws and in total environmental expenditures. Most experts agree that the quality of life has measurably improved in the United States over the past twenty years—most notably, in the area of public health. Still, serious environmental problems remain, many of which can only be solved at a high cost to society and the economy. For this reason, it has become increasingly clear that future progress will depend, to a large extent, on developing an economic incentives approach.

A "NO REGRETS" ENVIRONMENTAL POLICY

by C. Boyden Gray and David B. Rivkin, Jr.

The entire history of human civilization, in some sense, can be construed as an effort to break free from the environment, to be a plaything of nature no longer. These efforts have not been in vain. In particular, people today are much less dependent on the vicissitudes of global climate than their ancestors were. Nonetheless, climate has always had an impact upon global political systems and the security of international actors. For example, a general cooling and increase in rainfall in East Asia during the Middle Ages may have been partially responsible for the sweeping expansion of the Mongol tribes.

Modern societies, of course, are more complex, better organized, and often possess "safety nets"—characteristics that have ameliorated the effects of environmental upheavals. Still, such effects can be quite dramatic, both in the short- and long-term. For example, as *U.S. News &*

C. BOYDEN GRAY *is counsel to the president.* DAVID B. RIVKIN, JR., *is associate general counsel, Department of Energy.*

World Report noted, the August 1988 monsoon floodwaters in Bangladesh

> killed several thousand people, leveled 2 million homes, devastated 4 million acres of cropland, disrupted 25 million lives and cost the impoverished Asian nation $1.5 billion. Had this destruction been wrought by a military invasion, Bangladesh would have gone to war. It was instead an environmental blitzkrieg.

While the capabilities of modern societies have grown, so have the complexity, intractability, and urgency of environmental problems they face. Unilateral action may address some problems in the short term, but is fundamentally incapable of providing a long-term solution to global environmental problems. Countries acting alone can do little to mitigate, for example, marine pollution, rain forest destruction, and the decline of biodiversity. Moreover, unilateral steps by one state or a group of states may discourage action by other countries, which could attempt to "free-ride" on the efforts of more responsible states. This, in turn, is certain to undercut any program, as the "good environmental citizens" come to resent the free-riders.

The myriad difficulties in reaching an effective international agreement on environmental policy are nowhere more apparent than in the area of global climate change. Predictions of dramatic and disastrous shifts in the earth's climate are not new. In the mid-1970s, some scientists predicted an impending ice age. In the 1980s, attention shifted from cooling to warming. Most futurists rerouted their predictions and claimed that the earth faced not another ice age, but an inexorable global warming. The looming crisis will allegedly result in an unprecedented rise, perhaps as much as 9°F, in average annual temperatures. Vast temperate grain belts could turn into deserts, great coastal cities could be flooded as the polar ice caps melt, and tropical areas could suffer unprecedented droughts resulting in mass starvation and population dislocation.

The "greenhouse effect" is the stipulated cause of this projected disaster. This term describes the trapping of the sun's heat by water vapor, layer clouds, and other phenomena in the earth's atmosphere. The greenhouse effect is not inherently bad. Without it, the earth's surface would never have warmed enough to support life. However, some scientists argue that over the last two centuries, this beneficial natural effect has been dangerously magnified by human activity. The burning of fossil fuels has been releasing increasingly large amounts of carbon dioxide—a principal greenhouse gas—into the atmosphere. Recently, a number of other greenhouse gases have been identified as important in the greenhouse effect, including methane, nitrous oxide, and various naturally occurring trace gases, as well as the synthetic chlorofluorocarbons (CFCs) that have depleted the stratospheric ozone.

A few facts have been established. First, the levels of greenhouse gases in the earth's atmosphere—particularly carbon dioxide, methane, nitrous oxide, and CFCs—are rising. For example, the CO_2 level was about 280 parts per million (ppm) at the beginning of the Industrial Revolution, and is now about 355 ppm. Second, these gases do cause a greenhouse effect, trapping the sun's heat, warming the planet, and allowing life to continue. Third, although temperature trends over the last 100 years do not always correlate closely with changes in the atmospheric concentration of greenhouse gases, the average global temperature has risen approximately 1°F over this period. Global warming is certainly possible, and its potential impact on human civilization cannot be ignored.

Still, this does not add up to a massive climatic disaster. Unfortunately, many in both the domestic and international communities have accepted the global warming trend and its expected results as an axiom. Indeed, fidelity to the global warming disaster thesis has become a defining issue and a litmus test of true

environmentalism. Adherents to this position call for revolutionary changes in human behavior. Specifically, they demand that carbon emissions into the atmosphere be immediately capped. This approach—in a modified form with emissions being capped around the year 2000, albeit with some tinkering involved—has been embraced by a number of leading industrial countries, including Germany, Great Britain, and Japan.

Unfortunately, the debate has acquired distinct ideological overtones, and the more skeptical scholars have been branded as heretics and cranks. Nevertheless, some reputable scientists deny that any discernible warming is taking place, if a sufficiently long period of time is considered. They point out that all of the existing global warming computer models—known as general circulation models—are inherently flawed. They cannot explain temperature trends over the last century. Models that fail to explain the past hardly qualify as oracles for the future.

The global warming skeptics also point out that numerous natural forces mitigate against a rise in global temperature. The earth cools its surface with air currents and storms that transfer heat from one region to another. Further, much remains unknown about the roles of the earth's cloud cover and oceans—two key variables in shaping climate. Depending on the behavior of the clouds and oceans, the warming trend can be either greatly magnified or totally suppressed.

Moreover, even those who accept the premise that some warming may be expected have expressed doubt that a few degrees warming would necessarily constitute a catastrophe:

> [The] most feared consequence of global warming, dramatic sea-level rise, is also the least certain. . . the kind of sea-level rise that would inundate islands and reshape continents hinges on the Antarctic ice sheet's melting. At first glance, it appears obvious that if the planet warmed, the ice would melt. But the world is not so simple. In a warmer world, the atmosphere would hold more water vapor and storm patterns would shift. The net result could be a lot more snow—and larger glaciers—for Antarctica.[1]

The distribution of the warming trend throughout the year is another important variable. It appears that if any discernible warming has taken place at all, it has produced

---

[1] "The Whole Earth Agenda," U.S. News & World Report, December 25, 1989, p. 58.

warmer winters rather than hotter summers. Warmer winters would not melt the Arctic ice cap. More climate research is needed to resolve the many questions surrounding global climate change. Some estimate that up to two decades of intensive research on global climate change is required before major policy decisions can be made.

At a more fundamental level, the debate over global environmental change raises an interesting and important philosophical question. For many, the ideal environmental policy seeks a balance or equilibrium with nature. In this view, human beings should limit their impact on their natural surroundings in order to preserve as much of nature as possible in its original state. The most radical proponents of this thesis, known as "deep environmentalists," consider human beings a blight on the earth's face, disrupting a pristine state of nature.

The folly of these assertions is self-evident. All life on earth, not just human life, produces by-products that in some sense "corrupt" nature. Moreover, nature has never had an original state in any meaningful sense. Trying to preserve the status quo for its own sake is both fruitless and foolhardy. Indeed, scientific opinion has begun to shift from a vision of nature as a perfectly balanced system thrown out of kilter by human intervention to the realization that the "natural state" of the environment is one of continuing flux. In particular, in dealing with issues of global climate change, it must be remembered that the earth's climate has never been static.

Bush Administration Policy

The Bush administration, despite the claims of global warming doomsayers, is not ignoring this issue. Uncertain science and divisive politics have made for a difficult dilemma: What approach ought to be taken to reduce the allegedly excessive greenhouse effect? There are several possibilities, mostly costly, including adaptation, reforestation, and shifting away from the use of fossil fuels to alternative sources of power. Alternative energy sources offer great promise, and have been aggressively pursued by this administration in the 1990 Clean Air Act Amendments and the National Energy Strategy (NES) legislation. The NES specifically seeks to increase the use of renewable and nonfossil sources of energy. The real issue, however, is the pace of shifts in U.S. energy policy and the extent to which policy should be shaped by global climate change

imperatives as opposed to other environmental and energy security considerations.

The resources available in the United States, and in the world community in general, for addressing environmental problems are limited. Global climate change is one among many serious environmental challenges that face the human community. It would be irresponsible to commit disproportionate resources to solving a quandary whose very existence and severity are still uncertain, and thereby draw resources away from more concrete problems. For example, because of the magnitude of Eastern Europe's environmental disaster, a dollar spent there could yield more definite, tangible, and certain benefits than a dollar spent reducing carbon dioxide emissions in the United States.

In view of the uncertainties underlying the global warming debate and the limits on available resources, the administration has embraced a balanced policy of adopting those environmental measures that reduce greenhouse gas emissions while providing concrete environmental benefits. This approach has been termed a "multiple objective steps" or "no regrets" policy. Actions taken in this area should be based upon the long-term outlook, "taking into account the full range of social, economic, and environmental consequences of proposed actions for this and future generations."[2]

Further, a realistic approach to the problem must be a comprehensive one that, based on the best available scientific model of global climate change, reduces all greenhouse gases to the extent necessary by manipulating their differing sources and sinks (carbon-absorbing and -storing elements such as trees or oceans). All greenhouse gases should be addressed, including carbon dioxide, methane, nitrous oxide, halocarbons (which include CFCs and related hydrochloroflourocarbons), and tropospheric ozone. The complex interplay of sources should be considered as they affect the "net emissions" of greenhouse gases, that in turn influence climate processes.

"No regrets" is not tantamount to a "wait and see" approach. As a result of efforts already in place, in the year 2000 the United States will have an aggregate level of greenhouse gas emissions equal to or below the 1987 level. Furthermore, with the enactment of the

---

[2]America's Climate Change Strategy: An Action Agenda, *The White House, February, 1991.*

administration's NES proposals, aggregate levels of greenhouse emissions are projected to remain below the 1987 level through 2030, even accounting for new economic growth.

Absolute scientific certainty then is not a prerequisite for taking action. Rather, research should be aggressively pursued and the action taken should make sense based upon the current state of knowledge in this area. This will be an interactive process. As more is learned about global climate change and its dynamics, efforts to adapt to it can be increased, decreased, or redirected.

Assuming that scientific uncertainties about global warming are resolved sufficiently, and that a comprehensive approach is formulated, it is imperative that any solution be global. Worldwide cooperation is essential. For example, while in the past the developed world has been responsible for the release of most greenhouse gases into the atmosphere, the developing world is rapidly catching up. By the year 2025, the developing world is projected to account for nearly as much carbon emission as the industrialized world—approximately 5.5 billion tons versus 6.7 billion tons in the Environmental Protection Agency (EPA) baseline scenario. Even significant reductions in industrial country carbon emissions would still leave total carbon emissions and, more important, total greenhouse gas emissions close to projected baseline trends. Thus an agreement among the industrial powers addressing only carbon emissions is less desirable than one that also includes limitations for developing countries. The benefits of any such agreement among industrialized powers alone would therefore appear to be negligible. Policies with more leverage, such as technology development efforts, may be more attractive.

Fortunately, a number of international organizations are now working on global climate change issues. The United Nations Intergovernmental Negotiating Committee, an ad hoc group charged by the U.N. General Assembly with negotiating a framework convention on global climate change, held a series of meetings in February 1991. The Intergovernmental Panel on Climate Change, formed by the United Nations Environmental Program in 1988 to study and assess the issue of global climate change, met in Geneva in March 1990 and completed its first assessment report in August 1990. And preparations are underway for the United Nations Conference on Environment and Development in June 1992.

Agreement on an appropriate and successful strategy, however, will not be easily reached. The interests of the world's countries differ dramatically. Countries in relatively temperate climates that do not have extensive areas of low-lying coast may receive little benefit from a program addressing global warming concerns. In fact, some countries could benefit from an overall rise in global temperature, insofar as it might open up new territories for agricultural cultivation. However, the burdens that an effective global warming policy would entail can be readily quantified. The burdens, like the benefits, will not be evenly distributed. Countries that depend most heavily on fossil fuels like oil, coal, or natural gas for their energy needs will be the hardest hit. Because the carbon content of fossil fuels varies considerably, opportunities and limitations on fuel switching will also be an important determinant of relative burdens. Countries with abundant supplies of cheap coal and limited supplies of inexpensive natural gas will bear larger burdens than countries in which greenhouse concerns can provide a pretext for replacing subsidized coal with readily available natural gas. Countries in the developing world may not be in a position to make radical changes in their energy policies.

A successful regime must spread the burdens equitably among all members of the international community, while persuading all countries that participating in the effort is in their best interests. Goals should be chosen that reflect the benefits and costs of activities involved. Assuming that a credible case for implementing deep reductions in greenhouse gas emissions is made, under a comprehensive approach differing levels of "net emissions" of greenhouse gases could be set for each signatory and incorporated into an agreement. Countries would be empowered to pool or share obligations in order to improve the cost-effectiveness of agreed "net emissions" reductions or other agreed measures. This would grant maximum flexibility to signatories in meeting their obligations, based on their own domestic circumstances. Each country would tailor a combination of source and sink regulations to minimize economic and social disruption. Each signatory would choose those institutional enforcement mechanisms most conducive to its constitution, social structure, and cultural tradition, thus preserving its sovereignty.

Another critical environmental issue is the wholesale and continuing destruction of the

316

earth's rain forests. Deforestation has major repercussions for the world's environment, including possible effects on the global climate. Trees absorb carbon dioxide from the air, acting as carbon sinks, storing CO_2 in their trunks, branches, and roots. When a tree is cut down and burned, the carbon dioxide stored during the growth process is released, directly adding to the amount of greenhouse gases in the atmosphere. Large-scale deforestation also leads to the loss of topsoil, which reduces the earth's precious stock of arable land. Despite the penchant for dividing environmental problems into neat categories like "air pollution," "water pollution," or "waste disposal," most of these issues are as interrelated as is the environment itself. Indeed, increased carbon dioxide emissions and depleted topsoil are only two of the ramifications of disappearing rain forests.

Some estimate that up to two decades of intensive research on global climate change is required before major policy decisions can be made.

The tropical rain forests of Africa, Central and South America, and Southeast Asia, are a priceless environmental resource. While they cover only 6 per cent of the earth's surface, they contain as much as 50 per cent of its estimated 10 million species of plants and animals. It is impossible to predict the cost to humanity if these habitats and species are lost. Many species remain unidentified, and may never be found if the destruction continues. For example, Hugh H. Iltis, a botanist at the University of Wisconsin, points to *zea diploperennis*, a form of maize discovered in southeastern Mexico. The plant contains a gene for perennial growth which, if genetically engineered into other plants, could well increase agricultural yields in marginal areas. The entire species, however, apparently exists within a ten-acre area—it could be destroyed in a few hours. It is impossible to know what opportunities for improving human welfare are being forever eradicated with the destruction of the earth's rain forests.

The global environment, of course, is remarkably resilient. Life on earth has survived a number of cataclysms far more devastating that any human intervention. Scientists estimate that there have been at least 5 mass extinctions of animal and plant life in the past 600 million years. Each time, however, life on earth has rebounded in strength. Today, the environment is probably more diverse than at any time in the past. This diversity has enabled nature to replenish itself again and again. Now this diversity is threatened. The pace of extinction is greater now than at any time since the disappearance of the dinosaurs, and, by some estimates, a million species will disappear within the next quarter century—one every 15 minutes. It is impossible to predict exactly at what point these new extinctions will begin to undermine nature's ability to preserve and replenish itself. Brinkmanship, however, should not be the goal. Human survival is ultimately linked to the maintenance of the earth's ecological chain.

Saving the rain forests and the endangered species of the world will not be easy tasks. To begin with, Western aid alone would not stop the destruction of these resources. To encourage conservation, proper economic incentives and the protection of private property rights are necessary. An ambitious Tropical Forestry Action Plan, unveiled in 1985 with much fanfare by the World Bank, the U.N., and other organizations, appears to be foundering on political and bureaucratic shoals. The time is ripe for new thinking on rain forest preservation. Unilateral action also often proves inadequate in wildlife preservation. Further, like global warming, the benefits and burdens of such an effort will not be evenly distributed among the world's states. In the case of rain forest preservation, the countries of Central and South America may well ask why they should forgo the development of their most important natural resource for the good of the global environment. Nineteenth-century Americans, for example, gave little thought to global welfare when they swept away the forests of North America.

Another environmental problem that has received too little attention from a world focused on global climate change is the desperate ecological condition of the emerging democracies in Eastern Europe. Over the past 40 years, the central planners of the communist bloc paid scant attention to the problem of pollution. Until the democratic revolutions of 1989, the extent of the Soviet bloc's environmental problems was a forbidden subject. The emphasis on production quotas and reliance on antiquated technologies have taken a frightful toll. The former territory of East Germany is widely considered an environmental disaster area, and the city of Leipzig is the largest single source of carbon dioxide in the world. In one small town outside Leipzig, four of five children develop either chronic bronchitis or heart ailments by age seven. The situation in eastern Germany will be difficult to remedy—more than 80 per cent of its energy comes from lignite, a high sulphur, dirty brown coal that puts out less heat per unit than the more efficient varieties used in the West. Yet lignite is the principal fuel for the entire former East Bloc.

In Eastern Europe, Poland confronts the worst overall pollution problem. In the steel producing areas of Silesia, men in their 30s and 40s are dying of cancer, heart disease, and emphysema. Stretches of the Vistula River are so polluted that its water cannot be used even for industrial purposes. Close to 40 per cent of the forests in the "rust belt," an industrial area stretching across eastern Germany, Czechoslovakia, and Poland, has been damaged by acid rain. In Hungary, the once blue Danube now runs dark with pollution. Bringing Eastern Europe up to Western environmental protection standards may cost $250–300 billion, according to conservative estimates. Western Europe has realized that the East European environmental problem is really a problem for the entire Continent. To aid in this comprehensive effort, the Bush administration has created a regional environmental center in Budapest to provide the emerging democracies with technological and financial aid.

For its part, Western Europe, while certainly ahead of the former Soviet bloc countries, is no environmental paradise either. The magnitude of environmental problems currently facing the European Community (EC) dictates that they cannot be solved through the action of one, or even two, European states. The North Sea has become a virtual drainage basin for pollutants from Denmark, Germany, the Netherlands, and the United Kingdom. Pollutants are also carried from landlocked countries like Switzerland down the Rhine River into the North Sea. The Mediterranean Sea has been called by some a "communal sewer." Acid rain has become a serious problem for the industrialized areas of Western Europe.

The world's tropical rain forests and much of Europe face serious, concrete environmental problems. These cases illustrate that it may be more cost-effective to address pollution problems abroad rather than those at home. In the case of Eastern Europe in particular, the West has had considerable experience in dealing with similar problems. A dollar spent cleaning up air pollution in Poland may well yield a greater return than a dollar spent on further limiting emissions from the already well-controlled West European industrial sources.

The American Experience

Although global environmental challenges loom large, it is important to acknowledge and learn from American environmental achievements. These accomplishments are both an inspiration and a valuable source of learning. The United States is on the cutting edge of environmental technology, and its corporations, universities, and governmental agencies contain the world's most advanced scientific information about the environment. With respect to environmental solutions, the United States has much to offer the world.

Despite complaints about its allegedly cavalier attitude toward environmental protection, the United States is a world leader in its commitment to environmental policy. Recognizing that any sound policy begins at home, American efforts to ensure a good environmental quality of life have been particularly impressive. The vast number of existing environmental laws in the United States continues to grow. In addition to a variety of state laws and local ordinances, federal government programs regulate such matters as air and water quality, handling and disposal of solid and hazardous wastes, and disposal of toxic substances. The focus of environmental statutes is broadening, shifting attention to substances that pose indirect or long-term threats to humans and natural habitats.

The United States ranks high among industrialized countries in total environmental expenditures. According to the Council on Environmental Quality, such spending now exceeds $115 billion per year (in 1990 dollars)—roughly 2 per cent of the U.S. gross national product compared to roughly 1.5 per cent in the EC. Approximately two-thirds of this amount is spent on air and water programs. The EPA estimates that the cost of complying with federal air and water pollution–control regulations was $52 billion in 1981 alone (in 1988 dollars). Between 1981 and 1990 the nation will spend more than $560 billion in pursuit of clean air and water.

Most observers believe that, all in all, the quality of the environment in the United States has vastly improved over the last two decades. These improvements pertain primarily to public health, though progress has also been registered in such areas as the preservation of the environment and the protection of aesthetic values associated with it, such as atmospheric visibility. Particularly strong progress has been registered in air quality.

Despite considerable progress, serious environmental problems persist. Moreover, the remaining problems are highly complex and costly to fix. The solutions are uncertain and involve a complicated calculus of benefits, risks, and costs. Questions about what constitutes the acceptable level of risk and how to balance health- and technology-based environmental standards remain particularly vexing. These factors suggest that additional environmental improvements may be gained only at an increasingly high cost to society and the economy—a disheartening realization. Nevertheless, there is much to learn from both positive and negative aspects of past environmental experience, offering lessons on making environmental gains more efficiently and with fewer transaction costs.

In the past, excessive emphasis has been placed on rigid command and control methods for improving environmental quality. Likewise, environmental debates have often been unduly polarized, and dominated more by sloganeering than by scientific analysis. Environmental realism is an important virtue and has to be embraced by Congress, the executive branch, and the environmental community.

Past experience also suggests that various environmental objectives may be contradictory. Reductions in different toxic compounds, or benefits to one aspect of the environment stemming from a particular control technology, may inflict stress on other environmental media or goals. Finally, it must be acknowledged that the various non-environmental pork-barrels that have frequently shaped environmental statutes have proven inordinately costly.

The Bush administration recognizes that, budgetary resources aside, a new approach to environmental improvement is required. As President George Bush stated on April 18, 1990, "To those who suggest we're only trying to balance economic growth and environmental protection, I say they miss the point. We are calling for an entirely new way of thinking to achieve both while compromising neither."

Specifically, the administration seeks to base its environmental actions upon sound scientific, economic, and policy analysis. When amending existing environmental statutes, or enacting new

ones, it tries to act in a coordinated, rather than piecemeal, fashion. To avoid the acrimony of past environmental debates, it also seeks to foster a dialogue between industry and the environmental community, so that solutions acceptable to all can be found. A great strength of the administration's environmental policy is its basis on a partnership between the government and the private sector. Certain private companies and industrial associations have begun policing themselves, establishing standards of environmental behavior tougher than those required by federal and state laws. Meanwhile, private citizens and organizations—the "Thousand Points of Light"—have pursued environmental causes as part of their daily lives. The resulting environmental policy is dynamic and politically sustainable.

In the regulatory area, the administration emphasizes flexible, market-based approaches that feature diverse trading systems with built-in compliance incentives and that allow the bulk of pollution reductions to come from the sources that can accomplish them in the most cost-effective fashion. The administration also is committed to the principle of cooperative federalism, whereby the federal government, states, and local governments participate as full-fledged partners in developing environmental standards as well as in monitoring and enforcing them. All of these traits have been demonstrated in the administration's successful handling of the Clean Air Act, which languished in Congress for more than a decade until the president made it his top environmental priority.

Any global program that does not take into account the legitimate value of the nation-state is doomed to failure—and rightly so.

On the international front, the United States has also had a number of recent successes. These include the Enterprise for the Americas Initiative, a major package of economic initiatives involving Latin America that features an innovative plan to encourage "debt-for-nature" swaps and creates trust funds from certain debt payments to support long-term environmental programs; the economic summit meetings in Paris in July 1989 and Houston in July 1990, at which the president promoted a range of environmental initiatives; various bilateral agreements to provide technical and financial support to Eastern Europe through the environmental center in Budapest; assistance to new democracies and developing countries in drafting their environmental laws; a first-class research program including geological surveys and studies of natural hazards worldwide; air quality programs in Poland; efforts with the Soviet Union to create a wilderness park in the Bering Sea; agreements with Japan, South Korea, and Taiwan to monitor the adverse effects of driftnet fishing on marine mammals; and, perhaps most important, efforts to strengthen the Montreal Protocol.

The 1990 London amendments to the Montreal Protocol were both environmentally aggressive and historic in character. The United States, along with 92 other countries, has agreed to phase out chemicals that deplete the ozone layer by the turn of the century, while providing a program of technical and financial assistance to ensure that developing countries participate in this important task. A number of industrialized countries, including the United States, will contribute money to a special fund to be administered by the World Bank. For the next several years, these monies will be used to finance the research necessary to determine what industrial projects have to be reoriented to implement the CFC ban.

Of all the world's various environmental and economic problems, energy use and its consequences figure most prominently. Today, the world as a whole depends on oil, natural gas, and coal for most of its basic energy needs. These sources of energy are nonrenewable and at least oil and coal pollute the environment on a grand scale. Yet energy supply is the lifeblood of modern economies. The events of the 1970s demonstrated the importance of natural resources in the world's strategic balance of power. To take one example, the severe disruption to oil prices caused by the 1979 Iranian Revolution and its aftermath probably cost the economies of Organization for Economic Cooperation and Development countries about $1 trillion, causing unemployment to rise from 17 million to 29 million between 1979 and 1982. Given this nexus, any environmental strategy must include a sound energy policy. The administration's recently released NES, featuring an ambitious alternative fuels program, is a good example of balancing environmental, economic, and energy considerations.

The most important lesson to be drawn from domestic and international experience is that effectively resolving transnational environmental issues requires a comprehensive approach addressing all aspects of pollution at the same time, whether they be air-, water-, or ground-based. In fact, attempts to control one form of pollution in some cases have led to an increase in another form, resulting in net environmental degradation. "Cross-media" approaches propose protecting entire ecosystems, rather than focusing on individual environmental issues.

Moreover, any responsible international environmental program must take into account not only strict environmental needs, but also the need for economic and social stability. As EPA Administrator William Reilly pointed out in the Fall 1990 issue of *Policy Review*, without a stable and growing domestic and world economy, the international community will have neither the means, the will, nor the opportunity to overcome current environmental challenges. Thus, sustainable development must advance both economic and environmental values. If the "solution" to global environmental problems works to undermine global political and economic stability, the program may leave the world worse off. For example, while fledgling democratically elected governments are well aware of their pressing environmental problems, some are reluctant to make costly clean-up commitments that might adversely affect their own economic status, imperiling the transition to democratic and open societies.

International experience also has yielded valuable lessons. Internationally, a command and control emphasis is simply not feasible, since countries that do not agree to a particular environmental regime cannot be forced to comply. Military intervention would not be seen by the majority of states as an acceptable alternative, and economic sanctions have proven ineffective. In fact, economic sanctions could exacerbate the problem because economic pressure could spur the violators to develop their resources as a matter of survival. Global moral disapproval may be laudable, but it will not insure compliance.

Creating a supranational organization to monitor the process would have dubious benefits. In advocating such an organization, many environmentalists tend to denigrate the value of the nation-state. At best, they see national sovereignty as an inconvenience, and at worst, an all but insurmountable obstacle to effective global environmental policy. However, environmentalism is not the only value worthy of protection. Being environmentally responsible does not require abandoning other important values, such as national self-determination. The modern nation-state is a manifestation of the bedrock principle of national self-government.

National sovereignty is especially important to the developing countries. Many of these countries have only recently achieved their own independence. They are not likely to welcome suggestions that their interests should again be subordinated to "metropolitan" concerns. Any global program that does not take into account the legitimate value of the nation-state is doomed to failure—and rightly so. Thus, to have an effective policy, it is essential to forge an effective partnership among national governments, the U.N., other international organizations, domestic nongovernmental organizations, and businesses. Likewise, helping the developing world with financial and technological aid is not merely a handout—in many respects it may be the most efficient and effective means of addressing many international problems.

Given the magnitude of environmental problems, as well as the formidable resource constraints on the international and domestic levels, an economic incentives approach may well be the only realistic one.

The economic incentives approach can take a number of different forms. Today, the most familiar of them is the "emissions trading" program that is the centerpiece of the Clean Air Act's curbs on acid rain. Here, emissions levels of certain pollutants are established by law. A company that reduces its emissions below the legal standard at one location is allowed "credit" for the surplus reduction. These credits may then be used against higher emissions at other locations, or may be traded or sold to third parties. This allows the polluting parties to reduce emissions to a mandated level in the most efficient manner, while at the same time encouraging firms to reduce their emissions more than they would otherwise be required to do.

Other strategies include pollution fees or taxes or charging firms for emitting pollutants, so that the environmental cost of producing a particular product is reflected in the ultimate cost to the consumer. Such charges give the polluter a powerful incentive to reduce the level of pollution as a means of reducing production costs. Enforcement flexibility is also essential: Serious environmental offenders must be brought to justice, while law-abiding businesses remain free of excessive paperwork, bureaucratic delays, and burdensome regulatory micromanagement. As chairman of the Task Force on Regulatory Relief, then Vice President Bush recognized these objectives as early as 1983. Today, the Competitiveness Council is responsible for similar work under Vice President Dan Quayle.

Market approaches encourage polluters to clean up their operations, function more efficiently, and develop new pollution control technologies. The best feature of the system is that each pollution producer is allowed, within broad limits, to determine which emissions reduction strategy is the most efficient for its particular circumstance. On the international level, each country should have the same flexibility in crafting environmental solutions for itself. This will accommodate the earth's diverse political and cultural systems, while still achieving real environmental advances. Respecting this diversity is critical. Progress on global environmental issues will only be achieved by demonstrating to the developing world, and to the emerging democracies of Eastern Europe, that sound environmental policies are in their national interest and will provide better lives for their citizens.

Although the gulf war will probably be remembered as a political and military triumph, many analysts believe that it will also rank as one of the most ecologically destructive conflicts in history. Although Kuwait has been liberated—and the flow of oil assured, at least for the short-term—the region has been blackened by hundreds of oil fires, which have contaminated the atmosphere. In addition, marine life has been poisoned, huge quantities of toxic substances have been released into the ozone, and famine and health epidemics loom possible. In fact, Kuwaiti officials report that the environmental dangers may actually exceed the material losses of the war. Sadly, the international community spared little expense in routing the Iraqis from Kuwait, while moving far more slowly in addressing the ecological consequences of the conflict. The gulf war shows, quite clearly, the importance of developing a mechanism to deal with ecological problems stemming from military conflicts. It also reveals that war brings with it a host of environmental problems, which underscores the importance of finding peaceful means of resolving disputes.

MILITARY VICTORY, ECOLOGICAL DEFEAT

Iraq was not the only loser in the Persian Gulf War.
The region's air and water quality, along with its plants and animals,
may not soon recover.

BY MICHAEL G. RENNER

Military historians are likely to remember the recent Gulf War as a modern-day *blitzkrieg*, a triumph of "smart bombs" and other high-tech wizardry. However, while the fighting was brought to a swift conclusion, the onslaught against the environment continues with undiminished ferocity. The Gulf War now ranks among the most ecologically destructive conflicts ever.

Kuwait is liberated, but the region has been transformed into a disaster zone. Hundreds of oil fires are severely polluting the atmosphere; oil deliberately spilled onto the ground and into the Persian Gulf is tainting aquifers and poisoning marine life; attacks on refineries, petrochemical plants, and chemical and nuclear facilities have likely released substantial quantities of toxic materials; dam-age to public utilities and roads could trigger health epidemics and famine; the massive movement of troops and their heavy equipment has imperiled an already fragile desert ecology. Kuwaiti officials think the environmental damages may be more severe than the material losses of the war.

But the disparity in the response to the military and environmental aspects of the conflict could hardly be more pronounced. To force Iraq out of Kuwait, no expense or effort was spared. An alliance of more than two dozen countries was carefully crafted, the United Nations machinery for collective security was thrown into high gear, and hundreds of thousands of soldiers and huge amounts of equipment were ferried halfway around the globe.

By contrast, assessing and tackling the

From *World Watch*, July/August 1991, pp. 27-33. WorldWatch Institute, Washington, D.C. 20036. Reprinted by permission.

ecological consequences of the conflict has been a much lower priority. For example, the effort to contain and clean up the massive oil spill in the Gulf in February was hampered by lack of money and poor coordination among various Saudi government agencies. Attempts to monitor the impacts of oil fires and to put them out also seem woefully inadequate. An air-quality testing lab in Kuwait has not been repaired, and fire-fighting equipment has been slow in coming.

The Gulf War demonstrates the need for the international community to set up a mechanism to cope with the ecological damage arising from armed conflicts. In a broader sense, though, it shows that wars and environmental protection are incompatible. Although international environmental-protection agreements are necessary, the most important step that can be taken is to work for peaceful means of resolving conflicts.

Towering Inferno
Kuwaiti officials estimate that as many as 6 million barrels of oil are going up in flames every day—almost four times the country's oil production per day prior to the Iraqi invasion, or 9 percent of the world's petroleum consumption. Some scientists, includ-

---

Roughly 10 times as much air pollution was being emitted in Kuwait as by all U.S. industrial and power-generating plants combined.

---

ing Paul Mason of the British government's Meteorological Office, believe the volume of burning oil is smaller. Beyond dispute, however, is the fact that immense clouds of smoke block the sunlight and turn day into night. In April, daytime temperatures in affected areas were as much as 27 degrees Fahrenheit below normal.

Fire fighters have never confronted so many fires burning simultaneously and in such close proximity. By May, workers had put out only 60 of the 500 to 600 fires, primarily the smaller and more accessible ones. Experts estimate that it will take at least two years to extinguish all of the blazes. By that time, Kuwait may have lost as much as 10 percent of its 92 billion barrels of proven oil reserves—either through combustion or structural damage to its oil reservoirs.

The atmospheric pollution resulting from these fires is almost unprecedented, comparable only to large-scale forest fires and volcanic eruptions. Assuming a burn rate of 6 million barrels per day, as much as 2.5 million tons of soot may be produced in a month—more than four times the average monthly emissions in the entire United States in 1989 (the last year for which data are available). In addition, more than 1 million tons of sulfur dioxide and approximately 100,000 tons of nitrogen oxides may be released each month.

The clouds of oil smoke also contain large amounts of toxic and potentially carcinogenic substances such as hydrogen sulfide, benzene, and other hydrocarbons. Overall, according to a U.S. Environmental Protection Agency (EPA) estimate in March, roughly 10 times as much air pollution was being emitted in Kuwait as by all U.S. industrial and power-generating plants combined.

The stew of contaminants makes breathing a hazardous undertaking. Rare is the news story about postwar Kuwait that does not mention the sore throat from which virtually everyone seems to suffer. Kuwaiti hospitals are filled with people fallen ill from exposure to the air pollution, and doctors advise those with chronic respiratory problems not to return to Kuwait. Although considerable uncertainty persists concerning the long-term toll on human health, many air pollutants are thought to cause or aggravate a wide range of conditions, including blood disorders, respiratory problems such as asthma and bronchitis, coronary ailments, cancer, and possibly genetic damage. Scientists now acknowledge that prolonged exposure to even low levels of smog—the product of reactions between nitrogen oxides and hydrocarbons in the presence of sunlight—may cause irreparable lung damage. Young children and the elderly are particularly at risk.

Because Kuwaiti oil has a high sulfur

content, acid rain—of which sulfur dioxide is a principal component—is expected to afflict the Gulf region and adjacent areas. Acid deposition (which does not always require rain) is known to destroy forests and reduce crop yields. It can also activate several dangerous metals normally found in soil—including aluminum, cadmium, and mercury—making them more soluble and therefore more of a threat to water supplies and edible fish. "Black rain"—soot that is washed out of the skies or eventually falls back to the ground—is coating people, animals, buildings, and crops with an oily, black film.

The effects of air pollution depend not just on the quantity of contaminants released, but on atmospheric conditions that change with the seasons. Summer is a particularly bad time for pollution in the Gulf because of diminished air-cleansing winds and rains, and increased atmospheric inversions that trap pollutants under stagnant layers of air.

The Geography of Pollution

The densest smoke is found over Kuwait, eastern Iraq, and western and southern Iran. In Kuwait, scientists with the British Meteorological Office recorded 30,000 soot particles per cubic meter of air, 1,000 parts per billion of sulfur dioxide and 50 parts per billion of nitrogen oxides at an altitude of 6,000 feet—about 30, 20, and 10 times, respectively, the levels in a typical city plagued by air pollution.

As far as 1,000 miles away—in parts of Bulgaria, Romania, Turkey, and the Soviet Union that border on the Black Sea—smog levels caused by the oil fires are as serious as the smog found anywhere in Europe under normal conditions, according to Paul Mason. A much larger area—from the waters of the Nile to the snows of the Himalayas—is susceptible to acid rain and soot fallout, according to the Max Planck Institute for Meteorology in Hamburg, Germany (see map on page 31).

The burning of such large amounts of oil over long periods could generate enough soot and smoke to diminish solar radiation, thereby lowering daytime temperatures and reducing the amount of rainfall. One ounce of soot can block about two-thirds of the light falling over an area of 280 to 340 square yards. In Kuwait, the amount of solar energy reaching the ground is at times reduced by more than 90 percent. Reduced photosynthesis combined with the deposition of soot and other toxic materials could imperil crops.

Whether such an effect would extend beyond the Gulf region depends on how high the soot climbs and how long it remains there. That, in turn, depends on a range of factors, including the combustion characteristics of the oil fires, the size of the soot particles, and general atmospheric conditions. Intense fires, such as those involving hydrocarbons, create convective currents that give smoke a strong updrift. The finer the particles, the higher they rise, the longer they stay aloft, and the more efficient they are at blocking sunlight, according to Paul Crutzen, director of atmospheric chemistry at the Max Planck Institute for Chemistry in Mainz, Germany. Many small particles appear to be present in the smoke clouds, according to scientists from the British Meteorological Office who gathered samples from a plane in April.

The soot would need to rise to about 35,000 feet for the jet stream to pick it up and carry it around the globe. During April, the smoke plume was reported to be hovering at altitudes of no more than 12,000 feet, with small quantities found as high as 20,000 feet. But the same hot summer weather that helps create temperature inversions near the ground could cause greater updrafting and thus make some of the smoke climb higher. By early May, the U.S. National Oceanic and Atmospheric Administration (NOAA) reported that soot levels at about 20 times above normal readings were recorded at the Mauna Loa Observatory in Hawaii. Presumably, the Kuwaiti oil fires, some 8,000 miles away, are the source of the soot. Despite the elevated soot levels, NOAA does not expect any "significant" environmental impact in North America.

At the same time that it is potentially causing a short-term cooling, the Kuwaiti oil conflagration is also contributing to the long-term phenomenon of global warming. It may add as much as 240 million tons of carbon to the atmosphere in the course of a year—about 4 percent of the current global annual carbon release. This is comparable to the amount produced by Japan, the world's second-largest economy and fourth-largest emitter of carbon dioxide from fossil fuels.

Since carbon emissions need to be slashed by at least 20 percent by the year 2005 just to slow climate change, the Kuwaiti oil fires send us another step in the wrong direction.

Nothing in human experience could help model and predict the precise consequences of the Kuwaiti oil blaze. The Gulf region thus has become a huge air pollution laboratory. Unfortunately, the subjects of these dangerous pollution experiments are people, plants, and animals.

Oil on the Water

The oil spilled into the Gulf waters is posing a severe test for marine ecosystems. Estimated at more than 3 million barrels by the Saudi Meteorology and Environmental Protection Administration, the Persian Gulf oil spill roughly equals the largest in history—the Ixtoc well blowout in the Gulf of Mexico in 1979—and is 10 times the size of the Exxon Valdez accident.

Following spills during the eight-year Iran-Iraq war, the Persian Gulf was already a highly stressed environment in poor condition to withstand additional ecological assaults. A relatively shallow sea, it is essentially a closed ecosystem with only a narrow outlet to the Arabian Sea through the Strait of Hormuz. Because Kuwaiti oil is of a "light" variety, up to 40 percent of it may have evaporated. The warm waters of the Gulf allow the remaining oil to decompose fairly rapidly, but significant amounts will foul shorelines or poison the sea bottom. The Saudi government was apparently ill-prepared for dealing with a disaster of such magnitude. By early April, only about half a million barrels of oil had been recovered, and it was clear the focus of the effort was to protect the country's desalination plants.

Considerable harm to Gulf fish and other wildlife—including porpoises, turtles, and seabirds—seems inevitable since many nesting and spawning grounds have been soaked in oil. At least 14,000 birds were killed along the Saudi shore. Some areas are so contaminated that they had to be declared off-limits to fishing, threatening the livelihoods of commercial and subsistence fishers. The Saudi shrimp industry, for example, has been wiped out and is considered unlikely to recover before the end of the decade. Extensive damage to coral reefs and sea grasses also has occurred, according to the EPA. If large quantities of plankton are killed, the entire ecosystem may be threatened.

Desert Wasteland

The presence of more than 1 million soldiers with their immense arsenals has placed severe strains on the already fragile desert ecology of Kuwait, Saudi Arabia, and Iraq. Normally inhabited only by Bedouins, the desert of the Arabian peninsula cannot bear such a massive burden. Desert vegetation is sparse, but it helps to stabilize and protect the soil. Tanks and other vehicles have disrupted and compacted the soil and destroyed plants whose root systems are often close to the surface. As a result, the ground in many areas has been rendered susceptible to accelerated erosion. Seeds that lie dormant for large parts of the year, but which spark to life during spring rains, were likely affected.

If a significant portion of the desert vegetation is destroyed, dry spells might be lengthened and the ecological balance could be tipped into long-term decline. It may take hundreds of years for the desert to recover from the massive pre-war maneuvers and the tank battles, according to John Cloudsley-Thompson, an expert on desert ecology at the University of London. The Libyan desert, for example, still bears heavy scars from World War II combat, as do portions of the Negev in Israel from fighting in 1967 and 1973, and parts of the Mojave in southern California from maneuvers in the early 1940s.

The military presence has additional consequences. The armed forces routinely handle massive amounts of highly toxic materials to maintain and operate their tanks, jet fighters, and other pieces of equipment. Experience on U.S. military bases suggests that these substances could severely contaminate underground water supplies (see "War on Nature," May/June 1991) if they're not properly handled. The inhospitable Saudi environment, with its blistering heat and gritty sand, forced the allied troops to use special lubricants of a more toxic nature, according to the U.S. Congressional Research Service, and generally larger amounts of hazardous materials than in more moderate climates. Exposure to even trace amounts of these chemicals through drinking, skin absorption, or inhalation can cause cancer, birth defects, and chromosome damage, and may seriously impair the function of the liver, kidneys, and central nervous system.

Another long-term peril stems from unexploded bombs and mines littering large parts of Iraq and Kuwait. The U.S. Air Force says it dropped 88,500 tons of explosives. The Pentagon generally assumes a 10-percent dud rate, meaning that almost 9,000 tons of explosive material must be cleared. Even an intensive recovery effort will likely fail to detect many of them, as experience from previous wars suggests. Gar Smith reports in *Earth Island Journal* that as much as 20 percent of the 1 million land mines laid by Iraq may remain undetected after cleanup efforts. Clearing the bombs is extremely difficult. Some of the "smart bombs" can only be disarmed with special tools and techniques that may be unavailable to Iraq. According to a report by the San Francisco-based Arms Control Research Center, some of these bombs are magnetically triggered. Any metal tool, such as a farmer's hoe or plow, could detonate them.

Chemical Warfare

The veil of military secrecy and post-war chaos in Iraq have precluded a full assessment of the effects of allied air attacks on Iraq's chemical, biological, and nuclear facilities and its refineries and petrochemical plants. Many of these facilities are located close to civilian population centers along the Tigris and Euphrates rivers. The incineration of materials produced and stored at these installations may well have generated a variety of deadly toxins, including cyanide, dioxin, and PCBs.

Reports in the German press, including such well-respected newspapers as *Frankfurter Rundschau* and *Handelsblatt*, suggest that toxic vapors escaped following air raids on chemical facilities, killing scores of Iraqi civilians. The nerve gases tabun and sarin, which Iraq has admitted possessing, evaporate rapidly and thus do not pose a persistent hazard. But another agent in the Iraqi arsenal, mustard gas, which is a mutagen and a

carcinogen, is much longer-lived. A spokesman for the Patriotic Union of Kurdistan, an Iraqi opposition group, asserted in early February that allied attacks against chemical and ammunition plants led to widespread contamination of water resources.

Victor or Vanquished?

Sadly, the environmental disaster in the Gulf was preventable. In the months leading up to the outbreak of armed conflict, the alternatives of resorting to military force or relying on economic sanctions were debated, but the latter option was given too little time to work. Sanctions may have been less swift and certain than force, but would likely have spared many lives and avoided the tragic environmental effects.

That Saddam Hussein would set the torch to Kuwait's oil wells was no secret; he repeatedly threatened to do so if attacked by the U.S.-led coalition. The U.S. and British governments even commissioned studies about the potential environmental impact of such an act, but proceeded with their military plans anyway. The responsibility for the environmental destruction lies with Saddam Hussein's regime, but the devastation was either underestimated by the allied governments or considered an acceptable price of victory.

With such results, it is difficult to distinguish between victor and vanquished. Indeed, the war's ecological impact extends far beyond the battlefield, blurring the distinction between the combatants and countries that were not party to the conflict and had no say over its course.

In light of the Gulf War's ecological devastation, the time has come for the world community to consider creating a stronger convention for the protection of the environment in war. The existing United Nations "Convention on the Prohibition of Military or Any Other Hostile Use of Environmental Modification Techniques" is tailored to proscribe use of the environment as a weapon. A 1977 amendment to the 1949 Geneva Protocols prohibits means of warfare that are intended or expected to damage the environment and, in consequence, jeopardize the health and lives of the civilian population.

Neither agreement, however, includes any enforcement mechanisms and both were ignored by the belligerents in the Gulf War. Establishing such mechanisms, including trade embargoes and other nonviolent sanctions against offenders, would be an important first step. Next, lowering the threshold at which the prohibitions apply and making more explicit what acts they cover would give them more practical meaning.

But even a strengthened international code is of limited value. The conduct of war and the protection of the natural environment are fundamentally incompatible objectives. War on the environment is, unfortunately, nothing new. From the Punic Wars in the third century B.C. on, armies have poisoned wells, salted soils, and destroyed crops to foil the enemy. However, over time, the environmental impact of warfare has grown as sophisticated technology has boosted the firepower, range, and speed of weapons. In addition, modern industries present many high-profile targets whose destruction can wreak environmental devastation on a vast scale.

It was after the dawn of the atomic age that nations gradually came to realize that nuclear arsenals, if used, would destroy what they were supposed to defend. Now, in the wake of the Gulf War and its immense environmental toll, conventional warfare, too, may come to be seen as a less-acceptable means of settling conflicts. ●

Michael G. Renner is a senior researcher at the Worldwatch Institute. His work focuses on the links between military activities and the environment.

Chapter 26

Energy and National Security

Article 26.1.   Bush's Pro-Nuke Energy Strategy

In this article, the author assesses the Bush administration's national energy strategy, which calls for an accelerated emphasis on oil exploration and nuclear power. The president views oil as the kingpin of his proposal, calling for expanded drilling offshore and in the Alaska National Wildlife Refuge. The administration's main "alternative" is nuclear power, which the president sees as a viable option. In addition, more than $430 million is earmarked for research, development, and other industry subsidies in fiscal year 1992. This represents more than twice the amount set aside for renewable energy. The Department of Energy also advocates "streamlining" the licensing process for nuclear power plants which, according to the president's critics, will exclude the public from the process. The fight is far from over, contends the author, who insists that the fate of the administration's proposals will ultimately be decided by the voters, who will, in all likelihood, continue to oppose the construction of new power plants and weapons production facilities.

■ THE TURKEY THAT WON'T DIE

Bush's Pro-Nuke Energy Strategy

HARVEY WASSERMAN

Homestead, Fla.

Nestled in a lush tropical cove at the northern tip of the Florida Keys, the Turkey Point power plant stands as a national symbol for the fight over war and energy that could dominate the post–gulf war 1990s. For in the wake of George Bush's assault on Iraq, the issues of nuclear power and atomic warhead production have become more thoroughly intertwined than ever. Both industries are trying desperately to inaugurate a modernized generation of production plants. And the fate of both may very well be determined within the next two years, in far-flung places like the lagoon at Turkey Point.

Consisting of two atomic reactors (both now shut) and two oil burners, Turkey Point thoroughly embodies the Bush Administration's national energy strategy. Announced at the White House in late February, just before the gulf war ground attack, the Bush strategy calls for accelerated emphasis on oil exploration and nuclear power. Even the sparse conservation measures apparently favored by Adm. James Watkins, Energy Secretary, were summarily dismissed by White House Chief of Staff John Sununu.

For the Bush Administration, particularly in the wake of Iraq's defeat, oil remains at center stage, with demands for expanded drilling offshore and in the Alaska National Wildlife Refuge. The Administration's main "alternative" is nuclear power. More than $430 million is set aside for research, development and other industry subsidies in fiscal year 1992, which is twice the amount set aside for renewable energy sources. The Department of Energy (D.O.E.) also calls for "streamlining" the licensing process, shorthand for excluding the public. A hearing is now required both when a construction permit is granted and when the reactor is completed and about to go on line. The Nuclear Regulatory Commission, which is supposed to oversee reactor construction and operation, is now in court attempting to delete the second hearing. "The industry doesn't want to face public scrutiny after they've built a plant," says Michael Mariotte of the Nuclear Information and Resource Service, which sued the N.R.C. on the issue. "They want to walk in with plans and a site and sail through, even if there's a meltdown at a similar plant, an earthquake at the site, a bankruptcy at the utility. It's totally undemocratic and outrageous."

Last November the U.S. Court of Appeals for the Washington, D.C., Circuit agreed, and unanimously ruled in N.I.R.S.'s favor. But the Administration and the nuclear industry are now pushing Congress to pass legislation that would omit the second hearing. "The industry believes that no utility company will begin the process if it has to face the public after the reactor is built," says Mariotte. "They can't stand the uncertainty." Indeed, the current consensus is that after financially catastrophic delays at Seabrook, New Hampshire, and other sites around the country, Wall Street would never fund another commercial reactor project.

Harvey Wasserman is the author of Harvey Wasserman's History of the United States. *As senior adviser to the Greenpeace Nuclear Campaign, he was co-planner of a recent national conference on nuclear power and weapons.*

From *The Nation*, May 20, 1991, pp. 656-660. *The Nation* magazine/The Nation Company, Inc., © 1991.

The fates of both nuclear power and warheads have never been more vitally intertwined.

But Bush has an answer: funding by the producers themselves. Buried in the Administration plan is a provision to allow nonutility producers to sell large quantities of electricity into the national grid, free of state regulation. In essence, this is an end run around local public utility commissions and allows multinationals like General Electric and Westinghouse to build their own reactors and then market the juice without worrying about local scrutiny. In partnership with nuclear construction companies like Bechtel and Stone and Webster, G.E. and Westinghouse could use tacit participation by a pronuclear utility like Florida Power & Light to site their own reactor and fire up. Bechtel and Westinghouse's recent purchase of a controlling share of a Michigan reactor from the utility that originally ordered it may be a sign of similar moves soon to follow.

The strategy is crucial now because the industry is desperately seeking salvation in a new generation of reactors. "The consensus is that this last batch of nukes was a failure," says Mariotte. "The industry needs to shed the images of Three Mile Island and Chernobyl, and the general belief that it's an economic turkey. They seem to think a vaguely different design with an 'inherently safe' label can help them do that."

There are now just under 120 reactors in the United States either licensed to operate or still in the active pipeline. That's down 880 from the 1,000 Richard Nixon predicted in 1974, in the aftermath of the first oil embargo. In fact, there have been no orders brought to completion since Nixon's prediction.

That has spelled disaster for the industry, which has seen a generation of scientists drift away, and which can barely sustain the personnel pool needed to operate and maintain the reactors now in service. "A few more years without a new order, or the prospect of a mass revival, and the industry is just plain out of business," says Scott Denman, director of the Washington-based Safe Energy Communication Council. "They can't sustain themselves on hollow dreams."

But with the ascent of John Sununu and the Persian Gulf blitzkrieg, the industry is stirring. Its Washington-based P.R. front, the U.S. Council for Energy Awareness, has been pumping out $20 million a year in print and electronic hype. The latest ads claim nuclear power has saved Americans some 4.3 million barrels of oil since 1973. But even with oil at $30 per barrel, the best the industry can claim to have saved us in two decades is about $130 billion—not much when compared with an investment variously estimated at between $500 billion and $1 trillion.

The reactor makers also claim to save the United States as much oil as it imported from Iraq and Kuwait. But less than 6 percent of the oil the United States uses goes to produce electricity, and much of that is residual "trash" oil from the gasoline refining process, which has no other use and is imported

from Venezuela. "Even going nuclear for 100 percent of our electricity would make barely a dent in our oil addiction," says Mariotte. "Their whole argument is specious."

Also specious is the idea that a substantial number of new reactors could come on line soon. Given what has happened to date, no utility is about to order a first-generation plant. An "enhanced" model is being built by G.E. and Mitsubishi in Japan, but it remains unproven.

The industry's hopes lie instead with a new generation of reactors, for which four preliminary designs are in circulation. None have been brought to the construction phase. Robert Pollard, a former N.R.C. official now working for the Union of Concerned Scientists, says nothing firm will be ready for licensing for three to five years. At least five years of construction would follow, probably more. So even under optimum industry conditions, no new-generation plants are likely to open in this century.

But the industry is desperate to get one ordered, and that's where Turkey Point comes in. The reactor makers have named Florida as a prime state to get a new plant built. Florida Power & Light is supportive, and Florida Senator Bob Graham, who chairs the Senate Subcommittee on Nuclear Regulation, is generally in favor of nuclear power. Michael Wilson, former chair of the Florida Public Service Commission, has publicly invited the industry into the Sunshine State, where former Governor Bob Martinez, who appointed Wilson, slashed funding for solar-energy research.

Many Floridians believe, however, that Turkey Point is aptly named. Its two reactors are shut at least until November to install emergency diesel backup generators. Local activists charge the money could be better spent on solar alternatives, and they may sue. As Joette Lorion, director of the Center for Nuclear Responsibility, says, "Both of the pressure vessels that surround the reactor cores are severely embrittled due to radiation damage, which makes them susceptible to meltdown."

A bitter battle over Turkey Point would almost certainly dampen the ardor of Florida Power & Light or any Wall Street backers for a new reactor in Florida. Attention might then focus on the Tennessee Valley Authority or North Carolina's Duke Power, both of which have ardently pronuclear C.E.O.s. The T.V.A.'s Marvin Runyon has already threatened to restart construction on six mothballed reactors.

But both areas also present problems. "If they're scared out of Florida the industry's going to have its work cut out for it anywhere else," says Mariotte. "It's easy to buy print ads and win votes in Congress. Actually getting these plants built is a whole other story."

That's where the D.O.E.—and atomic weapons—could come in. Throughout the 1980s, while global debate raged over the potential for an East-West nuclear conflagration, the actual machinery for building nuclear bombs slipped into disrepair. From the swamps of South Carolina's Savannah River complex to the deserts of the huge Hanford site along the Columbia River in Washington, from Fernald near Cincinnati to Rocky Flats outside Denver, the seventeen U.S. warhead production facilities have degenerated and are approaching collapse. Radioactive emissions have exceeded even lax D.O.E. standards, with lethal impact downwind.

A spate of damaging news coverage about the health problems of people living downwind from the plants has helped force the D.O.E. to reconsider how it builds bombs. When Watkins took over, his staff estimated the cost of cleaning up the warhead production sites at roughly $60 billion. Last year a Government Accounting Office study put the figure at $125 billion to $155 billion. In March the Office of Technology Assessment estimated that the cost could go as high as $155 billion.

In the meantime, the D.O.E.'s ability to maintain its atomic arsenal has come into question. The military has admitted to being "awash in plutonium," with enough stockpiled and available from obsolete warheads to maintain the arsenal for decades. Tritium, however, is another story. A key element in advanced warhead design, the radioactive gas decays quickly enough to require a constant supply. Arms-control advocates have suggested allowing the arsenal to decay automatically along with the tritium, which would yield a decline of about 5 percent per year in available megatonnage. The D.O.E. doesn't like the idea and wants to build at least one new tritium production reactor, most likely at Savannah River.

With its New Production Reactor as the centerpiece, the D.O.E. has presented an overhaul plan it euphemistically terms "reconfiguration." The idea, it says, is to create a weapons-production complex "which is smaller, less diverse, and less expensive to operate." New equipment would be brought on line at five or six key facilities, with the rest being abandoned. The process would begin around 1996, end "well before" the year 2015 and cost in the range of $6.7 billion to $15.2 billion. The result, say weapons planners, would be an infrastructure capable of maintaining a downsized supply of warheads at a level between 15 percent and 70 percent of the current 20,000, depending on arms-reduction negotiations.

The proposal has aroused widespread fears that if sites like Fernald and Hanford are taken out of production, the D.O.E. will also abandon its cleanup plans. Degradation of the industry as a whole could have an impact; the D.O.E. is already complaining of a shortage of qualified personnel to staff the cleanup effort. The problem is particularly critical at Hanford, which continues to be mentioned as a potential national repository for radioactive waste. Within the next year alone, for example, as many as thirty retired submarine reactors may be headed toward burial there.

Indeed, the tendency merely to walk away from abandoned production sites and turn them into dumps will be hard to resist. But the D.O.E. may also use reconfiguration as a cover to save the commercial reactor industry, using national security as a pretext for developing a new generation of prototype reactors. The department has already floated the idea of using an advanced reactor to power the Portsmouth, Ohio, enrichment facility, which currently uses as much electricity as Cleveland.

In any case, hundreds of millions of dollars have already been spent preparing for the New Production Reactor. The 1992 D.O.E. request for it is $550 million, and the design is due to be chosen by December 31, 1991, with the betting strong on a high-temperature, gas-cooled model, usable as a prototype for a new line of power plants.

But, as always, politics will determine the choice of sites. "Grass-roots opposition at the weapons-production sites has had an enormous impact on D.O.E. planning," says Robert Alvarez, a staff member for Senator John Glenn's Committee on Government Affairs. "Watkins sees those letters from the people living around the plants, and they are taken very seriously." Thus the Savannah River plant in conservative South Carolina is not only the likeliest target for the New Production Reactor but will probably be the center for the entire future of nuclear-warhead production.

And the fates of both nuclear power and warheads, of the new generation of reactors and of reconfiguration, have never been more vitally intertwined. With both industries at life-or-death turning points, we can expect the mass media to churn out even more hype about the need to keep our atomic power plants and our nuclear warheads ever at the ready.

But the ecological and economic costs have also never been more obvious. For one thing, despite resistance from the Reagan and Bush administrations, which cut the D.O.E.'s solar research budget from $770 million in 1980 to $219 million in 1992, renewable energy has made several major breakthroughs in the past several years. Photovoltaic cells, which convert sunlight directly to electric current, and which could decentralize most of our electric supply, are coming closer to mass application. And a large-scale solar thermal facility northeast of Los Angeles has come on line, producing electricity at 8 cents per kilowatt-hour with 95 percent reliability, a record far exceeding anything the nuclear industry can offer. Windmills at Altamont and two other major California sites now generate enough electricity to power San Francisco at 5 cents per kilowatt-hour, well under half the cost of new nuclear capacity. Experts on North American wind patterns conservatively estimate that within the next two or three decades the United States could derive 20 percent of its electric supply from wind—as much as we now get from atomic reactors. With both wind and solar thermal technology, capital costs and time frames for new capacity are less than half of even best-case scenarios accompanying new-generation reactors. Major advances in energy efficiency could do even more.

The case for nuclear power has also suffered a new setback in Japan. There, in the midst of a massive push for more plants, mechanical failure and operator error resulted in a flooded steam generator and a serious radiation release, followed by the inevitable cover-up and scandal.

In the United States, the fight continues to rage over both power reactors and weapons production at far-flung sites like Turkey Point and Rocky Flats. Ultimately the reverberations from those battles find their way to Congress, the White House and the national media. For the next few years, it will be the ground war in places like the swamps of South Carolina and south Florida, the hills of Tennessee and the flatlands east of the Rockies that will determine the fate of nuclear power and weapons. Whatever the result, the fallout will be with us all for a long time to come. □

Richard Miniter analyzes the impact of the gulf war on oil prices, noting that most of the pundits proved wrong in their predictions that the conflict would send oil prices through the roof. True, oil prices increased in anticipation of the war, but plummeted with the success of the air war. Although oil industry spokesmen forecast significant price increases, they, too, proved to be wrong. The price of gasoline did rise—on average of twenty-five cents per gallon—but the oil shock turned out to be relatively painless, as few consumers had to wait in long lines and most service stations did not run out of gas. Interestingly, some policy experts raised a 1970s shibboleth when they revived the argument of "energy security"—meaning, that it might be in the interests of the United States to review its commitment to Israel and grant some foreign policy concessions to the oil kingdoms. The logic of this argument escapes the author, who contends that OPEC is far more responsive to markets than to politics. If rationality prevails, the gulf states will refrain from using their oil weapon. If not, it is pointless to sacrifice America's foreign policy interests in the hope of future oil deliveries.

After the War

THE OIL SHORTAGE THAT WASN'T

True or false: The Arabs hold
Western foreign policy hostage
to our need for oil.
False—unless we make it so.

RICHARD MINITER

FOUR MONTHS ago, nearly everyone expected that if fighting began in the Persian Gulf oil prices would go through the roof. As the January 15 deadline approached, the price of oil climbed in step with mounting fears of an impending oil shortage. On the first business day of 1991 oil was $28.44 per barrel. When the New York Mercantile Exchange closed on January 16—just hours before the bombs started falling—oil prices had hit $32 per barrel. But the first casualty of war turned out to be high oil prices: when

Mr. Miniter is an environmental-policy analyst at the Competitive Enterprise Institute in Washington, D.C.

U.S. commodity markets opened the next day, the price of oil had fallen a sharp $10.56, to $21.44 per barrel—just about where it had been on August 1 of last year ($21.54). The price of oil plummeted when traders realized that the air war was going well and that oil stocks in industrial countries were at record levels.

That was the last thing the pundits had expected. "Failing a last-minute Mideast miracle, higher gasoline prices over the next few days look like a sure bet," the *Wall Street Journal* worried on January 16. "Prices will definitely go up," Bill Ligon, manager of the Texas Service Station Association, told the *Journal*. Though the price appears stable, a significant

threat to oil supplies "will wake up the market pronto," said Cheryl J. Trench, executive vice president of Petroleum Industry Research Foundation.

It was not surprising that people believed these predictions. The dramatic increases in gas prices after Iraq invaded Kuwait had made a deep impression on many Americans, and they expected a similiar price rise when warplanes filled the skies of Iraq.

Prices in Perspective

THE AUGUST price rise should be put in perspective, however. Gas prices were set to rise *before* Iraq invaded Kuwait. OPEC had reached an agreement in late July to

From *National Review*, April 15, 1991, pp. 36-38. © 1991 by National Review Inc., 150 East 35th Street, New York, NY 10016. Reprinted by permission.

raise the price of crude oil some 40 per cent. If hostilities had not begun, industry analysts calculated, the price of gasoline, heating oil, and other petroleum products would have gone up by 10 cents per gallon anyway.

It was the embargo on Kuwaiti and Iraqi crude oil that set off the sharper price rise. The embargo dislocated about four million barrels of oil per day and was the greatest oil shock to America since the 1956 Suez crisis. The U.S. lost only 1.6 million barrels per day during the 1973–74 Arab oil embargo, and 3.7 million barrels during the Iranian crisis in 1979.

What's remarkable is how relatively painless this current oil shock was. True, gasoline prices increased by an average of 25 cents per gallon, but most consumers did not have to wait in long lines, and most service stations did not run out of gas. The reason is that this time we did not have an "energy policy."

Still, one relic of the 1970s did come back to haunt us. Some policy-makers began again to talk about "energy security," meaning foreign-policy concessions to oil kingdoms. In the 1970s America was repeatedly pressured by "experts" to back away from its pro-Israel stance in order to "guarantee" its supply of oil. The influence of this factor can be found in the U.S. sale of F-15s and AWACS to the Saudis, the quiet toleration of Saudi interference with U.S. arms shipments to North Yemen, an anti-Egypt tilt during the Egyptian–Saudi rivalry, a somewhat pro-Arab tilt in the Arab–Israeli conflict, a pro-Iraq tilt during the Iran–Iraq war, and the current intervention in the Persian Gulf.

Would appeasing Arab interests in fact make U.S. oil imports stable? Hardly. Oil prices are stable because markets work and because what the Saudis really want is not short-run high prices but long-run price stability. This is because, as former Saudi oil minister Ahmed Zaki Yamani explained to his countrymen in 1981, "If we force Western countries to invest heavily in finding alternative sources of energy, they will. This would take no more than seven to ten years, and would result in reducing dependence on oil as a source of energy to a point which will jeopardize Saudi Arabia's interests."

This policy occasionally puts the Saudis at odds with their neighbors. Yamani made this clear in a recent *Time* interview. When asked about Iraq's oil strategy, Yamani responded: "I wonder if Iraq has a strategy. Saddam may only have temporary oil policies, depending on his large financial requirements."

Those who believe oil sheikhs are less interested in riches than in making political statements are deluding themselves; those who say that political concessions are necessary to keep oil prices low are simply trying to peddle an agenda which includes price controls at home and concessions to the PLO abroad. The strangest people echo this regulatory agenda. When asked recently what the U.S. should do, Yamani said: "Well, I think you should encourage exploration. You have to establish good relations with the producers and have a stable supply of oil for yourself and the Western alliance. You have to be more cautious about how to consume energy."

Why would Yamani urge Americans to seek non-Saudi sources and consume less oil? If his advice were taken seriously it would cost the Saudis billions. But Yamani knows how to reinforce the prejudices of Westerners. And he knows a plea for "good relations" and a "stable supply of oil" will subtly remind Americans of their interest in Saudi Arabia.

But while Yamani has consistently told the West what it wanted to hear, he has sung a very different tune at home. During the 1981 AWACS debate, Yamani told Leonard Silk of the *New York Times* that his country "has been moderate in [its] demands on the price of oil because Saudi Arabia desires military hardware from the United States." Yet at a press conference in his own land, Yamani said: "I see no connection between the OPEC price decision and the AWACS issue. . . . Certain OPEC [members] refused to lower their prices to reflect market realities."

Throughout the 1970s America repeatedly overpaid, with diplomatic concessions, for an already precious commodity. One "expert" pushing the political-concessions line was Walter Levy, who consistently made predic-

tions in the pages of *Foreign Affairs* which just did not pan out, such as: "Around the mid 1980s or early 1990s, when the specter of imminent oil shortages begins to haunt the world, the opportunities for large advances in the real price of oil are almost certain to become decisive."

Levy made this prediction while acknowledging that the price of oil fell 20 to 25 per cent in real terms from 1974 to 1978. He attributed this to "restraint exercised by Saudi Arabia with the support of Iran and a few other OPEC members." Levy argued that OPEC had allowed its profits to be trimmed by one-quarter out of the goodness of its heart.

Nor was Levy the only one who got it wrong. George W. Ball, a former U.S. under-secretary of state, has a history of urging closer ties with Arab oil producers and warning that catastrophe would come if his advice wasn't followed. In 1973, Ball worried that "the U.S. import bill for oil may be something like $18 billion by the early 1980s." He said this was "a very alarming figure," and that our import bill should be closer to $6 billion. By 1980, the U.S. import bill was over $100 billion—and the economy didn't collapse.

Ball told a roundtable discussion group in September 1973 that OPEC countries will earn more in oil profits than they could ever "need." By "almost any projection," Arab states will have "earnings far in excess of their absorptive capabilities." While Ball feared that all the oil kingdoms combined could spend no more than $40 billion a year, Saudi Arabia alone spent $200 billion on public projects between 1975 and 1980.

Despite a record of failed prophecies, Ball continued to push his view that political pressure must be applied to Israel to ensure a stable oil supply. "Unless we make prompt and serious progress toward solving the Palestinian problem, we can expect to see our energy needs increasingly held hostage to our Middle East policies," Ball wrote in 1980.

The Saudis' Little Gift

THE VIEW that political forces wholly controlled the price of oil led to some interesting opinions. It was widely reported in 1980, for example, that the Saudis increased oil production as an "Independence Day gift" to President Carter. The market explanation is less exciting, but built on solid evidence. Supply and demand drive oil prices; politics can only cause short-term price spikes. After both the 1974 and 1979 price increases, oil prices fell sharply in real terms. As a result of the twin price spikes in 1979, demand for OPEC oil fell and OPEC production had to fall with it, from a peak of 32 million barrels per day in 1979 to 24 million per day in 1981. As world demand continued to shrink, OPEC was forced to cut prices and squeeze profits.

During the war between Iran and Iraq, the oil production of those two nations was severely restricted. Yet this conflict did not touch off a supply shortfall or a price increase. Other oil producers, especially Saudi Arabia, took up the slack.

At least one of the warring nations feared that it would permanently lose market share. As early as 1981, Iran's oil minister, Mohammed Gharazi, threatened that even if the Islamic Republic "has to resort to force" to win back its share of OPEC production, it would, once the war with Iraq ended. History has a way of repeating itself in the Middle East: Iraq's dispute with Kuwait also involved OPEC production quotas, among other things.

Meanwhile oil-importing nations were working on the demand side of the equation. Oil that was used to make heat and steam could be cheaply replaced by burning coal and splitting atoms. France now meets about 80 per cent of its domestic electricity needs with nuclear power. (The U.S. failed to take full advantage of nuclear energy for political reasons.) While nuclear-power plants are large capital investments, once those costs are sunk the marginal cost of nuclear fuel is very low—currently corresponding to about $4 per barrel of oil.

More efficient cars also diminished demand for oil. In 1973 the average new car consumed 13 miles per gallon; by 1990 the figure was 27 miles per gallon. (Although that is not an unmitigated

good. Most cars become fuel misers by sloughing off weight, but lighter cars do not survive accidents as well as heavier cars.)

And yet some editorial boards still believe oil kingdoms are immune to market forces. A recent *Washington Post* editorial said: "Unlike the other leading oil-producing countries, Saudi Arabia, with its minimal domestic requirements and its enormous accumulated wealth, has wide discretion in deciding month to month how much to pump."

This theory of immunity to market forces led some Democrats, including Senate Majority Leader George Mitchell (D., Me.), to call for a return to the Carter "War on Energy Dependence." But that war produced only Pyrrhic victories. One battleground in those days was Beverly, Massachusetts. The high school there installed a solar-electric system in 1980 at a cost of $2 million, hoping to save $10,000 per year in electric bills. "This would have corresponded to break-even in two hundred years, but hopes of achieving it by the year 2280 were shattered two years ago when the contraption conked out," writes Petr Beckmann in a recent issue of *Access to Energy*.

When it became clear the Bush Administration was going to take pains to avoid the pitfalls of Carter's energy policy, not everyone was pleased. "Gone are the higher mileage requirements for gas-guzzling autos," wrote Tom Wicker in a recent *New York Times* column. "Gone are [new] federal regulations to impose energy conservation, any suggestion of government intervention in the sacrosanct private sector, all impolitic urgings toward consumer sacrifice." This echoes the common derision of Reagan's energy policy. "Oh, is there a U.S. energy policy?" Yamani said, neatly capturing the conventional wisdom. "I understand that your policy is no policy."

The policy-that-is-no-policy has been an unblemished success, however. Within the first year that Reagan removed oil-price controls and abolished over two hundred other energy regulations, oil consumption fell, oil prices fell in real terms, and domestic oil production increased for the first time in a decade. And the policy-that-is-no-policy produced no gas lines or fuel shortages. Even with the upheaval in the Gulf, American gas prices are now

less than 40 per cent in real terms of what they were in January 1981.

While the 1973 Arab oil embargo boosted oil prices, it was the national energy policy that created the other problems. Yamani is quick to point out that there was always "enough oil, a huge stock . . . The gas lines were not done by me."

The $40 a Barrel Question

ALL OF this raises the question: Can oil ever be used as a foreign-policy tool? Imagine that Saddam Hussein had become able to dictate Saudi oil policy. That would have given him control over some of the richest oil fields known to man. Saddam might then have expected to hold U.S. diplomacy hostage.

But don't bet on it. To inflict real economic damage, Hussein would have had to cut Saudi oil production by an amount greater than the unused production capacity of other nations—which is not easy or cheap. Meanwhile, other producers would have increased production to grab market share. During the recent embargo, world oil production from the North Sea and Venezuela increased to meet the demand. Revenues from the Saudi oil fields would have dropped by somewhere between $50 and $100 million a *day*. By contrast, the Saudis give about $70 million a *year* to the PLO and about $200 million a *year* to Syria.

Nor would Saddam Hussein have been in control of a majority of the world's oil. Even if Iraq had come to control the entire Arabian peninsula, Saddam would have had a little less than 22 per cent of the non-Communist world's oil supply.

Finally, the hope that the United States would have conceded, once the oil weapon was wheeled into battle, is faint. During the 1974 Arab embargo the United States did not yield to OPEC's demands. In fact, once the Saudis realized the December 1973 price increases would stick, they increased production for every month of the first quarter of 1974—despite their threats to cut production each month until Israel retreated from the occupied territories.

In short, if the Gulf states are rational they will not try to use the oil weapon, and if they become irrational, it is pointless to exchange political gifts for oil deliveries.

Despite the evidence, many policymakers refuse to learn the lessons of the 1970s. When the Carter Administration was repeatedly reaching out to Arabs and trying to "solve the Palestinian problem," no easing of oil prices occurred. The Reagan Administration was firm in its commitment to Israel, and oil prices fell. The moral of the story is not that closer ties with Israel create oil gluts, but rather that OPEC is more responsive to markets than to politics. □

Chapter **27**

Human Rights and Democratic Rule

Article 27.1.   Movements Toward Democracy: A Global Revolution

According to Dankwart A. Rustow, a democratic revolution is sweeping the world, leading the author to look for patterns in the changes that are occurring. In the process, he identifies four main factors that explain efforts to replace oppressive rule with popular government. First, totalitarianism, by its very nature, denies the kind of choice and orderly change that allows for the resolution of conflict, as witnessed by recent events in the USSR. Second, immediate circumstances, like illness, old age, or death of dictators, are responsible for toppling authoritarian regimes, as was the case in Portugal (1968-76), Tunisia (1987), and Paraguay (1989). Third, lost wars are notable in the demise of many dictatorial, particularly military, regimes—for example, Argentina's loss of the Falkland Islands/Malvinas war in 1982, which led to the ouster of the Argentine military dictatorship the following year. Fourth, economic incentives have played a prominent role in many of the recent changes. For instance, F.W. de Klerk moved to dismantle apartheid in direct response to the economic hardships imposed on South Africa by the international community. In Rustow's view, the world is safer today for democracy than at any time in previous history. The Soviet Empire has gone the way of the dinosaur, and so too will the few remaining communist and Third World dictatorships which, today, find themselves on the wrong side of history.

MOVEMENTS TOWARD DEMOCRACY
A GLOBAL REVOLUTION
DANKWART A. RUSTOW

Mr. Rustow is Distinguished Professor of Political Science at the City University of New York. From "Democracy: A Global Revolution?" by Dankwart A. Rustow, Foreign Affairs, Fall 1990, pages 75–91:

A tide of democratic change is sweeping the world, not only in the once-monolithic communist regions but also in a wave that started in Mediterranean Europe in the mid-1970s and spread to Latin America, Asia, Africa and, even, South Africa.

Remarkably, the current demise of communism and the movement toward democracy have come not in the aftermath of destructive war but in an unprecedented half-century of global peace. Indeed they come at a time when the Cold War has ended, regional conflicts from Central America to Southeast Asia have abated, and Europe, the very powder keg of global wars from the late eighteenth to the mid-twentieth centuries, has moved into a historic process of economic and political unification.

Why is all this happening? Why have communist and Third World dictatorships embarked upon their various moves toward democracy?

Factors specific to each country are obvious:

an ailing or aging dictator in Lisbon or East Berlin, economic setbacks in Brazil and economic successes in South Korea, Catholic priests providing safety for regime opponents in El Salvador and Poland, the insistence of a Soviet leader on fundamental restructuring at home and abroad. Taken separately, such stimuli for change toward democracy might seem no more than fortunate happenstances. Is there a broader pattern?

Looking back, three times in modern history the world has seen efforts to replace oppressive rule with popular government. The American War of Independence, followed by the French Revolution, set off proclamations of free republics in Europe and across Latin America; but then came Napoleon's military dictatorship, traditional monarchies were restored, and the new states of Latin America soon succumbed to *caudillismo* or other forms of feudal or military rule.

A century later, Woodrow Wilson sought to make the world safe for democracy; the empires of Russia, Germany, Austria-Hungary and Ottoman Turkey fell, but again the gains for nascent democracy in the successor states proved precarious.

The Allied victory in the Second World War removed the threats of Nazi tyranny and Japanese military conquest. American occupation policies in West Germany and Japan made a major contribution to the global spread of democracy. Colonies of European powers in Asia and Africa moved toward independence, but few of them developed any democratic traditions. Indigenous revolutions in China (1949) and the Third World (Vietnam, 1954; Cuba, 1959; Ethiopia, Angola and Mozambique, 1975; Nicaragua, 1979) seemed to elevate communism into a global alternative to democracy. And in response, the West's Cold War policies encouraged the buildup of military establishments from Turkey to the Philippines and South Korea.

A search for patterns in the recent transitions toward democracy may help suggest what is to be done this time to improve the chances for nurturing and sustaining democratic change.

PATTERNS OF TRANSITION

Democracy is a process of choice and orderly change that allows for resolution of the very dilemmas that have proved fatal to numerous dictatorships.

President Mikhail Gorbachev's commitment to glasnost and perestroika and his rejection of the Brezhnev Doctrine of military intervention in Eastern Europe were clearly motivated by his calculation that the Soviet Union could not continue to carry the triple burden of (a) being a leading superpower in military and space

technology, (b) presenting communism as a worldwide option by subsidizing wars throughout the Third World and continuing its own unwinnable war in Afghanistan, and (c) satisfying the expectations of its own people for better standards of living.

Elsewhere the immediate circumstances that toppled authoritarian regimes in recent years have varied widely, though even the specific factors in various countries make a pattern of sorts. As a dictatorship becomes more centralized and personal, the government becomes increasingly repressive, important information often fails to reach top officials, and alternatives for orderly succession become scarcer. Illness, old age or death of dictators thus were a major factor in the transformation of Portugal (1968–76), Tunisia (1987) and Paraguay (1989). The approaching senility of Erich Honecker hastened the demise of communism in East Germany, and the fact that Deng Xiaoping and most of his inner circle are in their seventies or eighties reinforces the expectation of further changes in China.

Lost wars have been another notable factor in the demise of many dictatorial, particularly military, regimes. Portugal's dictatorship was undermined by its inability to put down the anticolonial rebellions in Angola and Mozambique. In Greece the junta's plans to depose President Makarios of Cyprus by military coup provoked the Turkish invasion of the island and the fall of the junta in Athens (1974). The loss of the Falkland Islands/Malvinas war in 1982 led directly to the exit of the Argentine military dictatorship the following year.

Economic incentives have played an important role in many of the recent changes. The South African government of F. W. de Klerk moved to reconsider the apartheid policy in response to the growing hardships imposed by years of international economic sanctions. Conversely, Gorbachev and Deng each sought different ways to overcome decades of self-imposed isolation. The Soviet Union had more than held its own in the post-World War II competition in military and space technology; but communist countries had excluded themselves from most of the world's civilian markets, from efforts to satisfy expanding consumer needs, and from the international pattern of migration.

This policy of self-exclusion, symbolized by early decisions such as the refusal of East European countries to participate in the Marshall Plan and the building of the Berlin Wall, committed communist regimes to a sequel of undesirable choices. East Germany could stop the postwar mass exodus to the West, but could not prevent West German signals from being readily received on East German television screens. The resulting constant comparison of life-styles and economic levels forced the East Berlin government to be more repressive than other communist regimes, and increased the outflow of East German migrants as soon as neighboring communist nations relaxed their controls. For a brief period in 1989 a desperate East Germany even banned the import of Soviet newspapers, only to find a steady stream of copies of *Pravda* and *Izvestia* smuggled in from West Berlin.

Beijing found it difficult to be selective in the kinds of foreign contacts it wished to maintain. The Deng regime after 1979 had abandoned China's earlier policy of total isolation so as to catch up with Western advances in science and technology, but found to its dismay that students sent abroad to study computer engineering returned home to erect a statue of the "Goddess of Democracy" in Tiananmen Square.

TRANSFERRED BURDENS

Poland's communist regime under General Wojciech Jaruzelski, facing recurrent labor unrest and a high burden of international debt, had to choose between heavier repression or concessions to the opposition, and in the end preferred to shift the burden of responsibility for economic reform to Solidarity. Similarly, a cynical interpretation of the shift from military to civilian government in Latin American countries such as Brazil would suggest that the generals were content to run up astronomical foreign debts and let civilian successors worry about repayment.

In their economic performance, Third World dictatorships seem to be caught in a catch-22. If the economy declines under heavy burdens of rising prices, unemployment or foreign debt, the rulers will face growing opposition or violent unrest. If the economy expands with a thriving middle class and growing export sector, pressure mounts for political liberalization and change of regime. Thus the booming economy of South Korea under Park Chung Hee and Chun Doo Hwan gave rise to ever more insistent demonstrations for democracy. Chile's military ruler Augusto Pinochet, after presiding over a decade of relative prosperity, sought to strengthen and prolong his regime by allowing more leeway for opposition, only to see his presidential candidate overwhelmingly defeated in the free election of November 1989. In contrast, Taiwan under the successors to Chiang Kai-shek was one of the rare authoritarian regimes that avoided such upheavals by phasing in a steady program of political liberalization and, in December 1989, winning a solid legislative majority in free elections.

A major factor in hastening the transitions to democracy in the Mediterranean countries in the 1970s and 1980s was their desire to share in the higher living standards of the European Community, whose membership is open only to democracies. Additionally, the capitalist democracies controlled the international financial institutions, such as the International Monetary Fund and the World Bank, whose preference for lending to countries with more liberal regimes added to the human rights pressures of U.S. foreign policy since President Carter and of such organizations as Helsinki Watch and Amnesty International.

The Roman Catholic Church in Latin America and in countries such as the Philippines, Poland and Czechoslovakia has evolved into a consistent factor in favor of democracy. Totalitarian regimes typically suppress all secular associations not controlled by their own parties, but prove unwilling or unable to extend that same policy to religious organizations. Thus, churches can serve as privileged meeting places, priests can form a network of opposition information, and visits by the pope to South America or Eastern Europe can help to crystallize anti-regime sentiment.

International sports events have made an incidental contribution to this growing democratic climate. During a 1985 hockey game between the United States and the Soviet Union in Prague, the Czech audience expressed its preference by shouting "Go! Go! U.S.A. Go! Go! U.S.A." And a major consideration that prevented the South Korean military regime from suppressing the growing opposition movement in 1987 was the Seoul Olympics scheduled for the following year.

COMMUNICATIONS AND ECONOMICS

The most powerful impetus to change in this era has been the global trend of intensifying communication and economic integration. Whereas democracies have thrived amid this flood of messages and goods, dictatorships had difficulty isolating themselves from it. In the past half century, the portion of the world's agricultural and industrial production traded across frontiers has grown at a steady and cumulative rate. Travel, communication and commerce have advanced from railroads and steamships to supersonic airplanes; from typewriters to computers, satellite television and fax machines; from local stock exchanges to global electronic trading of stocks and commodity futures. And whenever regulatory restrictions were maintained, competition from less regulated economic locations—from ship registries in Panama and Liberia to banking in Switzerland or the Cayman Islands and stock trading in Hong Kong—has added to the pressure for liberalization and global integration.

In this novel setting an economic measure such as the Organization of Petroleum Exporting Countries' tripling or quadrupling of world oil prices in 1973–74 and again in 1979 had instant global repercussions; the availability of money deposits from OPEC for global lending by Western banks further aggravated the debt crisis in the Third World. Another side effect of the economic revolution of the late twentieth century has been the steady pattern of migration of workers from poorer to richer countries, such as from the Mediterranean to Western Europe, from the Caribbean to North America, and from Egypt to Kuwait and Saudi Arabia.

PROMISES OF DEMOCRACY

Whatever the impetus for political change in Warsaw, Beijing or Santiago, there was little doubt about its direction. Neither communist nor military regimes managed to hold out any viable ideological alternative. Democratic constitutions have long been accepted globally—at least on paper; democracy was a major theme in the official pronouncements of both communist and military dictatorships. Third World juntas commonly have claimed to be offering temporary emergency regimes that will restore full democracy after overcoming the effects of economic crisis or political instability. Communism has presented itself as the ultimate version of democracy, purged of its bourgeois defects of class exploitation and nationality conflict; Third World communist regimes, with tautological insistence, called themselves "people's democracies." The worldwide revolution of technology, communications and travel therefore not only spread the awareness of democratic life-styles, but also helped expose this hypocrisy of "democracy" in communist and Third World countries. Thus, when communist regimes started tottering, four decades of their own Cold War propaganda left little doubt in the minds of the citizenry that capitalism and democracy were the logical alternative.

Authoritarian rulers often adopt limited moves toward liberalization so as to appease the opposition or strengthen the support for their own regimes, only to find that they have set off a process of change that cannot be halted. As soon as there is margin for disagreement, some leaders of the government's own party are sure to stake their political futures on criticism and further liberalization. And once such disagreements have arisen among the regime's military commanders, any reversion to a policy of repression may be difficult or impossible.

In South Korea the government of Chun Doo Hwan had long resisted the opposition's demand for direct presidential elections. But by mid-1987 Roh Tae Woo, whom Chun had designated as leader of his Democratic Justice Party, conceded that opposition demand—and Roh proceeded to win the first direct election later that year because of an unforeseen split between the two major opposition leaders.

Once the government offers its citizens half-free elections with a limited choice of candidates, the ensuing election campaign is sure to expand the previous agenda of public debate. Once the press is allowed even minimal freedom to report and compete for readership, enterprising journalists are sure to explore any latent issues of popular discontent and weak spots of government performance.

In Turkey the military had seized power in 1980 after years of parliamentary deadlock and mounting terrorism, but promised to restore democracy as soon as feasible. Their own plan of banning former politicians and sponsoring new government and opposition parties soon went awry, as Turkish voters opted for a third party, and former politicians went on "nonpolitical" speaking tours. By 1989 Turkey had returned to full democracy with a lively free press, intense partisan debate and maneuvering, but little of the political violence of the 1970s.

It was a division within the military that led to the downfall of Ferdinand Marcos' dictatorship in the Philippines (1965–86). Appeals from Jaime Cardinal Sin, mass defections from the pro-Marcos military forces, and the U.S. offer of exile for Marcos and his entourage secured Corazon Aquino's succession.

In suppressing the June 1989 demonstrations in Tiananmen Square, the Chinese hard-liners had to rely on army units from remote parts of the country. A similar dilemma of military indiscipline might be faced in the Soviet Union if Gorbachev or a hard-line successor were to attempt to repress the forces unleashed by glasnost and the growing assertions of separatism.

THE POLITICAL CONSEQUENCES OF REVOLUTION

In assessing the prospects ahead, it is essential to note that the demise of an authoritarian or totalitarian regime in no way guarantees the instant advent of democracy. Russia's revolutionaries of February 1917 sought to replace tsarist autocracy with constitutional government, and soon found themselves under Leninist party dictatorship.

In more recent times, there have been bitter reminders that the outcome of the global democratic revolution remains far from assured: the victory of fundamentalism following the 1979 downfall of Iran's shah; the cruel repression of prodemocracy demonstrations in Beijing; growing unrest in the Soviet Union; and the many earlier failures of democratization in Latin America. In Romania the less-than-free elections of May 1990 merely replaced one communist regime with another under a different name, inaugurating a new phase of violent confrontation. In Latin America newly elected governments are grappling with the deep-seated economic problems that have confounded military and civilian governments before them.

Recent events thus pose, with renewed urgency, the questions that political philosophers and social scientists have addressed since Rousseau and de Tocqueville: "What conditions make democracy possible and what conditions make it thrive?" Indeed the recent global wave of transitions or attempted transitions to democracy amount to a unique laboratory experiment to test any hypothesis suggested by the historical growth of democracy in Western countries and earlier attempts at transition in the Third World.

NATIONAL IDENTITY One such hypothesis is that an unquestioned sense of national and territorial identity is a highly favorable precondition. Democracy means government by the people; but, as a British political scientist observed, "the people cannot decide until somebody decides who are the people." History shows that such decisions have commonly been imposed by force or devised by diplomacy, and confirmed by the evolution of governmental institutions and social relationships within those borders.

In most of northern and western Europe, national boundaries were established in the monarchic wars of the thirteenth through the seventeenth centuries, and within those boundaries political regimes were gradually broadened from monarchic to aristocratic to democratic. By contrast Italy and Germany did not resolve their problems of territorial identity until the mid-nineteenth century—and their attempts at parliamentary democracy quickly succumbed to fascism.

The peaceful democratic evolution in countries such as Australia and New Zealand benefited from their insular boundaries, and also the aspirations for freedom and equality of their lower-class immigrant populations. Israel had undergone a similar, but far from rapid, development within its 1948 boundaries; but when that earlier territorial identity was thrown into question by the occupation of the West Bank, Gaza and East Jerusalem after 1967, disagreements and deadlock within the Jewish population, and martial law and violent unrest in the occupied Palestinian territories, severely hampered that earlier democratic evolution. By forcing two nations to coexist in violent conflict, the post-1967 de facto borders have prevented any wholesome democratic evolution for Israelis and Palestinians alike.

While territorial identity and national homogeneity clearly are favorable preconditions for democracy, there are exceptional countries, such as Belgium, the Netherlands, Switzerland, Canada, India and Singapore, where democracy has evolved despite profound linguistic or religious divisions. The key factor in such countries typically has been a decentralization of many administrative functions, including education, to more homogeneous subunits—a pattern that Arend Lijphart has described as one of "consociational democracy." It is noteworthy that the de Klerk government has sent missions to Canada, the Netherlands and Belgium in order to study the possibility of adapting such institutions to South Africa in a post-apartheid era.

The colonial boundaries inherited by tropical Africa have created few states with linguistic unity or even linguistic majorities; and amid this scarcity of clear territorial-national identities it is no coincidence that Africa is the region where progress toward democracy has remained most precarious. Only in a few countries, such as Botswana and Nigeria (after the bitter experience of the civil war of 1967–70), has something resembling a "consociational" pattern been adopted.

ARAB DISUNITY The Arabic-speaking world in the postcolonial era found itself divided into more than 20 countries, from Morocco and Mauritania to Somalia and Oman—a circumstance that discouraged the development of democracy and instead fostered fantasies of wider unification under military leadership from Egypt's Gamal Abd al-Nasser to Libya's Muammar al-Qaddafi, Syria's Hafez al-Assad and Iraq's Saddam Hussein.

It would seem doubtful that ethnically divided countries such as the Soviet Union or Yugoslavia can proceed toward democratization until their problems of national identity are resolved. Recent guerrilla wars in countries such as the Philippines, Peru and Nicaragua, although often clad in ideology, have been largely based on ethnic differences. Even in Czechoslovakia, the recent communist demise gave rise to symbolic conflicts, such as the Slovaks' insistence on hyphenating "Czecho-Slovakia."

One of Gorbachev's most challenging tasks has been the need to conceive a more genuinely federal future for what otherwise is sure to become the "Soviet Disunion." Soviet Russia is the only colonial empire that survived the decolonization of the mid-twentieth century; as soon as glasnost and perestroika gave rise to free expression and genuine electoral alternatives, national conflict (as in the Transcaucasus and Central Asia) and secessionist aspirations (as in the Baltic states) came to the fore. Such nationality conflicts are aggravated by memories of the Stalinist policy of forced resettlement of entire ethnic groups—in glaring contrast to the official fiction of the Soviet Union

339

as a voluntary confederation of equal nationalities.

The end of decades of repression by totalitarian bureaucracies brings out accumulated political frustrations and economic hardships. There is a widely felt need for group action—amid a vacuum of social organization and experienced leadership. In the resulting restlessness and confusion, people take out their resentments on those who seem "different"; hence the most reliable identifications prove to be those within linguistic or ethnic groups.

In sum, the breakdown of totalitarianism creates an unexpected level of tension and conflict. As long as some of these conflicts concern the identity of the future decision-making units, democratic evolution will be severely hampered. Certainly conflicts continue in established democracies—indeed the very method of political decision-making by voting among rival candidates and parties puts a premium on expressing latent conflicts. But the democratic way is to settle those conflicts by discussion, and that process is facilitated when the citizens speak, literally, the same language.

THE PROBLEM OF DEMOCRATIC EXPERIENCES

In the typical Western country it was the growing strength of the lower classes in the wake of the Industrial Revolution that forced the ultimate transfer of power from oligarchic to democratic regimes. In Western Europe in the nineteenth century (and indeed in England in 1640–88 and in the United States in the Jacksonian and Civil War periods) the major choice was between achieving broader political participation by peaceful compromise or by violent upheavals. Either way, the process was one of gradual evolution: universal and equal suffrage (even for males) was not achieved in most Western countries until the late nineteenth or early twentieth centuries.

The typical Western country thus went through a three-phase process of democratization: a preparatory phase of organization of competing parties amid deep-seated and unresolved class conflict; a decision phase when major compromises on political participation and procedures were adopted; and a habituation phase when politicians and citizens at large came to accept these procedures.

In contrast to this phased, if mostly unplanned, historical process in the West, recent developments in Eastern Europe have reversed the preparatory and decision phases. There is unquestioned agreement, at least in the abstract, that democracy must be the government of the future, but no prolonged experience of struggle and compromise to prepare for effective democratic decision-making. The very experience of seeing regimes such as Latin American military dictatorships and now East European communism come and go is likely to beget cynicism and hence a lack of positive involvement. If to this is added economic hardship—due to drastic anti-inflationary measures in Latin America or fast-track transitions to capitalism in Eastern Europe—cynicism may become tinged with despair.

Whereas most Latin American countries have had earlier experience with democratic government, more than forty years of communism in Eastern Europe and over seventy years in the Soviet Union have left a complete vacuum of relevant experience in the conduct of organized, competitive politics. In 1989 a Solidarity leader in the newly elected Polish parliament reported, "When we introduced the idea of discipline, everybody said no, that's the old communist system." And when Solidarity leader Lech Walesa, in preparation for his own presidential candidacy in mid-1990, stated, "Poland needs a president with an axe in his hand, a tough determined man, set in his ways," one of his critics noted sarcastically that axes seem more appropriate for woodcutters than political leaders.

In East Germany the postcommunist vacuum was filled, at least temporarily, by an inrush of West German politicians and organizations; West Germans (including native East Germans returning from decades in the West) will clearly have a continuing role in building the necessary political and economic infrastructure in the eastern parts of the country. Poland, whatever the current altercations, is fortunate to have the experience of the Solidarity trade union as a political network that survived a decade of illegality and persecution. Hungary may benefit from its period of economic decentralization under the post-1956 communist regime. Czechoslovakia has a tradition of 20 years of successful democracy (1918–38) to draw upon—although few of today's Czech and Slovak adults have more than childhood memories of that period. By contrast, there are few such resources to be drawn upon in Romania, Bulgaria or Albania.

The most urgent political need throughout the newly proclaimed East European democracies clearly is for dismantling the communist apparatus of centralized control and replacing it with a nonpartisan bureaucracy and stable, competing party organizations. Equally daunting are the tasks of alleviating the long-standing economic frustrations of the populace, privatizing the economy in the absence of any recent patterns of private ownership, and developing a new system of social benefits along the West European or Swedish socialist models.

PAST EXPERIENCE

For new democracies in the Third World, the priority task is to establish civilian control over the armed forces. Throughout the Third World, there has been a glaring discrepancy between the armed forces' function of external defense and their domestic political activity. Aside from Argentina's abortive 1982 attack, which led to the Falkland Islands/Malvinas war, Latin American military forces have fought no external wars since the War of the Pacific (Chile, Bolivia, Peru) of 1879–84 and the Chaco War (Paraguay, Bolivia) of 1932–35. Similarly the massive flow of arms into the Middle East has produced few international effects but a prolonged Arab-Israeli stalemate; the destruction of Lebanon; and, after eight years of war and perhaps a million casualties, a shift in the de facto Iraq-Iran border by a few miles or yards here and there.

On the domestic scene, however, arms have been available throughout the Third World to overthrow elected civilian regimes or to fight bloody and inconclusive guerrilla wars against fellow citizens. By the 1970s military coups had displaced civilian governments in a majority of the countries of the Asian periphery, the Middle East, Africa and Latin America. And, of course, what drew the soldiers into the political arena was not their own strength but rather the weakness of the political system. As Hobbes observed in the aftermath of Britain's seventeenth-century civil war, to hold political authority is "to trump in card-playing, save that in matter of government, when nothing else is turned up, clubs are trump."

COSTA
RICA
By the late 1980s, most Third World military regimes had yielded to elected civilians, and regional conflicts and civil wars were on the verge of settlement. Third World leaders, Latin Americans in particular, thus might wish to look closely at the courageous example of Costa Rica, which in 1949 abolished its army, and where economic and educational achievements far outrank those of its Central American neighbors.

Similarly the superpowers and other developed countries might make a signal contribution to world democracy by agreeing to phase out their arms exports to the Third World and converting their present arms industries to producing machinery needed for economic development in the new democracies. But since arms exports to the Third World are a highly competitive business, their conversion to civilian uses obviously should be coordinated not only between the Soviet Union and the United States, but also among other major arms-exporting countries such as France, Britain, West Germany and, perhaps, China, Brazil and Israel.

In countries such as Mexico, Brazil, Nigeria and the Philippines prolonged military or one-party rule has engendered a pattern of patronage and corruption throughout the economy— aggravated in countries such as Colombia by the de facto military enclaves established by drug lords. Third World countries that have moved from military or authoritarian rule to democracy, in addition to establishing civilian control over the military and developing a democratic party system, thus must put an end to endemic government corruption and (in countries such as Argentina) save their currency from four-digit inflation.

The weakness of the political party structure in some Latin American countries is in part due to the fact that right-wing economic groups did not seriously support democratic parties, knowing that if the left needed to be counteracted they could rely on the military to mount another coup. Recently, however, there are some indications that after years of economic mismanagement by military establishments, businessmen in countries like Brazil and Uruguay, and perhaps Argentina and Peru, may be ready to involve themselves more seriously in democratic politics.

In building up their civilian democratic institutions, countries of Eastern Europe and the Third World will have to choose carefully among alternative constitutional and electoral systems. Centralized government may facilitate sweeping economic and political reforms, but carefully devised federal structures may alleviate ethnic and regional tensions. Presidential government brings with it the dangers of demagogic election campaigns and weak party organizations; it needs to be carefully balanced with such institutions as federalism and judicial independence. Parliamentary government, on the other hand, can strengthen party responsibility, but it crucially depends on a respected and politically neutral head of state and a workable party system.

Among the major voting patterns, the Anglo-American system of plurality elections in single-member districts tends to foster stable two-party systems, but risks creating permanent regional minorities. By contrast, proportional representation of party lists makes for a proliferation of parties and recurrent parliamentary deadlocks, which threatened democracy in Weimar Germany in the 1920s and in Turkey in the 1970s, and paralyzed the political process in Greece and Israel in recent years.

INVESTMENT ADVICE

Since most new democracies of the late twentieth century were established in the wake of major economic failures by the preceding communist or military regimes, one of the first needs is for economic advice, investment and aid, for which there is a well-established (and by now hummingly busy) network, such as the International Monetary Fund and the World Bank, and private consultants. It would also be useful if some of the eminently successful newly industrialized countries such as South Korea, Taiwan and Singapore could provide similar advice. Of more direct political relevance are institutions such as the Konrad Adenauer and Friedrich Ebert foundations (affiliated respectively with West Germany's Christian and Social Democratic parties), which have been providing assistance for newly formed right- and left-of-center democratic parties in developing democracies. Following the June 1990 summit meeting in Washington and Camp David, White House Chief of Staff John Sununu agreed to travel to Moscow at President Gorbachev's request to provide expert advice on how to run a presidential office in a democracy. Generally the most useful service that the liberal democracies of Europe, the United States and Japan can provide to the world's struggling new democracies would seem to be the exchange of such technical information.

INTEGRATION

West European leaders, while proceeding with their own plans for closer economic and political integration, will also be engaged in growing economic and political contacts with Eastern Europe. And in the decades ahead an enlargement of the European Community to include other countries of Western and Eastern Europe (such as Sweden, Austria, Finland, Poland, Czechoslovakia, Hungary) as associate and eventually full members may be expected. This European example of economic and political union since the 1950s could serve as a model for Latin American countries in strengthening their processes of economic recovery and transition to democracy through regional cooperation and integration.

James Bryce wisely noted in 1921 that "one road only has in the past led into democracy, viz., the wish to be rid of tangible evils." Incipient democracies in former communist countries and the Third World must learn to deal forthrightly with their particular set of economic and political problems, and experienced liberal democracies should stand ready to provide needed advice.

What must be kept in mind in all these new contacts among private experts, government officials and international organizations is that democracy is a process of communication and an instrument of choice that offers alternative solutions to a given problem. Situations that confront rigid dictatorships with insoluble dilemmas thus allow democracies to show themselves at their best as mechanisms for change, specifically for orderly change among parties in power.

Thus democratic parties may have leaders subject to old age, illness or incompetence—but will be allowed to resolve such leadership crises while in opposition. Similarly, economic crises are bad for any government, democratic or dictatorial, but they give democratic voters an incentive to transfer power to the opposition. Thus the Great Depression replaced right-wing governments with the Labour Party in Britain, the Social Democrats in Sweden, and the Democrats and Roosevelt's New Deal in the United States. Democratic governments that take the country into a binge of uncontrolled inflation are likely to be defeated by an opposition party that promises sweeping reform.

Democracies not only can choose their governments, they also can learn from one another. And by helping to resolve the urgent economic and political problems of nascent democracies, the growing network of advice and technical assistance will further emphasize the global character of the current movement toward democracy.

Deng's China for the moment is still excluding itself from this worldwide movement toward liberal democracy. National rivalries and conflicts of secession in the "Soviet Disunion" may pose a major danger to regional peace. And in many of the newly proclaimed democracies of Eastern Europe and the Third World, the road ahead is bound to be arduous and bumpy in many places. But there are no current equivalents of Napoleon, Hitler or Stalin to challenge the democratic movement in the name of any alternative principle.

The world, in what promises to be more than a half-century of global peace, has become safer for democracy than it was in 1945, 1917 or at any previous time. And that global character—and the cumulative effects that may be expected to flow from it—are clearly the most important assets of the current democratic revolution.

In this article, the author examines the issue of human rights, arguing that in spite of legislation adopted in the 1970s committing the United States to consider human rights as a major factor in American foreign policy, it has only been applied at the discretion of the administration in power, or when Congress has been willing to bar aid to governments on a selective basis. For example, in the Carter years, the administration placed strong emphasis on human rights. During the Reagan and Bush administrations, however, the termination of aid usually only occurred as a result of congressional insistence. Overall, compliance with human rights laws has been at best sporadic. Although the Left has traditionally championed the cause of human rights, recent history suggests that the Left has often been hypocritical in its stance. For instance, instead of condemning the abuses of the Sandinistas in Nicaragua, the Left chose either to deny those abuses or compare them with other repressive regimes. Likewise, the Left has been equally reluctant to denounce abuses by Castro's government in Cuba, abuses by Black African governments, or abuses even by the Soviet government. Its failure to do so neither serves the human rights cause nor the Left. Principle demands that the Left condemn human rights abuses, whether they be committed by friends or enemies.

■ HUMAN RIGHTS AND POLITICS

A Matter of Principle

ARYEH NEIER

In principle, concern with human rights has no politics. Indeed, it could be said that politics—that is, efforts to advance one's own cause or the cause of one's allies, or to retard the cause of one's antagonists—is antithetical to concern for human rights. George Bush, Saddam Hussein, Yitzhak Shamir, Deng Xiaoping, Augusto Pinochet, Mobutu Sese Seko or anyone else would protest abuses of human rights against themselves or their friends. Similarly, they would denounce such abuses by their enemies. Yet, by itself, this hardly adds up to a commitment to human rights. Such a commitment also requires a readiness to oppose abuses when they are committed by one's allies or those with whom one sympathizes politically; and a willingness to defend human rights when the victims are one's enemies or political antagonists, or when denouncing abuses may play into the hands of one's political opponents.

That said, it must be acknowledged that most of the energy that has gone into the human rights movement worldwide and helped it to become a powerful force in world affairs is generated by politics. It is not that principled advocates of human rights do not matter. In defying state power in defense of human rights, an Andrei Sakharov, a Fang Lizhi, a Paulo Evaristo Cardinal Arns of Brazil or a Gibson Kamau Kuria of Kenya may have enormous impact. Yet it is also the case that those who are politically motivated will seize on the efforts of even

Aryeh Neier is executive director of Human Rights Watch and writes the "Watching Rights" column for The Nation.

From *The Nation*, April 22, 1991, pp. 519-522. *The Nation* magazine/The Nation Company, Inc., © 1991.

the most principled defenders of human rights for their own purposes. When Amnesty International published its recent report on Iraqi atrocities in Kuwait, for example, George Bush seemed to commit that report to memory and repeatedly cited Amnesty's findings in interviews. Yet Amnesty's reports on Iraq prior to August 2, 1990, and its reports on some nations in the military alliance against Iraq have had little impact for lack of a powerful political constituency eager to exploit those reports for its own political purposes.

Until the early 1980s, most of the political energy available to the human rights movement was supplied by the left. Although some organizations concerned with human rights internationally were founded long ago, and Amnesty International was established in 1961, it was only in the 1970s that the movement started to become a force, first in Europe and then in the United States. In this country, it drew most of its support at the outset from some of those on the left who had opposed the U.S. role in Vietnam and from those who were outraged at the U.S. part in the 1973 coup led by Pinochet against Salvador Allende in Chile. The abuses that characterized the Pinochet regime—extrajudicial executions, "disappearances," torture and political imprisonment—became the main focus of the human rights movement.*

As accounts of Pinochet's brutalities circulated, a few Democrats in Congress—former Representatives Don Fraser and Tom Harkin (the latter is now a senator) and Senator Edward Kennedy foremost among them—sponsored legislation to prohibit U.S. military and economic assistance to governments that practiced such cruelties. They succeeded in overcoming the opposition of President Gerald Ford and his Secretary of State, Henry Kissinger, by enlisting support from members of Congress of both parties who were then discovering the

---

*As used here, the term "human rights" refers only to civil and political rights. In much of the world, human rights also refers to economic and social rights, and some have also argued that such matters as the right to a decent environment and the right to peace should be encompassed by the term human rights. The issues raised by these varying definitions of human rights are important but require more extended discussion than is possible here.

343

human rights cause because of their interest in the dissident movement that had been emerging in the Soviet Union since its invasion of Czechoslovakia in 1968. Also, some conservatives supported the laws barring foreign assistance on human rights grounds because of their general hostility to the use of U.S. tax dollars to support other governments.

The legislation adopted in the mid-1970s committed the United States to making the promotion of human rights internationally a major factor in our government's foreign policy. That legislation focused on the physical abuses associated with regimes such as Pinochet's. Governments that "practice" such "gross abuses" are ineligible for U.S. aid except to meet "basic human needs."

In actuality, of course, such legislation has been enforced only at the discretion of the Administration in power, or when Congress has been willing to bar aid on a case-by-case basis. During the Carter Administration, when some in government were struggling to reassert a moral claim for U.S. foreign policy after the degrading failure in Vietnam, compliance was demanded primarily by the White House. Subsequently, under Reagan and during Bush's first two years, the termination of aid on human rights grounds has most often taken place because the Administration deferred to Congressional pressure or because of legislation focusing on the abuses of a particular country. Throughout, compliance with human rights laws has been at best spotty.

The most intense battle over compliance took place in the early days of the Reagan Administration over aid to El Salvador. Reagan and his Secretary of State, Alexander Haig, had made El Salvador the test case for demonstrating that the United States could defeat a left-wing insurgency. Opposition to U.S. aid to the Salvadoran government, led by the left, focused on its human rights record, then among the bloodiest anywhere in the world. For a while, it seemed the opposition might prevail. The way that the Reagan forces capitalized on elections in El Salvador in 1982 to turn the tide in Congress, on the editorial pages and with the public also helped redefine the human rights issue and end the domination by the left of the politics of human rights.

By most criteria, the elections that took place in El Salvador on March 28, 1982, were preposterous. The left did not participate. Six top leaders of its political arm, the Democratic Revolutionary Front, had been kidnapped from a public meeting on November 27, 1980, and murdered. Any others bold enough to campaign could have expected a similar fate. Also, the military arm of the left, the Farabundo Martí National Liberation Front (F.M.L.N.), called for a boycott of the elections and threatened to attack voters. The far right won but was not allowed to take the presidency.

Its leader, Maj. Roberto D'Aubuisson, the leading suspect in the March 24, 1980, murder of Archbishop Oscar Arnulfo Romero, would have embarrassed the United States and jeopardized U.S. aid, so the military selected a nonentity who had not taken part in the campaign, Alvaro Magaña, and made him President. Some observers doubted that as many votes were cast as claimed by the Salvadoran authorities, and two years later, those doubts turned out to be well founded. An electoral official revealed that the parties that did take part had agreed to inflate the total by more than 25 percent while maintaining the proportions of the actual vote.

Yet those elections were a great victory for the Reagan Administration. In addition, they played a crucial part in suggesting a way to co-opt the human rights issue that had caused so much difficulty in its first year in office, when the Administration had been embarrassed by the Senate's refusal to confirm the President's first nominee for the post of Assistant Secretary of State for Human Rights. That much of the left did not speak out against abuses of human rights by governments aligned with the Soviet Union, particularly in the Third World and above all in Nicaragua, aided Reagan and company in gaining control over some of the political capital of the human rights cause.

Those elections in El Salvador were important because they produced television scenes and newspaper photos of great numbers of ordinary Salvadorans standing in line for hours under the hot sun to cast their ballots. Never mind that their choice was limited, that voting was required or that too few polling places were provided, thus forcing them to stand in long lines. What mattered was that the people of El Salvador seemed to take the process seriously. That the F.M.L.N. had threatened to attack them for voting, of course, only made their readiness to stand up for their democratic rights more impressive.

Three months later, Reagan delivered an address to the British Parliament in which he embraced the human rights cause and equated it with democracy and elections. Previously, electoral democracy had been one of many goals of those promoting human rights, though not among their most urgent concerns. The speech was Reagan's most important statement of the right's new definition of human rights. He praised the bravery of the Salvadorans, argued that the elections refuted the charges of widespread human rights abuses and contrasted the elections in El Salvador with the refusal of the Sandinistas, who had taken power in Nicaragua in July 1979, to hold elections until 1985 (they were eventually moved up to November 1984). After being severely castigated for his Administration's support of military dictatorships in Latin America, the Philippines and elsewhere, Reagan was turning the issue around, depicting the Sandinistas as villains for their abuses of human rights. At times thereafter, Reagan and his associates used human rights abuses that they attributed to the Sandinistas as their foremost argument for the *contra* war.

By and large, the left's response was either to deny those abuses or to belittle them by comparing the Sandinistas with the Salvadoran and Guatemalan regimes supported by the United States. Neither response was wholly persuasive. The Reaganites could occupy some of the moral high ground that the left previously had to itself. Yes, the Reaganites exaggerated greatly, and those exaggerations had to be exposed. But Americas Watch tabulated hundreds of murders and "disappearances" of draft resisters and suspected *contra* or Miskito rebel collaborators during the Sandinistas' decade in power. By the standards of El Salvador or Guatemala, those are not large numbers, but by any standard of decency, the Sandinistas deserved denunciation. Most of the left failed to denounce those abuses, however, because to do so might seem to accept the distortions of the Reaganites and to legitimize the war to overthrow the Sandinistas.

Much of the left considered that its responsibility was to denounce vigorously abuses by right-wing regimes because those were the governments that enjoyed U.S. support. Much of the left has failed to denounce Fidel Castro's systematic abuses of human rights in Cuba, because this could appear to justify the U.S. campaign against his regime that has included invasion, efforts to murder Castro and a long-term embargo. Much of the left has failed to denounce abuses of human rights in Vietnam because of the misery that the United States inflicted on that country. Much of the left has failed to denounce abuses of human rights by black African governments out of guilt over the history of racism in the United States or out of unwillingness to appear to support South African propaganda about the consequences of black self-government. Much of the left failed to denounce human rights abuses in the Soviet Union out of a desire not to provide ammunition to cold warriors. Viewed politically, none of this may be irrational. However, viewed from the standpoint of concern for human rights, it has no more to commend it than the willingness of the right—for example, the editorial page of *The Wall Street Journal*—to denounce the abuses of a Castro while remaining silent about, or acting as an apologist for, the abuses of the Salvadoran military.

Some on the left have been more willing than most of those who speak out on human rights to denounce Israel's abuses against the Palestinians. Yet because those who have been vocal on this issue have often been susceptible to the charge that they have not also denounced abuses by the enemies of Israel, their effectiveness has been impaired.

The cost to the human rights cause of the failure of much of the left to act in a principled way has been considerable (it must be noted that there have been honorable exceptions to this broad-brush criticism of the left, among them those associated with the Campaign for Peace and Democracy). This failure helped to make it possible for the right to reshape human rights discourse and to prevail in some measure with the Reagan definition. The equation of human rights with electoral democracy has helped to deflect criticism on human rights grounds of a number of democratic governments, particularly in Latin America and East Asia.

Unfortunately, the physical abuses that were previously the main focus of attention to human rights have been widespread in some of those democracies. Yet during the second half of the 1980s, for example, most efforts to call attention to the disastrous human rights situation in Guatemala were effectively countered by that government's lobbyists, and by the Reagan and Bush administrations, by citing that country's electoral development. During that period, some liberals in Congress who had reputations as proponents of human rights vied with the Administration in their effort to demonstrate support for the government of President Vinicio Cerezo, both because he had been elected democratically and to reward him for his role in trying to end the *contra* war in Nicaragua. They succeeded in providing Guatemala with more U.S. aid than the Administration had requested. Thereby, they signaled to the Guatemalan military, which retained most actual power, that there would be no penalty for its gross abuses of human rights.

If there is a lesson in all this it is that the left's failure to be principled in its advocacy of human rights served neither the human rights cause nor the left. Whether it will serve the left politically in the future if it is more principled from now on, I cannot say; but only a principled approach will serve the human rights cause. ☐

Chapter 28

The Rise of Terrorism

Article 28.1.   10 Steps Against Terror

Admiral Stansfield Turner, former Director of the Central Intelligence Agency, outlines ten steps to combat terrorism, among them: that assassination is neither an appropriate nor an effective counterterrorist tactic; punitive military attacks can and should be used, but only sparingly; covert actions should be undertaken, even though the probability of success is low; rescue operations must be considered, but will continue to prove risky; media restraint could prove beneficial, but modest restraint is the most that can be expected; and legal recourse is the option most compatible with American societal values. The secret of dealing with terrorism, advises Turner, is selecting that option or combination of options, pro-legal and pro-active, that will have the greatest impact on the terrorists while minimizing threats to basic societal values.

I N THE FALL OF LAST YEAR I CALLED ON the chairman of the KGB, Vladimir A. Kryuchkov, in Moscow.

Chairman Kryuchkov told me that the KGB had made many mistakes in its past, but that he was intent on operating it in a manner compatible with a democracy. When I asked whether there were any prospects for cooperation between the KGB and the CIA against terrorists, he responded that the Soviet Union was willing to go to great lengths to cooperate with the US. He was interested not only in exchanging intelligence but in undertaking joint operations against terrorism.

While Chairman Kryuchkov made no acknowledgment of any Soviet involvement with terrorists, he was forthright in saying that the reason he wanted to work with the US was that terrorism has become a serious problem inside the Soviet Union. He noted that today's terrorists are well organized, professional, and adept at new technologies. He was worried about the possibility of nuclear terrorism.

I believe he was saying the Soviets realize that, if they hope to control domestic terrorism, they cannot ignore terrorism abroad. For instance, in December 1988 Soviet terrorists, using 30 schoolchildren as hostages, commandeered an Aeroflot aircraft and had themselves flown to Israel. With the United States facilitating communications, the Israelis disarmed and arrested the hijackers when they arrived in Tel Aviv. The price for continued assistance of this sort will be reciprocity and cooperation.

Kryuchkov also suggested that the Soviet Union and the United States promote a consensus within the United Nations on standard punishments for terrorism. I pointed out that the UN had never been able to agree on a definition of terrorism and suggested that perhaps at least our two countries could do that, now that we no longer were competing in the third world. He agreed.

Meanwhile, the potential for terrorism to increase is there, but terrorists are not invincible; the bygone Zealots, Assassins, and others were suppressed in time.

Today many countervailing strengths come from the very fact that the United States and more and more other countries have democratic systems. But this means that governments need public understanding of the options for curtailing terror—and the wisdom to avoid actions that might undermine the democratic process they are defending.

I have searched US history for common threads, which, it turns out, go all the way back to the founding of American government. I was not surprised to find that much of the common wisdom about dealing with ter-

From *World Monitor*, July 1991, pp. 46-50. Reprinted by permission.

rorism does not accord with what presidents have actually done.

There are 10 options that I call pro-legal or pro-active. Presidents and public must understand the strengths and the pitfalls of each one. My views on these are:

1. Assassinations are neither an appropriate nor an effective counterterrorist tactic.

The lure of assassination is that it seems surgical and final. In reality, it is neither. If US authorities attempted to kill a foreign leader, they would logically turn to foreigners to do the deed or to help their own people get away safely; thus the Americans would lose control. Because an assassination would be a major foreign policy choice, it would require an order by the president, who would then be embarked on a game of dirty tricks in which America's opponents are likely to be far more ruthless and persistent than Washington.

Assassination is morally repugnant to the majority of Americans. It is always dangerous to counter terrorism with terrorism. A nation can lose what it is defending in the process of defending it.

Still, most US administrations, when frustrated beyond measure by a Khomeini in Iran or a Qaddafi in Libya, will be tempted to consider assassination. I believe the US needs a law, not just the present presidential executive order, prohibiting assassination. The rationalization that the deliberate killing of an individual can be classed as "justifiable homicide," not assassination, would be more difficult to maintain against a law than against an executive order.

I believe, though, that such a law should be limited to peacetime. Targeting specific leaders in wartime, when the country has determined openly that widespread killing is justified, is quite different from a president's making a secret political decision to take someone's life.

2. Punitive military attacks are a remedy to be used, but sparingly.

It is futile, even irresponsible, to advocate consistent use of force against terrorists. The record shows the American people will not accept it. For instance,

Ronald Reagan unleashed only one attack—the one against Libya in 1986—despite repeated provocations.

A principal inhibition on Reagan was the reluctance to take human life outside the due process of law or war. Even the advocates of punitive force tacitly acknowledge concern about the killing of innocents when they talk of employing "surgical attacks." But we know how low is the probability of punitive attacks being surgical. In Libya, though the US employed a particular aircraft because of its accurate bombing system, some bombs hit the French Embassy.

Perhaps the best argument for exercising the punitive option is that doing so reinforces all other options. Allies, for instance, are more likely to be cooperative if they believe a country really will turn to the use of force. Terrorists are more likely to come to terms for the same reason.

In short, between "never" and "always" there is some ground for the occasional use of punitive force.

3. Judicious covert actions should be undertaken, even though the probability of success is low.

There are a number of covert techniques that can be effective against terrorists, such as infiltrating an organization and making its plans go awry; feeding disinformation to groups to mislead them and perhaps cause them to terrorize one another; and toppling governments that sponsor or provide support to terrorists. Maneuvers like these present formidable challenges: Jimmy Carter's efforts to change the complexion of Iran's Khomeini government never made headway; Reagan's attempt to use arms to advance the position of moderates in that same government ended in a giant con game.

We must take into account that these actions come under even less scrutiny than other secret government operations. Who, for instance, will make the judgment that the people Washington supports to overthrow a government will do so within Washington's bounds? Who will determine the cost if Washington's disinformation feeds back into America's own media? Washington should not ignore covert actions just because there are such risks, but it must weigh the prospects for success against the threat to American values.

4. Rescue operations must be readied, but will continue to be highly risky for the United States.

A government that values its citizens will try to maintain a capability for rescuing them if they are taken hostage. And a rescue operation will be tempt-

Admiral Stansfield Turner, US Navy (ret.), former Director of Central Intelligence, is the author of "Secrecy and Democracy" (1985). He adapted this article from his new book, "Terrorism and Democracy," © 1991 by Stansfield Turner, published by Houghton Mifflin Company, Boston. Reprinted by permission.

ing because, if it is successful, it will solve the problem instantly.

But rescue operations carry high risks. Many former hostages say they were afraid of being killed during a rescue attempt, either deliberately by their captors or accidentally by the rescue forces.

Because such operations are complex and often demand feats approaching the heroic, they can fail through (1) poor execution, as with the 1975 US assault on Koh Tang Island (to search for the crew of the hijacked merchant ship Mayaguez) and the 1980 Desert One operation (to rescue hostages in Iran); or (2) bad timing, as with TWA 847 that had been hijacked to Beirut in 1985 and the ship Achille Lauro that was hijacked in the Mediterranean in the same year.

Maintaining competent rescue forces will always be difficult for the US military, because it is expected to have such a wide range of capabilities. At one end it must deter thermonuclear war, and at the other outwit a handful of 20-year-olds who have seized an airliner. Presidents and secretaries of defense would do well to make periodic inquiries about the readiness of rescue forces and to order unannounced tests of them, as a modest amount of such high-level attention to low-level operations will advance the day of readiness.

5. Improved intelligence, especially by human means, is always desirable but seldom achievable.

There is a danger that overemphasis on improving human intelligence as an antidote to terrorism could lead to the neglect of technical intelligence systems. Satellite photos revealed who was probably behind the third terrorist bombing in Beirut. National Security Agency electronic intercepts produced the clinching evidence about the terrorist bombing in Berlin that sent US bombers over Libya in 1986.

When President Bush's Commission on Aviation Security and Terrorism recommended more attention to human intelligence, it called intelligence the "first line of defense." This was misleading. The number of times US intelligence has given operationally useful warning of impending acts of international terrorism is so low that it can hardly be termed a line of defense. At most it is a soldier in the battle.

That is not to say Washington should not sustain a major intelligence effort against terrorism, but if a president counts too heavily on it, he will be disappointed and may ignore important alternatives. Washington must also be careful that agencies, in their zeal to track down terrorists, do not intrude on the privacy of Americans except as provided by law.

6. Restraint of the media could be helpful, but very modest self-restraint is the most to be expected.

Publicity for their cause is usually one objective of terrorists. Almost any media coverage plays into their hands. There are also situations in which counterterrorist efforts are hurt by reporting, as when the hijackers of TWA 847 were tipped off that Delta Force was on the way to the Mediterranean; or when too many details are printed about hostages.

But erring on the side of the openness that keeps government accountable is preferable to governmental control of sources of information. The media face difficult decisions. Would publication of the information harm the national interest? Or is an administration attempting to bury a political embarrassment or to use secrecy to do something the public might reject?

Administrations that appreciate the media's dilemma will think carefully before attempting to manipulate them. (It is not only terrorists who attempt manipulation of the media.) In building credibility and understanding about terrorism, administrations would do well to conduct simulations of terrorist incidents with media participation. Each side could learn to appreciate the other's considerations.

7. Economic sanctions should be used against state sponsors of terrorism, even though they will be effective only after a considerable time, if at all.

Unilateral economic sanctions can have only limited effect. Someone else will usually fill whatever gap the US creates and take the business away from Americans besides. The Congress in 1985 strengthened the hand of presidents by authorizing them to bar imports from or aid to countries that harbor or otherwise support international terrorism. Such measures are useful tools.

Americans tend to believe there must be something they can do to solve any problem, and just forcing other nations to decide whether to honor or reject US requests for sanctions can help. These countries must evaluate what they believe to be their responsibilities; over time, their assessment can help make them more reliable.

8. Defensive security is unlikely to receive sufficient attention or money.

Recent history in Beirut shows how difficult it is to persuade Americans to take security overseas seriously. Within 17 months Americans were struck by three bombings, largely because of lack of physical

348

preparedness. Once the Congress and the administration became committed to the construction of better physical defense in Beirut and elsewhere, the bombers lost interest.

In 1985, in the wake of TWA 847, Congress passed the Foreign Airport Security Act, directing the secretary of transportation to assess periodically the security of 247 foreign airports. President Bush's Commission on Aviation Security and Terrorism noted, though, that "severe FAA [Federal Aviation Administration] personnel shortages generally limit the depth of these assessments to interviews and observations....Inspectors do not substantively test the operational effectiveness of security procedures." A modest increase in resources would allow for rigorous inspections and make useful a provision of the 1985 act that permits the suspension of air services to any airport where conditions threaten the security of aircraft, crews, or passengers.

9. Deals are an option that Washington must be ready to employ.

The platitude that no one should ever make deals with terrorists because doing so inevitably leads to more terrorism is factually incorrect. We have seen deals that did not lead to a repetition of events; for example, Lyndon Johnson's gaining release of the crew of the USS Pueblo in 1968 by agreeing to a false confession when the North Korean captors demanded a confession that the ship had intruded into their waters on a spying mission. Except for Gerald Ford, every president since Johnson has been involved in at least one deal.

In the wake of the political explosion that followed the exposure of Reagan's arms-for-hostages deals with Iran, politicians have become leery of any talk of deals. The reality is that presidents will make them, so Americans had better learn to differentiate between a deal that is acceptable and one that is not.

And presidents, instead of stating categorically that they will never cut a deal with terrorists, should stimulate discussion of all possible alternatives. Then, if a deal provides clear advantages for the United States, they would be in a better position to accept it without appearing weak.

10. Legal recourse is the option most compatible with American societal values.

Legal recourse against terrorists falls into two categories: apprehending terrorists, and isolating states that support terrorism. Apprehending the terrorists themselves serves as a warning to would-be terrorists that they are likely to be caught. Despite the examples of suicide drivers, most terrorists prefer not to be killed or jailed.

Isolating a nation by means of political con-

demnation can be telling over the long run, though it seldom has an immediate impact. For instance, in October 1980, when the Iranian prime minister visited the United Nations to seek that body's denunciation of Iraq's invasion of his country, he found a total lack of sympathy, because for 11 months Washington had been reminding the world that Iran was holding US diplomats hostage. That must have given impetus to the pragmatists in Iran who wanted to put the hostage issue behind them.

Legal means are by far the preferable way of dealing with terrorism. They do least violence to democratic values, even if some efforts to arrest suspected terrorists violate legal principles.

When Americans forced down the aircraft carrying away the hijackers of the Achille Lauro, they broke international law against air piracy. In my view that was reasonable, as the rights of the culprits would have been only slightly abused had they been innocent.

The secret of dealing with terrorism lies in selecting the option or mixture of options, both pro-legal and pro-active, that will have the greatest impact on the terrorists while minimizing the intrusions into societal values.

My appraisal of the effectiveness and the risks associated with each of the ten options will certainly not be shared by everyone. No individual's judgment is necessarily right and another's wrong; it depends on one's view of the seriousness of the threat.

It is all too easy to be misled by an immediate threat. Jimmy Carter's fear for the American hostages in Tehran led to unwarranted optimism about the rescue mission. Ronald Reagan's concern over the US hostages in Beirut led to a flouting of the Constitution. In each instance, the responses of the president damaged America's national interest. Noel Koch, a former Pentagon official involved with countering terrorism, stated, "Most of the damage to US interests done by terrorism has been self-inflicted."

But there may be times when Americans choose to pay a high price. They might do so in response to two forms of terrorism they have not had to face: widespread terrorism at home, as the West Germans and the Italians experienced in the 1970s and 1980s with the Baader-Meinhof gang and the Red Brigades, and nuclear terrorism.

Fortunately, international terrorists have hardly ventured onto US soil—because of the excellence of the FBI and the law enforcement system, and because they found it easier to attack Americans abroad. Terrorists may move to the US out of desperation if America and its allies close in on them. Washington would then have to rely on more difficult measures. One would be stringent inspections at international airports and other points of entry, with all the inconvenience that involves for Americans who travel abroad. Another would be intrusion into citizens' private lives by law enforcement officials ferreting out terrorists who had slipped by. Much the same would be the case with nuclear terrorism.

However, thus far, terrorist groups have not shown great interest in acquiring nuclear weapons or materials. Governments must be concerned, though, with countries that support terrorism, like Libya and Iraq, and also aspire to nuclear capabilities. Again, tightening entry inspections at airports, ports, and border crossings would be one recourse. Military defenses against delivery by aircraft or missiles would be another.

The major effort, though, should be directed toward preventing the acquisition of nuclear capabilities by such nations. This will require worldwide, highly intrusive controls and inspection procedures, something possible only with the wholehearted support of all responsible nations, large and small.

That returns us to the importance of Washington's working for heightened international cooperation against all forms of terrorism.

Americans should set their sights high in the hope that the burden of terrorism they are currently carrying will be a blessing in disguise by helping usher in a new era of world cooperation that will reach well beyond the suppression of terrorism itself. **WM**

Article 28.2.   Should We "Take Out" Terrorists?

The author explores the issue of political assassination, arguing that it is time to debate the merits of this option. Presently, there are no statutory prohibitions against assassination, although a number of laws impact on the subject. Unlike previous presidents, the Bush administration has chosen not to issue its own executive order on assassination, but has said that it will abide by the previous administration's ban. Despite this fact, several top administration officials favor limiting the all-encompassing nature of the existing ban and to exempt certain categories of deadly force. In the author's view, a compelling case could be made for eliminating a madman like Adolph Hitler or even, for that matter, a leader like Saddam Hussein, who is guilty of any number of crimes. In most cases, assassination is an ineffective tool, as it is both difficult to accomplish and laden with potential problems. As for Saddam, those closest to him stand the best chance of removing the Iraqi dictator. Clearly, he has the most to fear from his own inner circle. It would be far more prudent if they removed him than if some other power or outside force attempted to do so.

Should We "Take Out" Terrorists?

You can't talk about it in polite company. It's the "A" word—assassination. Its very mention makes many Americans squeamish, uncomfortable. We don't even like to think about it.

Public opinion polls indicate that under certain circumstances most of us feel that dropping bombs from a B-52 onto an unseen enemy is morally acceptable. On the other hand, most people cannot justify selectively killing an enemy with a name and a face, even if he is a madman or a terrorist responsible for the deaths of innocent Americans. To many liberals, moreover, the term assassination conjures up visions of the Vietnam-era Phoenix program and an interventionist foreign policy.

Humorist Dave Barry once suggested we abolish the Department of State and replace it with a new department called "The Department of a Couple of Guys Named Victor." Instead of "sending hundreds of thousands of our people to fight hundreds of thousands of Iraqis all because of one scuzball, I'd say 'Victors, it would not depress me to hear that Saddam Hussein had some kind of unfortunately fatal accident in the shower.'"

Barry's simple logic is difficult to dispute. Indeed, the recent Gulf War raised anew the issue of assassination, or what some today prefer to call "selective targeting." If, as President Bush said, our problem was not with the Iraqi people, then it clearly had to be with the Iraqi leadership, namely Saddam Hussein. On January 21 the president even called it the "war against Saddam." Thus, it was not surprising that some Americans, among them Senator Alfonse D'Amato (R-NY), wanted to know why the United States did not attempt to kill Iraqi dictator Saddam Hussein instead of fighting a war that cost the lives of more than a hundred American soldiers and tens of thousands of Iraqi troops.

Ironically, last fall, Air Force chief of staff General Michael Dugan was fired by Defense

> "No employee of the United States Government shall engage in, or conspire to engage in assassination."

Neil C. Livingstone

Secretary Dick Cheney for allegedly divulging US war plans, including the assertion that the United States would not only go after Saddam but, in addition, his family and even his mistress. This was in direct contradiction to statements by Cheney and Chairman of the Joint Chiefs Colin Powell, who dismissed any suggestion that the United States might attempt to eliminate Saddam. Articulating the administration line, on January 20, 1991, commander of allied forces in the Persian Gulf, General Norman Schwarzkopf, denied that the United States had "a policy of trying to kill any particular individual."

But some Americans remained unconvinced, and that popular barometer of contemporary culture, the tee-shirt, certainly indicated that it was time for the debate over assassination to come out of the closet. Last fall, during the US buildup in the Persian Gulf, tee-shirts began to appear showing Saddam in the crosshairs of a sniper rifle, and others with mottos like "Saddam, Make My Day" and "Dead Meat" beneath his picture. *Soldier of Fortune* magazine even distributed a target with Saddam's face on it and directions on how to mail it, after shooting it, to the Iraqi embassy in Washington.

However, Saddam disappointed many of his detractors and survived the war. Today, therefore, we are left with a number of questions. Should more effort have been expended to kill him? Would it have been the right thing to do morally, legally, politically? Could we have done it, even if we wanted to?

Restrictions on Assassination

There are no statutory prohibitions against assassination, although a number of laws, such as the Hughes-Ryan amendment, indirectly impact on the issue. In reality, however, the ban on assassinations is entirely voluntary, the product of a succession of executive orders issued by recent presidents.

The prevailing Executive Order, number 12,333, was promulgated by President Reagan and prohibits assassination as an instru-

From *International Counterterrorism & Security*, May/June 1991, pp. 11-16. Reprinted by permission.

ment of national policy. It has its antecedents in Director Richard Helm's 1972 ban on assassination by employees of the CIA. In 1975, President Ford extended the prohibition to all employees of the Federal government in Executive Order 11,905, which stated that, "No employee of the United States Government shall engage in, or conspire to engage in, political assassination." The word "political" was dropped under President Carter, and the ban applied to any form of assassination (Executive Order 12,036).

President Reagan, in Executive Order 12,333, regrettably adopted the far too inclusive language of the Carter Adminstration. This turned out to be a mistake since it drew no distinction between the assassination of political leaders in peacetime—which was the intent of the act—and the targeting of a foreign leader during time of war or conflict. Nor was there any attempt to exempt the use of deadly force in conjunction with anti-terrorist activities.

This was a source of major contention after the April 1986 raid on Tripoli. Administration critics charged that Libyan strongman, Muammar Khadafi, was the actual target of the raid and that this violated the assassination ban. The administration denied the accusation, but did acknowledge that it was aware that Khadafi might be killed since his compound, the Azzizia Barracks, was a major command-and-control center and a primary target of the operation. Indeed, there was enough reason to believe that the United States might actually get Khadafi that the National Security Council (NSC) drafted a statement—to be issued on his death—explaining away the Libyan dictator's demise as "fortuitous." Khadafi was not killed in the raid, which made the debate moot, and subsequent efforts by some in the Reagan Administration to clarify aspects of the assassination ban were shelved as a result of the Iran-Contra scandal.

Breaking with past precedent, the Bush Administration has not promulgated its own executive order dealing with assassination, but rather has indicated that it will be bound by the previous administration's ban. Nevertheless, there is interest by some in the administration to limit the all-encompassing language of any new executive order and to exempt certain categories of deadly force.

CIA Director William Webster, for example, has called for more latitude in interpreting the ban on assassinations. He recommended that Congress permit the CIA to assist efforts to overthrow foreign dictators, even if it might inadvertently cause the individual's death. In the event that the dictator was killed in the subsequent coup attempt, it would not be considered assassination since his death was not the primary goal of the operation. This issue grew out of the refusal by congressional intelligence panels to go along with presidential findings authorizing efforts to either "snatch" Panamanian dictator Manuel Noriega or to help coup plotters overthrow him. In both instances, faint hearts in Congress were worried that something unfortunate might happen to Noriega and that this could be construed as a violation of the president's ban on assassinations.

Humanitarian Intervention

A good case can be made for eliminating a leader engaged in massive human rights violations—the so-called "Hitler exception." Wouldn't the world have been better off, say proponents, if Hitler had been assassinated, sparing perhaps millions of lives?

The same argument could have been applied to killing Saddam Hussein. His list of crimes is long. The Iraqi dictator's forces invaded Kuwait, in what only could be described as naked aggression, and plunged the entire region into war. Kuwait was looted and Kuwaiti citizens kidnapped, tortured, and murdered. Foreign nationals, including Americans, were abducted and dispersed throughout Iraq as "human shields." POWs were brutalized in blatant violation of the Geneva conventions. Unprovoked Scud missile attacks were launched against civilian targets in Israel, a non-belligerent, and Saudi Arabia. Iraq deliberately created an environmental catastrophe with the massive release of oil into the waters of the Persian Gulf and by setting Kuwait's oil fields ablaze. None of this takes into account Saddam Hussein's support of international terrorism and the use of chemical weapons against Iraq's Kurdish minority. In view of these travesties, many make the case that there is a moral imperative to protect the innocent and spare the world such depredations, even if it involves assassination.

Assassination in Wartime

There is no such thing as assassination in wartime, say many legal scholars, who apply the term only to "treacherous murder" in peacetime. The commander-in-chief of enemy forces is a legitimate target, they contend, especially if the military objective is to destroy the adversary's command-and-control structure. As the undisputed commander-in-chief of Iraqi forces, Saddam Hussein was, in every respect, the most important figure in his nation's command-and-control structure and, therefore, an appropriate target of coalition forces.

In cases where open hostilities do not exist,

the issue is more complex, but no less clear. Article 51 of the United Nations' charter guarantees the "inherent" right of self-defense to countries under armed attack. Terrorism, clearly, is a form of armed attack, and nations such as Libya, which is a principal state sponsor of international terrorism, must bear the consequences of its aggression. This is precisely what happened in 1986, when US military aircraft attacked Libya in response to its participation in the so-called La Belle Disco bombing and other terrorists attacks. A good case can be made that Colonel Khadafi was a legitimate target, since he personally bore responsibility for such terrorist attacks and that the United States was engaged in the lawful exercise of its right of self-defense.

In the Talmud it says, "If someone comes to kill you, rise and kill him first." This raises the issue of whether the United States must wait until first attacked, and suffer the resulting casualties, before it responds. Obviously, many people—especially the victims and their relatives—would disagree with any policy that did not provide for the preemption of terrorist attacks. In the aftermath of the Libyan raid, a number of senators, including Robert Dole (R-Kansas), introduced legislation authorizing the president to undertake any measures—presumably including assassination—deemed necessary to protect US citizens from terrorists. Unfortunately, the legislation died in committee.

Rules of Engagement

Delta Force commandos have a little ditty that goes, "Two to the body, one to the head, makes you good and dead." It's really a shooter's creed, reminding Delta operators—when taking down a plane or rescuing hostages—that they should hit the adversary with two body shots and then go for a head shot just in case one of the terrorists is wearing body armor. Given the extraordinary shooting skills of US anti-terrorist commandos, any terrorist hit by three rounds and not wearing body armor is, in all probability, going to be dead.

Liberal critics have argued that rules of engagement (ROE) that call for commandos to pacify a situation with such deadly dispatch amount to little more than assassination. Military experts, on the other hand, counter that anything less would place hostages at great risk. A wounded terrorist can still detonate a grenade or explosive device.

There is also the issue of turning the hunters into the hunted, and dispatching anti-terrorist commandos to snatch or even eliminate, as a form of preemption, known terrorists that cannot be brought to justice any other way. Under the existing assassination

As the undisputed commander-in-chief of Iraqi forces, Saddam Hussein was, in every respect, the most important figure in his nation's command-and-control structure and, therefore, an appropriate target of coalition forces.

ban the use of commandos in peacetime to strike at a terrorist cell or to disrupt an ongoing terrorist operation could, under some interpretations, be proscribed. Critics contend that if terrorists are simply ambushed without giving them a chance to surrender it amounts to little more than murder. The British SAS, for example, has been publicly accused of behaving as a "death squad" in connection with a number of successful operations it has carried out against the IRA.

As a result of the Gulf war, the debate over assassination is likely to intensify, with new focus on issues such as the executive ban on such killings, rules of engagement, and presidential accountability. All such considerations aside, the question still remains: Was it possible to kill Saddam?

Locating Saddam

The Israelis keep very close track of many key Arab officials. They continuously monitor, for example, the movements of PLO chairman Yasir Arafat, and on their computers usually can punch up his whereabouts at any given moment. Similarly, they generally can find Saudi King Fahd, Jordan's King Hussein, Morocco's King Hassan, Egypt's Mubarak, and other key regional leaders, along with many of the most notorious terrorists. By contrast, they have found it more difficult to keep track of Syrian strongman Hafez al-Assad. But the most elusive Arab leader of all, they say, is Saddam Hussein. Even prior to the Gulf War, Israeli intelligence sources reported that they were able to fix his whereabouts—on an average—only three days a week, and then rarely more precisely than within a radius of one or two blocks.

Any real effort to kill Saddam requires reliable information about his exact location at a given time. Unlike Western leaders, Saddam's daily schedule is secret, and in recent years he has made few public appearances. Saddam's paranoia is well-founded. He has countless enemies and there reportedly have been more than a dozen serious attempts on his life, including incidents in 1982, 1984, 1985, and 1987. The 1985 incident took place in Tikrit, his hometown.

Stories about the heavy-handed nature of the security surrounding Saddam are legion. After his trip to Iraq in early 1990 to meet with Saddam, Assistant Secretary of State John Kelly described security in Baghdad as the most pervasive he had ever witnessed in his twenty-five year career as a diplomat. Although Kelly was in an official car accompanied by representatives of the foreign ministry, guards at three separate checkpoints thrust their guns into the vehicle and checked their documents.

353

Saddam, Kelly told a *Washington Post* reporter, was surrounded by bodyguards during the entire meeting. Even the dictator's own interpreter was so frightened that his hands trembled.

CNN reporter Peter Arnett covered the war from Baghdad and was unexpectedly offered an exclusive interview with Saddam. But before he was taken to the meeting, five men—presumably members of Saddam's security force—took him to a room in his hotel and "asked me to undress completely, and began checking every pocket and seam of my clothing. My wallet, watch, pen and notebook, handkerchief and comb were put into a plastic bag and taken away. They were even reluctant to return my trouser belt until I objected." Arnett goes on to say that he "was taken into the bathroom and my hands were immersed in a disinfectant carried by one of the group. This was either an extreme form of security, or else, I mused, Saddam Hussein has a Howard Hughes-like phobia of germs. Then I was escorted back to the lobby, and instructed neither to talk to nor touch anyone."

Saddam, after all, is a former assassin, and he learned at a young age the lapses and mistakes that can get a man killed. After successfully assassinating a prominent supporter of Iraqi leader Abdul Karim Qassem in Tikrit, Saddam—then only twenty-two—was selected to command a team of Baathist gunmen tasked with murdering Qassem. Because of a breech in security, Saddam and his confederates knew the exact route of Qassem's motorcade and almost succeeded in their mission.

Today, the cornerstone of Saddam's security is his unpredictability and lack of routine. This was demonstrated on the morning of January 17, when Saddam was filmed touring a Baghdad neighborhood to inspect war damage. From the film clips broadcast on Iraqi television it appeared that his visit was a total surprise to local residents. Instead of a forty or fifty-car convoy and hundreds of bodyguards, Saddam's entire party apparently consisted of one or two cars and a few trusted bodyguards. Needless to say, this is often the best kind of security. By avoiding the temptation to make every movement a major production, and by keeping his entourage to a minimum, Saddam effectively reduces the chances that there will be a breech of security or that conspirators will be able to lay a trap for him.

When he goes anywhere, Saddam's movements are masked by phony communications traffic, and it is reliably reported that he employs many doubles. Saddam rarely travels outside of Iraq, and his last known trip be-

Saddam, after all, is a former assassin, and he learned at a young age the lapses and mistakes that can get a man killed.

yond the Arab world was in 1976, before he became president. He spends most of his time in various bunkers and command-and-control centers, shielded by tons of concrete.

There are approximately 5,000 men in Saddam's personal praetorian guard, and they are the best-paid and best-treated component of his entire military. But even they are not completely trusted. Indeed, he has layers upon layers of secret police, each watching the other for any sign of treason or conspiracy.

His inner circle of bodyguards—a mere handful of men—are among the most powerful figures in Iraq, with absolute authority to protect their leader with whatever means they choose. Highly paid and motivated, they swear personal loyalty to Saddam, and he reciprocates their devotion by placing their well-being above even that of family members and senior government officials. When Saddam's son killed one of his father's favorite bodyguards in circumstances that are still not fully confirmed, the Iraqi dictator moved swiftly to make his priorities absolutely clear. Not only was his son temporarily banished from Iraq, but there are reliable reports that he was condemned to death for the murder, and that his father let him sweat for a time in prison before commuting the sentence and shipping him out. Actions like that impress bodyguards.

Despite the formidable security around him, Saddam remains vulnerable to plots hatched by his inner circle, say knowledgeable observers. In the past, however, he has always moved ruthlessly at any sign of trouble or disloyalty, often killing not only the actual conspirators but every member of their families. And death does not come easily for those accused of plotting against Saddam. Horror stories abound of the terrors waiting in Saddam's torture chambers. A former minister of health suspected of not being one-hundred percent behind Saddam was sent home to his wife in a small black canvas bag, chopped into little pieces. In liberated Kuwait, coalition forces have found a wide array of instruments used by the Iraqis to torture members of the Kuwaiti resistance and other perceived enemies. These include truncheons, hammers, power drills, razors, broken bottles, pliers used to pull fingernails, saws, planes used to shave away skin, and devices to administer electric shocks.

So institutionalized is torture in contemporary Iraq that one of Saddam's former foreign ministers reportedly used to wander down into the basement of his ministry, dressed in his tuxedo, to torture hapless prisoners as a way of getting him in the mood to visit his mistress.

Operational Choices

It is clear that there were only two ways of "taking out" Saddam. One was to get lucky and simply hit him by accident. American warplanes allegedly almost did just that when a fifty-vehicle convoy bearing Saddam was bombed on the highway to Basra. Unfortunately, he escaped without a scratch.

The second, and more deliberate, method of killing him would have required a Herculean effort to locate and then target him with the best weapon available. The Israelis and some of the coalition nations had "assets" in Baghdad capable of tracking Saddam during the crisis, but it became extremely difficult to communicate with them after the onset of hostilities. In addition, US special operations forces penetrated Baghdad both before and after January 16. However, since Saddam's movements were almost impossible to predict within the clutter of bogus communications traffic, it would have been extremely difficult to ambush him. Similarly, it is doubtful that any member of his security force could have been "turned" and persuaded to take out his leader.

Only if Saddam's location was absolutely fixed, could an assassination attempt—with cruise missiles or snipers—be mounted. In view of the difficulty locating Saddam when he was moving about, the most likely scenario was to hit him when he returned to his bunker. Constructed by the West Germans, the bunker under the presidential palace reportedly cost $80 million and could withstand a direct nuclear hit, although this clearly is open to question. Whatever its actual strength, there is little doubt that it is extremely formidable, as are the other command-and-control bunkers Saddam uses throughout the country.

There were a number of methods of attacking the bunker available to military planners, including cruise missiles and other so-called "smart" bombs launched from US war planes. However, many planners doubted that such weapons could have successfully penetrated the lower reaches of the main bunker, although they probably would have worked against most of the other command-and-control facilities. In all likelihood, more devastating weapons would have been required to destroy the main bunker, such as 15,000 pound bombs developed by the United States during World War II to pulverize Nazi bunkers. Such bombs, delivered by C-130s, were used against the Republican Guards' fortifications in southern Iraq.

In addition, the United States has developed various technologies to deal with super-hardened Soviet missile silos; technologies that could have been employed against Sad-

One of Saddam's former foreign ministers reportedly used to wander down into the basement of his ministry, dressed in his tuxedo, to torture hapless prisoners as a way of getting him in the mood to visit his mistress.

Those with access to Saddam stand the best chance of toppling the Iraqi dictator. Just as during the war, he has the most to fear from his own inner circle.

dam's bunker. In this connection, the weapon given the greatest chance of success was an enhanced radiation device, or so-called mini-nuke, which can be used to attack a relatively small area with great effect. The use of a fissionable weapon, however, would have represented a major escalation of the war and been accompanied by a great deal of international criticism of the United States.

One senior US scientist involved in many key weapons programs even recommended a new version of an old German technology developed during World War II. His plan called for large metal "spears" with "smart" guidance systems to be dropped from 30,000 feet on Saddam's bunker. He calculated that the spears would develop so much velocity that they would pass through at least fifty feet of solid concrete.

British or American special operations forces also could have been sent against the bunker. Special ops units could have fought their way into the bunker or attacked it with explosives. Lethal chemicals could have been pumped into the bunker's ventilation system. Such an operation, however, would have been extremely risky to the forces involved.

Conclusion

As this is written, Saddam Hussein is fighting for his life. There are Shiite uprisings in southern Iraq and the Kurds are struggling for control of a number of cities in the northern part of the country. The coming weeks and months will tell whether Saddam Hussein's regime survives. Despite public denials, the United States and its coalition allies, not to mention the Iranians, are providing both direct and covert aid to Saddam's opponents.

Those with access to Saddam stand the best chance of toppling the Iraqi dictator. Just as during the war, he has the most to fear from his own inner circle. All it will take is for one member of his Revolutionary Command Council to draw his gun and pull the trigger. Indeed, there are unconfirmed reports that Saddam was wounded in the hand in early March during an unsuccessful attack by a senior member of his government.

Even if he weathers the current storm, Saddam must still contend with the Israelis, who won't soon forget the Scud attacks on their civilian population. Indeed, as Defense Minister Moshe Arens and other Israeli officials put it, retaliation is inevitable, and they will choose the appropriate time, place, and method. Few doubt that their target will be Saddam.

Neil C. Livingstone is a Washington-based national security expert.

Article 29.1.   Terror for Profit: The Colombian Cocaine Connection

Carl H. Yaeger analyzes the inner workings of the Colombian cocaine connection—more specifically, the infamous Medellin Cartel—which is said to be the wealthiest and most powerful supplier in the world. In recent years, the cartel has increasingly resorted to violence and terrorism as a means of protecting its drug profits. During the past three years, for example, the cartel has orchestrated the assassinations of a Colombian ambassador, a minister of justice, an attorney general, more than fifty judges, at least thirty journalists, and over four hundred police and military personnel. During the course of its twelve-year existence, it has also claimed credit for hundreds of other murders, many of which resulted from organizational feuds and the creation of drug distribution networks in the United States. According to experts, the cartel presently earns between $2 billion and $4 billion a year from drug trafficking. For these reasons, the destruction of the cartel is uppermost on the minds of Washington and Bogota. The article examines the background of the cartel, U.S.-Colombian efforts to stem the flow of drugs, the cartel's counterattack, the impact of the Colombian government's war against the cartel, the cartel's worldwide campaign of terror, the feud that is now taking place within the cartel, and recent U.S.-Colombian efforts to curb the power of the cartel. Ultimately, argues the author, the Colombian cocaine connection can only be broken by cooperation and interdiction, as well as by drastically reducing the demand for drugs in the United States.

Terror for Profit

THE
COLOMBIAN
COCAINE
CONNECTION

by Carl H. Yaeger

On January 13, 1987, Colombia's Ambassador to Hungary, Enrique Parejo Gonzalez, miraculously survived an assassination attempt. The Ambassador's would-be assassins were not left-wing Hungarian terrorists. They were a group of Colombian hit men sent behind the Iron Curtain to execute a death warrant placed on the ambassador years before. Gonzalez had been targeted for assassination when, as a Justice Minister, he supported a 1979 US-Colombian extradition treaty which allowed for suspected drug traffickers to be

From *International Counterterrorism & Security*, May/June 1991, pp. 18-24. Reprinted by permission.

extradicted and tried in US courts. After receiving numerous death threats, Gonzalez requested assignment in Budapest where he thought he could find refuge from the organization which sought his life—Colombia's infamous Medellin Cartel.

Since 1977 the drug barons of Medellin, known as "The Mafia" by the locals, have increasingly gained notoriety as the wealthiest and most powerful suppliers of cocaine in the world. Their profits are estimated to be somewhere between $2 billion and $4 billion a year which, were it legitimate, would place the cartel among the Fortune 500 list of companies. These earnings are astonishing even considering that the cartel supplies as much as 80 percent of the cocaine flowing into the American market.

What is equally incredible, however, is the extent of violence and terrorism that the cartel has used as a means of securing their coveted profits. In the last three years alone, the drug lords of Medellin have crippled Colombia's justice system by assassinating one minister of justice (in addition to the attempt on Gonzales), one attorney general, more than fifty judges, at least thirty journalists, and more than 400 police and military personnel. In addition the cartel has orchestrated hundreds of murders during its twelve year existence due to feuding and the establishment of distribution networks in the United States. Given these figures and the predominance of the cartel in world drug trafficking, it is no wonder that government officials in both Washington and Bogota want nothing more than to see the total destruction of the organization.

Violence in Colombia

Despite its relative economic success, Colombia is one of the most violent countries in the western hemisphere—possibly even in the world. In 1987 there were 16,200 homicides reported in Colombia—the highest ratio of killings per capita among countries not at war.

Part of Colombia's increasing violence is politically-motivated. Since 1958, Colombia's political system has been formally democratic. Yet the restrictive political procedures adopted under the bipartisan National Front agreement have denied access to the mainstream Liberal and Conservative party elites. In addition, Colombia has one of the most skewed patterns of income distribution in Latin America. Together these conditions have fostered decades of violent guerrilla warfare. Colombia is home to the oldest Marxist guerrilla organization in the hemisphere, the Colombian Revolutionary Armed Forces (FARC) and at least eight other guerrilla organizations including the 19th of April Movement (M-19). All told, there are over 15,000 guerrilla soldiers currently active in Colombia.

There is also considerable violence from the right in Colombia. A recent government finding identified 138 paramilitary groups and right-wing death squads. The targets of these organizations are mostly peasant and labor union leaders, intellectuals, journalists, and leftists suspected of collaborating with the guerrillas.

Background of the Cartel

The background of the Medellin Cartel really begins with a brief look at Colombia's historical involvement in narcotics. For thousands of years, Colombia's indigenous people have cultivated and chewed cocaine. As for marijuana, it was introduced much more recently to Colombia via Panama in the first decade of this century. Colombia's first involvement in drug trafficking began with marijuana in the mid-1960s as a result of the demand in the United States. By the early 1970s, Colombia had become a major source of marijuana for the US market, earning at least $1 billion annually. Still, Mexico reigned as the predominant supplier of marijuana to the United States until 1975, when joint US-Mexican efforts along the border and against Mexico's domestic producers slowed down much of its industry. Colombia, with its relatively corruptible government and ideally suited terrain, soon emerged as the new epicenter of marijuana reaching the US market.

The cocaine industry in Colombia began in the late 1960s when individual smugglers, or "mules," transported a few kilos at a time from southwestern Colombia to Cuban drug lords in Miami. The real growth of Colombia's drug trafficking, however, took hold in 1977, in the city of Medellin. It was here that Carlos Lehder Rivas, who served time in a US prison for marijuana smuggling and car theft until 1976, and Jorge Luis Ochoa teamed up to revolutionize their industry. By replacing the "mules" with private airplanes capable of transporting hundreds of kilos, the future drug barons formed the embryo of what is now referred to as the "Medellin Cartel."

The cartel quickly became Colombia's most powerful drug trafficking network. By 1978, they had dominated the South American side of the market and had begun fighting for control of the wholesale distribution network in the United States. By eliminating the Cuban middlemen and installing their own personnel, the Colombians not only improved their profit margins, but they disposed of many Cuban informants who had ties with the CIA and Drug Enforcement Agency (DEA).

A major step in the solidification of the cartel took place on November 12, 1981, when M-19 guerrillas kidnapped Ochoa's daughter and demanded $1 million in ransom. Realizing their profits had made them vulnerable to extortion, Ochoa and Lehder called together a meeting of the leading drug traffickers at Ochoa's restaurant, "La Margarita," on the outskirts of Medellin.

One of the consequential decisions made at this convention was the formation of an organization called "Death to the Kidnappers" (MAS). Each of the traffickers reportedly contributed $7.5 million to MAS which had the sole purpose of ending any further attempts at extortion by guerrilla organizations. How this objective was to be accomplished is largely unclear. What is known is that Pablo Escobar, who was put in charge of security for the cartel, employed an estimated 200 gunmen, known as "Sicarios," and created two schools for training assassins.

In addition to forming a common security network the traffickers planned out an intricate distribution system and agreed to collectively build and operate a huge cocaine laboratory complex on the Yari River in Colombia.

Since then the Medellin Cartel has expanded its operations, influence, and profits in leaps and bounds. Cartel revenues were estimated to be around $1.5 billion in 1980 and $2.5 to $3 billion by 1985, leading Forbes magazine to list members Jorge Ochoa and Pablo Escobar among the richest men in the world. By reinvesting these profits, the group purchased bigger and better airplanes, boats, sophisticated electronic communications devices and radar to escape detection. Technical superiority, however, has not sufficed the Medellin bosses. Many, like Carlos Lehder, have bought interests in local radio stations and newspapers. Pablo Escobar and others have created a following among the people by regularly handing out cash to the poor, building a local zoo, providing low-income housing in the slums (still known as "Barrio Escobar")—even purchasing sports teams and stadiums throughout Colombia.

In the political arena, the Medellin bosses have contributed substantially to local and national campaigns. Lehder even created his own political party and ideology (a mixture of Colombian and Latin American nationalism spiced with fascism). Escobar was elected, in 1982, as an alternate congressman on a Liberal Party slate in his home state of Antioquia. The Medellin group even financed their own nationwide publicity campaign against the 1979 US-Colombian Extradition Treaty. Despite these political activities, it is widely believed that the Medellin traffickers do not seek any ideological/political objectives other than protecting their profits and themselves from prosecution in Colombia or extradition to the United States.

The most powerful tool of the Medellin Cartel has been its systematic campaign of murder and intimidation of government officials. The cartel's complex network of "Sicarios" are trained by the cartel to very efficiently carry out the wishes of their superiors. Some of these men will fulfill an assassination contract for as little as a few hundred dollars. The favored armories of the "Sicarios" include US-made M16 automatic rifles and Israeli-made Uzi sub-machine guns, complete with silencers and infrared sights for nighttime assassinations. In effect, the Medellin Cartel has paralyzed the country's justice system and subdued all other efforts which aim to slow its momentum.

US-Colombian Efforts

The first significant anti-drug assistance from the United States came in 1973, when Colombia received some $6 million over four years to train 600 Colombian law enforcement officials. Corruption and general inefficiency within the government and military led to a virtual standstill of any real progress Colombia's anti-drug efforts.

When Reagan took office in 1981, the situation in Colombia was mixed. On the one hand, a US-Colombian extradition treaty had been signed in 1979 that would allow Colombian traffickers accused of crimes in the United States to be extradited and tried in American courts. On the other hand, the Colombian army had recently announced its refusal to continue US-assisted anti-drug efforts in the vital region of Guajira due to corruption and an upsurge in guerrilla activity elsewhere in Colombia.

The declaration by the Reagan Administration of a renewed commitment to curb drug trafficking—the so-called "war on drugs" of 1981—seems to have been unimpressive to the Colombian government. In 1982, Colombia's President Betancur refused on national grounds to honor the 1979 extradition treaty preferring to try Colombian traffickers in Colombian courts. This blow was softened considerably when, in 1984, a joint US-Colombian raid on the cartel's laboratory complex on the Yari River seized 27,500 pounds of cocaine with a street value of $1.2 billion.

In retaliation, the Medellin kingpins put out a contract on Rodrigo Bonilla—Colombia's Minister of Justice. Despite increased security measures and a bulletproof vest given to him by US Ambassador Lewis Tambs, Bonilla was assassinated six weeks later. President Betancur acted swiftly by abandoning his previous opposition to the extradition treaty and implementing a surprisingly effective crackdown on the cartel.

The United States enthusiastically embraced Betancur's offensive with increased aid. For the next two years ten Colombians and three foreigners were extradited to the United States. Betancur's administration also beefed up eradication programs and succeeded in seizing more narcotics than all of his predecessors combined. This US-supported Colombian crackdown even forced the "Mafia's" bosses into hiding in Panama.

The Cartel's Counterattack

While in exile in Panama, the cartel leaders embarked on an extensive plan to proliferate new routes and to corrupt government officials throughout the Caribbean and Central America. They began by strengthening already existing ties with Panamanian dictator General Manuel Noriega. According to US intelligence estimates, Noriega received a payment of $4 million in exchange for a "safe haven" for boats, planes, money, etc. In addition, the cartel established ties with both the Sandinistas and the Contras in Nicaragua, then with Honduras, Belize and Mexico. In the Caribbean, the cartel reinforced connections in the Bahamas and Jamaica while developing new relations in Cuba, Haiti, and several smaller island countries. The result has been an overwhelming expansion of connections, havens, and trafficking routes that have tied the interdiction efforts in knots.

Next, the Medellin Cartel transformed their cocaine processing complexes into small-scale, mobile operations that could be dispersed throughout Colombia's dense terrain. This decentralization of the Medellin network has frustrated the once successful sweeps and confiscations by the Colombian army.

As if these steps were not enough, the Medellin leaders stepped up the use of bribery, intimidation and murder to insulate themselves against prosecution and/or extradition. Between 1981 and 1986 over fifty judges, including a dozen Supreme Court justices, were killed. Many judges who refused to be bribed were bombarded with death threats.

Terrorist activities such as these were often contracted by the drug lords to the various guerrilla groups within Colombia. The cartel has formed many such alliances with terrorist groups within Colombia, particularly in remote areas where drug cultivation and refining activities overlap with guerrilla operations. The guerrillas are paid in weapons and money in order to keep the government occupied and divert the army away from its attacks on the cartel's operations.

These arrangements have often been mislabeled as the new "narcoguerrilla" and "narcoterrorist" alliances, but it is more accurate to describe them as temporary marriages of convenience rather than as strong bonds. These ties will probably never be permanent due to the fact that the goals of the traffickers and guerrillas are fundamentally incompatible. The guerrillas are mostly Marxists who seek to overthrow the Colombian political system while the traffickers are true-blue capitalists who want to protect their profits and assure themselves immunity from prosecution.

The relationship between the Medellin Cartel and M-19 guerrillas is especially interesting. The initial contact between the two groups was the kidnapping of Ochoa's daughter in 1981. With the organization of MAS, the cartel and the M-19 were, to say the least, not on good terms. For years there were untold casualties between the two sides. Then in November 1985, in a self-serving reversal of policy, the cartel reportedly paid the M-19

The cartel has formed many alliances with terrorist groups within Colombia, particularly in remote areas where drug cultivation and refining activities overlap with guerrilla operations.

guerrillas $1 million to storm the Palace of Justice in Bogota. Some fifty heavily armed terrorists seized the building and took a large group of government officials and Colombian citizens hostage. Among this group was the President of the Supreme Court, Alfonso Reyes Echandia, and eleven other senior judges. In response President Betancur not only refused to negotiate, he demanded the immediate release of the hostages. The terrorists' reaction was to throw Dr. Reyes's body into the street with a warning that more would die if any attempt were made to attack the building. Twenty-four hours later the army drove an armored car through the doors of the Palace of Justice. In the ensuing confrontation 100 people died (including all of the M-19 force), and the hostages were burned to death, tied to their desks. A few of the terrorists crowded into a bathroom and blew themselves up in a group suicide.

In the aftermath it was pointed out that all of the murdered judges had been involved in processing the extraditions of Medellin traffickers for trial in the United States. During the siege the terrorists had made reference to the 1979 extradition treaty, including a legal argument against it. In the end the real beneficiaries of the tragedy were the drug lords whose criminal records were destroyed when the building went up in flames.

The Continuing Saga
Since President Virgilio Barco's inauguration nearly three years ago, there has existed a virtual stalemate between the Medellin network and the government. Barco's forces made sporadic raids on the cartel's complexes, including one, in February 1987, in which Carlos Lehder and fifteen of his bodyguards were arrested (Lehder was later extradited to the US, tried and sentenced on July 20, 1988, to the maximum term of life imprisonment without parole). But the government's efforts have failed to bring any significant reduction in the volume of drugs smuggled into the United States.

Likewise, the drug-related violence has continued to plague Colombia, especially its system of justice. In June 1987, Colombia's Supreme Court reflected the government's fear of violent reprisals when it ruled that the 1979 extradition treaty was unconstitutional. President Barco rejected this notion, but the extraditions were suspended indefinitely. Five months later Jorge Ochoa was captured and arrested, only to bribe his way out of jail within a month. Claiming that Colombia had assured him of Ochoa's extradition to the United States, former Attorney General Edwin Meese protested the release, calling it a

"shocking blow" to international law enforcement. Then on January 25, 1988, Colombia's Attorney General Carlos Hoyos Jimenez was shot to death on the outskirts of Medellin.

Hoyos' murder was typical of the way in which the cartel carries out its brand of terrorism. The attorney general had just spent a week in Medellin investigating a group of officials, including two judges, suspected of accepting bribes for Ochoa's release. Hoyos and two bodyguards were headed for the airport to return to Bogota when, suddenly, three jeeps and a car forced Hoyos' Mercedes off the road. Instantly, a group of men jumped out and blasted the Mercedes with sub-machine gun fire. The two guards were quickly and brutally killed while Hoyos sustained serious wounds to the head. The gunmen then dragged Hoyos out of his car and kidnapped him. A few hours later his bullet-riddled body was found in a nearby farmhouse.

After the vicious slaying, a man claiming to represent the cartel called a Medellin radio station and reported that the attorney general had been executed for "betraying his country" by supporing the 1979 extradition treaty.

The Cartel's Worldwide Terrorism
A year before his murder, Attorney General Hoyos commented on the assassination attempt on Ambassador Gonzalez, stating that "No one is safe anywhere against the vengeance of the mafia." Indeed, the ability of the cartel to inflict its terrorism throughout the world is a most frightening reality for those who oppose the Medellin gangsters. Recently, a Colombian judge, who attempted to prosecute one of the drug lords, took refuge in the United States to escape the wrath of the cartel. Within weeks of secretly relocating, the judge received a horrifying telegram which stated, "We are capable of executing you any place on this planet—you will not survive." That the cartel can make such claims is largely explained by their vast and complex network of international connections, not only in this hemisphere but in many locales throughout the world.

Through these contacts, whether they be government officials or others involved in the drug trade, the cartel has a means of tracking down virtually anyone. In places where there are no established contacts, the cartel can use bribery to achieve its objectives.

The terrorism and violence of the Medellin Cartel has frequently spread northward into the United States. In early 1985 Carlos Lehder publicly announced that he would pay $350,000 to anyone who could kill or capture the US DEA chief. Later that year, Lehder gave an interview (that was subsequently aired

Indeed, the ability of the cartel to inflict its terrorism throughout the world is a most frightening reality for those who oppose the Medellin gangsters.

on national television) in which he called out for discontented military officers and Marxists alike to join him in the "cocaine bonanza...the arm of the struggle against America...the Achilles' heel of American imperialism."

Upon Lehder's extradition, cartel leaders made numerous threats against the United States. One of these, which has not yet been fulfilled, was to kill five Americans for every Colombian extradited to the United States.

Although such threats are often mere terrorist rhetoric, the cartel has shown a bold willingness to kill on American turf. In 1979, after the cartel had established itself as the leading drug trafficking network of South America, the syndicate began a massive effort to gain control of wholesale distribution in the United States. In order to break into the new market, the cartel went to battle with Cuban-American drug lords in south Florida. This period of violence, known as the "cocaine wars," peaked in 1981 with a reported 101 murders.

The Feud
Once in control of the Miami-based wholesale market, the Medellin Cartel agreed to let its main competitor in Colombia, the "Cali Cartel," take control of New York's drug trade. The popularity of crack cocaine, however, has made the New York traffic more profitable, leading the Medellin gang to break the deal. The result has been a vicious feud between the drug lords which has taken place not only in Colombia but in New York City. Former Mayor Ed Koch, NYC's DEA chief, and special narcotics prosecutor Sterling Johnson are but a few of the US officials who have received death threats from the cartel.

Anti-drug officials in Colombia are wishing the drug cartels good luck in their feud. As long as the rivalry continues, say these officials, the cartels will kill each other off. In the first eight months of 1988 there were over eighty murders reported in Colombia—all attributed to the feud. One case occurred in August 1989 when Medellin gunmen fire-bombed the local branches of a drugstore chain and a radio network owned by Rodriguez Orejuela—one of the Cali bosses. Several Cali hit men were killed in the attack.

Police also benefit because the cartels often attack each other by tipping off the authorities. Upon bribing his way out of jail, Jorge Ochoa claimed that the Cali Cartel had provided the information leading to his arrest. In retaliation the Medellin bosses tipped off US officials to a major shipment (four tons) of Cali cocaine on its way through Florida.

Another encouraging development took place very recently when US officials cracked down on a billion-dollar money-laundering operation, known as *La Mina*, which handled a large chunk of the Medellin Cartel's profits. Called Operation Polar Cap, it was an interagency investigation involving the FBI, the DEA, and the IRS. The investigation began with an undercover money-laundering operation by the FBI in Atlanta. After hearing that *La Mina* could get drug money by wire from Los Angeles to Panama within forty-eight hours, the undercover agents expanded their investigation using electronic intercepts, surveillance, and the pursuit of financial paper trails. In the crackdown agents seized a half ton of cocaine and $45 million in cash, jewels, and real estate. In all, Operation Polar Cap has brought charges against 127 people, two banks in Colombia and Panama, and civil action has been filed that could seize an additional $412 million. Attorney General Dick Thornburgh called the investigation "the largest money-laundering crackdown ever carried out by the federal government."

Although the recent crackdown will cause some damage to the traffickers, it must be remembered that the Medellin Cartel is extremely resilient. Over and over again, US and Colombian officials have seized tons of cocaine worth billions of dollars in street value. Cartel leaders, such as Lehder, have been extradited and feuding has taken many of the traffickers' lives. Yet through it all, the Medellin Cartel goes about its business almost nonchalantly. The traffickers are estimated to have at least three times as much financial power as they did in 1981 and are trafficking more cocaine than ever before. More worrisome, however, is the fact that over the years the cartel has developed an incredibly intricate network of worldwide connections and channels of distribution.

Recent US-Colombian Response
The efforts of the Colombian government during the 1989-90 year to curb the power of the Medellin Cartel has been gratifying. A series of bold and spectacular assassinations of government officials and politicians who opposed the cartel clearly put the Colombian government in a position where it had to wage war for its survival.

Army sweeps through the jungle have destroyed many cocaine labs. The removal of Panama's Manuel Noriega has hurt cartel distribution and money-laundering efforts, but the drug lords have shown a remarkable ability to survive. Cocaine labs have been moved to the jungles of Venezuela and Guyana. New coca fields have been planted in Ecuador, and new alliances have been formed with new

In early 1985 Carlos Lehder publicly announced that he would pay $350,000 to anyone who could kill or capture the US DEA chief.

terrorist groups such as Ecuador's Viva Alfaro, Carajo!, and Peru's Sendero Luminoso.

The cartels have launched a new war of terrorism within Colombia. The Andean nations under siege by the drug traffickers—primarily Colombia, Bolivia, and Peru, along with the United States—have worked up a regional and global strategy at the February 15, 1990, summit meeting at Cartagena, Colombia. Presidents Barco, Bush, Garcia, and Paz all agreed to cooperate in the areas of exchanging information and intelligence, money laundering, asset seizure, and extradition. The summit declaration also urged all countries to ratify the United Nations Convention Against Illicit Traffic in Narcotic Drugs and Psychotropic Substances.

The Soviet Union has also joined the anti-drug fight since the cartel has targeted Russia as a new market area. Cocaine has been flooding the country through new distribution channels in Spain. The Soviet Union has reportedly sent teams of *Spetsnaz*—Soviet army special forces—to Peru to train the *Cinchis*, elite units of Peru's Civil Guard, to combat the Sendero Luminoso terrorists in the Huallaga Valley. It is here where most of the world's coca is grown.

International cooperation against the drug lords is a step in the right direction. Over the past decade joint actions have made a dent in the cartels' ability to spread their deadly business throughout the world. However, cooperation and interdiction are only one half of the equation. The violence and terrorism of the Medellin Cartel will continue—despite world efforts to the contrary—until the demand for drugs in the United States is drastically reduced.

Carl H. Yaeger is counterterrorism specialist and a former US Army intelligence officer. He currently teaches political science at Utah Community College.

The Soviet Union has also joined the anti-drug fight since the cartel has targeted Russia as a new market area.

Article 29.2.   Sowing Violence in Peru

In recent years, America's appetite for cocaine has steadily increased, to the point that it has turned the remote Huallaga Valley of Peru into an armed camp, where drug lords and rural peasants work side by side to supply the needs of American consumers. Many U.S. and Peruvian officials are reluctant to finance the Andean military to eliminate the scourge, fearing that such aid would strengthen the already powerful military and threaten the fragile civilian government which is struggling to reform the country. According to most experts, sending weapons to Peru's military would inevitably lead to direct involvement in one of the ugliest wars in the hemisphere, where the dreaded Shining Path, a Maoist guerrilla movement, has waged a brutal ten-year battle to overthrow the government and establish a totalitarian regime modeled on Mao Zedong's revolutionary China. The U.S. government hopes that the Peruvian military will succeed in "taking control" of the Huallaga and, in the process, force the farmers to either refuse to grow coca or else pull up their coca and plant other crops instead. At present, no one is betting on the outcome.

Sowing Violence in Peru

BY ROBIN KIRK

General Jaime Rios likens his job to the one that faced General Norman Schwarzkopf, commander of the Allied forces in the Persian Gulf. "The Americans that come here to visit tell me that after General Schwarzkopf, I have the toughest job in the world," Rios says, relaxing in his peaked-roof bungalow in the Huallaga River Valley of Peru.

Physically, they are nothing alike. Schwarzkopf is a burly mountain of a man; Rios is lean and lanky, his face toasted by the intense tropical sun. Instead of desert fatigues, he wears a high-tech jungle-warfare outfit, comfortable despite the 100-plus degree heat.

But that outfit, like Schwarzkopf's, is made in the United States. Rios commands the *Frente Huallaga*, or Huallaga Front, the 100-mile-stretch of the Valley where more than 65 per cent of the coca leaf refined into U.S.-bound cocaine is grown.

America's appetite for cocaine has turned these rolling green hills, veined with the earth-red rivers that feed the Amazon, into a modern Wild West where justice is in the hands of those with the most cash and the greatest firepower. Portly men in embroidered white shirts and Italian loafers disappear into the bush with briefcases. Bodies putrify along the roads, some with placards around their necks: DEATH TO SNITCHES AND TO ANYONE WHO REMOVES THIS BODY.

According to reliable studies, up to 220 Cessna flights leave the Huallaga's innumerable clandestine—and public—air strips during dry months. Each can carry up to 880 pounds of *pasta basica*, meaning an annual export of 302 metric tons of purified cocaine. Air Taxi Iberico in Tarapoto has a motto fit for the times: DON'T ASK US WHERE WE GO, JUST TELL US WHERE YOU WANT TO GO.

Robin Kirk is an associate editor at Pacific News Service and contributes frequently to U.S. newspapers and magazines from her base in Lima. This report was made possible by a grant from the Fund for Investigative Journalism.

It is here that the United States thinks it can—and must—win the "war on drugs." To do so, American officials are forging an alliance with the Peruvian military. The drug war has replaced the Cold War in the plans of the U.S. Southern Command, which has already sent trainers, weapons, and supplies to Colombia and Bolivia under the International Narcotics Control Act (INCA).

For the past year and more, shadowy characters with experience in Vietnam, Teheran, and El Salvador have circled around the "Super-Base" at Santa Lucia on the banks of the Huallaga, the $3.5 million headquarters of "about twenty" Drug Enforcement Administration agents, heralded as "the new inter-American center for the struggle against drug-trafficking."

Many in Peru and the United States question the wisdom of financing Andean militaries to fight drugs. Although these nations are at least a decade past their military dictatorships, the men in uniform remain powerful. Strengthening them, rather than civil authorities, may tip an already fragile standoff.

Sending weapons to Peru's military means direct U.S. involvement in the dirtiest war in the hemisphere. Shining Path, the Maoist guerrilla movement of Peru, began its war in 1980 and has gained notoriety as the most brutal insurgency in modern Latin American history. Its aim is to establish a totalitarian state modeled on Mao Zedong's revolutionary China.

In the Upper Huallaga Valley, Shining Path has formed an alliance with coca growers, giving protection in exchange for a lucrative cut of the estimated $1 billion

From *The Progressive*, July 1991, pp. 30-32. Reprinted by permission from *The Progressive*, 409 East Main Street, Madison, Wisconsin 53703.

made every year off the sale of *pasta basica*, the gray alkaloid cake leeched out of coca leaves for shipment to Colombian refining labs.

The Middle Huallaga Valley is controlled by the smaller, Castro-style Tupac Amaru Revolutionary Movement (MRTA), which also charges area businesses a "war tax." More than 40 per cent of Peru's territory, including the Huallaga Front, is in a state of emergency, meaning that official control has been ceded to the military.

To combat guerrillas, the security forces have unleashed an equally brutal campaign whose daily features are torture, "disappearance," and extrajudicial execution. For four years in a row, the United Nations has put Peru first on the list of countries that "disappear" their citizens. According to the National Coordinating Committee for Human Rights, 246 Peruvians "disappeared" in 1990, putting the ten-year total at more than 3,000.

The U.S. State Department's own 1990 human-rights report singles out Peru's military for their ferocity. Nevertheless, according to U.S. officials, the Peruvian military will provide the "security frame" needed before crop substitution and police antidrug actions can take place.

General Rios says human-rights complaints are a plot funded by drug-traffickers to attack the army. Without help—and soon—he says, coca and insurgency are bound to grow. The Frente Huallaga command base has not yet come under attack, but military and police vehicles are often ambushed by guerrillas.

One of Rios's predecessors was seriously wounded in an MRTA assault last November. Since assuming command in January, Rios himself has been attacked unsuccessfully three times. In May, the MRTA carried out its most ambitious operation, simultaneously attacking five police stations over a twenty-mile area, including the station ten minutes' walk from General Rios's bungalow.

Of the $100 million slated to be sent to Peru, $30 million is for the military. The rest is for "alternative development." But not one dime will be issued until "security" is assured.

The accord has taken more than a year of comic diplomacy to work out. Last year, the U.S. embassy led hundreds of Peruvian and international journalists through a Potemkin Village of cocaine set up at Santa Lucia, to impress on them the idea of "narco-terrorists," meaning just about everyone living within Huey range of the base.

Lifelike huts, each with authentic-looking "narco-terrorists," were stops along a winding trail near the airstrip long enough to land the biggest U.S. Air Force cargo planes. Other props included coca bushes, harvested leaves spread out to dry, and pace pits where the cocaine alkaloid is stamped out in a murky bath of lime and kerosene.

But when newly elected President Alberto Fujimori decided not to sign a military-aid accord, arguing that those "narco-terrorists" were really coca famers struggling to survive, the "Santa Lucia Drug Experience" was abruptly closed.

Fujimori insisted that guerrillas, not drugs, were Peru's main problem. A political newcomer without an organized party, Fujimori made it his first act upon taking office to ally himself with the military, Peru's most powerful institution. During one week, he received so many honorary medals that the lapel of his pin-striped suit sagged with gilt-encrusted metal.

What he needed was guns—guns and more guns, boots, rockets, rations, uniforms, bullets, better salaries, and helicopter fuel, to revitalize Peru's flagging war against the Shining Path.

"We need the coca-growing farmers' support, to win them back to the system," explains General Alberto Arciniega, a key Fujimori adviser. "Targeting them would simply push them into the arms of the guerrillas."

Coca farmers insist they have little choice. The village of Cacatachi, for example, used to be the best rice producer in the province. A pleasant clump of blue adobe buildings, Cacatachi is in a fertile valley that empties into the Huallaga. But prices didn't cover costs. To ship rice out on one of the two disastrous roads that link the jungle to the coast is an exercise in futility. The government, which used to buy the rice, still has not paid for last year's harvest.

Not that it matters any more, according to Cacatachi mayor Roaldo Archenti.

"Inflation has made the amount that they owe us into a barbarous joke," says Archenti, a son of Italian immigrants. "There used to be over 15,000 acres planted in rice here. Now, there's not even 2,500. Many farmers have moved down to Tocache to grow coca."

Despite years of antidrug efforts, which included forced eradication and broken promises of development aid, land under coca cultivation has steadily grown. According to Peruvian estimates, there are at least 500,000 acres planted with illegal coca in the Huallaga Valley, which means at least 1,500 metric tons of *pasta basica*.

Most of Peru's coca is now grown "outside" the Upper Huallaga. The village of Huacayacu—I've changed the name of the village and its mayor—is fifty miles by tortuous road from Tarapoto in the Middle Huallaga. Four years ago, farmers opened up new hillside plots for coca. Huacayacu's 3,000 acres produce approximately 200,000 pounds of *pasta basica* per year, sold in an open-air Saturday market for the equivalent of $145 a pound, or $1,300 per villager per year. That is triple what Peru's nurses and teachers make.

"We are in an impossible situation," explains Mayor Severo Constanza. "We're not going to let ourselves die of hunger."

In fact, Peru's economic reforms depend on a cheap and plentiful supply of dollars shipped in bales from the Huallaga—$4 million a day, which the Central Reserve Bank buys. Fujimori's predecessor, populist Alan Garcia, spent the country into bankruptcy, leaving Peru blacklisted with international lenders and with only unsellable gold artifacts, dating from Peru's colonial splendor, in the Central Reserve Bank vaults.

However, economics is Fujimori's weak spot. He needs international credits to keep reforms afloat. The United States has made it clear that negotiations with the International Monetary Fund and other lenders depend on this accord. No drug war—no credits.

For signing the accord, the United States has thrown Fujimori some plums. The United States now admits funding the fight against guerrillas. No longer are coca farmers considered "narco-terrorists," but entrepreneurs in search of a free market.

Three separate "accords," the most important of which covers military aid, will probably be negotiated, signed, and implemented in secrecy. The United States will be the sole arbiter determining how and to what degree Peru complies.

U.S. officials believe the Peruvian military will now "take control" of the Huallaga—the navy of the rivers, the air force of the skies, and the army of the land. Then the Drug Enforcement Administration and police will just say no to coca. Farmers who do not choose other crops will be compelled to pull up their coca; and like a bad dream, the crack nightmare of the American inner city will vanish.

But the Huallaga Valley has a new sense of tension and fear. The drug economy has always shown an ability to adapt to circumstance, popping up in new and more inventive ways. For instance, although the Peruvian air force has forced thirty-two small planes to land in the Huallaga since January, the supply of *pasta basica* has not notably diminished. Drug-running Cessnas, equipped with the latest equipment, simply fly at night, evading the government's outdated Tucanos.

The military and police have never cooperated. In fact, units often face off at gunpoint, in a hail of mutual accusations

Coca's Environmental Impact

Coca farmers who refine their own *pasta basica* stand to increase their profits substantially. However, the price they pay in health is often high. Last year, Huacayacu's children began falling ill with strange gastrointestinal disorders. Studies revealed that the diseases were linked to high concentrations of kerosene, lime, and sulfuric acid in streams used for drinking and cooking.

These are all chemicals used to make *pasta basica* in makeshift pace pits, often next to streams.

Mayor Severo Constanza has gained the help of the High Jungle Research and Development Center for a potable water project to eliminate contaminants.

"We know that this is not the best way, but we have no choice," he says. "I believe the U.S. and Peru can come to an agreement, but it must be democratic and without using arms."

Chemical contamination from the refining process isn't the only problem for coca growers. Farmers cultivate coca on steep hillsides, causing erosion. The herbicides used to protect the plants also seep into the ground, then inevitably into waterways. Jumps in prices mean that farmers slash open new fields, adding to deforestation.

The U.S. Embassy has highlighted the ecological damage wreaked by coca-leaf refining. However, the United States continues to support the idea of chemical eradication with Spike, a total vegetation eradicator strictly controlled in the United States. Recent reports from the Upper Huallaga Valley have also hinted at the possibility that the United States, in coordination with the Peruvian police, is carrying out secret experiments with coca-killing fungus. According to coca growers near Santa Lucia, planes are dumping a substance over coca bushes. Within days, the plants begin to die.

—R.K.

---

about corruption. The district attorney's office in Tarapoto rarely receives a drug case. As one official explains, most are quickly "arranged" with police—by payment of a stiff bribe.

However, the office is overwhelmed with human-rights cases. According to Horacio Garcia, the legal adviser for the human-rights office sponsored by the Catholic Church, it receives thirty cases a month, mostly "disappearances." Half "reappear" bearing horrifying tales of torture—shocked with electrical charges, hung with their arms tied behind their backs, pushed out of helicopters, shut in metal containers placed in the jungle sun.

"The general denies that they are detained at the base, but we have hundreds of testimonies," comments Garcia, an elf-like man with a shock of white hair. "The ones who are eventually handed over to the police are often in bad shape. The police commander takes them immediately to the hospital for an evaluation, so that if they die in custody he won't be blamed."

Unlike cases of torture and disappearance, charges that military officers skim off the drug trade—$10,000 per landing, according to rumors—are taken seriously, Rios says. He claims he showed a list of officers tried and convicted of taking bribes to General Maxwell Thurman, head of the U.S. Southern Command, when Thurman visited the Huallaga Front in February.

But unfortunately, like the lists of officers the military claims are tried for human-rights violations, Rios's list is not available to the press. Recently, the U.S. Army made its first "good faith" gift to the general—500 M-16 rifles, now being lugged around Rios's command center by diminutive Peruvian recruits.

"With this weapon, I could pick off that man at the defense perimeter," Rios says, motioning toward a soldier crouched in a weed-choked trench 100 yards distant. He has detailed crews to fix the Outer Highway, ritually washed away every year by intense rains. But he gives this "development" phase six months, and if he gets no results, things will change.

"The next six months would be very different," he comments dryly. "The subversives may take that as a sign that I am weak. But I will show them differently." ∎

SELECTED BIBLIOGRAPHY—SECTION VII

Alexander, Yonah, and Joshua Sinai. *Terrorism: The PLO Connection*. Bristol, Penn.: Crane Russak, 1989.

Ali, Sheikh R., and Jeffrey M. Elliot. *The Trilemma of World Oil Politics*. San Bernardino, Calif.: Borgo Press, 1991.

Commoner, Barry. *The Poverty of Power: Energy and the Economic Crisis*. New York: Bantam Books, 1977.

Donnelly, Jack. *Universal Human Rights in Theory and Practice*. Ithaca, N.Y.: Cornell University Press, 1989.

Dreze, Jean, and Amartya Sen. *Hunger and Public Action*. New York: Oxford University Press, 1989.

Ehrenfeld, Rachel. *Narco-Terrorism*. New York: Basic Books, 1992.

Ehrlich, Paul R., and Anne H. Ehrlich. *The Population Explosion*. New York: Touchstone Books, 1990.

Forsythe, David P. *The Internationalization of Human Rights*. New York: Lexington Books, 1991.

Franck, Thomas M. *Human Rights in the Third World Perspective*. London: Oceana Press, 1989.

Garst, Rachel, and Tim Barry. *Feeding the Crisis: U.S. Food Aid and Farm Policy in Central America*. Lincoln: University of Nebraska Press, 1990.

George, Susan. *How the Other Half Dies: The Real Reasons for World Hunger*. Savage, Md.: Rowman & Littlefield, 1977.

Gever, John, Robert Kaufmann, David Skole, and Charles Vorosmarty. *Beyond Oil: The Threat to Food and Fuel in the Coming Decades*. Cambridge, Mass.: Ballinger, 1987.

Grmek, Mirko D. *History of AIDS: Emergence and Origin of a Modern Pandemic*, Princeton, N.J.: Princeton University Press, 1990.

Gupte, Pranay. *The Crowded Earth: People and the Politics of Population*. New York: Norton, 1984.

Harris, Jonathan. *The New Terrorism*. New York: Simon & Schuster, 1983.

Kirkpatrick, Sidney D., and Peter Abrahams. *Turning the Tide: One Man Against the Medellin Cartel*. New York: Dutton, 1991.

Laqueur, Walter. *The Age of Terrorism*. Boston: Little, Brown, 1987.

Lernoux, Penny. *Cry of the People: The Struggle for Human Rights in Latin America*. New York: Penguin Books, 1982.

Pachavri, R.K. *The Political Ecology of Global Energy*. Baltimore, Md.: Johns Hopkins University Press, 1985.

Patton, Cindy. *Inventing AIDS*. New York: Routledge, 1990.

Pryer, Jane, and Nigel Crook. *Cities of Hunger: Urban Malnutrition in Developing Countries*. Oxford: Oxfam, 1988.

Rosenbaum, Walter A. *Environmental Politics and Policy*. Washington, D.C.: Congressional Quarterly Press, 1991.

Rubenstein, Richard E. *Alchemists of Revolution: Terrorism in the Modern World*. New York: Basic Books, 1988.

Sabatier, Renee. *Blaming Others: Prejudice, Race, and Worldwide AIDS*. London: Panos Institute, 1988.

Schlagheck, Donna M. *International Terrorism*. Lexington, Mass.: Lexington Books, 1988.

Schneider, Stephen H. *Global Warming: Are We Entering the Greenhouse Century?* San Francisco, Calif.: Sierra Club Books, 1989.

Sederberg, Peter C. *Terrorist Myths*. Englewood Cliffs, N.J.: Prentice-Hall, 1989.

Timberlake, Lloyd. *Africa in Crisis: The Causes, The Cures of Environmental Bankruptcy*. London: Earthscan, 1985.

Turner, Stansfeld. *Terrorism and Democracy*. Boston: Houghton Mifflin, 1991.

Vance, Cyrus. *Hard Choices*. New York: Simon & Schuster, 1983.

Wardlaw, Grant. *Political Terrorism: Theory, Tactics, and Countermeasures*. New York: Cambridge University Press, 1982.

Warnock, John W. *The Politics of Hunger: The Global Food System*. New York: Methuen Publications, 1987.

Index

ARTICLE EVALUATION FORM
THE BROWN & BENCHMARK READER IN
INTERNATIONAL RELATIONS 1992

We are very much interested in knowing your responses to the articles in this edition of *The Brown & Benchmark Reader in International Relations*. Please rate the articles using the following scale:

1. **Excellent: definitely retain this article**
2. **Good: possibly retain this article**
3. **Fair: possibly delete this article**
4. **Poor: definitely delete this article**

Your ratings count! Please fill out this form and mail it back to us as soon as possible. Simply fold the form in thirds so the address is on the outside, staple, and mail. It's that simple! Thank you!

Rating **Article**

TITLE

____ 1.1 What Is the National Interest?
____ 1.2 Imperialism and the Gulf War
____ 2.1 Nationalism Is Not Necessarily the Path to a Democratic World
____ 2.2 Yugoslavia: The End of Communism, The Return of Nationalism
____ 3.1 China: The Unfinished Revolution
____ 3.2 Unpromised Lands
____ 4.1 The Soviet (Dis)Union
____ 4.2 Soviet Disunion
____ 5.1 Reaching Out to Moscow
____ 5.2 Balancing the New Order
____ 6.1 After the Cold War: What Should the U.S. Do?
____ 6.2 Uncle Sam as the World's Policeman: Time for Change?
____ 7.1 Defining the New World Order
____ 7.2 The Meaning of the New World Order: A Critique
____ 8.1 The Destiny of South Africa
____ 8.2 Mobutu Sese Seko: "I Have a Clear Conscience"
____ 9.1 India: The Seed of Destruction
____ 9.2 Hongkong — The Case for Optimism
____ 10.1 Reforming the Nonreforming Regimes
____ 10.2 The One Germany
____ 11.1 As the World Turns
____ 11.2 From Horror to Hope
____ 12.1 Remaking the Mideast
____ 12.2 Revolution, Reform, or Regression?: Arab Political Options in the 1990 Gulf Crisis
____ 13.1 Has the CIA Become an Anachronism?
____ 13.2 The KGB: Still a Potent Force
____ 14.1 Re-Arm the World
____ 14.2 Fueling the Fire: How We Armed the Middle East
____ 15.1 The Nuclear Threat: A Proposal

Rating **Article**

TITLE

____ 15.2 Iraq and the Bomb: Were They Even Close?
____ 16.1 After the Battle
____ 16.2 A Defense Industrial Strategy?: Yes, Preparedness Requires It
____ 17.1 STARTing Over
____ 17.2 Is the Soviet Union Prepared for Peace?
____ 18.1 The U.N. in a New World Order
____ 18.2 Closing Time for the U.N.?
____ 19.1 A New Role for NATO
____ 19.2 United States Security Policy and ASEAN
____ 20.1 The Rise and Fall of the Third World
____ 20.2 Why the Third World Goes Hungry: Selling Cheap & Buying Dear
____ 21.1 It Won't Go Away Alone
____ 21.2 Go Slowly on Debt Relief for Third World Nations
____ 22.1 Capitalism Isn't All It's Cracked Up to Be
____ 22.2 The Big Split
____ 23.1 World Population Continues to Rise
____ 23.2 Population: Red-Hot Realities for a Finite Planet
____ 24.1 World Hunger Amidst Plenty
____ 24.2 AIDS: New Threat to the Third World
____ 25.1 A "No Regrets" Environmental Policy
____ 25.2 Military Victory, Ecological Defeat
____ 26.1 Bush's Pro-Nuke Energy Strategy
____ 26.2 The Oil Shortage that Wasn't
____ 27.1 Movements Toward Democracy: A Global Revolution
____ 27.2 A Matter of Principle
____ 28.1 10 Steps Against Terror
____ 28.2 Should We "Take Out" Terrorists?
____ 29.1 Terror for Profit: The Colombian Cocaine Connection
____ 29.2 Sowing Violence in Peru

(continued on next page)

BUSINESS REPLY MAIL
FIRST-CLASS MAIL PERMIT NO. 1070 MADISON, WI

POSTAGE WILL BE PAID BY ADDRESSEE

ATTN: Political Science Editor
WCB Brown & Benchmark
25 Kessel Court
Madison WI 53791-9042

والبارمار ساسال السابار

_____

2. (FOLD HERE)

Name: _____ Date: _____

_____ Instructor _____ Student   _____ Full time _____ Part time

Institution _____

Department (if applicable): _____

Address: _____

City: _____ State: _____ ZIP: _____-_____

Institution phone #: (_____) _____-_____

COURSE INFORMATION:

Course for which this book was used: _____

Was a text used with this reader? _____ YES   _____ NO

If yes, which text(s)? _____

_____

1. (FOLD HERE)

Instructors, did you use the Instructor's Resource Guide? _____ YES   _____ NO

Comments on the IRG:

Please rate the effectiveness of the following:

	Effective/ Useful							Ineffective/ Not Useful	
Abstract summaries that preceded the articles	1	2	3	4	5	6	7	8	9
Key Terms	1	2	3	4	5	6	7	8	9
Discussion Questions	1	2	3	4	5	6	7	8	9
Selected Bibliography	1	2	3	4	5	6	7	8	9
Instructors Resource Guide	1	2	3	4	5	6	7	8	9

Overall comments: